BOWERMAN

AND THE MEN OF OREGON

RODALE

LIVE YOUR WHOLE LIFE™

Every day our brands connect with and inspire millions of people to live a life of the mind, body, spirit — a whole life.

Bill does a victory lap with the team after the 1967 PAC-8 Championships in Eugene. *Photo by* ROGER JENSEN

BOWERMAN
AND THE MEN OF OREGON

The Story of Oregon's Legendary Coach and Nike's Cofounder

KENNY MOORE

RODALE

© 2006 by Kenny Moore

Printed in the United States of America

Rodale Inc. makes every effort to use acid-free ∞, recycled paper ⊙.

BOOK DESIGN BY Susan P. Eugster

Library of Congress Cataloging-in-Publication Data

Moore, Kenny
    Bowerman and the men of Oregon : the story of Oregon's legendary coach and Nike's cofounder / Kenny Moore.
       p. cm.
    Includes index.
    ISBN-13 978–1–59486–190–1 hardcover
    ISBN-10 1–59486–190–0 hardcover
    ISBN-13 978–1–59486–731–6 paperback
    ISBN-10 1–59486–731–3 paperback
    1. Bowerman, William J.   2. Track and field coaches—United States—Biography.
3. University of Oregon—Track and field.   4. Nike (Firm)—History. I. Title.
GV697.B68M66   2006
796.42092—dc22   2005035749

Distributed to the book trade by Holtzbrinck Publishers

| 2 | 4 | 6 | 8 | 10 | 9 | 7 | 5 | 3 | 1 | hardcover |
| 2 | 4 | 6 | 8 | 10 | 9 | 7 | 5 | 3 | 1 | paperback |

RODALE
LIVE YOUR WHOLE LIFE™

To my three great mentors,

Oregon track coach Bill Bowerman,

Sports Illustrated *managing editor Gilbert Rogin,*

and Oscar-winning screenwriter Robert Towne,

whose iron standards infuse these pages

Bill sits in the President's Box, Hayward Field's east stands, where he often called team meetings.
Photo by BRIAN LANKER

CONTENTS

Acknowledgments

ONE OF BILL BOWERMAN'S STERNEST COMMANDMENTS WAS TO GIVE CREDIT where credit is due. If I obeyed completely, this note would take up half the book because writing it required the help of hundreds—a magnificent, trusting relay team—to carry this endeavor to conclusion. The following few are those without whom the book simply would have been impossible:

Bill Landers, who first gained Bill Bowerman's permission to proceed on his biography and taped days of memories from Bill and his family, friends, enemies, colleagues, and athletes. Landers's knowledge of Bowerman's life and character guided each chapter from an unwieldy mess to a clear stage on an epic journey.

Heidi Rodale, who was drawn into the Bowerman story when her runner son Alex was inspired by Steve Prefontaine—an abiding personal connection that enabled her to be the best publisher possible.

The Bowerman family. Bill's sons Jon, Jay, and Tom patiently answered every question with well-supported history, documents, and lengthy personal accounts. Barbara Bowerman bravely went back through her seventy years with Bill with the zeal of a detective-psychologist. I will always recall her at age ninety, ordering me to stay behind the wheel while she jumped out to swing open every cattle gate crossing on the ranch roads around Fossil, Oregon.

Jeff Johnson, who gave Nike its name. Jeff willed himself back from a stroke to go over every page for accuracy. "Reading this book," he reports, "saved my life." He returned the favor with extraordinary insights into Nike's formation and growth.

Contract editor *Roberta Conlan*, who first met Bill Bowerman in 1968. Bobbie applied her gifted editorial mind with professional rigor, doggedly overseeing my transit from good intentions to credible, weight-bearing sentences.

James Fox, the spirited head of Special Collections and University Archives at the University of Oregon's Knight Library, and his astute team of curators: *Linda Long, Heather Briston, Leslie Larson, Bruce Tabb, Normandy Helmer, Marilyn Reaves, and Melissa Anderson*. All were a striking blend of energy and mindfulness as they helped me and assistant *Connie Johnston* review the huge volume of papers Bowerman assigned to the Library. Among the 35 boxes in the collection, many books and dissertations remain to be written about Bill Bowerman. James Fox and company stand ready to point the way for future authors.

Faithful friends *Jim and Mary Jaqua, Ron and Mary Beth Seiple, Kip Leonard and Jody Miller, Josh and Nancy Reckord.* Their leaping into every breech kept the project rolling through torrential rains and mounting, unplanned years.

Finally, my apologies to dozens of Men of Oregon (Jim Grelle, Dave Steen, Jere Van Dyk, Vic Reeve, Archie San Romani, and Dick Miller spring to mind.) for having to dilute the humor, pace, and detail of their stories by mashing them into the confines of these few pages.

— *Kenny Moore*
November 15, 2005

Men of Oregon

*"A guru gives us himself and then his system;
a teacher gives us his subject, and then ourselves."*
—ADAM GOPNIK

IN THE SPRING OF 1964, BILL BOWERMAN GAVE ME HIS SUBJECT AND STOOD back to see if I deserved it. Bowerman, then fifty-three, had coached six sub-four-minute milers at the University of Oregon and had won the 1962 NCAA Track and Field championship on the very field where he now stood, signaling me over. I was twenty, a sophomore two-miler, just finishing my first training run after being out with the flu. He put two fingers to my neck, taking my pulse from my carotid artery.

"Easy day?" he asked.

"Easy day. Absolutely."

"Twelve miles?" As if he were my physician, he tilted my head back so he could look me in the eye. He was six feet two and over 200 pounds, with a powerful upper body.

"An easy twelve," I said.

We had vexed each other that year. I had never won a race in high school, had never broken 9:15 for two miles, but was determined to run the 100 miles a week his good friend Arthur Lydiard assigned his New Zealand Olympic champions.

"Are you in this simply to do mindless labor," he said, "or do you want to improve?"

"To improve."

"You can't improve if you're always sick or injured."

"I know, but Bill, it was an *easy* twel . . . "

He closed great, calloused hands around my throat. He did not lift me off the ground. He did relieve my feet of much of their burden. He brought my forehead to his. "I'm going to ask you to take part in an experiment," he said with menacing calm. People five yards away thought we were sharing a tidbit of gossip. "For three weeks, you are not going to run a yard except in my sight. You will do a three-mile jog here every morning, and our regular afternoon workouts. If I or any of my spies sees you trotting another step, you will never run for the University of Oregon again."

"Bill . . ."

"Are we agreed?"

"*Bill . . .*"

"Agreed?"

As I was feeling faint, I submitted.

Some of my afternoons remained exactly the same. I was allowed our regular hard-day sessions of four three-quarter-mile repetitions at a 67-second-per-lap pace, then a five-mile run through the hills and rhododendrons of nearby Hendricks Park and four fast 110-yard strides before showering.

It was the easy days that were humiliating, reporting to Bowerman morning and evening on the sawdust trail inside the Hayward Field track, having him count my laps, barely feeling warmed up before he called, "Three miles. In. In."

I did not suffer this gladly. I was tempted to do secret, defiant runs, but he had enlisted the rest of the team and half the town; every friend was a possible traitor. And the potential cost was too great. No one who knew Bill Bowerman doubted he would back up his ultimatum. No one who knew me doubted that I desperately wanted to be an Oregon runner.

The mornings were the worst, running through fog that made our hallowed old field pass in and out of time. I saw the great meets of the past few years. Every time I trotted the north turn, I passed the low chain-link fence where I'd stood as a sixth-grader and watched Oregon's first sub-4:00 man, Jim Bailey, hurtle by, his spikes making a wonderful gnashing sound on the moist cinders, his expression inward, controlled, alien to the wondering boy. That was where my hunger began. From then on I wanted to run farther, to train more, to consume myself in transforming work, and so, like Bailey, to win.

I felt Bowerman's eyes. I should have avoided this ignominy somehow. I was hardly new to his ways. At North Eugene High, I'd been coached by Bob Newland, who had high-jumped and coached with him. Had it not been for Newland, I doubt that I would have survived to have any confrontations with Bowerman. I never won because I was late in maturing, not breaking five minutes for the mile until my junior year, and because teammates Harlan Andrews and Dave Deubner won successive state 880 and mile championships. Newland gently led me to see the merit of honest effort, of a race being a way to measure my hard-earned progress apart from winning, and so I had endured.

I also knew Bowerman was adamant about enforcing his principles because I was friends with his middle son, Jay. Bill Bowerman knew me as a skinny kid who helped Jay chop Christmas trees from their woods long before I improved enough to get his attention as a runner. That time came in 1962, when I finished fourth in the state meet's mile in 4:23.2, behind Deubner, who ran 4:11 that year, the best high school time in the nation. Bowerman told Dave, a brain, to go to Stanford because it'd be better preparation for medical school later. He invited me to walk on the team at Oregon and got me a terrifying weekend job in a ply-wood mill to pay for my dorm and fees.

My early experience with him actually led some on the team to hope I'd be some kind of liaison to Bowerman, because everyone found him inscrutable. No such luck. Even when he went out of his way to be welcoming, as at the annual team picnic at his house in September, it wasn't safe to relax.

For freshman runners new to the team, the intimidation started with his hill-side view, which spread to the snowy Cascades. Below, the McKenzie River carried fishermen in double-ended boats through spangled light. Beyond lay a soft-edged shire, stretching past farms to the mill town of Springfield and the university in Eugene. We were greeted by the platinum-haired, unexpectedly beautiful Barbara Bowerman, who guided us to tubs of corn, roasts of beef, wheels of pie. The sight closed our throats because standing behind them, mag-nanimously pouring cider, was our new coach.

Bowerman, inhaling the land, seemed in leathery profile to have been through some mythic struggle. He spit when someone called him *coach* because the foot-ball coach he most hated had demanded it. "Just call me Bill," he said, but few would, or could, at first.

We gathered in the living room. The house had no trophies, simply varnished fir beams, high windows, and a tall rock fireplace Bowerman had built himself. There was a woodstove in the kitchen, beside Barbara's spinning wheel, and a wire cage under the deck where Jay kept rattlesnakes for milking.

Bowerman stood. The river and mountain, behind him now, were filtered through Barbara's bonsai and sprays of orchids. This accorded with why we were here. We were to be cultivated, refined. Bowerman was about to ask us to put aside the things of a child. Not by accident did he begin, "*Men* of Oregon...

"Take a primitive organism," he continued, his voice oil and sweet reason, "any weak, pitiful organism. Say a freshman. Make it lift, or jump or run. Let it rest. What happens? A little miracle. It gets a little better. It gets a little stronger or faster or more enduring. That's all training is. Stress. Recover. Improve. You'd think any damn fool could do it, even. . ."

He turned, squinted, went far away somewhere and turned back. "But you don't. You work too hard and rest too little and get hurt. You yield to the temptations of a liberal education and burn your candle at both ends and get mono. Every angelic, lying face I see here is poised to screw up, to overtrain, to fall in love, to flunk out, to play the guitar until three in the morning in the Pioneer Cemetery . . ."

There were hoots. Senior Archie San Romani reddened.

"We have no hard and fast training rules," Bowerman went on. "The vicissitudes of life usually teach an intelligent person what he can handle. It does help to have someone wise in the ways of candles to steady you as you grope toward the light. That would be me.

"But I regret to inform you," he added, his tone not the least regretful, "you cannot just tell somebody what's good for him. He won't listen. He will not listen. First . . . first you have to get his attention."

A few upperclassmen nodded. Bowerman didn't have a central organizing principle. He had this, a central organizing parable.

"Farmer can't get his mule to plow," he said. "Can't even get him to eat or drink. Finally calls in a mule skinner. Guy comes out, doesn't even look at the mule. Goes in the barn, gets a two-by-four and hits the mule as hard as he can between the ears. Mule goes to his knees. Mule skinner hits him again, between the eyes.

"Farmer drags him off. 'That's supposed to get him to plow? That's supposed to get him to drink?'

"'I can see you don't know a damn thing about mules,' says the skinner. 'First you have to get their attention.'"

In the hush that followed, Bowerman's grin was not far from fiendish. This was his allegory, his rationale, his fair warning. He was our mule skinner, and all he would do to us—including booting us from the team to make a point—constituted the two-by-four he would use to crack open our mulish skulls, so that lessons might be inserted.

At the time, of course, I didn't know the details. Leaving that first meeting, I felt only baffled disquiet. Even men who had trained under him for years were edgy. "Bowerman," said Keith Forman, a 3:58.3 miler and a keen psych major, "is ruled by a need to unsettle, to disturb. The man lives to get to you."

And so we freshmen found. That first fall, Bowerman's urges seemed to war with each other. His own competitiveness was barely containable, but anyone racing in cross-country practice found himself working out alone. He affected countrified ways ("You run like a turkey in a plowed field.") but just as often

quoted scripture, the classics, or the *Epic of Gilgamesh*. He was a difficult, digni-
fied professor of kinesiology but cracked up at jokes that began "Two guys were
peeing off a bridge . . . " He raised funds for the Bach Festival, but when a trucker
kept flattening his mailbox, he booby-trapped it to puncture the guy's tires. For
twenty-five years, Oregon freshmen asked each other the same thing: Was Bowerman here to teach us to overcome a cold, hard world? Or was he one of its
coldest, hardest terrors?

In theory, as a coach, he should have been as interested in motivating the lazy
as in mellowing the mad, but he wasn't. He regarded that most frustrating athlete, the gifted but casual, as beyond real help. He would juggle their roommates
to give them an example of ambition but took no further steps to inspire. He
never gave a pep talk. "I'm sorry I can't make them switch brains," he said. "But
I can't."

That left him free to be absorbed by the eager. He examined and reexamined
what we ate. What we wore. What we did (and with whom we did it). He
rethought our gifts, our goals, and the blind spots that kept us from reaching
them. He took a personal interest not only in our roommates but also in our
classes, our jobs, our diet, even our women. Most of us he pushed toward
restraint. That would be hopeless with Dave Wilborn, so he pushed him toward
marrying. Dave went from 4:20 in April to 3:56.2 in June.

And yet, no matter how he permeated our lives, he always kept a kind of
officer-and-troops distance, never trading intimacy for intimacy. The better you
knew him, the less you could let down your guard. He confounded friend and foe
alike because he was completely unreadable.

Bowerman thought of himself as an educator. He scorned recruiting and
almost never gave full scholarships. "Anyone can be taught," he said, "those who
don't expect a handout best of all. I'd sure rather be teaching than blowing smoke
up some spoiled brat's ass."

He loved language and loved it if you loved it, too. When he forced those easy
days on me, I called him a tyrant and he would never let me forget that. Once
when I was too weak to trim some ripple soles he'd glued to my shoes, he took
the shears and felt my hands and called them "philosopher's hands." And later he
came into the sauna and put a big claw on my tender thigh and grinned that
fiendish grin and said, "Now, Kenny, *this* is a horny hand. Feel a truly *horny*
hand." I decline to call that "mentoring."

He didn't believe that a paternal concern for our feelings was his job. Athletes
who'd depended on father-figure high school coaches were always in for a shock.
When we were new, he'd assign a track workout and time us civilly enough yet

ignore us otherwise. Was our form correct? His only answer was to stonily lift his gaze to the swallows in their flight above Hayward Field.

"He speaks to us as does God," said my roommate, Bruce Mortenson. "Intermittently."

Disdainful of the leaden weight and nonexistent cushioning of running shoes in the 1950s, he had taken up cobbling and made us three-ounce spikes that lasted one race. We had no inkling that these were the beginnings of Nike's vast success, but we knew we had better shoes than anyone else. When Bowerman satisfied his academic curiosity about whether middle-aged professors and townspeople might be trained to actually trot a few miles, we had no idea jogging was about to inspire a sea change in American habits and health. But we knew there was only one man who could make both the professors and the mill foremen get out and run. Bowerman held our town together.

His training system rested on the deceptively simple truth that all runners are different. He might forget our names (he was famous for long and sometimes futile pauses when introducing even seniors at the Monday Oregon Club lunches), but he never forgot who strengthened more after intervals and who after long runs, nor whether we showed up fresh and ready for more work the next day or stiff and sour. In the 1950s he'd learned to tailor the nature and intensity of workouts—and especially recoveries—to individual needs and had been rewarded with Bailey's 3:58.6 mile in 1956, the first sub-4:00 on US soil. A steady green line of national champions and Olympians followed, from Otis Davis, the 1960 Olympic 400-meter champion, through Bill Dellinger, the bronze medalist in the 1964 Tokyo Olympics 5000 meters, to Steve Prefontaine, holder of all seven American distance records, from 2000 to 10,000 meters, at the time of his death in 1975. In the sprints, jumps, and throws, Bowerman was just as good. He coached NCAA champions in fifteen of college track's seventeen individual events.

O ur desire to join that lineage was almost demented. I, for one, was so wild to remake myself into a champion that I rolled my eyes at Bowerman's patient studies of our strides and metabolism, and especially his damn easy days. It felt demeaning to just rest. Work was righteous; rest was weak-willed, ignoble.

And so I rammed into a classic paradox. "To run a world record," said Australia's Herb Elliott, world record holder and 1960 Olympic 1500-meter champion, "you have to have the absolute arrogance to think you can run a mile faster than anyone who's ever lived; and then you have to have the absolute humility to actually do it." Elliott was a god to me then. I took him as an example of maniacal effort. But if that sentence urges anything, it urges balance. You must balance the arrogance of your ambition with the humility of your training. If that was a hint to rest more, I ignored it.

Bowerman understood that paradox—the need for both abandoned effort and ironclad control—because it was his own. He told us of being turned from youthful rebellion by Ercel Hedrick, the Medford School Superintendent, who terrified him into channeling his energies. Bowerman knew and loved and distrusted us as he had been known and loved and distrusted himself.

When he talked with us about goals and hopes, he asked us, though never in so many words, to balance the hunger that is in all runners with some grasp of what our predecessors had achieved. The thing was not to blindly disregard limits but to understand the odds, even as one refused to accept them. He asked us, then, to leave open a tiny window of possibility. "If you go out to race," he said, "and know you'll lose, there's no probability involved. You'll lose. But if you go out knowing you will never give up, you'll still lose most of the time, but you'll be in the best position to kick from on that rare day when everything breaks right."

He said that on May 4, 1964, when my three weeks of tyranny were over and he sent me out to run the two-mile in a meet against Oregon State. He said to begin no faster than 4:30 for the first mile and not to chase after their animal, Dale Story, the NCAA cross-country champion, who ran barefoot and was thirty seconds better.

Stripping down, our filmy, Bowerman-designed racing shirts and shorts made me feel battle naked. My sharpened steel spikes sank into the cinders with a gnash that evoked Jim Bailey years before. On the starting line, Story's shirt looked heavy, almost like wool. All of Bill's care in preparing me hit home, and I gave myself over to his plan. I hit 4:30 for the first mile. Story ran 4:19 and led by seventy yards. Bowerman, on the infield, said, "He won't hold it. See what you can do."

I began to gain, and the crowd, Bowerman's crowd, 10,000 strong, saw me coming and got up and called. With half a mile to go, I had no real will left. All control had passed to that thunder that would not let me slow. Into the last turn, Story still had ten yards. Then he looked back, his shoulders tightened, and I experienced for the first time the full savagery of my competitive heart.

I outkicked him by a second in 8:48.1, ripping twenty-seven seconds from my best, finishing in bedlam, crowd and teammates pressing the air out of me, shouting that everything was possible now, the Olympics were possible now.

Bowerman was there with wild blue eyes and a fiendish grin, and I knew what he would say. "See!" he'd crow. "I told you! You just needed rest!"

But he didn't. He whispered in my ear as he had when he strangled me. "Even I didn't think you could run that fast, Kenny," he said. "Even I."

He had given me his subject. I had found myself. It finally began to penetrate my thick skull that I had to rise above the world's fixation with sheer work. I had to attend to my own eccentric physiology. I accepted easy days into my life. I stopped counting miles.

Over the next eight years, the one long run he permitted me every ten days would turn me into the fourth-place finisher in the 1972 Olympic marathon. It was the lesson of my life, and it forces me now to consider—with a shiver— whether anyone besides Bowerman could have gotten through to me.

CHAPTER 1

That Wild Yearning

BOWERMAN MAY WELL HAVE BEEN AN INTROSPECTIVE SOUL, BUT WHO COULD tell? He spent long hours in contented silence, solving a huge range of problems, and he was brutally eloquent when dissecting others' psyches. Yet he kept the process of himself to himself. As Barbara Bowerman would recall, "I can't tell you how frustrating it was to love him and trust him, and know he loved me and trusted me, and still he would never tell me what he was thinking."

To get across what he deemed worth knowing, Bowerman's instrument, blunt or pointed, was the story. So it is to his narrative tales—what they celebrate, what they mock and loathe—that we must look for clues to his character.

In 1983, the editors of *The Wheeler County History* asked him to write about his family's founding of the town of Fossil, his boyhood home and the seat of the smallest, poorest county in Eastern Oregon. Bowerman chose to tell the story of his mother's grandfather, James Washington Chambers, who had grown up in Tennessee.

Along with his parents, Thomas and Letitia, and his four brothers and two sisters, J. W. Chambers lived at The Hermitage, the plantation near Nashville where General Andrew Jackson bred and trained racehorses. Irish-born Letitia Chambers was Jackson's cousin by marriage. The future president and his wife, Rachel, had no children of their own, but they took in family like laundry, turning out one starched, pressed relative after another. Bowerman bled for young J.W., subjected to such bark-bound, puritanical authority: "Being a very much younger brother in a family of Scotch-Irish," Bowerman wrote, "J.W. had plenty of opportunity to vent his rebellion."

In 1828, Andrew Jackson was elected the seventh American president and two years later signed into law the Indian Removal Act of 1830. Henry Clay rightly called the act an eternal stain on the nation's honor, but white settlers cheered and pushed greedily onto tribal lands. By the spring of 1832, the family member hungriest to go was fifteen-year-old J. W. Chambers.

"What took him," Bowerman asked, "on his quest for the new, the romantic, the dangerous, to what became the Oregon Territory?" Bowerman could only guess, but judging by the words he chose, he must have felt the answer in his bones: "A wild yearning for perfect freedom." One day, young J.W. just up and left, saying (as Bowerman loved to tell the tale), "I'm a-headin' West and just takin' ma pony."

The Chambers kid's way with horses found him a place among the voyageurs and trappers who mapped the great routes. Every so often a crumpled letter would get back to his family, describing the fish, game, and topsoil beyond the Rockies. Thomas Chambers who had wanted to cross the plains since he'd read Lewis and Clark's journals couldn't rid his dreams of the bounty his son described. By the early 1840s he had moved his family to Morgan County, Missouri, where they began assembling a wagon train.

In 1844, word of it reached the prodigal son. J.W., then twenty-seven, rode hell-for-leather to Missouri to lead the train, only to find a father who didn't exactly kill the fatted calf in welcome.

Bowerman put it this way: "As mountain men were wont to do when going to rendezvous, J. W. Chambers joined his buddies in a rip-roaring, trail's-end wingding. The head-of-clan Chambers, exercising Puritan logic, 'splained to J.W. that he was not fit enough nor mature enough to lead the train." To test J.W.'s fitness, Thomas asked whether his son's rebellious habits might accept something short of perfect freedom—namely, the settling influence of a wife. As Bowerman often told it, Thomas had someone specific in mind: "Meet the widow Scoggin," Thomas said. "And her five children. Husband died back East. Needs a man."

One can imagine the poleaxed J.W. taking a long look at the widow's fiercely bulging eye and hard-set jaw (she did look like Harry Truman) and growling, "By God, I'll do her." They married in 1844, and the Chambers wagon train departed on April 1, 1845, with J.W. riding scout beside his father. And J.W. did her well, for eight months and three weeks later, on the banks of the Willamette, Mary Greene Scoggin Chambers would give birth to Bill Bowerman's grandmother, Mary Jane.

But first they had to cross two-thirds of a continent. Half a million people traversed the Oregon Trail between 1842 and 1860, a number so vast as to suggest it wasn't all that hard. But it was bitterly hard. Men, women, children, animals, and wagons had to cover ten to fifteen miles a day for eight months or risk having a mountain pass named for them because they froze in it, like the Donners. One in ten died—50,000 in all—far more of them from cholera and accident than at the hands of Indians.

Almost all those who traveled the Oregon Trail were on the only trip of their lives. They'd sold their farms to outfit their wagons and teams. If they made it to the valley of the Willamette, a married couple was entitled to 640 acres, but meanwhile, that acreage existed only in the haze of carnival-barker promises. The land and friends they'd left behind were heartbreakingly real. It was, as one historian put it, "the experience of giving all to gain all."

It was a defining ordeal, a winnowing out of the nonindustrious, the nonenduring, the inflexible, the uncooperative. Those who completed the cross-country journey found that it concentrated traits in their new society that would last as long as the wagon tracks themselves, still plain to see today through the sage near Baker City in Eastern Oregon. If Bowerman was stubbornly ingenious, if Bowerman loved to tell a story, if Bowerman gloried in Oregon's vistas and fertility, well, Bowerman was pioneer stock and had a right to cackle, as he did, that "The cowards never started and the weak died along the way."

The 2,000-mile trek took the Chambers family seven months. On October 15, 1845, their train reached The Dalles, on the Columbia. They were less than a hundred miles from the mouth of the Willamette, but the way was blocked. The basalt cliffs where the Columbia Gorge slices through the Cascades north of Mt. Hood were impassable by wagon, and no flatboats were to be found. The family made their winter quarters about two miles from the Methodist Mission.

After they had built huts and corrals, Thomas Chambers led an advance party, including J.W. and his gravid wife, Mary, downriver by boat to find their promised land. They selected loamy pastures on the Tualatin River, a tributary of the Willamette, near what would become Hillsboro. They filed Donation Land Claim #41 at the new capital, Oregon City, and it was there, on December 22, 1845, that Mary Jane Chambers was born.

That winter, J.W. built the first flat-bottomed boat to make it through the Columbia rapids known as Cascade Falls and carried the families' wagons and belongings in a complicated series of ferryings and portages down the Columbia and up the Willamette to their 642-acre homestead on the Tualatin.

Western Oregon kept its promise. The grass stayed green all winter. The Chamberses were disoriented by the sight of their cows standing fat in the pastures in February. Once the weather cleared in June, the skies were cloudless until October. The Indians had used fire to keep much of the valley in grassland. The settlers' fields produced so much wheat it was soon being used as a means of exchange. They had given all. They had gained all. They were home.

Not that much peace crept upon the mind of J. W. Chambers.

In the Willamette Valley, the Chambers family had come to a place with California summers and English winters. The rivers coiling past mistletoe-clotted oaks and dark, befirred hills were swollen by five months of cold rain. The bone-chilling wet that drove Lewis and Clark to clinical depression on the Oregon coast did the same for J.W. He called the Tualatin area a "swamp" and often rode out looking to find better. Indeed, his father, Thomas, and several family members moved to Puget Sound in Washington.

But the "settling influence," as Bowerman put it, of J.W.'s wife and, eventually, seven children "partially took." For fifteen years, J.W. built warm, dry log homes and barns, helped his neighbors thresh their wheat, and reined in his wanderlust. He made a trip to the gold fields but didn't stay, returning home instead to raise and race his beloved horses. And he used the profits from the farm to order up a spectacular symbol of making it to the new land without sacrificing the refinement of the old: a grand piano for each of his daughters. "They were shipped around Cape Horn before the Panama Canal was built," wrote J.W.'s great-granddaughter Patricia Hoover Frank in 1983. "The girls learned to play them at school. Mary Jane played quite well and sang very well too. She often entertained overnight travelers or guests." (According to Barbara Bowerman, "There's a story that one of J.W.'s horses, named Foster, won $30,000 in a race. I don't know if that's apocryphal, but it would have financed the pianos and considerably more.")

In 1864, when Mary Jane was eighteen, she accepted the hand of Thomas Benton Hoover, who had been five when he traveled the Trail with his parents in 1844. A photograph from that time shows Mary Jane to be comely and clear-eyed. Many desired her, even to a deranging degree. "The first night in their own home, one of Mary Jane's former suitors set the cabin on fire," wrote Mary Jane's great-granddaughter, Georgia Lee Hoover Stiles. "Obviously they got out, for we are all here."

Barely. They lost all their belongings—except for the piano, which Tom and Mary Jane somehow managed to drag from the cabin to safety.

By 1869, the Hoovers had two children, Annie and Will. One day J.W., whom they hadn't seen in a year, burst in and shouted, "Finally, finally, Eden is at hand!" They had heard this before.

"Horses were J.W.'s life and cattle his cash reward," wrote Bowerman. "His restless spirit was always taking him back across the Cascades." On this trip he'd explored the canyons of a river flowing out of the Blue Mountains. The river was named the John Day, for a hapless man who had been captured and tortured by Indians, escaping with his life but without his sanity.

It was a cautionary tale, but one totally lost on the old mountain man J.W., now in his early fifties. He rode up the John Day with an Indian friend in 1868, returned in 1869, convened a family council, and said he'd seen over a million acres of rich, black loam and rolling hills. There were lush meadows, virgin timber, abundant springs and creeks. Bowerman liked the line in J.W.'s report that made for an equine heaven: "Shoulder-high in meadow grass, knee-high in bunch grass." Bunch grass endures after meadow hay has frozen. If your hills have clumpy, silvery bunch grass, your stock can last out any winter.

J.W. had surveyed some ranch-sized claims and ridden for home. Now he asked, who would come across and live with him in a land of milk and honey? The look upon the face of his wife, the formidable Mary Greene Scoggin Chambers, is lost to history, but her reaction isn't: She declined the invitation. "His wife," as Bowerman put it, "figured winning one wilderness home was enough."

But J.W. talked his daughter Mary Jane, her husband, Tom, stepson Woodson Scoggin, and horse-raising partner William Bigham into joining him in peopling the spreads he'd claimed.

Their 1870 trek, with covered wagons and livestock, first by boat to The Dalles and then into the interior on Indian trails, took almost three months, lengthened by their lugging along Mary Jane's piano. One wonders, as Bowerman did about J.W. fleeing westward at age fifteen, what made Mary Jane at twenty-four, her children four and two, so uproot her life. If their Tualatin farm was prosperous, it was also by then routine. The family yearning for freedom must have surged in her, too. She was her father's daughter.

They arrived at a crystal stream in a bowl of greening, juniper-dotted hills on April 26, 1870, named it Hoover Creek, and quickly built four log cabins with floors of whipsawed planks. They turned their animals out into the meadows and planted cottonwoods. From a white cliff, they cut slabs of soft rock that hardened in the air and let them make a fireplace in every dwelling. The mud-caulked cabins (all but one with openings for rifle barrels in case of an Indian attack that never came) were snug, durable, and had room for the piano.

J.W. wrote in his diary, "This is truly the promised land."

Sometimes the price of perfect freedom is perfect isolation. Mary Jane wouldn't see another woman settler for two years. When a husband and wife driving their hogs to market sought refuge at Hoover Creek, Stiles continued, "The two women on seeing each other broke down and cried, as they were so starved for friendship. They stayed up all night talking."

Tom Hoover petitioned for and won a road from The Dalles and settlers filtered in. In 1876, Tom and Mary Jane were sworn in as the area's first postmaster and -mistress and opened an office on their ranch. But what to call it? In their choice, they linked their lonely outpost with concerns greater than bunch grass and hogs. They seem, now and forever, thoroughly modern.

Not long after they had settled in, they'd heard a rumbling and had run out to see dust rising from the base of a ridge. Tom rode over and found that a landslide had exposed large bones that looked like nothing he'd ever seen. He sent word to a friend, Thomas Condon, who was becoming an eminent geologist. Condon came, looked, was stumped, and packed some off to New York. Eventually the bones proved to be ossified camels and elephants from the Tertiary period, some 60 million years before. Fascinated by the petrified remains and cutting-edge science, the Hoovers named their post office, and later the town, Fossil.

The connection with Condon was possible because the Chamberses and Hoovers honored learning in a way unusual in such a speck of a frontier town. Each generation of Fossil families sent many of its young away to good colleges. After seeing the wider world, a healthy number returned to keep the ranches thriving. Much of the land today remains in the hands of the original families.

Was J. W. Chambers, the cause of all the uprooting, satisfied with his new life? It's hard to know. A photo of J.W. in his thirties shows an unfurrowed brow and a coarse, dark beard that can't obscure eyes and mouth brimming with wit. In another image, taken some twenty years later, the beard is white-streaked, the mouth rigid, and the eyes squint beneath a ridge of worry. The photos seem to be of different men.

Twenty years on horseback will do that. But Chambers might also have been worn down by his failure to reunite his family. "Only once did J.W.'s wife come to Fossil country," wrote Bowerman, and the opinion she recorded in her diary read, "A more godforsaken place does not exist on this earth." She returned to the Tualatin Valley, where she died in 1890, at the age of eighty.

But Fossil grew. It grew because Tom and Mary Jane filled it with seven children: After Annie and Will came Hattie, Mary, Lizzie, Maud, and Thomas Jr., the last born in 1886 when Mary Jane was forty. From 1879 to 1883 they lived in The Dalles so the kids could attend a better school. But then they returned to Fossil, built a two-story house (it took seven men to get Mary Jane's grand piano into their upstairs bedroom), and never left again.

Tom started the town's first store and was elected mayor, justice of the peace, and county commissioner. "He gave a great deal to encourage the young people in the pursuit of healthful sports," the *Fossil Journal* would write. "While not a churchman, he helped in a substantial way to build every church in town. But the organization he loved more than any other was the Fossil Band, which he helped start in 1885 and of which he has ever since been an enthusiastic member."

Fossil flourished, but for years it had no doctor. Instead it had Mary Jane Hoover. She delivered babies, set broken limbs, treated burns, sewed gashes, and pulled teeth. "My favorite story, told to me by my grandfather Will," recalled Stiles, "had to do with a tooth extraction. She pulled the tooth all right and then cauterized the gum with a white-hot nail."

It's hard not to see in both Tom and Mary Jane the templates for Bill Bowerman. Bill would have Tom's openness to his community's calls, the same musicality, the same ecumenical approach to matters of faith, never letting religion's doctrine interfere with religion's comfort. Like Mary Jane, he'd be good at adapting simple tools to sophisticated uses, especially in the healing arts.

All the Hoover children had a vigor equal to the demands of ranch life. "Today we would refer to those girls as movers and shakers," wrote Stiles. "The boys were gentle and soft-spoken. When they all left the ranch each morning for the one-room schoolhouse on the Busby place, astride their favorite horses, their father would tell them not to run the horses. And just as soon as he was out of sight one of the girls would shout 'GO' and it was a horse race."

Tom Hoover's fear was only natural, because his father-in-law, still horse-besotted at fifty-nine, was killed by one. While racing with Indian friends, J.W. was thrown, suffered a broken neck, and died on July 11, 1877. He was buried on a westward-facing slope above the ranch where Tom and Mary Jane would raise their family. Bowerman, writing of his favorite ancestor's departure, wished tranquility on J.W.'s restless spirit and deemed it "fulfilling that, having ridden into the western sunset at age fifteen, he should close his book of life on his last ride."

Tom and Mary Jane bore up and went on after J.W.'s death. Their fourth daughter, Elizabeth, was born on September 21, 1878, and so missed knowing her grandfather by fourteen months. Lizzie, as all would call her, would grow into the most beautiful and headstrong of the gallopers to school.

Over the years, Mary Jane became smaller, wirier. Tom grew more florid. In a midlife photo, she is trim, her mouth straight and intelligent. Her liquid eyes have the power of an osprey's, but their focus is inward, as if she is saddened by what she has seen, or is about to see. Perhaps the picture was taken after January 19, 1896, when she awoke to find Tom dying of what news accounts called "apoplexy" but was surely a stroke. He was fifty-six.

The Condon Times's obituary needed a full page to list all that Tom had done and been and founded and named. "The burial ceremony was beautiful in the extreme," it said, "and visibly affected the great concourse of friends who were present." The funeral oration was delivered by Judge H. H. Hendricks, a brother Knight of Pythias. "Our brother belonged to no church," said Hendricks, who risked a little heresy in the Methodist-heavy town. "He professed no creed, but he had a faith in Him whose guiding hand is felt though unseen. To do good and be true, was his religion and there needs no other."

Lizzie Hoover was seventeen. She fought down as much of her own grief as she could to help her mother deal with the crush of the community's condolences and to console her sister, Maud, thirteen, and brother, Tom, ten.

Lizzie was a natural at both empathy and reaching out to hold her family close. Her spirits usually were so irrepressible that she seemed to physically vibrate with them. "I'll always remember Lizzie's hum, then chuckle, then hum," wrote Stiles. The deductive reader, knowing that one of Mary Jane's daughters will become Bill Bowerman's mother, may safely presume her to be Lizzie.

CHAPTER 2

Lizzie and the Governor

IN 1897, LIZZIE HOOVER FOLLOWED HER SISTER MARY TO OREGON AGRICULTURE College (now Oregon State University) in Corvallis. She threw herself into her classes, in part because she loved them, in part because she disdained the idea of going to college to find a man. "Her husbandry studies," Bill Bowerman would say, "were strictly animal." She fought off homesickness in a way her sports-loving father would have approved, by starring on the Beavers' women's Pacific Conference championship basketball team.

Lizzie took her degree in 1901 and returned to Fossil a strong, confident young woman whose next step was to find a man of substance who shared her ardor for the land and understood how inseparable she was from the burgeoning Hoover clan. So Lizzie took a back pew in the Methodist Church, studied the availables, and was unimpressed.

But soon someone mentioned a young lawyer up in Condon who was making something of a name for himself. William Jay Bowerman Sr. was born in Hesper, Winnesheik County, Iowa, on August 15, 1876, the oldest son of Daniel and Lydia Bowerman. The family came west when he was sixteen, in 1893—not by wagon but by the Canadian Pacific Railway—settling in Marion County in the central Willamette Valley.

Jay, as he was always known, was effortlessly quick, surged with ambition, and saw youth as no barrier. He whipped through Willamette University and took a law degree at twenty, before he was old enough to be admitted to the bar. He did farm work until he had aged enough to hang out his shingle in 1897 in Salem with John McCourt, a future Oregon Supreme Court justice. A year later, Jay enlisted in the Army, served in the short-lived Spanish-American War, and mustered out determined to live east of the Cascades.

In 1899, at twenty-three, he moved to Condon, about twenty miles north of Fossil. (The town had no connection with Thomas Condon, but would be the boy-hood home of double-Nobel Prize winner Linus Pauling.) Within five years, Jay was enjoying a lucrative law practice, owned a 560-acre farm planted in wheat and barley, was brokering vast real estate deals, and was running for the state legislature. A photo from that time is striking for the expressionless poise of his face and for eyes so observant they seem to follow one's every move. Jay's younger sister Mary, equally exceptional, took her M.D. from Willamette in 1903, moved to Condon too, and became the first female doctor in Eastern Oregon.

The juicy details are lost, but it couldn't have taken Jay long to meet tall, athletic, clear-eyed, crooked-nosed Elizabeth Hoover after her return to Fossil. All who knew him had to be astounded by how young Jay was. At twenty-five, only two years older than Lizzie, he'd achieved riches and renown. If Lizzie hummed with energy, Jay Bowerman's alpha-male presence more than matched it. He had a farm and a law practice. The legislature beckoned.

Lizzie found that she had a charismatic suitor. "Jay Bowerman," recalled attorney Jim Castle, who would work with him in later years, "was a very handsome man. You would introduce someone to him and he had the faculty of saying the right complimentary thing and thereafter it was the most colorful talk you ever heard." ("Colorful," in the parlance of the day, meant "suggestive.") Jay and Lizzie married in a rush in Fossil in 1903 and set up housekeeping in an imposing dwelling in Condon. There was no grand wedding trip because Jay had clients to serve and an election coming up. Their first child, Daniel Hoover Bowerman, was born January 21, 1906, in Condon. Mary Elizabeth (Beth) Bowerman would follow on February 26, 1908.

Jay pronounced himself the world's happiest man. Lizzie, as she had known she would, loved being a mother. She would have preferred to live in Fossil, within the bosom of the Hoover family, but the sheer joy of her babies made her content in nearby Condon.

And Condon was where Jay was going places. At twenty-eight, in 1904, he was elected to the State Senate as a Republican and began a precipitous rise in that body, which met at the capitol in Salem, far across the Cascades. A Mr. Hofer, whom Jay trounced in a primary, told the *Condon Times*: "To Jay Bowerman, life is real, life is earnest. As a poor boy in Marion County, he was not hunting soft clerical jobs. He mauled rails and hauled cordwood for a living. He has hands and arms and a physique developed by hard labor. When he talks to a campaign audience, he strikes telling blows straight from the shoulder. In the legislature, he was always dead in earnest for or against a proposition."

At age thirty-two, in 1909, Jay was elected president of the State Senate. None of this was handed to him on a tea tray. In fact, Jay had ferocious enemies to the south, in the town founded by his in-laws.

The differences between Condon and Fossil ranged from the geologic to the financial to the moral. Condon was surrounded by vistas of rippling wheat. Its grain elevators creaked with money. The masthead of the *Condon Globe* read "Condon: Largest Primary Grain Shipping Point in The United States." Fossil, tucked among its buttes and creeks, was really suited only to growing hay, subsistence farming, and grazing. So Condon was the seat of prosperous Gilliam County and Fossil the seat of hardscrabble Wheeler County.

Acrimony was fanned, as it so often is, by the hot breath of distilled spirits. Condon was not averse to a saloon. Fossil was intemperately for "temperance," voting that no rum should pass its lips. Every Oregon city and county battled in those years over whether to be wet or dry.

It was inevitable that Jay, a Condon wheat man, an attorney, a live-and-let-drink man, would be felt by many citizens of Fossil to be in league with the devil in all his guises. One accuser was James Stewart, editor of the *Fossil Journal*. On March 20, 1908, Stewart reported hearsay from a Mr. Searcy that Senator Bowerman had received the sum of $600 from the saloons of Condon for amending that city's charter in such a way that if Gilliam County voted to go dry, the town would stay wet.

However, as reported in the loyal *Condon Times*, the facts were these: Three years before, Jay Bowerman had been asked to draft the city's new charter. He had done so. It was amended and approved by all of Condon's citizens at a "mass meeting" and passed by the legislature exactly as amended, without a jot of Bowerman hanky-panky. Besides, every town's charter had a clause like that, even Fossil's.

Finally, Searcy, who'd started the whole fuss, filed an affidavit with the *Condon Times* swearing that he had said nothing about Bowerman receiving any $600 for anything. The charges against Jay were amply rebutted, but he was not a man to suffer accusation coolly, or at all. His "dead-in-earnest, for-or-against" temperament moved him to overkill.

On April 11, 1908, the *Condon Globe* (yes, the little town supported two argumentative papers) reported that "District Attorney A. J. Collier filed an . . . indictment, against James Stewart of the *Fossil Journal* for criminal libel alleged to have been committed against Jay Bowerman, [Collier's] political boss and benefactor. A bond of $1500 has been fixed by Judge Littlefield."

The parties met in court two weeks later in Fossil. The *Condon Times* reported that the case was continued "over vigorous protest from Senator Bowerman who requested immediate trial," adding snidely that Stewart had gotten the continuance "on the grounds that he had no evidence to back up his charges and where he is going to get such evidence in a month from now, or in six months from now is an open question."

What seems to have happened—since this was right before the 1908 Senate election, which Jay won—is that Jay settled for an apology and dropped the case. In subsequent elections, Jay's opponents didn't raise the topic of the incident against him. Apparently it wasn't felt to be especially high-handed in the rough-and-tumble civic discourse of Eastern Oregon, the cultural compost upon which Bill Bowerman's forebears flourished. (Indeed, Bill would inherit not only his father's eyes, but also something of his reflexive urge to sue.)

In 1909, Oregon Governor George E. Chamberlain resigned to take office as a newly elected US Senator. He was replaced as governor by Secretary of State Frank Benson who then fell deathly ill. Next in line for the governorship was the president of the State Senate, William Jay Bowerman Sr., who became the youngest man—at thirty-three years and ten months—ever to sit in the governor's chair.

For seven months, from June 17, 1910, to January 8, 1911, Jay ruled as if born to the job. Despite being essentially a caretaker, he chose the site of a big state hospital and developed a list of seven proposals for when he ran for election in his own right. Most of these were basic needs of the time, such as creating a state highway department and a central accounting system, but one was intriguing in that it might not be put forward by a twenty-first-century Republican. It was an employers' liability act, to provide, in case of injury on the job, "for prompt and complete compensation to the employee without cost to him." Jay was one of a classic Oregon breed, a moderate Republican, who well remembered his summers mauling rails.

The acting governorship allowed Jay to expand his interests and contacts statewide. So, in early 1911, he moved the family and his law practice to Oregon's largest city, Portland, to become partner in the firm of Fulton and Bowerman.

Lizzie, hugely pregnant at the time, wasn't exactly overjoyed by the move. She had never cared much for living in rented apartments in Salem when the legislature was in session (carousing legislators seemed wicked to her), and no Portland town house could equal the Hoover ranch back in Fossil. But she'd made a sacred promise to help her husband and she was sticking to it. She would cheerfully throw fine Sunday dinners for visiting politicos and be gracious to all, whether statesman or hack. This would take a certain self-discipline, but she was equal to that. The pioneer principle was that everyone pulls his or her weight. That's what's meant by character.

Thus it was that the birth of their twins, Thomas Benton Bowerman and William Jay Bowerman Jr., who arrived in Portland on February 19, 1911, flooded her with reassurance. The twins would be a perfect distraction from the world of logrolling and speechifying and plotting campaigns. The twins would be a worthy mother's parallel to Jay's success.

I n the fall of 1910, Acting Governor Jay Bowerman ran for the governorship against Oswald West, a Democrat from Astoria, whom Jay had known since they were stripling lawyers in Salem in 1897. After receiving the Republican nomination, Jay returned to Condon and a rapturous welcome. "As the train pulled into the station," said the *Condon Times*, "the racket was deafening. Mr. Bowerman, accompanied by his mother and Mrs. Bowerman, was driven down Main Street, being lustily cheered as the big car passed each corner."

In later life, West (who is honored in Oregon for abolishing the death penalty and preserving the state's coastline by declaring the beaches highways) would say the policy differences between the candidates amounted to little more than West being a smoker and Jay a chewer. But the *Condon Times* of November 5, 1910, evoking Eastern Oregon's belief that to the rest of the state it might as well be Manitoba, commanded its readers: "Go to the polls and cast your vote for the man from the wheat fields and bunch grass. Mr. Bowerman is a man of ability, a man of brains and an American. Mr. West is a light weight, a man chosen by a political machine and a Canadian. Which do you want?"

Jay carried the East but West won the race by about 3,000 votes. West would say, "Turned out there were a few more smokers than chewers" and go on to adopt almost all of Jay's proposed improvements.

The *Condon Times* was crushed, noting, "The defeat of the head of the Republican party was a complete surprise, not only to the Republicans, but to the Democrats themselves. Practically all the rest of the Republican ticket was elected."

The paper knew why Jay had lost, but could hardly mention it in that unforgiving era. West's victory was due to rumors that Jay was divorcing Lizzie.

Over the years, Jay had grown close to his young aide in the Senate, Wayfe Hockett, the daughter of a Grants Pass banker. Jay taught her the law and she passed the bar on the strength of his lessons. Lizzie was spending more and more time at home. "So the love match was made sitting there in the legislature," Barbara Bowerman would say, not unkindly, many years later. "When his wife didn't want to be there, here was someone who adored him."

Jay and Wayfe were so open about their affection that when he was elevated to the acting governorship, judiciary officials had asked Wayfe, not Lizzie, to accompany him to the swearing-in ceremony. Wayfe had declined because Jay had not yet obtained his divorce, and wouldn't until 1913. But so many knew the truth that a whispering campaign by the Democratic machine was lethal. "It was the dirtiest election," Wayfe told Barbara long afterward.

Lizzie didn't contest the divorce, but her resentment would not abate. She knew she'd kept her end of the deal, had sacrificed her wishes to his ambition. In return, she felt that Jay, that congenital luster after power and ownership and pleasure, had cared to sacrifice nothing. For the rest of her life, when Lizzie spoke of the split or of Jay's betrayal, it was always in terms of deceit, as in "That man never told the truth in his life."

Jay married Wayfe on November 3, 1914. They were a far better match, and would prove it by living a long, faithful life together in Portland and bringing up two daughters of achievement, Jane and Sally. He had, of course, sacrificed a great deal for his love. For the rest of his life he would be called "Governor" and judges and attorneys would leap to accommodate his wishes. But his career in elective office was over. He would wield remarkable influence, but it would be from behind the scenes.

Among a broad-minded populace in a more tolerant age, mere divorce wouldn't have destroyed a man's ability to ask for its votes. But this was Oregon in 1913. The lessons of the wagon trains were still fresh, and they were all about morals. Having faced death many times on the Trail, the first settlers were people of tremendous religious faith who raised their families accordingly. As Barbara Bowerman would put it, "The Hoovers were all Methodists. The schools were started by the churches and set the codes for society. Divorce was considered as bad as fornication."

So Oregon would not forgive Jay's breaking of faith. "Wayfe and Jay were haunted by guilt all their lives," said Barbara, who came closest to being an objective observer and would grow to care a great deal for Wayfe Hockett Bowerman.

Both sides of the family took the divorce hard. Long years later, a gaggle of Hoovers was dining at the University Club in Portland when the Jay Bowerman family came in. The whole Hoover family got up and left.

Since society went easier on a clearly wronged woman, Lizzie might well have gone home, grieved, and (in the manner of her grandmother, the widow Scoggin) found a man content to bring forth calves and children. However, as they were negotiating the divorce settlement, Jay had the gall to suggest that Lizzie might be the wayward one and wondered whether the twins were even his. And then something happened to make even that wretchedness seem little more than playground babble.

Lizzie had taken seven-year-old Dan, five-year-old Beth, and the twins to live in a Portland apartment building. Because little Tommy and Bill were well and truly into their terrible twos, Lizzie hired a nurse to help out. One morning, the nurse dressed the twins and took them for a walk. The elevator had wrought-iron accordion doors and an open grille through which passing floors were visible. When the elevator started down, Tommy's clothes or arm got caught on something outside the car's grating. In front of Bill and the screaming nurse, the little boy was pulled up and crushed against the edge of the compartment's iron ceiling. He died later that day.

As an adult, Bill Bowerman would have no memory of the accident. Nor did he seem to his aunts or uncles to have been marked by it. His wife was less convinced. "I've always wondered how it affected him, psychologically, seeing that," Barbara would say in a tone that was almost academic. Yet her next words would reveal her true horror: "Can you imagine how it affected that distraught woman, whose husband was already shaming her and leaving her? I cannot!"

Tommy's death made Lizzie cleave to her remaining children as few mothers have. She snatched them up, went back to Fossil, and, everlastingly embittered by abandonment and loss, raised them without the help of a man ever again.

The two-year-old Bill was imprinted with his mother's judgment. If his father had just kept his promise and taken care of his family, the accident would never have happened. Bill's twin, little Tommy, would have been alive to play with, to grow up with. On some deep, emotional level, Bill Bowerman may well have believed his father a murderer.

Barbara mused upon all these things for years and developed a theory. "Bill's inner conflict, wherever it came from, had to do with being uneasy about being a man. Like his whole family on his mother's side, he was ashamed of his father. As he grew and began to be prideful about his own manliness, it ran right into his mother's hatred of that very thing. She taught him that you beware of men. All men. They'll betray you. Maybe he became ashamed of his own masculinity. Bill never even spoke about it until after we got married—the divorce or his dying twin or his mother's trauma, or even that his father had just been governor when it all happened. Of course he was too young to remember any of it. But also, it was something you didn't discuss in that family. Talk about your deep, dark secret."

Lizzie was thirty-five and would earn her living by teaching. For that, she had to go back to Oregon State for her master's degree. Leaving the kids in Fossil with her younger sister, Maud, who'd married Weaver Edwards, she enrolled in Corvallis in late 1914. The Edwardses had no children of their own and Maud doted on Bill, but however splendidly her children were being cared for, Lizzie could not endure being apart from them.

So she soon brought them all to her. Her brother Will loaned Lizzie his own daughter to help out. "I was seventeen and I babysat the kids while Lizzie went to college," Dot Hoover Miller recalled many years later. "And then I went to Corvallis High School. I had a lot of fun. But Aunt Lizzie hated men. She hated men. She'd turned against them, every single one. Later, she'd never let Beth have a boyfriend. Poor Beth. She could have had a life, but she always had to live with her mother."

Lizzie—who exempted male family and friends from her disdain—wouldn't leave her kids, not then, not ever. If one child needed to go somewhere, the whole family went. She taught school in Fossil until Dan was in high school, then moved the family to Ashland because the schools offered a wider choice of subjects. They would go on to Seattle so Dan could attend the University of Washington's Journalism School, to Medford for Dan's first newspaper job, and to Eugene, so Bill could graduate from the University of Oregon while still living with his mother.

But that was far in the future. First, Lizzie took her master's in home economics in 1916 and the family returned to Fossil. Bill was five. Lizzie's brother Will had taken over the original ranch and other siblings had homes and families nearby. Lizzie and her kids lived in those houses, among those myriad relations, and young Bill started school. On his first day of first grade, the teacher asked, "Can you write your name?" Bill cried, "That's what I came here to *learn*!"—an early warning that he meant to go through life on his own terms.

CHAPTER 3

Wild Bill Meets a Mule Skinner

DURING HIS EARLY CHILDHOOD, BILL'S LIFE CENTERED ON THE HOMESTEADS. All the families had houses in town, where the mothers lived with their kids during school. Come summer they'd move out and work on the ranches, setting up big tents for the overflow.

"When we returned, years later," Barbara Bowerman would recall, "Bill's Fossil wasn't the little town. It was the original ranch of his grandparents' on Hoover Creek, eight miles away, where he carried water to the hay crews with a mule and slept under the stars."

At times, the boy Bill ran wild among the lava-topped buttes and pinewoods, as rebellious as only a fatherless child can be. Driving through the area in later years, Bowerman would point out to visitors some cramped little cave he'd spent the night in after running away from home. There were a lot of those caves. He seemed to imply that he was so fired by his own wild yearnings, so temper torn, that obedience had been impossible. But make the slightest suggestion that he might've been an unhappy child and he'd narrow his eyes and say, "Just the opposite." He didn't flee because he was miserable. He ran because he could get away with it.

Fossil has changed so little that one may stroll up Main, pass the Mercantile general store, its exterior unaltered, and retrace Bill's footsteps. After exploding from his fourth-grade classroom and the stucco grade school, he played workup with kids from the large Kelsey and Steiwer families on the weedy softball field that abuts the thirty-degree hillside at the town's eastern boundary. Behind the backstop, he worked beige claystone rocks from the crumbling gumbo and whacked them open to reveal 10,000-year-old leaves and ferns. People still do. This is the only Oregon fossil bed where one may remove specimens. (The hill is huge and has yielded only leaves—so far.)

Bill, born ravenous, would have bolted at the faintest call to dinner and raced down the hill. He'd have whooped past Uncle Will's white frame house on Main Street and skidded into the yard of whichever Hoover place Lizzie and her kids were occupying that year. Bill's appetite was mythic. Decades later, writing for the *Wheeler County History* magazine, Bill's son Jon told a story about his dad. "When Lizzie's children were small," Jon wrote, "some friends had gone to the Columbia River and speared a bunch of salmon. They had several on the table for Sunday dinner and while heads were bowed to say Grace, Bill stood up in his chair with a knife and interrupted the prayer by announcing, 'I'm gonna spear me a salmon.'" The reaction from the grownups was not surprising. "It was some time before young Bill could sit with his full weight let down," Jon wrote, but his fascination with impaling a big fish was undiminished. A few days later Bill called from in front of the house for his mother to come watch him spear a salmon. "Lizzie was busy inside," Jon wrote, "but her son was so insistent that she finally went out and found him teasing a rattlesnake with a willow branch."

On Sundays, Lizzie required Methodist rear ends to be on hard, oak Methodist pews. Bill would be squirming by the doxology, but leaped to add his voice to hymns. He attended well enough to the sermon if the preacher used a few barnyard similes. But readings from the King James Bible, when the strange power of the Psalms and Prophets poured over the congregation, left him open-mouthed with awe.

Patience for the young Bill's pranks ran deep. Fossil knew what Jay Bowerman had done to Lizzie and her children. It was hardly compensation for the ache of being fatherless, but the community spread a safety net under the three Bowerman kids. Lizzie had unlimited support in the hard things, the life and death things, so wild little Bill's antics were accorded some rolling of the eyes and clucking when a child of their own might have gotten the strap. "I was a shirttail cousin to everybody in that town," Bill often said with an amazement that never seemed to fade. He had no father, but he had a family. He had a huge family. He had a town of his own, eight blocks square.

Not that his grandmother cut him any slack. Bill knew her as an amazingly strong and observant woman. When he was eleven and Mary Jane Hoover was seventy-six, she asked him where he was going with that gunnysack.

"To pick apples with Ed," said Bill, ducking and trying for the door.

Knowing that not one tree in the neighborhood was ripe, Mary Jane acted, as we've come to say, preemptively. When Bill's partner in green apple theft, Ed Kelsey (who would one day be county sheriff), peeked in the window, there was Bill trussed to a kitchen chair with dishtowels. "That little bit of a woman hog-tied me!" Bowerman would recall proudly.

His mother was tough, too. One story passed down through the family told of Lizzie and the kids traveling by stagecoach from Fossil to Condon one winter. The stage was late due to heavy snow so, on a ridge called the Devil's Backbone, where the wind had swept the road clean, the driver tried to make up time despite a drop-off on one side. The frightened kids began screaming. The driver shouted down from the box, "Shut those goddamn kids up, they're spooking my horses." Lizzie hollered back at him, "Slow down those goddamn horses, they're scaring my kids!" As Jon Bowerman would write, "Lizzie could sit at a table with heads of state and diplomats and know which fork to use and how to talk to whom. But she could just as easily put a recalcitrant teamster in his place. She raised her kids the same way."

Wherever Lizzie and the children lived after their years in Fossil, they came back for the summer harvests. Throughout high school and college, Bill leapt at every chance to return. It wasn't that he romanticized farming. "A horse to him was hard, hot work," Barbara would say. "Bill had to pitch hay, and underneath those stacks they would find four or five rattlesnakes, so they kept their boots on. It was hot in summertime. But he gloried in that. The harvest was communal, the people going from one ranch to another, and he loved telling of the amounts of food, served 'promptly' at noon. When the whistle blew, crews came in, washed their faces in horse troughs and sat down to huge meals. Whenever, in later life, I placed before him a plate of food that seemed too much, he'd say, 'Trying to feed me like a hay crew?'"

Gradually the hard life of Fossil would turn Mary Jane Hoover into the image of Abe Lincoln. But it took eighty-nine years to kill her. She would live until 1934, when Bill was a year out of college. Indeed, Bowerman was reared by such strong women that one can search for a dynamic man in the mix and find none to compare. His favorite uncle was Will Hoover, who managed both the ranch and the Mercantile general store. But Will was more benefactor than disciplinarian. According to Mary Jane's great-granddaughter, Georgia Lee Hoover Stiles, "All Tom and Mary Jane's children went to college except the first, Will. He became the solid rock you hear about that looked after his widowed mother, trying to keep the ranch going and providing aid and comfort to his sisters and their children. You will be surprised how many lives he touched and how many today carry Will's first name through the generations, whether their last names are Steiwer, Bowerman, or Hoover."

Tom and Mary Jane had only two sons, Tom and Will, so the family tree is hung with Williams and Toms, Toms and Williams, twig after twig, limb after limb. Some Chambers/Hoover/Bowerman qualities come down the generations with eerie exactitude. Bill's three sons all fix the world with their grandfather's voracious gaze. Hold a photo of Lizzie at twenty next to Jon's elder daughter, also named Elizabeth, and people will swear they're not looking at resemblance but identity. There is that yearning gene that causes, when adolescence attacks, a fury to flee.

These are eccentricities, oddities that run through every clan. If the family serves as an object lesson, it is in its ability to jerk on its boots and buck 100-pound hay bales or break a bronc and then take a bath and make a beef bourguignonne and play the banjo and read a book and clean a fossil and teach the kids to do the same. To attain that Jeffersonian range is not just to be heir to Mary Jane and her grand piano. It is to prove that there is no necessary center of the world, no real need for New York or London or Paris. The great concepts, the logic, the math, the observations, the poetry, can be made to advance anywhere. A Nobel chemist can grow up in Condon. The ranch life of Fossil taught its children to close off no options, to presume nothing impossible.

Lizzie and Mary Jane formed Bill's lens on the world for his first twelve years. So as the character of the man who would mold so many other characters began to take shape, it included, as Barbara would note, a certain feminine indirection. Although he grew to look the part, Bowerman would never be a classic, macho, frontally attacking man's man. In his approach to the world he would take stock, give nothing away, circle to different vantage points, and keep an eye out for a sign of something he might exploit. But as a youngster, Bill was still so feral that before he could contribute anything to humanity, he would need to join the species. That humanizing would have to take place elsewhere—and with the help of a man, thank you very much.

As Bill finished sixth grade, his brother Dan graduated from Ashland High and headed to the University of Washington. Lizzie had planned to move the whole family to Seattle, but was offered a job in a Portland hospital. She agonized over the decision. Taking the job would mean having to split up her brood. But she wanted to put her own talents and education to work and, besides, they needed the money. So she accepted the post, fiercely hugged Dan good-bye, and looked around Portland for a school to tame her willful youngest.

Thus it was that Bill—"this free, hayseed, babied, coddled child," as Barbara would describe him—spent seventh grade in Hill Military Academy. Bill's ambivalence toward the military dated from that year. A photo shows him in uniform there, combed, polished, ramrod straight, with a face that repudiates it all. He hated it.

Bill shared this with his mother. Lizzie, acting on what her whole being urged her to do anyway, reunified her kids, packing up Bill and Beth and joining Dan in

Seattle, where Bill completed eighth grade. He'd now had to win new respect three years in a row, in Ashland, Portland, and Seattle.

And they weren't settled yet. By 1925, Dan was chafing. Vibrant with the impatience of all young Bowermans, he felt perfectly able to run a small newspaper. Yes, he was two years from a degree, but Lizzie believed him. They headed to the southern Oregon town of Medford, just a few miles from their previous home in Ashland, because Lizzie had spied an opportunity. Her work and frugality had let her hoard Jay's divorce settlement and alimony, and with it she bought a freshly launched Medford newspaper, the *Daily News*. Dan started right in as reporter and city editor. Bill, now fourteen, learned to help his brother in the production department.

Bill and Beth entered Medford High as a freshman and a senior, respectively. Bill was soon observed in playground battles. Beth had an equally familiar problem. Lizzie still allowed her no boyfriends and watched her with the relentlessness of the permanently charred. Beth dutifully trudged straight home every day and studied for hours, transferring whatever burgeoning desires she may have had into emulating her teachers. Four years later, she would graduate Phi Beta Kappa from the University of Oregon in education and go on to embody Lizzie's belief about how a woman's life ought to be conducted. She would teach and help others rear children, but she would have no truck with the deceiving-seducing gender. Years later Barbara Bowerman would liken Beth to a once-juicy grape, drying into a raisin.

All three Bowerman children revered their mother. She was all they had, especially during the years after leaving Fossil. The older two each found a way to honor Lizzie's wishes, albeit, in Beth's case, at some cost. Not so Bill.

At fifteen, Bill was as wild as his mountain-man great-grandfather had been at that age, as ungovernable, he would say later, as most of us are when the threat-assessment part of our brain is a few neurons short of a connection. But he was worse. Circumstance had conspired to keep him from confronting his inner demons, and as he grew closer to becoming a man, a species his mother had taught him to distrust, his furies began to intensify. He sometimes fought with such ascending rage that he seemed not to care if he was killed in the process. In his sophomore year, his brawling got him suspended from Medford High. Barbara, who wouldn't meet him for another two years, suggests that he may have been overly aggressive. "Not a bully, but it's the responder who gets caught."

Lizzie couldn't do anything with him. A teacher herself, she would have thrown him out of her own classes as summarily as his own teachers had. Beyond that, she was at a loss, because she recoiled from asking any man to intervene.

Finally, Dan did what his mother would not. He sat Bill down one day and told him he had an appointment at eight o'clock Monday morning with the superintendent of schools, one Ercel H. Hedrick. Bill, having no choice, nodded.

At the appointed hour, he was welcomed by Hedrick's secretary, given a chair, and told to wait. He sat and was ignored. By noon he was squirming. Barbara could imagine him in agony: "That energy all balled up, going over and over what they might do to him. Paddled or whipped? He could take that. Thrown out of school? He could live with that. Military school? He'd run away . . . "

Then, as Bowerman himself would always remember, "the voice emanates from the inner sanctum . . . '*Is that hell-raising son of a bitch still out there?*'"

Bill had barely crossed the threshold when Hedrick began hitting him with a profane list of his sins, delivered in a command voice that made his scalp crawl. Ercel H. Hedrick was then thirty. He had graduated from Oregon in 1916 and been a World War I Marine mule skinner and artillery officer. Standing above a stack of Bill's teacher reports, he said, "This is ridiculous. You're good in band, good in journalism, so you're not stupid, just a hell-raising son of a bitch."

Bill, by his muteness, could only agree. Hedrick studied the skinny, jug-eared creature. "Bowerman," Hedrick went on, "here's how life is going to go for you. You'll keep up this goddamned fighting and you'll not only be out of Medford, you'll be out of goddamn everywhere. Grants Pass, Ashland, nobody is going to stand for this shit. And that's the way it should be. You'll fight and I'll be rid of you. You'll fight and everybody else will be rid of you. Fight here, fight there, die in prison or on some barroom floor, I could give a royal, oozing shit. That's justice. That's just dying by your own goddamn sword."

Bill reddened, as if he could feel all those fights in his blood.

"The only thing wrong with that," said Hedrick, "is that you'll dishonor a goddamn worthwhile human being."

Bill's head came up. "Who?"

"Elizabeth Hoover Bowerman." Bill stopped breathing.

"You will bring eternal shame upon the name of your mother," intoned Hedrick. Bill's pallor became not of sickness but death.

"What . . . What should I do?" he finally croaked. "What do you want me to do?"

"Control yourself!" roared Hedrick. "Cut the crap and channel that goddamn energy! Go back to that school and be of use! Make your mother proud. Because I swear to you, Bowerman, I never want to hear your goddamn name again."

Bill stumbled across town, his system raging against itself. He thought of running away forever. He thought of killing himself. Neither would exactly thrill his mother. At school, he was escorted to class by a grimly silent principal, took his seat, and opened a book. The pages boiled before his eyes, but he willed the words into focus.

Like his great-grandfather, he learned to accept something short of perfect freedom. He began to channel. Systematically, he threw himself into his studies, sports, the band, drama, and the school paper. Hedrick's two-by-four between his eyes would be the lesson of his life. "Where would I be if they'd categorized me at age ten?" Bowerman would say fifty years later. "In jail or worse." Instead, he got nothing lower than a single B in his last two years of high school. "Hedrick got my attention."

Whether Bill swore to himself that he would never lose control again isn't known. But this was the beginning of the self-possession that would strike anyone who met him thereafter. Bill's turnaround was so dramatic that Hedrick would, in fact, hear his goddamn name again.

CHAPTER 4

Barbara

LIZZIE EXPECTED ALL HER CHILDREN TO BECOME MUSICALLY COMPETENT, SO AT Medford Bill went with the clarinet and joined the marching band. But he kept casting a covetous eye toward the gridiron, the one place he could hit and no one would complain. When he tried out during his freshman year, however, coach Prince ("Prink") Callison, noting his 105 pounds and clarinet case, said, "To the band!" The next fall he went out again. Callison took another look and said, "Back to the clarinet! Back to the band!"

Bill grew as if he willed it. Before his junior year he was nearing six feet and weighed 170 pounds.

There was a story he loved to tell: "End of summer I worked in the packing plant with a guy named Woody Archer. He was a sophomore at Oregon, and had played end for Medford. One of my friends and I were playing tennis on one court and using his balls and Woody was playing someone else using my balls.

"I got done and wanted to leave, so I said, 'How long are you going to be playing, Woody?'

"'What difference does it make?'

"'You're using my balls and I'd like to have them when you're through.'

"He walked over and said, 'These aren't your tennis balls.'

"'Well, that WJB doesn't stand for Woody Archer.'

"He made a fake like he was going to hit me, and I hit him right in the mouth. His feet flew out from under him, but he jumped right up again. We fought there for a half-hour. He never hit me any place except the top of my head. He was throwing roundhouse rights, and every time I'd crouch and uppercut him. Had him bleeding like a pig. The police came and we got taken down to the station to explain why we were fighting. There was no explanation. So they said, 'Don't fight in the neighborhood,' and let us go, and we had another one. And Woody didn't learn a damn thing. We got arrested again. And when school started, someone brought a message. 'Callison wants to know if you want to turn out for football now.' I'd beaten up the guy who'd been his starting end for two years."

Bill had jumped on a moving freight. Medford under young Callison had gone undefeated for four years. Bill began as a guard because that's where the depth chart was thinnest, and he played every minute of offense and defense. Later he would loathe platoon football, saying one can't understand the game without partaking of both sides.

When Callison asked if he could learn an injured center's plays, Bill said he'd already memorized everyone's assignment on every play in the book. Callison moved him to end, where he became the favorite target of a curly-haired quarterback named Al Melvin. The 1927 and 1928 Medford teams went undefeated and twice won the state championship by lopsided scores. In 1927, after Bill had kneed and hacked through Ashland for the winning touchdown, the losing coach asked Callison where this wildcat had come from.

"Got him off the band," Callison said.

Watching from the Medford bleachers in Bill's senior year was a fourteen-year-old sophomore, Barbara Young, who had just transferred from a cultured, all-girls prep school in Chicago. "I'd never even been in a school with men teachers," she would say. "Or boys running around loose." Back East her father had taken her to University of Chicago games, where she'd cared more about the fur coats and chrysanthemums. "But in Medford, I got to see these great big creatures in action, and I confess I exulted!"

She was not alone. "My Aunt Margaret and my folks were in the 'orchard crowd'—doctors and professional people who had pear ranches. Several had girls of my age, so after one football game, there was a dinner party. The Roberts girls gave it, at the Colony Club, where only the upper echelon belonged."

In her trepidation, Barbara skipped the football game to get a private dance lesson: "I'd hated dance school in Chicago—all white gloves and the boys and girls standing across a vast room, and the fear of not being chosen, and the fear of *being* chosen."

The Medford party dined at elegantly chic tables, each seating four. Maids distributed plates weighty with prime rib, baked potatoes, Waldorf salad.

"Just behind me, at another table," Barbara remembered years later, "was this football player. What caught my eye was that every time a maid would bring him a dinner, he'd thank her, and when she'd gone, he'd slip it onto his knee. Then he'd smile a beatific smile at another and get another dinner."

The boy, a tall senior named Bowerman, ended up with a meal on each knee and one on the table, all three of which he wolfed down by dessert, neatly stacking the plates before him.

When the dancing began, the boy came over. Standing there, he wordlessly offered Barbara his hand. She took it. Nothing at dance school had prepared her for what came next: "He was strong and sensitive. At first it was wonderful. But it was dead silence. Sepulchral silence. Now I know he grew up in a silent home. I was shy, but at least we talked in my family." Finally she couldn't stand it any more. "You must have been hungry," she whispered.

"Oh, no," he said. "Ate dinner before I came."

They danced on without another word. "He was always a great dancer," Barbara would remember, "always musical, always a graceful athlete." Barbara's nerves melted away and were replaced by a feeling new to her experience. "More than anything in high school I wanted acceptance. On that floor, with his hand at my back guiding me, I'd never felt so relaxed. I felt unconditionally accepted." When the music stopped, the two youngsters parted with awkward nods and rejoined their tables.

In the beginning, Barbara would say, she and Bill shared a similar sort of yearning: "At that age, we had absolutely no self-esteem. Both of us had been raised by stern parents. My mother had been brought up a hard-shell Baptist, all hell and damnation. Bill revered his mother, but she was full of expectations, and all Fossil had urged him never to let her down, because she'd had it so hard. I had seen him in classes, in the halls, and I remember that hungry look in his eye, that lonely look."

That first meeting did foretell a small part of their future. Bill and Barbara would love each other wholly, even as they remained mystified by each other. Their dance would often be as wordless as its first steps, each wondering what the other could possibly be thinking. But Barbara's uncommon gift was to be aware. It was just like her to notice the shenanigans of some guy sitting with his back to her. It was also like her to find the phrases to engrave an experience in memory, to name, to clarify. She would be the perfect balance to Bill's tactical taciturnity.

Barbara Young was born May 4, 1914. Her father, Ernest Hamilton Young, had been in the Signal Corps in World War I and taught flying in Texas. His oldest brother bought land in Chicago, made money, and started a family real estate company. As the youngest Young brother, Ernest didn't go to college, but simply joined the business. "He was a great salesman," his daughter would say, "for whom all things weren't just possible, but visible."

Barbara's parents were enfolded in the Young family prosperity: "We lived in different apartments on the South Shore, close in," she would say. "After we left the South, it turned to slums. I spent summers in a big old house on a lake in northern Illinois." Barbara attended the austere Mrs. Faulkner's Day School, run by three unmarried sisters. The school taught 200 girls from kindergarten through high school, preparing them for the Eastern women's colleges that would later be known as the Seven Sisters.

The family's religion was Christian Science, a creed that Barbara would almost surely have discovered even if she hadn't been born to it. Christian Scientists read and study the Bible with purpose, to strengthen a surpassing ideal. "Why are we here?" Barbara would ask years later. "To live in intelligence, to express intelligence. This is the force in us."

In the mid-1920s, Ernest Young was pouring all his energy and capital into developing a golf-course community called Valparaiso in the Florida panhandle. "For three winters we were down there," Barbara would remember, "with palms, and warm water. The adjoining town on the Gulf Coast was called Niceville. Wild pigs in the palmetto. Cows sauntered into our garden."

A cold wind shook this idyll to pieces. The venture failed and the Youngs headed west, to Medford, Oregon, where Ernest's sister lived.

In the Rogue and Applegate river valleys of southern Oregon, the clay soils and hot summers produce succulent tree fruits, especially pears. By the 1930s, 400 growers were picking 43,000 tons of Bartlett, Bosc, and Comice from 11,000 acres of orchards around Medford. The Medford pear boom attracted retired Midwesterners who ran what they called "ranches," as if they were always rounding up, branding, and driving to market herds of lowing pears. Barbara's Aunt Marg and Uncle Rupert named their ranch Sunny Cliff Orchard for the sandstone cliff above it. When the nation's economy plummeted, the orchard crowd offered a haven to needy relatives.

Barbara's family lived at Sunny Cliff for a month while Ernest looked for work. Then they moved to a nice house on Main. Despite their straitened circumstances, her parents insisted there would be no lowering of standards of respectability. Part of that was Ernest's adherence to the salesman's imperative—that when you are poor, you must never look poor. But, as his daughter would remember, "he never found a job appropriate to his . . . talents. My mother did work, to be able to keep up appearances. My aunt fussed so much about the house and keeping her pictures straight that it drove me nuts. I thought one married for freedom!" When Bill laid siege to this fortress, he would find a restless damsel.

The day after the Colony Club dance, during Sunday dinner at the ranch, the telephone on the wall rang. It was for Barbara. "I said hello and there was a long pause and then a hello back, and then a wait so long I thought the line was dead," she would recall. "And then, 'Could I drive out to see you?' I said, 'I'll have to ask my family.' And I did have to, all eight of them. Parents, uncles, aunts, cousins.

They all looked crosswise at each other, and even though he was a senior, because he was a football star, they said they guessed so, if he just came to the house."

When Bill appeared at the door, Barbara slipped out and they sat on the porch. Bill said nothing, just looked around, absorbing everything. Then he said, "Want to go for a ride?" So Barbara had to take him in and introduce him to everyone and ask permission. "Finally my father was so impressed with this big Medford football player, he let me go. We got in a coupe that belonged to Bill's brother, Dan, and drove the orchards, one of which, Hillcrest, is now on the national historic register."

Hillcrest Orchard deserves to be stamped into history, if only because Bill and Barbara got to know each other beneath the archways of its pollarded trees. Bowerman opened up, haltingly. He said he'd picked so many boxes of fruit from the passing branches that he didn't even like pears any more. He said he'd noticed her in the two classes they shared, French and Latin, and asked how it was that she'd parachuted into Medford from the mysterious East. When she told him, he said he was basically a farm boy from a little place called Fossil, across the Cascades. Barbara yelped and said she wanted nothing more than to live on a farm some day.

When Barbara said she wasn't so blasé that she didn't love a big, sweet pear, Bill said some were so juicy you had to take off your shirt before you sank your teeth into one. Barbara blushed.

"People go crazy over them," Bill said. "They taste these and never again like any others."

I think maybe we're trying to talk about more than pears here, thought Barbara. She let that sink in, then shouted her reaction: "I can't wait!"

"Our secret," Barbara would say later, "was that we gave each other social confidence. We were so shy. We wanted to belong, to a crowd or to someone. But in a flash I'd learned I could get along with boys, or at least this one remarkable boy, and I never wanted to be alone again!"

In later years, Bowerman's associates would snort when Barbara called herself shy. She was reserved, in the sense of not needing to talk or hog the limelight. But once launched, she often spoke in perfect paragraphs, with topic sentences and bravura, unexpected endings.

But at fourteen, still a truly coy maiden, she was sure her family back at the farmhouse would be frantic that the kids in the orchard were eating too richly of the tree of knowledge. The Youngs' opinion of boys in their daughter's life was not as harsh as Lizzie Bowerman's, but it was strict. When Bill and Barbara returned, however, all were relaxed and welcoming. Barbara always thought Bill's being a football player had this miraculous effect on her father. It seems equally likely that Bill had been raised by Lizzie to be rigidly respectful. He was simply an engaging, courtly young man. No matter how terse, when he did speak he was funny, and he reflexively shied from anything that might be threatening. All his adult life, he would put women on a pedestal.

In the following weeks, Barbara tried to take a good, clear look at young Bill. "At first, I really thought he was from the wrong side of the tracks," she would say. "They lived in a little hovel two blocks from the high school. His mother and sister looked as if they could barely buy clothes. But they had some money because Lizzie bought our old Plymouth from my dad. It turned out she had a $200 alimony from Bill's father, but she wanted independence, so she taught school and ran the family as a kind of corporate concern, with everyone working when they could. She decided what to spend. So they did not spend." It didn't help that the *Daily News* couldn't stay afloat. "When the paper failed, and she was too proud to ask for any more money from Jay," Barbara would say, "it complicated life a good deal."

Barbara learned of Bill's eminence at school. He was allowed to leave class five minutes early because he had to go downtown to put the school paper to bed. He was king of the football team. He sang with the Glee Club. He was on the honor roll. "It was staggering," Barbara would say. "In the spring, he showed up late for school in second period, all black and reeking of smoke, and was welcomed into class like a hero! He'd been out all night firing the smudge pots to warm the orchards, saving the new pears from a late frost. And he was mine! Pretty soon I felt I owned him. I remember lying spread-eagled on my bed with that easy feeling that you don't have to worry who you're going to the dances with."

Medford so loved its 1928 football team that when it qualified for a trip to Portland to play Benson High for the state championship, the town hired a private train. "We went up in the morning before the game, and came back in sleepers," Barbara would recall, "although there was no sleeping in our cars. Did we win? Handily! Thirty-nine to nothing!" Then Bowerman helped Medford win a second title, in basketball, beating Astoria 35-14.

Barbara would come to feel as if she lived an entire lifetime in the school year of 1928–29. "I was cheering from the stands when someone knocked his tooth out with an elbow during a basketball game," she said. "I took him to the dentist. We shared study hall, where I was often the recipient of cryptic notes, one or two words, and I never knew what they meant, like 'Rain today?'"

"During recess, we'd stand out on the corner and match pennies—heads or tails. He'd win all of them and loan me more, and win those. I had to get five dollars from my folks to pay off my gambling debts. I said it was for the movies."

Although her parents at first were worried about her being with an older boy, they were eventually reassured that Bill would not harm their daughter. "It got to be that it was one of those things. It happened, and it—us—was soon taken for granted," Barbara would say.

Bill was not the only one who found Barbara attractive, though, and she did, in fact, pencil in a few other boys on her dance cards. "In Medford," she would recall, "I quickly absorbed that girls who were two-timers were looked down on. But I accepted dates anyway, with boys my cousins knew. One was Farwell Kenly, who was going to Princeton. I felt so wicked going out with him that I gave his ring back at the end of summer."

By then Barbara felt as if she were caught up in a literal fairy tale. She'd given her maidenly handkerchief to her hero to bear into conquest—and discovered a new realm. "In Medford," she would say, "I found the two great loves of my life. Bill and Oregon."

Within a two-hour drive of Medford is every climate in the temperate zone except true desert. That year, Bill was usually off working somewhere during breaks from school, but Barbara, with family and friends, explored. They went west and camped on deserted Pacific beaches or mossy, spruce- and salal-covered headlands, where twenty people could picnic on a single old Douglas fir stump. They climbed lighthouses and looked out over the slowly surging, gray-green, kelp-thickened ocean. They swam and learned what all Oregon kids know: It is a cruel sea. If Poseidon can get you alone and unprotected for twenty minutes, he will kill you with cold. Or with a log rolling in the pretty waves. In winter, they skied and tobogganed the Siskiyou Mountains. In summer, they went northeast from Medford, up the jade and cream riffles of the Rogue River (it is considered uncool to call the blasting cataracts "rapids."), a stream distinguished by steelhead and seventy-pound Chinook salmon runs. They hiked complicated woods, going from heat-loving Madrone through spicy cedar, sticky Douglas fir, gothic Noble fir, fat-stogie Ponderosa pine, the trees changing at every bend or lacy waterfall. The sheer forces of this place, whether slope, surf, or storm, intoxicated her.

With Dan and Beth, Bill took Barbara to a Fossil haying and introduced her to an appraising, eighty-four-year-old Mary Jane Chambers Hoover, who surely sensed a fifteen-year-old kindred spirit. They toured the Wheeler County homesteads, and Barbara loved every horse, every barn cat. Bill even defused a raucous cowboy—and without resorting to old habits. "He was so courageous," Barbara would recall. "He always knew how to control any situation he found himself in, by intelligence if not strength. But he didn't like doing anything he didn't know how to do."

Well, sometimes he'd parlay a little knowledge into a lot more. "The football team had gone up to work on road crews at Crater Lake National Park," Barbara recalled, "and a ranger asked, 'Anybody know trees?' Bill didn't really, but he raised his hand and that summer he cruised the park timber and marked beetle-infested trees to be cut. And three of my girlfriends and I visited and stayed at the Lodge."

Crater Lake stuns everyone who makes the pilgrimage into cowed spirituality. If the ancient Greeks had passed there, it would have been an oracle. Only 7,000 years ago, the top half of 14,000-foot Mt. Mazama exploded with the energy of dozens of Mt. St. Helenses. A pilgrim coming over that granite rim today comes face-to-face with a huge open maw, six miles of hypnotic sapphire, and must fight the urge to leap and plummet. The crater's cliffs plunge 1,000 feet to the surface, another 2,000 to the bottom. Its waters seep through the rock of the grinding Cascades until they rise to begin the Rogue. A drink from Crater Lake is cold and clear, tasteless in its purity, a sacrament in remembrance of the fire and violence of creation.

Climbing awestruck through its gnarled firs and, later, skiing above the deserted lake would become the most intense of their intertwined memories. "Forever after, we went there," Barbara would say. "It would be ours."

It seems only natural. The greater one's sense of the human condition—and there is no more potent reminder than Crater Lake—the greater the urge to grab hold of a true friend. That's what Barbara felt she had in Bill and Bill in her. And they were right, but it would be years before they could turn to each other whenever they felt the need.

"The night he graduated from Medford, we went to a party," Barbara would remember. "He was going to work at Crater Lake that summer, and the next morning we talked about our life after that." Barbara's idea, she would say, came out of a clear blue sky.

"Couldn't we get married?" she began.

Bill said, "I'm going to college. I'm going to Oregon. Maybe pre-med."

"But what about farming?" Barbara bleated.

Barbara at seventy regarded Barbara at fifteen as tragicomic. "I was devastated," she would say. "I thought, *I've found Bill and he seems to have found me, so why do we have to go to school?*"

Never a cajoler, Bill didn't try to explain why college was right for him. Lizzie insisted that her kids get degrees, emancipating degrees. She had set the example herself after the divorce and scrimped until they were in tatters so he could afford to enroll. Moreover, Bill's high school résumé and football renown had won him eager acceptance from Oregon. And his coach, Callison, would join the Oregon football staff the same year.

So Bill and Barbara didn't exactly swear each other eternal love. "I realized, having read enough of them," she would say, "that if this was a real fairy tale, the path could not be smooth. I had to go through all kinds of agony before I got to heaven. So this is how it should be. I would have to go to college and be miserable."

The Young family cooperated and piled on her pain. They were moving to Southern California and dragging her with them. Two weeks later, her whole family went for the weekend up to Crater Lake, where Bill was working in the woods. One night after dinner, they cast back over everything they had shared in their year of destiny, as Barbara would call it. And then, she would remember, "two people, with the voices of Nelson Eddy and Jeannette MacDonald, stood on the rim and sang 'Indian Love Call.' It was chilling with power. It cemented the wonder of the place for us."

CHAPTER 5

The University of Oregon

IN SEPTEMBER 1929, BILL TOOK THE BUS THE 180 MILES FROM MEDFORD TO Eugene, got off on Onyx Street, and found the University of Oregon. Photos of the time suggest the campus had been recently logged over. The portly, Victorian hulks of Deady and Villard halls stood hot and unshaded in pastures dotted with Queen Anne's lace.

When he reached Fifteenth Street, he put down his bag and slowly pivoted from one wonder to the next. Strange, roofed grandstands—looking more like covered bridges than bleachers—hunched over an emerald football field and cinder running track. Behind the stadium, tussocky practice fields and embankments mounted to the rear steps of a blocky, new basketball arena. Ivy was just beginning to climb two-year-old MacArthur Court's concrete walls. The catacombs in its basement would be Bill's locker room, infirmary, laundry, classroom, and lair.

During orientation, Bill pledged the Beta Theta Phi house for its sporting tone and chance to sling hash for meals. He registered for the required freshman classes in math, English, and physical education. He also signed up for biology although he didn't expect to like it; high school chemistry had been the worst course ever. To his surprise, as he would recall, "the teacher, named Houston, made it live, made it pretty damned exciting. Houston said to me, 'You're a pretty good biology student.' And I said, 'Well, you are a pretty good teacher.'"

He took journalism too, but found he already knew the basics. The next year, he added business courses. His grades were good, but he begrudged accounting its nitpicking precision. "To this day," Bowerman would say in his seventies, "when someone whines, 'Your account is ten cents short,' I haul out a dime and give it to them."

He wrote weekly letters to Barbara, but sometimes urgency drove him to the Western Union office at Willamette and Oak. On September 28, 1929, he wired, "Pledged Beta. Glad you like school. Like see you. Bill." An April telegram read, "Easter Greetings, Sweetheart. Wish I might be with you."

The stock market crashed the second month he was in school, which didn't make finding part-time jobs any easier. "Bill split wood for a family named

White," Barbara would remember, "and when he knocked to say he was done, Mrs. White said, 'Please don't ever come to the front door again.' He had to get paid his twenty-five cents an hour out of the servants' entrance."

Any and all frustrations—Barbara's absence being the keenest—he jammed into freshman football. It would, of course, be forty years before the National Collegiate Athletic Association (NCAA) would let student athletes go straight from high school to a college varsity. Bill felt so at home, he didn't care. Prink Callison was now on the Oregon staff, and he kept an eye on Bill, kept him learning the game, using his head, thinking about what plays he would call and why, and, on defense, what the movements of one blocker revealed about the intentions of everyone else.

Callison was a remarkable teacher. In his six years of coaching at Medford he'd won forty-five of forty-nine games and brought much talent to Eugene along with Bill. Of the twenty-one players on Callison's 1928 Medford squad, eleven went on to play college ball at Stanford, Army, and Oregon State, among other schools, and two who came with Bill to Oregon would play professionally.

When these stout freshmen were thrown into scrimmages against the varsity, Bill at once grasped the nature of his head coach. Doc Spears was dictatorial, abrasively vocal, and resembled a bloodthirsty infantry commander. He loved to see the bodies fly.

"The varsity had a good team, almost in spite of him," Bowerman would recall. "Spears was cruel. Spears was a windbag." This intense dislike of blowhards had to be related to the loathing that came over his mother in the presence of aggressively powerful men. That detestation ran deep in Bill, and Spears brought it out as had few before him. The man's bellowing insistence on being called *Coach* turned Bill against the word forever.

As if to balance the scales, Bill made another acquaintance. A weathered gentleman in shirtsleeves and suspenders, while tightly taping Bill's ankles in the training room before practice, noticed they shared a name.

"But I hear people call you *Colonel*," said Bill Bowerman.

"Just call me Bill," said Oregon's head athletic trainer and track coach, sixty-two-year-old Bill Hayward.

Hayward had invented state-of-the-art splints, casts, straps, pads, slings, and braces to keep injured bodies in the lineup or allow them some movement and protection while they healed. The devices fascinated Bowerman, who got to know Hayward while listening to him explain the anatomy that his wire and leather prosthetics supported.

Hayward had been Oregon's track coach since 1903 and had coached two US Olympic track and field teams. Nevertheless, he was under orders not to scout fall practice for spring talent: It was Doc Spears's edict that no football player should run track. "That was stupid and I knew that was stupid," Bowerman would say. "But I didn't want to test how stupid Spears really was by challenging him on it and getting tossed."

Bill had never run an official race because Medford had no track or track team. But he'd usually finished near the front in wind sprints in conditioning and PE classes and had thought he'd like at least to try the 220. Hayward opined that the 440 might be better for him, but he'd understand if he didn't come out.

His first spring at Oregon, Bill learned that track could be more dangerous than football. Word came that his friend and quarterback back in Medford, curly-haired Al Melvin, who'd gone to a California college, had broken his neck in a high-jumping accident and been killed.

"Al was one of the guys who'd come out with Bill to see me at the pear ranch," Barbara Bowerman would recall. "One of the gang my cousins said were so corny and sweet they left goop marks on the porch. Bill took the loss to heart, then and forever. The safety of the high jump would always be an issue for him. Later, he was concerned about Dick Fosbury hurting himself jumping backward. He always made sure the jumpers had big, thick landing pads."

During Bill's second year, Lizzie coalesced her family again, moving up from Medford and renting a two-story house on Fifteenth Street, across from what had been known since 1919 as Hayward Field. (The honor to the track coach and trainer must've galled Doc Spears no end.) The place was so close to thwacks and grunts wafting from across the street that the entrepreneur that always simmered in Lizzie came to a rolling boil.

As Barbara would tell the story, "Bill's mom had her degree in home economics. It was the Depression, and all these impoverished football players were hungry, so she cooked for them. She reigned in that kitchen, turning out meat and potatoes and hot apple pies, threatening them with her chef's knife to keep them out of the cookie jar. They loved her. And she them! It ran so counter to her hatred of men that it was fascinating."

Bill, duly concentrating on football, became a starter midway through his sophomore year in 1930. On offense he played end or quarterback, which in the single-wing formation of the era called upon him to hand off and become the team's most vicious blocker. He threw an occasional pass. On defense, his quickening grasp of the game often got his legs to carry him to a point where a running back or pass was bound to arrive.

43

It would help when Spears let him use what he learned. In a huge battle against the hated University of Washington, played in Seattle, the defensive coach, a man named O'Brien, told Bill to watch for a certain move by one of the Husky receivers. At halftime, Bowerman would remember, "Spears grabs me and says, 'What the hell are you doing? I don't want you going out there like that.' But in the second half, O'Brien said go with that guy, so I stuck with him, and they drove down to our five-yard line and threw the ball to my guy." Bill picked it off. "There was only one Husky between me and the goal posts ninety yards away," he said, "and I think I ran over him."

Bill took it down the Oregon sideline. Washington tacklers gained on him all the way, but he collapsed across the line for a touchdown, a reward for O'Brien's reading of the opposition.

That night, in the hotel elevator going down to dinner, Bill's teammates were regaling him about his performance. Bill Hayward's voice came from the back of the elevator car: "Did you hear me?"

"What do you mean, hear you?"

"I was trotting with you down the sideline," said Hayward, "yelling, 'Lift your knees! Lift your knees!'"

Bill asked Hayward to help him work on his stride. Hayward agreed and they had a deal.

The next morning, in the bright kitchen of a tall house in a leafy section of Portland, the Jay Bowerman family was reading the Sunday *Oregonian*. Wayfe and the former governor were deep in the editorial pages; daughters Jayne and Sally, fourteen and thirteen, were poring over the sports section.

"Dad," said Jayne, "Bowerman's not that common a name, is it?"

"No, not really."

One wonders whether fifty-five-year-old Jay felt a little trickle of fear just then, because neither Jay nor Wayfe had ever told their daughters that he'd had a family before their own. Jayne turned the page so he could see a photo of Bill, his helmet off, his face full of easy, celebrant grace, and said, "Is there some chance we might be related to this beautiful man?"

"Jayne, Sally," said her father, after one of the more pregnant pauses of all time, "there's something I've been meaning to tell you."

The sisters froze at his voice. They turned to their mother and found her ashen. Wayfe looked to her husband, and to heaven and back, then nodded her acquiescence.

"He's your brother," said Jay. "Actually your half-brother."

Years later, Jayne Bowerman Hall would remember the moment first for its shock and wonder. She felt no resentment at being kept so long in the dark. Her father was a Bowerman, after all, and so never volunteered more than necessary. She and Sally demanded the whole story. Jay got it out amid disbelieving whoops ("three kids!") and questions. He omitted mention of the awkward timing of their marriage and the death of Bill's twin. Both Jay and Wayfe said they were sorry their daughters had to hear about it this way and apologized for not telling them sooner.

Jayne and Sally looked at each other and shrieked, "He's our brother! We got a brother! We gotta meet him!"

Jay, ambushed, had no choice. So, on a subsequent Friday his son came to dinner. And all apprehensions evaporated. "Bill was never anything but darling to me," Jayne recalled. "I felt he was this big star, but he asked if I'd like to go to lunch with him the next day, before their game. I almost swooned at the thought, but yes I sure could, and there we met some other godlike football players and he introduced me as his sister!" Bill loved the idea of having brand-new sisters. He, Sally, and Jayne became lifelong friends, even though Bill made no move to improve relations with his father.

Bill poured all these events into his letters to Barbara, including a clipping of the December 1930 story noting that he had won, by a technical knockout, the university's light heavyweight boxing championship.

The house on Fifteenth was becoming a little fraternity of its own. In the basement, in this Prohibitive era, a substance was mellowing intended to induce even greater brotherhood. One day the Teutonic lady from whom they rented walked by, stopped to converse with Bill on the sidewalk, and picked up a certain aroma. "If someone would just ask," the landlady said, as Bill was trying to sidle away, "I could teach someone how to make *good* beer." Bill sidled back

"And," as Barbara Bowerman would recount, "she proceeded to do so. Bill enjoyed chemistry and things like that almost as much as the home-brew reward at the end of it all." His desire to go to med school arose, Barbara felt, from a sense that "medicine was this grand combination of chemistry and PE."

The young Barbara Young, meanwhile, was adjusting to life in California. The Youngs had first moved to Westwood Village, near UCLA, where her father plunged gratefully back into high-end real estate. Barbara went to huge Beverly Hills High, where, she would recall, "nobody spoke to me the whole term." But it was not in Barbara's nature to sustain a mope. Slowly, the glories of where she was wore her down: "My family were always great driver-arounders. We drove to the beach and felt that ocean. We went to the desert when the flowers bloomed. My brother Jack and I did love that."

A year later, they moved east to Monrovia, where she fit in fine among the 400 students at Monrovia Arcadia Duarte High. She even took up with a football player. "He was neither an intellect nor from a good background," she would confess, "but basically I didn't want to be lonely ever again."

Her social possibilities skyrocketed the next year when Ernest Young discovered an estate in Covina, a hacienda with a red-tiled roof, persimmon trees, pool, barbecue pit, sixteen acres of orange groves, and a tennis court with a double row of roses all around it. They couldn't really afford it, but her father had gotten a great deal on the estate ("so he called it an investment") and they found people to live in the carriage house and take care of the place. Barbara was just starting at UCLA, and the hacienda was perfect for parties.

By then Barbara had been seduced by the new land. "I'd fallen in love with the nights of Southern California," she would sigh, remembering. "The stars . . . And the orange blossoms were so fragrant." It didn't take long before romance was of a different odor.

Lit by the glow of a huge bonfire at a pep rally the Thursday before the homecoming football game, the incandescent face of Barbara Young struck UCLA quarterback Mike Frankovich dumb. But not for long. Frankovich recovered, made an inspiring speech promising victory or death, then shoved through the cheers to make sure this blinding vision didn't escape again. He'd actually seen her before, when he had come to pick up one of her sorority sisters at the Tri-Delt house. When Barbara opened the door, Frankovich had grabbed her hand and said, "Where did *you* come from?" But she had torn free and retrieved his date for him.

Now she was trapped. They stayed the night at the dying bonfire, comparing their origins and family histories, and watched the sunrise while talking about their dreams.

Barbara returned to the house neck deep in what would become the quandary of her life. She was tremendously attracted to Frankovich. In strength and declarative sentences, in appetite and boldness, he was a match for Bill Bowerman. Football quarterback and a catcher on the baseball team, Frankovich was also a star in the UCLA drama and radio departments. He was handsome, hardworking, and so exemplary that he had been adopted by comedian Joe E. Brown to be a live-in role model for Brown's own kids. The Browns encouraged Frankovich and Barbara's friendship, and soon she was a member of the family.

Joe E. Brown, of course, is immortal for uttering the last line in *Some Like It*

Hot. When Jack Lemmon rips off his wig and says, "The reason I can't marry you is I'm a MAN!," the lascivious, undeterred Brown replies, "Well, nobody's perfect."

Even though that triumph lay thirty years in the future, Brown was already someone who could open every studio door to his ward. Frankovich would go on to have a producing career worthy of such a launching pad, working with David Lean on *The Bridge on the River Kwai* and *Lawrence of Arabia* and becoming head of Columbia Pictures. Even at twenty-one, he was sure such achievements lay ahead and he wanted Barbara to experience it all at his side.

Decades later, Barbara would reserve a special tone of voice for discussion of her most intimate topics or moments. She would use it with interviewer Bill Landers when she whispered, "I got in a little over my head."

She had told Mike all about Bill, but it would be two years before she told Bill all about Mike. At first, she didn't think this was any great betrayal. But time passed and she still couldn't choose. "I felt so conflicted," Barbara would remember at eighty, "that I hoped some third person, some even shinier knight would come riding in and carry me off, to solve this thing."

None did, so Frankovich, knowing that UCLA would play Oregon in Portland, sought to have the outcome really mean something. "If we win, if I beat Bill, will you marry me?" he asked. Barbara gave him an answer after the team had gone up to Portland. "I sent Mike a telegram saying I'd marry the winner," Barbara would blush to confess, adding, "I thought Oregon would win!" When it came down to it, she couldn't bear to watch, so she stayed in Los Angeles.

Jayne Bowerman, then fifteen, got her parents to invite Bill to dinner in Portland the night before the game. All were astounded when Bill walked in with the opposing quarterback. Although the two were equally magnetic to Barbara, they were temperamental opposites. As Jayne would put it, "Mike is a passer, an initiator. Bill is more of a catcher, a responder." Mike entertained everyone so thoroughly that Jayne could remember her own reaction vividly: "I hated that man because he hogged the limelight."

For Bill's father the attorney, this was a chance to see his son tested off the playing field. He had to be impressed. In quietly sitting back and beaming while Frankovich performed, Bill might have been following a script by Machiavelli. He already knew to keep his friends close and his enemies closer—where he could study them at will. Not for the first time, nor the last, Bill was doing recon.

The game itself was a brutal defensive struggle. Oregon led 7-3 with five seconds left, and UCLA was backed up on its own twenty-five-yard line. Bill, playing defense against Frankovich's final, Hail Mary pass, leaped, batted the ball away from the UCLA receiver, thought it hit the turf, but turned to see it drop into the hands of a second Bruin, who sprinted away from the fallen Bill to score. UCLA had won, 9-7.

But had Frankovich? When Bill called Barbara and told her the score, she cried out as if struck. Bill wondered why she was taking his loss so hard, but she couldn't bear to tell him. Ultimately, she couldn't bear to lose him and climbed back up on the fence.

Frankovich, however, was prepared to declare it to high heaven. As Barbara would tell it years later, "I thought Mike would keep the telegram under his hat, but no, that wasn't his way. Both Mr. Brown and Mike were always telling the papers about Mike, which was why the thing blew out of control."

Frankovich, a natural public persona, had no qualms about publishing her vow, even if she wasn't keeping it. "It was in the UCLA *Daily Bruin* that I'd promised to marry the winning quarterback. There was even a song about it, a phonograph record, which I later threw in the trash."

Bill, somehow spared hearing about all this, returned to what was becoming a mixed bag of studies. At the urging of the chemistry dean, he had taken physics and biology and found them so absorbing he began to think seriously of medical school. (He would actually end up a PE major, but with minors in journalism, business, and pre-med.)

Bowerman signed up for one other class, public speaking from Professor Glenn Starlin. Barbara had often teased Bill about how, when he was on the honor roll back in Medford, he'd stand up with the team at pep rallies and—when asked for a few stirring words—would say, "Do our best," and look at his feet.

Always a lover of stories, Bill had an ear for the ring and richness of language, from the barnyard to the chapel. Under Starlin's guidance, he quickly grew eloquent before a group, becoming a weaver of narratives with riveting beginnings, hysterical middles, and bewildering ends.

Barbara, who would hear these yarns in the years to come, was becoming a sophisticated audience. She majored in English, to one day write, but freely sampled other disciplines and found she liked philosophy. If she hoped to find something to soothe her conscience for allowing her two suitors to dangle on and on, she searched in vain. Even Gandhi had no advice for a woman with two irresistible forces trying to conquer her.

CHAPTER 6

Bill Hayward

AFTER THE DISASTROUS UCLA GAME, BILL LED THE DUCKS TO A 14-6 UPSET OF New York University, wrecking the Violets' hope of a national championship. Yet, as hard as he could hit, Bill had no wish to maim. And it seemed that everywhere he looked he saw carnage caused by his football coach being utterly and stupidly brutal.

Bill Hayward shared Bill Bowerman's view of Spears. Assistant trainer Bob "Two Gun" Officer once watched Hayward tenderly tape the separated shoulder of a halfback named Watts. Then Hayward walked Watts out to the field, flagged down Spears and told him, "No contact for Watts." Hayward came back to the training room and had barely sat down when Watts clattered in, bug-eyed from pain, his shoulder sticking out at a horrifying angle. Watts said Spears had put him in as soon as Hayward's back was turned.

After practice, Hayward told Officer, "I'm going up to see our great 'doctor,'" and mounted the steps to the coach's office. Officer heard a knock, Spears's muffled roaring, a sharp crack, then silence. In a minute Hayward came back in, rubbing his hand.

"Got any ice?" he said.

William Louis Hayward was born on July 2, 1868, in Detroit, Michigan, the youngest son of Mr. and Mrs. Thomas Heyward. (Hayward would change the spelling when he came West, arguing, irresistibly, "You spell *hay* 'H-A-Y,' don't you?") The family was Roman Catholic, of French Canadian descent, and lived in a large house on the edge of town. Hayward's earliest memory placed him in the lap of richly deserved attention.

"When I was five," he once told an interviewer, "I had nice, rosy cheeks and all the pretty girls used to make quite a fuss over me." In grade school, he was outgoing and competitive. "If a boy at school lifted some big weight, I'd lift a bigger one," he recalled. "I got a great bang out of robbing birds' nests and helping myself to other people's apples."

A gong of similarity with Bill Bowerman sounds here and never quite fades. Bowerman, too, would crow of winning a beautiful-baby contest. A signal parallel was their sparse fathering. When he was ten, Hayward's parents took off to Peru to run a rubber plantation and never came home. Hayward, his three sisters, and an older brother were taken in by their grandparents and raised in Toronto, Canada.

Hayward was bright but tempted away from studying by all things physical. At twenty he was six feet and 190 pounds and had mastered lacrosse so well that he played for a championship team, the Ottawa Capitals. But his genuine gift was the ability to lift those knees and fly. In the early 1890s he prospered as a professional sprinter. While traveling on a summer Caledonian Sports circuit that began in Rochester, New York, and ended in Halifax, Nova Scotia, Hayward once won five races in one day, at 75, 135, 300, 400, and 600 yards.

He had phenomenal incentive. Hayward's winnings topped $4,000 per meet, which accustomed him to his first fine clothes and exquisite fly rods. It would be ninety years before there was a better time to sprint for money. Before 1896 there was no modern Olympics to ban professionals. Neither did Hayward's earnings disqualify him from other amateur sports. Summers, he played lacrosse and rowed. Winters, he boxed, wrestled, and played hockey.

Hayward competed across the American West, and Bowerman recalled his telling of a match race in Spokane. Hayward had acquired a great prize—one of the first pairs of spiked shoes ever made. He didn't want the sight of them to prejudice the betting, so he warmed up with tall, striped socks covering their soles. These he whipped off at the start and won easily, dust rising, spectators' jaws dropping.

When his speed began to ebb, Hayward turned more fully to the sweet science, honing the punch he would use to such effect upon Doc Spears. He fought exhibitions with heavyweight champ "Gentleman Jim" Corbett until Britain's Bob Fitzsimmons took the title from him in 1897. Corbett then invited Hayward, a natural showman, to be part of a barnstorming vaudeville company.

One time, while training in Vallejo, California, Hayward was asked to spar with another contender, "Sailor" Jack Sharkey, from whom Hayward extracted a promise not to start slugging. But Sharkey immediately started swinging from his heels and wouldn't lay off despite Hayward's warnings. As Hayward would tell the story, "I reached behind me with one hand, picked up a baseball bat that was in a corner, and when he came after me I cracked him over the head—hard. He stopped all right, but he just shook his head and started swinging again. I wasn't around by then. I'd hit him and ducked out of the ring at the same time." Speed saves. And teaching speed would be the key to Hayward's life's work.

Hayward essentially started track coaching at the top. When a friend, world champion sprinter Walter Christie, became track coach at Princeton, he summoned Hayward to assist. The duo worked there for three seasons before being enticed away by the University of California at Berkeley, where they got a sluggish team rocketing. This was not lost on other schools. In 1901, Pacific University in Forest Grove, Oregon, lured him north. Hayward was pulled, as if by a Royal Coachman in his cheek, to Oregon's fly-fishing. "I came for a vacation," he would say, "and caught what they called the Oregon spirit. It's not serious, but it is contagious so they kept me here. I like everything in the state and everything I like is in the state so I stayed."

In 1903, an even smaller Willamette Valley college, Albany, hired Hayward away. He coaxed from its hundred-member student body a team that embarrassed the University of Oregon, a behemoth at three times that number. This had to stop, declared Virgil D. Earl, student manager of the Oregon track team (and later dean of students; Earl Hall bears his name). Earl overstepped his authority and hired Hayward in late 1903. It wasn't hard. "Wasn't Eugene nearer the McKenzie River, the greatest fishing stream in the world?" Earl would say.

At Oregon, Hayward coached and taught gym to both men and women and doted on his first wife and mother of his son, William Hayward Jr. Along about 1910, the first Mrs. Hayward, always a frail woman, died at an early age. The vagueness is because Hayward declared his personal life off-limits to all interviewers. Hayward grieved in silence and coached on. Never again would he consider changing schools.

In 1921, at age fifty-three, he married Bertina Orton, daughter of a prominent Eugene family. Their union sustained Hayward throughout his long life. After the overworked coach had a heart attack at seventy-one in 1939 ("I knew it was do or die against Oregon State," Hayward cracked in the hospital. "And I damn near died."), Bertina doubled her efforts for his comfort and protection. He would coach another eight years.

We dilute the word and usually demean the subject when we call someone a *character*. But Hayward's eccentricity invited it, and he didn't seem to mind. A true boxer, he loved cars, clothes, and monikers. Known as Blackjack in his running days, he later switched to Colonel to impress carnival crowds. He had never been in the service, but Colonel grew so natural he used it when signing the title page of an Oregon graduate student's thesis (which was titled "The Life and Times of Colonel William Hayward").

Hayward wasn't especially fatherly toward his charges and treated each one differently, characteristics Bill Bowerman would emulate. Hayward also preceded Bowerman in being a practical joker, and his habitual deadpan remark over a painful limb was "If it's bothering you, cut it off." The day Hayward complained of a headache, half the team shot back, "If it's bothering you, cut it off!"

When Bill met him in 1929, Hayward had coached several men of Oregon in four Olympics. He'd paid his own fare to London in 1908 to accompany versatile Dan Kelly, who'd tied the 9.6-second world record for the 100-yard dash. Kelly didn't make the final in the 100 meters but took the silver medal in the long jump, and Hayward was immediately pressed into service with the US team.

Hayward brought back a fine new camera, a trunk full of photos, and a pair of English waders that allowed him to drop a fly above the noses of more McKenzie trout. All his life, he held it truly, honestly immoral to fish with bait or lure.

At the 1912 Olympics in Stockholm, Hayward was the official US track coach, guiding such talents as decathlon champion Jim Thorpe. "Meeting King Gustave when he awarded the medals," Hayward would tell Bowerman, "destroyed my illusions of the grandeur of nobility. Terrible posture. Twelve-dollar suit. Buck-and-a-half straw hat." Sharing the ship home with Douglas Fairbanks and Gloria Swanson was more Hayward's style.

The German team found Hayward's organization in Stockholm so impressive they wanted him to coach them in the 1916 Games, planned for Berlin, but of course other, hotter heads in Germany prevailed, starting World War I. The Olympics were canceled. The Great War also wiped out the 1917 and 1918 Oregon seasons.

In 1920, the Games resumed in Antwerp, Belgium, and Hayward was again US coach. Oregon throwers Ken Bartlett (discus) and Art Tuck (javelin) made the team. Hayward recalled for Bowerman how Paavo Nurmi of Finland carried his own stopwatch in the 10,000 meters, running stoically to the first of what would be nine golds over three Olympics. "The Flying Finn," as Nurmi was called, struck Hayward as humorless; "The Grim Finn" was more like it.

The 1924 Olympics in Paris were retold in *Chariots of Fire*, with Britain's Harold Abrahams nipping the American Jackson Scholz in the 100 meters and Scottish missionary-to-be Eric Liddell running away with the 400. Hayward's coaching did help Scholz and Charlie Paddock come back to sweep the 200, and Oregon pole-vaulter Ralph Spearow (who had cleared a collegiate record 13 feet $1\frac{1}{2}$ inches earlier in the year) finished sixth in his event.

After Paris, Spearow, then known to his Cottage Grove flock as the "pole-vaulting Presbyterian pastor," was invited on a goodwill tour of Japan. "He saw people using bamboo poles for the first time," Hayward would tell Bill, "tried one himself, and broke the world record with 13 feet 10^1/$_2$ inches. But it was never accepted because the Amateur Athletic Union hadn't issued him an official 'travel permit' to compete there. They treated him like an outlaw." Bowerman would recall this as his first exposure to AAU obtuseness.

Listening to these litanies of the great, it dawned on Bill that Hayward had enabled, witnessed, or photographed about two-thirds of Olympic track and field history. There was no more experienced village elder, if the village was the Olympic one. Hayward urged his men to shoot for the Games as "the ultimate fellowship, the highest target."

When Bill appealed to Hayward for help with his football speed, Hayward again chuckled at how oddly he ran. Bowerman leaned forward and had such a hitch in his stride that teammates called him Hopalong. Hayward explained that you don't change your form by just holding yourself differently, but by strengthening the muscles you need to be more effective. He gave him "high-knee, fast-leg" drills that made him mimic a high-stepping drum major until his groin seized up. Gradually Bill began to sprint with his knees and chest higher, his hips tucked under him.

"Because of what he taught," Bowerman would say, "I went from one of the slowest players on the football team to the second fastest, behind only Paul Starr, our great sprinter."

For such drills, Hayward simply threw Bill in with his 1931 runners, who happened to be the best Hayward ever had. Besides Starr, they included Ralph Hill, a quietly confident distance runner from potato country near Klamath Falls. Bowerman liked Hill immediately. He'd cheered him on to a near world record 4:12.4 in the mile the year before (Nurmi had run 4:10.4 in 1923). He also observed the long runs that Hill took for stamina and saw how Hayward gave him different track workouts to build two very different things, raw speed and the ability to sustain it.

Hill was the first world-class miler Bowerman ever met. Recalling that Hayward had said Bowerman himself might be a 440 man one day, Bill ran what he felt was a hard lap. When the nausea and burn ebbed, he was able to lift his watch to his eyes: 63 seconds. "Just so's you'll know," Hayward chortled. "Ralph goes that fast for four laps."

"When I coached milers," Bowerman would later say, "I affected to be nonchalant about what they could do. But that took years. I was staggered by what Ralph could do. It just seemed impossible."

The force with which the young Bowerman connected with Hayward certainly had aspects of finding a long-lost father. Bill was grateful to have a guide to good form in his career as well as his stride. But he also came to revere Hayward because he was logical. It is not just the condescension of hindsight to say that sport in the 1930s was a miasma of ignorance. Doc Spears was no exception in putting arbitrary authority ahead of common sense. Hayward, by contrast, looked for the underlying reasons. He'd applied almost all his lessons to himself. He could whisper to a vaulter or jumper or hurdler the tiny changes that made all the difference. This fit with Bill's growing interest in the sciences and what we now term biomechanics, how the levers are moved by the muscles, how the body, properly aligned, performs at its optimum.

Hayward was a model healer—half doctor, half inventor. Bowerman began to mold himself into one too, with the same eagerness that he did high-knee drills. "I learned from the master," he would say. Hayward soon thought of Bowerman as a colleague.

There was one other parallel. Hayward and Bowerman both felt that high drama was part of a well-imparted lesson. In knocking down Spears, the coach seemed to be striking a blow for a greater good. And in early 1932, it turned out he really had. Others had joined Hayward in complaint and Spears was fired. For the coming football season, Bill's last, the head coach would be his old high school mentor, Prink Callison, who was fine with Bill's running track.

Bill rejoiced, although the college track season was over. Still, there was a big meet coming up. "Not that you'll probably ever run in one," Hayward said, "but you should never miss an Olympics. Got somewhere to stay in Los Angeles?"

Well, yes, as a matter of fact.

Every Christmas vacation he'd gone down to see Barbara and watch the Rose Bowl and he would also stay with the Youngs for a week each summer. So in the summer of 1932 Bill and Barbara went to the Olympics every day. "I surely didn't know it would be a foreshadowing of life to come," Barbara would say.

The 1932 Games, of course, didn't sneak up on anyone. Ralph Hill had been working for them for years. He didn't have a devastating kick in the mile, so Hayward had shaped his training to let him take on Nurmi and the other dour, dominant Finns not in the 1500 meters (the metric mile) but in the more wearing 5000. Hill figured that, coming from Klamath Falls, he'd be able to take the heat in Los Angeles better than Finns from the north woods.

Hill was right, which made for a historic battle. Nurmi was disqualified before the Games by the International Olympic Committee for taking expense money. But that still left Finns Lauri Lehtinen and Lauri Virtanen, multi-gold medalists whose best times were many seconds faster than Hill's. In the 5000 final they worked together, set a tough pace, and soon shook off the rest of the world—except Ralph Hill.

With a kilometer to go, Lehtinen surged, trying to break the American. He broke Virtanen. Into the last lap, Hill was only a meter behind. Bill, Barbara, Hayward, and 90,000 other Americans rose in the stands and called him home. In the last turn, Hill moved to pass, but Lehtinen went wide too, driving him out to the second lane.

Hill waited there, off his shoulder. Into the stretch, Hill kicked with all he had. As he came even, Lehtinen again veered outward, this time raking the taller Hill with his right elbow, catching his left arm and making him break stride. Lehtinen held the lead.

But Lehtinen could go no faster. Hill could. He gathered himself and drove on, now in the third lane. Lehtinen saw him, hurled himself out, too, and they collided again. They hit the line a foot apart, both timed at 14:30.0, but Lehtinen reached it first.

Barbara Young would still feel deaf from the booing two days later. Clearly, Hill would have won if the Finn hadn't interfered with him. The crowd howled for Lehtinen to be disqualified. He wasn't. European judges allowed this kind of roughness. The crowd knew what was fair and got uglier. Finally the announcer uttered the desperate cry for which the race would always be known: "Ladies and gentlemen . . . these people are our guests!" But it was only the sight of Hill going to Lehtinen, taking his hand, and the two trotting a victory lap that restored any calm.

Events could not have been crafted to better enthrall Bill with the Olympic empyrean. Before him was theory made flesh, the Games creating greater brotherhood among the combatants than the maddened horde. Moreover, he was being steeped in possibility. There was absolutely no reason that a flesh-and-blood friend, a potato-farmer-to-be, could not run with the finest ever. He talked for hours with Hayward and the gracious Hill about racing tactics and the nature of sportsmanship. Both would be needed in that other deadlock down the stretch—the struggle for Barbara's heart.

Barbara was a demon socialite. "I accepted everyone who ever asked me for a date, but was serious about only Mike and Bill," she would say. "Mike was in the news so much it's no wonder my sorority sisters were jealous." They pointedly gave her a beautiful, leather-bound copy of Flaubert's *Madam Bovary*, "who of course has all these pathetically overblown love affairs and dies a suicide."

Years later, Barbara said of Bill, "I really doubt our relationship would have survived if we'd gone to the same college. The interests I had were so disparate. But also, would Bill have endured what I put him through if we'd been at school together?"

In his letters and calls to her, Bill began sketching plans for after he graduated, and they always included Barbara. But in early 1933, something happened that would delay everything. Bill had joined ROTC as a senior because he needed the money, without realizing that in return for tuition help he was committing himself to a two-year obligation. He'd have to spend a fifth year at Oregon when he'd hoped to graduate in four.

Bill's reaction to this belated realization was apparently to reason that if he was going to be controlled by the military, he might as well really *be* military. Half a century later, Barbara unearthed a stack of 1933 letters from Oregon Governor Julius L. Meier to Senator Fred L. Steiwer and other politicians in support of Bill's appointment to the US Military Academy at West Point. All mentioned that Bill was the son of former governor Jay Bowerman. Yet although he took an exam and qualified, Bill never transferred to the Point. "It's another mystery," Barbara would say. In any event, nothing came of it. Bill stayed at Oregon. Although he had exhausted his football eligibility in the fall of 1932, he would have another season to run for Bill Hayward.

The next spring, free at last, he took full advantage. His stride was smoother and he learned that for a quarter-miler, how fast you run is almost unrelated to how you feel. "You're near death's door anyway afterward, paying off your oxygen debt," said Hayward. "You may as well make it worthwhile." Bill was soon knocking at the door of a 50-second 440.

He broke through when Hayward taught him finesse. "Sprint the first 110 yards," was his advice. "Then float the second 150, then sprint again in the last turn. After that, it's who slows down the least." Bill obeyed and eventually ran times in the high 48s for the 440. He was an emotional relay-team member. "He was almost always better in our mile relay than he was in his individual races," said George Scharf, a teammate who would become a lifelong friend.

Bill was also trying to uphold the Bowerman family honor by graduating Phi Beta Kappa, as his sister Beth had done. He would have made it, save for one class. "His French teacher gave him a D," Barbara would lament. "Why? To demonstrate not caring about football players." Bill took extra business courses he knew he could ace to bring up his GPA, but missed the cutoff by a hair. Given the hours he'd spent at part-time jobs, it was a considerable achievement.

About this time, Jay Bowerman summoned Bill to his law offices in Portland.

When his solemn, curious son was standing silently before him, the former governor stood, shook his hand, and said, "Son, you have the grades. I've seen you with people. You have the talent to be a fine attorney. And I'd like to help you become one." There was surely a Bowerman-length pause as Bill considered. Jay was only fifty-seven, but Bill could see that he was aging rapidly. "The biggest help you can be to me, sir," Bill said softly and evenly, "is to go straight to hell."

He turned, walked out, and began a life in which he would have little further contact with his father.

Bill graduated in June 1934 in business, but with enough science and math credits that Oregon's School of Medicine, in Portland, admitted him. No scholarship came with it, however, and he didn't have the tuition, nor would he accept anything from his father.

"The Depression was deep," Bowerman said later. "I didn't have a plateful of choices." After much canvassing, he was offered a position teaching and coaching for eighty dollars a month at Portland's Franklin High School. He elected to take it for a year and salt away the money. The medical school saved him a place in the next year's class.

At Franklin, he taught science, coached football, assisted in track—and chafed. "Everything you did, you did by the numbers," he would remember. He had a number of run-ins with the principal over his disciplinary methods. "Marijuana is not new, you know," Bowerman would say, looking back. "Kids would go out to these shacks and I'd chase them out of there, then their mothers would call the principal. I don't know if they were selling or what. But kids wouldn't show up in my classes, and I'd go look. I'd find one out there and I'd drag his ass out and say, 'Get back in school.'" This was not allowed, said the principal, because the handbook specified that teachers had to confine their discipline to the campus. "That wasn't the kind of school I went to," Bowerman told him.

Bill's sense of being in limbo could only have been intensified by the death of his grandmother, Mary Jane Chambers Hoover, in Fossil, on September 29, 1934. He couldn't get away for the funeral, but Lizzie, Dan, and Beth filled him in. The stories flowed for days. Mary Jane had raised the town just the way she had raised him. Whether she had to hog-tie, cauterize, or serenade, she was the tough, hard, proper, educated, musical soul of Fossil in its youth. Dozens walked away from the service sure that Mary Jane was pressing some lesson on him or her still, to be more civil, to watch your language, to study harder, but also to always have a little wild yearning in you, a shot of pioneer spirit, for those of pioneer stock.

It made Bill miserable to compare his heritage with his dreary, nowhere job that was so resistant to any pioneering. Besides, things in LA were not good.

Mike Frankovich had graduated from UCLA two years before Bill did from Oregon and went off to do sports radio in Canada. As Barbara discovered "how nice it was to have two people who were both *away*," she also realized that she preferred "the quietness of Bill rather than the . . . un-quietness of Mike, at least to live with."

But each time Frankovich returned to LA he applied gentle pressure, and Barbara began to yield. "I graduated in 1935 and Mike and I decided we were engaged," she would recall. "We had a ring made." Meanwhile, she was living at home while going to business college and resenting the change after four years of being free to come and go at UCLA. "So one night when Mike was back from Canada, I called him and said, 'Come get me!' I told my folks I was going to spend the night in the Tri-Delt house." When Frankovich hopped out of the car, he took one look at her and said, "Let's go to Reno and get married."

"I threw a bag in the car and we took off," Barbara would remember. "But he stopped to run in and tell the Browns, and while I sat there, I thought, 'I'm not doing this, not this way,' and turned us around."

Frankovich, so near to victory, pressed on, and eventually Barbara wrote a letter to Bill saying she wasn't going to marry him. "Mike took me to the post office and made sure I mailed it," she would remember. Having made the decision, Barbara's reaction was not one of peaceful relief. "I went home and cried for two weeks," she would say. "I didn't want to marry either of them. I loved them both too much to give them up!" But Frankovich had called the newspapers, so when Barbara changed her mind again, "we had to call them back, call it all off."

But Bill had received that letter and had begun to accept the reality of losing Barbara. In so doing, he may have stumbled upon the way to keep her. A few weeks later, when she got word to him that she'd broken it off with Frankovich, he didn't react quite as he had so many times before. "Bill and I started writing again, kind of coolish letters," Barbara would say. "In one of them he mentioned that he was taking another woman skiing at Crater Lake!"—their sacred place.

"The reason Bill Bowerman married me," Barbara has maintained, "was his sense of competitiveness." Of course, that's true. But in the end it was Barbara who most couldn't bear to lose him. She and a girlfriend whipped up to Medford. In a week, she had him back.

But times were hard, and the rule in those days was that the groom had to have $1,000 in the bank and a job that paid $100 a month. "Bill was making $80 a month teaching at Franklin," Barbara would say, "but he hated that job so he wasn't ready to marry then, and I had to go back down to LA. A lot of this was decided without words. A lot of life with Bill was like that."

A voice from the past, a profane, commanding voice from the inner sanctum, came to the rescue. Medford school superintendent Ercel Hedrick heard that goddamn Bill Bowerman was out of Oregon and coaching. Hedrick called Bill to say he'd been recommended to coach the Medford football team. "I'm very flattered," Bill said, "but I have one more year teaching and then I'm entered in medical school." Hedrick persuaded him to come to Medford to talk it over.

"So I drove down," Bowerman would recall, "and he said, with a lot of profanity thrown in, 'You're a Medford product. You know how I like to run my schools.' My schools. I reminded him about med school. He said, 'Here's a point you may be interested in. I know in Portland you get paid $1,000 for the year. We pay $1,500. We hire people one year at a time. Hell, you may change your mind and stay after a year. Think that over and let me know tomorrow.'"

Bill called Barbara and asked if she thought she could live in Medford, Oregon. She screamed and said yes. "And since that moment," she would moan down the years, "Bill has always blamed me for his not being a doctor."

It would be a year before they could marry. That summer Bill moved to Medford, reported to Medford High, taught history, and, at age twenty-four, head-coached his first season of varsity football.

The departing coach, Darwin "Brute" Burgher, had hardly been forced out. A gentle man, his nickname pure irony, he'd gone 36-5-3 in five seasons and won the 1933 state championship. Burgher would build a dynasty of his own at Boise High in his native Idaho. Bowerman learned that the best Medford players had graduated and those remaining were far from massive. He talked with assistant coach Ed Kirtley—eleven years his senior. They decided to return the offense to Prink Callison's single wing, which Bill knew well, in the hope of opening up the passing game.

Bill rented a house with friends Russ Acheson and Otto Frohnmayer, then a young attorney. "We had a bachelor threesome," Frohnmayer would say, "Bill, Russ, and I, and that's where I learned to drink Scotch whiskey. Russ was a coach too, came from Bend. Bill was always our practical joker. He'd look at any ordinary slimy thing and think how to get it under your pillow."

The 1935 Black Tornado team, as Medford became known, (they were the Tigers when Bill was in school) was often outweighed by fifteen pounds per man. But what they gave away in heft, they took back with a rapidly converging defense, allowing only 20 points all season while scoring 190. Bowerman's diagnostic gifts were paramount, enabling him to spot opponents' flaws and teach his players to exploit them. Medford was undefeated at 7-0-1, the only blemish a scoreless tie against the alumni.

After the season, Hedrick had him in to talk. "We've got to have a good football team if we want to win a goddamn school-funding election," Hedrick said. "And you did that, and I'm proud and I'm grateful. Now it's high time Medford had a goddamn track around the goddamn football field." He gave Bill a list of building contractors the schools used. Bill thanked him, tucked it in his briefcase, and said he'd be back after his wedding.

Bill and Barbara married on June 22, 1936, in the wedding chapel at Forest Lawn in Pasadena. Bill's white suit was tailored by the Portland shop that made his ROTC uniforms. Barbara carried Cecil Turner pink roses from her family's gardens, cuttings of which she would plant in the dooryard of her new home. Her train was three times the length of her dress, and for the photographs she had to stand on a platform to let it fall properly. In one picture, Barbara's expression is both idolatrous and relieved; Bill's is calmly, not to say smugly, triumphant. But to gaze into Barbara's eyes, Bill had to be posed on a high box. He seems to be testing a rocket pack, hovering four feet above her billowing train, an image of literal, bounding joy.

CHAPTER 7

Medford

AT THE AGE OF TWENTY-FIVE, BOWERMAN HAD UNIFIED THE TWO GREAT PROJECTS of his life, his work and his love. He was full of plans, animated by the freedom to coach as he knew best. Financial survival had given way to professional ambition: He wanted to add a track program and begin to impart Bill Hayward's bottled-up knowledge.

After a month's honeymoon at a borrowed house in California's San Gabriel Mountains (where Bill studied nearby tracks), the newlyweds drove slowly up the east side of the Sierra. Upon reaching Medford, they unloaded their wedding presents at a little rental house near the school and opened a bill for $125 for life insurance. "How do we pay this?" Barbara gasped. "Why," Bill said, "we go to the bank and borrow enough to tide us over."

Barbara was horrified: "We never borrowed in my family." So she took over the budget for the rest of their lives, monitoring every penny with unexpected zeal. "He thought I was spoiled, and always had everything," she would say, her tone allowing for some truth in that, "but a lot were hand-me-down clothes."

Bowerman earned a princely $125 per month from Medford High, on which they lived comfortably. They even saved a little—although they sometimes differed on exactly what they were saving for. Bill once spent the fund intended for the births of their sons on a movie camera and projector. "A son is just a son," he would say, "but a camera can teach someone to high-jump."

They spent their honeymoon summer planning how to lay out the running track. Bowerman organized the whole facility down to the landscaping. Then it was right into coaching football, scouting, and managing assistants. In his first two years, he also taught history and coached basketball—a sport he disliked, Barbara would say, "because you couldn't control it out there."

Bowerman's subsequent football seasons revealed him to be as humane as Doc Spears was bloodthirsty. This was not lost on a young man—Robert Warren Newland—who would benefit from and complement Bowerman's gifts perhaps more than anyone else. Bob Newland, said by Hedrick to be the most versatile athlete to come out of Medford High, would follow Bill as Medford track coach, direct three US Olympic Trials, and be the 1976 and 1980 US Olympic track and field team manager. In 1936, Newland was a freshman quarterback and high jumper—and all eyes.

"In practice, a lot of coaches like to hear the bodies collide," Newland would remember. "Not Bill. He taught us how to hit, but we really only did it in the games. That way we kept all those fine athletes who like to play football but hate getting beaten up every day."

Nor did Bill call the plays from the sideline. "That was the quarterback's job," Newland would say. "He always encouraged us to think and react on our own. But man, there was an aura of dead certainty when we talked about game plans. He was such a student of the sport that we were absolutely convinced anything he suggested would go all the way." The Medford practices, in the golden light of Newland's memory, were almost seminars, with players putting forward ideas and Bowerman judging their soundness.

In later years, watching Bowerman watch a football game from the sideline was to know what it had been like in those teaching huddles. He'd observe in silence for a time, then direct your attention to how a guard, say, was lining up slightly differently before different plays, telegraphing whether he would charge ahead to block or pull back to protect the quarterback with subtle shifts in his balance, nothing obvious until you knew what you were seeing.

Then Bill would bet you quarters on whether a play would be a pass or a run, to be divined from the posture of the poor guard. Then (having taken all your quarters) he'd watch to see whether any opposing players were able to read these blaring signals as well and, if so, would pronounce them "well coached." Finally, he'd list five things the guard could do to falsely telegraph one play and get the better-coached defenders out of position to defend another, turning the exploited into the exploiters.

"Football players," you'd say, "obviously can't afford to be dumb."

"But they are," he'd say. "A lot are. They don't realize what their own eyes are telling them." At such times, he seemed to brim with a cunning spirit—not fiendish, not driven, just the natural habit of a man who couldn't look at an angleworm on a wet lawn without thinking how to get it in your mouth.

Thus his high school football teaching stressed clear explanations and the exploration of possibilities. This led to Bill and Barbara's often being awakened at 4 a.m. by gravel striking their screen door—tossed by assistant Ed Kirtley, who'd been seized with an idea for a new play. ("And in the morning," Barbara would recall, "on the kitchen floor, there would be all the marks, lines, abscissas from this act of creation.")

In the nine seasons Bowerman coached Medford football (six before the war and three after), his teams would win fifty-nine games, lose thirteen, and tie eight. Every year he forged fresh unity. When the Black Tornado traveled to big games, Bowerman took Medford water along so the team wouldn't have to drink anyone else's impurities. It was the night before such a crucial game, Bob Newland would remember, that Bowerman imposed an 11 p.m. curfew. But starting quarterback Newland happened to know a lovely young lady in that city and lingered so long with her that he had to sneak back into the hotel.

As Newland would tell the story, "I got into the elevator okay, and when the door at our floor opened, I was sure Bill or Ed Kirtley would be there, but the coast was clear. I tiptoed down the hall, eased open the door to my room, and got inside. Sighing with relief, I stripped off my clothes in the dark and lay down on the bed—right on top of Bill Bowerman, who'd been waiting there all the time." Curfew not being a hanging offense, Newland was allowed to play, and Medford beat Coquille 6-0.

Barbara didn't bemoan the hours sports took Bill away, because Medford turned out to have a bracing cultural life. For one thing, Bowerman's mule skinner of a boss, Ercel Hedrick, was married to a terrific writer. "I dearly loved Helen Hedrick," Barbara would reminisce. "They lived a block away with four kids. I was awed by them both. She wrote stories about the West for *The Saturday Evening Post* and *Esquire.* She wrote right there among the clotheslines, laundry, dogs, cats. She was the most intriguing person I'd ever known. When Marian Anderson came to sing, no Medford hotel would house her, so Helen Hedrick took her in."

In rapid succession, Bill and Barbara had drawn to them almost a salon of kindred spirits. Two houses away were the Frohnmayers—Bill's bachelor housemate of the past year, Otto, and his wife, MarAbel—who had been married within two weeks of Bill and Barbara. "I don't think a person has more than half a dozen close friends," Bowerman would say in his eighties, "and Otto is one of mine. We've been through so much that I call him once a month just to bullshit and run things past him. Otto is meticulous about the rules of the game."

Born in 1905 in southern Germany, Otto was six months old when his parents brought him to a German colony in Portland. According to Otto's son David, "My grandparents watched the rise of Bismarck and didn't want their sons being cannon fodder for Prussian militarism. Dad did smelt fishing to earn his tuition and worked at the Eugene Hotel to put himself through college and law school."

Otto Frohnmayer watched Bowerman with fascination. "Once he sets out to do something, he sees it through," Frohnmayer would say, so when Bill lost a game, "his mind would be on what went wrong." Otto was also moved by Bowerman's humaneness: "Bill never played a man who was not in top physical shape. The minute he sensed a man was injured, the man came out. I've seen him lose track meets because he didn't think that one of his runners was in the right physical or mental shape to double back."

Admiration ran both ways. "Otto Frohnmayer," Bowerman would observe, "established himself as the wisest counsel in Medford. I always ran my decisions by him." One had been the question of medicine. "He should have been a doctor," Frohnmayer would declare. "I think if it hadn't been for the fact that Barbara was a Christian Scientist, he might have done it. And he would have been a tremendous doctor. He'd have been one who studied diseases and what causes them and what's the cure for them because that's exactly what he's done in all the other things that he's been into."

It doesn't seem far-fetched to see, in Bowerman's eighteen-hour days of coaching and teaching, the sleep-deprived routine of the medical student he might have been at the time. His instincts, always, were to ameliorate. Otto would tell the story of a steep hike into the Seven Lakes area, a trek he wasn't in shape for: "I was really tired, and then we all drank some particular liquor, I can't remember what it was. I went to sleep, and when I awoke I got the shakes." When it got worse, he mentioned it to Bowerman, who diagnosed dehydration. "So he got me a lot of water, and the second night I had a perfect sleep. He was the kind of guy who knew what to do for you. Bill wouldn't want it to look like he had any real feelings, but he was very deep in lots of ways, very thoughtful."

Dave Frohnmayer found his father and Bowerman an unlikely pair: "Bill the raconteur, the athlete, the ecumenical man, interested in music, medicine, science. Dad the complete lawyer, but not an athlete, even though he was six foot three and had great physical strength. He'd always had to work, not do sports. Bill introduced him to the outdoors, to trout fishing. And the musical side of the family was definitely my mom's."

Where the two seemed to match up was in their senses of humor. MarAbel Frohnmayer would remember bridge games in the early years when "these two miserable husbands would pass the cards under the table." The men would tuck the cards in their socks. "We had a system," Otto would confess. "I would send him three cards of one suit and he would send me three cards of another. The three-cards-in-the-shoe pass!"

Son David treasured other memories. "Dad had that great, southern German sense of humor—earthy isn't a strong enough word—and Bill and he egged each other on."

It is delicate work to ease Bowerman's language onto the page. Most allusions deserve to remain with the cows and the outhouses. But others are literature, such as when he observed with satisfaction to the Oregon Club that "some women are born great, some attain greatness, and others have greatness thrust into them." He loved multi-entendre, mega-entendre. In team meetings, he liked to use a lurid opening ("I am not a virgin . . . "), a pregnant pause, and an anticlimactic finish once he had your attention (" . . . at making mistakes. But in this case, Mr. San Romani, I bow to your overwhelming superiority.").

In any case, Bowerman practiced an iron double standard, never once swearing in front of Barbara when they were alone. His profanity didn't arise out of frustration. It was expressive art. It was poetry. One of Dave Frohnmayer's early memories is of listening, "with hope in my greedy heart," to his father and Bill on the phone. "Mother had instituted a fine for swearing, so Dad said he'd give us five cents per cuss word when he slipped up. So we couldn't wait for Bill to call. It was worth forty-five cents!"

In the spring of 1937, Medford High fielded a track and field team for the first time in fifteen years. Bowerman told boosters that he believed track to be "a developer of football and basketball stamina and speed," but of course he loved it for its own sake. In search of jumpers or sprinters, he gave tests to PE classes and junior high schools and soon had a winning squad. When a junior high principal didn't feel PE and sports was top priority, Bill told Hedrick, "This violates your golden rule on how never to lose a school bond levy." The man got the message.

In his eight track seasons at Medford, Bowerman would win three state championships and eight Hayward Relays team titles. But track is a sport—and a story—of individuals.

In 1938, Bill heard that up little Wagner Creek, living with his grandparents, was "an orphan so hungry he ran down a jackrabbit to see if he was fat enough to eat." Bowerman drove up and talked the grandparents into letting Ray Johnson enroll at Medford. "Okay," they said, "but he can't drive our car any farther than Talent."

So Johnson began getting up at four in the morning, taking their car to tiny Talent and hitching a ride on to Medford before school. He walked and jogged the whole twelve miles many times. Johnson was indeed fast in the short sprints, but—it taking one to know one—Bowerman made him a quarter-miler. Johnson responded with times of 50.8 seconds as a sophomore, 49.5 as a junior, and 47.8 as a senior in 1941. That would be the fastest high school 440 run in the United

States during the decade of the 1940s. Johnson also starred on the football team in 1938 and '39, but Bill kicked him off during his senior year so he wouldn't hurt himself and lose a sure track scholarship. Johnson ran well at the University of Southern California and said of Bowerman in 1985, "I respect and love that man. You may quote me."

Another boy weathered a slightly different experience with Bowerman—one that may have taught Bill something, too. Al Gould, who would go on to a sports writing career, moved up from Ashland after eighth grade and, as he remembered it later, regarded Medford as "comparable only to an unescorted visit to hell." Meeting Bob Newland eased the transition. "He and I spent much time together, including mowing the lawn of one William J. Bowerman, for which we split a small fee."

Bob Newland's father, Bill Newland, was brewmaster at the local brewery and an ingenious problem solver. He had built two hurdles in the Newlands' backyard. Gould described them as being "on rockers, with webbing across the top, as opposed to the unforgiving wood of hurdles of that day." Gould and Bob Newland developed credible form by practicing over them. "But when we got to high school, Bowerman was our PE instructor. In the gym he placed two of the monstrous standard hurdles and demonstrated the correct form. Trust me, you don't want to drop your trailing leg too soon, not if you want to dance at the prom that evening."

In the act of proving to Bowerman that he could hurdle, Gould tore open his trailing knee. "I stopped the tiny flow of blood and retired to the dressing room. Bill came by, looked at the knee, patted me on the shoulder, and said, 'We'll have to work on that form a little.' I grunted and never approached a hurdle again in anger or in peace."

Gould wanted to escape to baseball, but Medford had no team. As the sports editor of the *Medford Hi-Times* he campaigned for the return of baseball to the school. Bowerman, who wanted no siphoning of talent in the spring, was opposed. Gould enlisted the aid of the sports editor of the *Mail Tribune* (the paper that had essentially driven Lizzie and Dan Bowerman's paper bankrupt), whose father had played two seasons for the Philadelphia Phillies. Finally Bowerman gave in and baseball returned in the spring of 1940. Thirty years later, Bowerman would recognize Al Gould in a hotel and call out, "There's the guy who tried to scuttle my track program at Medford High!"

With all of Bill's coaching and teaching, Barbara got to see more of her man in the winter than any other time of year—after football, before track. It was then that they found their way back to their special place. The Bowermans would go up to Crater Lake with a carload of food and, thanks to a friend who was a ranger there, have the whole park to themselves. "We stayed at Annie Springs," Barbara would recall, "and the ski from the lake rim to Annie Springs was six miles of powder. That was how Bill first got into mountain skiing."

Perhaps not coincidentally, Barbara was soon pregnant. Keeping pace down the block was MarAbel Frohnmayer. The Frohnmayers were delivered of their first child, Mirajean, in 1938. A month later Barbara gave birth to a son, Jon.

Life in Medford in those years was so good that, in the memories of all involved, it would seem like no time at all until war clouds thickened. "We were in Eastern Oregon with Jon," Bowerman would recall. "On the Sunday, we were driving back to Medford and heard the Japanese had come on in and dropped the bombs on Pearl Harbor." Looking over at Barbara, Bill simply executed a U-turn. "I just drove right to Vancouver Barracks and took a physical, and went back to Medford for a month while they decided what to do with me."

Because he'd been in ROTC and the Army Reserve, he was made a second lieutenant and assigned to Ft. Lawton, near Seattle. The camp was essentially a staging ground for sending troops to Alaska, where an invasion was expected.

"But they classified me limited duty," Bowerman would remember with disgust. "I've got a scar on my left eye. I got it when I was a boy, ten or twelve, playing mumblety-peg. All it did was nick it. Hell, I could see like an eagle. But they gave me theatre officer, athletic officer. I was doing everything except washing the dishes."

Their second son, Jay, was born December 17, 1942, a year into Bill's war. Barbara would remember her husband "chafing at the bit, wishing he could go with the men he was always sending off."

CHAPTER 8

The Tenth Mountain Division

JAY'S BIRTH WAS NOT THE ONLY SIGNIFICANT EVENT FOR LIEUTENANT Bowerman that December: He finally got an assignment he could sink his teeth into. In January 1943, the family left Ft. Lawton and drove to Southern California, where they found a little house for Barbara and the kids on the beach at Topanga Canyon.

Bill then took a train to Camp Hale, near Leadville, Colorado, elevation 9,500 feet. Arriving in February, Lieutenant Bowerman was sent to the just-forming Eighty-Sixth Regiment, which was joining the Eighty-Seventh Regiment in making up what would become the US Army's Tenth Mountain Division. (The Eighty-Fifth Regiment would be activated in July.)

Commissioned at Ft. Lewis in December 1941, the Tenth had been created to give the United States a counterpart to the Finnish soldiers on skis who had been so effective against the Russians in the 1939–40 Winter War. With Charles Minot "Minnie" Dole using his National Ski Patrol to recruit for it, the Army would assemble the nation's best skiers, climbers, forest rangers, even falconers. It would then wash out huge percentages of them to find and anneal the toughest for mountain combat.

Its first volunteers had vacated college ski teams and resort slopes worldwide to become the cadre that would teach those next in line. Indeed, the Tenth's very first officer was former Oregon ski coach Paul Lafferty. So when Bowerman sensed he could be stuck showing movies for the duration, he had begun a vigorous correspondence with his fellow Beta. Bowerman would never be a great skier, but his years at Crater Lake had taught him the basics, so Lafferty expedited Bill's transfer to the Tenth's mountain training center at Camp Hale. It didn't hurt that Bill knew a little about mules; they were to be the unit's prime means of supply.

By the time Brigadier General George Price Hays took formal command of the division in late November 1944, the 14,000 men of the Tenth had survived three years of Darwinian trial. In Hays, who had won the Congressional Medal of Honor in World War I and had commanded an artillery division on D-day at Omaha Beach, the Tenth had a leader fully capable of welding its smart, polyglot, outspokenly independent troops into an effective tactical weapon. During his first meeting with his officers and noncoms, Hays would earn an approving roar with the remark, "Hey, if you're going to risk your life, you might as well do it in good company."

Lieutenant Bowerman was made a platoon leader in First Battalion, C Company. Among the lifelong friends he would gain from the Tenth was another Bill, Bill Boddington, the CO (commanding officer) of A company. They bonded for a host of reasons. Both were over thirty, far more seasoned than the usual lieutenant. Boddington, too, had employed his connections, having pleaded with Minnie Dole in a New York elevator for a slot in the ski troops. And Boddington twice had been on the US Olympic men's field hockey team. In fact, during the Berlin Olympics in 1936 he had come within a few feet of Adolf Hitler. "There was a reception," he told Bowerman, "and we all marched in and he gave us the old Nazi salute. I was so close I could have reached out and hit him."

"Well," said Bowerman, "let's get you another chance."

They were classic Tenth material. As Barbara would describe it, "The Tenth was like an Ivy League club—a mixture of Regular Army leaders and citizen soldiers, some from expensive colleges. Occasionally officers objected to noncoms coming in the officers' club. But some corporals were world-class heroes to men like Bill, who were only officers because they'd been in ROTC. Bill would host these great skiers and be frowned upon by the colonels."

Camp Hale's barracks housed 17,000 men and 3,900 horses and mules. On clear days the view was glorious, but the little Pando Valley was so hemmed in by peaks that the air grew polluted from coal smoke and troop trains. Bill and his men coughed for weeks with "the Pando hack." General Lloyd Jones, the Tenth's first CO, took over in July 1943. He later developed a bronchial condition that worsened in Camp Hale's smog and was replaced by General Hays in 1944.

Bill and his men learned military skiing and snowshoeing. Testing the equipment and themselves, they climbed peaks, rappelled cliffs, and struggled through deep powder under huge rucksacks. The attrition rate was inhuman. In eighteen months, one sergeant trained 1,100 men to get 184 for his company.

The men of the Tenth got to try out the first snowmobiles and snowcats. They fired "pack howitzers," 75 mm cannon that would break down into six parts—one per pack mule, with more mules to carry ammunition. That arrangement required 1,200 mules per battalion. Bowerman became an S-4, the regimental supply officer, and Boddington his assistant. "I was the proud owner of 200 mules," Bowerman would remember. Fortunately, some champion rodeo cowboys had been sent to help.

In April 1943, Bill wrote Barbara to come stay nearby. She threw the boys and a playpen in the back of their Ford station wagon and soon found lodging in Glenwood Springs, thirty miles away. The men could leave camp on weekends, so from Friday afternoon to 4 a.m. Monday mornings Glenwood Springs was Party Central. "It was not the life we'd ever lived," Barbara would remember. "It was tremendously exciting. I indulged too, mildly." Barbara had never had a drink of alcohol until the war, never drank coffee until the war. "But it all heightened the drama," she would say. "Everything was important, everything could end tomorrow, so everyone savored. Most in the crowd were college kids." No account of the much-memorialized Tenth leaves out its love of song. The men belted out cadence chants while in the mountains and wrote and rewrote lyrics for the tunes brought by Austrian or Nordic skiers

In the din, Oregonians sought one another. Paul and Jeanne Lafferty were already old friends of Bill's, Paul as a fraternity brother and Jeanne because Bill had helped her through chemistry class. Lafferty's younger brother, Ralph, had gone to Eugene's University High when Bill was doing his student teaching at Oregon. During the week, Bowerman and Ralph Lafferty had the two front rooms in a Bachelor Officers' Quarters at Hale, where they'd booby-trap the hall with crisscrossed skis, Lafferty would say, "just to hear people crash when they came in late."

That summer, at age thirty-two, Bill felt he was in the best physical condition of his life. He ran in the Army and was the division champion in the 440. Against an all-black division with one Olympian, though, he was fourth. His best time in the service equaled his best at Oregon, 48.8 seconds.

In the fall of 1943, Bill was ordered to a six-week officer-training course at Ft. Benning, Georgia. He returned to Camp Hale a captain, in plenty of time for a physical ordeal that would surpass anything they would experience in the war. On March 26, 1944, the entire division, 12,000 strong, their long, flat-board skis tied atop their heads like little steeples, trudged out into the wilderness for maneuvers called the "D-Series." For six weeks they would bivouac and war game in the open, often above 13,000 feet. As soon as they were exposed in the snow-fields, a blizzard hit and it fell to thirty below. No fires were permitted. More than a hundred men with frostbite had to be evacuated in one night.

Bowerman, his metabolism burning huge meals as if he were on hay crew, was in his element. He stayed clearheaded in the high camps, even improving on the Army's way of supplying troops on ridges, leading his mules in shortcuts across the valleys. It was a matter of sheer survival. The men's boots froze to their feet and the ones who got altitude sickness were washed out. "But Bill just gloried in that," Barbara would say.

The division passed every test, endured every extreme, and marched singing into camp fit for war. But the Army in it's wisdom would leave the Tenth without a mission for a while yet.

That momentous spring of 1944, while the Allies were moving slowly up the Italian boot, while the Russians were crushing German lines on the Eastern Front, while the Normandy invasion, at terrible cost, made it a three-front war in Europe, Bowerman and his men felt doomed to shiver in Colorado, playing no part. Insult was added that summer when the men, so acclimated to cool mountains, were entrained to the hundred-degree heat and humidity of Camp Swift, Texas, thirty-eight miles east of Austin. "They had washed out those who couldn't stand the altitude," Barbara would observe. "Now they washed out those who couldn't stand the heat."

Their mules, meanwhile, were shipped off to Burma and Bowerman's men later had to break hundreds of new mules that had spent months in boxcars. "Mules that have been sitting around for a while are just like a bunch of kids," Bowerman would say. "They raise hell as soon as you turn them loose." Jon Bowerman, then five, would never forget: "Mules were stampeding up and down the street, and the Missouri and Arkansas mule skinners were running around yelling things you could hardly understand and it was better if you didn't."

Then, late in 1944, with the Germans dug in for the winter in the mountains of Italy, someone figured out how to put the Tenth to work. They finally had a mission and they were shipping out across the Atlantic. Bowerman's Eighty-Sixth Regiment had two weeks' notice. For Barbara, this good-bye was the most daunting test of her positivism. She could hardly believe her prayers would keep him safe.

Just before they went overseas, Bowerman was made a major, a staff officer at division headquarters in S-2, intelligence. Then he developed a hernia and had to go into the hospital. He was not there very long and was well on the mend, but when he got back to headquarters, Ralph Lafferty would recall, "the chief of staff, a West Pointer he'd offended somehow, said they were full, so he had to go back to supply, and all those mules."

The 2,000 troops and thirty-five officers of the division's Eighty-Sixth Regiment sailed from Hampton Roads, Virginia, on December 10, 1944. At sea, their orders were revealed, and applauded. They were going to Italy. On December 23, they landed at starving, bombed-out Naples and took a rusty Italian freighter north to Livorno.

In January 1945, the Tenth took up positions beside the Fifth Army, which was stalemated against the Germans in a valley in the Apennine Mountains, central Italy's corrugated spine. The Allied forces' main objective was highway 64, the north/south road connecting Pistoia, which they held, and Bologna, which they did not. If the next ten miles of mountains could be taken, including a series of three peaks—Monte Belvedere, Monte Gorgolesco, and Monte della Torraccia—the road into the vast, flat Po Valley would be open and the Germans would have to retreat to the Alps. Four times Allied infantry had taken Mt. Belvedere. Four times they had been thrown back. The American Fifth Army could neither shell the Germans off the heights nor break through their lines below.

When Hays reported for duty, Major General Lucian K. Truscott, recently given command of the Fifth, informed him that the Tenth's assignment was first to capture Mt. Belvedere, "then proceed by stages to capture all the high ground to a position east of the town of Tolè." When Hays asked Truscott, "Who is going to share the bullets with us when we attack?" Truscott answered, "No one."

Hays soon determined that the key to a successful assault on Mt. Belvedere and points north lay in first taking a $3\frac{1}{2}$-mile-long, 2,000-foot-high mass of shale and scrub oak—the Mt. Manzinello-Pizzo di Campiano Ridge, later code-named Riva Ridge—which overlooked Mt. Belvedere. From Riva Ridge, the Germans could rain artillery and mortar fire down upon the Allies. Indeed, the Germans had been so successful in stopping the Fifth's advance that they regarded their positions on Riva Ridge as impregnable.

Hays sent the best scouts in the Eighty-Sixth to find out if that was really the case. One was eighteen-year-old John Skillern from Eugene, Oregon. "Skillern was a hell of a soldier," Bowerman would recall, "He was one of my recon men and he was so good that he got bumped up to sergeant. 'Course he was just a kid. Every time he absorbed too much Chianti he'd screw up and we would have to make a private out of him again. But he reconnoitered that thing."

At sunset, before Skillern and the others set out, Bowerman put his binoculars on the east face of Riva Ridge, a connected series of peaks that wouldn't look out of place in Wheeler County. The side facing him across the Dardagna River was an eroded cliff, 1,500-feet high, climbable in a place or two, but mostly brittle shale, scree, waterfalls, and ugly ravines, all glazed with slippery ice. At the top were Germans with their binoculars trained on him.

The next day, Skillern and the other scouts returned safely. "Skillern came back and said it wasn't impregnable at all," Bowerman would recount. "He'd impregnated it himself. He'd impregnated the hell out of it. There were no Germans up there at night."

Over the next few weeks, as more patrols identified five routes to the top and even strung ropes up a few bad spots, the men of the Eighty-Sixth studied models of the ridge and worked out transit times and deadlines in preparation for the planned night attack, the most difficult of military operations.

At 7:30 p.m. on February 18, 1945, with guns unloaded so no accident would give them away, in single file, 700 men of the Eighty-Sixth's First Battalion began to climb. Their orders were to control the ridge by daylight. To illuminate the ridge without giving their positions away, the division shone searchlights not on the ridge but on nearby clouds, creating artificial moonlight. The significance of this was grasped by no one on top, although the Germans did spot one company and fired on it. The Americans had the discipline to not shoot back, and the defenders left the area without sounding the alarm. After a few nerve-racking hours, men began to crest the ridge, help their fellows up, load their weapons, and prepare to make their presence known.

At dawn, a heavy fog rolled in, obscuring the advancing Americans as they went from bunker to dugout to gun emplacement, waking Germans with grenades or turning their own machine guns on them as they emerged. But the men of the Tenth were relatively few and facing a battle-hardened corps scattered over miles of ridgeline. The Germans regrouped almost instantly. The four minipeaks composing the ridge all saw desperate combat for their possession.

It was one thing to take Riva Ridge. It was another to hold it against the mortars and artillery and tenacious counterattacks of the Germans, who flooded up the gentle west slope. The experience of Lieutenant James Loose, a platoon leader from Cleveland, was typical. The Germans attacked Loose's platoon all that day and four times that night. By their second night on the ridge, his men were out of grenades and almost out of ammunition. They had to call in pack howitzer artillery to within ten yards of their own foxholes to keep from being overrun. Loose's platoon accounted for twenty-seven German dead. Each of his men received the Bronze Star, Loose the Silver.

Bowerman all this time was helping load climbing teams with ninety-pound packs of ammunition and rations for Loose and the other fighters. A few embattled US units on top, who'd been told they'd be relieved and resupplied after twenty-four hours, weren't reached for eight days.

Meanwhile, even before the Eighty-Sixth's assault on Riva Ridge began, the division's remaining regiments, the Eighty-Fifth and Eighty-Seventh, had begun moving into place against their primary objective. Traveling only under cover of darkness, they made their way to the long mass of rock, shaped like an undulant caterpillar whose three peaks were Mt. Belvedere, Mt. Gorgolesco, and Mt. della Torraccia.

The Germans were no longer subject to surprise. They had been fortifying this ground all winter and were fanatically determined to stop the Allied drive. As the Tenth's first 400 men slogged across a muddy slope on Mt. Belvedere, parachute flares popped above them and the night became as blinding day. The German 1044th Regiment opened up with everything they had. Worst were the mines, sending men spinning and clawing, screaming for a medic.

But the Tenth held discipline. In small clumps, they kept climbing, avoiding the minefields as best they could, pouring their own fire into the bunkers. As Bowerman would tell it, "My friend Jack Hay, from the University of Montana ROTC, was commander of the Third Battalion, and he took Mt. Belvedere." On Mt. Gorgolesco, Staff Sergeant Hugh Evans led a small party and took that summit. "Della Torraccia was the worst," according to Thomas O'Neil of the Eighty-Sixth. "Only about thirty percent of our men made it to the top." Still, the few who made it held the summit against counterattack. By dawn on February 25, the Germans had withdrawn to the north.

"But the rest of the Army was sitting on their asses to see how the mountain boys did," Bowerman would remember decades later, with scarcely dimmed disgust. "They weren't ready to move. So we sat there for another six weeks. And the next time it was tough."

The struggles for Riva Ridge and the Apennine mountains cost the Tenth 203 dead, 686 wounded, and 12 missing. They'd taken 400 prisoners and killed many more men than they'd lost. Before Mt. Belvedere, Ralph Lafferty would recall, "Regular Army guys would see your Tenth Mountain shoulder patch and want to fight you. We were college boys coming to play war." After Belvedere, that hazing stopped cold.

They had made themselves known. If General Truscott and his subordinates were amazed by what the untested Tenth had accomplished, the German high command was equally astounded. Field Marshall Albrecht Kesselring would later write that the attack "might imperil our whole operational plan for the spring."

Bowerman fully intended to assist in that imperiling, but first he had to help collect the fallen and transport them to Graves and Registration. Ralph Lafferty would remember bodies "contorted like twist-ties" strewn on a hillside and troops, on orders from the regimental commander, stuffing them into mattress covers. The CO, Lafferty would say, "knew how terrible it is to morale to see your friends in pieces."

As Bowerman followed the collection squads, he somehow mastered an essential skill: to register the deaths of comrades in grisly, unforgettable detail without being wrecked by it. No one he returned to after the war felt that he had been scarred by his immersion in brutality. Unlike the many for whom war is defining, Bowerman didn't find himself as a man on the battlefield. Rather, he made the war his job and treated its risk much as he treated the Regular Army bureaucracy. He held his nose and got on with it. When the war ended, he would be the first one out the door.

After Mt. Belvedere, the division didn't simply sit and wait. There were weeks of fluid, vicious fighting, pressing ever northward. Its three regiments leapfrogged, blended, and passed through each other according to terrain and enemy movements, all to prepare the tactical ground for one last, overwhelming offensive. Bowerman was often out in a jeep observing, tailoring supplies to the needs of the moving units. His favorite jeep driver was Sergeant Joe Litecky from Minneapolis. "Our minds worked alike," Bill would say. "He was my guardian angel, getting us out of some places we both sensed we shouldn't be in."

April 14, 1945—one day after the death of President Franklin D. Roosevelt—would be the bloodiest day for the Tenth, with more than 500 lives lost. The Allies carpet bombed the German positions in the last line of hills south of Bologna and the Po and shelled them with cannon fire. Still, when the Allies attacked, resistance was greater than any they had ever faced. The German artillery and mortars were devastating. Mules carrying ammunition were hit and the ammunition exploded. On a hill near Castel d'Aino, a platoon from the Eighty-Fifth's Third Battalion, just taken over by Second Lieutenant Robert J. Dole, was ordered to capture a prisoner on night patrol. "We took them by surprise," said his sergeant, Stan Kuschick. "And then there was a firefight. A minefield, protected by German machine gun fire, blocked our movement. Bob, in a gutsy move, led the platoon up front with two scouts. Machine gun fire killed the scouts and hit Bob. I saw he was barely alive. He looked gray." Dole, later US Senator from Kansas and the 1996 Republican presidential nominee, was at first paralyzed from the neck down. He would spend forty months in Army hospitals and lose the use of his right arm.

Days later, Ralph Lafferty went down. An executive officer for his battalion, he had just taken over a company because its commander was badly wounded. "I got two doses," he would recall, "first from mortar fire and about twenty minutes later someone stepped on a mine, an S-mine, that kicks up in the air and breaks and sprays balls of shrapnel." In all, Lafferty took fragments in his chest, hand,

and—he was sure from the pain—heel. "I was carried out of there on a door by two German prisoners. They took me to our medical collection station, which wasn't far because as we attacked they moved right behind us."

But they could only bandage and drug him. He was forced to stay there during German counterattacks. He didn't feel life slipping away, but he was still bleeding and far from any real help. "I knew you could take a surrette of morphine every four hours," Lafferty would say. "I had a stopwatch, and every four hours I would notify the medic of the time. I was pretty faint. I was naked by then. They strip off your clothes to see what happened to you. I was just in a blanket."

Out of the night leaned a familiar face. It took Lafferty an instant to believe it. "I don't know how Bill found me."

Bowerman had been doing "the usual roaming," anticipating the supply needs of units that were coming up from the rear, if it could be called a rear. The fighting was so fluid that some hills were safe while others were receiving shells from the huge German 88s. Bowerman spoke with the medics and said to Lafferty, "Let's go. Let's move you now."

Bowerman didn't have Sergeant Joe Litecky with him, so he ran out, flagged down a jeep, and ordered the driver to help him load Lafferty in the passenger seat and stand clear. Violating a standing order, he took the wheel himself. "Officers absolutely were never permitted to drive," Lafferty would say.

"We had something of a trip," Bowerman would recall. He knew where he wanted to go, back where the offensive had begun, on the lower slopes of Mt. della Spe, where there would be a medical transfer unit. But the road had so many convolutions and switchbacks that he had to drive cross-country in places, using his sense of where different American units were and were not. At one point he had to pass under some tracer fire across a canyon. He would look over at Lafferty to see if his color was still lifelike and, seeing that it was, tell them both to be patient. Eventually he made it out. An ambulance took Lafferty on to an Army surgeon operating in a schoolhouse near the town of Pistoia.

Lafferty's telling of this story would still have morphine's calm clarity forty-five years later. "I remember seeing a big garbage bucket of arms and legs in the waiting area," he would say. "The surgeon asked if I needed blood, and I said I didn't think so. I felt pretty good. I was concerned about my hand. I couldn't get it to open. They said, 'Don't worry about your hand, guy. We got more to worry about than that.'"

The surgeons took out a rib to remove all the shrapnel that had lodged in Lafferty's chest and abdomen. "I got hit at 2 p.m. and was operated on at 10 a.m. the next day, and that would have been a lot longer were it not for Bill. I sure give him credit for getting us moving right then. If he didn't save my life, he sure improved the odds."

Lafferty finished out the war in a Pistoia hospital. His heel hurt so much that he was amazed to find no wound there. The doctors finally convinced him they hadn't missed any metal and sent him home. A year later, after he was out of the service, the Army shipped home his gear. When he put on the boots, one felt odd. "In that heel, just under the insole, was this big ball of shrapnel that had come through two inches of rubber and stopped just in time."

If he had to choose, Bill Bowerman would later say, he would take saving people and supplying people over killing people. But the Allied offensive was on the verge of shoving the Germans into the Po Valley, and Bowerman's fighting merit had not been lost on his superior officers. "My contention," Bill would often say, "is this division was successful because they were all outdoorsmen. They all could read a situation and they could act."

As a prime example of that ability, Bowerman was asked to leave supply duty and take command of the Eighty-Sixth's First Battalion. He accepted. A few days later he earned his highest decoration. As he would tell the story, "We were on reconnaissance, going down the road in a jeep. At the end of the road was a building. And we took fire from there and my Jeep went right over and we dropped off the road into a ditch. We got our asses back out of there. This is when nobody knew who was where, what areas were friendly or not. All we knew is we got shot at. So we headed back up the road to warn our guys and see if we can't get somebody with a bazooka. I don't know what the hell I was going to do with a bazooka."

En route he flagged down an American tank with a jammed turret. The gunner could shoot but not maneuver. Bill talked him into attacking the house with machine guns. "So I get up on his tank and we go down the road and he's firing his machine gun and I'm riding behind the turret, and Jesus, the Krauts, it looked like somebody kicked an anthill. They hit the ditch running and hit the other side of the road running. And my tank guy fired his cannon at them, and about that time, here came a guy out from the house and started waving his arms. He turned out to be an American colonel. So I rescued an American colonel by accident. They had captured him somewhere, and he was so glad to see us he recommended me for a Silver Star. It was purely an accident, but I took it."

As the Germans retreated through the fertile Lombardy Plain, they tried to blow every bridge behind them to delay their pursuers. So for Bowerman's First Battalion, speed was everything. On April 30, the lake towns of Nago, Riva, and Torbole fell to the Americans. In Torbole, Bill Boddington got out ahead of the attack and had to lie in a ditch for two hours while the Third Battalion fought their way toward the town. He watched the Germans retreat to Trento and Bolzano, higher up. Beyond, the snowy Alps rose in a beautiful wall to the Austrian border, an improbable battleground.

I n the town of Riva, while getting his bearings, Major Bowerman got a call from Regimental Intelligence saying they had captured a German colonel on his way across the Brenner Pass. After hearing what the colonel had to say, Bowerman did what he'd been told to do in officer school—"use initiative appropriate to the situation." He ran out and grabbed a captain, a couple of lieutenants, and an interpreter, Staff Sergeant Julius Keller. He told them that he'd heard a few Germans were in the mood to surrender. "Come on," he said, "let's get a few Lugers." Bowerman had promised Bill Hayward that he'd bring him one of the German pistols.

With Bowerman driving, they headed up the road toward Brenner Pass. They were stopped at a German Army checkpoint about fifteen miles outside of Riva. With Keller translating, Bowerman told the soldiers he was on the way to a meeting with the German high command and they let him through. Keller began to suspect Bowerman was out for more than souvenirs.

A few miles later they were stopped at an SS checkpoint. This time simply mentioning the high command was not enough. Keller quietly told Bowerman that the SS (for *Schutzstaffel*, the Nazi party's storm troopers) was a political arm that thought it should dominate the army. When Bowerman insisted that the SS lieutenant call the commanding general, the lieutenant replied, "I cannot call the general. I am only a lieutenant."

As Keller would tell the story in a memoir thirty years later, Bowerman, "drawing himself up to his full height of an All-American football player, which he was, answered, 'I am a major and I order you to call the general and tell him a group of American officers would like to talk to him in his headquarters.'"

Rank worked wonders. The lieutenant phoned the general, who agreed to talk with the major. With Keller interpreting, the general (who "sounded very friendly") said that he would send a staff car to bring the major and his interpreter to headquarters. The jeep and the other Americans would have to wait. It was a calculated risk, but when the staff car arrived fifteen minutes later, Bowerman and Keller got in.

The car took them to the fifteenth-century Castel Toblino, where Keller took note of the intimidating number of armed guards. Convinced they would have to make an escape, he tried to memorize every turn and every door. And he tried not to worry about the disgraceful state of his uniform. At least Bowerman "made an impressive figure," he would write, "over six feet tall with shoulders nearly as wide!" Noticing empty nail holes where pictures had once lined the hallways, Keller whispered to Bowerman, "They are getting ready to move!"

At length they arrived in front of the general, a fatherly looking man in his late sixties. Bowerman addressed him immediately. "General," Keller translated, "you surely know you cannot resist our air force, artillery, and troops standing by to blast you off the map. Do you want to avoid this bloodshed? We come to you with an offer to accept your surrender."

"It was like a movie scene," Bill would write to Barbara. "The general's office was a large room and there were staff officers all over the place. The general informed me that he had 4,000 men in that area. So I went with him to look over his troops in all the little villages. It was quite a deal."

In the end the general admitted his situation was *hoffnungslos* (without hope), but declared that he had no authority to surrender on his own. He said he had already sent a messenger, a colonel, to headquarters to ask for such authority and had to wait for the colonel's return.

Bowerman gave the general until ten the next morning. At that point, he said, "whether you have received orders or not, you will march your troops in orderly columns without arms down the road. If you do not, we will attack."

But the general was afraid his men would be shot by the Italian partisan resistance. "So we finally arranged that his troops would keep their arms and the next day I was to send men to disarm the partisans," Bill would write Barbara. "Then the Germans would move down and be turned over to our commander."

Bowerman and Keller were escorted back to their jeep, where their comrades had traded cartons of cigarettes for Lugers. Only then did Bowerman explain what had moved him to take such a chance. "Regimental Intelligence had grabbed that messenger colonel," Bowerman would remember. "We knew they knew it was hopeless. We knew it was over."

And it was. Shortly, another message came through the battalion switchboard. The Germans had signed the surrender in Caserta, near Naples. The entire war in Italy was over.

"Delirious celebrations started in the street, dancing, singing, rifle-fire in the air," Keller would write. And the next morning it was a hungover group of mountain soldiers who took custody of the 4,000 Germans of the Fourteenth Army who came marching down the road as Bowerman had specified. "It was," Bill wrote Barbara with Bowerman understatement, "a rich experience." Three weeks later, Hitler committed suicide in his bunker in Berlin and Europe was at peace.

Nineteen thousand two hundred and ten men served in the Tenth Mountain; 978 were killed in action, 3,882 wounded, and 28 taken prisoner. One of the last entries in its official history reads "4 May 1945, Lt. Col. Jack Hay's 3rd Bn of the 86th reached Resia Pass in the Alps on the border of Italy and Austria." That farthest reach of the unit was to liberate some champagne for Bowerman and friends and to assign a few mules to feed starving people.

In later mule-related tales, Bill loved to say that when the war ended, the Army records showed that he had 200 mules, but there were 201 in the corral, so he shot one to balance the books. The truth according to Barbara was a little softer: "After the Italian war ended Bill turned loose a lot of mules, and peasants grabbed them up. Then a week later he got an order to turn them in. Bill shrugged and said, They're gone. So that was another time he was worried whether he'd be praised or brought up on charges."

Bill was aboard a troopship bound for America in August 1945, when atomic bombs were dropped on Hiroshima and Nagasaki, but Japan had not yet surrendered. The troops were given a month off until their next assignment, so Bill headed for Medford, where Barbara and the boys were waiting.

Barbara, so unshakably positive, was beginning to doubt. She had received a telegram saying Bill would be home for a month and then shipped out for Japan. "Talk about your good news/bad news," she would say. "I knew the South Pacific was a horrible place to be . . . Then suddenly, bang, it was over. The Empire of Japan surrendered as his plane touched down at the Medford airport."

That night the citizen soldier became pure citizen again. The next day, he strode onto the Medford High football field and asked Al Simpson if he needed an assistant. He told his principal to pencil him in for his usual classes. And he dropped a Luger on his superintendent's desk and said he'd gone a whole war and never heard anything more profane than what Hedrick had taught him in the tenth grade.

And after a month of doing all these things, he was absent without leave. "I was supposed to go back to Camp Swift," Bowerman would say, "because I'd been renamed Division Supply Officer. I was going to have to check in all our trucks and equipment. I had my orders in hand. Everybody did. I didn't even respond."

One blustery day, when the pear leaves were blowing across the fields, a pair of soldiers with MP armbands hailed Bowerman at practice to say he was under arrest. "Yeah?" said Bowerman. "For what?"

The MP, who was from Portland, answered, "Because you refused to obey an order to return somewhere in Texas where your people were to reassemble to be disbanded."

"You think you are going to take me back to Camp Swift," said Bill. "In the first place, I'm not going. In the second place, you are going to look pretty funny. I've got four Bronze Stars and a Good Conduct Medal. I've got a Silver Star for gallantry in action. In the third place, the war is over. I'm a schoolteacher. I'm back here teaching school. In the fourth place, if you try to take me out of here we'll have a riot and you'll get arrested, right here in my Jackson County."

"Well," said the MP, "I'm going back to the Adjutant General's office."

Where someone must've taken a look at Boweman's service record, for the Army wrote that he could officially muster out at Camp Carson, in Colorado. One of Barbara's favorite photos shows him there, holding up his honorable discharge papers. His medals would arrive in the mail a couple of years later.

Bill Boddington, to his chagrin, wound up taking over Bowerman's supply duty and having to check everything in. "God, it's amazing we stayed friends," Bowerman would say. Spared, knowing how blessed he had been, he was ready to do right by the life he had so amply defended.

CHAPTER 9

First Principles

IN THE MONTHS SOON AFTER HIS RETURN, BILL SAVORED EVERY MOMENT OF peacetime normality. As town and school welcomed back their favorite educator, he was touched to find that the Medford High yearbook had dedicated its past issue to him, its editors writing that his addresses to teams and assemblies "always left us laughing" and praying for his safe return. That winter, he took over as head track coach, resuming the top football job the following year.

One evening after Jon and Jay were in bed, Bill placed on the kitchen table a battered split of G. H. Mumm champagne and a German pistol. He had promised Bill Hayward a memento and had brought back this gun, but Hayward, realizing how special it was to Bill, had refused to accept it. The champagne was another souvenir, liberated from the wine cellar of an Italian castle. Contemplating it that night, Bill asked Barbara if she wanted to open it.

"Do you?"

"I don't want to drink to something bad that's over," said Bill. "I've done that enough. I'd rather drink to something good."

They put the bottle away, saving it for a special occasion. It would become a kind of metaphor for their lives. "We had, to be sure, numerous special occasions, but none seemed so at the time," Barbara would say more than a half century later. "It would remain in our closet through the years, the unopened bottle and the gun that Bill Hayward didn't take." The best was always yet to come.

One of the good things that came relatively soon—but not without a certain Bowermanesque flourish—was son Tom. One day in 1946, Bill, Barbara, Jon, and Jay were having a Sunday picnic on the Rogue River. "I was on a sandbar," Barbara would recall, still shaky about it decades later, "and heard the screams of my child. I looked up and saw four-year-old Jay going past all alone in the canoe."

Other people heard the commotion and several dived into the river to swim after him. Then Bill, who'd been hiding in the bottom of the canoe, rose up and got his laugh. The very pregnant Barbara was "not amused." She went into labor for a grueling day and a half to produce their third son and vowed never to go through it again.

Bill's heart-stopping practical jokes aside, Oregon's rivers and lakes were a favorite venue for outings with the Bowermans' much-loved neighbors, the Frohnmayers. David Frohnmayer, who was five when Bill came home, would remember "this tall, rangy guy hugging my dad and grabbing us all up and taking us everywhere, on Christmas tree hunts, fishing, everywhere outdoors." For three glorious summers, the families would camp at Cultus Lake. There were two lakes, really—big Cultus and little Cultus—accessible only by way of a dusty road that went right through a creek. The cars were crawling with kids: four Frohnmayers, three Bowermans. "We camped on a sandy beach," Dave Frohnmayer would say. "There were no cabins, no motors, just us and the lake and huge silence of the forest."

No motors, but they did have rowboats and Bill's canoe. Otto Frohnmayer would recall one evening when the kids were out on the lake and the wind came up. "We were afraid, with no way to get out there. But Bowerman says, 'Ah, they'll take care of themselves.'"

While the other grownups fretted, Bowerman blew a bugle to call the kids back. "But the wind was against us," David Frohnmayer would recall, "so it was dark when we made it in." Facing the glares of the adults, David showed he might have some future in advocacy. "I can only paddle so fast against the wind," he said. "You just needed to be patient."

Bill and Barbara would be as proud of the Frohnmayer brood as they were of their own. Mira, the eldest, and Philip, the youngest, would become professional singers. The middle two—David and John—would follow their dad in earning law degrees and then work for two administrations in Washington, DC. David, who would write speeches for the Nixon administration, would prove an invaluable ally some years later when he served as Oregon Attorney General. John would become chairman of the National Endowment for the Arts in the first Bush administration, a turbulent experience he would describe in his book *Leaving Town Alive*. The account would offer some insight into the Frohnmayer family ethic of remembering "who you are and what you represent," an ethic that also requires, as he would write, "the internal gyroscope that ultimately forces you to say, 'There are some things I will not do.'"

Rich in stalwart friends at home, Bill was also fortunate in his professional friends. Bob Newland, one of his former students, would reappear to be his right-hand man in the collaborative world of Medford high school sports. After the war, Newland returned to take his bachelor's (and later master's) in education at Oregon, the first in his family to graduate from college. Hedrick hired him to teach and coach at Medford in 1947, and his blond crew cut and deceptively open face began showing up in team pictures beside Bowerman's.

From a longtime Medford family, Newland was steeped in Medford sports since fourth grade. Remembering how crucial an outlet it had been for his own athletic energies, he helped Bowerman introduce age-group track meets to the summer schedule. Saturday mornings, kids from eight to eighteen would vie in two-year age brackets for shiny blue, red, and white ribbons in the 100, 440, 880, mile, high and low hurdles, discus, shot put, long jump, and high jump. Bowerman, Newland, and assistant Tom Ragsdale ran the meets with the emphasis on fun and teaching. The most talented became future Black Tornado stars. The parents whose kids dragged them to rake the long-jump pit became lifelong supporters.

Newland projected calm and sweet reason. He was a superb organizer with a mind for detail and dissecting a project into its logical steps. But what distinguished that project was his ability to find and put the right people into the places on the team or faculty or, later, Olympic Trials Organizing Committee that made it all hold together—and left those people feeling as if they'd had all the brilliant ideas.

Underneath all that organization, Newland could be both corny and sharp. Behind his desk was a plaque with the Grantland Rice homily, "For when the One Great Scorer comes To write against your name, He writes—not that you won or lost—But how you played the game." Just below that was "Do unto others as they would do unto you, but do it first."

Bowerman and Newland would pack a lot into the brief time between Newland's return to Medford and Bowerman's moving on. Medford's 1947 football team was struck with incessant injury, but remained undefeated until the playoffs, when it went down to Ashland, 27-19. In the spring of 1948, Bowerman coached the track team to his eighth Hayward Relays title, although not another state meet win.

The two men overlapped at Medford for only one year because, up in Eugene, Bill Hayward was on the verge of retirement and who but Bowerman would be his replacement? Newland would take over as Medford head track coach and eventually he would make his way to Eugene as well, where he and Bowerman would quickly renew their collaboration.

After more than four decades at Oregon, Bill Hayward was weary. Before the war, he had attracted a great sprinter, Mack Robinson (Jackie's brother), who was second to Jesse Owens in the 1936 Olympic 200 meters, and two meters, and two world record holders, George Varoff (indoor pole vault in 1937) and Les Steers (high jump in 1941). But the magnitude of World War II's departure from Olympic ideals had depressed him. The 1940 Olympics, planned for Tokyo, had been cancelled, and in 1941 he told an interviewer he didn't believe the Games would ever be resumed. "The Olympics take brotherhood among nations," he said, "and we don't have that now." He began hiring assistants to spread his workload, but university officials made no move to suggest retirement, so he soldiered on, keeping his eye out for talent.

One of the talents he found for Oregon in 1946 was a young 4:42-miler, Peter Mundle, who attended University High. At Oregon Mundle majored in math and, during his freshman year, was coached by Hayward. He dropped his best time by eighteen seconds, to 4:24. Hayward's crucial lesson? "Pace yourself! He had me run 65-second 440s," Mundle would say, "and if I didn't hit between 64.9 to 65.1, it was 'Do it again.'" The lesson took: "From then on, I really had a sense of what different speeds felt like. People would say I was easy to run behind, because I never varied my pace." Mundle would go on to run under Bowerman, an experience that would have lasting effects on both runner and coach.

Bowerman, at about this time, began to get feelers from his alma mater about a job. In 1946, football coach Jim Aiken was let go amid scandal and the athletic department was restructured. Oregon's first professional athletic director, Leo Harris, was hired in 1947. A 1961 profile in *Old Oregon*, the university alumni magazine, would call him "a person who stirs unwanted emotions in the mildest breast. His friends are ardent, his enemies passionate; his detractors are offensive, his supporters defensive. There are few non-partisans."

Harris, with the gravelly voice and haircut of a drill instructor, would be a huge force for good at Oregon. On his first visit to the campus he'd seen that the 20,000-seat Hayward Field had its limits as a football venue and that something bigger would have to be built. Over the next twenty years, he would campaign to make that happen. But first he wanted to find a head football coach of unquestioned integrity to replace Aiken. One suggested candidate was Bill Bowerman of Medford High.

Harris checked Bowerman out, invited him to visit, and offered him the position, saying that he needed Bill's reputation, his ethics, and his ability to connect with the faculty. Bowerman, who liked the blunt Harris immediately, said he was flattered and excused himself to think it over. He walked downstairs in Mac Court, took a seat on one of Bill Hayward's training tables, and said he'd just been offered what he'd long wanted—a springboard to university coaching.

His mentor told him, "Bill, college football coaches lead a miserable life." With that, Bowerman's direction was essentially sealed. He went back upstairs and declined. But he told Harris that if they ever needed a track coach, he was their man. Later he would explain his decision: "A lot of football players can't stand being alone out there with no one to hide behind. And track men have a higher general level of intelligence than football players." Of course there was more to it. Bowerman was rejecting our most military of sports. He wouldn't reject the team concept, far from it—but his would be a team of irregulars.

In 1947, Hayward finally formally retired. His assistant, John Warren, served for a year of transition, but Hayward insisted that Leo Harris offer the position to Bowerman. Harris did so, and Bowerman accepted. But Harris, who in every waking moment tried to fortify Duck football, added a condition: Would he also coach the freshmen? Bowerman agreed, the first of a career's worth of little compromises with Leo Harris that would serve both men and their university well. "I would have done a lot more than that to take Hayward's place at Oregon," Bill would say.

In September 1948, the Bowermans arrived in Eugene. They moved into Quonset-hut faculty housing across Agate Street from the track, met congenial professors, and felt instantly at home. Not long afterward, Bill Hayward died. "It was as if he'd taught until he was completely used up," Pete Mundle would recall, "then said, 'Good-bye, world' and was gone." In so doing, Hayward made sure that Bowerman would be free of his own long shadow.

Before the war, that thoughtful teacher Lizzie Bowerman had sent a letter to Hayward. "I have asked my son which of his instructors he considered had done the most for him," she wrote, "and without a moment's hesitation he named you. I am sure there are many boys who feel the same as Bill does, and I hope they have told you so. You are a teacher who is a friend and who imparts a spiritual development and inspiration."

Bill had done as his mother had hoped. He'd told Hayward what he meant to him several times, in several contexts. So that week, as eulogy followed eulogy and masses of men that Hayward had escorted from boyhood returned to voice their gratitude, Bowerman was content that he had spoken while the man was alive to hear it.

He took from his scrapbook a photograph of Hayward, in shirtsleeves and suspenders, leaning on a hurdle. He had it framed behind glass, to preserve what Hayward had written on it: "Live each day so you can look a man square in the eye and tell him to go to hell!! 'Bill' Hayward." Then he hung it in a little alcove outside his office door, where he would see it at the beginning and end of the day. And where anyone waiting to speak with him might pause and reconsider.

When Bowerman took over the Oregon track program, he had only two full scholarships to give each year. He divided them into quarters and eighths, pressed Leo Harris for more, and gradually reached eight or ten. But a track team can have as many as sixty men on it, so he needed to find ways for his athletes to support themselves.

"One of Leo's golden rules," Bowerman would remember, "was No One Will Solicit for Individual Sports. And that was appropriate, a good policy. So I asked him before I went out to beg funds for the department whether I could solicit jobs for the track athletes. He said, Get all the jobs you want."

So in about 1952, Bowerman began a town-gown partnership that would become an Oregon sports tradition for the next twenty years. He talked Harold Jones, the owner of some half-dozen mills, into hiring Oregon athletes to work weekend shifts. Jones would supply about a hundred weekend jobs in his various mills and Bowerman would find athletes to work them. "That helped baseball, helped me, helped swimming," Bowerman would say. "I was the straw boss. The guy slated for each job had to come to my office by Wednesday to check his name off."

The job roster—a sheet of yellow legal pad taped on the wall behind Bowerman's desk—listed the name of the mill and the athlete's shift assignment. "Day" ran from 8 a.m. to 4 p.m., "Swing" from 4 p.m. to midnight, and "Graveyard" from midnight to 8 a.m. In those days, the mills ran almost nonstop, three shifts around the clock. In the early 1960s, the starting wage was $2.40 an hour. (Jones sold his operation to Georgia Pacific in 1965, but that would have no effect on Bowerman's relations with the foremen who accepted athletes on the dryers, conveyors, and putty-patching lines.)

The mills, which made interior plywood paneling, offered two shocks to the collegiate soul. One was how hard the work was. Deafening machines seized green, Douglas fir logs, blasted their bark off with jets of water, cut them into twenty-foot lengths, fitted them onto a huge lathe that "unpeeled" them into a river of veneer flowing away down a conveyor belt. Other blades chopped the wet veneer into four-by-eight-foot sheets that were dried in a block-long dryer that ran all day every day except one shift—Sunday graveyard—when some pitiful organism had to blast out the splinters and sawdust that had caked up the bottom and become a fire hazard. The cleaner had to lie on his back to drive a six-foot steel nozzle ahead, forcing the dust and debris in front of him out the far side. The steel rollers a foot above his nose were a steam-heated 300 degrees. Even with goggles and three bandannas around his face, the cleaner always went home with a neck full of splinters.

The other shock was how hard the men were. Many had come west from Arkansas during the Depression. Some were fatherly, cheered us from our east stands during meets, and said that the mill was no life to aspire to and our education was the way out. And some were rabid white supremacists, so cynical they were toxic to stand within ten feet of.

The bleakest conceivable introduction to the real world, the mill must have compromised the athletes' training to a degree. Certainly most of Bill's men, once bloodied by the mills, wanted no part of them. But the jobs offered much-needed assistance and, in return, taught a greater set of lessons. Among them were those of the marathon, of not giving up, of finding out what others could endure and then, once a little calloused in both mind and body, whether one could measure up.

The mill jobs also taught stewardship. When Bowerman spoke of the mill, he made it clear that if anyone screwed up, he was screwing up for everyone—for the team, for the entire arrangement between university and mill owners. Anyone who was too sick to work had to get his own replacement. The shifts had to be covered. If the assignment was to be the night watchman on a holiday, when the conveyors were stopped and the mill empty, carrying a heavy, leather-covered clock (into which every hour the watchman stuck metal keys hanging at different places around the mill, so it would record on a paper strip inside that he'd made his rounds), that watchman did his duty until he was relieved.

I was one of Bill's athletes who drew that graveyard watchman job on Christmas Eve my senior year. I'd done a long run that day, and so had been tired to start the shift, but I'd made it through, and as soon as my relief came I could head for home. But no one came. Who my replacement was or what happened to him I have suppressed. I was alone with a multimillion-dollar mill spread over a dozen blocks hissing and rumbling in my incompetent care. I called every athlete I could think of who worked the mills. No luck. I called my house to say I wasn't coming home Christmas morning. I did not call Bill Bowerman. I just kept doing my rounds, drinking coffee, trotting outside in the frost, doing wind sprints, slapping my face, imagining races to summon the emotion to keep going.

My father showed up at noon with turkey and stuffing in tinfoil. He said I had to be making a killing on double overtime. I was beyond caring. At four in the afternoon, someone arrived for the swing shift and I went home. Double overtime was about $5 an hour, so on my sixteen-hour Christmas I made $80 before taxes. This was when tuition was $110 a quarter and room and board in the dorms $235.

Even as he looked for ways to help his athletes pay for college—and learn the tough lessons of hard work and responsibility in the process—Bowerman was furthering his own education. As homage to the breadth of Bill Hayward's knowledge, he set out to learn one discipline he hadn't mastered, distance running. And Pete Mundle would be his guinea pig. In truth, all who ran for Bowerman would carry that baton, but Mundle was the leadoff.

Bill began by having Mundle, then a junior, ease off the "hard day every day" schedule he had been following. "Slacking off" was what Pete called it and, contrary to Bill's expectations, he did not run well that season. In his senior year he trained the way he'd heard Paavo Nurmi did—and set the Oregon two-mile record at 9:32.4.

Bowerman pounced on this. For the track and field class he taught, he asked Mundle to write a term paper on the Finnish training techniques. Mundle found that the Finns did a lot of intervals—repeated short runs on the track—with controlled recoveries. His research also turned up the information that Mihaly Igloi of Hungary, who coached record-breakers Sandor Iharos and Lazlo Tabori, had his runners do intervals not once, but twice a day.

Czechoslovakia's Emil Zátopek, who had won the 1948 Olympic 10,000 meters in London, was already demonstrating the power of this kind of training. Zátopek was renowned for doing as many as forty hard 400-meter laps every day, with 200-meter recovery jogs. In the 1952 Helsinki Olympics, he would become the only man ever to win the 5000 and 10,000 meters and the marathon in a single Games, all in record times.

Repetition work was revolutionizing running, at least in Eastern Europe. The science of it was first explored in the 1930s in meticulous research by Germany's Woldemar Gerschler. Working with physiologist Hans Reindell, Gerschler showed that dozens of repeated 200s increased the pumping power of the heart better than any other exercise. Gerschler called his method "interval" training because, he said, the cardiovascular improvement occurred in the rest interval between the hard sprints. He and Reindell would not allow a runner to begin the next repeat until his pulse had returned to 120 beats per minute. If this didn't happen within ninety seconds of the end of the prior repeat, the workout was deemed too difficult and would be adjusted. In late 1938, Gerschler began coaching Rudolph Harbig, who would run 800 meters the following July in a world record 1:46.6, a record that would stand for sixteen years.

So, yes, intervals worked. But there was a catch. Runners often improved their times dramatically for a few weeks or months, but then tore Achilles tendons, or one weird day woke up with bones that seemed to have aged forty years in the night and devastated by the conviction that running was infantile and meaning-less. Such runners had gone (and the word is too feeble) *stale*.

Runners who overdose on intervals can often need months before their sys-tems are once more able to handle the lactic acid stress of repeatedly going in and out of oxygen debt. Then, six weeks later, they can be devastated all over again. Bowerman likened the pure interval syndrome to climbing a peak. The higher one went, the faster one raced—until one pitched over a cliff into black, sour uselessness.

Bowerman wondered how to responsibly administer intervals to college milers. Mundle's findings contained a clue. The Hungarian coach, Igloi, who would emigrate to the United States after the 1956 Hungarian revolution, put his men through twice-daily sets of intervals, sometimes two and three hours' worth, but he would not let them run a serious step except in front of his deeply judgmental eye. If he saw a hint of stiffness, for example, he would reduce the work until the runner was ready again. In the United States Igloi would train Jim Beatty to the first indoor sub-4:00.

Bowerman was so impressed by Mundle's research and racing that he would use the term paper as the basis for all his work with endurance men. Although he would tailor workouts to the specific creatures in front of him and would experiment until he died, from 1950 to 1952 he puzzled out most of his solution to the great problem of how to train for the middle distances.

There are only two training questions, both simple and haunting. What should I do and how much should I do it? Because a miler needs both the speed to race and the stamina to cover the distance, that miler's coach must choose from a vast continuum of possible work—from long, slow runs to all-out sprints, from rigidly timed repetitions on the track to go-as-you-feel romps on a beach or forest trail (often called *fartlek*, Swedish for "speed-play"), from one workout a day to three, from twenty miles a week to 200. In other words, choose from zero to infinity, from indolence to madness.

It was good that Bowerman wasn't a miler himself. He could approach the problem not with the wishful thinking of ambition but the objectivity of a phys-ical scientist. He sensed that the answer had to include not only the right type and amount of work but also the right type and amount of rest to keep a runner from illness or injury. If he erred, he wanted to err on the safe side of that cliff, so he decided to train and race his men to seasonal peaks but back off before they crashed. Moreover, he aimed to train them for their training—by having them do slower, strengthening, "base" work in the off-seasons. Thus began his dismissive view of indoor track, which throws all-out racing into the middle of winter. Such races interrupt a sensible sequence of fall cross-country, winter stamina work, and spring intervals and races, intensifying toward the pinnacle, the outdoor national championships and international meets in June and July.

Intervals, therefore, would be central to Bowerman's program, but his runners would do them only two or three times a week. Penciled in on the rest of the days would be a steady Sunday run of ten to fifteen miles or an hour of *fartlek* on a hilly golf course. These rigors were separated by easier days: three- to six-mile jogs with stretching, form drills, some light weight lifting, pull-ups, maybe a swim, to allow the system to recover and keep athletes benefiting from their hard work. All this would add up, on average, to sixty miles per week.

Bowerman began exhorting Oregon runners to finish their workouts "exhilarated, not exhausted." As he timed them on interval days, he would scrutinize their form, grabbing a runner's throat and taking his pulse. He'd check the glint in their eye, sending the tight and dull to the showers, and especially those whose pulses weren't quick to return to 120 beats per minute. His credo was that it was better to underdo than overdo. He was adamant that he trained individuals, not teams, and he came to believe that group workouts could even be counterproductive. "The best man loafs, the worst tears himself down," he would say. "Maybe only one guy in the middle gets the optimum work."

All this was the genesis of his annual welcoming line to freshmen. "Stress, recover, improve, that's all training is," he'd say. "You'd think any damn fool could do it." In fact, interval training takes such care that to this day few coaches can consistently produce milers.

When Bowerman first articulated the hard-easy method, he was widely despised for it. The anthem of most coaches then was, "the more you put in, the more you get out." When Bowerman chided them—"Come on, the greatest improvement is made by the man who works most intelligently"—they were morally affronted. His easy days were derided. The intentional tailoring of stress to the individual was called coddling. Many coaches had their own personal "systems," to which the runners were expected to adjust. Bowerman had it all backward. (Indeed, his common-sense approach is still resisted by a minority, and probably always will be.)

This, of course, was not a matter of intellect, but of trying to monitor driving hunger, a hunger not confined to coaches. Driven runners really think 200 miles per week is doing them good. But if a coach wishes to rise above damn foolishness, he must celebrate optimum rather than maximum. And Bowerman did. He distanced himself from his runners' crazed yearning to do more. He saw when they needed to be snapped out of it and took royal pleasure in the snapping. Hammered by Hedrick to channel, Bowerman would hammer the demented to channel less. And if a runner couldn't forsake work for its own sake, that runner would be off his team. As for all the doubting coaches, there was only one way to reach them: Crush their runners with his.

Bowerman's first real talent came from Canada. Jack Hutchins from Vancouver would be a Canadian Olympian at 800 and 1500 meters and the progenitor of a tactic that Oregon runners would copy for thirty years. On his first jog around Hayward Field, Hutchins noticed that the track ran behind football stands on the south end zone, blocking the crowd's view of what went on back there for as much as eighty yards. Hutchins invented the great drama of disappearing behind the grandstand in fifth place and coming out in first while the crowd went wild. "I don't know if Bill taught that or not," Barbara Bowerman would say, "but you always looked for it afterward, the gap that grew and grew after the Oregon leader came out—the roar growing with it—until the chasers flailed into view."

Bill not only taught it, he exploited it. He shaped his runners to do it because an athlete had to sprint a minimum of 360 yards to pull it off. "Woe to anyone," Bowerman would say, "who sickens me with the sight of showing off so much for the backstretch goons that you tie up and get run down at the finish." He gave us a nine-tenths-effort 330 at the end of some workouts, and ordered pull-ups to make our arms and lats strong enough to keep our legs driving that far. We tested ourselves in time trials and discovered what a powerful thing it is to know from how far out we could kick. To have it grooved in muscle memory that the top of the backstretch is a thrilling place to sprint would win many races for Duck runners, at home and away.

As well as originating that long kick, Hutchins was a bridge to more Canadians like him. He brought 440/880-man Doug Clement from Vancouver. Later there would be shot-putter Dave Steen, miler Vic Reeve, half-miler Sig Ohlemann, and sprinter Harry Jerome. Bill loved the Canadians for their manners, Barbara would say: "They had that respectfulness that seemed built-in to British Empire people, except the Australians. Bill used them as examples." He also used the Canadians, along with the rest of the track team over the years, to help him build his house.

I n 1949, the Bowerman family scouted the rivers of Eugene in their aluminum canoe, looking for a place to call home. They responded to the McKenzie as strongly as Bill Hayward had, although more for its restoring beauty than its trout. The river coiled tightly against the Coburg Hills, only twenty minutes north of the Oregon campus. The forested slopes, though logged in places, were virtually undeveloped. Farms covered the loamy flats. One day they stopped the canoe to picnic on a point below a big hill of oaks. Eleven-year-old Jon looked up from his peanut butter sandwich and said, "What's that? Something white."

It was a picket fence, even though there weren't supposed to be houses up there. The whole family hiked up the hill and found that the fence ran around an old cemetery. Down an overgrown lane and through a hundred yards of woods, they emerged onto a little bench of sod and fern, framed by oaks. Below, the audible river marched right at them, as if to push into the mountainside, then swept past, taking the eye across the valley to the pastures and town beyond. "We're home," said Barbara. Bill grinned and silently nodded. He and his sons began pacing off where their house would go.

The owner, an orchardist named Pieterman, sold them sixty acres for $4,000—a sum covered by the first payment from the sale of their Medford house at the same time. The lot was remote and had no water or electricity at first. But a veterans' home loan gave them money to build a house. Professor Al Miller of the architecture school, after hiking the steep driveway that was the site's only access, designed the house to be constructable by a few men using two-by-fours instead of harder-to-wrestle solid beams. Bill's helpers were professors Bob Lacy, law, and Kenneth Ghent, math, and University High principal Ray Hendrickson. Both Lacy and Bowerman had flunked manual arts in high school, so the building rose on clouds of pride and amazement. The house was placed back from the cliff edge, leaving a small lawn that was soon replaced by a cement deck, and angled toward the southwest, putting the river straight ahead and sunset in summer off to the right. On the day in 1950 that the family moved out of the prefab in Eugene, one of their new neighbors, an old Norwegian master carpenter, hung the doors on their new home.

The track team pitched in on building the house, too, but for them this was only the beginning. Bowerman would always have some unfinished garden or pond or fence or shed or shop or tiny sawmill. Soon a runner's goal-setting session meant being handed a shovel, shown a pile of sand, and made to move it nearer a cement mixer before being rewarded with Barbara's lemonade and oatmeal cookies. These job assignments—whether at the house or around the track—were tests of moral fiber. Bowerman seldom said so, but failure to do a job and do it right was a mark on the wrong side of the ledger.

The greater reward, of course, were the notes on Bill's legal pad that sketched out the coming six months, concluding with the athlete's big race and the seconds per lap he'd have to run to have a prayer. In Bowerman's mind, a runner was always at some point in an annual unfolding. He was training, for example, at 4:12 pace in March in order to run at 4:00 pace in June. "The only way to get to point B is to start at point A," Bowerman would say, and he felt it so strongly that he gave names to those points. The speed a runner could hold right now was his *date pace*. The speed he hoped to sustain in the NCAA mile or 5000 meters was his *goal pace*. Interval days would contain some of each, blending the currently attainable with a taste of what was to come. If a workout was three sets of intervals, the runner might do one set at 60-second pace, the other two at 64.

One of the first freshmen to get the full—if still evolving—Bowerman treatment was Bill Dellinger, who was born in Grants Pass. Dellinger's running ability was discovered in a ninth-grade PE mile where, Dellinger would recall, the track and football coach yelled, "Holy smokes, kid, come here! I want you out for our track team!" Dellinger obeyed and was changed. "I'd been hanging out in bars with older guys and smoking cigarettes and chasing girls and trapping muskrats," he once said. "I found a different direction on that track team."

The Dellinger family moved to Springfield for his high school years and Dellinger kept running. Oregon wrestler and *One Flew Over the Cuckoo's Nest* author Ken Kesey, a year younger than Dellinger, would recall watching him from the window of the school bus as it pulled away: "Running to school instead of riding, rain or shine, the very sort of nut you'd expect to win the state cross-country title."

"Hey," Dellinger would say. "If Kesey called you a nut, you were free to be pretty weird."

Not that Dellinger gave much outward sign of nuttiness. At five foot nine, with a deep chest and strong, hip-twisting, head-rolling gait, he arrived at Oregon in the fall of 1952, attracted by Pete Mundle's progress and Bowerman's scary joviality. A prankster himself, Dellinger recognized a master. Mundle had returned to Eugene to work on a graduate degree in math, so he was around to help break in young Dellinger. Over the next two decades he would visit Eugene often and run with Bowerman's current crop.

Dellinger had never trained consistently in high school. He ran track in spring and cross-country in fall, but played other games in between. Not averse to the occasional beer, he sometimes had to lose a few pounds in the early weeks of training. But Dellinger was tough; he didn't need many easy days to come back from hard ones. And he was smart, quickly grasping the virtue of running even pace the way Mundle did. After two years under Bowerman, he found himself contemplating doing something he'd once thought impossible: run a swift mile.

The lure of the mile never fades, but in the early 1950s it was irresistible. A small handful of runners on three continents—Australia's John Landy, Wes Santee of the United States, and Britain's Roger Bannister—were coming ever closer to the record of 4:01.4 set by Sweden's Gunder Hägg in 1945 and to breaking the four-minute barrier itself. Dellinger, duly inflamed, set his heart on running the mile and nothing but the mile.

Bowerman and Mundle, seeing how fast he recovered from workouts, thought he should go farther. "Run a mile and a quarter with Pete, see how it is," Bill would say. Then the next week, "See if Pete will take you a mile and a half." In that fashion they got him up to racing two miles. In hindsight, Dellinger would come to see Bowerman's strategy as "a big part of my callousing process," a term he would use when he became a coach himself to describe the effect of toughening both mind and body.

Dellinger would eventually break world and American records for two and three miles, indoors and out. But it was in the mile that he struck the first championship blow for Bowerman's methods. Three weeks after Bannister's historic 3:59.4 at Oxford's Iffley Road track, Dellinger, a sophomore, stepped to the line for the 1954 NCAA mile in Ann Arbor, Michigan.

Obeying Bowerman's edict that "You don't win a mile by winning the first quarter," Dellinger began at a 63-second pace while the leaders flew away at 60. After one lap, he was last. He cruised past a few stragglers in the next half-mile, but was still ninth with a lap to go. Then Bowerman had the pleasure of seeing the calm, hard-muscled runner, his lemon shorts and green singlet easy to follow, moving through the field, gaining sureness with each man he passed.

Dellinger reached second place off the last turn. His reward for having husbanded his energy was being able to lift into a full sprint. Thirty yards from the tape, he shot past the stiffening, astounded Louis Olive of the US Military Academy and won going away in 4:13.8.

Years later, knowing what it would lead to, Bowerman would term Dellinger's mile triumph "my greatest and most satisfying experience." He may have felt Dellinger's victory was as much harbinger as vindication, but opposing coaches were far from threatened by one lucky win.

In the months following Dellinger's victory, Bill wasted no time in alerting talented milers to the University of Oregon. That August, he drove north to Vancouver and the British Empire Games to see the "Miracle Mile," the first head-to-head battle between the first two men under 4:00. Australia's Landy, the world record holder by then with 3:58.0, knew his best chance to win lay in upsetting Bannister's wait-and-kick strategy by sitting back himself, but he tore ahead at the gun nevertheless. The race had drawn such attention that Landy felt obliged to ensure a fast race. "Otherwise," he would say, "the sport might have suffered." The price of his nobility: Bannister outkicked him 3:58.8 to 3:59.6.

Bowerman absorbed the tactical lesson that in a race among equals the pace-setter seldom wins. But he went home without seeing a second Australian miler, because James J. Bailey had broken bones in his foot between the preliminary heat and the final. A gregarious spirit, Bailey would recall that a couple of Canadians took pity on him. "They said, 'Come on, you have to see Oregon, where we go to school.'"

So half-miler Doug Clement and pole-vaulter Bob Reed brought Bailey to Eugene and presented the hobbling Aussie to Bowerman's appraising eye. Bowerman heard that Bailey's fastest mile was 4:12 and that he was a five-time Australian 880 champion with a best of 1:51. Bailey's first impression of the Oregon coach was that he was "really strange," full of awkward pauses "where everything stopped and you didn't know what to say."

Still, Bowerman was a major college track coach and Bailey had never had a coach of any kind. The Aussie felt obliged to level with him: "Bill, I'm banged up. I'm twenty-five years of age. I've had more disappointments than successes in life as well as in running. I don't even know whether I want to run anymore after these bones knit."

Again, a pause. Bowerman seemed to be studying Bailey's muscular shoulders, hardly those of a gazelle. But Bailey's honesty had touched him. "We're prepared," said Bowerman at last, "to give you a foreign student scholarship. It would be entirely up to you whether you want to run again or not." Bailey accepted, figuring he could do it for a year and see.

At Oregon that fall. Bowerman made Bailey run with Dellinger and two-miler Ken Reiser. The workouts, Bailey would say, were "an absolutely shocking distance. Forty-five minutes! Continuous running! It would about kill me." Only his Aussie pride kept him going. "To stay with them, I'd say to myself, 'No Aussie man is going to be left by college boys.'"

The next spring, Bailey had the stamina to respond well to Bowerman's intervals. "I didn't think they were anything special," he would say. "Ten 440s, that kind of thing. I just ran with Dellinger and the team." The interval training also took effect almost without his noticing. His rainy, early season races against Oregon State and Washington were won in slow times. In the Pacific Coast Conference meet in Eugene he raced only the 880, which he won.

So when he and Dellinger lined up for the start of the 1955 NCAA mile in the Los Angeles Coliseum, they were scarcely noticed. The favorite was UCLA's Bob Seaman, who had run 4:01 as a sophomore and had both a kick and the ability to pace himself. Mid-race, Seaman set out to run away from the field. Dellinger and Bailey easily hung with and swept past him on the final turn, with Bailey winning in 4:05.6 and Dellinger right behind him in 4:06.4.

"I'd never broken 4:12," Bailey would remember. "And to go one-two, it put the school on the map. And then Ken Reiser won the two-mile! All of a sudden people were asking, 'Where were these guys coming from?'" As the world would soon learn, Bowerman hadn't developed a solitary prodigy. He was shaping a succession of them.

CHAPTER 10

A Friend, a Son, a Community

ONE DAY IN THE EARLY 1950S, AS BILL AND BARBARA WERE SETTLING INTO THEIR house, John and Robin Jaqua hiked up the next pasture to the east of the Bowerman acreage. Below them spread 1,400 acres of fields and row crops embraced on three sides by the river and dotted with a little town's worth of old buildings, buckling under blackberry. A sound between a voice and a squawk reached them. "*Private . . . private . . . property!*" To their left, a woman in jeans and plaid shirt had come out of the tree line and was advancing across the dusty hillside. John, a young lawyer who'd been farming about twenty miles south of Eugene, raised a hand in greeting. The woman raised a gun in answer.

The Jaquas bowed and retreated. They made their way down the hill, passed an old cemetery, and came upon the Bowerman driveway, with Bill in it. John Jaqua had met him in passing at the Oregon Club, the athletic department's Monday coaches' lunches for boosters, but this would be the first conversation that gave them a sense of each other.

Bill led the visitors onto the deck and Barbara told them about the farm that had caught their eye. It belonged to Alex Seavey, the profligate son of James Seavey, who had begun the J. V. Seavey Hop Company around the turn of the twentieth century. Hops, used to flavor beer, are the flowers of vines and grown on wires twenty feet high. Picking them takes a crew, so for forty years, summer laborers had pitched tents, built huts, and stayed the season. The dilapidated barns, store, and dance hall were remnants of those times. Then artificial flavorings cut the demand for hops. When Alex took the place over, he mortgaged it to the hilt and drained it of value. But the bleaker things grew, the more the Seaveys dug in. Anyone ignoring no-trespassing signs was turned away by one or another vocal Seavey, often armed.

John Jaqua made discreet inquiries and soon learned the extent of Alex Seavey's debts. To an intermediary, a state policeman whom the Seaveys called daily to report trespassers, Jaqua said, "When he goes broke, bring him in to the office." It took a year, but Seavey showed up. Were the Jaquas serious? Were they? Robin visited Barbara and asked, since they had small children, whether it was true that the area was crawling with rattlesnakes. "Oh no, don't worry! Don't worry at all!" said Barbara.

So the Jaquas closed the deal in 1953. One of Robin's brothers, Chuck Robinson, visited the property and wrote the rest of the family, "John and Robin have finally found a place that makes Tobacco Road look like Park Avenue."

But the neighbors were generous. "Bill Bowerman helped me set up my water system," John Jaqua would remember. "That's when I realized how strong he was. He picked up this huge roll of plastic pipe and carried it out from the culvert like it was nothing. I said to myself, 'This is not someone I'd choose to be on the wrong side of.'"

It was a great joy that the swimming hole had passed into friendly hands. Both families took their kids there for a celebratory dip. Barbara arrived in a bathing suit and heavy rubber boots.

"Why the boots?" asked Robin.

"Snakes," Barbara said.

"I thought you said not to worry."

"You don't have to worry! Just wear boots!"

In fact, because the hills held caves and the fields supported many mice, the area was a natural for snakes. In 1961, John Jaqua was driving home one summer evening and saw Bill's car stopped at the Bowerman driveway, dust rising. Bowerman had a thick-bodied, hissing, writhing diamondback pressed to the gravel with a clipboard.

"Need any help?" asked Jaqua.

"Nope," said Bowerman. "Just taking him a while to quit."

In the *Register-Guard* that week there was a photo of the clipboard and the seven-foot snake, the largest ever killed in Lane County. Bill's achievement was not universally acclaimed in the family. Had he let the monster live, budding biologist Jay, then seventeen, could have milked it for four times the venom of any of the other rattlers he kept in a cage, sending their venom to antivenin labs.

Bowerman and Jaqua both contained elements of the citizen-farmer, loving the land but not letting it isolate them from the wider world. Each admired the other for a quality they shared. Bowerman would describe Jaqua as "the greatest sizer-upper of a situation I ever knew." Jaqua sized up Bowerman thusly: "He knew you very well before you ever knew him."

As Otto Frohnmayer would declare of Bowerman, "He can be very cold about people he doesn't respect, but if he picks you as a friend, he is a friend." And Bowerman would have good reason to respect his new neighbor. Bill was staggered by it when he grasped what John had done and survived in the war.

As a Marine pilot, Jaqua had shipped out to New Caledonia in the spring of 1943, along with his good friend Jim Boyden, to fly dive-bombers and torpedo planes called TBM Avengers. After surviving three six-week combat tours on Guadalcanal, they began an assault on Rabaul in late fall. This major Japanese staging base—five airfields and a port—was surrounded by towering volcanoes riddled with tunnels and antiaircraft batteries.

Every raid on Rabaul resulted in allied losses; Jaqua's craft was hit several times. At length, the US high command decided that Marine fliers should lay mines at the entrance to Rabaul's harbor. "This was a night operation and we had to fly down the channel in a single file at 200-feet altitude and 200-knot air-speed," Jaqua would recount in *Navy Wings of Gold*, written by F. Willard Robinson, another of Robin's brothers. "We had to fly through an alley of fire, right between those fortified volcanoes." With all the searchlights on them, they were blasted from every direction.

The squadron's last mission took place on Valentine's Day, 1944. From Jaqua's point of view, the assignment served no purpose: "We had already destroyed the base and all the ships that hadn't been sunk were gone." But orders were orders; the planes took off. That was the last time Jaqua saw his friend Jim Boyden. The searchlights were blinding, the enemy firestorm horrific. Boyden didn't make it back. "To lose my best friend on the last mission we flew, after three tours of combat, in a useless attack, was devastating," Jaqua would say. "A terrible experience I will never forget." Only ten pilots, Jaqua among them, returned to San Francisco in the spring of 1944.

Although hospitalized with an ulcer, Jaqua's reprieve from war was temporary. He was next ordered to join the staff of Admiral Harry W. Hill, then based in Coronado, California. One bright note was that Robin was able to join him for the several months that he remained stateside. The following February, Robin gave birth to their first son. They named him James Boyden Jaqua.

In early 1945, John sailed on the admiral's flagship as an air support officer, coordinating fighters, bombers, and air-to-ground rockets during the invasion of Okinawa, the largest and most costly operation of the war in the Pacific. "Coordinating" meant going ashore and calling in planes to release rocket fire during the cave-to-cave assaults on the Japanese. "Marines moved right into the face of the caves and fired the caverns with napalm," Jaqua would recall many years later, his lawyerly choice of words no mask for the horror. "It was terrible to see a Japanese soldier running from a cave, his whole body on fire, only to collapse and die on the rocks."

After Okinawa fell, at the cost of 12,500 American lives and 100,000 Japanese, Jaqua was put on the staff planning the invasion of the Japanese island of Kyushu. In August, when Japan surrendered, he sailed home a major with seven Air Medals, the Battle Campaign Medal with five stars, and the Distinguished Flying Cross, "for undue bravery in pressing his attacks through intense enemy fire."

After graduating from Oregon Law School in 1950, Jaqua took over the Eugene law firm of a deceased uncle, bought a beautiful farm, and began a neighbor-to-neighbor partnership for the ages. Neither Bowerman nor Jaqua spoke of all they had witnessed in the war. Both exuded an almost tangible sense of good fortune.

Both also were not always contained by the bounds of civil propriety. Jaqua, like Otto Frohnmayer, loved the humor of the barracks and the barnyard. He would often appear on the Hayward Field infield after work, where Bowerman would be timing someone's workout, and he'd whisper some sophomoric, grotesque joke. (A mild example: "Kid's sitting in an outhouse, but there's no paper, just a hole with a sign, 'To clean fingers, put here.' So he wipes with his fingers and sticks 'em in the hole and a kid outside with a hammer *hits* 'em and the sitter pulls 'em in and *sucks* on 'em.") Bowerman would laugh so hard he'd double over and drop his stopwatch.

Robin Jaqua was more than equal to the tenor of McKenzie View Drive. One year, on the eve of the neighborhood's annual picnic, which the Jaquas hosted, Barbara called in a panic: "We can't come! Last night a dog came in and killed all our chickens, and we shot the dog, and now we're afraid someone at the picnic will ask, "Has anyone seen my husky?'" Robin blanched; they were taking care of their son Stephen's Norwegian elkhound. "You've killed our Stephen's dog!" she cried. "But never mind. At least now you can come to the picnic!"

When Bill got out of the car, he was solemn. Robin felt awful. "He'd been proud of those chickens. He'd worked days on that coop." Bill walked up to her and said, "Robin, Robin . . ." (unendurable silence) "*I like your attitude!*"

Barbara Bowerman would describe Robin as "a philosopher of nature, half poetry, half metaphor." That would be the metaphor of Jungian archetypes, the stories and structures common to all traditions and psyches, a discipline in which Robin would earn her doctorate at Oregon and then study further at the Jungian Institute in Switzerland—just the person with whom to discuss child rearing.

Topic A: Jon Bowerman. In his early his teens, Bill's oldest began to bully the four-years-younger Jay. When Barbara separated them, Jon was contemptuously rude. Barbara asked Bill to talk to his son. Bill merely said, "They'll outgrow it." Shocked, she suggested that Jon needed limits and help. Bill replied, "I can't talk to him unless he asks for help."

Barbara simply did not understand this; Bill had no qualms about intervening with his athletes. Robin Jaqua suggested that Bill's enduring anger against his father had inevitably affected his notions of fatherhood. It had not been his own father who scared Bill straight, after all. It had been Ercel Hedrick. Barbara still didn't see why Bill couldn't just act like Hedrick and lay down the law to Jon the way he did to the Oregon runners.

Decades later, Barbara would put that question to me. All I could answer—and it was no answer—was that we were not his kids. We were, in that phrase he took from medicine, in his care. And the necessary distance of a doctor was a part of that. He didn't love us as sons; he cared for us as patients, administering to our needs. He could issue edicts and hammer us as we needed it, but he couldn't hammer his loved ones. Or at least he couldn't until he absolutely had to.

Although Barbara may not have thought so, Bill was equally distraught. The only time John Jaqua ever saw Bill Bowerman with tears in his eyes was when he came to say how stumped he was about Jon.

In the mid-1950s, fourteen-year-old Jon mouthed off at school and was suspended from Coburg High. In an echo of J. W. Chambers becoming a mountain man, he ran away to be a trapper on the river.

He didn't actually stay away for long. But he was out again every morning at four. Getting upriver in a borrowed, old pickup, he'd put the canoe in at Mohawk and float down to the house, setting traps. In the afternoon he'd hitchhike back upstream and collect his catch—beaver, muskrat, an occasional mink. Back then fur buyers would pay $30 for a big beaver pelt, $25 for a mink. "It took three or four hours to scrape a beaver pelt," Jon would recall. "I was convinced I was gonna make a living as a trapper."

Bill watched him boiling his traps to rid them of human smell before heading out to set them again. He could only admire his work ethic. Son and father regarded each other, each feeling the other measuring, pushing.

When it came to his athletes, Bill had ways to make sure someone wanted to be on his team. He had a genius for finding the person's weak spot, hazing and hectoring on some point of the athlete's training or his classes or his associates until he demonstrated acceptance of Bill as the ultimate judge, the tribal village elder. With no corresponding process to apply to his son, Bill was stymied. Still, he knew about hardheaded men, being one himself. He gave Jon time.

Eventually they began to talk of practical matters. Jon fiercely wanted to be financially independent and to play football. The trapline wasn't paying enough to cover that. So they arrived at an arrangement. If Jon went back to Coburg High he could play there and work summers in a plywood mill. Jon would in fact earn his way in the world from the time he was sixteen. "We made our peace," Jon would say. "I came back and finished high school."

In truth, it wasn't quite that simple. When Jon was suspended from Coburg a second time, Bill took him into the parental bedroom. "The only time we ever went in there was for discipline," Jon would remember, "and I was so scared I was afraid, seriously afraid for my life." Usually Bill would get out the Bible, turn to Exodus, and read the part about honoring thy mother and thy father. This time, though, he just sat there: "The silence went on so long I actually wanted him to hit me."

In the end, Bill did have to hammer a loved one. Quietly and calmly, he said to his firstborn son, "I'm going to tell you what Ercel Hedrick told me when the same thing happened to me at Medford: 'It is never, ever going to happen again.'" And it never did.

Engaging his sons in fatherly heart-to-hearts may not have been Bowerman's strong suit, but he was a master at engaging the rest of Eugene in his projects. Almost from the moment he took over at Oregon, he'd been amassing loyal contacts and assistants. First, he'd trained a new generation of officials to conduct meets on schedule. One of them, camping buddy Ray Hendrickson, who'd helped him build his house, developed into the finest starter of sprint races in the nation.

Hendrickson's other job was being principal of North Eugene High School, where his gruff baritone, Norse countenance, and icy eyes beneath haystack brows easily intimidated brash teenagers. Hendrickson's choice of vice principal delighted Bowerman: It was Bob Newland.

In the ten years since Newland had replaced Bowerman as track coach at Medford High, his teams had won the state championship nine times, been second once, and won eight Hayward Relays titles. At North Eugene, Newland technically would be the guidance counselor, while math teacher Denny Davis was the official track coach. But it was Newland who guided the runners, among whom I was lucky to count myself.

No man could out-organize Bob Newland. When he, wife Carolyn, and fellow Medfordite Tom Ragsdale threw themselves into putting on Bowerman's summer age-group all-comers meets—the direct descendant of the meets they had organized in Medford—they were soon a Eugene institution. Each week, as many as 600 kids dragged their parents out to Hayward Field, fostering, as it had in

Medford, not only a growing pool of young talent but also a rising tide of adult supporters for Oregon track.

In 1956, Bowerman and friends decided they needed to start a track club to fund sending Oregon grads to big meets or to put on big meets in Eugene. The first president of the Emerald Empire Athletic Association (EEAA) was Dr. Ralph Christensen, then head of Sacred Heart Hospital. (In 1965 the EEAA would change its name to the Oregon Track Club.) "Chris" Christensen, as Bowerman called him, reached out to the professional community. Soon the club was holding its monthly breakfast meetings at a pancake house. Christensen would also be instrumental in hooking Bowerman up with medical experts who would help him improve his own and others' fitness: orthopedic surgeon Don Slocum, who collaborated with Bowerman on academic papers, used high-speed photography to do early biomechanical studies of running technique; arthroscopy pioneer Stan James; and cardiologist Waldo Harris, who would help Bowerman evaluate the effects of exercise on the heart.

The EEAA's first major project was to stage a track meet in October 1956. The US Olympic Committee wanted to give the US team heading for Melbourne in November a competition to sharpen its members in what is ordinarily the off-season for northern hemisphere track athletes. The only catch was that the USOC would not put up any money for the meet and neither would the university.

"Here's what we do," John Jaqua told Bowerman. "You get in writing how much it's going to cost. I will go up and down Willamette Street and get pledges, backed up by promissory notes. We'll take those to the bank and get a loan guaranteed by those notes." Bowerman quickly found that they needed $50,000. Jaqua canvassed Eugene business owners and reported to Bowerman that he had ten $5,000 pledges. "Which was wildly premature of me," he would later admit. "But I got them eventually."

Expenses covered, Olympians flooded the town in October. Jaqua also came up with a way to boost attendance. As he would recall, "Our pledgers, I happened to know, were such cheap bastards that they didn't want to honor their pledges. So we gave them piles of tickets to sell instead." The tactic worked like a charm. "We had a massive crowd out at that thing," Bowerman would remember. "It was a great meet."

It was to be the first of many.

CHAPTER 11

A Dynasty Begins

IN THE 1952 FIELD STUDY THAT WOULD BE HIS MASTER'S THESIS, BOWERMAN looked at the scholastic achievement of freshman athletes. He was not greatly surprised to find that trackmen on average earned GPAs a tenth of a point or two above those of football players.

Pete Mundle, whose senior term paper had sparked Bill's thinking on training for the middle distances, was a case in point. After graduating, Mundle had lived for a year in England and had trained under Chris Brasher, who had helped pace Bannister to the first sub-4:00 and would win the 1956 Olympic steeplechase. Brasher's coach was Bill Coyne, and Mundle brought back their steeplechase techniques, including a little pause at the top of the water jump barrier to effect a leap out and not up. Up is bad because it is followed by a plummet straight down, transforming a soaring antelope into a crumpled egret wading out of the water as the rest of the field escapes.

The steeplechase became Mundle's best event, although he would try for the 1952 and 1956 Olympics not only in the steeple but also in the 5000, the 10,000, and the marathon. He never made the US team, but drew solace from the fact that his Oregon teammates did: "I know I helped by competing with them."

In the winter of 1955–56, the best of those teammates, Bill Dellinger and Jim Bailey, trained with Olympian purpose, aiming for the Games in Melbourne the next November. At the 1956 Northern Division meet in Eugene, Bailey was as lean and impervious as a piece of machinery. Chest and arms held high, his face controlled, almost serene, he powered smoothly past the field on the last backstretch and won at a speed that seemed impossible to wondering sixth graders. Dellinger at least appeared to have feelings. He rolled his head a little, and in the last laps of the two-mile his neck and head turned a disturbing purple crimson, betraying the strain despite his unchanged, supple stride. In later years, when he coached Steve Prefontaine, Dellinger would marvel at how the naked need of Pre's final drives would bring the Hayward throng to their feet. But Dellinger's terrifying flush of effort elicited the same roars in 1956.

In May of that year, mile world record holder John Landy was to race in a special mile, during the USC-UCLA duel meet in the Los Angeles Coliseum. Both

Bowerman couldn't accompany them because the team had a dual meet that day, but he held a planning session with the two runners before they left.

Remembering how Bannister had stalked and out-sprinted Landy in Vancouver, Bowerman counted it as a plus that the Australian had not changed his tactics. Landy trained himself to be supreme at breaking away early and hanging on, thus forcing every opponent to make a decision in the first few strides after the gun: Go with him and burn, or wait and be left behind?

Bowerman didn't know how Bailey would react to 58 or 59 pace, but he did know that Dellinger couldn't take it; he just wasn't that fast. So he instructed Dellinger to finesse it: run 60s or 61s, and in the third lap go around people who'd gone out too hard. And Bailey? "In my whole career at Oregon," Bailey would say, "I can't remember Bill saying one word about tactics. I ran on instinct. I couldn't describe what happened in a race after it was over. It was the same in LA. I ran and reacted."

The formidable Ron Delany of Ireland and Villanova University, a future Olympic champion, was in the race too. Bowerman hoped that Delany would chase Landy and keep him from breaking free. If that happened, he told his two Ducks, "Don't lose hope in the last lap, because with Landy if you can get near, you can get by."

The race developed not at all as Bowerman had envisioned. Landy led, but not with any 59. He passed the quarter in a sensible 61. Delany stuck so close that his mincing stride seemed to threaten the Aussie's heels. Dellinger and Bailey ran a few yards behind, happy the pace was manageable. That didn't last long. Passing the half-mile in 2:02.3, Landy opened up. Only Delaney tried to stay near him for the next 220. By then, Bailey and Dellinger were fifteen yards back. On the turn Bailey moved ahead of Dellinger into third, but felt a twinge of doubt. He seemed too far behind and too tired.

With 550 yards to go, Landy broke Delany. The world record holder drove past three-quarters with a growing ten-yard lead in 3:01.5, having run the third lap in 59.2. Bailey was 3:03.1 with a lap to go, having reached the dying Delany's back. Passing him gave Bailey a great rush and he surged on after Landy. He caught his countryman at the top of the last turn and fought even at the 1500-meter point, where the time for both was 3:43.3. They had 120 yards to go.

Back in Eugene, schools and department stores had come to a halt listening to the race on KUGN. Seventeen-year-old Jon Bowerman, a senior at Coburg High, was competing in a track meet.

"They interrupted the meet to put the broadcast on the speakers," he would remember. "I can still hear us all screaming as they were on the last lap. 'Bailey pulling up! Bailey pulling up! Bailey passes Delany! Bailey passes Delany! Bailey's coming on! Bailey's passing Landy! Bailey wins!' It made us crazy. We ran our first laps too fast after that. We killed ourselves."

Bailey's 55.5-second last lap carried him across the line a yard ahead in 3:58.6, the first sub-four-minute mile ever run on US cinders. Landy and Delany ran 3:58.7 and 4:05.5. Dellinger finished fourth in 4:08.8. Huge, sequential pictures of Bailey coming off the turn and passing Landy ran in the *Register-Guard* the next day and were cut out and tacked up on my Dunn School sixth-grade bulletin board by a teacher who knew inspiration when she saw it.

When Dellinger and Bailey returned to Eugene, fighting through whooping students and athletic department secretaries to take refuge in Bowerman's office, he sat back and acted as if nothing unusual had transpired. But he couldn't pull it off for long. Finally, he jumped up and said, "You're Olympians now."

He meant this, of course, simply in the sense that they had acquitted themselves well against the finest on the planet. In fact, while the mile was enough for the Australian selectors to name Landy to their Olympic team, Bailey had to run the 800 and 1500 in later Aussie trials to qualify for both in Melbourne.

"I always had to prove myself more," he would recall glumly. "For weeks before the Australian Trials, Melbourne newspapers had been promoting the rematch between Landy and me as the Melbourne gentleman against 'the Rugby Ruffian' from Sydney, the bad boy of Australian track."

When he stepped onto the field for the finals in Melbourne, 50,000 hostile spectators were chanting, "Beat Bailey! Send him back to America!" Bailey won both the 800- and 1500-meter trials, but in Melbourne he was injured and didn't make the 1500 final. Ron Delany won it with a late, panicky sprint in 3:41.2, the equal of a 3:58 mile. Six yards behind, Germany's Klaus Richtzenheim outleaned Landy for second, both timed in 3:42.0.

Although he would come back to race in the 1957 season, James Bailey's finest sporting moment would remain his great mile in Los Angeles. But thousands of his countrymen never forgave him for beating Landy, their idol. After graduating from Oregon, Bailey would take a job representing Jantzen knitwear, an Oregon firm Bowerman had put him in touch with, and make his life in the United States.

Dellinger, for his part, had no trouble winning the 1956 US Olympic Trials 5000 in an American record 14:26.0. But Melbourne would be a miserable epiphany. Overcome by heat, he did not finish the race, which was won by twenty-seven-year-old Vladimir Kuts of the Soviet Union. Dellinger—twenty-one and the youngest in the field—was shocked at the huge gap between his training and that of runners from the rest of the world, who trained not only year-round but twice a day. "No wonder my 14:26.0 was almost a full minute behind the world record of 13:35—a time I felt was absolutely impossible for me to run."

He and Bowerman returned sobered. They had more to learn. A couple of years later, Bill would hear about a New Zealand coach named Arthur Lydiard, whose runners could carry a five-minute pace or better for ten miles. Intrigued, Bowerman began writing to Lydiard to find out about building that kind of strength.

B owerman already had more raw material at home to work on. In 1955, high school talents Dick Miller, George Larson, Phil Knight, and Jim Grelle had entrusted their fates to him. Knight and Grelle were the two best half-milers in Portland their senior year. Known to his family and friends as "Buck," the tow-headed Knight would endure other nicknames at Oregon. Jim Bailey, for one, used to call him "Albeeeno" because he was so fair. But then came a time when Phil took a carload of teammates to the Glenwood Drive-in on an evening when entry was a dollar a car. Grelle saw the marquee and said, "Look, we're being taken on 'Buck Night' by Buck Knight!" Phil was "Buck" from then on.

Quick of wit and a devilish mimic of other runners' strides, Grelle in 1956 had not been beaten in the 880 for three years, but Bowerman was leaning on him to move up. "Why suffer twice as far?" Grelle would say. But Bowerman nagged, telling him he wasn't fast enough to be a great half-miler, that even he, Bowerman, could beat him in a 220. When Grelle called him on it, Bill said, "Okay, I'm going to race you. We're going to line up here in staggered lanes and you can't look back. Look back and you're disqualified and I'm the winner."

"You're going to cheat. You're going to cut across the infield."

"But you won't know unless you look back, and then you're eliminated and I win anyway."

This went on for years. "Anybody who thought he was fast was supposed to race Bowerman and he made the rules," Grelle would say. "So we never did have a race."

Finally, after losing an 880 as a sophomore in 1957, Grelle bowed to the inevitable. Bill took him to the NCAA meet in Austin, Texas, and put him in the mile. Grelle didn't know mile tactics, but Bowerman told him it was simple: "See that Villanova guy? That's Ron Delany, the Olympic 1500-meter champion. I want you to follow that guy. Do what he does." Grelle found the pace not too bad and got on Delany's shoulder. "We work through the field and with 200 left Delany goes to the front and I get into second and we finish that way. And I go over to Bill and say, 'Wasn't that great? I got second! I ran 4:07!'" The following week, Bowerman took Grelle to the Oregon Club—where he stood him up and apologized for making such a tragic mistake. Everyone wondered, What mistake? And Bill said, "I forgot to tell him to win."

In 1958, Grelle ran 4:01.7 for fourth in the AAU Nationals (behind new Aussie sensation Herb Elliott's 3:58.0) and qualified for one of the Cold War's great events, the United States vs. USSR dual meet in Moscow.

There, beneath the glare of Nikolai Khruschev and 80,000 others in the Moscow stadium, all emanating grim negativity, Bill Dellinger made the 5000 meters "the event of the meet," as *Track and Field News* would deem it. Dellinger and teammate Max Truex of the University of Southern California and the LA Striders were up against Pyotr Bolotnikov and Hubert Parnakivi. Bolotnikov, who would be the 1960 Olympic 10,000-meter champion, would rank number one or two in the world for the 10,000 in every year from 1957 to 1962 except for 1961 when he fell to fifth; he would also rank in the top ten in the world for the 5000 during the same period. Parnakivi, a newcomer, had beaten Bolotnikov that year in the USSR Championships.

The Soviets led through sheets of rain on a heavy track, but the Yanks hung tough. Bolotnikov tried to run away with two laps to go, but escaped no one. Parnakivi then shot ahead at the bell, but couldn't shake Dellinger. Bill went for the lead on the backstretch, failed, went for it on the last turn, failed, and went for it all down the home stretch. He couldn't get the last six inches. Both were timed in 14:28.4.

In the 1500, with 400 to go, Grelle would remember, "there was *no* cheering." The disgusted silence was because he was winning. Grelle could hear his own footsteps as he outkicked Jonas Pipyne, 3:46.7 to 3:47.3. Despite the lack of encouragement from the crowd, Grelle took a victory lap and then headed for the showers. There he came upon Dellinger having a well-earned soak in a tub that looked big enough to dive into. "How's the water, Bill?" Grelle asked. "Just fine," Dellinger answered. So Grelle stripped, jumped right in, screamed, and popped straight back out, almost hovering in the air. The water was about 150 degrees. Dellinger, who had eased in a bit at a time over half an hour, "laughed so hard he about croaked," Grelle would recall, adding, "He's told that one a few times."

Dellinger's pranks were solidly within the Bowerman tradition, but Bill Bowerman's were even more devious. One of Grelle's favorite Bowerman stories involved a pair of twin quarter-milers, Dave and Don Christian, who were heaven-sent for a Bowerman scheme that had been germinating since the days of Jack Hutchins.

In 1958, Bowerman concocted a plan to enter one of the twins in the half-mile and hide the other one behind the end zone seats that briefly blocked spectators' view of the race. One twin would float along at the back of the pack for a lap. He'd step off in the turn and his twin would get on and smoke around the field, winning by fifty or sixty yards and breaking the world record.

The twins ordinarily would have done anything for Bowerman, but they worried about whether they could get away with it. What about the turn judge back there? Bowerman said he'd distract the judge during the switch, or if the judge caught on, he'd just persuade him to shut up for a while. Then, after the crowd was floored by the new world record, Bowerman figured he'd say, "Wait, we had a little mix-up. It's all a mistake. Dave got confused by what Don was doing. They thought they were in the relay."

In the end, the brothers couldn't bring themselves to do it. "But they practiced it in workouts a couple times," Grelle would remember, "and it looked great. From the stands it just looked great."

Something else that looked great from the stands in 1958 was sprinter Otis Crandall Davis. Born in Tuskaloosa, Alabama, Davis had had a stint in the service before being lured to Eugene in 1957, at the age of twenty-five, by a basketball scholarship. As it turned out, however, Davis rarely got into a game. Basketball coach Steve Belko asked Bowerman to take Davis off his hands, saying that yes, he had springs, but also an uncanny way of "going up when the ball is coming down and coming down when the ball is going up." Bill got Davis out to Hayward Field and tried him in the high jump and then, eventually, the sprints, once Davis mastered the starting blocks.

In the summer of 1958, we kids fought to carry those battered steel blocks for Davis during the all-comers meets. We instantly adored this gentle, bemused black man, the first most of us had been anywhere near, save for some gospel singers who came through at church. He let us cluster around as he measured how far back from the line Bowerman said each foot should be. He let us hammer in those blocks. When he crouched into them, he seemed heronlike, a folded-up Erector set. Thus were coach, runners, and admirers agape when Davis leapt up and sprinted 9.6 for the 100-yard dash and 21.5 for the 220. He ran high and proud, almost too much so, his back arching as he came down the stretch, his head tipping back, as if his joy made him look to heaven.

Since Bowerman wasn't content to merely find a sprinter, he thought of the

440. The following spring, he took Davis to Fresno State to run his first quarter-mile. On that track, the 440 was run around only one turn (there was a 220 straightaway before hitting the curve), so Davis took a little walk just to see how far this was. As Davis would tell the story many years later, "By the time I got back to Coach I was nervous as a cat. So Coach—I always called him *Coach*, and for some reason he never minded it from me—Coach Bowerman volunteered to massage me before the race, to calm me down. He got that balm all over my legs and was massaging closer and closer to the parts of which I was very proud, and I realized why, why . . . this man truly IS a great track coach! Then I felt the full heat of that salve, that Atomic Balm, and I think I ran so fast because I wanted to get back to the locker room and get it off."

Davis ran 48.6 for his first 440, a few tenths of a second from the school record. "So then I had an event to learn, and Coach said, 'Oat'—he always called me *Oat*—'Oat, that was my race too.' So I trusted him about how to run it."

A quarter-mile is 440 yards, about two-and-a-half yards longer than the 400 meters raced internationally. It is also about 100 yards farther than a man or woman can truly, physiologically, sprint. Thus it is won by the athlete who slows down least. Bowerman taught Davis to go hard from the start, reach virtually top speed, then "float" down the backstretch, maintaining his form and cadence without straining until, somewhere in the turn, he should "light out for home."

Davis soon got a feel for the crucial float. And there was a handy standard of greatness to measure him against. The University of Washington's Terry Tobacco was a Canadian Olympian and a sub-47-second man. Before their 1959 dual-meet race in Eugene, Bowerman walked Davis around the track himself, observing that if both men ran their best times, Tobacco would beat Davis by fifteen yards. He noted that Tobacco would be two lanes inside him and that, because of the stagger, Davis wouldn't be able to keep an eye on him in the first turn. "Here's how it will go," said Bowerman. "You sprint the first turn, then float, and in the middle of the backstretch, look left. Tobacco is going to be flying by. See if you can't go with him, maybe make a dent in his lead in the last hundred."

The race began. Davis sprinted, floated, and looked left as instructed. No Tobacco. "So Otis slowed down," Bowerman would remember. "Otis *waited*, let Tobacco pass him and get five yards ahead, then came back and beat him in the stretch." Davis, when he was able, made his way to Bowerman. "Worked like a charm!" he called. "Now that," Bowerman shouted back, "is coaching!" But he knew what he'd seen.

The next day Bowerman came to Davis and said, "Oat, Oat, we got something else for you to do. It might be that you have a date with destiny in a place called Rome." Davis thought, "Oh no, here we go again," without really grasping what Bill was talking about.

Someone else thinking about Rome was Bill Dellinger, who had joined the Air Force after graduating in 1956 and soon found himself stationed at a remote radar station on Washington's Olympic Peninsula. He was eighty miles from anything like a track, but he did have access to a hard, level beach.

"Bill mailed me interval workouts to do," Dellinger would recall, "so I did them"—did them in a character-illuminating way. He knew that his stride was about six feet, so he counted steps. "I would count to myself each time my right foot touched down until I reached ten. I'd put one finger out to keep track. Twelve fingers would be one 440. I ran up and down that beach doing everything from 220s to 1320s by counting, for eight months, without ever stepping on a track or knowing how far I was running or how fast."

When he returned to Eugene in 1958, he ran a mile time trial in 4:05. That year he broke American records in the 1500, two-mile, three-mile, and 5000 and had his great race in Moscow. "The funny thing was," he would say, "when I got onto the track it took me only ten fingers and two strides to do a 60-second quarter. I'd been running everything fifteen percent too far."

Dellinger not only was the first Bowerman runner to win an NCAA mile, he was the first to do what the Russians and Brits and Germans who'd beaten him so badly in Melbourne did: continue to run after leaving college, when most Americans quit. He proved that a runner's prime years were in his late twenties. Over two consecutive weekends in February 1959, he broke the indoor world records for two miles (8:49.9) and three miles (13:39). At twenty-six, he, too, was looking good for Rome.

As if two Olympic candidates weren't enough, there was also Bowerman's first extraordinary high school recruit. Dyrol Burleson, from Cottage Grove, was the best high school miler in the nation in 1958, running 4:13. Oregon State hired his high school coach, Sam Bell, in hopes of attracting Burleson. (Bell would coach national champions Dale Story, Morgan Groth, and Tracy Smith in Corvallis and the first American to break thirteen minutes for the 5000 meters, Bob Kennedy, at Indiana University.) But Burley, as all called him, never wavered. He came to Oregon with complete trust in Bowerman.

When Burleson was a freshman, Grelle was a senior and the country's best college miler. The freshman craved a race. "But Bill kept us apart that whole year," Burleson would say, still frustrated decades later. Bowerman protected Grelle because Burley could cover a relay 440 in under 48 seconds and would always have the edge coming down to the wire.

Bill made Burleson wait until the 1959 National AAU 1500 meters in Denver. Ravenous by then, Burley left Grelle standing during the last 100, beating him 3:47.5 to 3:48.4. That win qualified him for the United States vs. USSR meet, held that year in Philadelphia, where he won the 1500.

The following spring, during a dual meet on April 23, 1960, I was sixteen and on the hurdle crew when Burleson whipped around Stanford's brave, pace-driving Ernie Cunliffe off the last turn and finished in 3:58.6. It was Hayward Field's first sub-4:00 and it broke Don Bowden's American record by a tenth. I was left shaking uncontrollably and with a fixed idea of how a runner had to look. I have it still. It is Burleson's leanness, Burleson's quad muscles like bridge cables, sliding and jumping under the thinnest sheath of deeply tan skin.

Davis, Dellinger, and Burleson peopled my daydreams as the Olympics approached. Could three real guys from just down the road have any chance against the world's best?

CHAPTER 12

Rome

ALTHOUGH BILL WAS NOT ON THE OFFICIAL US COACHING STAFF FOR ROME, HE would spend every day at the athletes' Village, meeting with the Oregonians who had made it to the Eternal City. The cognoscenti knew there was only one Duck with a medal chance, the twenty-year-old prodigy Dyrol Burleson. Burley exuded invincibility. Back home, he emptied the sauna by coming in chewing a sprig of poison oak. So competitive he could seem vulpine, he drove opponents ahead like caribou, thinning them out, waiting, glittery-eyed, before feasting on the last lap. "Burley kind of kept to himself," Grelle would remember, "and did secret workouts, even though we were all on the same team."

Burley was different. He had one of the few full scholarships Bowerman allowed, so there was no energy-draining job in the mill for him. He also was never hazed by Bowerman, never felt at cross-purposes with him. "Bill was always very . . . kind to me," Burleson would say, almost apologetically. "Never any pranks. Of course I obeyed his every request. I had supreme faith in Bill. I never wanted to lose a race for him. And I can say I did that." Burleson would be undefeated in college competition, taking three NCAA mile or 1500-meter crowns.

And it was the crowns that mattered, not the times. After his seemingly effortless 3:58.6 against Stanford's Cunliffe, fans couldn't help asking how fast he'd have run if he'd blasted off with half a lap to go instead of 100 yards. (The world record was Herb Elliott's 3:54.5.) "It doesn't matter," Burleson would say and mean it. "I don't run for time. I run to win. That mile was a credit to two men, and I'm not one of them. It was a credit to Bill for preparing me so well and a credit to Ernie for setting such a tough pace."

Burleson's belief in Bowerman was such that he raced with his cheeks weirdly puffed out, as if trying to blow a walnut through a soda straw. In Bowerman's painstaking study of the physiology of exercise, something had caught his attention. Air pressure in the lungs affects how readily oxygen molecules hop across the alveolar membrane to be grabbed by red blood cells. Bowerman reasoned that if more pressure means more molecular hopping, a runner applying back-pressure when exhaling could force a little more oxygen into the system. Was this true? I have no idea. It would make a good PhD thesis. But Burleson did it, and that was good enough for me and many other Oregon runners. We still make noise when we run, blowing like horses, our lips flapping.

Otis Davis, whose struggles were painfully obvious, was also following Bowerman's advice—and learning from every race. Because he had a swayback and a high rear end and a way of arching his spine like a bow when he got tired, Bowerman taught him to run with his hips tucked under him, to keep his trunk perpendicular to the ground. "We did drills for that," Davis would recall, "high knee and stomach crunches. He never really tried to change me, just adjust me." Bowerman found ways, too, to assure Davis he was world class. When Davis graduated in 1960, Oregon president O. Meredith Wilson handed him his diploma and said, "Good luck in the Olympics." Davis thought, *What has Coach been telling people?*

First he had to make the US team. The 1960 Men's Olympic Trials were jammed into two July days in Stanford Stadium. The semi and final of the 400 were the same day, and after the semi Davis felt too tired to race. He bent into the blocks aching, repeating Bowerman's last words, "Oat, you can only do what you can do." At the gun, Cal's Jack Yerman and Abilene Christian's Earl Young rocketed away. At halfway, Davis was last. And then it came to him—"and I mean, came to me in a religious sense," he would declare—that he had better move up. He obeyed, caught sprinter after sprinter, and just edged Colorado's Ted Woods for third. He was on the team, barely.

Other Oregon runners had found the Trials ho-hum by comparison, with Dellinger running easily to qualify in the 5000 and Burleson and Grelle going one-two in the 1500. The 1960 team would also include Bowerman's first Olympian who wasn't a runner. Saying, "The more milk you have, the more cream that will rise," Bowerman for years had taught a PE decathlon class as a way to keep an eye out for talent. Up had floated Dave Edstrom, who could hurdle, leap high and long, and put the shot. Bill taught him the other six events and Edstrom made the decathlon team behind UCLA's Rafer Johnson.

A second set of Ducks would race for Canada, led by a nineteen-year-old freshman sprinter, Harry Jerome, who had tied the world 100-meter record of 10.0. Coming, too, was 800-meter man Sigmar Ohlemann, perhaps the smoothest strider ever to leave Eugene spectators agog. "Who on earth is that?" Robin Jaqua had cried upon seeing his tan, his grace, his amber waves. "Oh," said Bowerman, "our transfer from the School of Nordic Gods."

The weather in Rome was volatile, the daytime heat sending up evening thunderheads, but Otis Davis was glad about one thing: the 400-meter rounds were a day apart. The 400-meter semifinals had revealed two favorites, and he was one of them. Feeling no need to hold back, Davis had won his semi in an Olympic record 45.5. The other heat was won by Germany's brush-cut, oak-thighed Karl Kaufmann in an eased-up 45.7.

Kaufmann had not been beaten in two years. "You could see why," Bowerman would say. "Great sense of pace. Stamina of a half-miler. Man after my own heart. He was going to keep close to the leaders and run right by them at the end." So Davis's instructions were to use his effortless float and not make a big move in the last turn as was his habit. Bill told him to "save enough oomph to make it a two-man race all the way down the stretch."

The afternoon of the final was overcast and calm. Davis was in lane five; Kaufmann was inside him, in lane two. So the German would be the one aware of who was doing what on the first turn. At the gun, South Africa's Mal Spence went out maniacally, hitting the 200 in 21.4. Davis and Kaufmann, eyeing each other, were absolutely even in 21.8, four yards back. "Perfect," said Bowerman. He and Barbara were sitting almost above the finish line, and he felt that the hard part for Davis—mastering his excitement—was over.

It wasn't. "Into the second turn, seeing the others," Davis would say. "I was filled with emotion. I swore if they were going to win this they were going to have to come over me to do it. I ran on that emotion. I put everything into it. I moved at the top of the turn."

"Moved" is not the word. Davis ripped through the 100-meter curve in 10.8 seconds and came into the stretch with a lead of seven yards over Kaufmann. Bowerman and 90,000 others came to their feet to see if he could keep it. Kaufmann gained all the way, and the nearer the line, the faster he closed as Davis, back arched, head rolling skyward, desperately tried to hold together.

Davis felt a string touch his chest and right shoulder. He looked left. There was Kaufmann diving across the line, actually biting the tape, a perfect lean, the price of which was a descent to the cinders. "He landed flat on his face," Davis would say. "I thought I'd won but I couldn't tell. So we had to wait."

The officials peered at the finish photo for a quarter of an hour. Davis put on his sweat top, took off his shoes, paced. The nine runners in the next race, the men's 1500-meter final, were trotting around on the backstretch and still the verdict hadn't come. Two of those finalists—Jim Grelle and Dyrol Burleson— were having a hard time concentrating. "I couldn't believe it," Grelle would remember. "This is Otis, my teammate from Eugene, who has just appeared to win the quarter-mile? Finally the announcer says, '*Results, 400 meters . . .* ' And they go through fifth place, fourth place, third place . . . and there's a long pause. Then '*In second place, from West Germany . . .*' So you knew." Davis, standing in the middle of the infield, started jumping up and down. ' *. . . In a new world record time of 44.9, the Olympic champion . . .*'" The crowd was screaming so loud Grelle couldn't hear Davis's name.

In the tenth 400-meter final of his life, Otis Davis had won the Olympic gold. Kaufmann also was timed in 44.9, as both became the first to crack 45 seconds for 400 meters. Bowerman's reaction, he would confess later, was "eighty percent ecstasy, twenty percent unworthy." The perfectionist in him felt that if Davis hadn't disobeyed and exploded through the turn, he wouldn't have crawled down the stretch and might have run a tenth or two faster. "But you can't blame a guy for being brave," Bowerman would add, "and did he ever make it work! He may well have been second if he'd run the way I told him."

On went the tumult. "I have this picture," Barbara Bowerman would remember, "of Otis jumping up half his height, and the odd memory of someone grabbing me from behind, planting a firm kiss on my cheek, and saying, 'I've always wanted to kiss the wife of a coach whose athlete has just won a gold medal!' And the kisser, whoever it was, was swept away by the shouting crowd. I never found out who he was."

Suddenly, even as the crowd kept roaring, came the command "Fifteen-hundred-meter men, to your marks." Burleson and Grelle, still in happy shock over Otis's win, began what would be an epic contest. France's monkish Michel Bernard took the lead and passed 400 meters in 58.2. When he slowed slightly, reaching 800 in 1:57.8, Australia's Herb Elliott could contain himself no longer. Falcon-beaked, white uniform stark against his mahogany tan, he flowed past, running 55 pace so smoothly that watchers at first wondered why the world's best milers were letting him go.

Grelle knew. "I was turning into a spectator, it was so fast," he would say. He was in eighth. Burleson was just ahead, in mid-pack, and doing all he could to stay there. Three hundred meters after taking the lead, Elliott had twenty-five yards on Istvan Rozsavolgyi of Hungary and was still pulling away. Bowerman was so riveted by the sight that he had to will himself to look back at his two Oregonians. "Their only real hope was for it to be slow and tactical," he would remember. "That was how Grelle got through his semi. And Burley could kick with anyone if he could stay close to him. Well, Mr. Elliott removed himself from any chance of that."

Herb Elliott was then twenty-two and had never been beaten over a mile in his life. In 1958, he'd had a great year, taking the mile record to 3:54.5 and the

1500 to 3:36.0. In 1959 he'd gotten married, run a few races, barely won, and gone home to prepare for this effort.

Elliot was coached by a rude visionary named Percy Cerutty, who demanded that his runners become "Stotans," half Spartan and half stoic. Intervals were but a part of his system. Cerutty added intense weight lifting, killing sand hills, and a philosophy that edged toward the sacrificial. "Thrust against pain," he told Elliott. "Pain is the purifier. Walk toward suffering. Love suffering. Embrace it." John Landy had found this a bit much, but Elliott was a perfect vessel.

America's first sub-four-minute miler, Don Bowden of Cal, had visited Cerutty's training camp at Portsea, outside Melbourne. "Cerutty had Elliott doing *fartlek*, hills, and sand dunes, which gives you the strength to run one fast mile after another," Bowden would say later. "That's what I always tell people about the Olympic Games. You have to get through the heats. It's not the fastest athlete who wins, it's the strongest. And in 1960, Elliott was the strongest."

Bowerman stood and watched that strength carry the runner into the last lap. For an instant it seemed as though Elliott had gone wild too early. Then Elliott looked to his right. Cerutty had fought through guards, cleared a moat and fence, and was madly waving a towel outside the track, their signal that he was running a record pace. Elliott drove on toward his true limits.

Elliott, the man who gave actual words to the great paradox of arrogance and humility, was enacting it. The arrogance was making his move with 700 to go, impossibly early to start blasting at 55 pace. The humility was now, knowing with every step the suffering to which his move condemned him. For 300 meters he took it, embraced it, held it in, slowing only in the final yards. He finished with his head sagging back and eyes shut, not collapsing but reaching the tape utterly empty. His time was 3:35.6, a world record, the equivalent of a 3:52.6 mile. He felt no joy. "Only relief," he would say, "blessed relief."

Michel Jazy endured, as he would put it, "the tortures of hell," to finish second, twenty yards back, in a European record 3:38.4. Rozsavolgyi took the bronze in 3:39.2. Burleson, sixth in a US record 3:40.9, had acquitted himself well. Grelle hung on for eighth, at 3:45.0.

Later in life, Burleson would reveal a melancholy fact: "I don't remember my victories. Only the losses. The losses I see every step of." But he would not be haunted by Rome. "I was too young. I'd run as hard as I could. I'd done my best. I'd set an American record. I knew I'd be a lot better. And I'd seen a great run."

Burley had been part of a momentous, front-running race. But, secure in his own finishing speed, he was disinclined to learn from or to emulate Elliott's tactics. After Elliott retired (a meteor, it was said, who had burned himself out with

"By God, I'll do 'er."
Bill's maternal great grandfather, J. W. Chambers
married the widow Mary Greene Scoggin (*right*) so his father would let
him join the wagon train to Oregon. *Collection of* BARBARA BOWERMAN

Bill's maternal
grandmother,
Mary Jane, and
husband, Thomas
Benton Hoover, would
have five more children
after Annie and Will,
shown here, including
Bill's mother, Lizzie.
Collection of BARBARA
BOWERMAN

The original homestead on the Thomas Hoover ranch, seen here in 1875, became the site of the first Fossil Post Office. *Collection of* BARBARA BOWERMAN

Shortly after graduating from Oregon Agriculture College, Lizzie Hoover met up-and-coming attorney Jay Bowerman.

OREGON STATE UNIVERSITY ARCHIVES (Lizzie); *Collection of* BARBARA BOWERMAN (Jay)

Bill Bowerman and his twin brother, Thomas, were born February 19, 1911.

Collection of BARBARA BOWERMAN

After her divorce from Jay Bowerman and the death of her son Thomas, Lizzie Bowerman raised Beth, Dan, and Bill with help from her Hoover kin.

Collection of
BARBARA BOWERMAN

Bill Bowerman glowers
in captivity—seventh grade
at Hill Military Academy in
Portland, Oregon.
Collection of BARBARA BOWERMAN

In 1928, the fall of his
senior year at Medford High
School, Bill was a football
player and Big Man on Campus.
Collection of BARBARA BOWERMAN

Barbara Young, a sophomore transfer student, met Bill at a dance that fall.

At UCLA, Barbara was swept off her feet by Mike Frankovich (*second from left*), protégé of comedian Joe E. Brown (*far left*). Brown's son Don is at right.

Members of the 1934 University of Oregon Mile Relay Team flank Oregon president Arnold Bennet Hall. From left, Sherwood Burr, Bill Bowerman, Hall, George Scharpf, and Howie Patterson. © UNIVERSITY OF OREGON ARCHIVES

Bill and Barbara seem to hover
in mid-air after their wedding in
Pasadena, California, on June 22, 1936.
Collection of BARBARA BOWERMAN

In the winter of 1944, snow blankets
Camp Hale in Pando Valley, Colorado.

PHOTO BY HUGH EVANS *in* Soldiers on Skis, *by Flint
Whitlock, copyright 1992, Paladin Press, Boulder, Colorado*

Barbara and Bill with sons Jay and Jon and their Airedale in Texas before Bill shipped
out to Italy with the 10th Mountain Division in 1944 *Collection of* BARBARA BOWERMAN

Bill admires his Army discharge papers at Camp Carson, Colorado, in October 1945.

Collection of BARBARA BOWERMAN

Bill clowns around with Otto
Frohnmayer during a camping
trip after the war.
Photo by DAVID FROHNMAYER

Bowerman succeeded the legendary Bill Hayward (*left*)
as Oregon track coach in 1948. *Collection of* BARBARA BOWERMAN

The Bowerman house takes shape on McKenzie View Drive in 1950.

Collection of BARBARA BOWERMAN

Bowerman (*front row, far right*) sits with his first Oregon varsity track and field team in 1948. Next to him is Peter Mundle, with whom he developed his training methods.

© UNIVERSITY OF OREGON ARCHIVES

Members of the 1955 Oregon cross-country team flank their coach. Bill Dellinger is second from left, Jim Bailey third from right. *Collection of* BILL DELLINGER

Jim Bailey runs the first sub-four-minute mile on American soil, 3:58.6 to defeat John Landy in the Los Angeles Coliseum in 1956. *Collection of* BILL DELLINGER

Bill works on his rubber asphalt research in the late 1950s. *Collection of* BARBARA BOWERMAN

Bill presses the air out of Dyrol Burleson while congratulating him on Hayward Field's first sub-four, 3:58.6, in April 1960.
© UNIVERSITY OF OREGON ARCHIVES

The Bowerman-coached athletes who qualified for the 1960 Olympics line up on either side of Bill: From left, Jim Grelle, Dave Edstrom, Sig Ohlemann, Harry Jerome, Bill Dellinger, and Otis Davis. *Collection of* BILL DELLINGER

his intensity), Burleson's attitude seemed justified. The world's milers were all mortals compared to Elliott, and well within Burleson's range. Yet his valuing victory more than records ("I'd rather win in 4:10 than lose in 3:54.") and not exploring how fast he could cover his distance would leave Burleson vulnerable when he was faced with someone he had to run away from the way Elliott had run away from him.

Sig Ohlemann's physical beauty didn't get him past the semis in the 800, and the heavy favorite going into the final was Belgium's world record holder, Roger Moens. But as Moens roared off the last turn, he went yards wide to force Jamaica's George Kerr even wider. This freed a muscular man in the startling black of New Zealand from where he'd been boxed on the rail. Peter Snell saw the opening and lunged for it. At the finish Moens was out in lane three, looking over enraged as Snell, the Games' biggest surprise, beat him in 1:46.3.

Word of Snell's victory spread to the warm-up area. His Kiwi teammate, Murray Halberg, gave a little yip as he put on his spikes for the 5000. Halberg, the opposite of the mesomorphic Snell, had lost much of the use of his left arm as a result of a rugby accident in his youth and carried it tucked to his side as he ran. The British Empire three-mile champion and a 3:57.5 miler, he had a race plan not unlike Elliott's. "And he executed it beautifully," an admiring Bill Dellinger, brought low by the flu and forced to watch from the sidelines, would say. Halberg laid off the early pace and struck with three laps to go, blasting away with a 60-second circuit. Although Halberg, too, sagged near the end, he held on to win in 13:43.4.

Bill Bowerman, who had gone to the warm-up track to be near Otis Davis before the 4 x 400-meter relay, soon noticed that the two New Zealand champions had the same coach. Bowerman went over and offered his hand to Arthur Lydiard, the forty-three-year-old ultramarathoner with whom he'd been corresponding for a while. "What wonderful work," Bowerman said. "Got anyone else I can bet on?"

"As a matter of fact I do," said Lydiard. "Another fellow from my neighborhood named Magee, in the marathon." A few days later, Barry Magee took the bronze in the twenty-six-mile race in 2:17:18, two minutes behind the world record 2:15:17 of Ethiopia's barefoot Abebe Bikila.

Lydiard wasn't kidding about the neighborhood. Snell, Halberg, and Magee all belonged to the same track club in Auckland, and Lydiard, besides being their coach, was their milkman. "I never before nor afterward saw Bill so awed," Barbara would say, "as he was by Arthur's runners taking three medals, two gold.

They found themselves immediately and lastingly congenial. Arthur was a great talker, loved to share both his methods and opinions with any interested listener, and Bill always appreciated challenges by worthy opponents."

Lydiard's influence on Bowerman, and ultimately the planet, spread in a widening circle. First, he'd experimented on himself, finding that marathon training not only made him a better marathoner, but also able to withstand speed work as never before. Snell, Halberg, and Magee, despite being a half-miler, a three-miler, and a marathoner, all ran the same hundred miles a week for two or three months to condition themselves for weeks of hill drills and anaerobic "sharpening" work, as Lydiard called it, before presenting themselves at a starting line. Once there, the stamina they had built allowed them to carry their speed farther, no matter what the distance. This regime Dellinger rightly termed revolutionary. Of the two antipodean coaches, Lydiard and Cerutty, Lydiard would find his method the more widely adopted. "Marathon training" would rule like nothing since Zátopek's intervals.

But Lydiard's influence didn't stop there. In teaching his neighborhood to run, in telling it to "train, not strain," as he put it, Lydiard also found that any body, old or young, female or male, post-cardiac or Olympian, once gotten out trotting, would be the better for it. Lydiard would have to take Bowerman into *his* care before Bill would really believe that. For the time being, the two parted friends, both feeling they'd met a colleague with whom they wanted to keep in close touch.

Otis Davis concluded the Games by anchoring the US 4 x 400-meter relay. "After Jack Yerman, Earl Young, and Glenn Davis's legs," Bowerman would recall, "Germany was still right on the Americans' butt. Germany being that old seeker after revenge, Karl Kaufmann."

Davis took the baton, accelerated in a cinder spray, and hit the backstretch a couple of yards clear. Then he floated. Kaufmann saw that, drove hard with his arms, caught Davis, and went wide. He had fallen for a trap. Otis hit the gas, held him wide around the turn, and ran away from Kaufmann in the stretch. The Americans set a world record of 3:02.2.

Otis's reaction to his wins and records (after his jumping for glory) was a quietly abashed disbelief. But this gave way to an enduring sense of rightness. "I leaned a lot on my faith," Davis said in later years. "It had carried me to the miraculous. I came to feel I was destined to do what I did."

To the Ducks who had not medaled in Rome—among them Canada's young Harry Jerome, who had been kept from the 100-meter final by a hamstring cramp—Bowerman delivered part two of his standard speech about success and failure. They already knew the first part. We usually heard it on the team bus before a meet. It began, "When the ancient Greeks went out to battle, their mothers told them, 'You come back carrying your shields in triumph, or you come back being carried upon them.'" (It was a parable that often garnered puzzled looks. "Damn hard, those Greek mothers," hurdler Mel Renfro once said.)

So Bowerman would add, "Some of you are going to do better out there today than you think. Some of you are going to do worse. But no one is going to be borne home a corpse. So afterward, we will be able to talk about what happened, and why, and take some direction from it." And so, on the bus or plane home, after some had done better and some worse, Bowerman would sit with us in ones and twos and talk about the whys of our mistakes, the nuts and bolts of botched relay passes or getting boxed in, but also the whys of our wins, how we had nailed good javelin form or kept our trailing leg in tight over the hurdles. In Rome, though, he said, "Soak this in, breathe it in, sip the wine, take home a pocketful of cinders. You're Olympians and you live to fight again."

After watching Rome's bittersweet closing ceremonies, the athletes mingling and dancing without regard to nation, Bill and Barbara headed north, spending a couple of days driving through Northern Italy, visiting places Bill had been during the war. "He felt great affection for what he always called the *paisanos*," she would say. "He knew they had suffered terribly from the impositions of three different armies occupying their homelands. He felt good that he had intentionally let all the Tenth's mules loose as some small reparation for what our troops had done. He seemed to enjoy stopping on hillsides, just looking down on tidy farmlands, watching children playing and people going about their business." After the destruction wreaked here by steel and explosives, the man who loved being on hay crew smiled to see that life had returned to its organic basics—the figs and prosciutto, the Valpolicella and cheese and pesto.

They went on up to Germany to see the Munsingers, who lived about twenty minutes along the autobahn from Munich. Heinz Munsinger had been liaison to the Austrian Army when Bill had gone to the German headquarters with translator Julius Keller. "Keller translated my advice that Munsinger ought to go back and make the Austrians surrender or a lot of people were going to be killed," Bill would say. "Munsinger did go back and there was no more resistance." They got to know one another some in the chaotic weeks right after the surrender, but would not see each other again until 1960.

However, they had kept in touch. After Bowerman had returned to Medford, he found postwar American track shoes were, as he elegantly put it, "Crap. Crap. Crap. Crappy, hard leather, crappy ten ounces per shoe." The racing spikes of

Germany's Adidas were far superior, but punitively priced. Munsinger had repaid Bill for his kindness during the war by becoming his importer, sending Adidas in the sizes Bill ordered and negotiating a discount for them. When Adidas finally balked at that, Munsinger helped get Bowerman the right to distribute Adidas in the United States. But that didn't last long. Bill didn't want to sell shoes. He wanted to train runners.

So, in Bavaria in 1960, they talked of shoes and the future. Bill told Munsinger that Adidas were so expensive he'd been forced to take up cobbling. He showed him a pair of spikes he'd made for Burleson, and Munsinger was impressed. As the two veterans looked out over the Black Forest toward the Austrian Alps and lifted their steins to old times and better ones to come, what was more natural than the thought of a German Olympics someday? "Wouldn't that be grand?" said Munsinger. "To prove to the world we have come full circle from savagery."

CHAPTER 13

Innovation

THREE YEARS BEFORE BOWERMAN SHOWED MUNSINGER THOSE RACING SPIKES, when his trickle of discounted Adidas imports was drying up, he'd found himself in the campus shoe shop, picking up some reheeled pumps for Barbara. After he paid, he stood there going over the shoes' every crevice and seam until the elderly repairman asked if something was wrong. "Nothing's wrong. They're fine," Bowerman said, and then stepped back and took in the shop, the worn, incoming shoes, the neat bags of repaired ones, the mallets and punches, the sheets of fragrant, fresh leather. He observed until the proprietor's mood worsened.

"I don't want to demean your artistry," Bowerman said finally, "but how hard is it to make a pair of shoes? I mean really?"

"You cannot make your own shoes!" erupted the repairman. "Trust me. You cannot make shoes without a factory."

"Let us stipulate that you are absolutely right. Of course I can't make shoes. But if you were going to make a shoe, and you had the right equipment, how would you go about it?"

Bowerman said later it was wonderful to watch the man morph into "a grouchy professor of cobbling science 101."

"First," the repairman said, "I'd make a mold, called a last. Make it the size and shape of my foot. Then I'd cut pieces of leather and sew them together over the mold, making an upper. I now have the top half of a shoe. Toe in front, heel in back, tongue covering the arch of the foot, holes for the laces to hold in the sides. Then, zoop, zoop, I sew a sole over the whole bottom, add a heel, and I got a shoe."

"Sew or glue?" asked Bowerman.

"You can glue. Sewing lasts."

"Okay," said Bowerman. "Now how would you get spikes sticking out of it?"

"Spikes?"

Bowerman happened to have with him an Adidas sprint shoe. From the sole beneath its toe box sprang four glinting daggers. The repairman turned the shoe every which way, running his fingers inside, savoring the intelligence that had produced it. He put it down and stood back.

"You, sir," he said, "are on your own."

Bowerman went home, turned on the band saw in his garage, and cut open that shoe and dozens of others, learning their anatomy. The essence of a racing shoe, he realized, was its spike plate, the steel or dense plastic part embedded under the forefoot, into which spikes were screwed or welded. Merrily reverse engineering, he bought an array of lasts and leathers, cannibalized a few spike plates and set about assembling custom-made uppers for them.

His workshop at home began to resemble the cobbler's shop. It wasn't long before he could make decent-looking shoes using rubber contact cement instead of needle and thread. "I wasn't after a shoe that went a hundred miles," he would say. However, one of his hopes was quickly dashed. "I wanted the shoes as light as if I drove nails through your bare feet," he would recall with some relish. "But I discovered that a runner exerts so much leverage that spikes would just bend or tear off unless the shoe gripped them like iron. That's why all the spike plates were in one solid piece."

Spike plates ultimately would constitute most of the weight of Bowerman-made shoes, because he was soon working with very wispy materials. He obsessed about weight for a simple, mathematical reason: If a miler has an average two-yard stride, he takes 880 steps in his race. Save an ounce from his shoe and you save him 880 ounces—fifty-five pounds of hard labor. At the time, American shoes weighed from seven to ten ounces—half a pound on average. Even the lightest Adidas weighed five ounces. "I beat that by two ounces pretty quick," Bill would crow.

In his first trials, split calfskin worked best, but he tried anything that caught his eye. The material had to be light and strong, but not too flexible or, when real running force was applied, it would come off, as he would so delicately put it, "like a new lamb through the placenta."

It was Bowerman's recollection that the first Oregon runner for whom he made a pair of spikes was Phil Knight in 1958. "They were a white, rubber-coated fabric, the kind you'd use for a tablecloth you could sponge off," he would say thirty years later. "Buck Knight put them on one evening at the practice track and jogged around, and I didn't know whether he was going to laugh or cry at these things. Buck tended to keep his own counsel." Just then Otis Davis happened by and did a double take when he saw the shoes Buck had on. Somehow he got the shoes away from Buck, put them on, and ran off into the night. "All you could see of the thief was these white, white, shoes, taking long, long steps," Bowerman would remember. "You could hear him yelling that he liked them and he'd keep them and be grateful forever."

During this period Bowerman was coming out with a new experimental shoe every week. His best shoes used kangaroo skin—light, stretchy, but resilient enough to hold its shape. (After a while, though, kangaroo skin was hard to get. In the early 1970s, the United States would ban the importation of kangaroo products under the Endangered Species Act.) He tried velvet, deerskin, snakeskin, testing them on lower-value guinea pigs such as his middle son.

When Jay Bowerman, a promising half-miler, was a sophomore at Coburg High he wore custom-made racing spikes: a spinach-green suede upper with elastic instead of laces and 1¼-inch spikes riveted to a translucent nylon plate that was glued to the shoe. "I used foot powder to get them on since they had that elastic across the tongue and fit like ballet slippers," Jay would remember. The shoes worked well enough: Jay got third in the 1959 state small-schools meet, running 2:05.2.

The first big win for Bowerman's homemade shoes came at the 1959 Pacific Coast Conference meet. Favored in the 440 was Bobby Stanton of the University of Southern California, who had beaten Otis Davis a few weeks earlier at the Oregon–USC dual meet. But Otis, wearing the white shoes he'd nicked from Phil Knight, blew Stanton off the track. "I think," Knight said later, "a seed was planted that day."

Bowerman never forced his shoes on anyone. His credo was "Be true to your feet." If a runner felt more competitive in Adidas or Puma, Bowerman had no problem with his wearing those brands. But word of the Ducks' odd footwear got around. "As you lined up for your race in a dual meet," miler Jim Grelle would remember, "guys would look at your feet and say, 'Oh, weird, what are those?'" The Ducks would allow as how their shoes were lighter than the clodhoppers the other guys were wearing, pointing out that the work of lifting an extra two or three ounces 900 times over the course of a mile ("That's a hundred pounds right there!") might be the difference between winning and being an also-ran. "People got to kind of hate us because we had better shoes," Grelle would say. "You couldn't buy anything like what we had."

Custom fit meant just that. Bowerman would draw an outline of a runner's foot, measuring the circumference at different places and making notes on each drawing. "Grelle: thin ankle, size 10½, a heel that extends," for example, or "Otis Davis: 10½, but real wide ball of the foot." Then Bowerman would make a plastic shoemaker's last of each runner's foot, sanding it down or building it up with wood putty until, as Grelle would say, "it was exactly you." Socks defeated the purpose. They might be acceptable in cross-country because the race was long enough that blisters would be a problem. But in a mile, a blister wouldn't make itself known until the race was over anyway. The aim was always to take just a little more weight off and to have the shoe fit more snugly.

Bill's designs grew organically over time. Breakthroughs were brilliant, but rare. He made regular trips to the Tandy Leather Shop to see what had come in. One time it was some beautiful red suede that was tanned cod skin. His immediate (and seemingly logical) thought was "Fish skin is probably the ideal leather for when it's wet." He made a pair for his son. "Logical or not, he was wrong," Jay Bowerman would remember. After a lap around the wet infield grass, the shoes had soaked up a half-cup of water each and had stretched from size 9 to size 12. "I was running with these great, soggy, floppy things in front of my toes, like oversize gym socks," Jay would say. "When the shoes came off, my feet were a deep, lustrous red."

Access to the shoes that worked was strictly monitored, for reasons both practical and psychological. Bowerman would make his runners hand over their featherweight shoes right after their races, keeping each pair in a box labeled with the runner's name. "You get these back next Saturday," he'd say. Grelle would remember begging to wear the shoes in time trials, but Bowerman was unrelenting. "He got us thinking, *Man, when I get those things on, it's gonna be magic*," Grelle would say. "Magic shoes on Saturday."

The most successful purveyor of Bowerman footwear, of course, would be his first collegiate guinea pig, Phil Knight. Probably because of his shyness, Knight's commitment to running wasn't patently obvious to Bill at first. So, even though he was good friends with Knight's father, Bowerman exerted characteristic pressure on the son. "Bill made me pay my dues," Knight would remember.

Hazing kicked in during winter term, with Bowerman frequently wondering aloud whether Phil really wanted to be on the team. "I couldn't do anything right," Knight would say. One time Bill scheduled a three-quarter-mile time trial on a day when Knight felt terrible, achy with flu coming on. But he went out to the practice track anyway, only to find that Bowerman wasn't there. He waited fifteen minutes, felt worse, and was just heading up to Mac Court when Bill showed up.

"Where do you think you're going?"

"In. Feel awful."

"Phil, who would you say is the coach of this track team?"

"You are."

"Well then, you go in fifteen minutes."

Knight couldn't believe it: "He was contradicting everything he'd taught us about not running sick and making it worse. I knew it was just to make me acknowledge that his word was law, no matter how arbitrary. But that didn't make it any easier to take. I was so mad I ran a personal record."

Bowerman clicked the watch, noted the time, mildly observed, "You don't look that sick to me," and walked away knowing a great deal more about Knight's command of self.

"When I hung in," Knight would say, "he saw character, and that was the end of it. Later, it was funny to watch him hazing other guys the same way—funny after you'd been through the cycle."

Jim Grelle would describe Knight as so quiet that he "probably took his schoolbooks on a date," and drawing Knight into college-boy pranks was nearly impossible. But Grelle claims to have managed it once. During their senior year, 1959, after Oregon beat Washington State in a dual meet in Pullman, a bunch of guys that Grelle swears included Phil "went out looking for fun."

They came across a yellow school bus with the door open and the key in the ignition. Grelle got the bus started and the whole crew piled in, Phil protesting all the way. "I'm driving," Grelle would recall, "and the bus is long and tips up on two wheels on turns, and guys are standing up hanging on, and I'm honking, and Phil yells, 'Stop! Let me out! I'm a CPA! I want a career!' Finally, we realized this is not a huge city. People had had enough time to call the cops. So we left the bus in the middle of an intersection and ran back to the dorm. And you know what? To this day, Buck Knight will try to tell you he wasn't there in that bus that night."

Knight, in ways slow and inevitable, would have his revenge. "As a freshman," he would say four decades later, "I had to make one hell of an adjustment. I had to go from being a good high school competitor to a locker room with three Olympians in Dellinger, Bailey, and Grelle. Four, if you count Burley coming in my senior year. If you ask where Nike came from, I would say it came from a kid who had that world-class shock administered at age seventeen by Bill Bowerman. Not simply the shock, but the way to respond. He attached such honor to not giving up, to doing my utmost. Most kids didn't have that adjustment of standards, that introduction to true reality."

Knight said this at a quiet lunch with Barbara Bowerman in 2001. Barbara leaned over and said, "It always bothered Bill having you and Jim Grelle in the same class."

"Not as much as it bothered me."

"But he always cared," said Barbara, patting his wrist.

"He lied to me about my splits once," said Knight, "to encourage Grelle."

Knight had a perfectly respectable career at Oregon, running bests of 1:53 in the 880 and 4:15 in the mile. He won a couple dual-meet races and a small cross-country meet when Bowerman didn't send the big guns for some reason. "My racing was spotty, with a lot of ups and downs," Knight would recall. "Bill and I never quite got the formula for how to train me. We were close, though. Maybe in one more year . . . " He left that hanging, as do many who go on, unrequited, to other things. Knight graduated from Oregon in 1959. Masking his relentlessness with his quiet demeanor, he would not rest until he competed to the ultimate level in something.

The time since Bowerman's return from the Games in Rome had been filled with the usual plethora of duties, but he had not forgotten Arthur Lydiard in New Zealand. Snell and Halberg's coach hadn't written for months, so Bill had asked why. In April of 1961, in a seven-page, handwritten letter, Lydiard poured out his heart in answer.

Upon returning from Rome he'd found the small factory he managed a month behind schedule and had had to work sixty to eighty hours a week. "Then, on the athletic side, the rest of my time was fully taken by everyone thinking I could make them Olympic champs overnight. I became completely jaded mentally and physically." Lydiard was trying to earn a living to put his kids through college, but had no time to spend with them. "I could get no let up," he wrote, "so I took the only course open. I tossed my job in and took on a milk round with my phone number unregistered. I am on my own at night on the milk round and it has helped me to settle down and think." He still loved running "better than anything," Lydiard continued, "but for an amateur coach it got too big for me. This whole business has mushroomed and I am not in a financial position to do anything about it. Sorry if I have bored you with all this, but I had to explain to someone and I think you will understand, Bill."

"You have no idea," Bowerman wrote back, "how well I understand." Bill was coaching fourteen events and had so many good throwers, sprinters, and hurdlers coming on that he was feeling oppressed. To solve both their problems, he extended an extraordinary offer and sign of respect: "Presently, in the University of Oregon, I have ten of the finest runners in the United States. It would be a great thing for me and for these young men if they could come under your direction. Seven have run the mile under 4:10, five under 4:05." Bill suggested finding Lydiard something in public relations with one of the lumber companies. "I envision finding some kind of appropriate employment where you can earn a reasonably good living between the hours of 10 o'clock and 3 o'clock. You could devote your morning and late afternoon to the training of out-of-school or in-school runners. There is no doubt in my mind that if you were here, our runners would reach their full potential." Before Bowerman could find him the kind of position he'd described, however, the Rothmans cigarette company made a similar offer and Lydiard stayed in Auckland. Bowerman would train his embarrassment of riches by himself.

Those riches were making themselves known in the service of another of Bowerman's innovations, one that would become a hallowed Oregon tradition. Only five weeks after Burleson's American record mile of 3:58.6 in 1960, Jim Beatty had improved it to 3:58.0 at Modesto. On May 24, 1961, word rippled around town that Burleson might take a crack at getting it back that evening. It had to be in the evening. Virtually all sunny afternoons in the Willamette Valley are accompanied by strong winds from the north, frustrating anyone trying to hold a pace through Hayward Field's backstretch. But when the sun sets, the wind dies. A warm evening takes on extraordinary stillness. This, Bowerman and Burley planned to exploit.

Four thousand people had somehow found out. As they arrived, they saw Burleson warming up with a young man in fuzzy, green and white EEAA club sweats. This was Archie San Romani, who had transferred as a sophomore to Oregon from Wichita State University and was serving out his ineligible year before joining the varsity. San Romani possessed a regal lineage. His father, Archie San Romani Sr., had finished fourth in the 1936 Berlin Olympic 1500 meters. Archie had run 4:08.9 in high school, four seconds faster than Burley had, and Bowerman was coming to believe he never had a runner more talented. Archie's raw 220 speed was phenomenal, his acceleration amazing, his stride all grace and economy. On that day he was in no shape to challenge Burleson, but he had vowed to make his first effort at Hayward Field unforgettable.

Bowerman took up his bullhorn and addressed the packed west stands. "It's come to our attention," he said, "that with the longer days, and the fragrance of the peony in the land, students have begun strolling into these old stands, we can only presume to study. So we of the sporting department have arranged a short program for your diversion. We hope it meets with some approval."

For a record to count, it had to be set in an official meet, with five events. So a 100-yard dash and high hurdle race were run and the high and long jumps contested. Then announcer Wendy Ray introduced the milers, the runners trotted out of a bullpen on the infield, and the race was begun.

San Romani's judgment was perfect, putting in one 59.5 quarter after another, for 1:59.0 at halfway. Burleson, leaner than ever, shadowed him. San Romani slowed slightly in the third quarter. Burley drifted with him for a while, but then Bowerman said to go around. Burleson did and was on his own. The time at three-quarters was a second or two over three minutes, but Burley was a great kicker and with the crowd emitting the sound of ten he came home in 3:57.6, taking the American record back by four-tenths of a second.

On that day Bowerman got a glimpse of the future. "Eugene, Oregon," he would say, "had all the attributes that let Paavo Nurmi, Gunder Hägg, and John Landy set records in Scandinavia. We had the calm air. We had the demanding crowd." The Oregon Twilight Meet was born.

CHAPTER 14

The 1962 Season

OF ALL THE INSTITUTIONS THAT HAVE BECOME SHADOWS OF THEIR FORMER selves, traditional dual meets are the greatest loss. For the crowd, a dual was the equal of a football game, the score seesawing, the battle for each place crucial. For the combatants, each race or throw or leap was charged with duty to home, to cause, to sacrificing for the holy good of humiliating Oregon State University. Or USC.

In the spring of 1962, the University of Southern California had not lost a dual meet since 1945, racking up 129 victories in those seventeen years. Moreover, under coaches Dean Cromwell and Jess Mortensen they had won the NCAA team championship twenty-one times between 1926 and 1961. There has been no comparable dominance in any other sport before or since. *Sports Illustrated* senior writer Tex Maule, who'd been following Bowerman's milers in the indoor season, sensed the brawl to come and arranged to document it.

It was as if Bowerman had been born, raised, and sent to war in order to learn how to win dual meets. These contests took recon, lightning-quick adjustment, occasionally even disinformation. A dual is scored five points for first place, three for second, and one for third. The mile relay was five points for the winner, a pitiless zero for the loser. The way to conquer, thus, was less with outright victories than with depth. Team A could win thirteen of fifteen events, but if Team B grabbed all the seconds and thirds and then swept the last two events, it would win the meet by a single point. Bowerman, therefore, looked to engineer one-two-three sweeps.

On that hot, dry day in the LA Coliseum, the total possible points in the fifteen events was 131. The first one to reach 66 would win. Over breakfast, Bowerman acknowledged the power of USC's intimidating history, its crowd, and its 1932 Olympic stadium. "But we can make all that go away," he said to his team. "All we gotta do is get 'em quiet."

The first race was the mile. "We wanted to take one-two-three to start it off," Bill would recall later with great satisfaction in the telling. "Their miler was sure he could get second. So we entered our big guns, Burleson and San Romani, and a good steeplechaser, Clayton Steinke, whose best mile was about 4:08. The problem was how to help Steinke beat the SC guy."

The Ducks slowed the early pace so Steinke could keep up. With a lap to go, the Oregon men moved into a wing, with San Romani leading, Burley off his shoulder, Steinke off his shoulder, and the USC runner "boxed in the pocket," as Bowerman would put it. With 300 to go, Steinke blasted off and built a twenty-yard lead down the backstretch. "When the USC guy got out and went after him," Bowerman would say, "Burley and Archie held him outside. He was so frantic to get past them he had to sprint out in the third lane all around the last turn. He burned out, died in the stretch, and our guys exploded away from him and caught Steinke and we got our sweep."

To counter, the partisan crowd of 12,393 looked to the javelin. USC was sure to go one-two with world-ranked Jan Sikorsky and Dick Tomlinson. Sikorsky's opening effort was 230 feet 4 inches—10 feet farther than the best Duck had ever thrown.

Next up was sophomore Les Tipton, overflowing with "exuberance to do well," as he put it. Tipton stepped onto the runway, regarded the vast stadium, inhaled, snorted like a wide-eyed mustang, ran, reared back, cocked his hand too much, and hit the tail of the javelin on the runway behind him. Thrown off balance, he tried to adjust, slapped the shaft against his back, got his feet tangled up, and released the implement as if he were fighting off some attacking creature.

The spear went maybe twelve feet. From the crowd came a voice: *"Way to go . . . SPASTIC!"* Laughter mounted into shrieks.

Bowerman, as was his habit, was sitting across the way with a manager handy. "I got him to get Lester to come over," he remembered. "He'd actually done the right thing. When he got all askew, he didn't want to tear his arm apart so he'd done that goofy flip. I told him, 'Hey, just play like you're in practice. Think through your technique and throw it about three-quarters effort and see what happens.' He got a grin on him and went back out."

When Tipton took the runway for his second attempt, people in the crowd called, "Look, look, here's the spastic again!" And so every eye in the stands was privileged to see him run with deliberation, draw back the shaft, send it out without a shiver at an angle of eighteen degrees, and watch as the air lifted it to a steady thirty-three.

Let us freeze it there and explain. The javelin is not thrown for meat; it's thrown for distance. To do that, it must become an airfoil. To do that, it must be fired through a tiny hole in space with graceful surety. If the shaft vibrates, it's been compromised. If it goes a few degrees too high, it will stall, sicken, and drop, scattering officials. But if all the force of the run can be made to flow through the planting of the opposite leg, through the twisting hips and turning trunk and gathering, waiting, waiting shoulder, and final snapping arm into the shaft in a straight line, and if that line bears the proper relation to the horizon, then all the transferred energy will be revealed in soaring flight. By the time the javelin's point stabs the turf, the crowd will have risen up and borne it along on astounded breath.

That's what Tipton's throw did. It stuck at 238 feet 4 inches, 8 feet past Sikorsky's—and 20 feet farther than Tipton had ever thrown in his life. The crowd screamed for Sikorsky to come back. "Sikorsky was a heck of a thrower," Bowerman remembered, "but he was trying so hard to get it over the fence that he kept launching it straight up in the air. He never did get off a decent one, and our John Burns—who'd been hurt—got third, so we went one-three and got a 5-point swing."

The quiet that Bill had mentioned in the meeting was attained.

Then came the half-mile. "I hardly ever double," Bill would recall with grim relish. "But we doubled. We came back with Burleson, San Romani, and a fresh Sig Ohlemann. Another nine points. They were trying to figure out what hit them." The glorious pall deepened in the two-mile, as Ducks Vic Reeve, Keith Forman, and Mike Lehner ran away from USC's Julio Marin in the last lap.

"Well, it finally happened," began the *Los Angeles Times* article by Al Wolf. "USC lost its first dual meet in 17 years Saturday afternoon at the Coliseum. Bill Bowerman's mighty University of Oregon team, not even working up a sweat to score in some events, ran, jumped and threw to a 75-56 victory. The last time anybody saw the Trojans drop a dualer was on May 12, 1945, to California. The way those Ducks performed Saturday, it may be that long before somebody comes along to beat them. Oregon broke USC's back in the 880, mile and two-mile runs, sweeping all three races for 27 points. The visitors demonstrated all-around talent, though, by winning nine of the 15 events and sharing a first place in another. Jerry Tarr won both hurdles, the 120-yard highs in 13.9 and 220-yard lows in 23 flat, defeating Rex Cawley in the lows. Harry Jerome won both sprints in 9.6 and 20.8."

Who were all these guys? One was Harry Jerome, who had recovered from the hamstring cramp that had kept him from making the Olympic 100-meter final in Rome and gone on, as a sophomore, to place second in the 100 in the 1961 NCAA meet. Jerome exhibited less sprinterly braggadocio than any others of that breed. In fact, he was quite shy. Miler Keith Forman, who was in the same class, found Jerome to be kind: "He didn't race to crush the ego of the other guys. He raced to run faster than the other guys." Jerome's fellow Canadian, shot-putter Dave Steen, concurred. "After he pulled his hamstring in the semis in Rome," Steen would recall, "one of the Canadian national magazines ran a head-line: 'Jerome Quits.' That devastated him. There was nothing more unlike Harry than playing head-case sprinter games, faking injuries and things. He knew him-self very, very well, and it hurt him to think people would think he'd quit."

Jerome's form was perfectly aligned, with no look of all-out effort visible in his all-out efforts. If he had a trademark, it was when he swept off the turn in the 220, even with the field, and then simply lifted—torso, hips, and knees high—moving away with the certainty of a machine while the competition, suddenly poor flesh and blood, stiffened and flailed.

Bowerman, because of Jerome's gifts, reversed the colors of the team's racing shirts and shorts, changing the shorts to green and the shirts to yellow, the brightest lemon on earth. "By God, if Harry gets half an inch of his chest ahead of Bob Hayes," Bill said, "I want those judges to see it." He made the green equally bright, "the green of sunlight through new oak leaves in May," as he described it one May on his deck over the river, pulling down a limb, demonstrating.

If Jerome arrived with all his potential brightly in evidence, the other domi-nant force on the 1962 team slipped into town almost unnoticed. Jerry Tarr came from Bakersfield, on a partial football scholarship, as a 14.4-second high hurdler. His first spring, 1961, he cut that by half a second and narrowly won the NCAA highs in 13.9.

"I didn't know how lucky I was," Tarr would say later, "to be dropped into a school of hurdle training that Bill had been polishing since the Middle Ages."

Well, at least since 1954. That year Bowerman returned from Pakistan, where he'd been doing coaching clinics for the State Department, with the idea of stretching elastic across the top of the hurdle as a more forgiving barrier than solid wood. Soft-top barriers were not idle babying, but a commonsense approach to training any animal. "You hit your horse on the nose every day," Bill would say, "pretty soon he's going to remember and shy away. A hurdler will do the same if he hits that hurdle in practice and it hurts. Now, if he hits it in a meet he doesn't feel it because he's got adrenaline working for him."

Bowerman actually began using a less expensive loop of canvas instead of elastic, and that year Doug Basham dropped the school record from 15 flat to 14.4. "I never had a year after that, using the soft hurdles, that I didn't have somebody under fourteen seconds," Bill would say. In 1962, he had four guys under 14: Tarr, Mike Gaechter, Harry Needham, and Mel Renfro.

Renfro, a brilliant athlete from Portland's Jefferson High, had done 13.5 over the thirty-nine-inch high school hurdles (college hurdles were forty-two inches high). Bowerman would coach Renfro only his sophomore year, but would declare him "a great football player and athlete, one of the best to go through this institution." Upon graduating in 1964, Renfro was promptly drafted by the Dallas Cowboys and would go on to become a Hall of Fame defensive back and punt returner.

Bowerman often worked with the sprinters and hurdlers at the top of the backstretch, where he would offer a primer on technique. A lot had to do with the angle of the runner's torso as he bucked forward, lead leg lifting and shooting out toward the hurdle. "Some hurdlers drop their heads completely as they dive toward the barrier," Bowerman would intone. "Some of them fall on their faces because of it. But, gentlemen, neither should you look up in the sky. So what we do, we look at our crotch. We try to keep our shoulders level and peer forward right out under our eyebrows. We do not dive head down because we will hang our balls on the hurdle if we do."

Tarr was big—six feet one and 195 pounds—and had exceptional speed, but exhibited a flaw. "Bill finally got me to tuck in the foot of my trail leg, keep it as close to my butt as possible," said Tarr. "When I swung it wide it slowed me down. He told me fifty times that once I got that, I was world class."

Tarr got it. Every week in 1962 he was faster. He won the highs and lows against USC. In a subsequent meet in Eugene, he came to the track ten minutes before the highs with a headache, eased gingerly into the blocks, came to the set position, blew over the hurdles in a school record 13.6, coasted to a stop, put an ice bag on his head, and was led back to bed. This had to do with his not yet having mastered life under Bill. Tarr had played cards until two in the morning at his Sigma Chi house, soaking up beers. His frat brothers had rousted him out and half-carried him, hungover, to the meet. They'd brought along the ice bag.

Monday, Bowerman had Tarr come in to his office and closed the door. "I'm hearing things," Bill said.

"What things?" asked Tarr.

"Sightings. Appearances in the east side of town [this meant Springfield's ruinous, logger-heavy taverns]. Where there's smoke there's usually fire, so I'm asking you to knock it off."

"You can't tell me how to live."

"No, but I can say who is welcome on the Oregon track team."

"You're serious? I'm the national champion."

"I'm serious. Don't let me hear any more."

He didn't. And at the Coliseum Relays in LA in May, a clean and sober Tarr cut his best to 13.3, just a tenth off the world record.

The Coliseum Relays were not the only event that May to keep Bowerman's 1962 team occupied. For nearly a year, Bill had been plotting how to counter the coup scored by his friend Lydiard's New Zealand national team.

In Dublin, Ireland, on July 17, 1961, Kiwis Gary Philpott, Barry Magee, Murray Halberg, and Peter Snell had chopped the world record for the four-mile relay from Hungary's 16:25.2 to 16:23.8. As two-miler Vic Reeve would remember, "Bill started planning the assault right then, running different combinations, seeing who could do what."

Reeve was one of Bowerman's prized Canadians. He'd shown up in Eugene at age eighteen, at a 1959 summer meet between Oregon and British Columbia. "When I ran 4:14 in the mile and finished ahead of George Larson," Reeve would recall, "Bowerman came over and asked what college I had in mind. I asked what kind of chemistry department he had. He said, 'I'll set up a tour.' It was a fine department, and my best Burnaby South [BC] High School friend, Dave Steen, was going too, so it was easy. I had a dozen college offers, but Bill was the only track coach who cared about my academics. In fact, he gave me his old dissection kit that he'd used in his biology classes in his pre-med days."

When Reeve got his best mile down to 4:03, Bowerman put him in the pool for the four-mile-relay attempt. Also in the pool, and in Reeve's class, was Keith Forman, who'd run 4:26 for Portland's Cleveland High. Forman had received a dose of Bowerman essence on a 1959 recruiting visit.

"Bill met me at the door of the Athletic Department," Forman would say, "and showed me around. Leo Harris's office was empty, except that on the carpet was a pretty fresh, pretty obvious deposit of dog doo. Bill's eyes lit up and he ran out and came back with an Adidas box. He put it over the excrement, sat down in Leo's big chair with a big grin and we started chatting about my running. I didn't know until later that Harris had a curly-tailed dog. I have no idea what Bowerman's joke was going to be. But when you're eighteen and want with every bone in your body to run for him, a thing like that works on your mind."

Undaunted, Forman signed on. He couldn't have known Bowerman didn't see much promise in him. Over Bill's career there were three runners he would liken to bumblebees. This was a perverse badge of honor. "Engineers can prove," he'd say, "that a bumblebee, with its heavy body and little bitty wings, can't fly. *But nobody tells the bumblebees.* And they fly just fine. Keith Forman's rump was too big. He was not a classic miler, but he didn't know that and I never told him and he ended up running just fine." (The other two bumblebees were Alberto Salazar for his low, choppy back-kick stride and me for my knocking knees.)

With training, Forman's great, muscular legs became leaner and dramatically faster. As a sophomore, he took third in the 1961 NCAA mile at Franklin Field in Philadelphia, behind Burleson and Kansas's Bill Dotson. By early 1962, Bill's four best horses were juniors Reeve, Forman, and San Romani, and Burleson, a senior.

Bill began looking for an appropriate time and place to go for the four-mile-relay record. After a couple of false starts, he got the West Coast Relays, held in Fresno every May, to switch the race to high noon, the calmest hour in the interior valley. But the rest of the team was committed to a Seattle dual meet against the University of Washington, so Bowerman couldn't be in Fresno to watch. Freshman coach Chuck Bowles accompanied the milers.

Fresno's track was hard clay, so hard that Forman would describe it as "carved out of the natural ground." The big events of the Relays were in the evening, so not many people were there to witness what transpired at noon. San Romani led off. Only one other team was in the race. Archie tucked in second, but after a lap he heard "sixty-three . . . sixty-four . . . " and felt sick. He had run so well against USC that he'd been sure he could approach four minutes, but he'd let the first lap dawdle. Shooting ahead, he blasted his last three-quarters in 2:59 for a 4:03.5 mile.

Reeve was up next and San Romani had given him a sixty-yard lead. Reeve took off wildly, churning a 58, and his team yelled to slow down before he died. He did—but then had to come back hard in the last half-mile. The uneven pace took its toll. Primarily a distance man, Reeve made it down what he called "the lengthening tunnel of oxygen debt" in the stretch and handed off to Forman. He'd run 4:05.2.

Forman powered on, alone. From the end of the first lap of the first leg to the last lap of the anchor leg, each of Bill's runners raced just himself and the clock. The only person who had someone ahead to shoot for would be Burley, when he was lapping someone. Forman drove to a controlled 4:02.5.

Their split time with a mile to go was 12:11.2. To break New Zealand's world record, Burleson needed just a 4:12 mile. "This was a rare moment for him," Bowerman would say later, "the goal being more than just winning."

Stirred by the efforts of his teammates, Burleson ran with huge purpose. "Looking back," he would say in 2004, "that was a highlight of my life." He ran his anchor mile in 3:57.7 and crossed the line in 16:08.9.

Four young men from one college had removed 14.9 seconds from a standard set by a national team containing two Olympic champions. It was such an astonishing margin that it would start destiny's wheel turning. After this, the two great teams coached by the two great friends would have to race.

While the milers cavorted in Fresno, Bowerman led the rest of his Ducks into Husky Stadium for their dual against Washington. Bill cheered them with news of the record. And he noted that in the Washington school paper, "they're pissed about our not bringing our whole team." He passed the paper around. Somebody said, "Well, if they feel we're only sending 'a skeleton crew,' maybe we oughta unload on 'em!" So they did. They destroyed the Huskies, 98–46.

The Ducks were on a roll. Two weeks after that, Renfro, Tarr, and Gaechter, the three football player-hurdlers, anchored by the pure sprinter Jerome, won the 440-relay at the Modesto Relays in 40.0, tying the world record. And Forman won the mile in 3:58.3, becoming the fifth American to break four minutes. They had the longest relay record. They had the shortest. They were ready to take on the world.

Or at least the NCAA.

Some eighteen months earlier, Bill had pried from Leo Harris the funds to widen Hayward Field's track so that the school could bid to host the national collegiate championships. As night follows day, the NCAA rules committee, which happened to be chaired by Bowerman, awarded the 1962 meet to Bowerman on Bowerman's first try.

The nascent Oregon Track Club leaped into action. Bowerman would be the official meet director that June weekend, but Bob Newland assumed most of the organizational duties, assigning me, at eighteen, a coveted spot on the hurdle crew. My crew, wearing stiff white ducks and sweatshirts from the Oregon PE Department, worked frantically to keep the meet on schedule, but we never lost track of the score.

At that time, the nationals awarded points for the top six places, on a 10-8-6-4-2-1 basis. Jerome began by placing second in the 100, behind the 9.4 of Villanova's Frank Budd, then came back to win the 220 in 20.8. *Eighteen points.*

Burleson almost disdainfully pulled ahead of Kansas's Bill Dotson in the stretch to win his third straight NCAA mile, in 3:59.8. Forman was fourth. *Fourteen more points.*

Jerry Tarr won the 120-yard highs in 13.5 and came back to win his first ever 440-yard hurdles in 50.3. *Twenty more points.*

Mel Renfro placed second to Tarr in the highs, then trotted over and took third in the long jump behind Oklahoma's Anthony Watson and Ohio State's Paul Warfield. *Fourteen more points.*

That would have won it right there. But Dave Steen placed fifth in the shot put, Mike Lehner and Clayton Steinke were third and fourth in the steeplechase, Les Tipton was fifth in the javelin, and 5-foot-8½-inch Terry Llewellyn tied for second in the high jump at 6 feet 10¾ inches. *Twenty-one more points.*

The only Oregon contender to be cut down was Vic Reeve in the three-mile. He was wearing a new pair of Bill's kangaroo racing spikes. "It was like running barefoot," he would remember, "but one of the Boyd twins from Oregon State made it a point to try to spike me during the first laps. He came down on the back of my foot, with his spikes parallel to my Achilles tendon. They went through my heel and tore the shoe off. I was left bleeding on the side of the track, my own shoe ripped asunder. I never wore Bill's spikes after that. Adidas were heavier but they protected you better."

On the infield the final day, as the triumphs mounted, the crowd grew intoxicated in its hunger for more. But the great Oregon outpouring of emotion was so unlike meets elsewhere that after a while most of the other coaches leaned back and simply marveled. They would remember the crowd that day—the crowd that Bowerman's nurturing of the community had created—not as partisan, but as Olympian.

Oregon won with 85 points, more than the next three teams combined. USC's Sikorsky did win the javelin, in a bit of revenge on Tipton's home ground, but no one noticed. Bowerman seemed to be everywhere, at his beatific best, calming, congratulating, in full command. The next day, however, he had trouble controlling his emotion when he opened the Eugene *Register-Guard*. There was a photo of Renfro and Tarr midway through the highs, "both looking just the way they were taught," Bowerman said, "peering out under their eyebrows."

CHAPTER 15

The AAU Dictatorship

THE DAY AFTER THE NEW FOUR-MILE-RELAY RECORD WAS SET IN MAY 1962, Bowerman had written Lydiard and proposed they get the Oregon team down to New Zealand in December and January to race during the Kiwis' summer season. Lydiard was all for it. Both began planning, but each cautioned the other that their respective amateur track governing bodies—in Bowerman's case, the Amateur Athletic Union of the United States—would be obstacles. Bill was the first to be right.

Amateur rules and rulers had permeated Bowerman's sport since 1888. Each year, college coaches trained their athletes to a summer peak—and then were required to hand them over to AAU officials for international competition. This meant not just the Olympics or Soviet–American dual meets, but any competition for which an athlete stuck a toe out of the country.

The AAU had this authority because it owned the franchise. Both the International Amateur Athletic Federation (IAAF) and the International Olympic Committee recognized the AAU—and only the AAU—as the national governing body of track and field in the United States.

Under such leaders as Chicago industrialist Avery Brundage (who rose to be IOC president in 1952), the AAU was as controlling as a battering spouse. It kept the athletes paupers, because the amateur code ("that vestige of aristocrats," Bowerman called it) decreed that only athletes who didn't benefit financially from their competitive efforts were pure enough to take part in the Olympics. How pure? "A cheap hotel, a red-eye flight, and three bucks a day" was how Steve Prefontaine would put it on one of his more gracious days. Accept anything more from a meet director, endorse a product, even work as a coach and the AAU would destroy your amateur standing and end your career.

Anxiety about what the AAU might do was not paranoia. In 1954, the AAU banned Kansas miler Wes Santee for life for taking extra expense money from one of the AAU's own officials. In 1962, shortly after hurdler Jerry Tarr won the highs in a meet record 13.4, beating defending champion Hayes Jones, he signed with the Denver Broncos "for ten grand and a Buick," as Burleson would recall. Tarr was cut by Christmas and when no other teams called, not only was his

140

football career over, but he was forever barred from competing in track and field. In 1963, an anxious Otis Davis wrote Bowerman from where he was teaching in Fresno, saying, "My proposed book is well under way, but if I want to keep my amateur standing, would I have to omit instructional workouts for kids?" In other words, would that be considered enriching himself by coaching? Bowerman wrote back that Davis could leave the workouts in "if you emphasize this is for recreation, not competition." In 1971, when mile world record holder Jim Ryun was a junior at Kansas majoring in photojournalism, he was asked by *Sports Illustrated* to shoot a photo essay of other Olympians training for the upcoming Games. The AAU's track and field administrator, Ollan Cassell, informed Ryun that he'd lose his eligibility if he took the pictures because it would be turning his "athletic fame to personal gain." Ryun withdrew from the assignment.

The AAU surveillance system required that any invitation to compete in an international event had to come first to the AAU office in New York. If the invitation was approved, the AAU sent a "travel permit" on to the athlete. In 1954, Bowerman got a letter from the director of the New Year's Eve Midnight Road Run in São Paolo, Brazil, inviting Bill Dellinger to take part in the race. Bowerman told the race director he'd have to go through the AAU, but when it got to be late in the fall term and he hadn't heard anything further, he called Brazil. The race director said he'd sent the invitation three months earlier. Bowerman called Dan Ferris, the honorary secretary and de facto chief of the AAU, a pink, white-haired little boulder of a man who sat in the office at AAU House in New York. "Ferris was always very pleasant," Bowerman would recall, "but he said, 'I never received their letter.'"

Bowerman asked around and learned that every coach with a decent athlete had had a similar experience. It wasn't just incompetence, the coaches felt—it was greed. "The AAU always wanted to know how much money a race director would cough up to send 'our' runners," Bowerman would growl. "If the AAU didn't get a cut, the invitation just never made it through." Dellinger stayed home. But Bowerman remembered.

The hypocritical rules of "amateurism" were only part of the problem. The AAU governed not only track and field, but as many as sixteen sports. College athletes who'd made national teams returned from European meets with horror stories about incompetent support staff or officials for whom the trip seemed to be sheer boondoggle. In 1969 the US team competed in three major dual meets in Europe. Food and lodging were fine in Stuttgart and London, but between those two stops came Augsburg, site of the United States vs. West Germany contest. The US team and coaches stayed in the *Zur Post* hotel, six floors with no elevator, four to six tiny beds to each dank, claustrophobic chamber. Sewage stained the walls and carpets of many rooms. As for meals, "We had brown food and green food," hammer thrower George Frenn would recall. "The brown was salad and the green was meat." The $3 per diem wouldn't buy replacement groceries in the markets.

At a team meeting, the coaches confirmed that the official chief of mission was the AAU's secretary, Dan Ferris. But he wasn't staying at the *Zur Post*. Sprinter Charlie Greene, Oregon shot-putter Neal Steinhauer, and Steve Prefontaine, then just out of high school, tracked Ferris down and found him breakfasting on eggs and fresh orange juice at his immaculate hotel with views of the cathedral. Ferris said that he doubted the team's quarters were truly unsanitary and that nothing could be done in any case, so the athletes should endure without complaint. The team sent a telegram to the Nixon White House, saying conditions were impairing American competitiveness and demanding that Ferris and the AAU be rebuked and reformed. The telegram went unanswered.

Bowerman would liken the AAU to a dictatorship. Its governing board of twenty-five had a representative from each sport's association and one or at most two from the NCAA. "I was on both the AAU and United States Olympic Committee boards," Bowerman would say, "but the AAU always had the majority. That was written right into both AAU and USOC constitutions."

Bowerman, suspicious of any bureaucracy, was hardly a natural politician. Yet he was magnetic at meetings of his peers, the college coaches. He was respected for producing good athletes and he respected other coaches who did the same, especially those who taught as well as they recruited. In the 1950s, after he had coached Dellinger and Bailey, he was elected president of the National Track Coaches Association (which included high school and junior college coaches as well). He and his colleagues felt they had less and less ability to look out for the welfare of their best athletes.

Bowerman and the coaches nursed a plan whereby American track might shake off the yoke of AAU domination. Finally, in 1961, after being denied yet another request for AAU votes proportionate to their programs, they voted to form the US Track and Field Federation (USTFF) to try to supplant the AAU. Since colleges produced almost all the finest athletes and had all the facilities, the coaches felt sure they could prove to the IAAF that they should be given the chance to govern what they created.

First, they quietly lined up top Olympians for support. That summer, some of Bill's correspondence took on a subversive, burn-this-message tone. In August

1961, he wrote to Ed Temple of Tennessee Agricultural and Industrial State University, coach of Wilma Rudolph. "This is confidential," he began. "A group of coaches is considering forming a United States Track and Field Federation. Please do not discuss this with the newspapers or anyone else. What we wish to know is will you as one of the coaches in the NCAA be interested in joining us and would Wilma Rudolph be interested in joining? The athletes who have already indicated interest are Rafer Johnson, Bill Dellinger, Max Truex, Hal Connolly, and Parry O'Brien. We need Wilma and we need you." Both Temple and Rudolph were supportive.

Bowerman kept Arthur Lydiard in the loop. "You may or may not know we are having a down and out fight with our national AAU here in the US," he wrote in September. "I am one of a committee of five coaches that has led and instigated this. Arthur, the objective of the college coaches is to take international competition and running of track and field completely away from the AAU." The AAU obviously wasn't going to sit still for this, so the coaches were casting about for a way to demonstrate AAU malfeasance to higher authorities. He already had letters, Bowerman told Lydiard, indicating "that Dan Ferris . . . was down-right dishonest." Ferris apparently had assured an American ambassador in one country that a certain athlete would be invited there, but had not sent it on to the athlete himself "and tried to send one of his own pick" instead, as Bowerman wrote. "He [Ferris] denied that he knew anything about it, but I have a copy of the Ambassador's letter. Also his reply to the Ambassador. I need copies of your information because if necessary, we're going to take this to our United States Senator for investigation purposes."

The senator in question was Wayne Morse, a Bowerman friend who'd been dean of the Oregon Law School when Bill was in college. In another possible tack, Bill said in a memo for the record that the new federation hoped to use the US State Department to increase their clout with the international bodies.

In the fall of 1961, the coaches' group, with the support of the top fifty track athletes and the NCAA as a whole, announced the federation's formation. At first, the AAU treated it as the bleating of a disgruntled few. "This uproar," Dan Ferris fumed, "has been stirred up by about five percent of the track coaches." In fact, when polled, over ninety percent supported the federation's challenge. "This is a power play by the NCAA," Pincus Sober, chairman of the AAU's track and field committee, thundered, "to take over amateur athletics in this country."

"The NCAA," answered its executive secretary, Walter Byers, "has no desire to control all track and field activity in the United States. We do feel that we should have proportionate representation on any governing body. We do not have that under AAU rule." Until they did, the body would stick with its coaches.

The Byers quote appeared in a January 22, 1962, *Sports Illustrated* story by Tex Maule entitled "The Coaches Take Over." Maule made it seem almost a fait accompli. "Track meets are run on college facilities by college coaches," Bowerman was quoted as saying. "They [the AAU] talk about their junior development program. They don't have any. Do you know of any track in this country owned and operated by the AAU?"

Maule outlined the USTFF's plans to hold its own competing national championships at the LA Coliseum the same weekend as the AAU nationals in Walnut. Hal and Olga Connolly, Jim Beatty, and Dyrol Burleson all said they would compete at the Coliseum. "By the time this thing is set up," Olympic shot-put champion Parry O'Brien was quoted as saying, "the AAU will realize it can't beat the federation. It would be a stupid and senseless thing for the AAU not to join the track and field federation."

"If the AAU survives at all," Maule concluded. "It will be as a considerably weakened member of several larger organizations."

Maule's prediction did not come to pass. The coaches' "takeover" had depended on showing the fairness of their cause, and they had done that well. But the AAU didn't have to prove anything to anybody, didn't need to worry about being caught in double-dealing, didn't even need the goodwill of a single athlete. All the AAU had to do was pull rank. It simply passed along word from Avery Brundage that the IOC and IAAF would never bend, would never admit the new group, and there was no force on earth that could compel them to.

The athletes knew how true that was. The plain fact remained that any athlete who wanted to make the US team for international competition had to qualify through AAU meets. Burley, Beatty, and all who had come out for the federation had to run those meets or be reduced to running time trials for the rest of their careers. The coaches didn't have anything like the leverage for which Bill had searched. Athletes and coaches couldn't sue. They couldn't do a thing, because Brundage and the IOC answered to no one.

It probably wasn't sheer coincidence that the AAU then tried to keep one of the ringleaders of this failed revolt from taking his four-mile-relay team to race in New Zealand. First the AAU informed Dyrol Burleson that he would not be going to New Zealand unless he raced in the 1962 AAU national championships, a week after the NCAA meet. Burley'd had no plans to run the AAU meet at all, because a class he had to attend fell on the day of the preliminary heats for the mile. Bowerman tried to finesse the issue by putting Burley in the AAU three-mile instead, but, as Bill would put it, "that just made for more misery." As he would describe it in a letter to Lydiard, "Burley went through the motions, but he was in no mood at all to run. He dropped out at the end of two miles."

Meanwhile, Lydiard drafted a formal request for the specific Oregon runners who had broken the Kiwis' record and for their coach. At Bowerman's prompting, he included Leo Harris as official team manager. (Harris had been hearing from Bowerman for so long about the glories of New Zealand that he wanted to see it for himself.) Lydiard sent the invitation to the AAU office in New York, sent a copy to Bowerman, and awaited further orders.

Bowerman, once burned, crafted a plan to bring in real muscle. When it got to be November and he still hadn't received anything from the AAU, he called Lydiard. "I don't think we're going to hear," Bill said, "so why don't you send a letter and a copy to our governor, Mark Hatfield, and another to our State Department?"

Lydiard did just that. Governor Hatfield was more than a fan. He was a javelin official at Oregon meets, though he never liked it made public. Prepped by Bowerman about Dan Ferris's tactics, Hatfield and a State Department official called the AAU. As Bill would tell the story, the callers asked Ferris, "Are we or are we not sending these fine young men down to race the New Zealanders who have requested them?"

Ferris said, "Well, uh, we have a *better* team of other runners."

Hatfield replied, "Oh, really? Has somebody broken Oregon's world record? Somebody better than Archie San Romani Jr.? Better than Keith Forman's 3:58? Better than Dyrol Burleson's 3:57?"

"The AAU was pissed," Bowerman would recall with satisfaction. "But there was nothing they could do. We were cleared to go. They even let Leo Harris be our mission chief."

CHAPTER 16

Jogging

In mid-December 1962, while his milers crammed for final exams before the Christmas break, Bowerman formed an advance party of one. Leaving Leo Harris to accompany the team in a few days, Bill took off across the Pacific. Twenty-five hours later, his Pan Am 707 descended over the wind-scoured Hauraki Gulf. "Beautiful place, New Zealand," he wrote in the first of a series of articles for the *Oregon Journal*. "Green hills, pastures intermingled with trees, the coastline literally thousands of coves and inlets."

Soon he was being shaken by the strength of Arthur Lydiard's grip. The compact little coach ran every day and usually got in twenty pull-ups as well, yet derided weight lifting for runners. This was one of the few differences between Lydiard and Bowerman. In defense of weight lifting, Bill would point out that folks still pitched hay and cut wood in New Zealand: "If we did that," he said, "we wouldn't have to lift weights."

Bill was stiff after the long flight. As a remedy, Lydiard suggested he call for him the next morning, a Sunday, and take him on an easy run. Lydiard drove them to a rolling, pastoral expanse called Cornwall Park, swarming with a couple of hundred runners. "I thought a cross-country race was going on," Bowerman would recall, "but they were men, women, children, all ages, all sizes." Lydiard told him he'd begun this Auckland Joggers Club about a year earlier. "We found that the best thing for my champions was also the best thing for everyone else," Lydiard said, "a good, long Sunday romp. Different packs go different distances. You'll manage in the slow pack."

Bowerman was then fifty years old and, as he described it, "I was used to going out and walking fifty-five yards, trotting fifty-five yards, going about a quarter-mile and figuring I'd done quite a bit." Lydiard indicated something in the distance and told Bill the run was headed to One Tree Hill, which Bowerman estimated to be about a mile and a half away. As he would later tell the story, "We took off and it wasn't too bad for about a half-mile, and then we started going up this hill. God, the only thing that kept me alive was the hope that I would die." For the rest of his life, Bowerman would utter his truism "The hills will find you out" with genuine feeling.

Lydiard had vanished ahead. Bowerman dropped to the back of the last group. "Everyone had left me," he would say, "except one old fellow moved back and said, 'I see you're having trouble.' I didn't say anything. I couldn't. Then he said, 'I know a shortcut.' So we took off down the hill and got back about the same time as the people who covered the whole distance."

Bowerman's savior was Andrew Steedman, who was then seventy-three. Steedman kept stopping and waiting for Bill, encouraging him to keep going. "It gave Bill the bloody shock of his life," Lydiard would remember. "He was nearly in tears when I got back from my own run." A second jolt was discovering Steedman's medical history. "I'm a coach of athletes," Lydiard would remember Bowerman saying. "And that old guy has had three coronaries and he had to wait for *me*. From now on I'm into training."

Bowerman didn't need a two-by-four twice. He would run almost every day during his six weeks in the country. He pumped Lydiard for information on how running en masse, this heresy that middle-aged people are trainable, had spread. Lydiard told him all his original joggers (the word was simply the one he employed to command runners to trot as slowly as possible) were, like Steedman, post-cardiac patients.

"They came to me a few years ago," Lydiard said, "kind of pleading to exercise. Their general practitioners were scared to death of letting them do anything. I asked some sports medicine experts. Anyone with a whit of coronary training knew those hearts were muscles. Those hearts had to be exercised."

So Lydiard had bravely, blithely told his trusting subjects, their first time out, to try to run a mile or so, while closely attending to how it made them feel. No one died. What didn't kill cured, or at least transformed. Before Rome, Lydiard had been talking up the benefits of running for the average New Zealander. "After his guys came home with gold medals," Bill would say, "the media engulfed him, and he used that. He said, Look, the principles of training work the same for everybody."

Lydiard's famous dictum was "Train, don't strain," and he enforced it with the talk test. If you couldn't carry on a conversation, you were going too fast. "It followed," Bill said later, "that the best way to keep people active was to give them someone to talk to. So Lydiard combined conditioning with companionship by telling people to run in slow, steady groups, or 'jogging' clubs. Hell, whole communities, from toddlers to grandmas, jogged on weekends and holidays." It was a slightly fitter Bowerman who greeted his milers when they arrived at the end of the week.

Travel, as it does, opened eyes. And ears. At the formal welcoming banquet, the host dignitaries gave speeches of welcome. Oregon's team leader, Leo Harris, delivered something stuffy in return. Then his wife, Zoë, was pressed for remarks. She, an impulsive woman who hadn't traveled widely, stepped to the mike and yelled, "We're so happy to be here! I won't bore you with a speech! I'm saving all my energy so I can root for the team! Root for the team! *Root for the team!*"

Instant, hysterical bedlam. The Oregon runners learned why and joined in the whooping laughter. *Rooting*, wherever Britannia has ruled, means exactly what one imagines. Bowerman shook and wiped away tears. Zoë sat down, happy to see that people appreciated brevity in this country. Somehow, she would pass the ensuing weeks feigning not to hear Keith Forman or Archie San Romani always saying, "we gotta look for the root cause" or "root that out before it gets too rooting big."

Despite wet weather, the first race, a four-mile relay at Auckland's Western Springs Stadium, was sold out. Judged on best mile times, the teams were even. But Bowerman knew the Kiwis were racing sharp, having just come from the British Empire Games in Perth, Australia. Besides, Peter Snell had earlier that year taken the world record to 3:54.4.

Knowing Snell would surely run last, the task for Oregon was to give its own anchor a big enough lead to hold him off. Bill had an idea. He'd conclude with Keith Forman. "Bill thought I would need twenty yards to beat Snell," Forman recalled. "That was three seconds." By anchoring with Forman, Bowerman was free to put his champion, Burleson, on the third leg against someone who had to be far weaker than Snell, someone Burley could run away from by those priceless twenty yards. Lydiard saw through this plot and chose young John Davies—second to Snell in the Perth mile—to foil it.

Bowerman had hopes for a new record, but on race day an inch of rain fell three hours before the start, turning the track into a sticky, slick gumbo. The race was run at night and the stadium was poorly lit, a murky setting that did not bode well for Oregon's leadoff man, tall, bespectacled Vic Reeve. "It was slop, puddles up to your ankles on the inside lane," Reeve would remember. He was matched against the shorter, stockier Bill Baillie, who would win Kiwi titles at every distance from the 880 to six miles.

Reeve set the pace, the better to make out the two-inch pegs that marked the curb. "I was just trying to hold it together and not slip." They passed three-quarters in 3:12.

"The first leg between Bill and Vic had all the tension of the duel that had been anticipated," Snell would write a few years later in his book *No Bugles, No Drums*. "The crowd kept up a continual roar which swirled to fever pitch on the last curve as Bill overtook Vic. Swinging round into the home straight, they were neck and neck."

Swinging was the word. Baillie swerved left and slammed into Reeve. "He just decided to cut in on me," Reeve would remember some forty years later. "He hit me with his arm in midstride and threw me off balance. My shoe slipped in the mud, caught on one of those pegs and down I went. All I could do was pick up the baton and sprint after him. He'd gained forty yards, six seconds. After that, it was catch-up." Snell remembered the crowd being shocked into silence. "The race in a split second was ruined," he wrote. "Vic got up and ran on, but with a big gap between the teams, it became a dreary procession on the wet track with no chance left of a decent time."

Snell made that a little too foregone for accuracy. "Archie lost ten yards to Murray Halberg," Bowerman wrote in his account to the *Oregon Journal*. "But then Burley made up twenty-five on John Davies and Keith Forman's race was tremendous. He closed from twenty-five yards to six on Peter Snell to make it close at the finish."

Bowerman tried to put the best face on the Baillie-Reeve collision for the readers at home. "Vic was not fouled but he was 'squeezed,'" Bill wrote, adding that "a good New Zealand medic joined me in cleaning up Reeve's many lacerations—shoulder, knee, back, and elbow. He was stiff but OK." Bill also managed to perceive a silver lining. "It rains alike on the just and the unjust," he wrote. If the weather had been fine and the track as fast as it had been on the preceding Sunday, he observed, "our record might be gone."

The Oregon team was slated to compete as individuals in several meets around the country before concluding with a second, grudge-match four-mile relay in Nelson, on the South Island. The next races were in geothermally blessed Rotorua, south of Auckland.

Bowerman told Vic Reeve to go find their hotel's ballyhooed thermal spring and soak his sore knee in it. Arriving quietly, pushing aside giant ferns, Reeve surprised the stark naked Zoë and Leo Harris. "Give us a goddamn minute!" explained Leo. Reeve did. Then, decorously swimsuited, they all soaked together. Reeve concentrated on the pain in his knee to keep from exploding. "I kept wanting to say 'un-rooting-believable,' but I couldn't get it out."

The Rotorua meet was on December 26, which, across the Commonwealth, is the holiday known as Boxing Day. Snell awoke feeling unsteady from one too many Christmas toasts the night before. He was to race Burleson that night over a mile. Here was Burley's chance. Conditions for the race were frigid: thirty-five degrees with a raw wind. Reeve led and the wind took it out of him. When Davies jumped him at three-quarters, Forman went with him and Snell was third. In Snell's written account of the race, "Burleson was still pinning all his faith on his finish and tagged along behind me. I sprinted to win, Burleson was second, and John third." Given the cold and the wind, Snell's time was a remarkable 4:05.

The third meet was on the South Island, on New Year's Eve, in the little township of Waimate, which had a fine grass track. The weather had finally broken and a crowd several times the town's population turned out. Snell faced Burleson in an 880. Bowerman clocked Snell in 53 for the first quarter and observed that he slowed on the turn, where San Romani jumped him. "A figure came hurtling past," Snell would write. "This shook me back to awareness. I struggled to close the few yards that Archie had opened up, and at the top of the straight, he, Burleson and I were all together." San Romani faded slightly. Burleson did not. Bowerman judged that Burley had closed "to chest-width at the finish."

"He was apparently so frustrated in his desperation to beat me," Snell wrote, "that as we crossed the line he grabbed at my right elbow with his left hand."

"Both of them were diving at the tape," Vic Reeve would recall, "and I remember Burley physically *pulling* himself ahead of Snell." But that wasn't until after they had crossed the line. Snell had won again, in 1:48.0. Bowerman would characterize the race as "a diller."

Bill pondered all this as he reviewed the Oregon strategy for the last race, the score-settling four-mile relay in Nelson, a pretty town set among apple orchards. The grass track was smooth enough for lawn bowling and the weather dry, but windy. Keith Forman was running strongly, "really coming into his own, tougher every race," so Bowerman kept him at anchor and told Burleson that if he could give Forman twenty yards they'd win.

"This race," wrote Snell, "was to decide what the Auckland fiasco had not, which of us was the better team. But we New Zealanders didn't want to run the risk of another flop and would hustle the pace along. This attitude seemed to be shared by the Americans, with the exception of Burleson."

Bill Baillie led off again for the Kiwis. But this time, as if to atone, he led all the way, sheltering Vic Reeve, who got close off the last turn but couldn't quite get by. Baillie (4:07.5) passed the baton to Murray Halberg four yards before Reeve (4:08.2) reached San Romani. "In the wind," wrote Snell, "Bill's time was a little slow and it was obvious that this race could again turn into a tactical battle with victory as the only consideration."

San Romani was a true miler with a wonderful kick. Halberg, the Olympic 5000-meter champion, knew that and set out to destroy it. "Archie had a tough assignment," Bill would write in his *Journal* account. "After one lap, Halberg tried to get away but Archie hung on. On the backstretch of the fourth lap, Archie glided up and shot by. He was too far out for a full sprint and Halberg closed to his shoulder. Archie glided away again and handed off to Burleson five yards ahead." San Romani had run 4:04.0 to Halberg's 4:05.0.

As soon as the batons changed hands, a shocking thing happened. Snell would call it "an incredible display of negative running." As Snell would tell it, "Burleson, with a best time of 3:56.8 to his credit, actually slowed down to a near-walk to force John, who had yet to break four minutes, into the role of pacemaker. We all knew how Burleson liked running from behind, but in our eyes this deliberate go-slow was a ridiculous waste of the lead his teammate had struggled to give him. It was impossible to see just what Burleson's thinking was. Did he believe he could open up a race-winning lead on John in the last lap or was his interest only in preserving his own prestige?"

Well, both. Burleson was gambling that if he hid behind and cut loose around an exhausted Davies in the last lap he'd get the requisite three seconds for Forman. But Davies had no intention of cooperating in his execution. He calmly began running gentle 66s.

Bowerman, who wanted Burleson to pass Davies hard and run his guts out the rest of the way, was exasperated. "They loafed through three and a half laps," he wrote.

Davies ran through the three-quarters in 3:17 and led into the back straightaway before Burley attacked. Davies had not only been coasting, he'd been psyching himself up to react the instant Burley came into view on his right. When he did, Davies rocketed with him. "They put on a 220-yard dash, which Burley won by four yards," Bowerman wrote irritably. "So he left Keith Forman the task of beating the world record holder with a four-yard lead."

Snell recalled it being only two, and he was probably more accurate than Bowerman. Burleson's split time was 4:11.2 to Davies's 4:11.0—meaning that Burley's tactics had actually cost the Oregon team a couple of yards. But there was no gamer runner than Forman. "Keith took up the challenge that Burleson had dropped," continued Snell, "by running the first lap in 58.7, but the wind took its toll and he reached the bell in 3:04.7."

Forman would not crack. "He ran a terrific race," Bowerman wrote for the *Journal*. "He gave Peter Snell all he wanted and almost burned that great sprint out of him. Snell tired on the backstretch but just edged past in the last 25 yards."

Snell won by two yards in 16:25.5. His mile had been 4:02.0 to Forman's 4:02.4. Both teams were fifteen seconds slower than Oregon's record.

"A thriller for the 12,000 here in Nelson," Bill wrote with remarkable restraint, "but had we had our yardage—oh well." The race had been so close, even with Burleson's antics, that Snell concluded, "New Zealand *still* wasn't sure which was the best team."

Sure or not, it was about time to go home. After six weeks of daily jogging, Bowerman had lost ten pounds and three inches from his waistline. Before they left the South Island, Lydiard coaxed him into running to an abandoned ghost town. He wasn't quite candid about the distance. "He told me this run was five miles each way," Bill would recall, "but a sign said twelve. But we went at my pace—a slow, comfortable jog—crossed a creek a few times, running up this canyon, and sooner than I thought, without any of the distress I thought I'd have, we were there. Then we went back the same way." Bill had managed over twenty miles in four hours.

"It was a mark of his determination and of the value of a sensible approach that he went from no miles to twenty in four weeks," Lydiard would recollect years later. "We sent him home a jogger."

When Bill came down the ramp in Eugene, Barbara shrieked that he looked ten years younger. The next morning Eugene *Register-Guard* sportswriter Jerry Uhrhammer, who had been following the tour, phoned to ask Bowerman to sum up his experience. Bill told him that the competition was great, but the biggest thing that had happened was his realizing that his idea of exercise was "way, way, way low." In New Zealand, thousands of people jog, Bill said. "Their women jog, their kids jog, everybody jogs." Uhrhammer asked, "Do you think we could do that here?" And Bowerman said, "Why don't we find out?"

So Uhrhammer's article contained Bill's invitation to anyone of any age to come to the Hayward Field practice track that Sunday and hear more about it. On February 3, 1963, two dozen citizens showed up. Bill spoke about good shoes and loose clothing, and everyone did a mile of trotting the straightaways and walking the turns. The next week, the total grew to fifty. Bill explained how the talk test keeps exercise fun. He was surprised to see about a quarter of the folks were female. The third week, two hundred loosely bundled souls appeared and did a mile or two. Uhrhammer wrote a follow-up piece, mentioning that *Life* magazine planned to send a photographer to document this bizarre activity.

The following Sunday, Vic Reeve would remember, "Bill timed us in an interval workout, and as we were warming down, he said, 'Hang around, you might see something unusual.' We started to notice people showing up. A lot were in street clothes, housewives, professors, some kids, some quite elderly. They kept coming and coming, going around the track. In half an hour they completely covered it, jogging and walking. And they kept coming." Even in New Zealand, Reeve and the others had never seen such a mass of runners. "That was the start of the American jogging movement," Reeve would say, "right there, that morning."

The crowd peaked at somewhere between 2,000 and 5,000 human beings that day. The mass scared Bowerman silly: "I knew someone was going to die right there." He urged everyone to go home and jog with friends in their own neighborhoods "until we get a better handle on this thing." He went to his office and called Dr. Ralph Christensen, who put him in touch with Eugene cardiologist Waldo Harris. "We can't take all these old guys out there," Bowerman told Harris. "We'll kill them."

Harris and Bowerman quickly taught each other their specialties. Bowerman laid out the theory and practice of preparing four-minute milers. Harris explained how much stress untrained cardiovascular systems might be able to handle at different ages and weights. Finally they wrote a training program based on running at a speed of 45 seconds for 110 yards, which is twelve-minute-mile pace— slightly faster than a brisk walk. Harris and Bowerman did a little pilot study, giving physical exams to four hefty Oregon faculty members and monitoring them through three months of gradually increasing mileage. All four completed the study safely.

Bowerman's dean in the PE department, Charles Esslinger, approved a larger study. Bowerman and Harris recruited 100 middle-aged subjects, almost all male, through the Central Lane YMCA. These they split into ten groups of ten that jogged three times a week. Each group was assigned an Oregon varsity runner, each of whom made ten bucks a week jogging with his group, explaining workouts, advising on form, and panicking when someone fat turned purple. Everyone survived, but a few subjects did turn out to have heart conditions. Harris sent those to a walking study group.

Just as he experimented upon incoming freshmen, Bowerman assigned different kinds and dosages of trotting to the test subjects. He found that, like his college runners, some responded better to interrupted work, some to steady running. Bowerman and Harris found dramatic weight loss among the overweight and a general feeling of well-being among the joggers. "Almost without exception," Bowerman would say, "they began to feel more tigerish." The likes of fifty-five-year-old Texaco gas station manager Gordon Sherbeck and seventy-year-old radiologist Dr. Larry Hilt underwent remarkable transformations.

Having been sedentary all their lives, they went from five miles per week to twenty after the three months of the study and ultimately became marathoners.

The varsity athletes who headed the jogging groups found this transformation more amazing than their own racing success. Obviously, even athletes were gripped by the conventional wisdom of the time, namely that physical decline was inevitable as soon as one reached middle age, if not sooner, and that such decline was useless to resist beyond middle age.

Originally a nation of pioneers accustomed to hard physical labor, America in the mid-twentieth-century had become a society that actively condemned adult fitness. It may be hard for anyone born after 1960 to believe, but runners in those days were regarded as eccentric at best, subversive and dangerous at worst. During the day, cars would routinely swerve to try to drive a runner off the road. And running at night was deemed suspicious enough to warrant being stopped by a police cruiser and held until phone calls ascertained there had been no burglaries in the area.

It was against this background that Bowerman's converts began to appear on tracks and in parks. The second study showed nothing but benefits for its 100 subjects and confirmed the effectiveness of the distances and speeds they'd run. Bill was deluged with letters from people and groups who had heard of the jogging phenomenon and wanted information. "Our country is not nearly so vigorous as it was twenty-five years ago," Bill wrote to his old Auckland jogging mate, Andrew Steedman, with whom he'd struck up a lively correspondence. "We have much to learn from you people and I am going to do my best to get the word around." He began to organize his thoughts. In reply to another correspondent in January 1964, Bill declared that fifteen or twenty minutes a day of jogging is an ideal way to provide "needed exercise for the average middle-aged American," adding, "To procrastinators who complain that they cannot afford the fifteen or twenty minutes a day, I echo the words of Arthur Lydiard: 'You cannot afford not to take the time.'"

As the mounting questions began to swamp Bill's secretarial support, he and Harris in 1966 knocked out an eighteen-page pamphlet. Its main points echoed various letters Bowerman had written: Don't compete, build up slowly, keep it fun, and be good to your feet and joints. Demand for the pamphlet was so great that the following year Bill got jogger pal and Oregon vice president Jim Shea to help expand on it. The farsighted Barbara Bowerman insisted that the book be inclusive of women.

Still quite thin at 127 pages, including the story of the New Zealand trip, the book was called *Jogging*. It had a bright red cover. It would sell a million copies. "The book," Shea would say, "I regard as Bill and Barbara's gift to Everyman. They really did help start it all."

After jogging caught on and millions took it up, after Dr. Ken Cooper's book *Aerobics* confirmed and quantified the need for exercise, the old animosities toward it began to ebb. Society inched toward a tipping point where the old constraints on eccentric behavior—or at least this eccentric behavior—fell away. As Dr. Duncan MacDonald, who would break Steve Prefontaine's American record in the 5000 meters, once put it, "The exact moment came when the drivers who wanted to run us off the road now had aunties or nieces who ran, and that fuzzed up the question of who was the enemy."

A great movement had been pent up. Exercise had been calling to us from our genes, from our childhoods, but not from our culture. Now it could. Frank Shorter would help, winning the Olympic marathon in 1972 and showing that Americans could master real distance the same as anyone else. That would begin not a jogging but a running boom and the phenomenon of mass marathons, such as those in New York and Boston, whose starting fields today number in the tens of thousands.

But none of that could have come about without Bowerman's bringing the flame back from New Zealand. Naturally, the first person he sent a copy of his book to was Lydiard, who opened it and roared. Bowerman had inscribed it:

"To the Best Rootin' Team in the World"—Bill Bowerman

CHAPTER 17

The Birth of BRS

AFTER TAKING HIS OREGON DEGREE IN 1959, PHIL KNIGHT SPENT A YEAR ON active duty in the Army Reserves and then returned to Eugene for a time before heading to graduate school. The military's kiss-ass/kick-ass command style left him with fresh appreciation for how his track coach exercised authority.

"I worked up a little speech about what Bill meant to me," Knight would say, "but when I went in to give it, I kind of choked getting it started. Somehow he grasped my intent and made it to me instead, a speech about what I had meant to the team and the University."

Then Bowerman delivered the final line: "Never underestimate yourself."

Knight would deem that moment "my true commencement ceremony."

He arrived at the Stanford Graduate School of Business not at all clear about what aspect of commerce might stir his competitive heart. His Oregon major had actually been journalism, a choice not unrelated to his father's being publisher of the *Oregon Journal*, and Knight had written sports stories for the *Oregon Daily Emerald*. "One editor did a column saying all these great Oregon runners would run even better if they trained in a warm climate," Knight would recall years later. "Bill had me write a counter story." Knight upheld Bowerman's view that the Oregon winter is just cold and wet enough to make a man out of you, but not so frigid that your lungs freeze and you can't train. "I concluded," Knight would say, "that all a bliss state like California does is spoil you."

Stanford, in the form of a small business class taught by Frank Shallenberger, would change his life. "Shallenberger started by defining the type of person who was an entrepreneur," Knight would remember, "and I realized he was talking to me." Shallenberger assigned the class to imagine a brand new business, describe its purpose, and create a marketing plan to make it competitive. Knight's business-major classmates each had ten ideas before they were out the door; his own head remained vacant. Then, pondering in his room, he looked at a new box of Adidas, resented again how much they cost, and it hit him.

"Being Bowerman's guinea pig," Knight would say, "I had naturally absorbed why Bill had to make our shoes. American running shoes were still made by off-shoots of the tire companies, cheap and terrible. They cost five bucks and gave you blood blisters after five miles. Adidas was taking advantage. And at $30 a pair, Adidas was making a killing."

Knight proposed a new company that would import first-rate athletic shoes not from Germany but from Japan, where his research had shown skilled labor was far cheaper. The paper—"Can Japanese Sports Shoes Do to German Sports Shoes What Japanese Cameras Have Done to German Cameras?"—sketched out a track-shoe distributorship in the Western states and projected sales to high school and college teams of up to 20,000 pairs a year.

Shallenberger's class was Knight's "aha!" moment. He received his MBA in 1962, knowing both his nature and his direction. He promised his father, Bill, that he'd take a job with a Portland accounting firm, but first he sold his car, got a loan from that same father, and took a tour of the Far East.

He went to Japan in the fall of 1962 and soaked in a *furo* (hot tub) of its thought and business practices. He visited the temples and gardens of Kyoto. "After I had been there a while," Knight would say, "the love affair with the East began. I was quite taken with Japanese culture and its people." He didn't formally study Zen Buddhism, but found his developing aesthetic stirred by the spare simplicity of Japanese design.

And on the Tokyo University track near the site where the 1964 Olympic stadium was rising, Knight contemplated the shoes on the fastest feet. They weren't Adidas, but some looked pretty good. He canvassed the sporting goods stores of Tokyo and concluded, as he would put it, "that the best hope for US exports lay with Onitsuka Company." Onitsuka made a brand called Tiger. Knight discovered their factory was in Kobe, a seaport near Osaka. "So I made a cold call on them."

This was in early 1963. On the train down, in the bar car, watching jovial men exchanging business cards, he realized with a jolt that if he wanted his overture to be taken seriously in this culture, he had to be seen not as a lone eagle but as part of a respected company. His eye traveled out the train window, across incomprehensible Japanese billboards, came back in and rested on the bottles of the different brands of beer that were arrayed above the bar. One was Suntory Blue Ribbon. He had another little "aha" moment.

In Kobe, he found Onitsuka's wooden factory buildings, asked to speak with someone in the export department, and was ushered into a conference room. After a short wait, a six-man team of Onitsuka executives crowded in. All bowed and shook hands. Knight said he'd been on the Oregon track team with Bill Dellinger and Dyrol Burleson, who were going to be winning medals in Tokyo in two years. Not only that, his Oregon coach, Bill Bowerman, had taught him track-shoe design. He proved his expertise by complimenting the quality of the Tiger models he'd seen in Tokyo.

After he sensed the Onitsuka men had assessed him, with nods and glances, as a rather knowing *gaijin*, or foreigner, Knight blurted, "Why don't I distribute Tiger shoes in the United States?" Silence and searching looks. The senior executive politely explained that their practice was to deal company to company; what might be the name of Knight's firm? Knight hesitated not at all. "Why, Blue Ribbon Sports of Portland, Oregon," he said. "Sorry I'm all out of cards. Boy, does your country ever eat up business cards."

"Ah *so*," said the Onitsuka people and proceeded to show Knight their line.

Onitsuka's sales were almost all in Japan; in the United States they were selling only wrestling shoes at the time. The staff brought out pictures of new spikes and flats they hoped would fly in the American market. Knight said they looked great (one leather flat actually did) but he couldn't place an order until he'd seen the actual shoes. The execs said they wouldn't have them for weeks. Knight said he'd order samples then, made his exit, and continued his Asian tour. From Hong Kong, he wrote his father and asked to borrow $37 for the samples.

Later that year, Dick Miller, Knight's best friend from the Oregon team, was living in Seattle and working for General Electric. "After he got back from Japan," Miller would remember, "he was all excited. He said, 'Hey, I'm in the shoe business. Look at these things. They're called Tigers. I faked out the company. I'm the US distributor. Come in with me.'" Miller saw that despite Knight's flippant language, he was serious about this venture. "'How much will it take?'

"'Six hundred dollars each. Twelve hundred dollars total investment.'

"I begged off," Miller would say much, much later, his tone manfully, even gaily resistant to what might have been. "I'd just gotten married. I had to think for two."

In December 1963, Knight was living in Portland and making $500 a month working for the accounting firm that would become Coopers and Lybrand. At last, a box of Tiger shoe samples cleared customs. "Twelve pairs for fifty dollars," Knight would recall. On January 20, 1964, Knight sent Bowerman two pairs of, as he wrote, "the hot new shoes coming out of Japan. The spike [shoe] weighs just under six ounces, which compares favorably with Adidas. If you feel the shoes are of reasonable quality, you could probably save a little money since I wouldn't make a profit on shoes I sold to you. Costs I think $4.50 on the flat and $7 on the spike."

Bowerman ran his fingers in and out of the shoes and was struck by their width. "The Japanese made them as fat as banjos," he said later, "but the leather was good, the construction was good. The potential was there, if they could use an American last." (As Knight would remember it, Onitsuka had made the samples on a version of an American last. "It was much narrower than their shoes for the Japanese market. But they were still a bit wide.")

On January 22, Bill wrote back: "I like the looks of your Tiger shoe. I've heard of these, but have never been able to get hold of a pair. If you can set up some kind of contractual agreement with these people, for goodness sakes, do it." Bill was already tinkering in his mind. "I have some ideas on a flat," he added. "I'll pass on some of my ideas to you, but, of course, I'll expect you to make some kind of an arrangement with cutting your old coach in, too."

Knight cut him in that very week, when Bowerman brought the Oregon team up to the Portland Indoor meet. Buck shared our soup, toast, and tea and honey prerace meal at the Cosmopolitan Hotel. When San Romani groused for the tenth time about the meagerness of our spread, Bowerman said, for the hundredth time, "A hungry tiger hunts best." Then he and Knight went up to his room to talk Tiger business.

An hour later they shook hands on a partnership. Bill would test and design the shoes and, if they deserved it, pitch them to other coaches. Buck, by virtue of a fifty-one to forty-nine percent division of voting control, would run the company. A few days later, with Barbara Bowerman and Robin and John Jaqua as witnesses (and with the Jaqua mantel steadying the papers), they signed their first written agreement, becoming jointly and severally responsible for a new entity, Blue Ribbon Sports. Their original investment was a little less than Knight had offered Miller, $500 each.

"I always felt a very personal connection to the birth of Nike," Barbara Bowerman would say, "because our original five hundred dollars came from a small savings account I had accumulated." The existence of this account she had hidden from Bill until then, she would say, because "I was well aware that he believed, 'If you have money, spend it; if you don't, do without.'"

Bowerman's hopes for the venture were high, as John Jaqua would attest. Over the years, Bill had approached shoemakers Spaulding and Rawlings with offers to show them how to make a track shoe, to no avail. "He knew Buck was bright," Jaqua would say, "and he knew if this worked out he could finally get some say in some actual shoes."

On January 30, Knight wrote his coach the good news: "With a hearty *ichi ban* Blue Ribbon Sports got off the ground on Monday with an order for 300 pairs of shoes." He added that with import duties, the shoes would cost a total of $4.06 per pair.

Then, with their deal barely a week old, Knight proposed to renegotiate. Under his signature he wrote in neat longhand, "P.S. I forgot to make it part of the original agreement, but I think it ought to be made explicit: There will be no pissing on partners in the shower."

Bowerman's joy in confounding his athletes extended, famously, to this: A team member would be in the Mac Court showers, which had six or eight nozzles along each wall, soaping his hair, eyes shut, and feel a warmth on his leg that didn't seem to be coming from the direction of the main stream. He'd rinse his eyes, turn, and there would be Bill's beatific smile. Bowerman didn't have to do this often before word got around. Athletes were wary in his presence anyway; in the shower they had to be on high alert.

Bill's proclivity to pee on legs was, of course, part of his ongoing character studies. Originating a new company, with the mutual trust it demands, required that he feel he'd tested Phil Knight.

And he had. Dick Miller would recall that Bill got Knight three times: "That's gotta be the record." As Miller would tell the tale, Knight tried to get even. "He found this trick gun where you flex your stomach muscles and it fires a blank cartridge. I went into Bill's office first, to distract him, but Buck was so excited he blew it up on the way in, down the hall!"

Did the peeing guarantee an effective partnership? No, but the peeing and practical jokes were inextricable from Bowerman's competitive ethos. He knew Knight would give the new venture the ceaselessness of a runner and the "top this" attitude of a prankster. Knight, for his part, knew he'd passed Bill's tests. "If someone else had sent those shoes," Knight would say, "Bill wouldn't have said the same thing about cutting him in."

Despite all the high hopes, Knight didn't quit his CPA job. He traveled to track meets and high schools in his spare time, selling Tigers out of the back of his green Plymouth Valiant. "Using a two-dollar commission, they really sold," he would remember. "We had no capital but we grew."

CHAPTER 18

Tokyo

THE TWO BRS PARTNERS SPENT 1964 IN THEIR RESPECTIVE PURSUITS—KNIGHT promoting Tigers at track meets, Bowerman readying his tigers for the big meets that would culminate in the Tokyo Games in October. Following their spectacular 1962 season, Bowerman's Ducks hadn't quite lived up to Tex Maule's prediction in *Sports Illustrated* that Oregon would "very likely dominate US collegiate track and field for the next decade."

Misfortune struck in December 1962, at the Commonwealth Games in Perth, Australia. Bowerman, who had been packing for the trip to New Zealand, got a call from the Canadian track coach about sprinter Harry Jerome: "Harry's quadriceps in one thigh had severed the tendon that attached them to the knee bone. The muscles rolled up like a window shade into a big bulging knot at the top of his thigh."

Shot-putter Dave Steen, who had also made the Canadian team, went to see Jerome in the Perth hospital. "I could feel the hole in his leg. Harry was devastated," Steen would remember. "Hands down, he was going to win that race. It was his return to international racing after pulling a hamstring in Rome." Jerome was flown back to Canada and within thirty-six hours had undergone an operation to repair the damage. He returned to school in February, but faced a full year of rehabilitation before it would be known if he could run again.

That year in the big meets, without Jerome, the rest of the team seemed almost to sympathetically sicken, nowhere more so than at the 1963 NCAA Championships in Albuquerque. There were no Oregon individual champions, though Steen took second in the shot to the haystack-shaped Gary Gubner of New York University with 61 feet 11¼ inches.

Dave Steen eventually reached a rare understanding with Bowerman. In the fall of 1959, Steen had come to Oregon a 48-foot shot-putter. By early 1963, he had taken the school record from 52 feet to the verge of 60. "Bill was an excellent teacher of the throws, technically," Steen would recall. "I did both shot and discus, and many were the mornings when he'd change out of the suit he'd worn to teach his classes, get into old clothes, and we'd spend an hour in the old indoor field-house area, mastering one element at a time. 'You can only think of one thing at a time,' he'd say. I thought that just meant me, but later I found it applied to most people."

To augment his weight training, Steen had the habit of crouching and straining isometrically against the tops of doorways. Eventually all the steel door frames in the athletic department were bent, their plaster cracking. Athletic director Leo Harris complained to Bowerman and Bill agreed to pay for their repair out of his track budget, but on the condition that the door frames would be strong enough to withstand Steen's isometrics.

Harris called in the carpenters—and the welders. When the workmen were finished, Steen happened by and heard one say, "Well, that's the last door frame Dave Steen ever bends." Steen paid a visit later and bent three new ones. Harris came to Bill again. "I'll fix them, I'll fix them," Bowerman said, "but not until Steen *graduates*."

Steen was grateful for that—and for the way Bill allowed the throwers to get attention. To preserve the infield for football, most colleges relegated the permanent concrete throwing circles to somewhere on the far side of fences—which meant nobody could see them. Bill invented the portable steel throwing circle. "On meet days," Steen would recall, "a tractor would bring out our four-hundred-pound discus and shot circles, drop them on the Hayward Field grass before 8,000 people, and we'd be just as much a part of the show as the milers."

The first major meet of the 1963 season was a triangular against USC and San Jose State in Eugene. On his first try, Steen hit 61 feet 9 inches, a school record and the first time he'd thrown over 60 feet outdoors. It was also the number-one throw in the world so far that year. Earlier, he'd had a cortisone shot for a sore elbow and since the elbow felt okay, he took three more throws. After the meet—"just sky high, with all the work having come together"—he was alone down in the training room when Bowerman came in. "I waited and waited for him to say something," Steen would recall. "Finally I said, 'I did okay today, didn't I, eh?'"

Bowerman lit into him. "What you did was really stupid. You had it won on the first throw. With your elbow, you should have taken that one and quit." He walked out.

Steen was flattened: "I remember calling my mother, and I broke down on the phone, really struggling with the purpose of my life there. If it feels this empty after all the devotion and time, what good was it?"

The next day, Bowerman called Steen on the phone and said simply, "I want to see you." When Steen got to his office, Bill got up and they went for a walk in the

Pioneer Cemetery across the street. "I want to apologize for what I said yesterday," Bowerman said.

"It was okay. It hurt, but you were thinking about my elbow . . . "

"No," said Bill, "I spoke too soon. I was thinking about your elbow. I should also have been thinking about what a great meet you had. You had a great throw. Accept my apology." Steen did so. Much later he learned that his mother had phoned his brother, Don, whom Bill had coached too, and Don had called Bill.

A week later Steen's father died. Bowerman drove him to the airport and said, "Go home, bury your father, take as long as you want."

"After I came back," Steen would remember, "he was even more . . . I hesitate to say fatherly, exactly. But when you have a confrontation and reach some kind of understanding afterwards, underneath it all, you grow much closer. That's the way we were."

At the NCAA meet in Albuquerque, Steen was among the minority of Ducks who had done respectably. Keith Forman was recovering from mononucleosis, "or something like it," he would remember. "Bill put me in the steeplechase and I ran miserably. Then he cornered me and reamed me out because obviously I couldn't be living right. I came away feeling dumped on. I thought I'd been doing everything the way he wanted." Archie San Romani, one of the favorites in the mile but suffering a similar energy drain, finished fifth.

Bowerman, of course, had his own suspicions. He had a habit of sending a runner to the doctor or dentist in the hope that a malady or abscess would be discovered, which, when cured, would yield a stronger runner. That September, San Romani came back from the dentist with gaping caves where infected, impacted wisdom teeth had been. Within a week he was feeling like his old self again. Vic Reeve tried to avoid such scrutiny, but he was not always successful. "Bill took note that I ate a lot," Reeve would remember, "and became convinced that I had tapeworms. I thought he must be joking, but he had my stool tested for the presence of parasites. None were found."

Few stayed tranquil under such attention. "Bill could make life a living hell," Reeve would say. "If you did things he disapproved of, you were inviting you knew not what." Reeve shared an apartment with San Romani and Steen that they hoped to keep off of Bill's radar. "Once he showed up at our apartment and quizzed the girls in the next apartment, one of whom would become my wife, about just exactly what they were doing with Archie, Dave Steen, and me."

Reeve was another of the few who had done well in Albuquerque. After the New Zealand trip, Bowerman had told him he needed more strength. "He put me on major foundation work that about killed me," Reeve would say. "A hundred 220s at 35-second pace in the morning and fifty slow 440s in the afternoon. Then an easy day, then heavy work again. I guess cumulatively it gave me strength, but the entire season I felt tired."

Oregon runners were, of course, to finish workouts exhilarated, not exhausted. But Bowerman occasionally tested certain physiologies past that point. Reeve's was one. This being a question of intuition, Bill didn't share his reasons, at least not with Reeve. But Reeve peaked when it counted, in the Albuquerque three-mile, finishing second to USC's Julio Marin.

Forman and Reeve exemplified how Bowerman would order similar men to do different work. After watching two of Arthur Lydiard's men win gold medals in Rome, he changed Forman's training. "We started doing 'out and backs,' half an hour steady out, a half hour back, then forty-five minutes each way," Forman would say. "After six weeks of long stuff, I was the second-best miler on the team after Burley. The improvement was so dramatic it changed my life. Before that, 'long run' on your workout sheet would be a long jog around the golf course."

Even though Bill constantly reassessed what seemed to suit each individual, there was no guarantee he'd be right. Had Bowerman had another year with both runners, he would say years later, he'd have tried for a more exact coupling of work with subject.

Why load such astounding intervals onto Vic Reeve? Perhaps because Bowerman had been keeping in touch with Jim Grelle, who had moved down to Los Angeles in 1962. Soon afterward, Mihaly Igloi moved his running colony to Santa Monica from San Jose and renamed it the LATC, which sensible observers felt stood for the Lactic Acid Track Club. On the day Grelle joined the team, Igloi had him doing thirty-five quarters.

Bowerman had first encountered Igloi's training methods in Pete Mundle's 1950 term paper. Now he would talk to someone training with Igloi himself. "You never really left Bill," Grelle would say. "If you were doing anything he found interesting, he'd give you a call out of the blue."

Igloi's approach was diametric to Lydiard's. The Hungarian scorned running slowly (saying it only made slow runners) and was contemptuous of easy days ("every day hard training must make"). His athletes ran intervals on the track, in spikes, twice a day, every day of their lives. And the workouts lasted two or three hours. Some of Igloi's men were addicted to this work. As Grelle would put it, "They were like little puppets of the theory that he had. They hung out there and were running junkies."

The four best LATC runners were Jim Beatty, Grelle, Bob Schul, and Lazlo Tabori, and their races were extensions of Igloi's dominion beyond the practice track. As Grelle would describe the process, five minutes before the start of a race Igloi would say, "Okay, Grelle, you take the second quarter, make sure you hit the half at 1:58, and Beatty take the third quarter, and it's every man for himself on the last lap."

The man who improved the most under Igloi was Beatty. In 1962, he had had one of the great seasons in running history. In February, he became the first to break four minutes indoors with 3:58.9 in Los Angeles. In the summer, he won the AAU mile, broke the world record for two miles with 8:29.8, and set five American records over a sixteen-day span: the 1500 in Oslo, the mile in Helsinki, the 3000 in Avranches, France, and the three-mile and 5000 in Turku, Finland. He won that year's Sullivan Award as the nation's top amateur athlete.

Nearly forty years later Beatty would still wax poetic about the transfer of mind to master. "Imagine never having to go to a workout and ask yourself, 'What am I going to do today?'" he would tell an interviewer. "Your mind doesn't have to question, 'Am I doing the right thing?' That element is eliminated. It's already charted for you."

Jim Grelle was less obedient. In the spring of 1963, he and Beatty were slated to run the 1500 at the Pan American Games in Brazil. Igloi was there, too, and before the start he gave Grelle and Beatty instructions as usual: They were to run 2:00 for the half, at which point Grelle was to take the lead and carry Beatty on toward a record.

To Igloi's surprise, Grelle objected. The only real contenders in the race were the two LATC runners and, as Grelle would put it, "We were closer than snot and Beatty was always coming out on top, by just that much." So, as Grelle would recall, he and Igloi "had a little argument." Grelle told Igloi he wanted to try to win the race, that he didn't care how fast it was, and that letting Beatty draft on him was not to his advantage. "He's a good guy, he's my friend"—here Grelle turned to Beatty—"but I'm not leading this race. You got it?"

Beatty said he got it. He led the whole race with Grelle breathing down his neck. The pace was moderate, but, as Grelle would say, "it takes a little bit of sting off anybody to press the whole way." Grelle got past Beatty in the last 120 and won by half a second.

Grelle and Beatty remained friends, but Igloi wouldn't talk to Grelle for a week. Grelle liked records and he liked to run fast, he would say, "but if it's a choice of winning or losing, I'll taking winning over going fast. And I know exactly where I got that—I got it from Bill Bowerman."

The Oregon runners soon learned from Grelle or the grapevine about Igloi's ways. We would sit in the sauna and debate the effects that this cult and its guru were having on its members. One view held that when the puppets got away from their master they'd disintegrate without him to think for them. Runners such as we were, however, trained to plan and react as independent entities, would be better prepared for the high-pressure meets. Bowerman bore this for a while and finally snorted, "Too much wishful thinking and not enough good recon. No one running as well as Beatty is a cultist. Surviving Igloi's work just shows the guy's toughness and adaptive energy. He's not going to shrivel up when he gets to the Olympics."

No matter what was said in the sauna, Dyrol Burleson refused to get worked up about any of it. He'd always been able to outsprint both Grelle and Beatty. After graduating in 1962, he'd stayed in Eugene to train with Bowerman for Tokyo—which both of them felt meant training for Peter Snell, now the world record holder. However, the closeness of the races Burleson and Snell had had lately (namely, the "diller" of an 880 in New Zealand) gave Burley faith in his current training and in his usual wait-and-kick tactics.

Then, in May 1963 came a race that argued otherwise. Burley was lucky not to be in it. It was the Modesto Relays mile. With a lap to go, Marine Lieutenant Cary Weisiger was leading the pack in 3:00, just ahead of Grelle and Beatty. Snell loped along in fourth, in 3:02. A huge US TV audience was getting its first real look at the beefy, five-foot-ten and 170-pound Snell. He had a weird, low arm action—a Kiwi thing, taught by Lydiard—that called to mind a man carrying heavy buckets. At 60-pace he seemed to overstride. Then he reached the last turn. Grelle was about to pass Weisiger when he glanced to the right. "Snell looked like he'd been lassoed by someone on a horse and *jerked* past us," Grelle would remember. Snell sprinted his last 220 in a ridiculous 24.5 and won, having eased up, in 3:54.9, a half-second short of his world record. Eighteen yards back was Weisiger, who finished in 3:57.3. Beatty and Grelle did 3:58.0.

All who witnessed this display were shaken. Snell was not only better than ever, Snell was better than anyone had ever been. With Tokyo less than eighteen months away, Burley had to take measures.

His choices were few. One was to reconsider the strategy that had allowed him to go undefeated at Oregon. But he chose not to do that. With Bowerman's guidance, he had devoted his training and persona to wait-and-kick tactics for one simple reason: It takes more energy to run at the front of a pack, forcing aside still air or a headwind, than to draft closely behind the leader. In a mile among equals, Landy against Bannister being the classic example, the pacesetter almost never wins. He exhausts himself protecting his stalkers while they husband their resources for a final attack. That's why in record attempts a rabbit is hired to take the pace for two or three laps and why the ultimate race without a rabbit—the Olympic 1500-meter final—often begins at an infuriatingly slow tempo. No one wants to lead.

Burley, confident of his own finishing speed, had thought that was going to be just fine—until Snell ran that 24.5 last 220 at Modesto. In response, Burleson didn't seriously contemplate changing his racing tactics. He thought of making his own kick more lethal.

Burley thought back to the New Zealand tour and Lydiard's telling him that Snell's speed at the end of a race was the product of stamina-building "marathon conditioning"—100 miles per week, including a rugged twenty-two-mile Sunday run in the Waitakere Range above Auckland. Burleson asked Bowerman if such a weekly long run could be incorporated into his preparations for Tokyo. Bowerman didn't see why not, as long as he built up to it gradually.

Burleson already had a distance day in his schedule, a fifteen miler on the hilly, piney, gravel road around Spencer's Butte, south of town. Indeed, he took vicious pleasure in using "the Butte" to introduce freshmen to the sensations of running long when unready. He had done it to Bruce Mortenson and me. Bowerman had warned us, saying, "Listen, Burleson is mean." But we were so honored we couldn't resist. An hour and three-quarters later he returned us to the campus. "You're carrion," said Bowerman. We were worthless for a week, but Bill said no more. We might have been hens deciding pecking order.

The following year, rooming together, Bruce and I embarked on what seemed even to us a quixotic quest—to find out how far we really could run. Adding a mile here and there to our Sunday jaunts, we worked up to twenty, then twenty-five, and finally thirty miles. So in October 1963 it was a different pair of runners whom Burleson demanded keep him company on his first really long run.

Bowerman bowed us all, along with two-miler Dan Tonn and 880-man Don Scott, into his moldy station wagon and drove up the Willamette highway until we reached a point twenty-six miles from Hayward Field. Once we were running, Bill drove ahead, to water us every five miles, to pick up stragglers, to watch and learn. Scott, a sophomore, wouldn't be allowed more than ten miles.

At ten miles, Bowerman fed us juice and took in Scott. "Everybody okay?" he asked. Everybody was, though Burley just nodded. I thought real distance was having a calming effect on him, the way it can. At twenty miles we reached Interstate 5, the shoulder of which we'd use for the last six. "Tough to creep along in the car and watch you on the freeway," said Bowerman. "Everybody make it home?" We all nodded. He looked from face to face, stride to stride, and left us.

A mile later, clouds covered the sun and the air cooled. Mortenson and I did a little surge together, testing our legs, finding relief in a different gear, and suddenly we were unintentionally thirty yards in front of Tonn and Burleson. We were alerted to this by a keening bark: "*We do not race in workouts!*"

Bruce and I turned. Burley was crimson, his gait stiff. I looked over at Bruce. He didn't want Burley as an enemy. He slowed to rejoin him through what had to be five miserable miles.

I, for some reason, just kept sailing away. That this was sweet revenge entered my mind, but I did not run on cackling for long. The rage in Burley's "*Get back here now!*" haunted me. Then there was only silence. Bruce looked at Burleson's face and wondered what other college I could transfer to.

The last mile was up East Fifteenth. Bowerman stood with water by his car. He noted my time and looked up the road. The others were blocks back. I sucked down liquid, trying to form some words. A sudden image—of having to dance around behind Bill to escape Burley—struck me as comic.

"What's so funny?"

"God, I hope it's funny." I gasped. "We have a situation . . ."

"Bill!" came Burley's cry. "Please tell that . . . that . . . sophomore we do not *race* in workouts!"

Bowerman emitted not a flicker. After a pause he handed Burley a Coke, turned, and said, "Mr. Moore, Mr. Burleson is correct. We do not race in workouts. We never race in workouts. Never have. Never will. Do we not agree we never race in workouts?"

"I sure agree," I said. Bruce and Dan agreed too.

Bowerman looked at the stricken Burley, beginning to cramp. "Good," he said. "I'm glad we got that settled."

When Bowerman told that story twenty years later, he allowed himself to show some of the pleasure he had concealed at the time. "That was the senior finally getting a lesson from the underclassmen," he said. "Sometimes the best teacher is Darwin."

Burleson was undeterred by hitting what marathoners call the wall. He ran frequent twenty-two-milers throughout that pre-Olympic winter. His stamina grew, but it would be spring before he could test his kick.

One of the toughest of life's transitions is that between Olympian and former Olympian. Bill Dellinger, now twenty-nine, refused to accept it. After not making the 5000 final in Rome, he had come home to coach and teach at Spring-field's Thurston High School. Bowerman felt Dellinger didn't need races; he needed to start from square one and build his fitness all over again.

Most of this training Dellinger could do himself, alone or with his high school runners. But every two weeks or so, Bowerman had him run a time trial, three miles at first, then four, five, and six. The pace was whatever he could handle at three-quarters effort. Having just seen that I'd grown stronger, Bowerman asked me to assist. I can still taste the volcanic grit from the old practice track as Dellinger and I alternated the lead every 880, slopping through the twenty-four laps of a Saturday morning six-miler in the rain.

We began these with 80-second laps (5:20-mile pace). Every two miles Bowerman would ask us to take them down, first to 77s, then 75s (5:00-mile pace). Each time we ran by him, he'd call our target and then our actual: "Okay, you should be 10:40 here and you're 10:38!"

Dellinger, three inches shorter, utterly balanced, splashed through puddles unslowed. Never did he give the faintest instinctive surge when I passed. He was there to do work that would make him faster and that was it. Bowerman seldom spoke, but we could feel his eyes upon us. "Keep it tidy" meant I should stop overstriding.

We would not kick it in at the end, but rather just be glad we had held the pace. As we drew on our faded old sweats and hoods, we had to manage con-flicting reactions. Dellinger would mask how hard running these pedestrian 75s felt to him, when his goal for the 5000 was 66s. I'd try to mask the fact that I'd just set a lifetime best for six miles. But he knew.

I'd ask about Dellinger's younger brother, Fred, who'd been a senior at Spring-field when I was a junior at North. Fred was more talented than Bill, more flowing, and he broke all of Bill's Springfield records. But he never went to col-lege. "Fred should have been born in Europe," Bill said, "where you can run for a club and not have to go to school to get coaching and competition." Over the years, we'd hear Fred was out doing some mileage or easy intervals, beginning again. But the mill jobs always took too much out of him.

One Sunday in February 1964, starting with 77s and finishing with 73s, we ran six miles in thirty minutes flat. We had toughened each other measurably. Sounding like my metallurgist father, I told him I felt annealed, tempered. "*Cal-loused* is the word," Dellinger insisted, "physically and mentally calloused."

"Hey, whatever you call it, thanks."

"No, thank *you*."

In April, he ran a solo three-mile in 13:27 (67 pace) and qualified for the Olympic Trials.

As the 1964 outdoor track season began, a familiar face reappeared at Hayward Field. Because of his long rehabilitation after his awful quadriceps pull in Australia, Harry Jerome had not competed in 1963, the year he could have graduated. With another year of varsity eligibility left (and having refrained from fulfilling the last requirements for his degree), he could run for Oregon in 1964. "Harry went into his first meet and I ran him a quarter-mile," Bill would recall. "He did about fifty seconds. You know, I thought, he's not good, but he's not bad. Could be a lot worse." Determined to bring Jerome back slowly, to let him build into his speed, Bowerman let him do only standing starts: "No explosive moves." Gradually he began to smooth out and run better and better. On the day he first went under 22.0 for the 220 in practice, he yipped as he coasted to a stop. "Holding together never felt so good," he said. "I believe I am back!"

He was needed. Oregon State, forty miles north in Corvallis, under Burley's old high school coach Sam Bell, was building deeper, better teams every year. Seldom was an Oregon vs. Oregon State meet not tight. Indeed, the Duck–Beaver rivalry was so intense we met twice a year. At the first meet that year, in Eugene, I ran my epiphany two-mile to beat Dale Story. If I hadn't won, we would have lost the meet right there. But then we lost the mile relay and with it the meet. We were short of points because, after watching Harry win the 100, Bill had pulled him from the 220.

When some poor soul at the Oregon Club had the temerity to question Bowerman's decision, he expanded on his reasoning. "According to one of the Biblical philosophers," Bill said, "when in a race, run all, but one takes the prize. So you do your damnedest to be that one. On the other hand, you keep a little perspective. There is short term and long term. There is choosing among goals of different value. If the Oregon State meet hangs on the 220 and Harry Jerome has had a little twinge while running the 100, you say, well, three years from now who's going to remember Oregon didn't win all its dual meets that year? And you sleep a little better knowing Harry didn't rip out his tendon again." In the rematch in Corvallis, Jerome won both sprints.

That spring, Bowerman gave Burleson his usual sharpening interval work and sent him out to test his finish in the big invitational races. On June 5, 1964, Burley (waiting and kicking) narrowly won the Compton mile from a great mass of men in 3:57.4. Archie San Romani broke four minutes for the first time with 3:57.6, in third, just ahead of Oregon State's Morgan Groth at 3:57.9. Afterward Burleson showed a sense of history, yelling to reporters, "Hey, the story of this race is back in eighth place." That was the gangly, head-rolling, seventeen-year-old high school junior from Wichita, Kansas, Jim Ryun. His 3:59.0 made him the first prep runner ever under four minutes. Ryun came from the same high school that San Romani did, Wichita East, and was coached by the same Bob Timmons.

Also on that historic night, eighteen-year-old Gerry Lindgren of Rogers High School in Spokane drove the pace hard in the 5000 meters, only to be destroyed in the last lap by Bob Schul's kick. Schul's new American record of 13:38.0 put him forty yards ahead of Lindgren's high school record of 13:44.0. From then on, Schul was a powerful favorite to win the Olympic 5000. From then on, Lindgren's gifts were known to be otherworldly.

A few weeks later, the NCAA Championships returned to Hayward Field. In that Olympic year, finishing in the top six in the NCAA or AAU meets qualified you for the preliminary Olympic Trials in New York City on July 4. The New York trials were preliminary because the Tokyo Games weren't scheduled until October, the final trials would be held in LA in September.

In the 10,000 meters, I was hoping to win but was sure I'd score in the top six. San Jose State's Danny Murphy strode to a well-paced win. I ran with ever-greater weakness, feeling lost and embarrassed in front of my pleading crowd, and wobbled in ninth. I sat in shock, watching the 100-meter final. Harry Jerome, making his comeback complete, won it.

Jerome and I bumped into each other later, walking up to shower off the mud at Mac Court. He noted my pitiable posture. "Well," he said, "we're in the same boat now."

"Harry, how the hell do you figure that?"

"We have to completely forget whatever happened to us today and give it our all tomorrow."

Later, as I stepped out of the shower at Mac Court, Bowerman's hand closed around the base of my skull and guided me onto our big scale by the training room. My best running weight was 144. The pointer bobbed at 136. "What do I have to do?" he growled, "shovel in every bite?" He marched me to the cafeteria and made me eat a big steak, two baked potatoes, and half a pie. The next morning he made me choke down two plates of French toast and a quart of orange juice. Finally properly fueled, I finished fourth in the 5000, qualifying for the Olympic Trials.

Afterward I sat at peace and watched a historic outpouring in the javelin. Les Tipton was leading with 249 feet 10½ inches. Teammate Ron Gomez was in second with 232 feet 9 inches. A third Duck, slender senior Gary Reddaway, was in last place. Reddaway had thrown 233 feet 11 inches early in the season, but then, in a cold rain at the Washington dual meet, his elbow had popped.

"I couldn't throw feathers after that," he would remember many years later. "Just the motion put a red-hot paring knife in the ulnar nerve."

Weeks went by and he grew no better. Bowerman knew this was driving Reddaway (the most devout of trainers) wild. He offered a parable. "The pole-vaulter Don Bragg was hurt going into the 1960 Trials," Bill told him. "He had no idea whether he could vault. The day of the final he sat there and waited. He waited while guys missed and went out. Eventually, the bar got to a height that would make the team. He found out whether he could vault by clearing that bar. He went on, of course, to win in Rome." Reddaway got chills at this and vowed to wait, to not wreck his arm with constant checking.

By the nationals, he'd gone six weeks without training and felt no better. Bowerman had him into his office. "If you don't want to throw," he said, "don't throw." Reddaway said he was throwing. He had waited as asked. It would kill him to never know how far the last throw of his college career would have been.

In the prelims he reached 219 feet 10 inches, which barely put him in the final. "But that massacred my elbow," Reddaway would say. "The next morning Bill sent me to Dr. Slocum, who irrigated my puffy joint with cortisone for ten minutes. I came back to the field with iodine all over my elbow." In the final, when Tipton and Gomez went into the early lead, it seemed to be a meet-turning development and brought appropriate thunder from the crowd.

Reddaway's first try was tentative, exploratory. His elbow, he sensed, wouldn't last long. It had to be now. "You read stories," he said later, "of huge adrenaline rushes, of people tearing the doors off cars to save people. I knew this was the last throw of my college life. I was crying as I stood back in the tunnel at the start of the runway. I just shook the spear, ran, and threw. Someone yelled, 'Don't scratch!' I stopped leaning over the line, barely controlling my balance."

Reddaway had put every foot-pound of his kinetic energy into the spear, and released it at the proper angle. It flew 246 feet 1 1/2 inches. He'd bettered his lifetime best by thirteen feet. He was in second place. When no one improved on that, Oregon had swept the javelin for 24 points. No team had ever taken first, second, and third in any event in the NCAA outdoor nationals. "If you want something bad," Reddaway would say, "and if it's reasonable, if it's genuinely, physically possible, then there's at least a chance you can get it."

Then Jerome was second to Bob Hayes in the 200 and San Romani took second in the 1500 behind Morgan Groth. In the steeplechase, five-foot-three, 117-pound Mike Lehner was second to Villanova's Vic Zwolak in a huge school record of 8:46.0. Clayton Steinke and I got fifth and sixth. We topped out at 64 points. Oregon was again national champion.

To be a track Olympian you must finish in the top three in the final trials. When there are several great athletes in one event, judgment day is guaranteed agony. Over the summer, Dyrol Burleson, Jim Ryun, Jim Grelle, and Loyola University of Chicago's Tom O'Hara would race each other three times. In LA in September, one of them would not make the team.

"In the AAU meet in Rutgers," Grelle would recall, "it was a fast pace, and Tommy O'Hara set a new American record in 3:38.1. Burleson was second in 3:38.8. It was the first time Burleson ever lost to O'Hara. I was third in 3:38.9, and Ryun was fourth in 3:39.0. All four of us broke Beatty's old record of 3:39.4." They were now the four fastest metric milers in American history.

A week later came the first Olympic Trials in New York. The top eight finishers would move on to the real trials. With a temperature of ninety-four degrees and ninety-four percent humidity, the pace was much slower. "Burley won," Grelle would say, "O'Hara second, Grelle third, Ryun fourth again."

Two months later, in the final trials at the LA Coliseum, it was the same four, plus Archie San Romani. (Jim Beatty, who was injured at the time of the New York Trials, was advanced on the strength of his great record to the LA finals in both the 1500 and 5000. But Grelle knew from training with him that Beatty couldn't do speed work and so would surely choose to run the 5000.)

San Romani was as blatantly talented as a runner could be. He had the most amazingly sudden acceleration. With his strong hips and hamstrings and low back-kick, he could scoot from 60 pace to 50 pace in two steps. His best 220 was just over 22 seconds, faster than Snell's. Bowerman once told John Jaqua that if he could have convinced Archie that a mile was a boxing match and not a race, he'd have never lost. "San Romani was a real nice guy, and a hell of a runner," Bowerman would say, "but he was not mean. Not like Burley was mean."

An hour before the start, San Romani was still trying to settle on his race plan. "I felt like an orphan," he would say years later, "because there in the warm-up area was my high school coach, Bob Timmons, who was great with strategy, but now his first allegiance had to be to Jim Ryun. Bowerman and I talked, but it wasn't specific, not like picking the perfect spot to kick. Just stay out of trouble, he said. I don't know if it was just me, but he seemed more tuned in to Burley and Grelle. Then I looked from guy to guy to guy and realized, *There is no one here who can outsprint me.*" He had his plan.

The race, befitting its Olympian gravity, was slow. "I felt smooth and easy," San Romani would say. "I wasn't even breathing hard at the three-quarters." In the middle of the backstretch, he struck. He instantly had five yards. As Grelle would tell it, "With 250 to go, Archie blasts off and tries to steal it. He's flying into the last turn and I decide I better get back up there with him because it's going to be a dogfight at the end."

Archie's fantastic acceleration had been achieved at equal cost. "I don't know what gave me the idea I could run a forty-four-second last lap," he said later. "I moved fifty yards too soon." On the turn, Grelle began to close it up. He could see Archie was in trouble. "Right behind me are Burleson and O'Hara," Grelle would say. "O'Hara hadn't raced for a month and Burley had been sick. I think to myself, *I can win this*. I go right on by Archie."

Grelle was on the rail, leading by a few inches. "We come into the last 110 and I can see Burleson on my shoulder and O'Hara on his shoulder. I poured it on, pedal to the metal, and they inched, just inched by me and had a yard lead."

Forty yards from the finish, with the sun casting their shadows ten feet up the track, Burley and O'Hara still had a yard on Grelle. "I'm still burning everything I've got," Grelle would recall, "and I see another shadow coming up on the outside. We hit the line and I see Ryun out there about four lanes wide. I lean and fall across the finish and he beat me by an inch—and I was not going back to the Olympic Games."

Burleson was first, O'Hara second, Ryun third, Grelle fourth, San Romani fifth. "If Archie had waited another fifty yards to sprint," Grelle would say, still shaking his head many years later, "we both might have made it. But he killed us off with that move."

In the 5000 trials, Jim Beatty had been able to train so little he needed a miracle to win. He didn't get one. He was out of contention by two miles. Bob Schul won easily, with Bill Dellinger a safe second. Dellinger was happy he hadn't had to put forth a huge effort that would keep him from resuming his training. "Bill and I had planned the whole year to peak in Tokyo," he would say. "Not peaking for the Trials had its risks, but once Lindgren went to the 10,000, there was no one left I couldn't beat on a bad day."

Tokyo would see three Oregon repeats—Jerome and Burleson, now two-time Olympians, and Dellinger, going to his third Games. Javelin thrower Les Tipton rounded out the Duck contingent.

The first of Bill's Ducks to compete was Harry Jerome, running for Canada. The 100 meters required four rounds over two days. Jerome executed solid starts in his heat and quarterfinal, winning both in 10.3. It didn't take the eye of Bowerman to see that he was going to have trouble with Bob Hayes. In the first semifinal, Hayes won in 9.9, a tenth under Jerome's world record, but it didn't count because he'd been blasted along by an eleven-meter-per-second tailwind.

In the second semi, the wind turned against the runners. Mel Pender of the United States got an incredible start, but slowed at eighty meters. "It felt like something tearing loose inside me," he told a reporter afterward. Jerome won that semi in 10.3 from Cuba's Enrique Figuerola. Past the finish, Pender went down screaming and was carried off on a stretcher. He had torn muscles attached to the lower ribs on his right side. The medical team packed him in ice and ordered him to scratch from the final. Pender refused, "I came for a medal and I'm going to run," he said.

Bowerman fretted that Jerome, witnessing such a reminder of his own past tears, would be affected in the final. But Harry was cool. "It's rare in a big race, especially in late rounds," he would recall, "when guys *aren't* going down like flies. I just told myself stuff like that is normal. As long as I felt fine, I wasn't going to hold back, and I felt fine."

The deepest hush in sport falls over the stadium before the Olympic 100-meter final. Hayes was in lane one, Figuerola three, Jerome five, and Pender (with eight injections of painkiller) eight. The start was almost perfectly even. After ten meters, Hayes, Figuerola, and Jerome had two feet on the rest of the field. Then Hayes kept right on going. He didn't even bother to lean at the tape because he was winning by two meters in a world-record-tying 10.0. Figuerola just held off Jerome's closing rush and took second by less than a foot. Both sprinters clocked 10.2. Mel Pender finished seventh and spent the next three days in the hospital.

Jerome accepted his bronze with joy, and the more he reflected the happier he grew. "That was my best race of the year," he said afterward. "I thought I was going to get Figuerola at the line, but hey, does anyone remember where I've been? I'm really pleased to get any kind of medal in such great competition."

Bowerman wished he could have a withdrawn a cc of Harry's self-control and injected it into Les Tipton's strong arm. Tipton had been second in the US trials and thrown well (270 feet) in training meets in the summer, but he was twenty-two and in his first international competition.

Taught by Bill to emulate the form of the great Russian champion Janis Lusis ("We used film loops of him. I'd studied and been in awe of him."), Tipton was unprepared to meet the flesh-and-blood man himself in the Olympic Village—to sit and have a hot dog with Lusis. "The thing for me was trying to comprehend where I was and what I was doing," Tipton would say. "Hot dog or not, nice guy or not, I didn't feel I belonged in the same company with the greats."

In the javelin's qualifying round, each athlete has three throws. The top twelve go to the final. "I went out there," Tipton would say, "with Lusis, Pauli Nevala of

Finland, Terje Pedersen of Norway [the first man to throw 300 feet], and all the rest, having made it larger in my mind than anything my neuropatterning could handle. I was so out of control I released one throw—my best throw—ten feet before I got up to the line." That would be galling because he missed the final by only six inches.

Bowerman, who was not an official US coach, couldn't send a message to Tipton as he had at the thrower's first USC meet, nor could Tipton come chat with him in the stands. After his event was over, he returned on the day Bill Dellinger ran his race: "I took a little heart knowing this was Bill's third Olympics, that you can get better at this." Tipton vowed to be back.

It was raining steadily on the day of the 5000 final. Seven former, current, or future world record holders stepped to the line, including the two favorites, France's Michel Jazy and the United States's Bob Schul. Bill Dellinger was there too, as well as Bill Baillie of New Zealand, Harald Norpoth of Germany, Kip Keino of Kenya, and Ron Clarke of Australia.

The night before, Bowerman and Dellinger had split a bottle of Sapporo beer and put their heads together. Clarke seemed the key to the race. In the 10,000 he had driven the pace all the way and been memorably outkicked by Billy Mills of the United States. Clarke did not want that to happen again, but, with all the fast milers in the field, neither could he dawdle. If Clarke set off at world record speed, which Dellinger wasn't sure he could handle, what should he do? Bowerman reminded him that he'd run some quick, speed-sharpening 200s the week before and that he could kick as well as most of the big names. Dellinger nodded and said, "But what if Clarke goes wild?" Bowerman reminded him that he was primed, as never before, to run a tough last 600 meters.

"But what if Clarke goes?"

"No one in this race knows himself as well as you do, Bill," Bowerman said. "No one else could have run intervals for a year on a lonely beach by counting his steps. So if Clarke goes wild, let him. At least let other people be the ones to go chasing after him first. You run like you did in your first NCAA mile, when you worked through the whole field. You run what you feel is right for you. You do that and I don't think any Ron Clarke is going to get very far in front of you. You do that until you get to 600 to go and you can make it hell for anyone to pass you after that."

The early pace was slow, and at four laps it was still slow. Bob Schul, near the back of the tight pack, watched Clarke beginning to move up. "Following him was Dellinger," Schul would write in his 2000 autobiography, *In the Long Run*. "Then suddenly [England's Mike] Wiggs fell in front of me! I jumped to the right and barely missed his leg as I landed. Wiggs's spike must have caught Dellinger's shoe, because Bill staggered slightly and then glanced over his shoulder. It happened in a split second and there hadn't been time to think."

Schul and Dellinger composed themselves and watched Clarke. What would he do? Clarke had realized that on the soft track he couldn't just run away. Yet he had to do something to weary the big kickers. So he surged. Off the turn he took off at a four-minute-mile pace. Jazy, Norpoth, and Baillie stayed nearest. Schul and Dellinger let them go. Then Keino went by and Schul wondered if he should be going, too. But after a hard 200, Clarke had to slow and the pack began to catch up. As they passed the start, Clarke looked over his shoulder. Schul thought he had to be demoralized to see how many were still with him.

Lap after lap, Clarke surged and slowed, the pack an accordion behind him. Dellinger remained about eighth, running absolutely even pace. "You probably couldn't see it through the rain," Dellinger would recall, "but I was almost smiling. Clarke not only was killing himself, he was hurting a lot of other guys. I thought Jazy was dumb to stay as close as he did." Bowerman, watching from under an umbrella with Barbara and being of identical mind, beamed for him.

With three laps to go, Clarke slowed and Jazy went around him into the lead. With two to go, Schul, in fifth, felt a great charge of late-race adrenaline as he neared Clarke in fourth. "I move up on Clarke's shoulder," Schul would write, "and look at him as we go into the turn (with 600 to go). At that moment, Dellinger flies by me and takes the lead."

"I imagined it happening just this way," Dellinger would say. "A brutal last six hundred, the distance I first won on the playground when the faster kids died. I imagined it a hundred times, and always winning." There were six men he'd have to prove that to. Jazy looked supremely smooth. Behind him, Norpoth, Keino, and the USSR's Nikolai Dutov were abreast, trapping Schul inside them.

At the bell with a lap to go, Jazy was in second. He looked right, saw Dutov coming up, and flew into an absolutely maniacal sprint. Jazy shot past Dellinger so fast he gained five yards in the next twenty.

"It was amazing," Dellinger would say. "I thought he had to be tired from the surging. He looked like Snell blasting off." (In fact, the following year Jazy would cut Snell's mile world record to 3:53.6.) Jazy hit the last backstretch with a yawning twenty meters over Norpoth, Dellinger, and Dutov. Bob Schul had finally gotten unboxed. Sprinting wildly, he made it past Dellinger and Dutov into third.

The gap behind Jazy seemed hopelessly huge. Schul got by Norpoth and began, incrementally but significantly, to gain on Jazy. With 200 to go, Schul could see Jazy was tying up, and there is no sight on earth that imparts greater drive to a runner. "Coming off the turn," Schul wrote, "I'm a step behind. I come to his shoulder as we fly down the final 100. Several times he glances over, eyes wide. With 50 to go I pass and pull away. For the first time in the race my legs are heavy but it doesn't matter now."

With that perfect last sentence, Schul roared on to win in 13:48.8. Behind him, the crazy brave Jazy had entered rigor mortis so completely that Norpoth and Dellinger ran him down too. The skeletal Norpoth just held off Dellinger for second place, 13:49.6 to 13:49.8.

It wasn't long before Dellinger was showing Bill and Barbara an embossed, beribboned emblem. "Finally something to take home after one of these Games," Dellinger said. He shared Jerome's perspective on his medal. "Whew," Dellinger said. "You know, Bill, there were some real good guys in there."

"Yes, there were," said Bowerman, patting him on the thigh, counting him among them. "Yes, there were."

Only the 1500 remained. Watching Jim Ryun struggle in the semifinals, Bowerman again regretted that Jim Grelle had not made the team instead. "Ryun had the fifth-fastest time going in, but didn't make the finals because he wasn't old enough or strong enough to run three races in four days," he would say. "Our Trials was one race, one day. Grelle would have made the final in Tokyo."

Grelle was 6,000 miles away, but he was furious at another man who'd beaten him. "Tommy O'Hara," Grelle would recall years later, "didn't train from the time he made the team at the Trials. He did not work out the rest of the month. It was party time. He didn't make it past the first round in Tokyo. He had the second-best 1500 time in the world. That's what ticked me off."

The only American to make the final was Burleson. He looked tan and fit and feral. At the gun Michel Bernard of France led, just as he had four years earlier in Rome. Burleson, remembering how Bernard had set a fast pace for Herb Elliott then, went right to second. They passed the first lap in 58, Snell easing along at the back of the pack.

After his hard first lap, Bernard slowed down. "He motioned the runner behind into the lead," Snell would write in *No Bugles, No Drums*. "This was tricky because the front isn't the position Burleson likes to be in at that stage. So there was a confused lull for 200. No one wanted to set the pace. John Davies had hoped to begin making it tough from 600 to go. He had to make it a hard race for his own preservation. So, entering the homestretch for the second time, he moved round into the lead a lap sooner than he intended."

Earlier that year, Bowerman had written to Washington State coach Jack Mooberry, a respected colleague, and asked, "How in the hell can you keep a guy from running what I would like to call a 'stereotyped' race? Burleson always runs the same kind. He's very mulish about it. I should take a club to him, try to get his attention as one would a mule. Everybody knows how he's going to run and of course when he gets against the good ones, they know what he's going to do, when he's going to do it, and all they have to do is do something different and they have him. I don't mean runners in the USA, but when he runs with a Peter Snell, all Peter has to do is wait for Burleson to move and then out-sprint him because he can." Because adding long runs to Burleson's training had not made him dramatically faster in the last half lap, Bowerman hoped that his letter to Mooberry "wouldn't be too damn prescient."

At 800 meters the time was just over two minutes. Snell moved to second behind his teammate and got boxed in. "With just over a lap to go, the field began jockeying for the all-important position for the run home—and I found myself trapped," he would recall. Burleson and Britain's John Whetton had him sealed against the rail. If Burley had blasted off at that moment, Snell would have had real trouble getting out. Burley could have hit the last turn with a fifteen-yard lead. The thought of doing so didn't enter his mind.

"Fortunately," Snell wrote, "it wasn't necessary to use the discourteous elbow-jolt so common in races of this kind. I merely glanced back to see who was behind me and extended my arm, rather like a motorist's hand signal to show my intentions. I breathed a sigh of relief when the athlete on my shoulder, John Whetton, with the manners of a true Englishman, obligingly moved aside. As simply as that, I was out."

Burley had missed what—with hindsight—was his main chance. "Into the back straight," Snell continued, "I was well positioned and unworried. With 200 meters left I threw everything into the final bid. As I let go, I had the strange feeling that this was just what all the rest had been waiting for me to do, as if it were an inevitable part of the race over which they had no control."

That was absolutely not true of Burleson. Snell's move shocked him to the core. It tore at him to discover he wouldn't win. When half the field ran by in pursuit of second place, he let them go. "I screwed up," Burleson said quite some time later. "I was real cocky, too cocky. I was an idiot. After Snell took off, second felt no different from last."

Snell ran his last 300 in 38.6 and won in 3:38.1. Josef Odlozil of Czechoslovakia took the silver in 3:39.6, Davies the bronze in 3:39.6. Burley came to life at last in the stretch and kicked in fifth.

Later, Jim Grelle would say, "Burley was easily the second-best runner in that race. He should have gotten a medal." Burley was man enough not to say that bronze or silver was crap in the company of Dellinger and Jerome.

Before they departed Tokyo, Jerome and Bowerman reached an arrangement whereby Harry would help coach Oregon's sprinters and do graduate work. Bill Dellinger announced that as of this beer he was retired as a runner and aspired to do college coaching. Bowerman said he should go for a position at Lane Community College. Burley said he planned to take his young family and train in Sweden for a year.

Bowerman, in considering Burley's race, thought it might've been a good thing that Snell was superhuman. "It kills Burley to lose anyway," he would say, "but losing to a horse like that, who knows, it might be easier." Still, for weeks, Bill would have recurring queasy regrets that he hadn't convinced Burleson to prepare some plan B, some searing long move, something to drive the race so hard that Snell's tired legs would rebel. The 1500 final was, after all, Snell's seventh race of the Games; he'd run four rounds to win the 800. Bowerman worried that he'd enabled thickheadedness. He'd *let* Burley be an idiot. He'd described, months before, how the race was going to go and he'd been right, yet he'd let his runner down, let his profession down, by not somehow intervening. "I hope," he finally said, "this becomes the world's biggest two-by four. I hope this will crack open that skull."

CHAPTER 19

A Curious Mind

THE GAMES OVER, IT WAS TIME FOR BOWERMAN TO DO A LITTLE SHOE BUSINESS. The *shinkansen*, or bullet train, whisked Bill and Barbara from Tokyo's chaos to the quiet of a small *ryukan* hotel in Kobe. Bill was carrying two pairs of track shoes he'd just finished, prototypes for the Tiger factory to produce according to his design specs and Phil Knight's marketing expectations.

The Bowermans were invited to tour the Tiger factory and meet with company founder and CEO Kihachiro Onitsuka, who quickly won Barbara over. "He was surprisingly informal and outgoing," she would say, "with a bubbling sense of humor. He and Bill were immediately congenial and grew to be good friends, almost familial, within the week."

The two men hit it off because they had so much in common. Onitsuka had begun the company fourteen years before, in a Japan crushed by defeat. He had commanded an Imperial Army training regiment and believed the virtues of war—teamwork, living for a cause greater than oneself—were also the virtues of sport. After the war, he had worked in a shoe factory, learned the craft, and then begun his own tiny shop to make basketball shoes. Barbara was touched upon hearing how he'd created his original lasts by melting candles from a Buddhist shrine and shaping them to his own feet. Onitsuka had come up with the shoes' suction-cup-like sole, which had let Tiger take over the Japanese basketball market, when eating *tako* sushi. *Tako*, of course, is octopus.

Bill returned to the factory several times to converse with designers and workers. He studied Onitsuka's cutting and stitching machines, absorbing how they performed the tasks he did by hand. One of the obstacles to importing Japanese products was translating English specs into their Japanese counterparts. Bill hoped the foremen and crew bosses would remember the big, warm *gaijin*, the better to do his bidding from afar. For years, though, whenever a Tiger shipment arrived in Oregon with products that had misconstrued his instructions, he would groan and wish he could snap his fingers and be back there on the shop floor.

Knight had enlisted Bowerman in starting Blue Ribbon Sports well aware that Bill would always be an overpowering critic of anything but a perfect shoe. Sure enough, when enough Tigers had been on enough feet for enough time, there were problems.

I am here to vouch for that. In 1965, with 250 yards to go in the only 880 of my college career, I didn't look back before moving wide and the spikes of my passing teammate, Butch Meinert, ripped open the outside of my right foot. I somehow finished, my Bowerman-made shoe twisted sideways, my foot spilling blood and taking on cinders. Bowerman supervised our team physician, Dr. George Guldager (whom he called *Gravedigger* for his heavy hand in such work), in cleaning out and closing the gash with seven stitches. For two weeks I couldn't run except a little in the pool. Then, tightly taped, I managed to win both the steeplechase and three-mile in the Pacific Conference Pac-8 meet in Pullman, contributing to our team title. On the plane home, Bill asked what I planned to do the next day. I said I was looking forward to a nice, long Sunday run.

"Fair enough," he said, "but you haven't done one in three weeks and you're pounded flat from your tough double, so I just want you to do ten miles."

I nodded and the next afternoon set out to run an easy twenty. At $10^{1}/_{4}$ miles, at the Coburg Shell station, I felt a funny ping and some pressure in my right foot. It quickly hurt so much that I couldn't run. I had to call my mother to come get me. The X-ray showed a clear white line across the third metatarsal—a stress fracture. No NCAA meet for me.

I went to Bowerman's office. Later he would crow to UCLA coach Jim Bush that he knew his runners so well that all one had to do was go a disobedient quarter-mile farther than he had ordered and the runner would break down. All he said to me was "You will lay before me the shoes you wore." I did. They were lightweight, blue and white flats, Tiger model TG-22. Bill ripped them to pieces right there, without benefit of any band saw.

He was incredulous. The shoes had spongy padding in the heel and under the ball of the foot, but no arch support whatsoever. "If you set out to engineer a shoe to bend metatarsals until they snap you couldn't do much better than this," he said. "Not only that, the outer sole rubber wears away like cornbread. This is not a shit shoe, it's a double-shit shoe."

(Unbeknownst to Bowerman, Onitsuka had actually designed the TG-22 as a high-jump training shoe and identified it as such in their first catalog. "It was us," Blue Ribbon Sports's first employee, Jeff Johnson, would say years later, "who sold it as a running training shoe. Our bad.")

Six weeks later, the day he cleared me to run again, Bowerman tossed me a pair of prototypes he'd made. All the issues with the TG-22 as a running shoe had been addressed. The outer sole was industrial belting. A cushiony innersole ran the entire length of the shoe, under a shock-absorbing arch support. That summer and fall I ran more than a thousand miles in different versions of those shoes, giving them back for weekly inspections, then testing prototypes that the Onitsuka factory made and sent back for Bill's approval. Early models still had two distinct pads and a heel so narrow that more than a few buyers turned ankles. After a year, the shoe was given the full-length midsole Bill had conceived and a wider heel.

Once the shoe went into production, what to call it? Adidas had the habit of naming models for upcoming Olympic cities, such as the Roma or the Tokyo. Knight thought that was smart, imparting an aura of currency. He and Bowerman at first named the new flat the Aztec, in honor of the upcoming Games in Mexico City, but had to give it up because Adidas already had a shoe named Azteca Gold. They brainstormed. Bill suggested the Aztec god Quetzalcoatl. "Trips right off the tongue," said Knight.

"Well, then who conquered the Aztecs? Who's that Spaniard responsible for 400 years of Montezuma's revenge?"

"Cortés," said Knight. "Hernán Cortés."

So in 1966, Onitsuka introduced the Tiger Cortez. I was elated because for years, I'd be able to go into a store and walk out with custom-made shoes. Buck and Bill were elated because people bought them in great numbers.

The Cortez made BRS a viable company. John Jaqua, who would join the board of directors, would recall the many times Nike tried to discontinue the Cortez. "But people kept wanting them, so they kept making them," he would say. "It was the first stable, cushioned shoe for the roads, a comfortable shoe, and so many people liked it that it was the first shoe that made running shoes acceptable in fashion."

That year I took my BA in philosophy from Oregon and was accepted at Stanford Law School. I'd worked in the plywood mill that summer to pay for room and board, and then found I'd won an NCAA postgraduate grant and a Stanford scholarship that added up to an extra $2,000. I whooped about this to Bowerman, it being the first time in my life I was more than fifty bucks ahead.

"Interesting," he said. "Buck and I have a shipment of shoes on the dock in Portland and need some cash to pay the duty. This might be a fine time for you to take a thousand or two in stock."

I distinctly recall the cartoon image that came to me, of dollar bills flying away on little wren wings. "Seriously, Bill," I said, "Man to man, what are the chances of the business really panning out?" Bowerman switched from venture capitalist to solicitous coach. "Kenny, here's how I see it. It's a good idea. Buck's a good partner. The Cortez is a good shoe. I wish I could guarantee we'll turn your two thousand into a lot more, but I can't. It's a risk. It's a risk." I thanked him and ran for the airport. I used my windfall for a Christmas vacation in Hawaii.

Running shoes were hardly the only recipients of Bowerman's inquisitive inventiveness. In the dog days of August and September, as his runners tested shoes (and themselves) on long runs, Bill would drive along with us, stopping at stores en route, then catching up and handing out sodas, juice, water, iced tea—whatever he could find to keep us hydrated. Bowerman kept a notebook on what each of us absorbed best on the run, mulling the fact that no single liquid on the market provided the body with all of the substances lost in sweat.

This was ten years before Gatorade. He already knew what electrolytes needed to be replaced—basically, potassium, calcium, and sodium. So he began experimenting. One time he mixed a scientifically sound concoction of warm lemonade (calcium), salt (sodium), mashed banana (potassium), honey, and tea (caffeine). I spewed it instantly.

"What do you think this is, the *Cordon Bleu*?" he asked. "If it makes you run faster that should be enough."

"Have you tasted it?"

He took a sip, smiled, and acted as if it was terrific. We waited to see him swallow. Surrounded, he blew out his mouthful, too. "All right, all right," he said, "it's sheep's piss."

To my knowledge, he never tried any other blends. From then on, when you called to say you were doing the twenty-six-mile loop from town past his house on McKenzie View Drive, he would go down and put a big glass jar of Barbara's lemonade in the mailbox, the halfway point. When Gatorade finally came out, Barbara recalled Bill drinking deeply of it and saying, "These people are geniuses!"

Nothing affected us that Bowerman didn't examine. If it was not our training, our feet, or our precious bodily fluids, it was our clothing. In the early fifties, he had observed Dellinger and Mundle returning from runs in the rain with their groins and upper thighs knotting from the weight of their bulky, waterlogged sweatpants. Bowerman bought white cotton long underwear and found it acted like a wet suit, keeping their legs warmer and freer longer. But in the following days, he would remember, he got calls from "shocked Eugene biddies" irate over the indecency of the attire, even if worn under regular shorts. Bill stopped the fuss by dying the long johns dark green, which in turn dyed the legs of the runners splotchy green.

Second only to his hours spent improving our shoes were those devoted to what our shoes ran upon. The sensual glory of sinking your spikes into and striding away over a groomed cinder track such as Hayward's was possible during about a third of the Oregon year. Even then, the surface had to be dragged and rolled and the lanes marked with lime. A fixture in my memory is Bill, his long overcoat flapping in the storm, driving a long steel rod into the lake that formed on the first turn during heavy rains, digging through the top layer of cinders so the water could drain into the gravel below. There were few places more likely to prod a man into thinking of something better.

He began small, with runways. He'd observed that wooden indoor tracks provided good spring and grip, although they had dead spots where the planks sagged between supporting joists. In 1956, for the Olympic training meet and decathlon trials, he'd worked with university carpenters to design temporary long-jump and pole-vault runways of strong, one-inch plywood elevated eight inches above the infield grass. They'd worked well, but the athletes' indoor spikes had penetrated nothing fancier than green-painted wood.

Afterward, he lugged home some four-by-six plywood panels, upon which he tried affixing assorted surfaces. "Tar was too sticky," he would recall. "Road asphalt was too hard. Tire rubber was too delicate. I wondered if I threw them together, would I get something useful?"

He bought a little cement mixer, added a gas-burning heater from a roofing company, and put in about equal weights of sand, rubber grindings ("buffings") from Wyatt's Tire Company, and liquid tar. Then he fired up the heater, let the mixer turn until the ingredients melted, shoveled the black, gooey, stringy, smoking mess onto the plywood panels, and smoothed it with a trowel as it hardened.

Soon he had a recipe that gave him material with a nice bounce. But would it endure? He had done all this in his driveway. Wondering how to test it, he looked out across the neighboring pasture—and paid a visit to the Jaquas. He came bearing gifts: half a dozen four-by-six panels covered with rubber asphalt. "We put them around our cattle feeder," John Jaqua would say. "They lasted through four years of excited hooves stamping on them."

In the mid-1960s, by such means, Bowerman put himself in the vanguard of the designers of a new generation of tracks spreading across the land, smooth, black, springy roads from which puddles could be swept and on which meets could be held in all weather. Yet Bill, even after our runways were rubber asphalt, held back from changing the ancient cinders circling Bill Hayward's field. "We have the luxury of a great groundskeeper," he said. "I think at its best, this track is as good as the best artificial ones, and it's easier on runners' legs."

It was a time of feverish innovation in surfaces, and Bowerman, if only to know what shoes to use on them all, had to keep abreast. "When it got hot," he said many years later, "the Grasstex brand would disintegrate. Spikes got clogged with crap that looked like little kid's modeling clay. Every year somebody was coming out with something different. When the 3M Company got a contract to put their Tartan brand of polyurethane in the Mexico City Olympic Stadium, I decided to wait and see how that went."

Bill didn't try to capitalize on his leadership in the rubber asphalt field, at least financially, but he was always proud of his research. He kept his mixer around for years, generating, when runways needed fixing, a few jobs for the daring. This was because rain would seep into the mixer. When it was turned on and its heater fired up, the trapped water would flash to steam and spatter its scalding contents far and wide, leaving lasting scars on anyone within range.

Bowerman had a few himself. In 1963, Charles Wade Bell of Ogden, Utah, had won the prestigious Golden West high school mile in 4:17.1. In July, he visited the Oregon campus. Keith Forman brought him to the track.

"There was a man at the end of the long-jump runway with a cement mixer full of rubber asphalt," Bell would remember. "We got closer and saw he had holes burned in his overalls and his boots were smoking. Keith introduced us and Bill crushed my hand and left it covered with hot tar."

Bell savored the aroma. He'd saved a newspaper clipping about Burleson's 3:58.6 mile in 1960 and had been reading about Bowerman's oddities ever since. "I'd concluded that Bill had coached more sub- four-minute milers than anyone," Bell would say, "and since that was what I wanted to be, Oregon was where I should go. But he exceeded my every expectation. He looked like he'd come through a disaster in a steel mill."

CHAPTER 20

Rites of Passage

ONE THING BOWERMAN DIDN'T PREPARE YOU FOR WAS HOW TERRIBLE OTHER coaches could be. When Dave Deubner, my old North Eugene teammate, first slipped on a Stanford uniform as a freshman in the fall of 1962, he'd broken the school three-mile record with 13:57. Head coach Payton Jordan congratulated him and said, "You're going to be quite an addition, Dave, as soon as I break your spirit." Deubner couldn't believe he'd heard right, and then thought Jordan surely was joking.

But he had, and Jordan wasn't. As a sprinter, Jordan knew little about middle-distance training, yet he enforced a "system" of his own. What had worked for half-miler Ernie Cunliffe (daily intervals and unquestioning faith) should work for all. When Deubner's physiology and scientific mind didn't adapt well to that, an all-too-familiar cycle, repeated by abused runners everywhere, began. Dave would conclude the fall cross-country season strongly, run a few promising races in early spring, go stale from all the intervals, run 4:15 in the heats of the NCAA mile, and not make the final.

Sick of this by his junior year and told by Jordan that he could use the Stanford track only if he did Jordan's workouts, Deubner quit the team. Later, having trained on his own for sanity's sake, he looked good enough that Jordan let him enter the 1965 Pac-8 mile in Pullman. Deubner placed a close second to UCLA's Bob Day in 4:03.2. Dave asked Jordan if he could run the NCAA mile. "Only if you do my workouts," said Jordan. Deubner did them, ran 4:16 in the heats, and didn't make the final.

Ten years later, Dr. David Deubner was managing the cancer research institute at Duke University's School of Medicine, so I guess you could say he had a little success in life. But he could have done all that and been a 3:54 miler as well.

Over the years Oregon runners would race and defeat more talented people whose coaches had, if not ruined them, certainly impaired them. Only gradually would we realize how training sensibly, especially taking easy days, was heresy to the zealots who believed the more you work the better you get.

When I went to Stanford Law School for a year in 1966–67 (before realizing I'd better be a writer), I watched a Jordan assistant named Jerry Barland put the cross-country team through unrelenting intervals. One day he politely asked me not to use the practice track unless I ran hard, because it was difficult for his men to see me only jogging barefoot on the grass for three miles and then beating them by more and more in local cross-country races. When I tried to tell him that I ran brutal workouts on the road and that these were my recovery days, Barland turned and walked away so calmly it was as if he'd been called to the phone. Later I realized that I'd been uttering blasphemy.

I wrote to Bowerman about it. "As a coach, my heart is always divided," he wrote back, "between pity for the men they wreck and scorn for how easy they are to beat." (Bill's competition was more against coaches than against individual athletes, and different coaches elicited different reactions. He never minded the score getting lopsided against Payton Jordan's Stanford, but he wouldn't run it up against Brutus Hamilton's Cal or Jack Mooberry's WSU.)

Two men on the 1965 Oregon team were responding to Bill's care by becoming hard to beat. One was Wade Bell, who improved to 1:48.0, in placing second to Oregon State's Olympic 800-meter man, Morgan Groth, at the Pac-8 meet. The other was shot-putter Neal Steinhauer, another of my North Eugene teammates.

Following his older brother, Neal went to Westmont College, a small, nondenominational Christian school in Santa Barbara. At six-foot-three and 170 pounds, his combination of long levers and quickness said one thing to coach Jim Klein—raw potential. Neal needed only to pack on some muscle.

Steinhauer hadn't really considered going to Oregon after high school because at the time his distances weren't even close to competitive. But when he came home to Eugene after a year at Westmont, he had, in his words, "mega-morphed" into six feet five inches and 240 pounds of springy power. He decided to be a Duck after all.

In his redshirt year, Neal reconnected with Dave Steen, now doing graduate work at Oregon, with whom he had trained when he was in high school. That winter, Steinhauer and Steen practiced in a cramped, dirt-floored room in the Oregon PE building. "The wall was fifty-five feet," Steinhauer would remember, "and I was hitting the concrete at the base of that, but I really didn't know how far I was throwing."

While he was waiting to be allowed to compete for Oregon, Steinhauer threw for the Emerald Empire AA. Neal became eligible just before the 1965 Oregon Indoor in Portland, but it slipped Bowerman's mind to get him varsity gear. Competing in his Westmont jersey, Steinhauer shocked two-time Olympic champion Parry O'Brien and went over 60 feet. As Steinhauer would tell the story, "The press all yelled, 'Who are you? What's Westmont?' I said, 'I'm a Duck, Oregon eligible.' 'Why no uniform?' 'I don't know, ask him.' I pointed over at Bill and I could see him redden. I had not exactly gotten off on the right foot."

Even though they worked together daily on technique, it would take them months to get comfortable with each other, because the change Bowerman knew Steinhauer most needed to make was the one hardest for him to accept. "His basic lesson, both in throwing and in life," Neal would say, "was *don't rush it*. Pace yourself. Take it slow in the beginning. In training, don't go too hard or fast for your body. Do what you can, and don't expect to get there all in one day."

Bill was telling this to a man who twitched and rumbled with joyous impatience. Rather than seek calm, Steinhauer whipped himself toward greater intensity, placing a huge sign over his locker that read *"YAGOTTAWANNA!!"* Bowerman felt he already wanted hard enough, too hard in fact.

"Bowerman's was the right lesson," Steinhauer would say years later. "It's what I teach kids now. I just wasn't there yet. I slowed down my *technique*, sure, but never listened in any deeper way."

Besides churning with yagottawanna-style belief, Neal was also a devout Baptist, which led him to play a part in a drama I will never be able to relate without mortification. The night before our 1965 triangular meet with San Jose State and Cal at Berkeley, Bruce Mortensen and I happened to read in the California campus newspaper that Bob Price, the man I would be racing in the mile, was deeply involved in Campus Crusade for Christ. It was entirely due to his faith, Price was quoted as saying, that he was running well. That same week *Time* magazine had come out with its funereal black cover asking "Is God Dead?"

I don't remember who put two and two together, but we ended up writing, on a little square of adhesive tape, in tiny letters you had to be three feet away to read, "Yep. God's Dead." Mortensen stuck this between my shoulder blades as I went to the start of the mile. The early pace was slow. I made sure to run in last. Price was in midpack. In the second lap I moved up and settled in right in front of him. I can still feel the frisson of anticipation, waiting there around the turn. Would he even see it? What would he do?

He saw it. Fired with righteous anger, Price tore into the lead and passed the half-mile running 3:56 pace. I was sure I had just made the dumbest move of my life. Fortunately (for me, if not justice), Price couldn't hold such furious speed. He began to stiffen even before the last lap. I caught up, went around, and won by quite a bit in 4:08.8. There is only so much the spirit can do to get you through oxygen debt.

I'll always remember coasting to a stop and suddenly being lifted in triumph and carried into the infield by my teammates' strong arms. Well, by one team-mate's strong arms, Steinhauer's. Only when I was roughly skidding on the grass did I realize that Neal had not lifted me in joy. He was enraged. I came to my knees gaping up at Neal's long brown arm, pointing down at me from an awful height. "Don't you *ever* do that again!" he thundered.

He had heard Mortensen cracking up during my last lap, saying, "It worked, it worked," and had asked what was so funny. Bruce had told him and instantly realized his mistake, but it was too late. Neal, his message delivered, turned away to find Price and apologize.

Not too many days later, as I sat in the Mac Court sauna after an easy run, Bowerman opened the door and saw that I was alone except for a rubber-suited wrestler trying to make weight. He came in with his keys and towel, sat down beside me, and studied the tortured, cherry-red face pouring sweat opposite us. "You know," he said finally, fixing the guy with a look, "there are good ways to do things and less good ways to do things . . . " The wrestler twisted and leaned back, trying to get more steam between himself and Bill's eyes.

" . . . And there are truly imbecilic ways to do things," he went on. "Every once in a while, you see someone do something so dangerous to himself and his university that even though it's not your place to say a goddamn word . . . "

"I'm out! Don't worry! I'm gone!" yelled the wrestler, lurching out.

When the door was shut I said, "Wow, way to go."

"I was talking to you."

"*Me?*"

"There are better ways to destabilize an opponent than mocking his faith."

I must have turned redder than the wrestler.

"I know," I finally was able to whisper. "I know now. It will never happen again."

I waited, torn between wanting him to leave it at that and wanting to try to explain. But he had elicited my promise. He would say no more.

Bowerman often quoted scripture in team meetings, but it was always par-able, never proselytizing. In the sauna, where the heat shortened and sharpened conversations, making you yell your last point before running for a cold shower, he seemed like Plato in ancient Athens, listening to different athletes' beliefs but volunteering little about his own, apart from a conviction that there were no atheists in foxholes. Once I asked if there were any agnostics. He just gave me a look, as if that was splitting one hair too many. When I learned of the foxholes he'd survived, I felt a fool.

Now, all I could stammer was "I'm not an atheist, you know. Logically, you can't prove God doesn't exist because we haven't looked everywhere."

"Big deal," said Bill. "The thing is, you can't know that people aren't experiencing what they say they are."

We agreed, for the future, to honor any and all religious expression as truthful reports from the heart.

After the decades had bestowed their perspective, Mortensen could chuckle about the stunt with Price. "Even if it wasn't the kindest idea," he would say, "it was a great *story*. It gave us all something to think about. It gave you a chance to grow up a little. And it was typical of how Bowerman taught. He gave us our workouts, our lessons, our tactics, but then he gave us the freedom to execute them ourselves."

Mortensen believed this flowed from Bowerman's not being a father figure. "My high school coach in Minnesota, Roy Griak, was like a member of the family," he would say, "looking out for us, keeping us from harm. Boy, was Bill ever *not* like that. He expected us to be independent adults and make our own way. I believe that gave us more self-knowledge. We could run well for the rest of our lives because of his teaching us to do it on our own. Bill once told me he was proudest that all his Olympians set their personal bests years after they were out of school."

Well, Bill was hugely proud of Mortensen during the spring of his junior year, because he led a thin Oregon team to the national championship. The 1965 NCAA meet was at California. That year I watched with a cane, my TG-22 stress fracture still healing.

In the steeplechase, Mortensen fought his way out of the pack and into the lead off the last water jump. Approaching the last hurdle, UCLA's Earl Clibborn, wild to catch him, misjudged his steps, slammed into the 200-pound barrier, and went down with a sickening crack. Bruce drove on to win in 9:00.8. Clibborn arose and staggered in third on a broken leg, proof that steeplechasers bow to no one in what they risk. Mortensen, normally the mildest of men, was fearless during his races.

Mortenson's win juiced Steinhauer into launching his shot with an insane scream that echoed across the bay. The steel struck at 62 feet 6 inches, and Oregon had another ten points. Gerry Moro took third in the pole vault for six and Wade Bell was fifth in the 880 for two. That totaled twenty-eight, normally about half of what a team needs to win. But in this meet, points were scattered far and wide. Bowerman did a quick calculation and gathered the Oregon mile-relay team. "Fourth or better," he said. "To win the team title, get fourth or better." Al O'Leary, Butch Meinert, Jim Wood, and Gordy Payne delivered as ordered, with fourth place for four points.

USC and Oregon tied with 32 each. "Ugh," groaned Bowerman, "I should have told them third." Mortensen was stricken. "I'd won the steeple, but I was in the three-mile too, the last day," he would recall. "If I'd been tougher and gotten 1 point, we'd have had it outright."

Bowerman would nod and acknowledge such natural regrets, but didn't seem to share them. He occasionally pointed out that victory is sweet, but you wake up the next morning and it has flown. Similarly, defeat dissolved. He tried to take a long view of it, as in his treatment of Harry Jerome. Occasionally his view was so long that it seemed a kind of enlightened disinterest. That was never more evident than in the question of who should coach Gerry Lindgren.

Lindgren was the greatest distance talent to ever come down the pike. In the summer of 1964, barely out of Rogers High School in Spokane, Gerry had become the first American to beat the Soviets in the 10,000 in the United States-USSR meet, had run 13:44.0 for 5000 meters (a high school record that would last forty years), and had placed ninth in the Tokyo Olympic 10,000 despite gimping along on a viciously sprained ankle. The victor, the United States's Billy Mills, would later say that a sound Lindgren would have won the gold.

Earlier that year, Bowerman had written to Washington State's Jack Mooberry, "You know if I can do anything to help you keep Lindgren I shall be more than happy to do so. I have every confidence that he would be in just as good hands with you as in mine. Let me know what your pleasure is. On the other hand, if everybody is after him and he's not going to go to you, I'll do what I can to get him."

Mooberry's pleasure was to accept, and Bowerman bowed out. Lindgren always wondered why he had never received a letter of enticement from Bowerman.

In January 1965, Lindgren enrolled at Washington State. Not being eligible yet for the varsity, he ran selected open events. Mooberry and Lindgren were shaping his 140 miles per week of training toward a rematch against Olympic 10,000 champion Mills in the AAU six-mile in San Diego. As usual, the AAU nationals would be the qualifier for the US team competing in Europe and the Soviet Union that summer. But as the meet drew near, word came that the NCAA would forbid collegians to enter the AAU meet.

Back in 1963, President John F. Kennedy had assigned General Douglas MacArthur to slam the two groups' heads together and solve this ridiculous conflict that would not die. MacArthur had cowed their leaders into a truce that allowed the United States to send a joint team of collegiate and open athletes to the Tokyo Olympics.

Now, the truce had come apart. The colleges began using their athletes as clubs. I was one. By April 1965, I'd run a winter's worth of thirty-mile runs and worked extra nights in the mill to afford a plane ticket to the Boston Marathon. I was ready to maybe scrape into the top twenty. Bowerman made me a pair of new flats. While I took a test run (a team rule, on pain of dismissal, being *Never try anything new in a big race*), he called the NCAA offices in Kansas.

Executive Director Walter Byers said the colleges were again trying to prove that the NCAA controlled the majority of the athletes. Since Boston was an AAU race, Byers said, it was now not "sanctioned" for college entrants. "If Moore runs," Byers said, "you must take his scholarship."

"Aha!" said Bill. "He doesn't have a scholarship, Walter. And he worked in a damn plywood mill to pay for this."

"Then we'll take his eligibility to compete for Oregon."

When I next saw Bowerman's face, it seemed not so much deflated as desiccated. He kept his fury contained, but it gnawed at him that his own group, his NCAA, was hurting his runner.

Looking back now, to my moral dismay, that was the end of it. The NCAA clearly was wrong to sacrifice my right to run for its hope of leverage in a dispute, but I never considered running and risking my collegiate career.

Two months later, Gerry Lindgren wouldn't be so cowardly. Again, the terminology was that the AAU nationals had not earned the NCAA's "sanction." The AAU saw no reason to seek such a blessing, because it alone determined the national team qualifying process. So the NCAA told Lindgren that if he ran he'd forfeit both scholarship and eligibility at WSU. Word got out that he was vacillating. Lindgren would remember getting calls from college athletic directors saying he had to take their word on this and not run or they couldn't guarantee his safety.

Lindgren ran. He and Mills fought a historic, seesaw six-mile battle, Mills winning with a diving lean. Both broke Ron Clarke's world record with 27:11.2. In response to Lindgren's spectacular defiance, Byers was preparing to notify WSU to strip him of his eligibility when Washington's senior senator, Warren Magnuson, held hearings to find out why this absurdity kept happening.

Gerry was the star witness, pale, scrawny, squeaky, and devastating. "I just couldn't believe all these men who said they had my interests at heart would really kick me out of my school for running a *race*," he said. "A race I needed in order to represent my country. I couldn't believe they'd do that."

If Lindgren had not become a hero in beating the Soviets the year before, he was a hero now. Yet Congress didn't pass any new law. It just threatened to, if peace wasn't restored and Lindgren left alone. The NCAA, revealing Byers's visceral fear of government interference, backed off. But the terrible balance remained.

Lindgren's defiant 6-mile was not the only epochal race at the 1965 AAU meet. The other was the mile. One of its protagonists was Jim Grelle, then in his mid-twenties. Mightily frustrated by how poorly O'Hara, Ryun, and Burley had run in the Olympic 1500, he had determined to keep running even though he had moved back to Portland and was essentially training alone.

Grelle would remember "running things by Bill on the phone, and combining Igloi's intervals with Bill's easy days." The combination worked. In 1965 Grelle would break the American record and beat the indomitable Peter Snell. He almost did it twice.

In their first race, in LA in June, Snell made his trademark move with 300 meters to go. But as he came out of the curve, he caught a glimpse of someone in white moving up strongly. Snell thought it must be Jim Ryun. They reached the tape in a dead heat and Snell took a desperate dive at it. As they slowed, Snell saw that the white shirt was Jim Grelle's Multnomah Athletic Club singlet.

Grelle, who'd been in far more close finishes than Snell, knew he'd lost another one. Both were clocked in 3:56.4. "It was exciting to get that close," Grelle would say. "But you could see Peter wasn't that fit."

In their next race, on a rough track in Vancouver's Empire Stadium, Grelle drove hard the whole last two laps. He reached the finish, turned, and saw he was a hundred yards ahead of Snell, who had a gastrointestinal bug and had dropped back early. Grelle, so determined to break away, had run 3:55.4 and taken the American mile record. The record lasted a week, until the AAU mile.

In that race, Snell was feeling much better and planned, as he would put it, to "sit on Grelle" until the last straightaway. He had not reckoned on the young Jim Ryun. With 300 to go, Ryun took the lead. "Grelle and I covered him comfortably to the 220," Snell would recall later, "where Grelle began challenging. He couldn't make it past Ryun and they ran together round the bend. I could get past Grelle but not up to Ryun."

The eighteen-year-old Ryun finished with his head rolled back. He won in a new American record of 3:55.3. Snell was two feet back in 3:55.4 and Grelle ran 3:55.5, even as he lost the record to Ryun. "I sold a few extra pairs of Tigers for Buck because of those races," he said later. "Snell and I agreed this kid was for real." Ryun's high school record would last into the next century.

A talent second only to Ryun's had grown up voracious among the woodlots and sloughs near Vancouver, Washington. Roscoe Divine was seventeen when he ran 4:10.5 for Columbia River High School in the spring of 1965. Washington, Stanford, and Oregon State, among many others, dangled offers of full rides. But Roscoe knew he was going to Oregon. He had met Bowerman after a 4:13 mile at the Portland Indoor. Bill had told Roscoe that Oregon would prepare him to compete in more ways than the physical. The remark stayed with him.

Tall and charming, with a quick, dazzling smile, Divine gave every appearance of being the preppy product of a stable home. But he had grown up poor, with a disabled father, and would have gone hungry had not the neighbors fed him. By the time he came to Oregon, his father was declining toward death and his mother was too pressed for time to come to meets. Roscoe felt very much alone and, as he would put it later, "I had a money complex."

Bowerman, believing Divine was a middle-class white kid, hazed and embarrassed him as he had Knight and Forman and me. Roscoe didn't respond well to that, his temper flaring when he felt his worth was being challenged. "If he'd peed on me in the shower," Roscoe would say, "I'd have hit him."

Yet on the track, Bowerman quickly found workouts that suited him and, during Roscoe's ineligible freshman year, he chose open races to season him in. In the spring of 1966, Divine took second to Jim Grelle in the Modesto Relays mile in 4:03.5 (but, as he would remind Grelle years later, he was "leading with thirty yards to go"). He was on the verge.

Divine didn't have the recuperative adaptive energies of a Grelle. He would never run a killing three-mile. But he came to a peak more dramatically than any other miler. Bill's late-spring intervals carved five pounds from his running weight and gave him an elegance at speed that was mesmerizing, at no time more so than during his first sub-4:00.

On May 1, Oregon long jumper Bob Woodell, class of '66, with twenty of his frat brothers, was straining to heave a platform of timbers on oil drums across a muddy lawn and into the Millrace, a languid, duck-filled campus stream. Sorority women waited to turn it into a float for the annual May Day fête. The platform unexpectedly rose, buckled, twisted, and toppled. Everyone ran but Woodell. It mashed him to the gravel. When the crowd lifted it off, he could raise his arms but not his legs.

"I was a paraplegic from that moment," Woodell would recall. "Crushed first lumbar vertebra. I spent seventeen days in Sacred Heart Hospital, a year in Portland hospitals." Before Woodell went up to Portland, Bowerman came to see him.

"He asked my permission to give a benefit meet for my expenses," Woodell would say. "In my drug-induced stupor, I thought he was saying he was doing a barbecue at the house and passing the hat."

It was a little more than that. On May 6, 8,000 of the faithful showed up at twilight and paid a dollar to witness the varsity go against selected alums. Paramedics wheeled Woodell onto the field on a stretcher, green blankets and white sheets cinched over his chest. Given an ovation, he worked his arms free and waved and shook hands with the athletes, giving them the strength that only comes upon us when we are running for a larger good. It was in that atmosphere that Roscoe Divine, Wade Bell, Jim Grelle, and Dyrol Burleson stepped to the line in the mile.

Bell would recall Bowerman's prerace instructions: "We've done a lot of work to make you ready," Bill said, "and you are, so here's how we're going to do this. Take over the lead on the second lap and keep the pace up all the way in." Half-miler Don Scott led early, reaching the quarter in 59.0. Mike Crunican brought them by the 880 mark in 1:59.0. Bell, following his orders, surged into the lead.

Everyone's supercharged nerves made for a tightly jostling pack. On the next turn, as they disappeared behind the stands, Grelle was kicked in the ankle so hard he lost the use of it and had to drop out. Down the backstretch of the third lap, Divine moved to second behind Bell. Burleson went with him.

From then on, historians agree, the noise of the crowd exceeded any previous sound heard at Hayward Field. "Wade made the race," Divine would say. "He took the whole third lap." The time at three-quarters was 2:59.0.

"I led all the way to the last backstretch," Bell would say, "when Burley took off around me, and then Roscoe." Burleson won going away in 3:57.3. Divine maintained form and finished in 3:59.1, becoming the second college freshman ever to break 4:00, after Ryun.

Bell, coming off the turn, felt, "I'm not going to make it." Panic drove him in, in 3:59.8. He was the eleventh Oregon man to go sub-4:00. The race was so exciting, and for such a good cause, that it overrode memories of Burley's 3:57.6 in 1961, and would be for many the emotional beginning of the Twilight Mile.

"At the end Bill gave my family $10,000, and that went a long way," Woodell would say later. "But the energy that came from being there so far overshadowed the money that I simply can't encompass it. It let me deal with all the issues that lay ahead."

One of those issues was that he would never walk again. At the time, Woodell was swearing that he would. When he finally came to terms with reality, Bowerman would be there for him again, to suggest a line of work.

Rallying to Woodell's needs cemented the 1966 team. A week later, athletic director Leo Harris told Bowerman that the sixteen Ducks whose marks qualified them for the NCAA nationals had to be cut to ten. Harris insisted the budget permitted only ten to be funded and that he was cutting back on all sports. He didn't say that it was because he had almost squirreled away enough money to begin building a new football stadium.

Bill broke the news in a team meeting, to uproar. There was a shout: "Go over the AD's head. Go to the president!" Bill said, "I cannot. I have sworn to respect the chain of command. Whatever may reach the president's ears, it *cannot come from me!*" Abruptly, looking from one team co-captain (me) to the other (Steinhauer) with a certain you-take-it-from-here nod, he left us.

That night, commissioned by our teammates, Neal and I paid an unannounced visit to the president's mansion on McMorran Street. The only lighted area of the house was the rear entrance, shadowed by rhododendrons. Neal, excited, ran up the steps and knocked, still rehearsing, bouncing on his toes, clearing his throat. Delicate Mrs. Flemming opened the door and froze. Neal, thinking she was the maid, said it was urgent that we see the president. His stirring baritone increased her fright so much that she seemed about to hurl the door shut, so he stepped in, lifted her by the armpits, and set her to one side. Her shriek brought Arthur Flemming from the kitchen, dinner napkin in hand. Neal said, "Mr. President we have an emergency . . . Uh, Kenny, you tell him."

After assuring Mrs. Flemming that Neal was under my control, we stammered out that the athletic director was making qualified teammates stay home from the nationals. Flemming noted a name or two, thanked us for our concern, and made no promises. We escaped, howling at our ineptitude.

A day later an expanded roster for the NCAA meet quietly went up, with sixteen names on it. On the plane to Bloomington, Indiana, Bill revealed that he'd bumped into Flemming at the Faculty Club and gotten the story. The president had called Harris and said that he hated to see a promising sprinter such as sophomore Mike Deibele get left behind and that he really hoped it wouldn't be necessary to do so. Harris had said, "Doctor Flemming, you are remarkably well informed about the minutiae of my department. Say, you didn't happen to come by this information from Bill Bowerman?"

"Mr. Harris, I most certainly did *not*."

Leo could never prove that Bill had gone over his head. We, having abetted an instructive insubordination, felt prepared to take on bureaucracies in later life.

After all that effort to bring the whole team to Indiana, we did worse than any Oregon squad had done in the nationals for years. UCLA, coming into its own under Bill's friend Jim Bush, won commandingly with 81 points. Brigham Young University took second with only 33. Deibele made it only to the semis in the 100. "The 'agony' of defeat was apt for me," Deibele would say. "It simply hurt for days. It didn't come from my teammates or Bill. He was evenhanded. He could see we were doing our best. It came from me." In later years, all Deibele would remember about Bloomington was that he and Dave Wilborn, who hadn't scored in the steeplechase, "went out and got gorgeous pieces of Indiana limestone for our rock collections."

Wilborn was one of two genuine milers Bill had attracted in two successive years—Wilborn in 1964 and Divine in 1965. Divine had blossomed first. Now, Wilborn was about to catch up. Dave had run 4:11.2 at Albany High, taking Burley's state record and dispelling the myth that Bowerman never lifted a finger to recruit. "He came up to Albany a couple times," Dave would say. "He sent letters too. He recruited!"

Wilborn had as much stamina as we, his elders, had ever seen in someone who was seventeen. In September 1964, before school started, he, Bob Williams, and I drove up to the Northwest AAU Marathon in Olympia, Washington. I won in 2:38 on a hot day. Williams had to stop after twenty-one miles due to blisters. Wilborn, despite it being ten miles farther than he'd ever run, set a national high school record of 2:48.

At five foot seven and 132 pounds, with a capacious chest and powerful upper body, Wilborn was driven both to attain great strength of will and to goad others to challenge it. Once he announced to a crowded dorm dining room, "From this moment on, drunk or sober, awake or asleep, until I say different, I will always be able to break two minutes for the half mile!"

This was greeted with jeers of disbelief but no outright dares. A month later, after his declaration seemed forgotten, after he'd run three hours out to Bowerman's and over Mt. Baldy, the crest of the Coburg Hills, and back to campus, after he'd wolfed down two pizzas and drained three pitchers at Pietro's, Divine and three-miler Damien Koch appeared in front of Dave's woozy, reeling face and said but one word: "Now."

"Oh, you fuckers! You fuckers!"

They drove him to the track. Dave put on his spikes, trotted around for thirty seconds patting his distended belly, and went to the line. He ran 1:54.5. "Don't play poker with me!" he yelled. "Not on this! I don't bluff on this!" He didn't even give them the satisfaction of throwing up.

Wilborn's constant trumpeting of his ability (guaranteeing the incessant threat of having to perform) surely had to do with his own deep doubts about his consistency. It didn't take a deductive leap to see this. It just took a mediocre interval workout. Dave got more and more depressed as a poor run or race wore on. He once smashed his stopwatch on the track a few yards after concluding a mile in California that was ten seconds slower than his target. Teammates had to pull him away because he was scaring the officials. "I've always been great at throwing fits," he would say.

Bowerman, in the fullness of time, addressed this. "After a bad dual meet," Wilborn would recall, "I was all hang-headed, and he put his arm around my shoulder and said, 'Dave, if this is the worst thing that ever happens to you, I envy you. You're going to have a great life.' God, I needed that. That was a great lesson. Of course it took some time before I came around. I liked to roll in it for a while."

Sports psychologists drone on about mentorship and strategies for overcoming established patterns of failure. And Bowerman was adept at getting field-event people to visualize specific keys to their technique in competition. He never seemed to do that with runners, yet he took callow youth and made men who could run as hard as it is given to men to run. What made him, with his great silences and intermittent consoling, a superior mentor, a better guide to distance's extremity?

The answer lies in the nature of that extremity. In every honest race, there is what you swear is a turning point. In memory it's linked with an overwhelming roar because it tends to happen as the crowd comes up and calls. Take it from a marathoner, though, the roar happens out on the unwatched road as well. It happens when all your ambition and prerace blood oaths scream at you to hold on against the pain. And the pain shouts them all down.

I feel a traitor to Bill and my brethren allowing the word *pain* to crawl out on the page. I want to brush it off. It's not the pain of a burning stovetop. It feels like weakness. It feels like weight that can't be borne, panic that can't be controlled. At that moment, two paths open. You can press on and do well. Or you can back off, regroup, and try to catch up. If you fail at the second, the temptation is to finish humiliated, like a POW broken by torture.

Bowerman (without ever pronouncing the word *pain*) taught that you redefine yourself a little with every honest, killing effort. You might not win, but you will have been brave. If you can admit that to yourself, bravery is a hell of a thing to build on.

You didn't have to do it every time. If he thought you hadn't been particularly noble in a race, he would sit on that information. At the semiannual goal-setting talks, he'd ask if you really desired a future, a career he could help to frame. And if you did, if he had your considered word on that, he might say fine, we can work on a few things, and maybe the next time you meet a Morgan Groth, you'll be a little better prepared to go out with 60s and make it hot for him. A little better prepared. Not a weak-willed coward every time it starts to hurt. A little better prepared. It made the fault, if there was one, the fault of one runner in one race, but he wasn't always going to be you. It made things reparable.

And we needed that because, as Dave would put it, "It isn't just 'classic Wilborn' to say 'I should have gone harder.' It's classic distance runner."

The truth, however, is that—as physiologists monitoring oxygen consumption, heart rate, and blood lactates have established—after that certain point, if you have fallen off the pace, you really cannot sustain your chosen speed any longer, no matter what you *will*. Bill retired before those studies came out, but he didn't need them. He knew we all had to be kept from trying to go harder and harder until we ran ourselves into sickness or tendon tears. He also knew that we wouldn't toughen miraculously from one race to the next. His working assumption was that we could be a little better prepared. Bill succeeded so often because he didn't drive us. He let us drive ourselves.

"I don't believe in chewing on athletes," he once said. "People are out there to do their best. If you growl at them and they're not tigers, they'll collapse. Or they'll try to make like a tiger. But the tigers are tigers. All you have to do is cool them down a little bit so they don't make some dumb mistake like running the first quarter of a mile in fifty-five seconds."

There are certain words that I always hear in Bowerman's voice. He taught them to us, maybe one per team meeting, dwelling and returning until we ran to the dictionary: "Jejune." "Germane." "Vicissitudes." His view was that intelligent men will be taught more by the vicissitudes of life than by a host of artificial training rules.

Not that he wouldn't give the vicissitudes a shove if he needed to make his point. He'd get quarter-miler Gordy Payne up at 6 a.m. after he'd come in at 5 from the San Francisco fleshpots and take him for a bracing run around Hamilton Air Force Base in Marin County, where we were staying on our spring trip, order him through endless 220s in the afternoon workout, and then throw him off the team when he bullheadedly went into the city all night again.

Watching, knowing this would arise in a team meeting, we would remind ourselves of Bill's long- and short-term temperaments. Once his mind was made up, that was it, but it didn't congeal instantly. He could say or do something unwarranted, cool off, reflect, and reverse himself. Team captains occasionally won leniency and a second or third chance for miscreants such as Payne if Bill remained in reflective mode. He could conclude, as he said then, that "the man was simply one hell of a competitor. Trouble was, he was competing against me," and give him another chance.

In treating us all differently, according to our needs as he saw them, Bill opened himself up to charges of being arbitrary. "I don't remember Burley ever getting in trouble much with Bill," Archie San Romani would recall. "Bill kind of gave him a long leash." True, but Bill once yanked on it ingeniously. In 1961, Burleson wanted to get married. Bill tried to talk him out of it, and when that didn't work, he engineered an informative evening. He asked Assistant Coach Jack Burg, who had two infants, to invite Burley over for dinner. When Burley got there, Burg (at Bowerman's behest) called to say that he was delayed, but he'd be there soon. Burley had to help Burg's wife, Kay, take care of two screaming babies. Bill cackled later to Jim Shea that Burley had developed different views about having a family while still in college.

So Bowerman was virtually unpredictable. We never had postmortems. He pondered how he felt, made his ruling, and sometimes, as Bob Woodell would say of his senior year, "we had a better track team of guys who'd been kicked off than ones still running."

Some of that was because the boot, or the threat of it, could be a teaching aid. Bill's ultimatum to force me to do easy days was such a case, as was his kicking 1967 Pac-8 steeplechase champion Bob Williams off the team for sweeping out his church. "If he'd just sat there and prayed," Bowerman would say a few years later, "I'd have encouraged him. But he was into too many draining extracurricular things." As soon as Williams convinced Bill that he'd accepted a life limited to running and school, Bowerman welcomed him back.

The problem came when Bill's judgment had hardened. Then there was no recourse. "He 'disappeared' guys," Grelle would say. "When he lost hope, you were gone for good."

Bowerman was, of course, a creature of discipline himself. His debt to the intervention of Ercel Hedrick always seemed fresh in his mind. So the respect he developed over the years for coaches Len Casanova, John Robinson, Bill Walsh, and John Wooden (and they for him) arose because they all lived for the rite of passage. All of them hugged or whipped lumps of raging, yearning, acting-out clay and rechanneled it, got it past all the juices of desire and sorrow and fear and lust, all the drunk-on-dopamine excesses of young men fighting themselves to be themselves.

Steeplechaser John Woodward, class of '69, would say, "We had what would now be considered a sociopath for a coach." Woodward knew Bill loved to bewilder, and when he was a freshman, he tried to be wary. "But during cross-country, a bunch of us went in the sauna, and after a minute Bill came in. He'd just gone out to cool off in the shower and had left his towel, which happened to be by me. He picked it up, and underneath was his big, heavy set of brass keys. They had been sitting in there for fifteen minutes and were now the same hundred and eighty degrees as the air." The quick intakes of breath around him told Woodward something was up. "But I was trapped at the end of the bench. Bowerman grabbed the keys and pressed them onto the top of my thigh." John struggled, but was easily held by the great burning hand. He and others Bowerman caught this way swear that Bill's expression at the moment of branding was never malicious or cruel. It was a gleeful, almost beatific face we all saw before he lifted his hand and shouldered out the door.

"What the hell was *that*?" Woodward asked his whooping fellow runners. "Welcome to the team!" they said. "Welcome to the team!" The red welt lasted for days, but left no scar.

Bowerman imprinted so many thighs over the years that when, in 1991, Phil Knight held a tribute dinner for Bill, he invited all the past Men of Oregon to Nike's Beaverton campus gym, built half a cedar-planked sauna, and hung Bill's keys and towel in view. One by one, we sat and were photographed with Bill there, and he signed the pictures later. I look at mine as I type. His grip on my opposite arm pulls me toward him irresistibly. His grin is as exalted as it had been years before, when it had been my leg beneath those fiery keys.

Even Woodward agreed that Bowerman was hardly a sociopath. His laying on of keys was an initiation rite, not unlike the ritual circumcision some African tribes use to make men out of boys. It gave Bowerman the authority of a tribal elder. And he used it to keep us—tigers or not—whole. "I always respected him," said Wilborn, "even at the times I didn't like him."

This is from the autobiography of Nelson Mandela, a cross-country runner himself:

> *The old man was kneeling in front of me. . . . Without a word, he took*
> *my foreskin, pulled it forward, and then, in a single motion, brought*
> *down his assegai [a spear]. I felt as if fire was shooting through my*
> *veins. . . . I called out, "I am a man!" A boy may cry. A man hides his*
> *pain. I had taken the essential step in the life of every Xhosa man.*
> *Now I might marry, set up my own home, and plow my own field.*
> *Now I could be admitted into the councils of my community.*

I would have loved to read that passage to Bowerman in the sauna. The next day he would have brought in a rusty spear.

CHAPTER 21

Lessons Inserted

As indelible as Bowerman's brand of tactile advice was in memory, it often took a while to register elsewhere. Some time might elapse before Bill observed anyone actually heeding it. By 1967, however, Bill's teaching was fully informing Neal Steinhauer. In January, Bill took Neal to the *San Francisco Examiner* Indoor Meet in the drafty Cow Palace. The meet promoters had built up the shot put, touting the prospect of seeing Randy Matson break Gary Gubner's indoor world record of 64 feet 11¼ inches. About Steinhauer Matson was unconcerned; Neal had never beaten him in three years of trying. "Indoor meets always gave a TV set for the winner and a transistor radio for second," Neal would recall. "Matson was not a funny man, but he tried once. The last time he beat me, he said, 'Gol' dern, Neal, I have never gotten a transistor radio.'"

Steinhauer, first in the throwing order, rushed his technique and threw 59 feet. "Then there was a trumpet fanfare and the lights dimmed, and spotlights spun around and they stopped all the other events for Matson's first throw. He did a 63." Bill called Steinhauer over. "Neal, you've got this," he said. "You're just too anxious. Just slow down, let it come."

On his second throw, Neal would say, "I was blurry-eyed the adrenalin was so strong. I pushed off, got my lead leg across well, turned well, waited, waited, and let it come."

The shot cracked down 66 feet 10½ inches away, a new indoor world record by almost two feet. The crowd exploded, but Matson had four throws remaining. Casual no longer, he grimly pressed too hard and didn't come back. Steinhauer thought, *I finally won a TV set!* Matson didn't stick around for his radio.

The record paid off in a dozen invitations. "Bill picked three indoor meets and we finally bonded on one of those trips," Neal would say. "I remember the exact moment. At the Mason Dixon Games in Louisville, we were in the Brown Hotel, sixteen floors, two elevators jammed with Army guys, and we stepped in there and this elevator took off like a rocket. Bill's legs buckled and he went straight to the floor in a squat. It was so crowded he couldn't get up, and we both started laughing. And at the top it stopped so fast it brought him to his feet! We came out of there hysterical. Things were always fine with us after that."

Perhaps the most elusive psyche for Bowerman to grasp was that of Jere Van Dyk. Their beginning was promising enough. From Hudson's Bay High in Vancouver, Washington, Van Dyk had 47-second quarter-mile speed, but he looked able to train to stretch it as far as the half-mile, maybe farther. When Jere was considering coming to Oregon, Bowerman told the young runner's father that Jere was so talented "I can make your son an Olympic champion."

But along with being talented, Van Dyk was boyishly beautiful. His sweetly wicked grin seemed ready for anything; his wink signified knowledge of all the sexy secrets. This was a hard impression for Bowerman to get past.

If Bowerman—or any of us—had only known how little we knew.

Van Dyk had been raised an evangelical Christian in a small Plymouth Brethren assembly in Portland. In 1956, when Jere was eleven, a young man named Jim Elliott, who had grown up among them, was one of five young missionaries killed by the members of the Auca tribe in Ecuador. Jere would forever remember the *Life* magazine photo of their bodies "lying in a stream, with long spears in their backs." The tragedy spurred many in Jere's community to become missionaries, the highest calling in their faith.

For the Plymouth Brethren, if one side of the coin was ministry out in the world, the other side was avoidance of all things worldly. "I was taught as a Plymouth Brethren to shun the world," Jere would say, quoting 2 Corinthians. "Come ye out from among them and be ye separate, saith the Lord." But as a high school senior preparing to choose a college, he was yearning to sample all that the world had to offer. "I definitely wanted to go to Oregon," he would say, "at least in part because it had a reputation as a party school. I didn't do those things, or live like that as a boy."

On the weekend that Van Dyk came to visit the Duck campus, he had a strange portent that he might not be suited to life as Bill urged it. When Jere arrived to meet Bowerman at his office, Bill was not there yet. Sitting behind Bill's desk was a half-miler named Ray Van Asten. "Whatever you do," Van Asten said, "don't come here. Don't go to Oregon. You'll hate it. You'll be making a big mistake." Van Asten, in his mid-twenties and a transfer student from Mt. San Antonio Junior College, had found Bill to be oppressively meddling. "I felt kinship with him," Jere would say, "because of his name and the race he ran. I thought he was an oracle." Jere chose Oregon anyway. He would spend his years there pushed and pulled by warring desires.

Van Dyk had a full ride, so he didn't have to work, and his father could afford for him to have a car on campus. These factors no doubt contributed to Bowerman's conviction that Jere lived the party life on campus. At one team meeting,

Bill told his assembled athletes, "You can either run and study or run and play around, but you can't do all three. You have to choose." It was an admonition many of us had heard before, but it jolted Jere to the core. "I thought he was looking right at me," Van Dyk would say. "The truth was, now that I was out in the world, I wanted to go to the Olympics, the ultimate athletic brotherhood. I wanted to study, *and* I wanted to meet women, sure. But oh, that I were the playboy he thought I was."

In 1966, when Jere and long jumper Tom Smith of Springfield were sophomores, they didn't qualify for their finals at the Pac-8 meet at Stanford. Bill then saw them coming back to the team's motel at 4 a.m. Four hours later, he woke them, but he didn't blast them equally. He blasted Jere for "corrupting" Tom. "Tom, Tom," Bill said, "don't let Jere drag you down."

If Bowerman seems to have been excessively hard on Van Dyk, perhaps it was because he perceived there to be a lot at stake. Bill treated him as he did the rest of us, with a little overkill because he could see that Jere was hugely talented and very bright. All the young Van Dyk could see, though, was that Bill was hammering him.

The news Jere delivered a few weeks later didn't help matters. "I went to him, before the start of the UCLA meet," Jere would recall, "and told him that the doctor had just told me that I had mononucleosis. It was from overtraining. But Bill thought I was playing around. I had tears in my eyes as he told me, behind the stands on the turn at Hayward, to go home. My season was over. I never felt very close to him again."

By contrast, Bill connected instantly with Arne Kvalheim of Oslo, Norway. In the summer of 1966, Kvalheim had run 1:49.0 for the 800 and 3:42.0 for the 1500. A sprinter from his track club was an MBA student at Oregon, and his club coach, Arne Nyto, knew Bill through the International Coaches Association. The two convinced Kvalheim to choose Oregon.

With the equivalent of a year's college credits because of superior Norwegian schooling, Kvalheim could run for the varsity as soon as he arrived in the fall of 1966. A long-striding, rangy guy with voluble wit, Kvalheim gave no conversational quarter, even as we mocked him for producing such lines as "I vant to vash the vindows of your Wolwo." It took Bowerman all of five minutes to see that Arne was not only capable in English but also funny, so he conceived a memorable introduction for an Oregon Club lunch.

"We have with us today," Bill told the crowd at the Eugene Hotel, "a great addition to our team and our university. Unfortunately, I learn that our Duck Club officers are unable to welcome this distinguished scholar to Oregon in the splendor of his own tongue. Therefore, on behalf of the club, it falls to me to say, '*Arne, Ge hingenin freckensillen abelskiver morenen, byorn ramemnen byurr ostanden formic, hanimi and furtritern!*'"

Kvalheim put his hand to his heart, touched, as if this gibberish meant he was getting the key to the city, and responded with a rapid-fire paragraph of thanks in high Norwegian. To which Bowerman nodded and humbly replied, "*Aay nabetenden. Beplucken, beplucken, abelskiversfurallen andfuralleenfree. Frjobyornaballen offender kayy!*"

They went back and forth like that until half the room was in tears and the other half standing in applause.

"Bill's great lesson for me," Kvalheim would say, "was the need to conserve energy, both technically, by running with shorter and more economic strides ('Save those long strides for the last lap.'), and tactically in races, by trying to keep a steady reasonable pace instead of being provoked by a fast early pace or surging along the way—especially when running against Gerry Lindgren."

In 1967 the team had three other prime milers, and Arne was soon fast friends with Divine, Bell, Wilborn, and Van Dyk. Arne dubbed them members of his Tjalve track club and said they were welcome in Oslo whenever they could make it. (One of the overlooked benefits of welcoming foreigners into college programs is that teammates suddenly have homes away from home for life.) On May 6, 1967, thirteen years to the day after Bannister ran the first sub-4:00 with 3:59.4, Kvalheim produced his first. Against Oregon State, he placed a close second to Divine's 3:59.0 in . . . 3:59.4. The one-two-three sweeps that he, Roscoe, Dave, Wade, Jere, and Mike Crunican scored in the 880 and mile gave Oregon a comfortable win in that year's Pac-8 meet in Eugene. One of Barbara Bowerman's favorite photos was of the team taking a victory lap with Bill. "He didn't want to, because he thought it would end up in the steeple water pit," Steinhauer would remember, "but he jogged with us, and stayed dry, and Barbara always liked it because he's both smiling and running."

Van Dyk's racing so well after being out with mono showed Bill that his potential was extraordinary and put Jere back in his good graces. Two weeks later, at the 1967 NCAA nationals in Provo, Utah, Jere's parents were sitting with Barbara as Jere joined Wade Bell for the start of the 880 final. Bill hadn't thought Jere had trained enough to survive the preliminaries, but there he was.

"In the final I was determined to follow Bowerman's instructions and do what he'd drilled into us," he would recall, "that when you pass someone, you go fast, jump him." So when he took the lead, he went out hard. "Trouble was, it was with 330 yards to go," he would say. "I held it into the final straightaway, thinking I could win the whole thing. With 50 to go, I died. My lack of training caught up and I went from first to last. But I was always proud of myself for going broke."

Bell won going away in 1:47.6, but his would be the only Oregon victory of the meet. In the mile, everybody was intimidated by Provo's 4,500-foot altitude and by Kansas's Jim Ryun, who beat Roscoe Divine with a 4:03.5. Dave Wilborn was fifth in 4:07.9. Kvalheim had been denied entry over a foreign student eligibility problem. In the shot put, Steinhauer placed second to an awakened Matson. Oregon's 40 points was second to USC's 86.

The milers quickly cast their eyes toward Bakersfield and the 1967 National AAU meet. There they would be joined by Jim Grelle, but not by Dyrol Burleson. One of Bill's greatest tigers had seen the writing on the wall.

After his post-Tokyo year in Sweden, Burley had returned to Eugene to win the emotional Twilight Mile at the Bob Woodell meet. He had then joined Grelle and a field that included then-freshman Jim Ryun in the mile at the 1966 AAU meet in New York. Ryun led the whole race, with Grelle and Burley tucked in behind him, then simply pulled away with 200 to go and won in 3:58.6. Burleson finished ten yards back in 4:00.0 and Grelle was nearby in 4:00.6. This would be Burley's last race.

Grelle believed Burley quit racing because the nineteen-year-old Ryun had just proved he was better than anybody else. Burleson was twenty-six and, in Grelle's estimation, couldn't cope with the idea of someone younger being so much better because he had always been the youngest. "So he quit prematurely as far as I'm concerned," the thirty-year-old Grelle would say.

Later that summer, with Bell's help, Ryun established his superiority with unmistakable clarity. In the mile at the 1966 United States vs. British Commonwealth meet in Berkeley, Bell rabbited, towing the field past the 880 in 1:58. Ryun flew away with a 57, hit three-quarters in 2:55, and ran a 56-second last lap. He finished in 3:51.3—cutting 2.3 seconds from Michel Jazy's world record of 3:53.6. The time was disconcerting, seeming to herald the coming of the 3:50 mile when minds had barely begun to adjust to sub-4:00. Ryun, having run it, had no problem believing he could better it, with a more even pace.

So in the 1967 AAU meet, on a clay track in Bakersfield, he took a shot at it. Ryun led every step of the way and took two tenths from his world record, with 3:51.1. In retrospect, this was Ryun's most extraordinary performance. Run essentially alone on a crumbling dirt track, it was the equivalent of a 3:47 run behind rabbits on Scandinavian Tartan, a time fifteen years in the future.

Five seconds back, Bowerman-trained men were flooding in. "I waited in the pack," Grelle would recall, "knowing Jim was going to go out and kill everyone. I just made it past Dave Wilborn for second in 3:56.1."

Wilborn had been only fifth in the NCAA mile, but in Bakersfield he had the kind of unrelenting pace he was born to run. So the first time he broke 4:00 he broke it big, with an Oregon school record of 3:56.2. Divine was not at full strength because he'd had to go home to Vancouver after Provo to put his failing father in a better care facility and returned knowing his father didn't have long to live. Roscoe still was fifth, dropping his PR (personal record) to 3:57.2, "but heartbroken. I could have done better."

Nine men went under 4:00, including high school senior Marty Liquori, with 3:59.8. The three Oregon runners who'd finished ahead of Liquori took him over to see Bowerman. Also there were Bell, who'd won the 880 in a meet record 1:46.1, and Van Dyk, sixth in 1:47.8.

"Where are you from, son?" Bill asked.

"Essex Catholic High School in New Jersey," said Liquori. "Coached by Fred Dwyer."

"A good man," Bowerman said. "Well, that's pretty far. You ought to go to school back there."

"I think I will," said Liquori. "I'm going to Villanova."

"We couldn't believe it," Grelle would recall. "They shook hands and that was that. I've wondered ever since whether Bill had been in touch with Jumbo Elliott at Villanova and knew he coveted him." If Elliott did, no letter remained in Bill's files. As Grelle would put it, "Bill wanted you to want to come." Had Liquori—who would be the second-greatest American miler of the Jim Ryun era—voiced that feeling, the distance from home would have mattered not at all.

Years later, Dave Wilborn would reread the leather-bound training log in which he had carefully recorded each day's workouts and feelings. The entry for Friday evening, June 23, 1967, shows a warm-up jog of twenty minutes, 3 x 165 strides, some stretching and high knee drills, more jogging, and a list of the finishers in the mile: "Ryun 1st in WR of 3:51.1, Grelle 2nd in 3:56.1, me 3rd in 3:56.2, Von Ruden 4th in 3:56.9, Divine 5th in 3:57.2 . . . " The page is free of any other notation.

Wilborn would find it remarkable that he had put no more emphasis on his fine race than on running a dozen quarters. "Why no 'On top of the world!'?" he would wonder. "Why no 'Finally, the goal after years of struggle'? The reason has to be that I always thought I was capable of more. So even 3:56 by then didn't seem like that much to celebrate. God, I want to go back and operate that body with a fifty-year-old head! It was always my head that set me back."

In any other year, the top placers in the swift AAU mile, including Ryun, would have gone on planning their Olympic training, confident that they knew how to prepare. But in 1967, things weren't so simple.

Earlier, Bowerman, despite his lack of favor in high USOC councils, had been asked to address how American Olympic athletes should train for Mexico City's 7,350-foot altitude. The Games were a year and a half away, and the IOC was catching hell from writers and medical people alarmed about the dangers to endurance athletes battling in atmosphere containing twenty-five percent less oxygen. Could lowland runners adjust to racing on tracks a mile and a half high or were they doomed to stumble along a lap behind Colombians and Ethiopians? If they could not adjust quickly, how long it would take them to catch up?

"I think it was one of those things that no one knew enough about to object to me taking it on," Bill would say. "The track coaches' association had already resolved to study altitude, so when the Olympic Track and Field Committee met, they said, 'Bowerman you're the one with the Tenth Mountain patch on your briefcase. You're our Olympic high-altitude training coordinator.'" This assignment had been engineered by Hilmer Lodge, chairman of the track and field committee and meet director for the Mt. San Antonio Relays. "We had to learn how to train at altitude and learn it fast," Lodge would say. "We also had to find a place for our Olympic Trials. If there was somebody better than Bill at interfacing between athletes, coaches, and doctors, he didn't raise his hand."

Bowerman canvassed all the colleges, ski areas, and municipalities at altitude, perused their responses, and cut the list to four. In July 1967, he sent teams of runners, coaches, and researchers to scout Los Alamos, New Mexico (led by Arizona's Carl Cooper); Flagstaff, Arizona (Harley Lewis of Montana); Alamosa, Colorado (Ralph Higgins of Oklahoma State); and South Lake Tahoe, California (Bob Tracy of St. Cloud State in Minnesota).

He wanted at least ten runners at each site, and got many of the finest. At Alamosa, a young physiologist named Jack Daniels monitored Jim Ryun, Tom Von Ruden, steeplechaser Conrad Nightingale, and other champions for as long as eight weeks. Von Ruden, fourth in the AAU mile in 3:56.9, got his altitude time down to 4:12. Ryun ran but 4:16.

Bowerman assigned seven Oregon runners to Los Alamos and went along himself. The Oregon runners were Roscoe Divine, Jere Van Dyk, me, Tom Morrow (another late-maturing North Eugene grad at Oregon, now below 4:04), Bill Keenan (Jim Grelle's brother-in-law and national high school record holder in the steeplechase), Steve Bukieda (a tough, dryly profane three-miler originally from Chicago), and Australian Gary Knoke (who'd placed fourth in the 1964 Olympic 400-meter hurdles in Tokyo). Gary had flown into Eugene from Sydney to start school and was shipped right out again to Los Alamos. Jere came still sprinkled with the luster of finishing fourth in the 800 in the Pan American Games in Winnipeg. Bill especially wanted him there because he was racing fit. The amount that he slowed would be attributable to the altitude.

We stayed in The Lodge, the historic timber structure that was all that remained of the old scout camp that had popped into Robert Oppenheimer's mind when the Manhattan Project needed to find true isolation. Los Alamos had piercing blue skies, chalky canyons dividing piney mesas, a daily afternoon lightning storm, 1,500 PhDs, the highest rate of twin births in the nation (we had no doubt why), and a good rubber asphalt track at the high school, elevation 7,350. Upon it, we were subject to the deepest scrutiny of our lives.

We ran time trials the first day—an 880, mile, or three-mile. I didn't feel that bad warming up, but after a lap of the three-mile, it seemed that cold, heavy lead was being injected first into my arms, then into everything else. I had clocked an easy 13:55 two weeks before at sea level. Here, I had to will myself to a dismal 15:15. Already acclimated, altitude native Web Loudat of the University of New Mexico beat me easily. "Oh, wow," we all gasped, "it's not psychological. It's real."

Los Alamos also had scurrying men in flapping lab coats. They had taken four cc of blood from each of us before we began. Now, to measure how our systems were handling lactic acid, technicians tackled us as we finished, steering us over to tables of needles and drawing four cc within ten seconds of finishing, four after a minute, and four more after five minutes. We were there for three weeks. Every Friday we repeated the drill. Our times, hemoglobin counts, and hematocrits (percentage of red blood cells) improved each time.

There were other tests, including a way of measuring lean muscle mass that gave some of us nightmares. For this we were taken into the depths of the Los Alamos National Laboratory, to a wing that contained a room-size metal cube about twelve feet on a side, inlaid with dials and gauges. Bowerman, forewarned, came along to watch.

"What we have here," said a scientist, patting the thick, welded walls, "is a human counter." ("Don't need it," said Steve Bukieda. "Eight of us here. All done.") "This cube is made of foot-thick, battleship steel. Inside, it's completely full of heavy oil. What that does is block all outside radiation. So when you're in here, any radioactive impulses we pick up will be from your K-40, the potassium isotope in your muscles." ("Uh, when we're *in* there?" asked Tom Morrow.)

The scientist touched a button. From the steel wall issued a hollow torpedo tube. We could see its polished metal interior, earphones, and a little switch on a wire. "That is the panic button." For those who weren't all that claustrophobic, it was easy. I dozed off during the few minutes that it took. Morrow came out wild-eyed, fists balled, ready to swing at the technician. It turned out our ratios of muscle to total weight put us up there with climbers and wrestlers. Gary Knoke, our sprinter, did best.

Before our final time trial, the medical researchers said they wanted to up the ante a little. All the samples they'd been taking were of our venous blood, blood that had come from the muscles and was loaded with lactic acid and carbon dioxide. But what did our arterial blood, fresh from the lungs, look like? It was decided that whoever won the three-mile time trial would submit to the usual venous needles in one arm and an arterial needle in the other.

Morrow, Loudat, and I ran together most of the way. When I kicked, canny Tom, skittish about that extra needle, let me win. I crossed the line and was grabbed and braced over a little fence, with technicians poking at both arms on the other side. Gasping, head down, surviving those first few seconds, I heard, "Oh shit!"

I looked up. The white lab coats of three doctors were being machined-gunned by crimson blasts from my wrist. The instant the needle had entered the artery the force of the blood had filled the syringe, blown it out of my arm and kept spurting. None of us, not even Bowerman, had thought to mention that my heart rate would be over 200 beats a minute.

"ARM! Stick up your ARM!" yelled Bowerman. The attendants held it up for me. Fortunately, when you completely stop after running all out, the faintness you feel is due to blood pooling in the body. When it did, the pressure in the artery decreased and the bleeding stopped. "You know," said Bowerman ever so gently to the spattered doctors, "I think I may know the reason they don't do arterial studies."

Except for that one little thing, I loved Los Alamos and wanted to stay. I'd run 14:30, forty-five seconds faster than three weeks before. How much longer could I go on improving? Besides, I still couldn't do long runs. Track work was getting easier, but a steady ten-miler to the ski area above 9,000 feet brought on nausea very much like altitude sickness. Clearly, to train as I was accustomed, with a two-and-a-half or three-hour run every ten days, was going to take more than three weeks to get used to. It was going to take months.

That, coupled with offers of part-time jobs and homes to stay in during the next year, convinced Bowerman that it made sense not for me to stay on right then, but for some of us to come back to Los Alamos in the spring, for the five months preceding the Olympic Trials.

The arrangement took some deck clearing. In transferring from Stanford Law School to the Oregon graduate writing program in the spring of 1967, I had lost all legal grounds for further student draft deferment. Bill wrote the Eugene draft board and proposed a two-part plan for the nation to get the most out of me: "Give him to me for another year, and I'll see that he makes the Olympic team, and we'll be strengthened that way. Then draft him and I have great confidence he will serve with honor in any duty assigned." The board actually bought it. Only in Eugene, Bill's Eugene.

It was the relief of tearing open the official envelope and seeing *2-S* in the little box that moved me to win my first national championship, the 1967 AAU Cross-Country, over 10,000 meters in Chicago's Washington Park in late November. It was also the first nationals won in Tiger spikes sold by Blue Ribbon Sports. In defeating out-of-shape 1964 Olympians Billy Mills and Ron Larrieu, it was not hard for me to imagine doing the same in the 1968 track Trials and becoming an Olympian myself.

That winter, Jay Bowerman beat me to it. Compared with the ordeal that his older brother Jon had been as an adolescent, Jay was a mellow soul. When he broke a couple of windows in a vacant schoolhouse and was found out, he learned his lesson. "Bill let me know he was not pleased," Jay would say, "but he finished up the discussion by saying that he'd been a bit of a hell-raiser when he was a kid and thought it was important for me to understand that there was a difference between raising a little hell once in a while and destroying something that might belong to somebody else. And that's where it ended."

Graduating from Oregon with a degree in biology in 1966, Jay went straight into the Army. He had been in ROTC and so had a two-year military commitment, but as a science major he was able to get assigned to the chemical corps instead of the infantry. He did basic training at Ft. McClellan in Alabama, then tried out for and made the US Biathlon program (shooting and skiing), which the Army conducted in Alaska.

"I figured that was as far as I could get from Vietnam, honorably." The Army, as it had Bill twenty-three years before, taught Jay cross-country skiing. "I had been a confident downhill skier and had worked on ski patrol at Willamette Pass," Jay would recall. "Eight years of year-round training had given me a fitness base. But to compete, I had to master cross-country technique."

The men's Winter Olympic biathlon is raced over twenty kilometers. The biathlete carries a rifle over his shoulder and stops four times to calm his pounding chest and shoot. In a month, Jay was the second-best shooter on the team. "Bill had taught me basic marksmanship when I was little," Jay would say, noting that he had also been "blessed with very good eyesight and steady nerves."

Aside from mastering cross-country technique, Jay's main challenge was the US biathlon coach. Sven Johannsen, a Swedish national, seems to have been as relentless as Mihaly Igloi and as controlling as Payton Jordan. As Jay would put it, Johannsen "subscribed to an old-fashioned work ethic that included ideas like 'train through your injuries and sickness—it makes you stronger.'" Johannsen proposed a summer training run of twenty-five to thirty miles a day for two weeks (with a rest on day eight) that would have crippled the team, but the commanding officer, after a discreet visit from a jaybird, decided they had no funds for it. Jay, having a father/coach who might have come to blows with Johannsen over such madness, was in a bind. "Bill and I did talk once by phone. He gave me good counsel to keep my head, try to keep my training as sensible as I could, and persevere."

The 1968 US Olympic Biathlon Trials were a series of six races in Wisconsin to qualify six men. Jay had come down with a cold and after five races, his cumulative score put him ninth. "In the final race, I let it all hang out," he would say. "I went right to the wall, figuring there was nothing to lose now, and I'd be able to go home and recuperate after it was over." He just squeezed into the final spot.

The team flew to Lillehammer, Norway, for three weeks of training before going on to the Olympics at Grenoble, in the French Alps. Still hacking and coughing "from having run my guts out in zero temperatures," Jay figured he'd take some time to recover, to be ready for Grenoble. But he got a blistering lecture and edict from Johannsen, who demanded that he ski a time trial to determine the four slots in France or go home. "I was so pissed off I went out and tore through the course and, not surprisingly, had a relapse that carried clear through the Games. I guess I should consider myself lucky not to get anything worse out of it. I did not race in Grenoble."

Back home in the Bowerman kitchen, this news was received with relative equanimity. "Bill and I were very pleased (I thrilled) about Jay's simply *making* the Olympic team," Barbara would remember. Bill, as contemptuous as he was of Johanssen's destructiveness, thought it remarkable that Jay had achieved this in a sport he'd taken up only two years earlier. The Bowermans thus began 1968 with a new Olympian in the house, and a cautionary tale of how bad coaching can be.

CHAPTER 22

Mexico City

THE CITY THAT WON THE RIGHT TO HOST THE 1968 US OLYMPIC TRACK AND Field training camp and final trials was South Lake Tahoe, California. Its casinos and town were on the lake, at only 6,230 feet, but twenty minutes away at Echo Summit, a Tartan track was being built at exactly the level of Mexico's Olympic Stadium, 7,347 feet. The area wasn't bad for long runs, but I'd have had to use trails or brave a busy highway, so Bill supported me in sticking with Los Alamos for three months, anyway.

Bob Williams and I moved to New Mexico from Eugene in March. We roomed for a week or two with families who'd volunteered to house "Olympic hopefuls" and did substitute teaching to earn our keep. In April, we came in from a long run to find our hosts had dropped their martini glasses on the carpet and were staring at the television in dread. Martin Luther King Jr. had been assassinated. Back in Eugene, the shock was such that Bill let the team vote on whether or not to go to the dual meet that week. "We voted to go," Mike Deibele would remember, "but it stunned everyone." It was only the beginning.

Track and field athletes, whether they liked it or not, would be caught up in the harrowing events of 1968. The central conflict over what it means to be American was erupting on more fronts than at any time since the Civil War. In January, the Vietcong's Tet Offensive had showed that raising US troops to 500,000 had not broken the North Vietnamese strength or will and forced Americans to examine the true character of the war. In March, President Lyndon Johnson announced he would not stand for reelection. On April 4, King was assassinated in Memphis. On June 5, after winning the California presidential primary, Senator Robert F. Kennedy was killed by Sirhan Sirhan in Los Angeles.

The rest of the year, the nation lived out the stages of its grief. Before there could be acceptance there was anger and denial. On the issues of both civil rights and the war, American ideals were slamming head-on into American reality. Arguments wrecked company picnics, weddings, and graduations. One side wanted to turn the nation from its folly and toward its founding principles of equality. The other side resisted, out of prejudice, out of a belief that anti-communism justified an unconstitutional war, out of a my-country-right-or-wrong patriotism. Each side galled the other by calling itself the true Americans.

All the while, militancy had been rising in the black community. "Nineteen sixty-seven," San Jose State quarter-miler Lee Evans would recall, "was the first year I was proud of my skin being black. We stopped referring to ourselves as 'colored' or 'Negro.' You were black or you were not black. An Afro haircut was a statement of black nationalism."

Evans's sociology professor, a charismatic discus thrower named Harry Edwards, taught a racial minorities class that grew from 60 to 600 in the 1967–68 school year, forging both tools and will to confront the treatment black athletes received away from the field. In the early fall of 1967, Edwards led a campus protest that threatened to disrupt a football game. "If they won't rent to us," he demanded, "why should we play for them?" University President Robert Clark canceled the game, but heeded their concerns and instituted equal-housing guarantees at San Jose State. A furious Governor Ronald Reagan reprimanded Clark for being "coerced" by Edwards.

Buoyed by his success, Edwards went national, calling sixty prominent black athletes, including UCLA's basketball star Lew Alcindor (later Kareem Abdul-Jabbar), to a November 1967 meeting in Los Angeles. There, he tested support for an Olympic boycott to protest racial injustice in America. He found a great deal. The group issued a list of demands to the US Olympic Committee, asking, among other things, that apartheid-practicing South Africa, then pressing for Olympic reinstatement, be denied it, that IOC President Avery Brundage resign because of his alleged anti-Negro views, and that a second black coach be added to the 1968 US staff, joining assistant track coach Stan Wright. If not, American black athletes would boycott the Mexico City Olympics. Thus began the Olympic Project for Human Rights.

Brundage, choosing a word that had been used to infantilize black men for centuries, said, "If these boys are serious, they're making a bad mistake. If they're not serious and are using the Olympic Games for publicity purposes, we don't like it." The head US Olympic track coach was Payton Jordan of Stanford. "There must be some coercion," Jordan said in disbelief, "to have an individual who worked so long [to qualify for the Olympics] change his mind in the middle of the stream."

Jesse Owens, whose four gold medals in the 1936 Olympics had made a laughingstock of Hitler's Aryan supremacy theories, sided with the authorities. Always polite and humble, Owens embodied being "a credit to your race." Because he had preached that enduring racial taunts silently, as Jackie Robinson and Joe Louis had done, eventually would lead to progress, Owens was chosen by the USOC to try to talk some sense into these young firebrands.

It was too late. The new black athlete intended to stand as an equal with whites and point out the ills that needed addressing. Jackie Robinson himself was with them. His brother Mack had been coached at Oregon by Bill Hayward and had finished second to Owens in the Berlin 200 meters. "I say use whatever . . . means to get our rights here in this country," said Jackie. "When for 300 years Negroes have been denied equal opportunity, some attention must be focused on it." *Track and Field News* surveyed black contenders for the team. Nine of twenty-seven said they'd consider boycotting.

Three months before his murder, Martin Luther King Jr. weighed in. "Dr. King told me that this represents a new spirit of concern on the part of successful Negroes for those who remain impoverished," wrote Reverend Andrew Young, then director of King's Southern Christian Leadership Conference. "Negro athletes may be treated with adulation during their Olympic careers, but many will face later the same slights experienced by other Negroes. Dr. King knows this is a desperate situation for the Negro athlete, the possibility of giving up a chance at a gold medal, but he feels the cause of the Negro may demand it." With King expressing sympathy, the boycott idea was something every thoughtful black athlete had to address.

Thus, when members of the USOC Track and Field Committee convened in early spring, they had to decide who would be in charge of coaching this volatile group during the long, hot summer of 1968. That person would have to deal not only with the tensions of ultimate competition but the emotions of men agonizing over whether to sacrifice years of effort to strike a blow for justice. Whoever was in charge would have to deal with Olympic and AAU officials who desperately wanted those men to compete and with a pack of reporters fanning the flames of every grievance.

The committee deliberated and decided that the man in charge would be not Payton Jordan, the elected Olympic coach, but Bill Bowerman. His plan for the athletes to live in trailers beside the new track at Echo Summit was accepted by acclamation. He was ordered to supervise every aspect of the camp that summer between the preliminary Trials in June in LA and the final Trials in September.

Bowerman, sobered, went back to Eugene and learned from team doctor Don Slocum that both senior Jere Van Dyk and junior Roscoe Divine had stress fractures. Bowerman redshirted Divine that season to focus his training on the Olympic Trials in September. And he put both of them on a regimen in the pool. "In 1968," Van Dyk would recall, "like every track season at Oregon except my freshman year, I spent a good part of the spring injured, trying to stay in shape. I got well, ran, got hurt again. Bowerman and I were becoming increasingly frustrated. I saw my Olympic dreams fading, returning, fading."

Van Dyk tried to live in the Theta Chi house and then in the dorms, where he and Divine shared a room. But both places were too noisy and the whole campus was filled with the emotions of that spring. Finally, he decided to move into a rented house off-campus, where he hoped he could sleep and get well. "Bowerman didn't like the idea," Jere would recall. "He thought I wanted to play around, and said I wouldn't eat right."

Jere had not given Bill much reason to believe otherwise. Earlier, Bowerman had sent word he wanted Jere to help escort some high school athletes around campus the weekend of the USC meet. "He didn't tell me directly," Van Dyk would say, "because he and I were hardly talking." But Jere, who couldn't bear the thought of watching the meet without being in it himself, opted to go to the beach with his girlfriend and another couple. "Nothing happened. I was still very much a Plymouth Brethren. But I was ashamed that I didn't do what Bill had wanted me to do, and I am sure he was angry and he had every right to be."

Jere sensed exactly how Bowerman would react to his excursion. Sex, per se, was not the defining issue with Bowerman. Bill said repeatedly that it wasn't the sex act that was the drain on performance; it was the long, sleepless nights consumed in pursuit of it. He once joked to John Jaqua that he was thinking of hiring Jerry Tarr to teach people on the team how to get laid and be home by nine.

In Jere's case, though, there may have been something even more basic going on that had nothing to do with whether he was playing around. Bowerman had given Jere a job to do and Jere had failed to do it. Assigning mundane, even menial tasks was a test of character that Bill often applied. Failing it might not cause Bill to disappear a team member, but it would lead to a kind of probation.

Even without Van Dyk and Divine in that spring of 1968, Bill was as deep in middle-distance men as he'd ever been. Wilborn, Kvalheim, and two Canadians, Terry Dooley and Norm Trerise, were all running near four minutes. But when Gerry Lindgren came to town for the Washington State dual-meet two-mile, Bowerman felt only one of them might be ready to stay with him. "I wasn't really trained for the longer races," Arne Kvalheim would recall, "but Bowerman needed someone to run them, and since I was the slowest over 200 meters of the milers at Oregon, and the oldest, he chose me to face Gerry in the two-mile."

The match was a heralded one. "It was the Oslo Arrow against the Spokane Sparrow!" Roscoe Divine would remember. Bill had told Kvalheim to stay away from Gerry, to let him lead by ten to fifteen meters to keep him from varying the pace. "I did this and beat him over the last lap," Arne would recall matter-of-factly. That lap occupied but 55 seconds and let Kvalheim set a new collegiate record of 8:33.2. "Gerry was the best NCAA long-distance runner in history until Pre came along," Kvalheim would say. "In all his years in college, I believe my two-mile was the only race in which he was ever beaten."

Van Dyk, inspired by Arne's win, tried to replicate his own swift return from injury the year before. Seeing Van Dyk's stress fracture finally healing, Bowerman entered him in the Pac-8 meet at Berkeley. "I took aspirin, warmed up, ran, and the pain was too great," Jere would remember. "I didn't make the finals. Bill told others—he never told me—that I was kicked off the team." Jere took this hard. "I was out in the cold," he would remember more than thirty-five years later, "banished, an ancient form of punishment, from my tribe, my family, the only place where I was happy."

But Jere had misunderstood. He had not been banished. Bill's message, via the team captains, had been only that Jere wouldn't be going with Oregon to the NCAA championships. It had been a judgment of Jere's racing fitness, not his soul. Believing otherwise, Jere took his degree, went home, and thought about what to do.

Up in Los Alamos my training had gone well, and in late May I came back to Eugene to confer with my professors. Bowerman grabbed me to be cannon fodder in a Twilight Meet four-mile-relay record attempt. He felt a varsity team of Terry Dooley, Norm Trerise, Arne Kvalheim, and Dave Wilborn could threaten the 16:08.9 record set by the great 1962 team. He planned to run them against an Oregon Track Club crew of Wade Bell, a year out of school, Roscoe Divine (recovered from his stress fracture), Tom Morrow, and me.

Bill put the best OTC men first and instructed them to lead so the varsity guys could draft along. He put Morrow and me on the last legs to serve, if the varsity fell behind, as easy targets for Arne and Dave to catch. I thought this was great because I harbored secret ambitions. My best was 4:04.4 from two years before, but my Los Alamos workouts showed I could do around 4:00.

Roscoe led off our OTC effort with 4:03.2. Wade followed with 4:01 and put our team sixty yards—eight or nine seconds—up on the varsity. Near the end of Wade's mile, Bill realized that even if Arne and Dave concluded with sub-4:00s, the varsity wouldn't get the record of the 1962 team.

Bill wanted to keep the record try alive, but thought that Morrow and I surely couldn't run the 4:01s that would take. But his two varsity studs, Arne and Dave, could. So Bill stepped onto the track, nudged Morrow aside, grabbed Kvalheim, and said, "We're switching teams. Take the baton from Wade." The incoming Bell was surprised to hand off to a member of the opposing team, but he did it.

Morrow and I were outraged at being made to go from the winning team to the losing one by executive order, but Tom couldn't complain for long because he had to take the stick from Trerise. I, on the other hand, had four minutes to fume before Morrow gave it to me. I got next to Bill's ear and informed him that a record set by switching teams in midstream was a travesty and would never be accepted. All Bill said was, "When you get the baton, you're going to be way back. So don't run."

"Don't *run?*"

"Wait until Dave laps you and then *pace* him his last three laps." Now I was a damn rabbit.

Arne finished with a 4:03.3 and passed the baton to Dave, who took off to roars. Tom Morrow came in ten seconds later, handed off to me and I just . . . lingered there. People in the crowd (not to mention Tom, heaving on the infield from the effort of getting that baton to me) yelled, "What's going on? Come on, Moore, run!" I would have, but Bill had a firm hand on my arm.

Finally, Dave completed his first lap and Bill let me go. I took off, fell in beside Dave, got a sense of the pace and gave him two straight 60s. He was 3:00 with a lap to go in his mile. And it hit me that there might be a way to salvage this ridiculous situation.

I didn't feel that tired. Someone must have started a watch when I finally began with Dave. If I didn't kick with him on his last lap, but just held this 60 pace, I might have enough left to squeeze out a sub-60 on my last lap and thus break 4:00.

And so it happened. Dave sprinted in beautifully, with a 3:57.5. I was twenty yards back, passing the line in about 3:00.5. Around the turn the bedlam died enough for me to hear announcer Wendy Ray saying, "A new four-mile-relay world record of 16:05! And thanks, everybody, for coming to a great meet!"

By the time I emerged from behind the first-turn stands, the backstretch was filling with people jumping out of the bleachers. I yelled and bounced off a few until it was hopeless. I finished with an 80. I saw a guy from the mill. "Geez, Moore, what is it with you? First you won't run, then you won't stop."

At this writing, the record book lists the "Oregon Track Club's" 16:05.0 as the fourth-fastest four-mile relay ever run, although it was never accorded official recognition. Keith Forman, one of the 1962 team who witnessed the charade, remains irate: "Bill's switch absolutely demeaned what we four did alone."

I have always agreed. Bowerman never offered anything like an apology. Years later, at a 1991 reunion and tribute to Bill, I recounted the story and ended by saying that the memory still stung. He simply produced the same fiendish grin he had when he was rearranging us. That had to have been the face seen in 1959 by Dave and Don Christian, the identical twins who had refused to switch places behind the stands: the face of Bowerman at play.

That was about the last time Bill got to loosen up in that momentous year, for his responsibilities were soon Olympian. In 1968, both the NCAA and AAU nationals qualified athletes for the first round of Olympic Trials, held at the Coliseum in Los Angeles in late June. The primary purpose of these first-round Trials was to select the pool of ten athletes in each event who would be eligible for the Lake Tahoe altitude camp and final Trials. But for incentive, the USOC said that the first placers in each event in LA would make the team to Mexico and only have to "demonstrate fitness" in thin air during the final Trials. Those victors, among them Villanova 1500-meter man Dave Patrick and Oregon State high jumper Dick Fosbury, could then focus on peaking for the Games, not for the final Trials.

Also at the LA Trials, the black male athletes held a meeting. Of twenty-six favored to make the team, thirteen said they would boycott. But top 100-meter men Charlie Greene and Jim Hines were adamant that they would compete. "It comes down to whether you're an American or not," said Greene, who would go on to a twenty-year career in the Army. "I am an American, and I'm going to run." To hold unity, the boycott was abandoned. Black athletes would take part in the Games, do their damnedest to win, and then, if conscience demanded, make a gesture on the victory stand. This was a huge relief to almost everyone but Harry Edwards. The athletes would be able to train with undivided purpose.

They would, that is, if they could survive their first weeks in sky camp. Because Bill had to be with the Oregon athletes at the NCAA and AAU meets and LA Trials, he couldn't monitor the contractors building the Tahoe track and attendant facilities. When Bowerman arrived, with Barbara, he was appalled. "The top echelons of the USOC had set this up, and we were on the edge of mutiny the second day," he would recall. "The food was unsanitary, meager, and awful. The best shot-putters in the world were getting eight hundred calories a day. There was an open cistern, and the drinking water was polluted by wood rats and bird droppings. The athletes said they would really rather wait to get their dysentery in Mexico." Bowerman called the USOC officials and threatened to resign if conditions weren't improved immediately. He got results. "I don't think that had as much effect as telling them I'd send all the athletes home too," he would say later.

"Bill Bowerman is absolutely frank," Yale coach Bob Geigengack, who had helped Bill pick the Tahoe site, once said of his friend. "If I ask him a question, I know he'll give it to me straight, regardless of whether I'm going to like what I hear. That bluntness is rare. Almost all of us will bandy words. We'll circumlocute. We'll try to soften the blow. Not Bowerman. In fact, when I think of Bill, I'm a little ashamed of being diplomatic. I wonder if I might have compromised somewhere."

At Tahoe, the athletes lived in trailers and nearby cabins, eating and lifting weights in prefab structures covered with taut, shiny fabric. There can never have been a more ethereal setting for a track. The clearing was at the base of a ski run. From the top of the hill, the scene below became a *bonsai*, an oval Tartan plate sweeping around an infield of granite boulders and the ancient trunks of High Sierra forest. The long-jump runway emerged from the woods, with Bob Beamon the most deerlike upon it.

On the high-jump apron, Bill renewed his acquaintance with Dick Fosbury, then an Oregon State junior. As Bowerman viewed the history of high jumping, Bill Hayward and Les Steers perfected the Western roll high-jump technique in 1940. "Then Fosbury, as a sophomore at Medford High in 1963, developed something better that rightly bears his name—the Fosbury Flop."

All high-jump styles, Bill would say, are gymnastic moves to apply the most upward force to the body's mass and let the center of gravity go a little *under* the bar while the jumper—in different sections—goes over. "A five-six jump used to be pretty good," Bill once said, "because everybody jumped with the scissors. It was like you hurdled the high bar, but lay back along it while you dropped your lead leg down and then lifted your trail leg over. The scissors wasn't the best, as Hayward proved with the roll, but the reason they used it was they jumped from one piece of hard ground and came down on another piece of hard ground. Fosbury couldn't have done what he did without improvements in landing areas. Coming down on the back of his neck on those old piles of wood shavings or sand—he'd have ruined himself the first time he tried it."

That fateful spring day in 1963, as Fosbury would remember, was at a dual meet at Grants Pass. The landing area was fat foam blocks held together with netting. His coach had been trying to get him to learn the modern variant of the roll, the straddle, but when he needed a clearance to stay in the competition, he reverted to the scissors style, with all its limitations. Except this time, as Fosbury put it, "My body found a way to remove those limitations. It wasn't out of some idea I'd had, or a model. It was by feel—and the need not to lose to guys."

Fosbury changed the angle of his approach, charging almost right at the bar. "And in the air, when I tried lifting my hips to keep from knocking it off with my butt, the natural, equal-and-opposite reaction was that my shoulders went back." When they did, it was easy for him to keep his legs together and lift them over the bar. And since he could safely land on his neck and shoulders, he had found a new way. Fosbury improved his personal record by 6 inches that day, and went on to win the 1965 state meet with 6 feet 7 inches.

He still has the telegram he got from Bill after that, saying that he'd love to have him visit his university. But when he replied that he wanted to be an engineer, Bill said, More power to you. "Oregon State was great for him," Bowerman would say later. "Where else was he going to study engineering? And he had a terrific coach there, Bernie Wagner, who was the best in the high jump."

"Bill's teams always brought out the best in Bernie," Fosbury would remember. "And that had a huge effect on all of us. The Friday before every Oregon meet, Bernie would have a team meeting and go through the scoring chart and compare our athletes with theirs, and we would always finish about 1 to 3 points behind on that chart. Just a little bit behind, so pressure was put on everyone equally to take up that little slack. You knew you'd be a hero if it was you."

As furious as those meets were, Ducks and Beavers were able to shake hands afterward and "have the camaraderie of knowing you gave your best," as Fosbury put it. Often, bonds grew. Now, in the Tahoe camp, the Beaver was hanging out with Ducks again.

Bowerman had found the Oregon Track Club contingent a cabin up a nearby side road. "And the Oregon athletes," Dave Wilborn would say, "were two orders of magnitude wilder than anyone else up there!"

Much of the tone for the OTC crew was set by one William H. Norris. As a Massachusetts high school mile star, his first choice of college had been Oregon. But Bowerman had returned his eager letter and high school clippings ("for your safekeeping") without any further invitation or mention of aid. So Norris had gone to Boston College and become a three-time Intercollegiate Association of Amateur Athletes in America (IC4A) steeplechase champion. But Norris was undeterrable. "Delayable," he would say, "but not deterrable." After he took his degree in business, he moved to Eugene in the fall of 1966, began grad school, and showed up in muddy cross-country workouts among Koch, Morrow, Williams, Kvalheim, Bukieda, Divine, and Wilborn.

Well, not among them—behind them. "I was in terrible shape," Norris would remember. "I was fifty yards behind even on slow half miles." But Bowerman noticed that this awkward, arm-thrashing, hip-rolling creature was staying a little closer each week. He also was taken, as were we all, by Norris's Boston Irish wit. By the end of the year, Norris was a proud member of the Oregon Track Club, with Bowerman as his coach and strategist. In 1968 he ran a best of 8:44 in the LA Trials steeplechase and qualified for Tahoe.

Norris was a great adventurer. He drove the "Green Ghost," a faded lime, International Harvester Forest Service vehicle with a bullet hole in the driver's side door. On foot, he and Wilborn covered remarkable distances on the trails: "We took six or eight hours to run in past Aloha Lake along the crest of the divide. Another example of having too much fun for our own racing good."

Meanwhile, I was being sensible back in Los Alamos. Earlier in the year, Bowerman and I had felt that the 10,000 meters was my best chance to make the team. But over the weeks at altitude, we realized that I might have a shot at the marathon as well. The trial to make the Olympic team in the marathon was to be held in August in Alamosa, Colorado. It was open to anyone, but the USOC had funded about twenty of the best American finishers in other marathons for two months of altitude training beforehand at Adams State College in Alamosa.

But it had taken me four months just to be able to cover twenty-six miles at 6:30 pace in training at altitude, let alone race it. That told us that two months wasn't going to be enough for any competitor to fully acclimate. I would have had five months by the date of the marathon trial. Bill and I decided that I should take advantage of that and race. There would be a month to recover before the 10,000 at the Tahoe Trials.

The Alamosa course was five loops around the little town, and so flat and open you could look across the fields and see back to the start. Australian Kerry Pearce, in it to impress his nation's Olympic team selectors, set a brisk early pace. Billy Mills and steeplechaser George Young let him go, but I went with him, thinking to put some pressure on the "two-monthers," the subsidized entrants. Pearce fell back at seventeen miles and suddenly I was way out in front of the Olympic marathon Trials. I got a little dehydration twinge in one hamstring with four miles to go, so when Young passed, I let him, and he won in 2:30. I held second in 2:31.

George Young, then thirty-one and a tough old friend of Bill Dellinger's, was the American record holder in the steeplechase with 8:30.6, but had never run a marathon before. Yet he lived high, in Casa Grande, Arizona, and had had the same thought as I—that fully acclimated guys like us would beat the two-monthers. We also felt we'd proved that track runners would be better mara-thoners than plodders, our term for pure road men. The only plodder to make it was a distinguished Minnesota eccentric, Ron Daws, who finished third in 2:33.

I was an Olympian—and even happier that the slot was in my fallback race. I flew home and gave my report to a beaming Bowerman, observing that the race had gone not to the plodders but to the swift. Bill corrected me on the lesson. "You and Young were the two guys most at home up there. That race went to the *calloused*."

I recovered so quickly that Bowerman let me run a rainy 10,000 against Gerry Lindgren a week later in Eugene's Olympic training meet. The Olympic sea-level qualifying time was 29:00, which took 70-second laps. Bill ordered me to begin no faster than that, regardless of Gerry's early rocketry. At three miles Gerry had carved out a ten-second lead, but he slowed and I caught up to him with a mile to go. The storm clouds thickened and the light was going. Hayward Field had no lights. Cars parked around the north turn hit their high beams so we could be seen battling on through the rain. On the last backstretch, I gave it everything I had and drove into the lead. Gerry stuck right with me around the turn and up the homestretch. I beat Lindgren for the first time, by two feet.

"I'm not in shape yet," he said. "I'll accept that," I said. We both had gotten the Olympic qualifying time, but still had to finish in the top three in the final Trials.

Barbara Bowerman would never forget the party that night, as people took refuge from the storm in Dean and Shirley Pape's huge house below Hendricks Park. She radiated relief and success—"my relief and Bill's success." A month earlier she had taken a reconnaissance trip to Tahoe with him and had felt real qualms about the entire undertaking.

"I wondered if he knew how much responsibility he had assumed," she would recall. "He had huge expectations and many doubts from the Olympic Com-mittee, not to mention other critics. He appeared to have made all the arrange-ments His Way, from choosing the site and placing the track in its little clearing in the forest, to the arrangement of this trip back to Eugene for most of the Olympic team to put on a special meet for the thanks and enjoyment of his home crowd. Yet he never seemed to lose a hair or an hour of sleep, just relying on his own careful preparation, loyal support from well-chosen assistants, and well-trained teams."

The training of Bowerman's two Olympic 800-meter candidates, Wade Bell and Jere Van Dyk, could hardly have been going more differently. At home in Van-couver, Van Dyk had been mending. Since he'd been on the Pan Am Team and had ranked seventh in the world in the 800 in 1967, he had successfully petitioned the USOC Track Committee to let him go to Tahoe. However, the USOC also told him that he had only two chances to run the Olympic qualifying time for the 800, in meets at sea level. "I wanted to go to Tahoe, of course," Jere would say, "but was scared, Bowerman being the training center coach. In early August I sat on the front porch with my parents and asked them what I should do. My mother said, 'You have to try.' My father was quiet."

Jere went with his mother. "Bill Norris and I drove down in his old Green Ghost, laughing and having a grand time, but I was as nervous as could be. When we got there, we checked in and saw Bowerman, briefly. He assigned me a job, as he assigned everyone a job in the camp administration. I was to guard the track for a time in the evenings."

Soon after he got to Tahoe, Van Dyk took his first shot at a qualifying time at a training meet at Mt. San Antonio College (Mt. SAC) and barely missed. "I was close," he would remember. "With another couple weeks I knew I could be ready. I honestly felt that I could make the team. Everyone thinks that, I know. I was sure all I needed was to get into the 800-meter finals, and then I would do it."

One thing that lengthened Jere's odds of making the top three was the fitness of his old friend and teammate Wade Bell. Wade had improved year after year and now held the American 800 record, at 1:45.0. New Zealand's Peter Snell had retired, so Wade was the early book favorite for Mexico. He handled altitude fine, had 46.3 speed in the mile relay, and had become a classic exponent of the long, Oregon-honed, 300-meter kick. He could bolt to top speed a long way out and just keep going.

Bowerman felt Wade needed socializing, though. He called him in once and said, "Wade, I've had a couple people talk to me about you. Seems you do a lot of *whistling* when you talk. When other people talk, you're looking around, whistlin', watching the birds . . . Now, Wade, I want you to look straight at people when you talk."

"It turned out," Bell would recall, "I'd been acting in this evasive way to reporters. But I'd only learned it from Bill when he watched the birds and wouldn't talk to us when we were freshmen." Bill would use that tactic and more with the newsmen prowling the training camp. Their handling was crucial, because Tahoe crackled with tensions, one of which was not knowing how to act on the question of race.

D ozens of coaches that year, including Payton Jordan, were quoted in *Track and Field News* as refusing to accept that the boycott proposal might be a response to real grievances. Most of these coaches worked with black athletes.

But the fact was that many had no shame about how racism permeated their work. John Carlos had discovered this at East Texas State. "Football coaches called a black receiver who dropped the ball 'Nigger' or 'Nigra' or 'Boy,'" he would recall. "The athletic department called a meeting of black athletes and told us, 'You don't like it here, you can leave.'" Carlos had, for San Jose State and Bud Winter.

Winter was the best coach of sprinters of his era. Tommie Smith, the 220-yard world record holder, would say of him, "Bud, this white, middle-aged gentleman, coached Lee Evans, John Carlos, Ronnie Ray Smith, and me at a time when we were all quivering with the politics of the black athlete, and never said a word to us about any of that. He left us free to live our lives creatively."

It was no surprise that Bowerman, great friends with Winter, was the same way. At Tahoe, Bill became a big, strong, smiling wall against the forces that wanted to get to the athletes. With their personal coaches he was collegial, with their families he was familial, with their shoe-company reps he was professional, with reporters he was expansively distracting.

With the athletes Bill was protective, refusing to carry any message that wasn't about the subject at hand, and the subject was track. "Coach Bowerman was a very important person in my career," Lee Evans would recall. Evans, who had transferred to San Jose State from San Jose City College in 1965, had seriously considered Oregon.

"I studied the history of my event and saw he had coached Otis Davis," Evans would say. "I felt I could have broken the world record in the 800 meters if I had gone there. So I sought Coach Bowerman out. Even after I went to San Jose State, I talked with him whenever I saw him at meets. It was in Tahoe where Bowerman and I became close." Bill timed Evans on the sprinter's two long interval days, 500s and 300s. "He was very interested in my schedule and seemed to really like my hard work. He got excited when I told him I wanted to break the world record in the 600 meters up there. We planned a 46.5 first lap, but Ron Freeman brought us around in 48.5. Bowerman thought I could run 1:12. I ran 1:14.3, which still stood for sixteen years."

Bowerman walked exuberantly away from Evans's 600-meter record and saw, coming through the woods, an ululating Sasquatch. It was Neal Steinhauer, showing up from the Army track team. Bill knew Steinhauer had slipped a disc and he wasn't expecting to see him. But in June Neal had gone to see Dr. Don Slocum in Eugene and had found some relief. Bowerman started him on easy throws, 50 feet at first, and he began improving a yard a week. As the Trials approached he was getting up near 67 feet. "But three days before," Neal would recall, "I blew out my ankle."

As bad as it was to end that way, it was worse for Van Dyk. "I was either late or didn't show up at my job one evening," Jere would remember. Bowerman sent discus-thrower Jay Silvester to tell Jere to come see him. "I recall being scared, because Jay seemed a changed person," Jere would say. "In five seconds, Bowerman told me to get out of the camp and go home. I left, my Olympic dreams crushed." For the second time, Jere had failed to do the job Bowerman had assigned him.

The US Olympic Track and Field Trials began without either Steinhauer or Van Dyk, on a schedule never before followed. Bowerman was tired of watching people make the US team and then—like Ryun in Tokyo—not be able to get through all the rounds in the Olympics because there were no rounds in our Trials. So he insisted with all his persuasiveness that they run the Tahoe Trials on the same eight-day schedule as the Olympics, with all the heats.

But before they could begin, there was a terrible meeting. At a grave assembly of athletes chaired by Bowerman and USOC track official Hilmer Lodge, the rules were changed. The need to address the rules flowed from realizing that different people were responding to altitude differently. Specifically, the distance winners at the sea-level LA Trials might not be able to place in the top six at altitude, let alone the top three. If we wanted to send the most competitive team, we'd send the top three from Tahoe, but if we wanted to be fair we'd honor the promise made to the winners of the LA Trials and take them no matter what. It was an awful bind, and it was only settled when LA 1500-meter champion Dave Patrick rose and said, "If I can't make the top three here I don't deserve to go." LA 10,000 champion Bill Clark bravely said the same. Bowerman would always remember their gallantry—especially since neither Patrick nor Clark made the team.

In the 1500 final, the pace was slow all the way, and Jim Ryun (3:49.0), Marty Liquori (3:49.5), and Tom Von Ruden (3:49.8) kicked in Olympians. Patrick was fourth. Roscoe Divine was fifth in 3:52.0 and Dave Wilborn ninth in 4:03.8. Roscoe felt uncrushed, not unlike like Burleson after Rome. He knew he was young yet, still only twenty.

Wilborn, the most pessimistic of milers, came away blaming himself. Heats and final had all pooped along slowly and concluded with furious kicks. He needed it hard all the way, but almost surely wasn't strong enough to drive the pace himself. In the end, what tormented him was that he had sat back and not tried. "It was my fault that it was slow," he would insist years later. "An individual is at fault if he doesn't take it out when he has to. I was also a basket case by the final. That was the most disappointing effort of my entire life."

Bill Clark was the subject of emotional cheers in the 10,000, but Tracy Smith, Tom Laris, and Van Nelson ran away from the field. I had a bad day and was seventh—and was never more grateful that I had the marathon slot in my hip pocket. In the steeplechase, Bill Norris didn't make the final, but Bob Williams did and finished a valiant fifth, in 9:17.2. Lee Evans won from Larry James and Ron Freeman in a world record 44.0 for 400 meters.

But another LA champion, Dick Fosbury, had driven his stuff to Medford, flown back, and learned to his shock that because of the new rule he wasn't guaranteed his spot after all. And the trip had left him far from springy. "In the finals, I wasn't jumping well, kind of hit-and-miss, and at seven-two, I was in fourth place, because I'd made it on my third try."

Three others had cleared too, Ed Caruthers, Reynaldo Brown, and John Hartfield. "The bar went to seven-three, a PR for all of us. I got psyched up, had a great jump, and made it. My coach, Bernie Wagner, said it was the best he'd ever seen me do. I was, I hoped, back on the team." But both Caruthers and Brown made it. If Hartfield cleared as well, Dick would be back in fourth. Hartfield turned away and began psyching himself up.

"Because seven-three was our OSU school record, Bernie asked the officials to measure and confirm the height," Fosbury would remember. "That took some time. When John turned back, ready to go for his last try, all pumped, the officials were in the way, still measuring. They took so long, John lost that emotional edge and missed. He ran off into the forest and I didn't see him again for years."

Watching were discus-thrower Al Oerter and decathlete Bill Toomey, both of whom had made the team. "You know what number the Japanese believe signifies death?" asked Oerter.

"Four."

"How'd you know?"

"What else could it be?"

A fter the final trials, people scattered and then reconvened in Denver to be outfitted. "There," Lee Evans would recall, "we learned that IOC president Avery Brundage had attacked the black athletes. He said we were lucky to be allowed on the team. If he hadn't come out like that, I don't think anything would have happened." What happened was one last, poignant meeting. "Imagine the eagles we had there," Evans would say. "And we were going to run. But what else could we agree to do?"

"It boiled down to a clash," Larry James would remember, "between the goal—doing good for all mankind—and the gold: the individual's self-interest. There was, shall we say, counseling back and forth to sort out the two." Finally Tommie Smith stood. "I hold no hate," he began, "for people who cannot make a gesture, whatever the reason. But I have to reserve the honor of Tommie Smith. I'm an American until I die, and to me, that means I have to do something. I don't know what I'll do. But we have to make worthwhile this last year."

And there it was left. As Evans would remember it, "We all went out and got haircuts."

Bowerman's view of the Olympic Project for Human Rights over the years was positive, because he and Bud Winter knew for a fact that Smith, Carlos, Evans, Freeman, James, Ronnie Ray Smith, Leon Coleman, Willie Davenport, Erv Hall, Vince Matthews, Bob Beamon, and Ralph Boston—regardless of whether they would have actually boycotted the Games—were brothers with the rest of the team in their purely athletic need to improve. They were good men with legitimate complaints. At every workout, Winter and Bowerman marveled over the mechanical perfection of the sprinters and hurdlers. It broke their hearts that these athletes would consider withholding that beauty from the wider world. The coaches' relief was almost equal to that of the athletes when the boycott was abandoned.

But if Smith, Carlos, and Evans thought Bowerman might feel even neutral about their cause, they needn't have worried. Bill understood that what they were doing was crucial for them, and felt as well that they were not just addressing American racism. They were also addressing the entire stultifying IOC aristocracy, which had supported the AAU's malfeasance for so long. If you were going against Avery Brundage, Bill Bowerman would be with you. Solidarity had beamed from of his face every day he worked with the San Jose guys.

"Bowerman, like Bud, never got involved in our politics," Evans would recall. "They did not hold our politics against us, either. I really believe the 1968 team was so successful because of Bowerman being the head coach before the Mexico staff took over after the Trials."

In Mexico City, Bill and Barbara watched the athletes he'd help prepare win more gold medals than any track team from any country in history. Jim Hines took the 100 in a world record 9.95. Tommie Smith took the 200 in a world record 19.83. Lee Evans took the 400 in a world record 43.86. Willie Davenport won the 110-meter hurdles in 13.3. Hines, Charlie Greene, Ronnie Ray Smith, and Mel Pender won the 400-meter relay in a world record 38.03. Evans, Ron Freeman, Vince Matthews, and Larry James won the 1600-meter relay in a world record 2:56.16.

In the field, Al Oerter won the discus with 212 feet 6 inches, Randy Matson the shot put with 67 feet 4³/₄, Bob Seagren the pole vault with 17 feet 8¹/₂, Dick Fosbury the high jump with 7 feet 4¹/₄, Bill Toomey the decathlon with 8,193 points, and Bob Beamon the long jump with a historic world record of 29 feet 2¹/₂. That totaled twelve gold medals in all, six with world records.

"I am convinced," Bowerman would say some years later, "that it would have been thirteen wins and another world record had not Wade Bell come down with Montezuma's revenge before the heats in the 800." Bell had lost seven pounds between the team's arrival in Mexico and when he ran.

"His workouts had been amazing," Bill would recall. "Only two men in the world had a chance against him, and their tactics in the final would have set him up perfectly. Wilson Kiprugat of Kenya went out hard, and Ralph Doubell of Australia sat on him. Wade would have gone by Ralph just as Ralph went by Kiprugat. Doubell won in a world record 1:44.3. Wade would have been the first man to crack 1:44."

As it was, Bell walked the streets of Mexico until dawn, trying to reconcile himself to the fact that microbes on a random piece of bacon had so destroyed his world.

After placing first and third in the 200, Tommie Smith and John Carlos mounted the victory stand, accepted their medals, and at the first strains of the anthem, bowed their heads and shot their black-gloved fists to the sky. They meant their unshod feet to represent black poverty, their black scarves and beads to signify black lynchings, their fists to mean black unity. Any resemblance to Lady Liberty lifting her torch was ironic, for Smith and Carlos were taking America to task for failing to extend liberty and justice to all. This was the gesture that Smith's honor as an American demanded.

Bowerman's first thought when he saw those arms go up was to realize who was who. Carlos was Harlem-born, skeptical, wary, a fountain of jive. His arm was so crooked he could have been hanging on a subway strap. Smith was a child of farm labor, a rule-follower, a ROTC cadet, a congenital improver of self and nation. His arm was ramrod straight.

Barbara Bowerman would remember a gasp, followed by silence among the people they were with. "I think Bill may have imposed that silence," she would say, "by ignoring what was a frightfully embarrassing public breach of etiquette. He continued to discourage any references to or chatter about the scene. That was his usual reaction to a mistake. He didn't believe in giving or receiving apologies or listening to any rationalizing."

Harry Jerome, who had concluded his racing career by placing seventh in the 100 meters, was interviewed by the Canadian Broadcasting Company about Smith and Carlos's action. "I agree with the principle of pushing for equal opportunity," he said. "But an act on the podium takes away from other athletes in the event." Harry felt that the USOC should have sat down with the black athletes and worked out an understanding. But he had spoken with Carlos, he told the CBC, "and he's more interested in proving his point than anything else."

Bowerman said later he had no sense that his nation was being shamed unfairly. He trusted Smith and Carlos to know the need for their gesture. He respected them for earning the place where they stood, from which no one could look away. He knew he was seeing not self-promotion but an act of conscience. It was so powerful he shivered at what it might cost them.

"Glad that's over," said a relieved Tommie Smith when he got back to the Olympic Village, one of history's more inaccurate preliminary assessments. It would never be over. He was still shuddering a little at the hate-filled faces he had seen in the crowd. "It was the fist that scared people," he said later. "Bowing wouldn't have gotten the response that it did." Avery Brundage and the IOC immediately banned Tommie and John from the Village. Ron Daws, Tom Dooley, and I helped stack the sacks of hate mail that began arriving the next day.

Three days later, Bill sent me out to run the marathon. "Any last words?" I asked flippantly as we chatted before the bus took me to the start. "Only what I told Grelle before the 1959 NCAA mile," he said. "It's never a bad idea to stick with the champ."

The champ was Ethiopia's Abebe Bikila, who, having won the 1960 Rome Olympic marathon barefoot and the 1964 Tokyo Olympic marathon in a world record, was setting out to win three Olympics in a row. I, amazed and idolatrous, rolled along happily at Bikila's side in the early miles. Bikila, protecting his line before a turn, even gave me an elbow. I wanted to say there was no way I'd ever drive him into the crowd lining the road, but knew no Amharic. He had tape above one knee. We had heard he'd been hurt.

After ten miles, Bikila turned and beckoned to an ebony wraith of a teammate, Mamo Wolde, the 10,000-meter silver medalist and a fellow officer in Emperor Haile Selassie's palace guard. Wolde wove through the pack to Bikila's side.

Thirty years later, Wolde would tell me what had transpired. Bikila had said he wouldn't be able to finish and ordered Wolde to win. "Sir, yes, sir," said Wolde, and took off. He won by three minutes, in 2:20:27, the greatest winning margin in Olympic history.

I got blisters. It turned out I had unwittingly disobeyed Bowerman's law to do nothing new in a big race. I'd wrapped the US trainer's new "breathable" adhesive tape around the balls of my feet, where it breathed in the lanolin I'd dabbed on my toes, came unstuck, and rolled up into ridges of fire. At seventeen miles, in sixth place, I sat down, took off my shoes, and ripped the tape off one foot. A crowd of *campesinos* surrounding me was instantly spattered with scarlet, not unlike certain doctors had been back in Los Alamos. The skin had come away with the tape. I did the other one, got my shoes back on, hobbled for about three miles until I bled out and went numb, then was able to pick up the pace and start catching people. Approaching the stadium, I was in fourteenth.

As I came out of the tunnel into the light, a vast cheer erupted. It was for Dick Fosbury, who had just cleared his winning height. He was galloping around so heedlessly I thought I'd have to dodge him when I passed by with 300 to go. But he heard me yell, "Way to go!," turned, and saw that a Mexican marathoner was forty yards ahead of me. "Get that guy!" he ordered, so I sprinted for him, the stadium screaming for the gringo to fail. The gringo got the forty down to three, but the gringo failed.

The Mexico City Olympics ran late into October. So when Bill and Barbara returned to Eugene, it was to rain, blazing maples, and football. The sense of the seasons hurtling by forced Bill to look ahead to the next Games—which the year before had been awarded to Munich, West Germany. An Olympics in Munich was exactly what he and Heinz Munsinger had thought in 1960 would be most fitting, to seal Germany's return to decency. Now Bowerman fired off a letter to Munsinger, asking how the German planning was coming.

CHAPTER 23

Enter, Prefontaine

AFTER MEXICO, BOWERMAN HUNG HIS SERAPE AND SOMBRERO ON A NAIL AND thought about how to make the best use of the next four years. The first entry on his list read, "Get more help at UO." Bowerman had had dozens of graduate assistants over the years, but never a fully paid position. He thought perhaps the time was right to remedy that condition.

By 1967, Leo Harris had amassed two million dollars in athletic department surpluses. Portland donor Tom Autzen chipped in another million, and that year the university built Autzen Stadium, solely for football, across the Willamette from the campus. Harris then retired, resentful that the stadium didn't bear his name despite his having labored for it since the 1947 day he'd taken the athletic director job. Hayward Field was now exclusively Bowerman's for track and field.

The new AD was football coach Len Casanova, a little easier touch than Harris had been. Bill won from Casanova a living wage for an assistant's position. "Bob Newland is the one I'd like to have had," Bill would say, "but hell, he was paid twice as much being North Eugene vice principal as I could offer."

Bowerman thought Newland was probably a better track coach than he was. "Of the records that my kids established at Medford," Bill once said, "and they were pretty damn good records, all of them were broken while Bob coached there, all except one, and that was Ray Johnson, the high school quarter-miler of the decade. Ray ran 47.8 and if that had been an Olympic year he might have been Olympic champion. Or if I had been smart enough to put him in the mile, he'd probably have been the first person in the world under four minutes."

Bowerman finally hired Bill Dellinger away from Lane Community College. "Bill was good in the running events. When he was at Thurston High, he'd tell his boys that when you get really fit, running's easy, running's like brushing your teeth," Bowerman said. "Of course that wasn't training. Training is like having your teeth cleaned an hour a day."

Dellinger would be the first of Bill's assistants to work directly with runners of distance. In the fall of 1968 Dellinger's assignment was significant, because entering his senior year at Marshfield High in Coos Bay was one Steven Roland Prefontaine.

234

That spring, as a junior, Pre, as we came to call him, had set the state two-mile record of 9:01.3. Bowerman, who'd coached Marshfield coach Walt McClure in the 880, had arranged for Arne Kvalheim and Roscoe Divine to drive down and take a ten-mile training run with Pre. "I had just beaten Lindgren with my 8:33 national record," recalled Kvalheim, "and Roscoe was in 3:57 shape, and this kid took us out on the beach and kept saying, 'Am I going too fast for you? Can you keep up?'"

They not only could, they felt like leaving him standing, but reined themselves in for the sake of their mission. Later they would learn that Pre was bursting with a cockiness that had been long suppressed.

Pre's father, Ray Prefontaine, a carpenter and welder, had met and married his mother, Elfriede, in Germany while he was with the occupation forces after the war. Elfriede spoke German around the home, so Ray did too. When Steve started school, he knew more German than English and suffered for it. "Kids made fun of me," he would say, "because I was a slow learner, because I was hyperactive, because of a lot of things."

In eighth grade, he found he could run well. All it took was being able to stand the discomfort of effort. His need to measure up, in the elemental ways demanded by his Oregon logging town and port, turned into a need to surpass. As a sophomore, he finished sixth in the state cross-country race, but not before wildly trying to steal the race from the favorites with a quarter-mile to go. Earlier, he'd announced to his folks that he was going to the Olympics some day. He knew it. He could feel it.

His mother, who'd grown up in a Nazi Germany where the last thing you wanted to do was stand out, blanched and ordered him to never talk that way again. She insisted that he was an ordinary little boy. His father gently, gradually explained to Elfriede that the great thing about this country was that it was okay to dream big, but some part of Elfriede never absorbed that. Later, when her son enumerated the errors of the AAU for eager reporters, it would gall and mystify her. Plenty of other people had the same problems. Why couldn't they be the ones who stood up and exposed themselves to authority's eye?

In fact, Pre's bluntness was pardoned by anyone who grasped how good he was. In his senior year, all boasts were quickly followed by proof. He broke the national high school two-mile record by seven seconds with 8:41.5. He was getting close to Kvalheim fast. But even though Dellinger came to watch many of his races and McClure was nudging him toward Oregon (and was training him with workouts that Bowerman had suggested), Prefontaine wasn't getting from Bowerman himself anything like the recruiting pressure he was getting from a hundred other schools. Finally, though, Bill wrote him a letter.

It was a handwritten note. "I could barely read it," Pre would recall. "It said if I chose to run at the University of Oregon, he had every confidence I could become the greatest runner in the world." Pre signed on. Then he and McClure hopped on a plane to Miami for the 1969 National AAU meet.

That's where I met him, the night before his three-mile. Having been drafted and temporarily assigned to the Army track team, I'd finished third behind Jack Bacheler and Juan Martinez in the six-mile and qualified for the US team going to Europe. Afterward, I'd gone to talk to the feather-footed guy in a Yale uniform whom I'd sat on all the way and outkicked with a violent, 26-second last 200. "Sorry about that," I said. "If I didn't make the team, it was infantry training and 'Nam for me."

"Jesus Christ!" said Frank Shorter, "Why didn't you say something? We could have worked it out. You didn't have to kill yourself like that." That was the beginning of a beautiful friendship.

Another commenced that evening, when Walt McClure hailed me in the cafeteria and introduced Steve Prefontaine, who seemed properly abashed to be dining in the company of Olympians. I said I'd heard great things about him and that Jerry Uhrhammer, the Eugene *Register-Guard* sports editor, had commissioned me as a stringer to file a story on the meet, so what were his hopes? "That I survive this *heat*," he said.

The three-mile was run in ninety degrees and eighty percent humidity. Lindgren and Tracy Smith ran away early and dueled to the line. Smith barely took it, though both were timed in 13:18.4. Pre began strongly but fell back to seventh with a mile to go. He looked doughy and white, not the kind of body to endure these conditions. But then he started passing people on sheer will and drove in fourth, in 13:43.0. Since Martinez in third was Mexican, Pre had made the national team.

"So," he asked the next day, "whadja write?"

I showed him: "Today, America's two best three-milers battled it out to the line, then turned and watched the future racing up at them." He kept that clipping in his wallet for a while.

I knew about his wallet because we were roommates on the European tour. One discussion in a hotel in Stuttgart, Germany, was so delicious I entered it in my notebook. Pre, Lindgren, Shorter, and I shared a single messy hotel room. For the sake of team relations (and in my case, atonement), we agreed to listen to steeplechaser Bob Price's Campus Crusade for Christ presentation. We were all there except Pre when Price came to the room and distributed little booklets. Page one showed how The Fall estranged man from God.

Lindgren held up a timid little hand. "Have I got this straight?" he asked. "Adam and Eve didn't know right from wrong until *after* they ate the apple?"

"Right," said Price. "The Bible says, 'and then they were ashamed.'"

"Okay, well, so how fair was that of God?"

"It was fair. God had told them not to eat it. They disobeyed."

"But they didn't know right from wrong yet. They didn't know they'd be ashamed until they were ashamed. It seems like blaming a puppy. You'd think He'd give them another chance, after they could feel shame."

"And God cut us off over that?" asked Shorter, who was in law school.

"Cast us out of the garden. And it's our job to repent and take Jesus into our hearts to get back, get right with God."

"It sounds more like God has to get right with *us*," said Lindgren.

"With us? Why?"

"He made generations suffer for our sinful nature when we didn't have a sinful nature. We had an ignorant nature. Wouldn't you give a puppy a second chance to learn? We deserve another chance!"

"You know what this was?" said Shorter. "Entrapment. Any fair-minded court . . ."

"Another chance!" said Lindgren. He began to chant. "Another chance!"

Price was saved by Pre, who burst into the room and started rummaging through his clothes.

"Steve, hey, you made it!" said Price, "We're talking about the most important things in eterni . . ."

"Bob, Bob, you're absolutely right," said Pre. "I know, I agree, and I promise I'll sit and listen, I will, I will, but not right now . . ." He found his wallet and checked his cash. "The hoods back in Coos Bay asked for switchblades and I found some great ones!" He ran out.

The silence was finally broken by Shorter. "Now, Bob," he said ever so gently, "remember when you talk to the kid about Jesus, he's going to be armed."

Prefontaine occasionally evinced a tough hoodlum front, implying that but for the grace of finding running he'd have been back dragging the Gut in his lowered Chevy with proto-gangsters. But he was so far from being a delinquent when I met him that I think it was simply a handy façade that let him reach out to hardworking friends and fans and be a riveting counselor of truly at-risk kids. He wasn't running to compensate for his upbringing or some gnawing inner failing. He may have begun that way, but ultimately it was wrong to think of him as running *from* anything. He was burning his abundant energy in the expressive art of all-out racing, driven by the innocent desire to be better and better and better still. He was running *for* something.

In the Western Hemisphere vs. Europe 5000 meters, he hung with Lindgren and East Germany's Jürgen May until the last two laps and clocked his best time to date, 13:52.8. We went on to Augsburg for the West German dual. Pre led all the way to the last turn, where the cadaverous Harald Norpoth exploded around him and won effortlessly.

Pre was mad from the instant he crossed the line. On the victory stand, while receiving their medals and pewter cups, Pre got into Norpoth's face. "I think it's *chickenshit*," he hissed, "for an old guy like you to let a little kid do all the work and humiliate him in the end." The crowd saw he was hot and started to jeer. Norpoth replied eloquently without a word, lifting his gold medal to the crowd and then holding it right under Pre's nose. This was a dual meet and the win was the thing, not politesse.

Six weeks later, Pre drove his light blue, jacked-up '56 Chevy the 108 miles up the Umpqua River from Coos Bay to Eugene to register at Oregon. He soon met a freshman classmate, then-javelin-thrower Mac Wilkins. Together, they strolled into Bill Dellinger's office to say hello and find out the time of the annual welcoming picnic at the Bowerman home.

Wilkins's intelligence shone from intense, inquiring eyes. If he did not always respect everyone he met, he hid it well. His demeanor away from a throwing circle or runway was always politely restrained. As Dellinger welcomed them and gave them material on academic requirements and class schedules, Wilkins spotted a glass-framed photo on the wall and realized what it was. "Wow," he said softly.

Dellinger saw where he was looking. "My finest hour," he said. "Tokyo, on the victory stand."

Pre went over, peered at Bob Schul hung with gold and Bill Dellinger hung with bronze, and started stabbing his finger at the picture. Wilkins thought he was going to break the glass. "That's the guy!" Pre yelled. "That's the chickenshit guy who sat on me in Germany!"

Wearing silver, of course, was Harald Norpoth, whom Pre by now had sworn to hunt down and defeat. "He's a smart runner," said Dellinger. "In fact, I like to think that picture is of the three smartest guys in the race. We didn't chase after Clarke when he tried to surge away, and we didn't try kicking from 400 out like crazy Jazy."

"I would have run like Clarke," Pre announced with conviction that carried down the hall. "I would have made it hard all the way!"

"Notice," said Dellinger, "Clarke isn't in that picture. Clarke got eighth."

Later, Bowerman asked Dellinger what all the excitement had been about. Dellinger sketched the scene. "Ah, with the talent," Bowerman sighed, "comes the temperament." He sighed that occasionally over the years, but more often in the Prefontaine era. The exchange in Dellinger's office had been Pre's first salvo in a debate over front-running.

That week, after an orientation run through Hendricks Park with some upper-classmen, Pre went with them to the sauna, where they discovered Bowerman already there. Still coming off his trip to Europe, Pre told how the AAU's Dan Ferris had put the US team in an unsanitary hole of a hotel in Augsburg, Germany, while Ferris himself lived high on the hog across town. As Pre was getting worked up, Bowerman stood as if he was leaving, but then sat down right next to him, covering his key ring with his towel. Many eyes noted the keys. Many glances were exchanged.

"Apropos of the AAU," Bill said, "I'm sorry to tell you that the USOC has again refused to recognize the NCAA-backed Track and Field Federation. The AAU is still our governing body. I don't know how those old men figure to keep from stagnating if they don't let in new blood." He stood again. "It's understandable," he said. "They're crotchety old men, those kings of Olympic House. They don't want to change. It hurts to change."

Bill slapped his keys on the inside of Pre's thigh. "Doesn't it hurt to change?" he asked in his merry way, pressing down as the heated brass did its work.

"Sometimes it hurts more," Pre finally shouted, "just to sit and take it!"

Bill hadn't expected this. As he went out the door, the others could see he was impressed. Pre, inspecting the welt, came to a realization. He turned on everyone there. "Oh, you fuckers!" he yelled. "You didn't warn me! What kind of teammates are you? You set me up!"

"Welcome to Oregon," someone said, when the hysterics had at least died down enough.

It apparently was a few days before Pre could feel it an honor.

Having both Dellinger and Prefontaine there that fall made for a change in the stress put upon cross-country. The Bowerman philosophy had always been that it was great to run over autumnal landscapes, but only insofar as it made you better at running over a vernal landscape, the track. The fall atmosphere was meant to be one of renewal and going back to basics, and for many years Bill didn't want to compromise the restorative nature of such training by peaking for major cross-country races. In his first dozen seasons, even though Dellinger and others had dominated Pacific Coast Conference meets, Bowerman had never sent a team to the NCAA cross-country championships. But in 1961, under Sam Bell, Oregon State did. Dale Story won the (then four-mile) individual race and the Beavers took the team title.

Spurred by OSU's success, Bill entered us in the nationals for the next three years. In 1963 and 1964 we finished second, to San Jose State and Western Michigan, respectively. The next year, the NCAA went to a six-mile distance over brutally undulant cornfields at the University of Kansas. Five of us were running strongly and thought sure we were ready to conquer. But some inexplicable weakening agent seeped into us all. Lindgren won, Western Michigan took the team with 81, and we were eighth with 229. Bowerman was so dismayed, and so concerned about the damage that repeated six-mile races can do to milers, that he didn't send a team to the nationals again for three years.

That all changed with Pre, and with Dellinger there to devote full-time to preparing the squad. Prefontaine and Lindgren, who had one season of cross-country eligibility left at WSU, produced three great races in 1969.

In the Northern Division, in Corvallis's Avery Park, Pre wore spikes and Lindgren flats. Pre won by getting away over the trail's sloppy turns and just holding on. They both wore spikes in the six-mile Pac-8 race on the Stanford Golf Course. Pre ripped off a 4:23 first mile. "We were never more than eight yards apart the whole race," Lindgren would say. "I'd try to shake him, and then he'd try to shake me. Neither of us could." They were still banging shoulders when they hit the line. Lindgren had won it, but they warmed down together, brothers in effort.

Race number three was the NCAA meet in New York City's Van Cortland Park. Lindgren and Air Force's Mike Ryan broke away from Pre in mid-race and consigned him to third place. Texas-El Paso won with 74, and Pre led an all-miler Oregon team of Mike McClendon, Roscoe Divine, Tom Morrow, and Terry Dooley to third in the team race with 111. "I don't know what happened," Pre said afterward. "I like a fast pace, but I just wasn't right today." Bowerman knew: "People don't appreciate how much a hard six-mile takes out of you, and that was his third that fall. The young man is eighteen. Mr. Lindgren is twenty-three."

As Pre and Bill assessed one another, Bill, for one, noted similarities. Both were from small towns. Both were blunt. Bowerman sometimes called Pre "Rube" for his hopeless candor, but did so with a wink because it applied to him too. "Or at least it did before I grew old and crafty," he said later.

How do you handle a hardheaded man? At their first goal-setting session, Prefontaine announced that it was great that Bill was the finest coach of milers, because that was the race he wanted to ultimately rule. Bowerman asked how fast he hoped to run. Pre said, "Three forty-eight."

Knowing that the record was 3:51.1, Bowerman kept his counsel, noting only that 3:48 was 57 pace. But over the wet winter and spring of 1970, he observed that whereas Pre was hugely gifted over longer distances and capable of fully recovering from most workouts with a single night's sleep (no extra easy days for him), he didn't have anything like the foot speed of a Divine or a Ryun. Speed, unlike stamina, can be improved only so much by training. Pre would never quite crack 50 seconds for a quarter-mile.

"But that winter," Bill recalled years afterward, "all he wanted to do was train for the mile, run the mile. It got to where on our spring trip to Fresno, when I put him in the two-mile, he didn't want to run it. 'I'm not a two-miler,' he said, 'I'm a miler.' I suggested that he might want to give some thought to which university he'd be running for if he didn't try this particular two-mile because it wouldn't be ours."

At that, Pre had turned and run out of the room. In fifteen minutes he was back. He said, "Okay. Fine. Got it," and won the two-mile in 8:40.0. After that one quick test of the waters, Pre never seriously defied Bowerman again.

In April 1970, running all alone in the WSU dual-meet three-mile, Prefontaine clocked 13:12.8, the fastest by an American in two years. He was a natural three-miler, and so good that any immediate concern about his kick was rendered ludicrous by the pace he could sustain. "The man was designed," Bill grinned many years later, "to run away with things."

Psychologically, Pre could not have been more opposed to the Burleson tradition of wait and kick. His bounding energy seemed to make it impossible to do other than drive hard all the way. His model in this was Australia's Ron Clarke, who broke seventeen world records between 1963 and 1970. The greatest was his 27:39.4 for the 10,000 in 1965, which hacked 34 seconds from the previous mark. Pre's favorite article of mine was a 1972 profile of Clarke for *Sports Illustrated*. In part, it read:

> *Ron Clarke was a front runner, yet not in the classic mold of an athlete who has no finishing kick and therefore must set a hard pace out of desperation. When he followed instead of leading, he outsprinted such fast finishers as Kip Keino and Harald Norpoth. Shunning expediency, Ron Clarke was a front runner out of principle. He accepted each of his races as a complete test, an obligation to run himself blind.*

"The single most horrible thing that can happen to a runner is to be beaten in the stretch when he is still fresh," Clarke said. "No matter who I was racing, I tried to force myself to the limit over the whole distance. It makes me sick to see a superior runner wait behind the field until 200 meters to go, and then sprint away. That is immoral. It's both an insult to the other runners and a denigration of his own ability."

(Some will wonder whether Dyrol Burleson, who never raced any other way, ever met Clarke in a dark alley. I have no idea, but I do know that Burley and Prefontaine never seriously discussed their defining tactics, which was fortunate.)

... Among distance runners, who understand something of what Clarke attempted, will be found his most thoughtful judges.

In 1966, Clarke spent a week in Prague with Emil Zátopek, who at that time was not yet cast into official disgrace for having supported the liberal Dubcek government. Clarke retains the whole of that week in softly gilded memory. He speaks of his boyhood hero's grace, his standing in the eyes of his countrymen, his unabated fitness and energy. As Clarke departed, Zátopek accompanied him through customs and, in violation of regulations, onto the plane itself.

"He stood by me and then slipped a little box into my pocket. He seemed embarrassed and clearly didn't want anyone to see what he'd done. For a moment I wondered what I was smuggling out for him. Later, when the plane was in the air, I unwrapped it."

The memento that dropped into his palm, inscribed, "To Ron Clarke, July 19, 1966," was Zátopek's Olympic gold medal from the 10,000 meters in Helsinki.

"Not out of friendship," Zátopek had whispered to Clarke as he turned to go, "but because you deserve it."

Pre got chills reading that, he said, because it gave words to the front-runner's creed. He also liked the article because I quoted him on the ordeal of the leader:

The follower has only to match the leader's pace. He enjoys a comparative calm in which he can relax and conserve his emotional energy for a final, unanswerable assault. Given these realities, few men running at the head of a pack can avoid the feeling of sacrifice. Steve Prefontaine, explaining the savagery of his bursts to break contact with his followers, said, "I hate to have people back there sucking on me."

In the fury of that hatred, in the success of that breaking away, Pre had brought something unprecedented to the Bowerman stable. Bowerman himself would have to come to terms with it.

By June 1970, Pre had gotten his mile down to 4:00.4, and it was time. The occasion, as it had been for so many before, was the Twilight Meet. Dave Wilborn arrived for battle in good shape. Roscoe Divine, now a senior in his last home meet in the lemon and green, had been running sub-4:00s almost routinely in dual meets. It didn't sit all that well with Divine that a self-absorbed kid who wasn't a true miler was the focus of attention in his event. As he warmed up, he recalled being tempted to run away from him on the beach. Maybe it was time to conduct a little demonstration.

The early pace was modest, 2:01 at the half. Pre surged into the lead and the crowd came up with him. The time was 3:00 with a lap to go. Divine was fifteen yards back in fourth, in 3:02. The cheers down the last backstretch were of two orders, first, the jubilation that Pre was obviously strong, was obviously going to go well under, and then the involuntary "OOOOHHs" as Roscoe caught up and rocketed past him on the turn. Pre ran his last lap in 57 and finished in 3:57.4. Roscoe ran his in 54 and won by eight yards in 3:56.3.

The race showed both how fast Pre was improving and how prodigious was Divine's ability. In a fairer world, it would have heralded great races to come for both of them. But as Roscoe trotted his victory lap with Pre, their mile pecking order now firmly established, he was aware of a faint stiffness above one heel. It would worsen. Due to the hard new urethane track put in the year before, he had partially torn a few strands of an Achilles tendon. He would undergo two operations to repair it over the next three years, but would never race well again.

The 1970 NCAA Championships were at Drake University in Des Moines, Iowa. Three days before the three-mile final, Prefontaine was relaxing, playing around the motel pool with teammates, when his bare right foot struck an unprotected bolt that had been left sticking up after cement work around the diving board. He came away with a gash between his first two toes that took a dozen stitches to close.

The semifinals were the next day. "He was absolutely incapable of running,"

Dellinger would remember. "He'd never have made the final. There was one hope. If sixteen or fewer three-milers showed up for the semis, they'd be cancelled and everyone advanced to the final, and he'd have two days to try to recover."

But rumor of the wound had spread, to potential ruin. "If the coaches of the other three-milers had known how bad it was," Bowerman would recall, "they'd have poured their guys into the race until there were more than sixteen, and that would've forced semis to be run and Pre would've been cooked. So it called for a little thespianism."

Half an hour before the semifinal, Pre put on racing shorts and shirt in his room, did some pushups to work up a sweat, was driven to the meet by Dellinger, walked gingerly into the warm-up area, checked in, and sat down in the clerk's circle, spikes at the ready, exuding twitchy Prefontaine eagerness. "Several contenders looked at him and jogged right on by, convinced he was good to go," Bowerman would remember. "They went to the mile or six-mile instead. And so there were only fifteen declared entrants. He got his two days."

Pre spent them with his foot packed in ice.

In the final, foot wrapped as tightly as Bowerman could pull on the tape, Pre ran without a hint of impairment. This too was great acting. He led, but made no effort to break away, each stride being one into the unknown. With two laps to go, two tough men, Minnesota's Gary Bjorklund and Villanova's Dick Buerkle, challenged. Prefontaine reacted instinctively, refusing to let them pass. He ran two 60s in a row to keep them back, winning in 13:22.0.

"There's nothing like a little discomfort here," he said, pounding his chest, "to take your mind off a little somewhere else. But I haven't looked at it yet. I'm scared to look at it."

When he did, in the shower (with Bill right there, because his great fear was that by running Pre would split the flesh between those toes), it was no worse. The 10 points for his win lifted Oregon into a 35-all tie with Brigham Young University and Kansas. It was Bill Bowerman's fourth national team title.

The subsequent week was a true test for Prefontaine. He could only jog lightly in preparation for the 1970 National AAU meet in Bakersfield, the qualifier for the US squad going to Europe. I was running there as well, in my second year on the Army track team, as was a transformed Jere Van Dyk, who had qualified for the mile. Jere, who thought of Pre as a younger brother, invited him into his room to wait out the 108-degree day before their evening races.

In the last two years, Jere had dealt with the distress of not making the 1968 Olympic team by first seeking the cultural offerings of Paris. But then, like a character out of Lawrence Durrell, he kept right on searching. "After France," he would say, "I hitchhiked to the Mediterranean. In Spain, I looked across the water and thought of North Africa. Wanting adventure and to escape the West and my failures as an athlete, I took an old boat across to Morocco. There I discovered the world of Islam, and felt God calling me into the desert, God who would make me strong enough to be a great runner, the runner I knew I could be." In the final months of 1968, Van Dyk hitchhiked across North Africa, sometimes subsisting on orange peels.

He went all the way to Turkey. "In the Istanbul youth hostel," he would recall, "I met a beautiful Israeli woman, and changed my plans." They headed for India in an old Volkswagen. But then Jere got word from his father that his draft notice had arrived. "I liked America and felt she had given me a great deal," he would say, "especially when I saw so much poverty on my trip. I turned around at the Iranian border, hugged Susan good-bye, and went home and into the Army."

Van Dyk did basic training at Ft. Lewis, near Olympia, Washington, where 50,000 troops per eight-week cycle were being trained for Vietnam. After a few contracted spinal meningitis, the Army issued pain-of-death orders that trainees were not to mix beyond 150-man companies. Ropes and cables had been strung up everywhere to keep companies separate on the streets. No group could enter a barbershop or lecture hall until all others had left.

One snowy night in early 1969, I was a melancholy squad leader, four weeks into basic training, marching my men past the Post Exchange, when I saw a familiar profile among a squad coming out. I shouted, he turned, and the intervening ropes meant nothing. We reached each other and hugged like bears in the snow, a *Dr. Zhivago* reunion, while our screeching sergeants tried to separate us and, failing, started hitting us and ordering our squads to drag us apart, doing everything but drawing their .45s. I remember us, our hats torn off, laughing at each other's scabbed, shorn heads. For some reason, they didn't throw us in the stockade. Well, I know the reason. We were jocks.

Because of that, Jere and I, along with Neal Steinhauer, Bill Norris, Les Tipton, and Mike Deibele, were all assigned to the Army track team, whose members gathered every March at heavenly Ft. MacArthur in San Pedro, California. Ft. MacArthur had a thick, parade-ground lawn for morning runs and a marina next door. We awoke to the sight of date palms and the sound of clinking sailboat masts. We were loosely coached by an old friend of Bowerman's, retired Oklahoma State coach Ralph Higgins (whom Steinhauer dubbed *Cold Chicken* "because that's what he sounded like on the phone! 'Hello, this is Col'

Chiggennnn.'"). Olympians Charlie Greene, Mel Pender, Tracy Smith, Bob Day, and Tom Von Ruden were assigned to the team, too.

Coach Higgins had a single motivating sentence, the truth of which awoke you at 3 a.m.: "It's later than you think!" He was talking about the cutoff dates for making the qualifying marks for the AAU or Interservice meets. If we failed, we went back to our Army units. If we made those marks, we remained on TDY— temporary duty—until we had competed in those two June meets. If we then made the US national team at the AAU meet, Army Regulation 635-10 said our unit, wherever it was in the world, had to give us time off to join it. While half a million Americans were under fire in-country, we were running footraces in France and Norway. In the parlance of the barracks, we had it dicked, man.

The effect of being in heaven and not wanting to descend to the inferno was that a lot of people did very well, especially Jere Van Dyk, who built such strength by 1970 that he became a dangerous miler, especially kicking off a slow pace. Thus he had qualified for the Bakersfield AAU mile, and had invited Pre in to relax and wait.

In that mile, the pace was slow and the pack rough. Howell Michael's 4:01.8 won from the 4:02.1 of South Africa's Peter Kaal. The crucial, team-making third and fourth places went to Marty Liquori (4:02.4) and Jere Van Dyk (4:02.5). Bakersfield showed what Frank Shorter had become. A year before, just out of Yale, he'd scraped onto the AAU team and not broken 28:00 for six miles. In the Bakersfield six-mile, he displayed the results of nine months' training with Jack Bacheler in Gainesville. He and Jack tied for first—holding hands, which infuriated AAU officials—in 27:24.0. Gary Bjorklund was third in 27:30.8, I was fourth in 27:54.4, and Gerry Lindgren was fifth in 28:05.0.

In the three-mile, Pre led into the last lap, but his post-wound lack of training caught up with him as Shorter (13:24.2), Rick Riley (13:24.4), Lindgren (13:25.0), and Bacheler (13:25.4) all outkicked his 13:26.0. He was worried that fifth place wouldn't make the team, but Bacheler was getting his entomology PhD and couldn't go. Because so many people had doubled, the head coach, the inestimable Dr. Leroy Walker of North Carolina Central, simply took the top five in both distances.

Three major dual meets were scheduled for that summer, against France in Paris, Germany in Stuttgart and the big one, the USSR in Leningrad. First stop was Paris, where we arrived at the Claridge Hotel on the Champs-Elysée at four in the morning. Paris being a city of some light, Van Dyk led us on a memorable run around the boulevards, arches, *ponts,* and *iles.*

Bill Dellinger races
at Hayward Field in 1960.
Collection of BILL DELLINGER

Otis Davis levitates upon
learning he has won the Rome
Olympic 400-meter dash in a
world record 44.9, in 1960.
Collection of BARBARA BOWERMAN

"Peering out under their eyebrows"
Jerry Tarr (*right*) and Mel Renfro place first and second in the 120-yard high hurdles at
the NCAA Championships, June 16, 1962. © PHIL WOLCOTT, JR., EUGENE REGISTER GUARD

Bill shows off his pool of runners for the 1962 attack on the four-mile relay world record:
From left, Bowerman, Clayton Steinke, Dyrol Burleson, Archie San Romani, Keith
Forman, Vic Reeve, Sig Ohlemann, and Mike Lehner. *Collection of* BARBARA BOWERMAN

Bill counsels shot putter Dave Steen in 1962. © UNIVERSITY OF OREGON ARCHIVES

Robin and John Jaqua (*left*) became Barbara and Bill Bowerman's neighbors in the early 1950s, the beginning of a lifelong friendship. © NIKE ARCHIVES

For a promotional photo taken on the Bowerman hillside in 1964, Bill leads a crowd of joggers that includes Barbara Bowerman and Robin Jaqua (*far left*).
© UNIVERSITY OF OREGON ARCHIVES

With 600 yards to go, Bill Dellinger (*USA*) takes the lead en route to winning the bronze medal in the 1964 Olympic 5000 meters. From right, Ron Clarke, Michel Jazy, silver medalist Harald Norpoth, gold medalist Bob Schul, and Kip Keino. *Collection of* BILL DELLINGER

The 1966 team gathers around injured Bob Woodell at the Twilight Meet Bowerman arranged to help with his medical expenses. © UNIVERSITY OF OREGON ARCHIVES

The 1968 high-altitude training camp rises above South Lake Tahoe, California.

Collection of BARBARA BOWERMAN

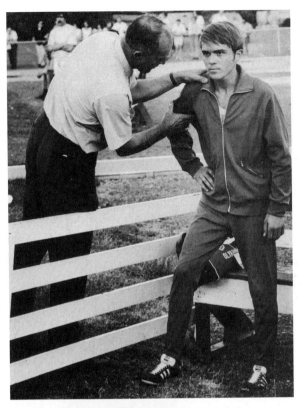

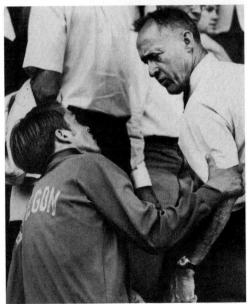

"There's not a picture where they're not asking, 'Who's boss here?'"

Bowerman slips in a word (*top*) before releasing Steve Prefontaine to run his first sub-four-minute mile in May 1970. Afterward, Pre grabs Bill's arm to press home his thanks. *Both photos* © JAMES DRAKE, SPORTS ILLUSTRATED

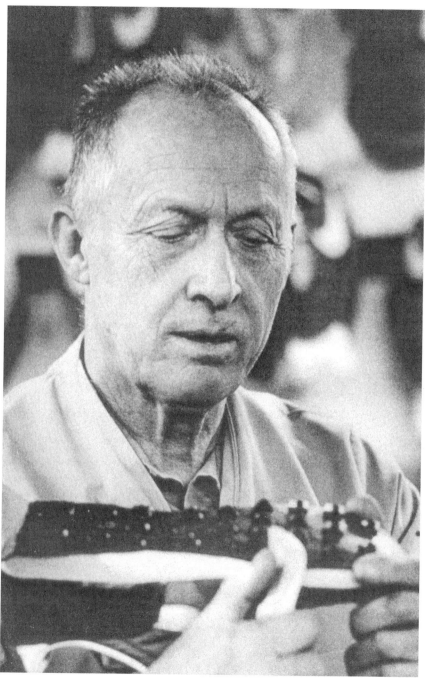

Bill whittles excess rubber from waffle shoe sole in about 1972.

Collection of BARBARA BOWERMAN

A mustachioed Steve Prefontaine grins in Bill Dellinger's favorite photo of himself with Pre, taken in 1973. *Collection of* BILL DELLINGER

Barbara Bowerman, Phil Knight, Bill Bowerman, and Penny Knight with the two Knight sons, Travis and Matt, relax after a Nike strategy session in the mid-1970s.

Collection of BARBARA BOWERMAN

Bill and Bill Cosby clown around at the Penn Relays in April 1993. *Photo by* JIM SHEA

Bill and Phil Knight cackle on the balcony of the Bowerman Building, circa 1994.

Collection of BARBARA BOWERMAN

Former Oregon Athletic Director Len Casanova (*left*) pays a call on the Tuesday Ad Hoc Group lunch in 1997. *Photo by* KENNY MOORE

Bill and Arthur Lydiard on their last visit, in Eugene in 1997.

Collection of BARBARA BOWERMAN

Bill and director Robert Towne plan the film *Without Limits* on the Bowerman deck in 1996. *Collection of* BARBARA BOWERMAN

Bill and coproducer Tom Cruise at the movie's opening in Eugene in 1998. *Photo by* JACK LIU

Bowerman expounds on the merits of his Dexter herd. *Collection of* BARBARA BOWERMAN

Bowerman feeds his sheep.
Photo by BRIAN LANKER

The Bowerman sons—Tom, Jay, and Jon—gather with their parents on Jon's ranch in July 1995. *Collection of* BARBARA BOWERMAN

Barbara and Bill were sweethearts for seventy years.

Photo by BRIAN LANKER

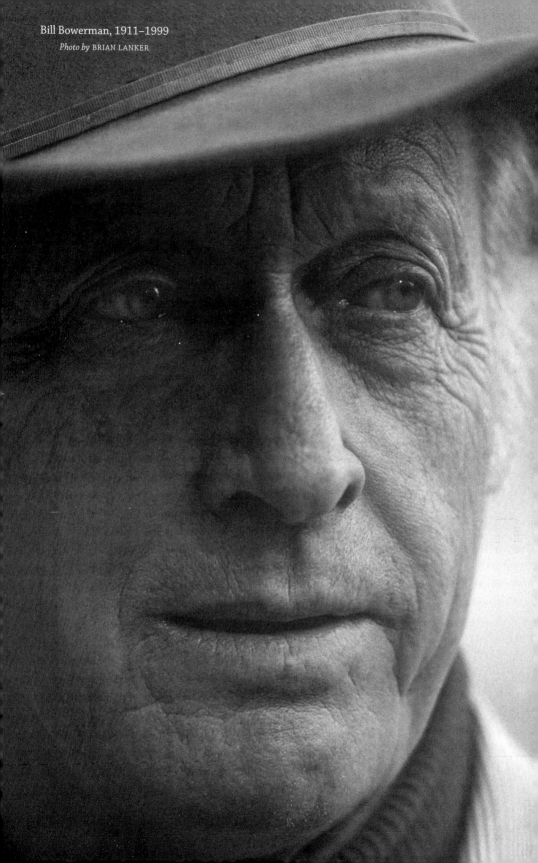

Bill Bowerman, 1911–1999
Photo by BRIAN LANKER

Prefontaine, who was still finding his training legs and wanted to be sharp for Stuttgart, didn't compete in Paris. Gary Bjorklund and I did, in the 10,000 against Noël Tijou and René Jourdan, who'd been fifth and sixth in the World Cross-Country meet and so were vastly favored. Frank Shorter's French let us decipher *L'Équipe*, the French sports daily, in which track expert Robert Pariente, whom we'd met, had written, "The improving young Bjorklund might be tough but Moore is a marathoner and therefore has *vitesse limitée* [limited speed]."

Tijou and Jourdan, perhaps having read that too, led all the way but didn't set a hard enough pace to get rid of Gary and me before the last lap. I kicked past them with a 26.5 last 200 and won in 28:47.6. The fates arranged that as I coasted to a stop, who should I see by the side of the track but Robert Pariente.

"*Vitesse limitée* enough for you, pal?" I panted.

"*Mon dieu!*" he moaned. "I have let down my countrymen!"

Years later, recalling Prefontaine during that week in Paris, Van Dyk said, "To me, there was always a kindness in him, a gentleness. He ran hard and was tough, but only on the track. He did not go around with a chip on his shoulder. He seemed relaxed without a great need to prove himself. Maybe I am idealizing him."

No, that was the nineteen-year-old Pre all right, at least whenever he wasn't racing Harald Norpoth. A few days later in Stuttgart he was doing just that, and I had a great vantage point because it was also my first race with Pre. I was tired from the Paris 10,000 and had to run another in Leningrad, so Coach Walker gave me a break and put me in the 5000. My tactical orders were to beat the second-best German, Werner Girke, for third place's 2 points, which I did.

Again, Pre led all the way. Again, the twenty-six-year-old Norpoth took off with 200 to go and won by thirty-five yards, 13:34.6 to 13:39.6. Again on the victory stand, Prefontaine growled, "Chickenshit then, chickenshit now, chickenshit forever," but Norpoth, who spoke accent-free English, pretended not to hear. After that, whenever Pre came home and talked about how he couldn't rest until the Europeans were truly beaten, we all knew he didn't mean the Europeans. He meant Norpoth.

If the German meet was personal for Pre, the Soviet-American one was public service for the entire US team. The Cold War was bitter in 1970, the second year of the Nixon administration, the sixth of Vietnam. We flew to Leningrad from Helsinki in a terrifying *Aeroflot* jet that never seemed to get above the treetops. Before we were allowed to disembark, armed guards came on with burlap sacks, into which we threw our passports as we filed out. Seventeen-year-old 1500-meter runner Francie Larrieu missed the sack with hers and they screamed at us to freeze until it was found. We saw that these perfectly uniformed, machine-gun-carrying soldiers, who had to be the most highly trained in their service, were sweating with fear. What monsters had they been told we were?

We were made to stay in the crumbling Sputnik Hotel outside of the city, the better to demoralize us. That was redundant. As Grelle, Burley, and Dellinger had tried to explain over the years, when you walk into an arena jammed with 65,000 malevolent Russians, as Lenin Stadium was that wet July weekend, you are oppressed by the gravity of the occasion. When their new sprinter, Valery Borzov, beat Ivory Crockett in the 100, the baritone delirium that followed let us know we were among enemies.

In the 5000, Prefontaine ran strongly, but was outkicked by Rashid Sharafyetdinov. He held second in 13:49.4. The track was gritty black. "That track," Pre said, "is a hard road." It was supposed to have some rubber mixed in with the asphalt, but you couldn't feel it.

Upon that road, Shorter and I faced Leonid Mikityenko and Leonid Ivanov in the 10,000, a distance at which the Soviets had never lost to Americans on Russian soil. Frank responded by running a race for the ages. Expressionless in his focus, he began with 66s, passing the mile in 4:25, world record pace. I let him go and found a tempo I could carry, 70s. But Mikityenko and Ivanov had no such luxury. The honor of Mother Russia demanded that they stay close. And they did for $2^1/_2$ miles, but then Frank glided away, running with a light, driving precision, passing 5000 meters in 13:55, a stunning pace, one held before only by Ron Clarke.

When the crowd—that great, educated Russian crowd—heard his split time, it came to its feet and thundered. Its love of track overcame love of country. It switched sides to roar Frank toward a record. At that moment, we both felt a weight lifted from our shoulders. I'd been laboring in fourth, a half-lap behind, but when the ill will evaporated, I felt free to run again. I caught Ivanov and set out for Mikityenko, who was dying ahead.

Frank was so gripped by the crowd's urging that he tried too hard to hold record pace. He would have destroyed Billy Mills's American standard of 27:17, but got a side stitch in the last mile and had to ease. He won in 28:22.8. I just made it around Mikityenko on the last turn to take second in 28:50.4. We not only beat them, we swept them.

As we four 10,000 guys did a weary victory lap, the sky over our heads filled with hundreds of hand grenades, flying end over end, lobbed from the crowd. They were cellophane-wrapped roses.

Everything had changed. What Frank had done was the single most dramatic example of sport catalyzing understanding I have ever witnessed. He was Van Cliburn making them cry with their own Tchaikovsky. His turning a stadium of indoctrinated Soviet citizens into 65,000 singing supporters should have let us see that the Cold War couldn't last forever. Eventually our two great peoples would get past our blood feud over whether central planning or the free market is better at distributing goods and services.

This outbreak of common humanity, ignited by a great run, gave those of us on that field reason to hope that other such outbreaks—ignited by sport or science or art—might overcome the fear indoctrinated into those soldiers on the plane. It would be no surprise that the thing it took to first pry open Communist China was ping-pong.

At the end of our lap, Mikityenko sat down on the grass, dug in his bag, pulled out enameled wooden toys—gifts from his kids—and handed them around. Prefontaine's eyes were alight. "These are so Russian," he said, "these dolls that fit inside each other."

"That's Russian *character*," Mikityenko said. "Many people within people, hidden."

"I believe that," said Pre. "After this crowd! God, won't it be something someday to get these out and tell our kids about this? Even though there'll be no way to really explain."

Some years later, Van Dyk, who had taken second in the 1500, would remember the Leningrad meet: "I keep a picture in my bedroom of me carrying the flag at the closing ceremonies. Pre is there, back in line, looking straight ahead, his hair combed, no moustache, his eyes wide open, bright and half-smiling, happy to be alive, happy to be there, as we all were. I will always love the memory of sitting in the infield with you and Frank and Pre after that meet, talking about what we were going to do in life. There are few things that can compare to being young and healthy and a part of a team that you want to be on, and doing well, as well as you could, and being proud."

When I finally made it home after a summer of racing in Scandinavia, I was discharged from the Army and resumed work on an MFA in creative writing at Oregon. It was a many-layered pleasure, then, to walk up the Bowerman lane, notebook in hand, for my own goal-setting session, now that I was back in his care. When I described the events of Leningrad, he was moved. "What a man this Shorter is!" he said. "His coach at Yale, Bob Geigengack, is a great friend, but he's never hinted Frank might be capable of this. I'm covetous of your being there when he turned that crowd. That's what it's for, isn't it? Boy, is that not why we do these things?"

I f you wanted to ask Bill Bowerman why he did things, then that fall of 1970 would've been a great time. What with coaching the national champion Oregon varsity and mulling a new shoe that might safeguard tendons such as Divine's on Hayward Field's new track, he had an overflowing plate. So why on earth did he accept the Lane County Republican Party's invitation to run for the Oregon State House of Representatives?

Was it simply a favor to politically connected friends, the bankers and mill owners who'd been telling him for years that his legacy as the son of a Republican governor and his spellbinding ways at Oregon Club lunches should be used to defend the GOP-held legislature against a rising Democratic tide? That was part of it. Many of those friends had given generously to his university. He was naturally grateful.

And Lane County was changing. As late as the 1940s, Oregon had been called "the Vermont of the West" (when Vermont defined Republicanism) by writer and later Oregon Senator Richard Neuberger. At one point, the GOP outnumbered Democrats in the legislature by an absurd fifty-eight to two. But Lane County is huge, stretching from the Pacific to the 10,000-foot Cascades, and with the arrival of cheap Bonneville Power Authority hydroelectricity, industry came to the woods and mills, employing men who voted ever more Democratic.

In 1954, Weyerhauser executive Robert Straub became the first Democratic Lane County Commissioner in forty years. In 1956, the father of one of my elementary-school chums, Charles O. Porter, became the first Democratic congressman in the history of the Fourth District.

As attractive Republican candidates grew scarce, the pressure on Bowerman mounted. Finally he relented, perhaps hoping that he could coast to a win on his reputation as a problem solver and educator. The statement he prepared for the 1970 Oregon Voter's pamphlet mentioned no desperate public need that compelled him to serve. After a short bio—he was a member of the President's Council on Physical Fitness and had organized the McKenzie River Protective Association in 1955 to clean up the river—he pledged to work to preserve the environment, end air and water pollution, relieve residential property taxes, and "ease tensions of student unrest."

Any other politician could have pushed all those causes effectively—except, perhaps, the last. Bill had seen several campus antiwar protests, including the February 1970 burning of a PE building that contained ROTC uniforms. He viewed them with a dismay that stopped well short of hysteria.

But many others did not. Tensions on campus had already led to tragedy. In 1968, Oregon President Arthur Flemming, having exhausted, he said, his political capital, had resigned to become president of quiet little Macalester College in St. Paul, Minnesota. He was replaced by a friend of the Bowermans, forty-seven-year-old Charles E. Johnson, an accounting professor and dean of the College of Liberal Arts.

War protests had so flayed feelings across the state by that fall that when obscenities appeared on a Students for a Democratic Society (SDS) flyer distributed on campus, the office of Governor Tom McCall was deluged with frenzied letters of complaint.

McCall, in what was not his finest hour, wrote acting president Johnson, "There's no one more fair on free speech than I, but after seeing its abuse in these and other recent instances, I'm afraid your way-out people are inviting restrictive sanctions by the Oregon legislature . . . . I plead with you to exert a measure of control so that a generally excellent campus climate is not drastically altered through an ever-gathering backlash reaction. Sincerely, Tom."

That would have been fine, except McCall released the letter to the press before Johnson even received it, triggering a storm of demands for Johnson to "clean up" the campus.

Bowerman seemed to have a muddy foot in each camp. The campus problems, he told journalism professor Ken Metzler (mixing a couple of metaphors), resulted from years of "running around in so many different directions that no one, least of all the man at the head of the ship, took the time to get rid of the accumulation of manure." But he also said Johnson's job would be easier if "so-called friends" [presumably his own friend McCall] would quit "taking potshots and throwing rocks at the university."

Things escalated from there. Johnson defended the students' right to free speech, but in that year when so many absolutely refused to grant their antagonists a shred of human feeling, he could never convince the most radical students of the strength of the backlash McCall had warned about. It was a virtually impossible job. Johnson, a perfectionist who believed in the rationality of both friend and foe, essentially consumed himself in a year of trying. He began to experience strange fugue states, coming to consciousness with torn clothes, finding he'd taken long walks of which he had no memory.

Another Bowerman friend, speech professor Glenn Starlin, said of Johnson, "This great, good, gentle man was cast in a modern tragic mold—he cared too much. He felt too deeply. As fatigue moved in, as disappointments overshadowed his solid achievements, despair replaced hope." On June 17, 1969, a few days after he was passed over for the permanent presidency in favor of San Jose State's Robert Clark, Johnson drove his Volkswagen up the McKenzie highway and, likely experiencing another fugue state, drifted over the centerline on a blind turn and slammed into an oncoming log truck. Johnson was killed instantly.

Governor McCall would be haunted by Johnson's death, once telling a reporter that he felt as though he'd murdered him. "I think he had tremendous disillusionment when he wasn't made the permanent president," said McCall. "I think he'd be alive today if he'd had that vote of confidence." It was a vote that McCall had withheld.

These were the stakes, then, in higher education in those years. It would have been a good thing, therefore, for the University of Oregon to have Bill Bowerman in the House of Representatives to reassure members from Pendleton or Medford or Coos Bay or Fossil that the school was not in the grip of Hanoi-loving traitors. When he ran to "ease tensions," surely he was hoping to chill the lawmakers as much as the students. And surely he also ran, though he never quite said so, to pick up the fallen standard of Chuck Johnson.

About the war itself, he and his state were similarly conflicted. Two of his heroes and friends, Senators Wayne Morse and Mark Hatfield, opposed it bravely. Morse was one of only two senators to vote against the 1964 Gulf of Tonkin Resolution authorizing war, presciently predicting a quagmire. Hatfield, who had seen the smoking, melted remains of Hiroshima at the end of World War II, never voted for a defense budget in his life. Such was the respect Oregon voters paid to independence that Hatfield was returned to Washington, DC, by greater margins each time he ran.

Nonetheless, Bill was a decorated member of the Greatest Generation, one of the thirteen million patriots who had dropped everything to fight a just war against an immediate menace. As easy as it was for him to imagine US Army generals being arrogant and ignorant, it was hard for him to accept, in 1970, that the war was unsalvageable.

He talked military matters with Colonel Embert Fossum, who commanded the university's ROTC department. "Fossum was an alumnus," Oregon Vice President Jim Shea would recall, "a big guy, craggy, the aging warrior. Actually, he was a rather sweet man with a wry sense of humor, who'd served both in World War II and Korea. I'd catch him and Bill at lunch at the student union and just listen to their warfare stories, or the japery of earlier UO days. (It was there I first heard the contradistinction between UO and OSU expressed as the difference between culture and agriculture.)

"The good colonel's program could be counted on as a refuge for a trackman with a shaky academic record who might otherwise be shipped to the Army and on to Vietnam. Bill always built bridges with faculty and others for the benefit of the program."

Bowerman felt Oregonians could disagree over the war. It was the intemperate character of the debate that he lamented. So, as his contribution, he ran for office. Unfortunately, to win he had to endure hours of panel discussions and questions on every issue from potholes to lumber prices. He tired of this in a hurry and stopped serious campaigning.

One writer said of his campaign that he didn't run so much as he jogged. Some felt the yellow and green colors at his booth at the county fair were a little overdone. As political reporter Mark Kirchmeier would see it, Bowerman's coaching fame was a big asset, "but one could overplay it and he did. Voters clearly respected, even revered him as a coach, but noticed that he wasn't taking the time to be a top drawer elected official." The *Register-Guard* would endorse eight of the nine Democrats in that election. Bowerman was the only Republican. "But," Kirchmeier would say, "about the strongest statement they could make was he was a 'team player.'"

Bowerman's opponent, Leroy Owens, was a Lane Community College professor who beguiled South Eugene matrons as easily as Oakridge mill workers. "He was a good-looking, personable guy who hustled and mastered legislative issues," Kirchmeier would recall, "and swamped the paper with letters to the editor with the tone of 'We want more than a jockstrap at the state Capitol.'"

Bill was a moderate Republican, not unlike his father the governor. "He was pro-education, live and let live on social issues, pro-choice," Kirchmeier would say. On the latter topic, he would recount a memorable exchange with Bill:

"Fall 1970, I'm visiting the UO campus and walking down the slope from Mac Court to Agate Street. I find myself walking beside legislative candidate Bowerman and I ask him, 'Mr. Bowerman, what is your position on abortion?' Bowerman puts his arm around me, a complete stranger, and as we walk, says, 'You remind me of a young woman who the other day asked me that very question. So I leaned toward her and said, 'Ma'am, do you have a problem you want to share with me?' Bowerman shrugged and smiled, concluding, 'I think I lost her vote.' His backwoods, borderline bawdy playfulness was completely innocent, but nothing that any rational Republican or Democratic politician would ever try on an incendiary issue like abortion."

Barbara felt there were two mistakes that cost Bill the campaign. One was that, at her urging, no Bowerman signs were planted on lawns (she felt it tasteless). "The second," she said, "was Bill's surprised answer to a question asked at a Republican candidates' rally. He had delivered a short, good, 'nothing to be against' speech when someone asked, 'What would you do if you find you don't like being a representative?' He answered directly and without a sign of thinking about his purpose, 'I'd resign.'"

Barbara realized then that Bill had stopped caring if he won. Indeed, at some point he had confessed to Tom McCall that he didn't think he was cut out for the politician's life. "You can't quit now," McCall told him.

It didn't help to be a Republican when there was a recession and lots of mills were down. Also a problem was word (from a *Sports Illustrated* story by Pat Putnam) that Bill had once wired a quarter-stick of dynamite to his mailbox when a trucker wouldn't stop hitting it and blew off a tire. The story, it turned out, was a typical Bowerman exaggeration. He had, in fact, booby-trapped his mailbox—with planks studded with big spikes that punctured the trucker's tires. Yet he told Putnam the dynamite version and never corrected the matter, even when it became an election issue.

In any event, Bowerman lost to Owens by just under a thousand votes out of 65,000 cast. It was quite possibly the first thing in his life, at age fifty-nine, that didn't go swimmingly.

Defeat, however, had freed Bill of his messy, good-idea-at-the-time distraction just in time. At its winter meetings, expressly rewarding his conceiving and managing the Tahoe training camp before the Mexico City Olympics, the US Olympic Track and Field Committee elected Bowerman to be the head men's US Olympic coach for the 1972 Games in Munich. Bowerman, who was in attendance, "was speechless," said University of Florida coach Jimmy Carnes.

Bill had long been ambivalent about the Olympic head coaching position because for decades one wasn't allowed the honor without acquiescence from the AAU. Back in 1961, in the midst of the push to set up the Track and Field Federation, Bill had written to Michigan's Don Canham: "As far as I am concerned, track and field is the biggest thing and, as far as seeing the Olympic Games is concerned, my preference would be to go with my friends, be a spectator, and enjoy the thing to the full. In other words, I would prefer not to be an Olympic Coach, even though I recognize it as the greatest honor that can come to a person in track and field."

Now that the honor had been extended to him by his colleagues, he was sobered. He accepted it in the spirit it was offered, vowing to shepherd and train the nation's best trackmen with even more care than he had in 1968. He mentioned how the Games' location in Munich was a great instance of peace overcoming the horrors of war, his war. And he added that he just happened to have some friendly nationals in place and could use their local knowledge for the good of the team. Then he went home and began pouring the ideas that were crowding his mind into the closest thing Eugene had to an Olympic movement, the Oregon Track Club.

The club almost immediately stretched its muscles by putting on the 1971 National AAU meet in Eugene and placing some new faces high among the finishers. The steeplechase showcased two, Wisconsin-born Mike Manley, who'd moved to Eugene and begun training with Bill after duty in the Marines, and Oregon senior Steve Savage, who'd run a 3:59.2 mile in the 1970 Twilight Meet. Manley's 8:27.6 and Savage's 8:29.6 put them second and third behind Sid Sink's American record of 8:26.4.

In the three-mile, Pre faced Steve Stageberg, who'd gone to South Eugene High and then to Georgetown University for its school of international relations. There, Stageberg had turned into one tough runner. Not that Pre's crowd felt that that was an entirely good thing. "We were both from Oregon, we were both Steves, yet he was the favorite, I the outsider," Stageberg would note, a little miffed at the one-sidedness of their introductions. "He got an ovation. I got little pitty-pats."

With two laps to go, Pre threw in a 63-second lap and shook off all pursuers except Stageberg. Down the last backstretch Stageberg went wide and almost got past him. The noise was two-thirds excitement and one-third disbelief. On the last turn, Pre began to inch away and won, 12:58.6 to 13:00.4.

Bowerman shook Stageberg's clammy, disgusted hand. "You just gave Steve a helluva lot closer call than anyone expected," he said.

"I should have won," said Stageberg. "I should have won."

"You'll have your chance. I'm sure of that."

The 1971 AAU meet—directed by Bob Newland—was conducted flawlessly and highlighted the growing sophistication of the Oregon Track Club. Not long afterward, the club received word from the US Olympic Track and Field Committee that if it cared to bid for the 1972 Trials, it was certainly welcome to try. So in mid-August, Newland and OTC board member Bill Rau flew to a USOC meeting in New York with armfuls of brochures and letters from Oregon officials. After Seattle dropped out, the choice came down to Los Angeles or Eugene.

LA made their presentation first. "They emphasized that they very much wanted the meet," Newland would recall, "and would run it on a two-day schedule, as had been done through 1964, to maximize attendance and therefore USOC profits. At Tahoe, of course, Bill had insisted on the full eight-day Olympic schedule, and that had worked out very well in terms of medals won."

When the OTC's turn came, Newland stood up. "Properly staged," he said, "a track meet is a thing of beauty. We feel we can do that on a Munich eight-day schedule."

While Newland sketched in the proposal, pointing out that the climate and elevation of Eugene duplicated that of Munich, Bill Rau overheard the LA officials chuckling that the Eugene plan was a box-office impossibility.

"How can interest be sustained for ten days," they whispered, "in a meet that could be run in two?" As promotions committee chair Bill Landers would later put it, "The Los Angeles promoters could not know what Bowerman and his friends knew—the inner workings of the Oregon track fan."

By a vote of thirty-nine to six, the committee awarded the Trials to Eugene. The athletes that Bill would be taking to Munich would select themselves at Hayward Field over eight days in July 1972. "Newland and Rau returned home," Landers would say, "with expansive smiles and nervous stomachs. There was work to do."

CHAPTER 24

BRS Becomes Nike

EUGENE'S PITCH FOR THE 1972 TRIALS WAS GREATLY ENHANCED BY BEING ABLE to claim one of the fastest tracks in the land. The eruption of world records on the Tahoe and Mexico City Tartan tracks in 1968 had finally convinced Bowerman to improve on Oregon's cinders. He approached the Donald M. Stevenson lumber family of Stevenson, Washington, and listed the virtues of artificial surfaces. They asked how much these cost. "Well," Bill said, "as with automobiles, there's a range." A Ford was rubber asphalt for $40,000 or $50,000. A Cadillac was the Olympic track—3M's Tartan—at $125,000. The Stevensons hung up.

"But they called back the next day," Bowerman would recall, "and said, 'Get the Cadillac.'"

He spent Cadillac money but decided against Tartan. He felt it was slipperier when wet than the urethane track of a company named Pro-Turf. Installation of Pro-Turf's liquid urethane over an underlying asphalt base was tricky, though. That base had to be level as a pond. Bowerman went to a friend, Eugene Sand and Gravel Company owner John Alltucker, who had certified Oregon's rings, approaches, pits, barriers, and runways for the NCAA and AAU meets. Alltucker came in with his crew and instruments and, as Bill would say, "put a road under our urethane that was level within a quarter-inch over a quarter-mile."

When the track was done in the summer of 1969, it was the color and abrasive texture of beach sand and let a runner stride out as confidently in a downpour as on a sunny day. Sprinters and hurdlers loved Stevenson Track's consistency. "Every step is the same as every other step," said the nation's best high-hurdler, Rod Milburn. "That's the key to hurdling." Its first world record was the 44.5 seconds it took UCLA's John Smith to win the 1971 AAU 440-yard dash.

But the track was hard. The disintegration of Roscoe Divine's Achilles tendon during the 1970 Twilight Mile was not the only injury. Bill soon ordered us to train more on the cinder practice track or the inner sawdust trail or to use flats. But flats weren't spikes, not at any appreciable speed. As Pre was fond of saying, "If you're going to run a damn fifty-seven-second quarter, you need damn spikes. Light ones."

So as a tongue returns to a canker sore, the Bowerman mind kept revisiting the idea of a forgiving spike, a spike with some cushion. One day, while demonstrating hurdle drills, he found himself scuffing his heel against the Pro-Turf substance. "I had a thought," he would recall. "If I made a racing shoe with a urethane sole, I would have urethane to urethane contact. Like on like. As with fish skin in water, this would either be very good or very bad, very slippery or very grippy." He procured a sheet of urethane, used it to sole a pair of racing uppers, put them on an unremembered sprinter, and sent him out to cruise a few turns. "Grippy or slippery?" he asked.

"Grippy. Definitely grippy."

"So at least I knew," Bill would say later, "that it wasn't entirely dumb to fool around with urethane. The real question was, What sole configuration would make it grippiest?" The smooth soles he'd fashioned were not much grabbier than other flats. "But you could have some kind of pattern of grooves or ridges," he'd say. "Should they be suction cups, or football cleats, or ripples, or what?"

Bill realized he needed a mold that he could heat. One summer Sunday morning in 1971, when Barbara was at church, his roving eye fell upon their waffle iron. He opened it and ran his fingers over its square little iron nubs. "They felt," he recalled, "halfway between spikes and cleats."

He absconded with the waffle iron to his shop, poured in some liquid urethane, turned on the heat—and bonded it shut. He hadn't put in the agent to release it. In any case, he realized, he wouldn't have gotten those little nubs. He'd have gotten a plastic waffle, with little holes for syrup and butter. No, the nubs he wanted were the reverse of a waffle.

Bill bought two more waffle irons. He replaced Barbara's and poured plaster in the second, making a mold that would yield nubs. He took that to a friend at Oregon Rubber Company and asked that molten rubber be poured in and pressed. The mold broke. He brought another. It melted. He brought a third, one he'd had a machinist create by punching nub-sized holes with an awl, one by one, into stainless steel. It held. Finally, he was able to peel off an eighteen-inch-square sheet of rubber nubs.

Using the same mold at home, he made his holy grail: golden sheets of urethane nubs. At last he was able to sole some experimental shoes—but for whom? Prefontaine, Manley, and I were at the Pan American Games in Cali, Colombia. But Geoff Hollister was back from the Navy. Bill called him.

Hollister was two years my junior and had been such a promising miler at South Eugene High that Bernie Wagner had offered him a scholarship to Oregon State. There was zero chance of him going, however, because he'd grown up even more imprinted by the sight of Oregon runners than I.

He was fourteen when he first set foot on Hayward Field. It was in the summer of 1960, on an afternoon when the US national team—Otis Davis among them—was working out before that year's Olympic training meet. Geoff gloried in the length of their leaps and throws, then collected autographs until everyone had left and he was alone with the hunched old grandstands and history. He slipped off his tennis shoes and socks, went to the starting line, and crouched there like Davis until he heard the report of a distant gun. Hollister ran a single lap as hard as he could. When he sank gasping onto the infield, his feet were burning. Hayward's cinders had abraded them down to their oozing quick.

Hollister had just enacted a microcosm of his varsity racing career. He had genuine talent in the mile and steeplechase, but became famous for his uncontrollable starts. We, Bowerman included, would wince and turn away from his ripping yet another 59-second first lap and then crawling in with yet another 4:09 mile. If Geoff had once begun with a conservative 62 and been able to use his considerable speed late, he could have approached four minutes. He seemed a classic case of wanting it too much.

Then, in the fall of 1965, when I was a senior and he a sophomore, he seemed to mellow out, gain more command. In cross-country, he was running better and better, always in our top seven, the number we took to the nationals. The race that Bill decreed would settle the spots on the team was the Northern Division meet, in the mud of Corvallis's Avery Park. Bowerman, knowing the going would be sloppy, made special shoes for Geoff.

The mire sucked them off twice. Geoff went back for the first. The second he left and ran on, finishing with feet almost as raw as they had been at age fourteen. He was seething. Bill himself had broken the nothing-new-in-a-big-race rule, but it was Geoff who paid. Bowerman left him off the team to the nationals in Kansas. "He wasn't in our top seven at division," was Bill's entire statement.

"The reason I wasn't in the top seven," fumed Geoff, "was Bill's stupid shoes!"

It made no difference that we all ran terribly at those nationals; Hollister wouldn't let it go. For months, he avoided speaking to our coach. He came to workouts, did them, avoided Bill's eye, and left.

In the spring, Bill cornered him. "You're still pissed at me for leaving you off that team," he said.

"You bet I am. What you did is hard to forgive."

Bill paused enough to make what came next a pronouncement. "Well then," he said, "it looks like you have a decision to make." He walked off. Geoff either had to quit the team or return to it in spirit as well as in body. Whether he truly forgave Bowerman is known only to Geoff, but he got back on the team in all other respects. Which Bowerman noted and accepted.

The next year, 1966, Phil Knight asked Bowerman to suggest a candidate to do what Phil himself had done during the company's early days—drive all over making Tigers known to teams and coaches, a job requiring boundless energy and morale. Bowerman said, Let me talk to Hollister.

Hollister would recall that it wasn't too long after Bill had given him the standard lecture about not doing too many extracurricular things that he called him in and said he had another job for him, selling shoes for Buck Knight.

Hollister had never heard of Knight, but called him up. They had burgers and shakes at the Eugene Dairy Queen, for which Geoff paid because Buck seldom had cash. Knight offered him the two-dollar commission that Grelle and others were getting. But he gave Hollister the whole of Oregon for his territory. Long before Hollister graduated, he was covering the state constantly, conducting running clinics in small towns and large, where he'd throw open the trunk of his little silver Moretti and sell the Tigers that tumbled forth to bedazzled, yearning young men not unlike himself. This was a perfect use for Hollister's native zeal. He felt part of a burgeoning mission to spread running, and the strength of that feeling made it happen.

Yet the work compromised Hollister's own training, and no one knew that better than Bowerman. Bill seemed to have written Geoff off as a future tiger, but knew that the very emotion he struggled to control on the track would carry him through the demands of the job. As it happened, Geoff was a better fit on Knight's team than on Bill's.

Hollister was Blue Ribbon Sports's third employee. The second was Phil Knight's sister, Jeanne, who shipped orders from the Knight family home, answering the phone in Phil's bedroom.

The first had been Jeffrey Owen Johnson, a bright, bookish romantic who grew up in Menlo Park, California, the son of an airline executive who'd begun an office-equipment company. Johnson was a middle-distance man with too little speed for the 800, so he dreamed of being a miler and two-miler, "Not that I had the strength either," he would say, "but it seemed a more reasonable dream."

Johnson at nineteen found himself miserable in the University of Colorado track program and looking to transfer. He applied to Oregon and Stanford and was astounded when both accepted him. He chose Stanford, but always wondered what Bowerman would have made of him. In the spring of 1962, he ran the prelims of the Stanford intramural 880. In his heat was a pale, blond, business graduate student in old Oregon shorts.

At the gun, Phil Knight led. The taller Johnson tucked in and studied him. Knight ran smartly and sprinted away from Johnson to win, 2:04 to 2:05, but Johnson felt he'd be able to take him in the final if he kicked on the backstretch. But before that final, Knight was disqualified, the rule being that anyone who had lettered in a varsity sport (as he had at Oregon) couldn't run intramurals. Johnson won unchallenged in 2:01.

Johnson took his anthropology degree in 1964 and entered UCLA's graduate school in that department. He took a series of jobs, doing social work for Los Angeles County and selling shoes for the Adidas distributor. Johnson was at a track meet at Occidental College, in Glendale, when he saw Knight again, and he uncharacteristically (Johnson was not the most social of souls) walked up and said hi. In the course of the conversation, Knight showed Jeff a bag of Tigers. When Jeff was convinced of their quality, Buck said, "I'm looking for guys who can help me sell them. Interested?" Johnson was, mildly, but had no time.

By early January 1965, however, Johnson was married and living in a Seal Beach apartment, with a daughter on the way. He called Knight and said, "I'm now free to do this. I'm not completely gung ho. I just haven't anything better to do at the moment." In February, he made his first major order, fifty-two pairs, worth $387.25. Some retailed for up to $11.95, and he got a $2.00 commission on flats, $2.25 on spikes.

He'd ordered four models, the TG-22 road training flat that would stress me unto fracture that year, the TG-23 Limber Up for cross-country, the TG-26A spikes, and the light, TG-4 road racing flat. Showing them around for the first time at a road race, Johnson took thirteen orders.

"It dawned on me that people needed these shoes," he would say. "I was doing them a favor. Tigers weren't as good as Adidas, but they were also not twice the money and five times as hard to get. That night I stopped worrying about selling shoes and started worrying about how to get them." He called Knight's office and found out there wasn't a single pair of TG-4s left in stock. So, with absolutely no guidance from Knight, he built a customer mailing list, got BRS stationery, took out a business license, ran mail-order ads in Long Distance Log, and learned rudimentary bookkeeping. He soon had the top LA road racers, including 1960 Olympic marathoner Bobby Cons, in Tigers.

That fall, Johnson realized he couldn't sate all of LA's desire for shoes during cross-country season if he didn't work full-time at it. He quit his social worker job and Knight advanced him $400 a month against commissions. It paid off. At the end of 1965, BRS's first full year in business, the company had retailed more than $20,000 of shoes. Many of those Johnson had sold in the LA area and by mail order. Gross profit was $7,260. The company's net was $3,240.

By 1966, Johnson was selling so many Tigers that his commissions were outstripping his advances. Johnson suggested two things to Knight, that he become BRS's first salaried employee and that he open a retail store. "I had to," Johnson said later, "if only to keep athletes out of my apartment twenty-four seven." Buck agreed to both.

"Jeff was a real shoe nut," Knight would say. "But it turned out he was also just bright as hell and really into this business, so he soon became a lot more than just the shoe peddler."

The first BRS store opened in 1967 at 3107 Pico Boulevard in Santa Monica, next to a beauty salon. Johnson was soon managing the retail store and mail-order operation, writing ads, and pushing shoes at races. Serious runners came to know his name almost subliminally, because he took exceptional photos at every major meet he could get to, which were gobbled up by *Track and Field News* and run with a tiny "Photo by Jeff Johnson" credit line.

That's what he was doing when I met him at the 1966 national AAU cross-country race at Pierce Junior College in Woodland Hills. After finishing fourth, I'd changed into my flats when he came over and pointed at them. "I sell all the Tigers down here," he said, "but this is the first time I've seen those."

"They're the Cortez," I said. "Don't they keep you in the loop?"

"I worked for the company two years before I had my first phone call!"

Years later, Johnson reflected on that cry.

"It sounds preposterous now, but it was true," he said. "Knight never communicated. The BRS 'office'—his house where he still lived with his parents—never called me and he was never there when I called it. I got to know his sister very well. Sometimes I'd learn about my company's top-of-the-line shoes by seeing them run by on athletes' feet. Later, dealers would show me my own line. The head office wouldn't alert me to a thing."

For the first six years after he joined the company, Johnson didn't set foot in Oregon, in part because in 1967 Knight sent him to establish an East Coast beachhead. Again, communication was comic. Knight hired John Bork, who'd been a world-class half-miler, to take over for Johnson in the Santa Monica store—but he didn't tell Johnson. It was a memorable moment for both when Bork strode in the store and announced he was the new manager.

"If this happened in any other operation than Buck Knight's," Jeff said later,

"I'd have been sick at seeming to be fired like that, all my work for nothing. But somehow I knew that just couldn't be."

It wasn't. Knight showed up the next day, embarrassed to find that Bork had gotten there first. "You just got a new job," he told Jeff, fanning out a sheaf of New England travel brochures. "A big shipment from Onitsuka is at sea, heading for New York Harbor. Cross-country season is two months away, and there's no way anyone but you could start up a new operation on the East Coast. Beat those shoes back there and be ready to go."

"I pick the location."

"You pick," said Knight. "Anywhere but Portland, Maine. We confuse our factory enough as it is."

Johnson drove across the continent, met the shoes in New York, U-Hauled them to an old house he'd rented by a funeral parlor in Wellesley, Massachusetts, and sold them all by October. He remembered the time as thrilling in its absorption. "The problems were obvious," he would say. "The solutions were, too. We just had to not let our growing pains kill us."

Johnson at least suffered those pains at a distance. Others were not so lucky. The first office Knight opened in Portland was a narrow storefront next to the Pink Bucket Tavern. Soon, as more stores opened around the country, a dozen green employees were receiving, packing, and shipping shoes. Penny Parks, a student of Buck's at Portland State who'd become his fiancée, sorted invoices. Knight's early hires were friends and family members who had no background in the tasks of importing and warehousing. Inventory counts rarely matched. The Onitsuka Company was shameless about shipping completely different shoe models than BRS had ordered, but no one kept track of the discrepancies. Business expenses were put on personal credit cards, ensnaring them all in thickets of IOUs.

Fortuitously, Bowerman had put into motion the wheels of a solution. "We were always trying to look for people who could help us above and beyond what they were doing," Knight would recall. "And one who saved us was Bob Woodell."

It had taken Woodell a year after his paralyzing accident to stabilize enough to leave the hospital. His weight had dropped from 142 to 95 pounds before slowly rebounding. After six months of bruising attempts to learn how to walk with braces, Woodell accepted its impossibility and sank into his wheelchair. During that summer of 1967, he battled the painful questions that erupt from loss and injustice and he fought them all down. He had always been a tiger, always upbeat. The reality of his disability could not overcome the reality of his psyche. "I am what I am and what the world has made me," he concluded. "I may never walk again, but I have a loving family and I can focus on what's important. I can live with that. I will live with that."

Bowerman had been keeping in loose touch. When he saw that Woodell had only been toughened by his ordeal, he picked up the phone and called Phil Knight. "Woodell says he thinks he wants to be a track coach," Bowerman said, "but he's had this accident, and I don't really think he can be a track coach and attend all the events you've got to go to out of a wheelchair. He's a hell of a bright and good guy. He might be good in the business."

So Knight called Woodell and explained that Bowerman was a partner in BRS. Only then did Woodell realize why the Oregon locker room was so thick with Tigers. "I'm looking for some good people to help the company grow," said Knight.

A few months later, Woodell began as manager of a new Eugene retail store dubbed The Athletic Department, which Geoff Hollister helped him open before departing to serve in the Navy. Hollister would always remember how Woodell growled at him when he tried to open a car door for him. Woodell's expectation to be given no special treatment was ferocious. But medical problems made him transfer to the Portland office in 1969.

He soon regained his strength, and more. When Knight and Woodell lunched together, they'd take Woodell's car, but only after Knight yelled, "Go!" and timed Woodell in rolling to the vehicle, opening the front seat, hurling himself in, folding his chair, and muscling it into the back seat.

The company was growing. "Sales were limited by how many shoes we had," Knight would recall. "Shoes were limited by how many dollars we had to order them." He and Penny Parks married in 1968. "I was still teaching accounting, but the next year, I told Penny if we sell $300,000 worth of product, I'm going to go full-time. She was pregnant and a little anxious. We hit $290,000. I said, That's close enough."

In the fall of 1969, Knight at last became a full-time employee of his five-year-old company. "There were nervous moments," Knight would remember. "Every time I brought a fresh letter of credit home and it said, 'Mr. and Mrs. Knight guarantee liabilities to the tune of $300,000,' Penny'd say, 'We don't have $300,000.' I'd say, 'I don't care. Just sign the thing.'"

As a full-time CEO, Knight centralized operations in Portland. For his top manager, he chose the meticulous and instinctively thrifty Bob Woodell, who promptly tightened ship. First, Woodell closed the Los Angeles warehouse and concentrated their product in a large Portland storehouse. He hired his mother, Myrle Woodell, who'd mastered warehousing at Pendleton Woolen Mills, to oversee it. Then Woodell reorganized BRS's bookkeeping to correspond to the fiscal year.

This all freed Knight to think more strategically. In December 1969, he took his annual trip to Japan and sat down with Kihachiro Onitsuka. He noted that Tiger shipments were continually late or contained the wrong shoes, which were harder to sell. Onitsuka told him that he was building two new factories to address the problems. The Onitsuka Company's total sales had reached $10 million, but were still mainly in the Japanese domestic market. So the founder had vowed to create a truly international company, an "Onitsuka of the World," he said. In charge of this aggressive dream he put an aggressive man, Shoji Kitami.

Knight and Onitsuka signed a three-year contract that gave Blue Ribbon Sports the exclusive right to market Tigers in the United States in return for selling only the Onitsuka brand. The contract would expire at the end of 1972.

During those years, Knight sold every cushioned shoe Tiger shipped him. This was because his thickheaded competition couldn't conceive that there was even a market for what the running and jogging boom was making essential— shock-absorbing road shoes. "That was the purpose of the Cortez," Knight would recall. "When we put that together, Bill and I sent over the components and said here, make this. They were kind of reluctant, but they finally did it. That was about 1967. That was the first innovation for the American market."

The amazing thing was how long it took other companies to catch on. "With the Cortez's cushioning," Knight would say, "we were in a monopoly position probably into the Olympic year, 1972. We had a great four-year run all by ourselves. Which gave us the sales volume to have a real company, kind of." Knight moved the administrative offices to Tigard, Oregon, and the shipping department into an old White Stag warehouse on West Burnside Avenue.

The company's success began to attract predatory eyes. Knight had always known this was a possibility. He had kept his best friend on the Oregon team, Dick Miller, in the loop. "When he really got going importing these Tigers," said Miller later, "and was working so hard to establish the brand, I told him, You don't have the trademark."

"I know, I know," Knight had said. That fact would always make him a middleman, ultimately at the mercy of his manufacturer. He was especially vulnerable because he couldn't get Tigers from any other maker. Therefore, Knight was acutely sensitive to any actions by Onitsuka that seemed to hint that the supplier was using its leverage for other than mutual benefit. But there never had been any. Just the opposite, Knight felt. Onitsuka had offered him advice as he might to a son. However, the Tiger maker's international growth was now Shoji Kitami's bailiwick.

"We had gotten people's attention," Knight would remember. "So a lot of American shoe distributors were going to Japan and telling Onitsuka, 'Well, if this two-bit outfit up in the woods in Oregon can do this kind of business, wait till you get somebody that's really in the business.'"

Onitsuka listened and sent Kitami to talk to Knight. In March 1971, they had a week of unsettling meetings in Portland. Kitami was carrying a fat file of what he termed market research and said it contained letters from distributors all over America promising to sell ten times in one state what BRS had been selling in the whole country. He said he planned to go around and meet with them and study the market.

Knight asked him not to go and said that if Kitami signed a contract with any of them it would be a violation of BRS's contractual right to exclusivity. Kitami would only promise that he wouldn't sign anything before he came back through Portland in two weeks. When Kitami stepped out of the office for a while, Knight slipped the Onitsuka executive's folder of distributor letters out from among his papers and put it aside. That night, he and Woodell read it. Kitami had eighteen appointments lined up in every major metropolitan area. All the distributors argued that the market was gargantuan and BRS alone could never meet it. Knight later slipped the file back into Kitami's papers.

Kitami made his trip and returned with an ultimatum. He had signed no contracts, but was ready to. The panting distributors needed exclusive territories, so to begin with, he said, Blue Ribbon Sports would give up New York and California. That was a fifth of Knight's business.

Again, Knight protested that it would be a violation of their contract. He also recognized it as a death-knell precedent. "If Onitsuka could say we don't care what that piece of paper says," Knight would recall, "they could carve up the entire United States and give it away to other distributors." Knight's company would have no reason to exist.

"After all these years," Knight said to Kitami, "after what we've been through together, isn't there some other arrangement we could come to?"

Kitami had been waiting for this. He said he would entertain one idea, a joint venture. A joint venture whereby "Onitsuka will own fifty-one per cent of the stock."

Knight was stunned. Onitsuka Company was clearly using its power of supply to take over Blue Ribbon Sports. Kitami added that Knight and Woodell would still have jobs, but would be supervised by Onitsuka executives.

"We have to talk," Knight said, "with Bill Bowerman."

After the initial shouting, when Bowerman and John Jaqua heard of Kitami's ultimatum from Knight, all three calmed down and came coldly to the same conclusion. The choice was between surrendering the company to Onitsuka or making their own shoes. Bowerman's phrase was "Find another hole to jump in." Bowerman did not accept that the company he'd cofounded was merely a distributor of other's creations. He had designed a shoe that let Onitsuka succeed in the American market. BRS had the right, he felt, to license that shoe to other manufacturers.

Knight agreed. And if they created a fresh brand, a trademark they did own, they would never be blackmailed by a supplier again. But meanwhile they had no other hole to jump into, no fallback factory—and they had debts they couldn't pay unless they kept selling Tigers.

So they played for time. Knight sent Kitami a letter masterful in its warmth and absence of substance: "I have spoken with Mr. Bowerman about your general proposal and he has been excited about the prospects." There would be no sign of anger. Knight told no other BRS staffers, not even Jeff Johnson, of the Tiger betrayal. Nothing would be said or done that might let Onitsuka deduce that they were mad enough to approach other shoemakers.

This was the time, Bowerman would say, "when John Jaqua proved what a great sizer-upper he was." Jaqua was certain from all he'd heard that their days of getting shoes from Onitsuka were numbered. "Go to Japan as soon as you can," he urged Knight, "and find somebody to make a whole new line." Knight heeded the advice, flying to Tokyo in October 1971.

A family connection was vital. Robin Jaqua's brother Chuck Robinson was a deputy secretary of state in the Nixon administration. Robinson helped cement Knight's relations with a huge Japanese trading company, Nissho Iwai.

Asian trading companies have little counterpart in the United States. They are the great business arrangers. Those in Japan specialize in different sectors of its economy (steel, autos, foodstuffs, and so on) and provide financial backing, shipping, and wholesaling, taking a small percentage every time. Often they do everything but actually make a product.

In Knight's case Nissho Iwai agreed to finance the first runs of the new brand. That gave Knight both the entrée and a loan of $650,000 to order 20,000 pairs of shoes to be manufactured by the Nippon Rubber Company. Without Knight's association with Nissho Iwai, the huge Nippon Rubber Company would never have bothered with such a gnat of a buyer. He ordered 6,000 pairs of the Cortez design, as well 10,000 pairs of tennis shoes and some basketball and wrestling models.

When those shoes eventually reached the US market, they couldn't very well be called Nippon Rubbers. They needed a name and they needed an eye-catching logo. The first time Jeff Johnson visited Oregon was for a spring 1971 meeting in which he, Knight, Woodell, and John Bork chose that logo from a stack of designs by a Portland State art student, Carolyn Davidson. Davidson had been instructed to shoot for something that offered both support, such as Adidas's arch-gripping three stripes, and "movement." It was impossible. "Support is static," she said. "Movement is movement."

So they separated form and function. They put the support in the shoe and chose the logo strictly for its raciness. They kept coming back to a fat check mark. Johnson, always a function guy, kept saying, "It doesn't do anything. It's just decoration." In lieu of anything better, though, they went with the check mark. "Maybe it'll grow on me," said Knight.

Johnson flew back to Massachusetts, where he'd built up the Eastern operation. He'd been impatient and distracted at the logo meeting "because only then had I learned the reason why we had to find a new supplier—Onitsuka's threats." Johnson had been depressed by Tiger's behavior. "They had the right to enter new relationships when our contract expired in 1972," he said years later, "but we had sold everything they had been capable of making for us, which was always less than we had ordered. What were they doing looking for a tenfold increase in sales?" Johnson thought the prospects of starting over with a new brand no one had ever seen before were grim.

But Knight had had a little longer to assess the situation. He amazed Johnson when he said in all earnestness, "Jeff, we have them right where we want them. Onitsuka is too slow to react to product development ideas we give them. They never ship what we order. And they'd probably yank the distributorship at the end of the contract in 1972 anyway. What we need is a brand we can control, because we have everything else, the shoes, the top runners. This is the best thing that could ever happen to us." Some of the vision in those words came right out of Knight's original paper at Stanford's business school. It was part of his strategy for beating Adidas in America.

Not long afterward, back in Massachusetts, Johnson got a letter from an old customer asking for a shoe made with "Swoosh fibre." This was a fanciful term

Jeff had invented in a 1967 ad for the nylon uppers of the Tiger Marathon model. Johnson sent the letter to Knight and noted that the word seemed to lodge in one's memory. Over the next few years, though no one recalled exactly why, the check-mark design became known as the "swoosh."

They were, of course, only half done. What brand name would be on the boxes that held the shoes with the swooshes? That was the question Woodell asked Johnson over the phone a few days later.

"Knight just came in," said Woodell, "and told me we need a name by 9 a.m. tomorrow because they're printing the boxes. But Phil says don't worry if you can't think of one because we've got 'Dimension Six.' I told him he can't use a dumb name like that. He said, 'Okay, come up with a better one.' Got a better one?"

"No," said Jeff, "but that's horrible."

"Sleep on it and call me early."

Johnson did. And while he slept, the memory of a Mainliner magazine article he'd read on the plane filtered through his subconscious. It had been about what made for a memorable brand name. The best were short and contained an "exotic" letter or sound: Kodak, Coke, Zippo, Clorox, Xerox, Kleenex. When he awoke at seven in the morning, his liberal arts education presented him with another, the ancient Greek winged goddess of victory.

He called Woodell. "I've got it!"

"What?"

"Nike!"

"What's a Nike? Spell it."

"It's the winged goddess of victory. Greek mythology. It has every hallmark of a great hallmark! It's short. It's got a catchy consonant!"

A gathering pause. "Got anything else?"

"No! No! This is it! Listen, Woodell, this is destiny, this is it!"

Woodell rolled into Knight's office. "There's a new one. 'Nike.'"

"What?"

"Greek winged goddess of victory. Nike."

"Sounds like a Jeff deal to me," Knight said. "What happened to Dimension Six?"

"Nobody likes that but you. This Nike thing would fit the shoes."

They had a 9 a.m. deadline to telex their choice to the factory. At five 'til, Knight typed it in. "Which did you pick?" asked Woodell when he was done.

"I guess we'll go with the Nike thing for a while. I don't like any of them, but I guess that's the best of the bunch."

The first Nike shoes began to trickle into BRS stores in Portland, Eugene, Culver City, and Natick that winter. They had vinyl swooshes stitched on the uppers. Of course, as soon as they sold a single Nike Cortez, they would be in technical violation of their agreement to sell only Tigers. But sell them they did. At the February 1972 National Sporting Goods Association trade show in Chicago, Jeff Johnson and the Blue Ribbon brochure said the new Nikes were "a parallel development to our Tiger line."

Dealers were confused about the new shoes but ordered some anyway, both to give them a try and out of loyalty to Johnson. Soon, back in Kobe, Japan, Mr. Onitsuka was reading that BRS brochure, airmailed to him by a prospective Tiger distributor. Shoji Kitami was on the next plane out.

Kitami hit Knight's office in March 1972. "What is this thing," he demanded, "called 'Nike?'"

Knight told him the new brand was a hedge in case the Tiger contract wasn't renewed. Surely that was reasonable.

"How many track and field shoes have arrived?"

"Just six thousand." (But by then he had more en route.)

Kitami headed to Los Angeles. Knight called his manager there, John Bork, and told him to use any measures necessary to prevent Kitami from seeing the Nike inventory. Bork tried to some extent, but Kitami said he was going to the bathroom, fought his way into the stock room, and started tearing open orange and black boxes. Finally he found a Cortez and grimaced with satisfaction. He had proof of BRS's betrayal and he knew what to do with it.

It wasn't long after that that John Bork went to work for Tiger.

On May 10, Knight, Bowerman, and Jaqua met with Kitami in Jaqua's Eugene law offices. Knight didn't know that many of the distributors he'd been threatening to sue for contract interference if they signed on to sell Tigers had actually insisted that Kitami formally terminate his contract with BRS before they'd sign with him.

Kitami said he was sorry Knight had breached their contract and handed him a letter from Kihachira Onitsuka that ended their relationship. Knight replied that the first breach had been Kitami's in lining up dealers behind his back.

John Jaqua softly said that disagreements such as this could often be settled if the desire existed to continue the relationship. But if Kitami had no wish to repair it, Blue Ribbon would proceed with legal action.

"We would still like Dr. Bowerman to continue to develop ideas for us," Kitami said blandly. Bowerman, as he put it later, "took the opportunity to educate him that that was never going to happen."

Kitami said that the offer of a joint venture, with Onitsuka being in control, was a very good deal for all concerned. Knight, finally free of the need to conceal his feelings, jumped from his chair, furious. Jaqua called a recess and hustled his two friends out into the hall. "You're not going to get any more shoes from them," he said.

As Kitami departed, Knight told him he'd see him in US court.

The next day Jaqua fired off a letter saying that if Onitsuka didn't continue shipping shoes, BRS intended to sue for breach of contract and to "enjoin within the United States sales of shoes developed by Dr. Bowerman and upon which there is a registered or common law trademark. These would include Cortez, Roadrunner, Tahoe, Simba, Jogger, Boston, and Olympia XIX." They would also sue for "damages for unauthorized use of the Bowerman name in worldwide advertising."

Kihachiro Onitsuka would testify later that he was unaware of Shoji Kitami's approaching other distributors without Knight's knowledge. But he didn't countermand his managing director's statements in Oregon. The rift would be irreparable. Yet Onitsuka the company couldn't simply turn ships around and sell the shoes they carried elsewhere. Many consignments made it into BRS's warehouses and stores. It was good that they did, because the new brand took a while to equal them in quality. However, it was not long until Blue Ribbon Sports was on its own.

"So that was when we started Nike," said Knight twenty years later. "There were some dark days in there." Yet reflecting on them made him summon the same words he'd used to encourage Jeff Johnson during the darkest. "Obviously in retrospect, that was the best thing that ever happened to us."

It was as a means of therapy, in that tense summer of 1971, when he couldn't share the Onitsuka threats with anybody, that Bill Bowerman began fooling with urethane and Barbara's waffle iron. When Geoff Hollister slipped on Bill's first test pair, he found that the "urethane spikes" on the balls of his feet seemed to grip almost regardless of what they touched, be it track, road, grass, or mud.

In the fall, Bowerman made me a pair and showed off his sheets of molded sole material. I, too, felt they had broader applications than just the track. I was so sure they were going to let me run away from Frank Shorter in the 1971 AAU cross-country race in San Diego that I got excited and ran the first mile in 4:19. Frank ran 4:30 for that mile and every other mile of the 10,000 meters, caught me at halfway and won. I got sixth. (Later, in the 1972 Twilight Mile, I ran a PR 4:03.2 in waffles, thought to be the fastest mile in a flat at that time.)

In December 1971, Shorter and I ran the Fukuoka Marathon in Kyushu, Japan. The week before the race, young Yoshihiko Hikita of the Onitsuka Company fitted us with Tiger's new Obori model of racing flat, named roughly for the Fukuoka Park in which we all trained.

We loved the shoes. Bowerman had not intimated a thing to me about Onitsuka trying to take over his company. In our blissful ignorance, Frank and I were unstinting in our praise for the shoes, Hikita (Frank would later hire him away from Tiger for his own clothing company), and Shoji Kitami himself, who attended the race.

It was only a great deal later that I learned that Bill had let me run in Tigers as part of the grand delaying strategy not to alert Onitsuka that there was a big break coming. Those pleasant hours with Kitami in Fukuoka were part of Buck and Bill's disinformation campaign.

Shorter won in 2:12:50.4, defeating Akio Usami and becoming a favorite for the Munich Olympic marathon. I got sick and crawled in twenty-ninth. When I got home, I showed Bill the new Oboris and asked how the company liked his nubs idea. "Buck doesn't seem all that taken by the waffle except for football shoes," he said. "But I'm convinced they're the thing to sole some road shoes."

Bowerman would revisit the idea a year or so later, when BRS board members would agree that training flats were the real market for the waffle sole and that, in fact, the waffle sole was the first really new product in shoes in half a century. But right then Bill had other priorities. "I'm discontinuing tests," he said. "We have an Olympic Trials to plan. We have a team to choose."

CHAPTER 25

Munich

"NEITHER THE AAU NOR THE UNITED STATES OLYMPIC COMMITTEE," WROTE Bob Newland in a paper he would deliver to the Eugene Round Table in 1974, "have any type of operations manual to assist a group receiving the honor of staging a national track meet. Each group evidently goes about running its meet while making the same mistakes all the others did." The Round Table, begun in 1912, assembles the town's academic elite and business people for purposes of mutual edification. Bowerman was the only UO head coach ever invited to join.

The Oregon Track Club, charged with producing Eugene's first Olympic Track and Field Trials, responded by leaving no possibility for error. "In January 1972," wrote Newland, "our organization table listed twenty-eight different committees, each with a chairman. The steering committee of OTC president Dale Pederson, vice president Ed Doll, treasurer Wayne Atwood, Olympic coach Bill Bowerman, and I felt it our responsibility to the incoming athletes to address their needs for legal, medical, banking, housing, food, meet information, transportation, hospitality, registration, and religious services." Since the Trials also included the twenty- and fifty-kilometer racewalks, the decathlon, and the marathon, each had its own committee. Oregon State University furnished officials for the decathlon.

The marathon course was two laps of the thirteen-mile loop along the Willamette and around Springfield used for the 1971 national AAU race. That had been Frank Shorter's first marathon. Tired of him always leaving me behind in the 10,000, I had talked him into trying my distance, in my town. At twenty miles we were together in the lead. I looked over. His stride told me nothing about how he was feeling. His question did: "Why couldn't Phidippides have died here?" he asked. I won by a minute in 2:16:48. Frank would not lose another marathon for five years.

For the Trials marathon, the track club wanted to use a new footbridge over the Willamette, but that meant crossing railroad tracks to return to Hayward Field. Southern Pacific refused to promise a slow freight wouldn't come along and chop the race in half. Bowerman spoke with Governor Tom McCall, who spoke with Southern Pacific superintendent A. W. Kilborn and the county parks department. One week before the Trials, a $400,000 tunnel under the tracks was completed and smoothly paved.

A less successful effort was to combine the men's and women's Olympic track Trials, which had never been held jointly. The protective coaches and officials on the women's side were leery of being overshadowed by the men. Newland had immediately written the USOC women's track and field committee and urged that the Trials be united in Eugene. "I said since we were doing the full eight-day Olympic schedule, the women's events would not only not get lost, they'd be needed, they'd be showcased," Newland would recall. "They wrote back that they already had their site picked, but I found out later they simply didn't believe me." The women's Trials were held in Frederick, Maryland.

"Many Knights of the Round Table were responsible for the success of the Trials," Newland would write. "Ray Hendrickson, our starter, is the best in the country. Dr. Bill McHolick and Mayor Les Anderson are our top high-jump officials. John Jaqua, our legal shark deluxe, keeps us out of trouble. John Alltucker and Jack Stafford make sure all is exact in measurement. Erhman Giustina is our fundraiser and expediter. George Hull and Lloyd Staples are our track inspectors, and we bask in the approval of our new University president, Robert D. Clark." Clark's support of Tommie Smith and John Carlos at San Jose State had been no barrier to his being offered the Oregon presidency. Bowerman would come to admire him for his scholarship as well as his courage.

The nerve center for runners was neither the track nor the athlete-thronged dorms. It was downtown, where flocks of ectomorphic, prominently veined competitors flitted through the Athletic Department store and were persuaded to stop, sit down, unlace, try on, and perhaps reconsider. Blue Ribbon Sports was taking exuberant advantage of its Bowerman-provided opportunity to introduce Nikes to the nation's finest. Its walls plastered with the *Register-Guard's* event-by-event Trials coverage, the little store was jammed even without customers. Jeff Johnson, Bob Woodell, Geoff Hollister, and the rest of the company had converged here to get shoes on feet.

Phil and Penny Knight were hot-pressing names on customized T-shirts to give to athletes along with their shoes. "How do you spell your first name, sir?" Phil asked a gnomic marathoner. "D-U-M-P," he said.

"Okay," Knight said, arranging the letters. "What's your last?"

"Nixon."

Thus did Tom Derderian run off in an emblem of the Trials' zeitgeist. Derderian, who later wrote the official history of the Boston Marathon's first 100 years, was camping on our lawn in nearby Lowell along with half a dozen other endurance men. Hollister's house was so full it was dubbed the Hilton. At Roscoe Divine's, Jere Van Dyk slept on a mattress with Gerry Lindgren.

Van Dyk, who had qualified for the 1500 meters, was again nearing odyssey's end. After being discharged from the Army in the fall of 1970, he had moved to Paris, run for the Racing Club de France, and studied at the Sorbonne, taking its famed *Cours de la Civilisation Française.* "I was exploring, a Plymouth Brethren in Paris," he would say. "I trained, ate, studied, read the Bible, and went to bed." In 1971, he'd returned to Eugene for the AAU nationals, walking onto Hayward Field, as he would recall, "wearing wide-wale green cords, loafers, a long, black corduroy coat, a silk turquoise scarf, and sunglasses." Marty Liquori walked over and said, "Liked your last movie."

Van Dyk ran that national mile in his blue Club de France singlet, placing third behind Liquori in 4:00.0. If he had hoped for a kind word from Bowerman, it was in vain: "Bowerman was nowhere to be seen." That fall, Olympic decathlon champion Bill Toomey and coach Pete Petersens (formerly of the Southern California Striders) began the Club West Track Club in Santa Barbara. They invited Van Dyk to join and he jumped at the chance to train during the pre-Olympic winter in what he thought of as Lotus Land.

Van Dyk's teammate and interval training partner, Jim Ryun, relished the warm, clean sea air. It was what he had come for. Ryun, who'd graduated from Kansas in 1969, was determined to redeem his loss to Kenya's Kip Keino in the 1968 Olympic 1500. He and his wife, Anne, had actually moved to Eugene in late 1970 seeking milder winters. He trained by mail, using workouts sent by his lifelong coach, Bob Timmons, from Kansas. But Eugene's pollen inflamed his allergies so badly that the Ryuns moved on to Santa Barbara. In May 1972, when the weather allowed, they moved back to Lawrence.

That same spring, at the West Coast Relays, Van Dyk faced his own internal struggle. Before the race he visited a former runner from his Assembly in Portland, who was teaching at Fresno State. "He had me get down on my knees and pray with him before my race," Jere would recall. "It was the worst race I ever ran in my life. I got last. I'd relied on God to run the race for me, to give me the strength to run. I didn't try myself. That worked for others, but no longer for me." Then, in the last lap of the Modesto Relays mile, someone's spikes raked Van Dyk's Achilles, ripping his shoe off. Not seriously hurt, he finished with one bare foot, and he was racing fit when he settled in at the Divine house for the Trials.

Could modest Eugene sustain interest for eight days in a meet that, as the LA promoters had scoffed, could be run in two? The answer came early. The first

morning's schedule had only a few 100-meter heats and the hammer-throw prelims, followed by four hours of nothing (when in Munich the women would be
competing). Six thousand Oregon track fans were equal to this. They arrived,
cheered, departed, picnicked, shopped, or floated the river, then filed back in for
the afternoon 800-meter heats, their number having doubled. All eight days
would be packed.

The Trials were a complete athletic success. In the 800-meter final, Ryun
seized the lead powerfully—too powerfully—with a lap to go. Bowling Green's
Dave Wottle ran him down and won in a world record of 1:44.3. Ryun faded to
fourth. For him it would be the 1500 or nothing. Eddie Hart and Rey Robinson
tied the world 100-meter mark of 9.9. Bob Seagren broke the world record in the
pole vault with 18 feet 5¾ inches. UCLA's Wayne Collett won the 400 in 44.2
from teammate John Smith, with Vince Matthews finishing third. Lee Evans, in
fourth, rounded out the relay team. "Safest gold medal on the team," he said.
"The 1600-meter relay."

The most emotional race for the town was the 10,000 meters. Jon Anderson
was the son of Les Anderson, Eugene's popular mayor, publisher of a lumber
market newsletter, and OTC high-jump official. Jon had attended Eugene's
Sheldon High, then, strangely intoxicated by the aroma of ivy, had gone to Cor-
nell. After graduating, he did a month of workouts with Bowerman, slipped on
our OTC green and yellow stripes, started cautiously in the 10,000 final, and
began moving up.

With six laps to go, three Florida Track Club runners, Shorter, Jeff Galloway,
and Jack Bacheler, were in command. But Bacheler was having a rare off day.
Anderson, sixty yards behind, was an emotional man, supremely equipped to
incorporate the crowd's frenzy into his own. He reached Bacheler's shoulder with
100 to go and sprinted in like Billy Mills in Tokyo, taking third and the last spot
on the team in 29:08.2. I yelled myself hoarse for him. When he came by on his
victory lap and hugged me, all I could croak was "You just changed your life!"

"The single greatest example of the crowd taking things into its own hands
I've ever seen," said Bowerman.

This meant, however, that five days later Frank and I had to run the marathon
trial in a way that would help Jack Bacheler—a great friend to all and mentor to
Shorter and Galloway—make the team. Frank and I set a tough, 2:12 pace to
turn the most eager chasers into wounded meat for Bacheler and Galloway—who
were running 2:20 pace—to gobble up. It took us thirteen miles to shake the last
guy, John Vitale, and then we coasted, our damage inflicted.

"My shining memory of those Trials," Frank recalled later, "was when we hit the track and I realized we could finish together and people would understand. We were running to get somewhere, literally and figuratively, not to compete. We were still training and this was to get to the Games. Finishing together showed we were still on our way."

We tied for first, in 2:15:58, and the understanding that Shorter described was such that no picky officials bothered to check the finish photo to see who had really won. They let the tie stand.

Anyway, the excitement was back in third place. Bacheler took it in 2:20:30, after he and Galloway had run through thirty men. Jack got an ovation out of moral relief—everyone knew how good he was and didn't want him to be shut out just because Jon Anderson had made it.

The crowd that last day numbered 23,000. They had not come to see us. They were there for Pre, and they rose to him in the last mile of the 5000 final, when he broke three-time Olympian George Young with ruthless laps of 63.4, 61.5, and 58.7 and cut seven seconds from his American record with 13:22.8. His great sense of theater led him to grab a "Stop Pre" shirt (that Gerry Lindgren had been booed for warming up in) and run 69-second victory laps in it. The sight of their champion parading the arena wearing the metaphoric pelt of the vanquished foe (Lindgren didn't make the team) made for atavistic hysteria.

Since Mike Manley had won the steeplechase in 8:29.7 and Steve Savage took third behind Doug Brown of Tennessee, five men—half of the team's distance runners—were Bowerman-trained.

Four of the top seven finishers in the Trials marathon wore Nike shoes. The brand's excellence was demonstrated, even though BRS's first attempts to make the word lodge in memory were failures. The lowercase letters on the box looked like "Mike" to a lot of people. And the swoosh in motion was hard to tell from the Puma side stripe. Art Simburg, the Puma rep, had lovingly cajoled and paid only sprinters to wear Pumas, but from the stands the mark of this "regional brand" looked so much like his own that Simburg kept exclaiming over how well Puma was doing in the distances. Finally Knight leaned over from behind and shouted, "That's not Puma down there. That's a brand called Nike!"

They wouldn't be Trials if dreams weren't broken. At the start of the 1500 final stood two men in the gray Club West uniform. Jim Ryun was a little self-conscious because, to minimize his exposure to Eugene's pollen, he had warmed up miles away in clean McKenzie air and taken a helicopter to the field. But Jere Van Dyk's unease was existential. "I felt like an outsider, no longer home. I was running on a different track, all-weather now, more modern—less pure than what we had known." In an echo of what Archie San Romani had felt before this race eight years earlier, Van Dyk wished he had someone to talk to, to give him encouragement and tell him how to run.

The night before, Jere had eaten in an Italian restaurant, alone with his thoughts. Dellinger had come over and told Jere he could do it, he could make the team. "I wished he were my coach," Jere would say. "He was the only person from Oregon I felt was on my side. I felt everyone hated me, with Bowerman leading the way." Yet Jere couldn't summon the strength to enlist Dellinger in advising him on the spot. "I didn't think to ask him," he said years later. "I was too solitary. I just figured that I was on my own."

We who thought we knew him never suspected that Van Dyk flayed his soul like this. In the evenings he was charming; in the mornings more chastened, but we never imagined him projecting such torment on Bowerman. His words seem one long yearning for reunion. Half of him wanted to transfer the burden that God hadn't assumed to Bowerman, to the only coach Jere could accept (otherwise he would have sought Dellinger's help). But Bowerman was as ignorant of this as we were.

Jere knew how good Jim Ryun was—"running with him was like running with a stallion," he once said—but felt that if he could just hang in there, he had the speed to kick in at the end. Van Dyk's tactic, therefore, would have to be to save that speed as long as possible. The modest pace was in Jere's favor, and with 600 to go he was in perfect position. He just had to be patient for another 350. But as he entered that stretch, the crowd came to full voice. Deeper needs assumed control.

Jere took the lead with 500 to go—and knew it was a mistake. "But I loved the roar of the Eugene crowd and wanted the people to know that I could do it, on my own, without Bowerman," he would recall. It wasn't enough to let him break away. Duke's Bob Wheeler got around him on the first turn of the last lap, and Dave Wottle and Ryun soon after. Jere got boxed in and others went by with 200 to go. He finished ninth, in 3:45.7. Ryun outkicked Wottle and Wheeler and won with a huge, uncharacteristic grin. At the line he thrust his arms out wide, crucified with joy.

"It was terrible after that, of course," Jere would recall. "My parents were there and I felt that I had let down my father, and didn't talk to them. They drove home and I wanted to disappear." Jere didn't disappear. He would go on to succeed in other arenas, becoming an accomplished international journalist and author of *In Afghanistan,* a book on his experiences living with the *mujahideen* during their struggle against the Soviet Army. Despite the emotional rollercoaster that seems to have been his career, Jere would not regret ignoring Ray Van Asten's oracular advice. "I am glad I went to Oregon," he would say more than three decades later. "I could not have gone anywhere else. My best friends in the world are track guys. I was never happier than when running the 440 or anchoring the mile relay and running, I felt, as fast as the wind."

Through all this drama, Bowerman abandoned his usual practice of watching from high in the stands. Instead, he was a presence on the infield, a genial general, welcoming new members to the team he was taking onward.

There, he pulled every string for them. Just as the 200-meter finalists were bending into their blocks, ABC wanted a delay for a commercial. Bowerman overheard the TV cameraman's walkie-talkie ordering him to run onto the track and take a slow shot of every tense face, thereby blocking the start until ABC was ready. The cameraman trotted to obey, but before he reached the track his camera refused to go any farther. He turned to see Bowerman standing on his cord. Bowerman nodded to starter Ray Hendrickson and the sprinters were sent on their way on time—meet time, not media time.

The last day's sellout crowd on July 9 brought total attendance to 141,100, the largest ever for an Olympic Trials, exceeding the 108,000 at Stanford in 1960. "Final ticket sales were $329,300," Newland would report, "with a net of $187,800.78. This was the most profit ever turned in to the USOC Track and Field Committee."

Bowerman wanted to put that profit to immediate use, but the USOC wouldn't hear of it. The USOC contract with the OTC expressly forbade the club from paying any athletes' expenses. Early on, having noted that stipulation with some disgust, Bill had solicited a pledge from General Motors for $50,000 to cover athletes' room and board. But the USOC had refused permission to accept it, saying that GM would have to put its money in the general pot and the USOC would decide where it went. GM withdrew the offer.

Bowerman then had petitioned the USOC on behalf of the athletes, asking that the top twelve or sixteen qualifiers in each event be reimbursed for their expenses and that machinery be set up to do it in the future. The USOC said there would be no reimbursing, not now, not ever. "Think of the horrible precedent that would set," said USOC Vice President Phillip O. Krumm.

"I've heard our officials make plenty of sanctimonious noises," Bowerman would tell me later, "when they were looking at a guy with a rap on him (boxer Bobby Lee Hunter) who might make their team, wondering if his morals were up to theirs—and then they won't pay back some fine athletes, some of whom weren't getting enough to eat."

So when the Trials were over, Bowerman took an idea to John Jaqua. "We're sitting on this $190,000 we made for our greedy USOC. Can't we use that for a little leverage? How about we seek an injunction preventing the Oregon Track Club from turning over the proceeds until the matter is adjudicated? We might lose in court but Krumm and [USOC President Clifford] Buck might cough up a little money for the athletes in order to get their hands on the rest."

"I salute your cunning," said Jaqua. "Let me think about it." When they spoke again, Jaqua had done some character study. "If you threaten somebody and they don't give in," he said, "you put yourself in a bad position. So our question is, if we sue, will these old AAU and USOC guys give in? My judgment is they have made their bones by not giving in. They don't give in on reforms urged by college coaches. They didn't give in on your gift from a big company. They don't give in enforcing the amateur code. Their entire reason for being is not to give in."

"So what do we do?"

"You give in. You give them a big, fat, beautiful check, and you are nothing but smiles."

"And? There's gotta be an 'and.'"

"And in two or three years you sweetly remind them where they got that check, and if they want the track fans of Eugene to write another one, maybe a bigger one, maybe a quarter-million for the 1976 Trials, there will have to be an adjustment or two, one being the athletes' expenses."

Bowerman, exultant that this was not defeat but rather the first step in a larger intrigue, gave in. He flew to Brunswick, Maine, where the men's team and staff was gathering at Bowdoin College before heading to Europe.

Dellinger stayed behind to oversee Prefontaine's increasingly rigorous preparation. "I can lose in Munich and live with it if I give 120 percent," Steve said, "but if I lost because I'd let it go to the last lap and got outkicked . . . I'd always wonder whether I might have broken away."

The Bowerman-Dellinger race plan would leave no room for that kind of regret. Conceived with Dellinger's experience in Tokyo in mind, the idea was for Prefontaine not to simply surge and slow, as Ron Clarke had done, but to free himself with inexorably faster laps late in the race. His battle against Young in the Trials, when he'd run the final mile in 4:10, was a dress rehearsal, but all involved knew he could run far faster.

Dellinger, both to enhance that ability and to know exactly what Pre could stand, put him through training to simulate that long last mile. There were three key workouts. One was four three-quarters in 3:12, 3:09, 3:06, and 3:00, with one lap recoveries, followed by a bunch of repeat miles. One was warming up, going to the line, and running, all alone, a four-minute mile. Pre did it in 3:59.0, changed shoes, and nonchalantly continued with his day.

The last workout gave him real concern. It was two essentially back-to-back runs of a mile-and-a-half in 6:30, with an 880 jog in between. These were brutal because the pace dropped every half-mile, from 70 to 65 to 60. No one could stay with him on both of these six-lap efforts, so Dellinger asked young Oregon miler Mark Feig and me to alternate halves. I drew the two-minutes-flat final 880 of the first run. Pre kept the pace, but you could see he was going all out to hold it. He finished and looked so chartreuse that Dellinger was about to say, Knock it off for today. Pre didn't let him.

"The next one will be easier," he said, and threw up a sticky yellow mass all over Dellinger's new Adidases. "Didn't give those last three Danish time to digest." The second one was easier.

Most of the team spent the last two weeks of July at the Maine training camp at Bowdoin College. It was ten days of scenic runs along the coast, clambakes with two lobsters per plate, uniform measurements, physical exams, and vaccinations. Bowerman introduced assistant coaches Stan Wright for the sprints, Hoover Wright (no relation) for the jumps, Ted Haydon for the distances, and Bruce McDonald for walks.

He also introduced head manager George Wilson. "The letter of USOC law," Bill said later, "is that the head manager outranks the head coach. That is a fact not widely appreciated. I didn't appreciate it one damn bit, but it meant that George Wilson and I had to get along." Wilson, technically a civilian, was deputy chief of the Army Sports Branch in the Pentagon and showed a worrying determination to stick to every nitpicking rule. But Bowerman, with the aid of the Tenth Mountain decal on his briefcase, soon had him eating out of his hand.

Bill so deferred to Wilson's authority—by insisting that he call all the team meetings and make all the official announcements—that Wilson quickly became uncomfortable. During a walk they took among the pines, Wilson told Bowerman that he saw the manager's role as handling the logistics of housing, feeding, and moving the troops. But the head coach's job—Bill's—was training, tactics, and inspiration. Wilson said he didn't want to overstep. Bowerman said he appreciated that, but he hadn't been. Wilson said it was hard for him to judge morale on a team of individualists. Bill said, "Let's ask."

The next day he opened a squad meeting by saying, "Gentlemen, I can report that the morale of the coaches and managers remains high. We are absolutely honored to be here. We have been trying to keep things flexible, and our first job is to convince you magnificent stud horses that we want to help, and not just tell you what to do. Olympic coaches don't do much real coaching, certainly not until they're asked. Do you know George Frenn?" He stopped and looked right at George. "You'd get a hammer in your ear if you tried to tell him anything he didn't want to know."

The laughter, including that of a burgundy, nodding Frenn, went on so long it was clear even to Wilson that the team was won. Bill listed a few Olympic champions that each assistant had coached. "But," he said, "all Stan Wright will do here is hold a watch on you. All I will do is measure your throws or heights. If you desire anything more, you have but to ask. I imagine some small wisdom will trickle out." The applause was full of the release of being understood.

The only exception to the tone of common purpose was in a meeting called by Dr. Dan Hanley, the USOC's chief medical officer. He affirmed, as we'd learned at the Trials, that drug tests would be given to the top six placers in every event in Munich. He listed the categories of stimulants and narcotics that were illegal under IAAF rules, the last being the recently banned anabolic steroids. Someone asked, "How effective are steroids?"

"To the best of our knowledge," Hanley said, "research shows anabolic steroids have absolutely no effect on strength or performance."

All the weight men got up and quietly walked out. Whether they took anything or not, the throwers' knowledge was, as it would be for the next several Olympiads, well ahead of the authorities'.

On July 29 the team flew to New York and took an overnight charter to Oslo, Norway, where we would prepare for three weeks before going on to Munich. On the plane, pole-vaulter Jan Johnson and Steve Prefontaine, who had become inseparable companions, softened the tedium with nips from a flask wrapped in a brown paper bag.

In Oslo we lived in the spare, functional, glass and birch *Panorama Sommerhotell* and trained at the Sports and Physical Education College of Norway, both on the shores of Sognsvatn Lake, a few miles north of downtown. The track was of Rekortan, the surface in the Munich Olympic Stadium. We were also free to use the European equivalent of Hayward Field, Oslo's Bislett Stadium. Most of the distance runners had raced in Bislett before, and visited Arne Kvalheim and his younger brother, Knut (who would break all of Arne's records at Oregon). We loved the sawdust and sand trails through the pine forest, used by skiers in winter, runners and hikers in summer.

Over the weeks in Maine and in Oslo, I had gotten to know and like javelin-thrower Bill Schmidt. I mentioned to him that when I was a kid, the javelin was the first image that riveted me at a track meet. He said I was not alone. "I think it's because the implement is clearly a weapon," he said. "The javelin is a great example of sport elevating mock conflict above war. But it's a real spear."

Schmidt proved that within days. One afternoon, I was running 300s on the Bislett track with Bowerman timing me. Nearing the end of a set, I looked left and saw a middle-aged banker, a local track club official, walking across the infield just as Schmidt launched a practice throw 240 feet away. The javelin struck the man in the abdomen and drove him to the turf. Bowerman was about the third person to reach him. Carefully, they pulled aside his clothes. The spear point had lodged in his hipbone but had missed everything vital. Bowerman stood over him and said in a voice that carried to the Frydenlund brewery, "You forgot your shield!"

Schmidt on the runway had been so focused on his target of a few square inches of sky that he never saw the man. He threw horribly for weeks after that, always searching downfield for wanderers.

In Oslo, we tried out what the USOC had sent us to compete in. When we'd first donned the attire back in Maine, none of us was wowed. "Our running uniforms have always been awful," Bowerman would say, "far too heavy, with stupid braid and elastic so strong it practically gives you constipation. The Olympic Committee has never seemed to know what it feels good to run in. I tried to explain to Marion Miller, the equipment man at Olympic House, that distance runners don't wear jockstraps any more. They wear a skimpy nylon bikini. He sent some samples and asked if they were what I had in mind. They were like Bermuda shorts."

In the end, Bowerman hated the thick, official racing shirts so much that he had alternatives done for those who wanted them. He found some kind of feathery knit material in Maine and ordered singlets made from it, but they arrived bearing heavily embroidered USA patches that outweighed the shirt and hammered the chest like a piece of Navaho jewelry. So Louise Shorter, Bobbie Moore, and Carol Bacheler spent hours unstitching the patches and ironing on a hot-pressed "USA" the "Dump Nixon" way. Most of the team's runners chose them. The shorts weren't hideous, just thick nylon. Shorter wore his navy blue Yale shorts. Bobbie dyed my weightless, green Oregon shorts the blue of our country's.

Pre, never one to mind an extra ounce or two, ran in his official issue for the two-day tune-up meet at Bislett. To rehearse going through the heats in Munich, he ran the 1500 on the first day and the 3000 on the second. He took a strong second in the 1500, running 3:39.4 to Pekka Vasala's 3:38.3. "I don't mind getting second to the best in the world," he said. And indeed, Vasala would be the Olympic 1500-meter champion. A day later, Pre won the Oslo 3000 in 7:44.2, which took ten full seconds from Jim Beatty's American record.

There was a quaint little tramline that got you back to the hotel in fifteen minutes. That night, Pre, Bobbie, and I happened to have a whole car to ourselves. Pre didn't hold back. "I know I could have taken the world record if my legs were fresh," he said. "I'm peaking perfectly. God, I wish we were racing the Olympics tomorrow! Nobody is running these times! I'm gonna kill them all. I know it. I feel it! I see it!"

His thighs were bobbing up and down. I asked him to consider the possibility that some wily vet like Tunisia's Mohamed Gamoudi was lying in the weeds like Dellinger did before Tokyo. "Not going to happen!" he said, wholly without reservation. "I am going to win that gold medal. Silver is crap. Bronze is crap. God, if I only got a bronze I could never go home to Oregon again! I am going to win that gold medal."

Soon after that, he came away from an interval session with a sore foot. So he had to watch when a tall, twenty-three-year-old Finn named Lasse Viren broke the world two-mile record at Bislett with 8:14.0 (passing 3000 in 7:43.6).

On August 19, we flew to Munich, bused to the impressive, banner-bedecked Olympic Village, and checked out our rooms in the United States' fourteen-story building. Groups of four or five would share apartments. We found everything comfortable and clean. But our coach was looking far beyond our creature comforts.

Within hours of our arrival, Bowerman was doing recon—political and otherwise. His half-sister Jane's husband, William Hall, a career diplomat, had told Bowerman to be sure to meet the American Consul in Munich. So he did. "I went over and put my card in and sat down with him and paid my respects," Bill would remember. "He said if you have any problems, don't hesitate to call."

Bowerman had no immediate problems to mention, but his recon wasn't finished. "Since the war I'd been conscious of security," Bill would say. "So I walked around the Olympic Village and saw there was none. As guards they had boys and girls dressed in pastels or Bavarian uniforms, not one with a weapon. The back fence was nothing, six feet, chain link, no barbed wire. The Germans were trying to erase memory of Hitler and Berlin in 1936. I went to Clifford Buck, our USOC president, to whom the Oregon Track Club had sent our fat check, and said we needed some real security on our building.

If we let visitors just walk in uninvited, the place would be picked apart."

Buck told Bowerman to write him a letter, which Bill did. "We should be able to keep out," he wrote, "thieves, harlots, and newspapermen." Buck sent the letter on to the Olympic Village Mayor, Walther Troger, who, Bill would say, "took rather strong umbrage." Troger informed Bowerman and others with similar concerns that the Munich Organizing Committee, under IOC member Willi Daume, was determined to minimize police or military presence. These were intended to be "The Happy Games," the ultimate statement of how peaceful and free life was in postwar West Germany. "Let's pray it stays that way," said Bowerman to all and sundry.

"The Germans were outraged that one of these whippersnappers from America would say their security wasn't good enough," Barbara Bowerman would recall. "So they went to the International Olympic Committee and complained about Bill and from then on, Bill was caught between the IOC and the Germans. But what happened then was something that happened to Bill strangely often his whole life. Something that started out simple became a great prophecy."

After all the pains of getting to the Games, some principled athletes, as in 1968, were prepared not to compete. The week we arrived, the IOC announced it had admitted Rhodesia to the Games, even though the nation practiced the same apartheid that made South Africa an Olympic outcast. The IOC had ruled that since Rhodesia's all-white team traveled on British passports (being part of the British Commonwealth), they were de facto British citizens and so eligible.

Reaction was swift and furious. Most black African nations issued statements that they would boycott the Games if Rhodesia stayed. On the evening of August 19, every US black athlete entered in a meet at Kempten, 100 miles from Munich, withdrew rather than take the field with the Rhodesians. The next morning, in the US quarters in the Olympic Village, we had a tense meeting of the full men's team. It was soon clear that our black members were united in their decision and that many whites, out of conscience or brotherhood, would support them.

"By admitting Rhodesia to the Games this way," said Bowerman, "under the flag of Great Britain, when Rhodesia has severed all ties with Britain over the issue of white supremacy, the IOC has committed a political subterfuge. If any of our athletes feel they cannot in good conscience compete against Rhodesians, I'll support them all the way."

We voted that a team statement urging the IOC to expel Rhodesia be given to USOC President Clifford Buck to deliver to IOC President Avery Brundage at the IOC hotel. It was by no means sure he'd get in. "I know the temper of these aristocrats," said 1964 Olympic coach Bob Geigengack, who'd planned the Oslo training camp and was a member of the USOC Track and Field Committee. "They will lock the door if they think they are going to be pressured."

Buck was allowed to present the team's appeal—barely. The IOC's sergeant-at-arms took the letter but sent the USOC president away.

While the IOC deliberated, we athletes mulled over what we would do if they let Rhodesia compete. There was eloquence on both sides of the issue.

"I don't have any question about which is more important," said triple jumper Art Walker, "my jumping in sand or the inhuman treatment suffered by the ninety percent of the Rhodesian population that is nonwhite. If that team stays, I have to go."

"I didn't have to pass a political test to come here," said George Woods. "I put the shot seventy feet. That's what I'm here to do, regardless of my sympathy for oppressed people. There are so many issues we could boycott over—the Russians' treatment of the Jews, the Nigerians' treatment of the Biafrans, the Pakistanis' treatment of the Bengalis . . . We're vulnerable ourselves over our Vietnam bombing. None of our governments is pure, so let's leave them out of it. When all those people who can't be athletes first have gone home, I'll be here, putting my shot."

In the event, we didn't have to choose. The IOC ousted Rhodesia. We were all free to be athletes first. But Avery Brundage, as would become painfully clear, would not forget.

Brundage was not the only one angry in Munich. Barbara Bowerman had made all her Olympic tour arrangements through their old friends Ehrman and Lee Giustina, who had just begun a Eugene travel agency, Lee World Travel. The Giustinas had signed up a great swath of the Oregon Track Club and other Bowerman friends across the nation, including Wade and Marie Bell. But when the group arrived in Munich, they were unmet. The Giustinas had entrusted their entire advance payments to a Bavarian agent who had taken all the money and invested it in a hotel that went broke before the Games began.

"He was being indicted for fraud," Barbara would remember. Meanwhile, they had nowhere to stay and no Olympic tickets. Eventually, another hotel was found—and tickets, too, at the lively Marienplatz. "All our men started going off every morning," Barbara would recall, "and every night when they came home they were more excited about who traded standing room tickets for seats on the fifty-yard line than what had happened at the track meet!"

Bill cracked that the din of ticket buying and selling in the Marienplatz was peaceful compared to what he heard as he was doing his job. "I went out to look at the marathon course with Arthur Lydiard," he would say later. "Beautiful course. Willi Daume conceived it. But it had loose gravel on miles of paths in the two parks, Nymphenburg and the English Gardens. The IAAF rule, of course, is pavement. I said, 'Sweep it!' They said they'd sweep and cover the paths with a 'special plastic.' But three days later it was still unswept. I complained through Clifford Buck and got more people mad at me."

Spared the brunt of these distractions, the athletes were peaking nicely. Bowerman and Dellinger timed Pre in his last tune-up, a two-mile time trial at dusk on the Post track outside the stadium. It happened to be ringed with off-duty soldiers. The sight of Pre churning lap after lap got them so excited they cheered him to an American record of 8:19.4. His foot was fine. He was ready.

The early track events were eye opening, especially if you were a 5000-meter runner studying your competition while they ran the 10,000. Lasse Viren was tripped and fell hard midway through the 10,000 final, almost taking Frank Shorter down with him. Viren arose forty yards behind, gradually caught the pack and went on to win from Belgium's Emiel Puttemans in a world record 27:38.4. Shorter ran an American record 27:51 and got but fifth. Pre sat with Dellinger and watched in silence. Viren was not ghostly and corpselike like Norpoth, but tall and ran with an eerie smoothness, the exact opposite of Pre's chesty power. You would never have guessed that Viren had covered his last 800 in 1:56.6. "Better hope that guy has shot his wad," Arne Kvalheim told Pre.

The occupants of our fifth-floor apartment, Anderson (whose PR of 28:34.2 didn't quite put him in the 10,000 final), Savage, Manley, Wottle, Shorter, and I, were doing okay. Then Dave Wottle came from amazingly far back in the 800, took the lead in the last five meters from the dying, diving Yevgeny Arzhanov of the USSR, and won in 1:45.9. Dave's parents came to the room and gave him a hard time because he had forgotten to take his golf cap off during the anthem and when he put his hand over his heart it happened to cover the "USA" on his uniform, as if he were some weird one-worlder who wanted to leave nations out of this. But we knew he was a true-blue Ohio patriot, so all-American he'd never even tasted broccoli.

In the javelin, Bill Schmidt rediscovered that perfect little keyhole in space just in time. The Munich final was a battle of titans, between Janis Lusis of the Soviet Union and Klaus Wolferman of West Germany. Wolferman won, 296 feet 10 inches to 296 feet 9 inches, that extra inch because 75,000 Germans expelled a unanimous "Whhoof!" at the moment the spear's grip shot past Wolferman's ear. Schmidt took the bronze with 277 feet 0 inches. "Guys tried to get into my head about hitting that gentleman," Schmidt said later. "I told them, You know, there's plenty of room on this spear for more notches." Bowerman finally felt free to introduce him as "Bill the Impaler."

Bowerman thus had stories to tell when he and Barbara slipped out of the Village for a lunch that would be a social triumph. Joining the Bowermans around the table were Mike Frankovich and Sydney Poitier and their spouses. Frankovich had been president of Columbia Pictures from 1963 to 1968, then returned to independent producing. He had maintained such respect for Bill, his erstwhile rival for Barbara's hand, that in the early 1960s, when his son by his first marriage showed talent in the middle distances, Frankovich had sent him to Oregon—where Peter Frankovich and Jay Bowerman were fraternity brothers. He'd met his second wife, Binnie Barnes, just three years earlier. "That lunch was the only time all four of us were together," Barbara would recall. "Binnie was a very composed British actress. I felt she was a little cool to me."

Once the pleasantries were out of the way, Bill was mightily impressed with the competitive understanding of Sydney Poitier. "Sydney volunteered to talk to the black athletes," Barbara would recall, "if Bill thought it was a good idea."

Bill thought it a great idea, because by then galling snafus had been mounting. US 100-meter sprinters Rey Robinson and Eddie Hart had qualified beautifully in the first-round heats but didn't show for the second-round quarterfinals and were eliminated. Bowerman would remember the dreadful unraveling: "The 10,000-meter heats were shifted from about 5 o'clock to 7 o'clock, and the 100-meter quarterfinals were moved forward, earlier than planned, but we weren't notified. Stan Wright used the original schedule in telling all three of our 100-meter men when to be back." Hart and Robinson were walking to the stadium and strolled through the press center on the way. They watched the telecast and heard the announcer say, "and in the 100 meters . . . " At first they thought it was a replay of their heat. But that fine OTC steeplechaser, Bill Norris, who was working as a photographer, told them it was live and they'd better move. He got them to the track, but it was too late.

Bowerman was furious, but the officials were adamant. "Only our third-best, Robert Taylor, ran," he would remember, "and went on to get the silver with 10.24 behind Valery Borzov's 10.14. It was terribly unfair."

There was more to come. For Jim Ryun, the two best places to run were out front or dead last. In the prelims, though, he found himself in the middle of the pack. With about 550 meters to go, he and Billy Fordjour of Ghana got tangled up and went down hard. Jim was dazed for several seconds, but then rose and sprinted after the field. Unlike Viren, however, he never had a hope of catching up. Ryun's Olympic Games were over.

In the men's 400-meter final, a US sweep seemed likely. Wayne Collett, John Smith, and Vince Matthews had the three best times in the world. But after 150 meters, Smith's hamstring knotted and tore. He went down on the track clutching it. Collett, his UCLA teammate and friend, saw that and hesitated for a step. Vince Matthews powered past to win, clocking 44.66 to Collett's 44.80.

Both immediately went to Smith, still writhing on the backstretch, helped him up, and carried him to the medical station. But this good deed meant that when they were summoned to the medal ceremony, they were neither jubilant nor dressed for it. The meet officials had taken their sweat suits with all the others to the practice track and they couldn't get them back. So when they got up on the victory stand they were still in shorts and T-shirts.

Then, during the *Star-Spangled Banner*, "Matthews and Collett made asses of themselves," as Bill would put it, "jiving around and talking, giving the impression they didn't want to be ramrod straight. That was unfortunate but no big deal. I felt they hadn't meant to be disrespectful during the anthem. Jesse Owens talked with them afterward and felt the same. He was arranging for them to apologize, but before they could, Brundage had Matthews and Collett suspended and sent from the Village."

"That tore at Bill," Barbara would say.

"You cannot expect on an Olympic squad of sixty to have everybody act like army privates," Bill said later. "They're great athletes. They're great individuals. The fact that some of them did things that the press objected to didn't bother me too much. They're vivid, alive, human animals. They're keenly interested, very competitive, and all different. So why not accept that and enjoy it?"

Bill wasn't going to let the matter die. He thought maybe the American icon, Jesse Owens, who'd opposed Smith and Carlos's gesture four years earlier, could help appeal to Brundage's better nature. He and Wayne Collett talked further with Owens and they decided to make a pitch to the IOC Council the next day.

That night, for the only time during the Games, Bowerman left the Olympic Village and went out on the town. Barbara's hotel put on a Bavarian dinner, so Bill didn't go back to the Village ("feeling guilty about it," Barbara would say) until quite late. He slipped into his ground-floor room and lay down. It seemed to him his head had just touched the pillow when there was a pounding.

Frank Shorter was the only one in our apartment five floors above who had heard anything. "I was out on our little balcony," he recalled later. "I'd dragged my mattress out there and had been sleeping there for a week or more. I heard a sound like a door slam." It brought him from fitful sleep to apprehensive alertness. "That's a gunshot." It was about 4:45 a.m.

A few minutes later came the pounding on the coaches' door. Bowerman groggily opened it. Before him stood an Israeli racewalker, Shaul Ladany, whom Bill knew slightly because he'd trained at the Tahoe camp four years before.

"Can I come in? Can I stay here?" asked Ladany puffing, pushing close.

"What for?"

"The Arabs are in our building."

"Well, tell them to get out."

"They've shot some of our people. I got out through a window."

"That," said Bowerman later, "changed the whole complexion."

As he reached to draw Ladany into the safety of the room, Bowerman was the first of the US delegation to know that we had become caught up in the modern Olympics' great loss of innocence.

Bowerman sat Ladany down on his bed, picked up the phone, and called the US Consul. "We've got a problem in the Olympic Village," he said. "I don't know what it is, but I want some security."

"What for?"

"Across the street from us, armed Arabs have moved into the Israeli quarters and we've got Jewish kids in our building, one the swimmer Mark Spitz and another the javelin-thrower Bill Schmidt."

"You've got it."

Thirty minutes later there were two US Marines at the US entrance and two in the halls. "We secured the building," said Bowerman. "But I got a call about 6 a.m. from the office of the International Olympic Committee. They said you've done it again, Bowerman, bringing Marines in here. We want to see you first thing in the morning. I said I'd be glad to be there."

By 7:30 a.m., German security forces had begun to flood the Village streets. What we would eventually learn was that eight members of the Black September faction of the Palestinian Liberation Organization, dressed in track suits and carrying rifles in sports bags, had scaled the back fence of the Village (with the unwitting aid of some American athletes sneaking in late) and forced their way into the Israeli men's quarters in Building #31, on *Connolly Strasse*. They shot and killed Moshe Weinberg, a weight-lifting coach, and mortally wounded lifter Yossef Romano. They took nine other athletes and coaches hostage in the two-story duplex. Nineteen Israeli coaches and athletes, including Ladany, escaped, some out windows after wrestling official Yossef Gutfreund screamed and tried to hold the door against the invaders. Once inside, the terrorists tied and gagged their captives, took up defensive positions, and at 5:08 a.m. tossed a list of demands from the balcony to a policeman. To show their seriousness, they threw Moshe Weinberg's body out the window onto the sidewalk.

The Black September spokesman went by the name Issa and said he'd graduated from technical school in Berlin. The terrorists wanted the release of 234 Palestinian prisoners in Israel and the Bader-Meinhof gang from German prison. They said they'd start killing captives at 9 a.m. if there were no releases. West German Interior Minister Hans-Dietrich Genscher told Issa he'd have to talk to both the Israeli and German governments and couldn't promise an answer in the $2^1/_2$ hours until 9. Issa said that would be too bad for the hostages.

West German Chancellor Willy Brandt called Israeli Prime Minister Golda Meir and relayed the Black September demands. Her response was short: "Under no conditions will Israel make the slightest concession to terrorist blackmail." The captives' families knew this would be the answer. The captives surely knew as well.

The Israeli position never changed. But the Germans, to buy time, didn't tell the terrorists. They kept saying the prisoners couldn't be located or that Israeli cabinet ministers were out of touch. Issa let the 9 a.m. deadline pass and reset it for noon, then 3 p.m.

Meanwhile, the area around Building #31 was sealed off. Tanks and troops took up positions out of sight behind myriad concrete walls and corners. But the Games themselves, said Munich Olympic Organizing Committee President Willi Daume, would continue until further notice.

News was slow to spread. In the early hours, before people fully understood the horror of the situation on *Connolly Strasse*, the machinery of the Games and the Village ground on, or tried to. So Bowerman, even though the place was becoming an armed camp, had to go to have his hand slapped by the IOC bureaucracy for bringing in a few Marines.

"I had one lucky break," Bowerman would recall. "Jesse Owens came by to help with the 400-meter situation. He went with me to the IOC staff office, too. They were, therefore, very polite."

The IOC people said they'd had a complaint from Mayor Troger's people about the fact that Bowerman had secured his building. Bowerman asked if they were aware of what had happened early that morning. "We have heard some rumor there has been some trouble with, with—whatever do you call them? The PLO or the Arabs?"

"Well," Bill answered, "I had an Israeli come into my quarters. When he told me what the problem was, I called the US Consul. And if it's trouble to secure a building when people are being killed, then I guess I'm trouble."

The staffers said they would look into this killing rumor further, but they understood his action. Bowerman and Owens escaped to try to reason with Avery Brundage.

This they did in the early afternoon, successfully petitioning to be heard by the IOC president and council members at their hotel. It was a small meeting, and Bowerman thought the IOC officials must not have been fully aware of the seriousness of the Palestinian terrorism because they were so focused on the quarter-milers' controversy.

In fact, Brundage had been constantly conferring with the German crisis team. He'd even suggested the 1920s Chicago police tactic of pumping knockout gas into buildings to overpower gangsters. The IOC president's ability to continue caring about runner decorum with Bowerman suggests a bizarre ability to compartmentalize. Or it suggests that Brundage, following the protests of 1968, was terrified of any further political use of the victory stand.

Brundage expressed his displeasure over Matthews and Collett. "He was very upset about this," Bowerman would say. "He wanted to know if I would apologize. I said sure. I said after all, they're here as terrific, bright young men representing their country. They just won the race of their lives. They're black. They're making a black salute or whatnot. They meant no offense. But if it offended you and you want me to apologize, by all means, please accept my apology."

Bowerman and Owens were pleased to see that both the council and Brundage swiftly accepted it. The suspensions would be lifted; Matthews and Collett would be permitted to run the 1600-meter relay—provided that the USOC also agreed to the decision.

Bowerman, Owens, and Collett hustled to USOC headquarters with the news and walked into a raucous meeting. "It was a mob in there," Bowerman would say, "Clifford Buck presiding." Bill told them he and Jesse Owens had just been to the IOC and cleared the way for Matthews and Collett's reinstatement. Buck replied that the USOC had already taken a vote. "The people involved in this episode," he said, "will not be able to run on the relay."

"I don't know how you reached that conclusion," said Bill.

"Well," said Buck, "they insulted the American flag."

And there it ended. "They were not prepared to listen," said Bowerman later, "to any explanation or apology from Wayne and Vince, or me. Avery Brundage and the stuffy IOC hierarchy had accepted my explanation. It was only our own USOC which would not." There would be no US entry in the 1600-meter relay.

Lee Evans's "surest gold on the team" had evaporated. He would never get to race a step in Munich.

Of course it didn't look like the rest of us would either. From our little balcony where Frank had heard the shots, Shorter, Anderson, Savage, Manley, and I could see tanks, troops, and emergency vehicles assembling 150 yards away, behind the blocky structure that housed the Israelis. We took turns on the terrace all day, nervously plucking seeds from a fennel plant there, grinding them into our palms, keeping vigil.

"Imagine how it must be for them in there," said Frank. "Some maniac with a machine gun saying, 'Let's kill 'em now,' and another one saying, 'No, let's wait a while.' How long could you stand that?"

Below, people played chess or ping-pong. The trading of Olympic pins continued. Athletes sunbathed by the reflecting pool. It seemed inappropriate, but what was one supposed to do? The scratchy, singsong notes of European police sirens sounded incessantly. Rumors leaped and died. There were twenty-six hostages. There were seven. The terrorists were killing a man every two hours. They were on the verge of surrender.

At 3 p.m. the dissonance between oblivious sport and imminent death finally became too great for the Olympic organizers. A friend in the press village called and said, "Have you heard? The Games are stopped."

"Stopped? You mean postponed or canceled?"

"Postponed for now. But they say it may be impossible to start them again."

I went back to the room, where Bobbie was waiting, and wept. I experienced level after level of grief: for the dead and doomed Israelis; for the marathon, those years of preparation now useless; and for the violated sanctuary of the Games. Until now, in my twenty-ninth year, I had believed the Olympics immune to the threats of the larger world. It was an illusion, but it had been the strongest of my life. I shook and sobbed as it was shattered.

I was not alone. Steve Prefontaine raged at the terrorists' blindness, at what he felt was their sheer, malignant gall. "These are *our* Games," he cried. "Anyone who would murder us for some demented cause just proves he can't understand what it is we do!"

When the Germans demanded that Issa prove that the hostages were still alive, Interior Minister Genscher and Mayor Troger were escorted to the second-floor room of Apartment 1 to verify it. "It was awful," Troger said later. "There was blood and they looked desperate. It was not easy to know that I couldn't do very much for them."

Would Troger reflect on Bowerman's warning to him about the Village's lax security? The haunted face he displayed in a 2002 ABC documentary suggested he had for thirty years.

German police needed to know how many terrorists there were. Troger emerged thinking there were, at most, five. There were eight. The Germans readied an amateurish team of riflemen in sweat suits to come down the airshafts from the roof into the building. But as they were about to begin the assault, the terrorists became observably nervous and it was called off. Then the Germans realized why. The ABC TV feed from a camera high on the tower over the Village was showing the track-suited riflemen on the roof. The terrorists had been watching their every move. The Germans would have been slaughtered.

The terrorists pushed back the deadline to 5 p.m. Just before that hour, Issa demanded a plane out to an Arab country. The Germans, under enormous pressure from Brundage to get this horrible struggle out and away from the precincts of peace, jumped at the plane idea, even though standard procedure for hostage situations is to contain and delay. They brought in two helicopters to take the terrorists and hostages to nearby Fürstenfeldbruck Air Base, from where, they falsely promised, a Lufthansa 727 would take the terrorists to Cairo and then deliver the hostages to Tel Aviv, Israel.

At 9 p.m., Bobbie and I tried to leave the Village. At the gates, the guards were letting no one in or out. Assistant coach Hoover Wright and his wife were also trying to get out. Someone who knew him shouted from the crowd, "Hoover, there's going to be shooting! There's going to be shooting." We went back through rising furor to the room.

After a few minutes, Dave Wottle came in from, to our amazement, a run. "I went out the back gate," he said. He'd covered a three-mile loop and returned to the rear of the Village, where his way was barred by ropes. He jumped them, and then the fence. "I heard some guards yelling 'halt' but I just waved without looking. After fifty yards I came to another group of guards. One recognized me and said, 'It's Wottle,' and they laughed." When Dave looked back, he saw five guards returning guns to holsters. "If I'd known they were so jumpy, I'd have walked around all night."

From the balcony a little after 10 p.m. we saw two large Iroquois helicopters lift off, wheel around, and disappear into roiling clouds reddened by searchlights. Shorter watched the sky long after the rest of us had finished our prayers for the Israelis' deliverance. "You know," he said with shaken softness, "I don't think it's over."

At Fürstenfeldbruck airfield, the German authorities were hastily preparing an ambush. Snipers knelt on three sides of the tarmac. A team of seventeen Bavarian and Munich policemen was assigned to be in the waiting plane, some hiding, some impersonating the pilot and crew. When Issa inspected the plane, as they assumed he would, they would kill him and the snipers would shoot the other terrorists.

All went wrong. There were only five snipers but eight terrorists. Worse, the helicopters would land precisely between two sets of snipers, so few could shoot without hitting others. Still worse, on the waiting 727, the German police team leader, Reinhold Reich, realized that their partial Lufthansa uniforms would fool no one. He polled his sixteen officers, who voted unanimously to abandon what they felt was a suicide mission. Everyone ran off the plane just before the helicopters landed at 10:35 p.m.

Issa and another terrorist did inspect the waiting plane, saw it was empty, and jogged back toward the helicopters. The German snipers began firing, killing two terrorists and wounding a third. The terrorists quickly shot out the field lights. The snipers had no night-vision goggles. For a chaotic hour, shots were exchanged in the dark.

The Germans failed to move in more forces. A police assault-team helicopter landed a mile away and sat there. Six armored personnel carriers coming by road got stuck in traffic among curious thrill seekers and reporters. The hostages had no chance of escape because they were tied inside the helicopters.

Finally, just before midnight, the armored carriers arrived and headed toward the helicopters and hostages. Seeing them, a terrorist machine-gunned the hostages in one helicopter. Another threw a grenade into the other. All the Israelis were killed. Issa was killed in the fighting that followed, but three terrorists were caught.

To add to the debacle, TV reporters had found their way to the airfield's locked outer gates. Before 11 p.m., someone with Olympic insignia—no one knows who—came to the fence and shouted, "All are saved!" That word went around the world. The German government spokesman repeated it. Newspapers printed it. Willi Daume brought the news jubilantly into the IOC council meeting.

It was not until 2 a.m. or later that the German armed forces returned with the truth. "They are all gone," said a stricken Jim McKay on ABC.

It would be hard to think of a scenario more hideously illustrative of the compounding effects of government, official, and journalistic irresponsibility. Those of us in the US building went to our beds at 1 a.m., shaken but relieved that our fellow Olympians had survived—then awoke to newspapers showing a picture of a horribly burned helicopter and headlines that said "Sixteen dead."

"If they loaded us all into a plane right now to take us home," said a devastated Prefontaine, "I'd go." Instead, Bill Dellinger, who'd vaulted a fence to get into the Village, persuaded Pre to come away into the countryside. He drove with Prefontaine for a full hour, well into Austria, where they stopped and inhaled truly Alpine air. To keep Pre from running himself to death as therapy, Dellinger had them take a jog together. This was September 6. Assuming the Games went on with only a day's postponement, the 5000 semifinals would now be on the 8th and the final on the 10th.

"I knew I didn't have to worry about Pre's bouncing back emotionally," Dellinger would say, "because he was so pissed that all this was giving Viren an extra day to recover after the 10,000." Dellinger goaded him a little more, pointing out that since he was, at twenty-one, the youngest in the race by two years, every veteran in there—say, defending champ Gamoudi or Harald Norpoth—was going down the list of entrants, coming to his name and writing him off as a cocky kid who was going to be thrown back into babyhood by the attacks. Personalizing it like that was working, Dellinger saw.

While Pre and Dellinger were in Austria, 80,000 attended the memorial service for the Israeli dead, held in the main stadium. Frank and I walked there from the Village. Russian soccer players were practicing on a field beside the stadium. Concession stands were open, smelling of sauerkraut. The athletes were given seats on the infield with no concern for nation. Frank, Jan Johnson, and I sat down amid Ethiopian runners and French vaulters. Bowerman, as was his habit, observed from high in the stands.

The music was Beethoven's *Egmont Overture*. The program seemed long-winded, not because it was boring (we were waiting for Brundage to say whether the Games would go on), but because it was in four languages, German, French, English, and Hebrew. The head of the Israeli team read out the names of the dead, all tough, combative men: wrestling coach Moshe Weinberg, weight lifters Yossef Romano and David Berger, fencing coach Andrei Spitzer, track coach Amitzur Shapira, shooting coach Kehat Shorr, wrestling referee Yossef Gutfreund, weight-lifting judge Jacov Springer, and wrestlers Zaev Friedman, Eliezer Halfin, and Mark Slavin.

Organizing Committee head Willi Daume spoke, pallid and shaky. Then eighty-four-year-old Avery Brundage stood before the podium. He had only a few days left in his twenty-year reign as IOC president. "Every civilized nation mourns ... " he began, and noted that the Olympic movement had never suffered such an assault. But then he thundered, "The Games have been subjected to *two* savage attacks! We lost the Rhodesian battle against naked political blackmail!"

I recall being blurry-eyed, staring down at the infield grass between my feet and wondering whether I'd heard right. Had Brundage actually just equated the murders of our fellow Olympians with his having to kick out that odious state?

In the car on the way to the stadium, he had shown his speech to IOC Executive Director Monique Berlioux. Even she, who knew him well, was shocked. "It was awful," she said later. "He'd almost ignored what had happened to the Israelis and written a political speech about the threatened boycott over Rhodesia. I said, 'You can*not* say that. It is a ceremony in memory of the murdered Israelis. This is impossible!'"

Brundage had replied, "I know what I have to do."

And after he had done it, after he had seemed to confirm all accounts of his towering racism and anti-Semitism, Brundage boomed, "The Games must go on! All events will be held twenty-four hours after originally scheduled!" And the crowd cheered.

Now, at decades' long remove, Brundage's defiant speech does not seem simply anti-Semitic. The man was a genuinely tragic character, his flaw and strength inextricable. He defined himself as the noble defender of the purity of the Games. Throwing out Smith and Carlos in 1968 was racist, but only incidentally so. Convinced he was defending the Games from political attack, he was blind to an act of conscience. In Munich, John Carlos himself cried out, "In 1968, we didn't hurt anybody. We just expressed our feelings. Can Brundage see the difference?"

No, he couldn't. There was no difference for him between outside agitators killing Olympians, deluding them into black-gloved gestures, or pressuring his IOC to keep out a country he'd decided to let in. All were attacks, and he fought them all with equal fury.

Walking back, Frank and I bumped into a pensive Bowerman. "If Avery is eighty-four," Bill calculated, "and he's been IOC president for twenty years, then he was sixty-four when he took over. I'm sixty-one. I can't imagine living like that for two years and not being made a madman. Let him go. He's done. He's gone. Let's hope the next guy, the Irish lord, Killanen, is halfway sane."

Back in our rooms we talked all this over. "The Games should go on," said walker Tom Dooley, "and they will. But for the wrong reasons. The Germans don't want any hitches in their organization. There are the financial considerations. Those people who applauded just want to see who will win the 5000 and the hell with the rest."

"What are the right reasons?" I asked.

"Just one. To stay together. Who wins or loses now is ridiculously unimportant, considered against these men's deaths. But we have to stay together."

Bowerman would never be more eloquent than in conveying that necessity. But he made no speeches. He called no big team meeting to address us on the subject of how to feel. He didn't want to preach. What he wanted to do was be there, physically with us, in ones and twos. He moved from room to room, shared with athletes the latest word on rescheduling the remaining events, and asked if people were okay. If anyone wanted to talk, he came in, sat down, and listened. If they'd had the reaction that Pre and I had, that our competitive urges were being sapped by our grief, he'd offer a word of context.

Some were easy. With shot-putter George Woods, who'd spoken so memorably about being an athlete first, Bill asked if it was still the case that when everyone else had gone off on some grand distraction, he'd still be here putting his shot. Woods nodded that it was. It wasn't as easy as he'd made it sound, but he was still here, still ready. "Good," said Bill. "Good." Woods went on to take the silver medal in the shot.

With high-strung George Frenn, whose parents were born in Lebanon, Bowerman observed that the terrorists in some ways were mirror images of Olympians. They were fanatics, prepared to die for their cause, their suffering people. But that from that suffering they brought forth death. "They surrendered to the cycle of violence," Bill said. "They were every victim become destroyer."

"Your point is we can't be like them," said Frenn, whose temper was known and respected. "Don't go into that cycle."

To George Young and Mike Manley, both teachers, Bill observed that if there was one place where war doesn't belong, it was here. "From 776 BC to 393 AD Olympians laid down their arms to take part in the Games." They knew there is more honor in outrunning a man than killing him.

And with me, he had an answer when I told him what Dutch 5000-meter runner Jos Hermens had said as he went home without competing: "If you throw a party and a gunman comes in and murders a dozen guests, you don't break out another keg and go on with the party."

"This is no party," said Bill. "This is the species' great moral advance. This is our answer to war."

With time and such reminders, we came not only to see that but also to feel it. "The day we watched as the hostages were held, and the day off for the memorial service," Shorter would remember, "we went through the stages humans must go through in times of brutal stress: from denial to anger, to grief, to resolve." Bowerman's person-by-person guidance had done much to nudge us there. The question became what to do with that resolve.

"We have to spread the word by our performance," said Shorter, "that barbarism only makes Olympians stronger. We have to say, 'This is as scared as I get. Now let's go run.'"

At 3:00 p.m. on the last day of the Olympics, sixty-nine marathoners heeded the gun, did two laps of the stadium track, swept through the marathon gate and out onto the roads. The day was hazy and humid. After a mile, I got caught in a jam on a corner and tripped. I curled into a ball until an opening appeared in the slapping feet and was up quickly, with a stinging elbow and knee and a thirty-yard deficit. Frank was among the leaders ahead, as was big Jack Bacheler.

Six miles from the start, I'd eased back up to the pack. We entered Nymphenburg Park. The paths were unswept. The yellow dust rising behind the official bus leading us was proof of that promise broken. Now, somehow, in a week with burning helicopters, it didn't seem that big a deal. We came to the first water station. Frank and I had spent a silly half-hour in the shower that morning shaking the fizz out of Cokes and pouring them into squeeze bottles. These were now arrayed on tables beside the path. An Ethiopian took Frank's. Frank took mine. I took nothing. He couldn't return my bottle to me because those prying eyes on the officials' bus knew it was against the rules to aid another runner. "Sorry," Frank said. Britain's Ron Hill and Japan's Akio Usami had been leading. After nine miles, Frank cruised through the front group, now down to eight. As we ran beneath maples lining a murky canal, he surged ahead.

Nobody went with him, though I considered it mightily. The strength of my race was my strength, meaning late stamina. I ran thirty- to thirty-five-mile runs every two weeks. Frank seldom went above twenty (though he often did twenty several days in a row). If we were together with four or five miles to go, I would have trained specifically for those conditions. To prevent me from being anywhere near him that late in the race, he used his superior track speed to bolt out to a big lead and then hang on. He had won the previous fall's Fukuoka race by taking off like this at halfway. But this move was with seventeen miles to go. It was hot. He seemed to have spurted too sharply. So we all let him go, assuming he'd pay for his profligacy later.

After the twenty-five-kilometer water station, with eleven miles to go, I was running second, beside the defending champion, Mamo Wolde of Ethiopia. He ran soundless of foot and breath, with his head tipped slightly forward. I sensed his presence only from that distinguished widow's peak floating above my left shoulder. We ran along boulevards, around statues, fountains, arches. But we were beyond noticing the scenery. Our universe was asphalt, tram tracks, and a faint blue line.

Mamo was knock-kneed and pointed his toes out slightly. I was knock-kneed and also toed out, both conditions being accentuated by fatigue. Once in a while our shoes brushed. "I'm sorry, I'm sorry," Wolde said each time.

At about that time, back in the stadium, the thirteen finalists in the men's 5000 meters were leaning over the starting line. Pre's plan was unchanged. With four laps to go he would begin a mile-long drive to run all pursuers off their feet. The field was the strongest ever assembled, the best being Gamoudi, Puttemans, Norpoth, Viren and his countryman Juha Vaatinen, as well as Britain's Ian Stewart and Dave Bedford. Bedford, the world cross-country champion, had earlier been vocal in his opinion that Prefontaine was a cocky little prick in need of quieting.

In the 10,000, Bedford had set a world record pace, but hadn't broken away and finished sixth. Now, he was doing no further favors. No one was. The USSR's Nikolai Sviridov and others led, but listlessly, and the pack remained a tight, worried clump. Many felt a fast pace was to their advantage. Vaatinen had run the last 400 in the 1971 European Championships in 52 seconds. Obviously he had to be exhausted or escaped from. But no one would sacrifice himself to do that. The mile passed in 4:30. Prefontaine had been 4:20 in the Olympic Trials.

Pre all this time remained in the middle of the pack, taking elbows and spikes. Everyone else's racing cowardice (or intelligence, depending on how they finished) was combining to create terrible luck for him. Never happy in a pack at the best of times, it was all he could do to keep his cool. He did so by visualizing how great it would be to be free.

They passed two miles at 8:56.4. It was almost time. On the homestretch with four to go, Pre cocked his head, moved out, and took the lead. They had been going 67 pace. He ran the next lap in 62.5 and followed with a 61.2. Only five men were in contention by then, Prefontaine, Viren, Puttemans, Gamoudi, and Stewart.

With 800 to go, Viren passed Pre, perhaps as a little psychological blow against the kid, who had to be feeling his blazing last half-mile. Puttemans went by too, as if he felt Pre was shot and was going to now fall back. Pre responded on the backstretch by charging past both of them and retaking the lead with 600 to go, just where Dellinger had led in Tokyo. He finished that lap with a 60.3.

At the bell with a lap to go, Viren passed him again, and Bowerman said later that he thought the Finn was sprinting too soon, that if Pre could tuck in and draft on his back, he could run him down late. But Pre wasn't hanging anywhere. As soon as they hit the backstretch with 300 to go, Pre moved out to pass Viren. But Gamoudi, who had done this to Billy Mills in the Tokyo 10,000, sprinted by, hit Pre so hard he drove him inside, and made his own charge to seize the lead. Pre was third with 250 to go.

Again, Bowerman felt that if he gathered and waited, he could catch them in the stretch. Again, Pre refused to wait. With 200 to go he went wide and got to Viren's shoulder. He gave a tremendous effort, his head going side to side, but couldn't get past before the turn. Gamoudi cut him off again and went back into second. The top three men ran the last turn a yard apart, praying that after all these moves and countermoves they would have something left in the stretch.

Only Viren did. He drew gracefully away to win in 13:26.4. Gamoudi was seven yards back in 13:27.4. Prefontaine died. At the line he was staggering. The madly sprinting Ian Stewart just caught him to steal the bronze in 13:27.6. Pre was clocked in 13:28.3. He had run his last mile in 4:04. Viren had run 4:02.

In the stands, Pre's girlfriend, Mary Marckx (now Mary Creel), didn't know what to do. "In the minutes right after the race I was upset," she would remember. "I didn't know how to reach Steve through the bowels of the stadium, so I started running up to the top of the stands. I was alone, crying. I couldn't imagine what he'd do. Would he kill himself? He'd been completely shut out, even of the 'horrible bronze' he'd disparaged."

At the top of the stadium there was a broad concourse. "You could walk all the way around up there," Mary would recall, "so I began, and there were Bill and Barbara Bowerman. I said, 'I don't know if he can take this. I don't know if I can help him.' Bill gently patted my arm and said it was a heroic effort, he couldn't have done any better. 'He's young.' Bill said. 'He's got a lot of races ahead. He'll be fine. Believe me, he'll be fine.'"

Mary felt a little better, but she knew her man. This was not going to be easy. Mortification, to use a word from her Catholic background, did not sit well with Steve Prefontaine. Bill and Barbara escorted her down to the "mixed zone," where the family and press could stand behind a barricade and visit with the athletes. There, Mary would say, "it seemed every third person was telling Pre that fourth in the world isn't bad."

Blaine Newnham of the Eugene *Register-Guard* was one of those people. "I know you feel bad," Newnham said, "but we've got to talk."

Prefontaine said, "I've got nothing to say," and headed for the darkest corner.

Newnham said, "Wait a minute, you've got to talk to me. What about all those people back in Eugene, the people at Hayward Field, Pre's People? They've lived this race for you, they can understand what happened and we've got to talk."

Mention of his people stopped him. Newnham asked, "How old are you, twenty-one? And you finished fourth in the world, how bad is that?"

"Well, that's not too bad."

Newnham said, "Did you run for third or second? No, you ran to win, you took the lead with a mile to go, you ran your butt off, and you finished fourth, now how bad is that?"

"No, it wasn't that bad."

"What he needed," Newnham said later, "was someone to put his arm around him, to kind of hug him and say it's okay, we understand. Pre's People understand. And so, goodness, he started talking, and twenty minutes later he was all pumped up again."

When Bedford came over to say he was the toughest little prick he ever saw, Pre shook his hand thanks and said, "How about us losers have a beer at the *Hofbrau Haus* later. Isn't that what this is supposed to be about?"

With six miles to go, Wolde and I were running in the English Garden. People shouted that Shorter was over a minute ahead. A hundred yards behind us was a pale little man in white. The day had cooled. Frank had once told me, "I've never really tied up, you know. I've never really died after getting a lead." I believed him now. Wolde and I were running for silver.

A mile later, on a rutted part of the path, a cramp shot up my right hamstring. Wolde passed immediately. He watched me hobble, clutching the back of my thigh for a couple of steps. His expression seemed to say this was all wrong, that he'd been expecting us to duke it out to the end. Then he turned and ran on.

I accelerated carefully to just below my previous pace. I couldn't risk a second attack. Karel Lismont of Belgium, the man in white, stormed past, running with his head down and a powerful arm action.

Mercifully, the park ended and we returned to level streets. I found a rhythm and began to move. There was no reason to look back. The last medal was disappearing ahead of me.

If it is run right, a marathon inflicts some damage. Muscle cells rupture. Joints, crunching together 22,000 times, wear away at tendons and cartilage. I ran it right, the crowd's approval roaring in my head, on a cushion of blood blisters. I tempted my twinging thigh, forcing the pace. But as the stadium neared, Lismont was out of sight and Wolde still had me by 200 yards.

Along the road outside the stadium, a final snafu was brewing. As Frank would learn later, a local high school student had hatched a prank with a friend, which they carried off with frightening precision.

The friend had a job during the Games of driving a golf cart around the outside of the stadium, delivering supplies to the concessions. He was thus familiar to all the guards. Just before Frank reached the stadium, the high school kid jumped on the cart wearing a track uniform and fake number. The friend drove unimpeded through the security and past the access tunnel to the track. The young imposter hopped off the cart and ran down the tunnel before anyone could stop him.

"He emerged about fifty seconds ahead of me," Frank would remember, "and accepted the roar of the crowd unique to the Olympic Marathon winner. By the time I emerged . . . to the silence, he had completed three-quarters of a lap and was one-half lap from the finish. I had turned right and was 100 meters ahead of him and never looked back so I never saw him."

Though robbed of a little of the immediate glory, Frank was the first American to win the Olympic marathon in sixty-four years. Crossing the line in 2:12:20, he put his hands on his head in amazement at what he had done. Shorter had taken all the sorrow and turned it into performance. Barbarism had only made him stronger.

Lismont took second in 2:14:32, Wolde third in 2:15:08, and I fourth in 2:15:39. Jack Bacheler hung on for ninth, in 2:17:39. Ours was the best finish by three runners from a single nation ever.

I walked the Munich infield trying to know how to react. The thought came of what Bob Newland would always tell us back in high school: "Lift up your head. You ran the hardest you humanly could."

Bobbie was there, holding me, and I came apart, pain and frustration forcing out tears. "I tried so hard," I said. In a few seconds I knew it was all right. She was more important than any medal and it didn't matter if I cried. I was amazed at having the moisture.

Prefontaine saw me in the tunnel and ran over. "Kenny, you have got to be proud!" he said. "Out of all the billions of people in the world you were fourth. I order you to be proud!"

I realized his race was over. "Pre, what did *you* get?"

"I got fucking fourth, man. It's the worst place you can ever finish."

That self-mocking, double-standard laugh showed he was on the way back. Pre went on to an uproarious evening downing steins with nonmedallists at the *Hofbrau Haus* and flew home the next day.

The instant his duties were over, the instant the last American trackman was safely signed out, Bill Bowerman walked from the Village, swung up and took a seat beside Barbara on a tour bus with the Giustinas and friends, and allowed himself to be driven to Switzerland.

It was a departure, Barbara would recall, with all too many echoes of their leaving Rome in 1960, going through these same Bavarian Alps and imagining, with hope in their hearts, what a Munich Olympics could be and signify. But now, the pinnacle of Bowerman's career had been savaged. Someone on board unwisely asked Bill how he had liked his prestigious position.

"Did I enjoy being the coach of the 1972 Olympic team?" he replied. "Worst experience in my total athletic career."

But it was also, as Barbara came to believe, the most necessary. Bill's problem-solving abilities under fire, his bringing in the Marines, his gifts for sizing up individuals and defending them against the bureaucracy, his putting the Olympic ideals into a few well-chosen words, all kept his Olympians safe and ushered a number through grief to the other side. No other leadership figure exhibited anything close to competence after the terror struck. When mortal pressure was applied, few besides Bill Bowerman acquitted themselves well.

So over the years, when he'd repeat his worst-experience-ever mantra, Barbara would demur and explain that it was the worst set of *events* ever, but a magnificent use of her man. Those of us who were there would attest to that. We'd have been lost without him.

CHAPTER 26

Transit and Sorrow

ON HIS RETURN FROM MUNICH, STEVE PREFONTAINE SETTLED IN FOR HIS SENIOR year. He lived, as he had for many months before the Games, in a metal trailer in a riverside mobile home park in Glenwood with three-miler Pat Tyson and now with Lobo, a German shepherd puppy he had rescued from the pound and trained to be an obedient running partner. He resumed photography and broadcast communications classes, his major.

Pre never questioned Bowerman's race plan in the Munich 5000. He complained to friends or coaches only of the slow pace and of Gamoudi's spikes, scratches, and punches. "If it had been 8:40 for the first two miles," he told *Track and Field News*, "I would have had gold or silver. It would have put crap in their legs. It was set up for Gamoudi and Viren." After watching the tape fifty times, I disagreed. I came to feel that if he'd let Viren lead the last 800 and made a single, all-out sprint with 250 to go, he'd have been second even as the race was run. His wild abandon was why he had been staggering blind before the line.

That autumn, as planned, Pre didn't compete in cross-country. Bill had him simply train as he felt, until the fire returned. Once, when Pre joined the team for some easy repeat miles at Laurelwood Golf Course, Bowerman asked him if he'd felt ill-served by their plan. Pre said, No way.

Bowerman had probed, wondering aloud whether maybe going hard the last two miles would have been better. That Bowerman, who seldom rehashed beyond a quick, postrace lesson, would bring it up seems a measure of his regret that Pre's incredible effort hadn't been rewarded.

It was a measure of how objective Pre had become that he told Bill no, he now realized those guys were good. If he'd led all the way, he'd have been vulnerable at the end, just like a Ron Clarke. He said there really wasn't much he could have done differently.

"Except be a different breed of cat," laughed Bill, "and run for third."

"Yeah, right," said Pre. "No chance of that."

Later, Bowerman was a little too rosy when he told Tom Jordan, Prefontaine's biographer, "He recognized he was a kid running among men and the longer distance races are men's races. I don't know of any distance performer who is not better at twenty-five than he was at eighteen to twenty-two, if he stays healthy. He recognized his time was ahead of him."

All this was true, and Pre voiced it too, though without his former obsessive sense of destiny. Still, Dellinger and Bowerman saw Pre wasn't bouncing back. He was moody, hopping from emotion to emotion. Mary Marckx Creel, who would call Munich "a turning point" in Pre's life, saw that, too. Pre began partying and drinking much more than he used to, Creel would say, and seemed to take running less seriously. It may have begun to occur to him, on some level, that he might need to consider making a living at something besides track. Creel came to feel he was resisting that possibility: "It took a lot of talking to get him back to being responsible again. I had to threaten to leave him."

Creel had known Prefontaine since February 1971, when he was a sophomore and she a freshman. They had met when he came to study in her dorm with a mutual friend, had seen blonde, dryly dubious Mary, and asked, in the manner of Mike Frankovich meeting Barbara Young, where she had been all his life. The relationship had blossomed after Mary told him she wasn't his type and he, taken aback, had set out to prove her wrong, whatever it took. It took paying some attention to politics.

"At first," Creel would say, "Steve was a pretty die-hard, conservative, rah-rah-USA guy." When they heard Senator Wayne Morse speak at a rally about ending the war in Vietnam, Pre was angry with the protesters because they alienated alumni, who then gave less money to the university and the athletic program. "He got mad," Creel would remember. "Then he got older."

Some of that aging took place in the Mac Court sauna in the spring of 1971. Arne Kvalheim, who had returned to get his master's in journalism, held up a soggy newspaper. The headline was "B-52 Missions, Tonnage Increase."

"The generals," Kvalheim read, "say we have not yet inflicted that level of pain, short of annihilation, under which reasonable people will see it's in their interest to accept our terms."

Pre closed his eyes, sick of the subject.

"So," asked Arne, "what would that level be in Coos Bay?"

"Beg your pardon?"

"How much would an enemy have to bomb before Coos Bay would give up?"

"Coos Bay would never give up."

"It would hate to, but there must be some point, if your bridges are gone, your mills are gone, your food is gone, half your families are dead, there's absolutely no hope of . . . "

"Coos Bay would never give up! They'd fight to the last man!"

Arne sat back. "Of course they would," he said. "Oslo would. Dallas would. No one would give up."

"So what's your point?"

"Just to wonder, in this war of yours, why you expect the people of North Vietnam not to fight invaders as hard as the people of Coos Bay. The more you bomb human beings defending home and family, the more they fight to the last man." There was a long moment of deepening hopelessness.

"It's not my war, Arne!" said Pre finally. "Stop calling it *my* war!"

Student draft deferments were ended in 1971 and the Selective Service System instituted a lottery. Pre drew a relatively low draft lottery number, which meant a correspondingly higher chance of being called. At that point, Mary Creel would remember, "For him, and a lot of his friends, the war got a lot closer to home." If Prefontaine had been drafted, he could have run for the Army track team as other Ducks had, but he told Creel he didn't want to have anything to do with the military.

"He knew he'd never be able to take orders," she recalled more than thirty years later. "If it was hard to take orders from Bowerman, whom he respected and loved in a convoluted way, how could he take them from some drill sergeant?"

In 1973, after more than two decades of quagmire, the US withdrew from Vietnam. The draft ended the same year, and young men of Pre's age could exhale and turn their attention to domestic issues.

Pre himself gradually began to remember that he loved running and winning, that the Olympics were not the only, or even the main, reason he ran. As he became excited about the possibilities of life again, Kvalheim helped keep the excitement in check. During one run, Pre proudly reported that Coos Bay was naming a street after him. "What are they going to call it?" Arne shot back, "Fourth Street?"

Tough as it was for Prefontaine to regain his former eagerness, it was tougher for Bill Bowerman. The man who had been such a rock for everyone in Munich came home exhausted and discouraged. He felt that "all the guff he had taken from the Olympic officials," Barbara would say, "defeated what he had tried to do there." He put up a good front for the sake of team and family, hoping the ancient rhythms of timing workouts and making shoes would restore his vigor.

Before they took effect, the city of Eugene's fire marshal informed the university that Hayward Field's west grandstand along the homestretch was no longer patchable. The 5,000-seat structure, built in 1919, would have to be torn down after the 1973 season. If the Oregon Track Club hoped to host further Olympic trials, new stands would have to be built.

Neither the athletic department nor the university had funds for this. Bowerman's boss was young athletic director Norv Ritchey, who had taken over from Len Casanova in 1969. Ritchey, a baseball man from tiny Yoncalla, Oregon, about forty-five miles south of Eugene, had asked Bill to be his assistant AD, and they had worked well together. Ritchey was sympathetic to building a new structure for the track program. But in a year of recession and Arab oil embargo, there was no money. Raising it would be an enormous task. "It was impossible," Bill said later, "to do justice to my coaching and to a big construction project at the same time. And we didn't have much time."

So, without a word of warning, he retired. After twenty-five years in the chair of Bill Hayward, Bowerman at the age of sixty-two announced that, effective the end of the year, he was leaving to do the greatest good for the greatest number by chairing a drive to restore the facility.

Ritchey asked Bill to help him find a replacement. "He said, give me three names," Bowerman would recall. "I put them in this order: Bob Newland, South Eugene High coach Harry Johnson, and Bill Dellinger. Dellinger was already on the job."

Ritchey didn't interview any of them. Instead, he sat with Bill and they made the selection jointly, without much regard, apparently, for the order Bill had ranked them. As they talked, it became clear that the need was for a candidate able to weather changing times. "Without question," said Ritchey in 2005, "the toughest decade for college coaches, presidents, and athletic directors was the 1970s." War protests bled into free speech and civil rights protests, which bled into hair and dress protests. President Clark and his wife Opal—veterans of Harry Edwards's campaigns at San Jose State—once disarmed an angry delegation of Black Panthers by bravely inviting them into the president's mansion for tea and cookies.

Every coach in every sport faced challenges to his authority. Bowerman confided to Ritchey that he'd had a few athletes announce that they ran for the university, but not him. He welcomed rigorous academic questioning (once he felt the questioner had earned the right to ask). But more and more often, he felt, young men sought confrontation for its own sake.

The job contender who benefited most from these concerns was Bill Dellinger. "Bill was clearly capable of handling the authority situation of the 1970s," said Ritchey. "Bowerman said, 'He can sure do it better than I can.'"

I, having been coached in high school by the winning and unflappable Bob Newland, remain surprised Bowerman hadn't judged Newland superior in adjusting to the new freedom. "I think," said Ritchey, "Bill felt Bob Newland might have had as little patience with that as Bill himself."

In any case, Dellinger was soon appointed. He was confident he was up to the job, but was sobered by the suddenness of his elevation—and by what an act he had to follow. "There is no way for me ever to be Bill Bowerman," he said. "I can only be Bill Dellinger carrying on the lessons and legacy of Bowerman and Hayward. Which I pledge to do until I drop." Dellinger and Bowerman divided their labor that last season. Dellinger took on more of the program's administration. Bowerman marshaled a great community effort.

At a breakfast meeting of the Oregon Track Club board, most of whom were still buzzing from the Olympic Trials experience, Bowerman announced that if they wanted to partake of such glory again, they had to have financing, blueprints, and contractors set to go in a year. University architect Jon Kahananui had made a preliminary estimate that the cost of new stands would be $600,000. Bowerman asked the OTC board members to join him in each pledging two percent of the target, $30,000 apiece, either their own or cash squeezed from other sources. He compiled a five-page, single-spaced list of every business or professional person in town. Beside each target cow was the worker who'd volunteered or been assigned to milk it. Bill scrawled an exhortation on a memo that said it all: "Give it or get it!" Their own giving, he stressed, was necessary if they were to go hat in hand to major prospects.

By November 1973, the total of pledges and checks exceeded the $600,000 goal. John Amundson, of the Lutes and Amundson architectural firm, had drawn up a cunning, steel-supported, 7,500-seat plan that matched the original stands' shape, but extended the roofed stands past the finish line and halfway around the south turn. Bids were sought from area contractors. Then, as Bowerman would put it, "like bad relatives the bids came in." The worldwide oil shortage had caused structural steel prices to leap. The lowest contractor's bid was $807,549. All the submissions had to be rejected and the project rethought.

Bill and committee didn't go back to the drawing board so much as they lifted their eyes to a resource being trucked past daily on Franklin Boulevard—immense laminated Douglas fir beams, the pride of the Oregon wood products industry. Bowerman and Amundson asked state and city building authorities to consider granting a code variance so such beams could be used in a new design. The appeal was granted.

Four major makers (Weyerhaeuser, Rosboro, Bohemia, and Duco-Lam) came through with majestic beams that were so strong they could be cantilevered out over the practice track in back and support a roof over the new stands that didn't need to look like an old covered bridge. Amundson abandoned the section around the turn and cut the design to five bays, seating just under 5,000. But the great change was the upturned angle of the roof. It would make those 5,000 feel as if they'd been sitting in an old parka for years and now the hood had been pulled back—they would see the Coburg Hills beyond the east stands.

The project was rolling, but to Bowerman's ongoing chagrin, it incurred pressure from every agenda in town. These included the university administration (even the redoubtable Robert Clark didn't want donors milked dry right before the start of a major endowment campaign), athletic director Ritchey (who loved free capital improvement, but wouldn't spend a dime of the department budget to put in decent toilets), coaches of other sports, the track club, businesspeople, and building contractors. Bill had to deal with them all. By February 1974, he was writing a memo to himself, asking, "Am I equal to the task of pursuing this project? I have the feeling that the various echelons of the university such as the Physical Plant, Business Office, Athletic Department, Development Fund, and other administrators wish that this project would go away."

His committee, and his nature, prevailed on him to continue. Few were better suited to plow through the morass. In much the way that Bowerman loved and distrusted his athletes, he loved and distrusted his university. Improving it was possible, but it was like hacking back blackberry thickets in a swampy pasture: You would come out bleeding. People would lie and prevaricate and stall and bluff and bluster and drive you mad with the intensity of how they felt things had to be done. And you had to not let them.

Bill detailed a tiny sample of his tribulations in a letter to Otto Frohnmayer. The focus of Bill's ire was the UO business manager. He was also no great fan of Bowerman's for reasons that seemed to stem from Bill's not giving the man's son a track scholarship. When the fund drive began, wrote Bill, "He indicated to me that he believed the Business Office and/or the Development Fund should take ten percent off the top for 'operation.' 'The practice,' he said, 'is similar to the Federal Grants.' I indicated that this would be done over my dead body."

Later, when pledges were falling short of the $679,617 low-bid contract with the V. A. Harding Company, Bowerman asked the business manager how much more was needed; $100,000 was the answer. Bill went to his pal, Seneca Lumber's Aaron Jones, who came through with that amount. Ten days later, the business manager told Bill that "an error had been made" and asked him to ask Jones for more. "I told him to go to Hell," Bill wrote. "I would find some other way, but I was not going to look like a fool or a beggar to a man who had gotten us off the rock." There was more, all irritating and, to Bowerman's mind, petty in the extreme, from "the man who thinks he is chancellor."

These aggravations explain Bill's fervor whenever he spoke to his teams about Oregon philanthropy. When the day came that we would want to spend our hard-earned money not on trips to Europe or home and family but on the very university out of which many were in jeopardy of flunking, he'd say, we had to promise him that we wouldn't write a check to the university's general pot. That was like writing a check to the USOC's general pot and expecting it to trickle down to the athletes. No, we'd write it to the Development Fund, a foundation that the university had set up to accept gifts for specified ends.

Bill made us swear we would direct our money to the business school, to the writing program, to the biology department for teaching fellowships, whatever we felt was important—even the track team. "That," he said, "is the only way to know and control where your gift is being spent."

The new stands, then, were a donation from the Oregon Track Club to the university via the Development Fund, which held and disbursed the monies as needed. The old stands were torn down, leaving a big hole filled with seep water. In the spring of 1974, the Oregon crowd would watch meets from only one side of the track, the former backstretch. It was hoped the new ones would be done before the rains set in that winter.

The restoration project took all of Bill's energy and time. He certainly wasn't retiring because there was no more talent to cultivate. Three-miler Paul Geis—who had transferred from Rice after being astounded to find at the Olympic Trials that a whole city cared intensely about what he did—was running so well in his redshirt year as to worry Prefontaine. And the talent wasn't only on the track. Mac Wilkins, Prefontaine's classmate, who had gone on to break the Oregon freshman javelin record with 257 feet, had switched to the discus after an injured elbow precluded his throwing the spear. He was now improving in his new event by prodigious bounds.

"I went to Oregon because my coaches in high school couldn't be honest with me," Mac once declared. "They told me, 'Football will make a man out of you.' When it didn't, I came to appreciate throwing, and I came to appreciate a man who hated to be called coach, because I didn't fit in well with people who demanded to be called coach." A fond Wilkins memory was Bill's repeated injunction: "Mac, never forget. No one will ever love you as much as your mother."

Bowerman and Wilkins quickly developed a certain collegiality. In one of Bill's PE classes, on coaching track, Mac was in the front row for the class on the javelin. Bill was demonstrating the rhythm of the five-step approach and the delayed, right-foot reverse that he called "the late cow turd." As Mac would tell it, Bill's demonstration "was so forceful that he farted on the plant of the left foot." Bowerman went on as if nothing had happened, but saw by Mac's look that he, at least, had heard. Bill's face turned red. He hissed, "Don't you say a word, Wilkins." But when Mac innocently asked, "Was *that* the late cow turd, Bill?" they both cracked up.

In 1973, in the steamy heat in Baton Rouge, Louisiana, Wilkins won the NCAA title with a meet record 203 feet 11 inches. Prefontaine concluded his magnificent college track career by fighting off sciatica and winning his fourth straight NCAA three-mile title, in 13:05.3.

At that meet, Pre's competitors noticed a change. Stanford three-miler Don Kardong thought that the defeat in Munich "seemed to bring out the warmth that had hidden behind that veil of invincibility." Western Kentucky's Nick Rose, who had not met Pre before, was unnerved when he did. "I was sitting in the shade of the medical tent and Pre came up and started talking," Rose would recall, "which really freaked me out because I hero-worshipped him."

With the wins by Pre and Mac, Bowerman's final varsity team placed second in the nationals with 31 points to UCLA's 52. But Prefontaine's service to his school was not over.

Early in the planning phase for the new stands, pledges were about $25,000 short of what was needed to pay for bulldozing the stands and architects' fees. "Norv Ritchey had the great idea of holding a restoration track meet on June 20, 1973," Bill Landers would recall, "that would have as its big hook our wonder child Steve Prefontaine racing Dave Wottle in a mile."

Pre had scheduled a stint in Europe with the U.S. national team as well as a slate of Scandinavian races. He'd planned to leave a week before the fundraising meet but his loyalty to Bowerman and Oregon carried the day and he agreed to the race. Dellinger, meanwhile, made the contact with Wottle at the NCAA meet in Baton Rouge. Pre followed up with his own phone call. "Come to Eugene before we go to Scandinavia," Pre said to Wottle, "and we'll try for a new world record mile. I'll lead and you'll get a great time." Wottle, a wait-and-kick miler and no fool, accepted that rare gift, a respected opponent setting a hard pace.

First, though, there were the AAU nationals to contest. There, in the dry heat of Bakersfield, the two seniors won again, Wilkins with 211 feet 11 inches, beating Olympians John Powell and Tim Vollmer. In the three-mile, an improving Dick Buerkle pressed Prefontaine all the way. Pre responded with a new American record, winning in 12:53.4 to Buerkle's 13:00.2.

Four days later, a crowd of 12,000 witnessed the Hayward Field Restoration Mile, double what attendance would have been without this duel. Prefontaine took over after the half and hit an eye-opening 2:56.0 for three-quarters. Wottle shot out to a ten-yard lead in the backstretch and held it to the end, which he reached in 3:53.3 to Pre's 3:54.6, both lifetime bests. Wottle had missed Ryun's record, but was now the second-fastest American ever. Bowerman exulted that Pre was fully, emotionally back. "He ran a great race," he said. "If Wottle had drifted five yards off, he'd have gotten whipped!"

The meet cleared $23,204. "How many world-class guys," Landers would say, "would agree to a race they knew they were going to lose? Would Burleson?" Afterward, Norv Ritchey congratulated Pre for his magnificent gesture. "Well, Pre," Ritchey said, "this is a great thing you're doing and it will repay every bit of grant-in-aid you ever received." Pre looked Ritchey right in the eye and said, "I did that the first race I ever ran at Hayward Field."

Pre then headed off on the Scandinavian tour, which was jammed with races, small and great. A week after the Eugene mile, he was outkicked by Emiel Puttemans in a 5000 in Helsinki, but finished in a new American record of 13:22.4. The next day, he ran a PR 3:38.1 in the 1500.

Then his schedule started to gnaw at where Prefontaine was weakest, his lower back. Facing down old ghosts, he returned to Munich to run his sixth race in fifteen days, a 5000 against Harald Norpoth in the United States vs. West Germany vs. Sweden meet. He led most of the way. "But when I wanted to bear down and step up the pace," he said later, "I couldn't. I wasn't tired, but my back would tighten up and I couldn't go any faster." Norpoth zipped around right where he always did (with 200 to go) and won, 13:20.6 to 13:23.8. Prefontaine heeded his sciatica and went home.

Pre always seemed most vivid when he'd just come back from somewhere because in his absence it was impossible to remember how intense he was. He ran hard, castigating those who didn't, and he loved hard—girls, kids, love, the rush of life. No matter what time he went to bed, he was up every morning at six and out the door doing six-minute pace. His morning ten-miler was to keep him from getting fat on the pizza and beer of the night before. His metabolism was so efficient he swore that if he didn't run, he'd gain four pounds a day, indefinitely. This of course needed proving. When he gained eight pounds in two days, we believed.

Not long after his return, running along the bike paths by the river with a mob of Oregon runners, Pre told the story of Norpoth's latest perfidy. Three-miler Dave Taylor whipped off his sweat top and sprinted ahead. On the back of his T-shirt he had had printed *NORPOTH*. Pre flew into a rage. He caught up to Taylor and began choking him, shouting, "If that skinny sonuvabitch, if he ever does that to me again, here's what I'll do to him!" Said Taylor, "He was beating me up on the run."

Nineteen seventy-three was a year for combat on all fronts. In March, Blue Ribbon Sports and Philip Knight filed suit against the Onitsuka Company in US District Court in Portland. They alleged that the Tiger maker had breached their contract by soliciting new distributors and demanding that Knight sign over control of BRS for the right to go on distributing Tigers. Knight also alleged that Onitsuka had infringed on BRS's trademark by selling the eight models that BRS had registered in the United States. He asked for $33 million in damages.

Onitsuka countersued, saying, essentially, that those were their trademarks and they hadn't solicited anyone until after BRS started bringing in those "Nikes." If Onitsuka won, BRS would lose the exclusive right to sell the shoes Bowerman had designed. "This lawsuit," Bill said, "is win or die."

After a preliminary struggle over jurisdiction, the trial was held in Portland. It took ten days in April 1974. I was called on to testify.

One issue was whether the Cortez represented such a momentous leap in shoe design that it could be patented. The BRS side presented me not only as the possessor of the feet that inspired the prototype but also as an expert on quality running shoes. (Because I'd been on US national teams from 1968 to 1973, all the major makers had pressed me to try their free samples.)

To test this expertise, the Onitsuka attorney arrayed eight or ten shoes in front of me on the stand. Starting from one end, he asked me to name each model and say when it was first available. The first few were easy, ordinary models of Adidas, Puma, Tiger, Spot-Bilt, or New Balance, but the two pairs on the end I had never seen before. I grew more expansive about the shoes I knew about, all the while thinking, *I'm going to look like an idiot when I have to say, Whoa, that's a new one on me.*

Perhaps it was a ploy to make me sweat, because right before we got to the mystery shoes, the lawyer gathered them all up and said, "We stipulate his expertise, your honor."

Then I was led through the tale of my broken metatarsal and how Bill created the Cortez so that would never happen again. On the question of patentability, Judge James Burns asked me directly whether the Cortez was such an extraordinary advance as to be one of kind and not degree. I somehow knew not to say absolutely yes. "All I know," I said at last, "is that I never broke my foot again." He seemed to sit back, satisfied. Later he would find that the design was protected.

The patent aspect was a side issue compared to the stunning Onitsuka claim that the Cortez had been designed not by Bill Bowerman but by a German professor years before. This fabrication was quickly disproved. Nike attorneys Rob Strasser and Doug Houser located the professor and took an affidavit from him refuting the Onitsuka claim.

Onitsuka's playing fast and loose with the truth would come back to bite the company. Strasser made that behavior (reflected in Shoji Kitami's offering in other testimony four different dates for when he found out about the Nike line) the heart of his argument, Onitsuka was "unworthy of belief," Stasser declared. When Judge Burns convened the court and issued his decision, it was clear he had listened.

"Based on careful observation of Mr. Kitami's demeanor on the witness stand and review of his inconsistent and false statements under oath," wrote Burns, "Mr. Kitami's testimony cannot be believed unless separately supported by other credible evidence."

Since there was none on the solicitation issue, and since the disputed shoe designs had been developed jointly, Burns awarded both BRS and Onitsuka the right to sell them. But only BRS could use the models' *names* because of common law trademark. Therefore, BRS was entitled to damages for Onitsuka's infringing upon those trademarks. Burns appointed a special master to assess how much BRS was due. Onitsuka appealed and sold the same shoe as the "Corsair," but in the interim, the Nike Cortez was the only legitimate Cortez. BRS had won. The company would live to sell Bill's creations.

And did he ever have a creation to sell. The waffle sole, the company had finally realized, was fantastic at cushioning feet on track and road. Bowerman had assembled a crack research and development team in Eugene, with himself, Geoff Hollister, orthotist Dennis Vixie, and Dr. Stan James, a gifted orthopedic surgeon who'd joined Don Slocum's practice and become Prefontaine's orthopedist. At James and Bowerman's direction, Vixie customized a waffle-soled shoe for Pre, with a beveled heel that he really liked. This was the forerunner of the Nike Oregon Waffle, a yellow and green cross-country racing flat that was released late in 1973.

The problem suddenly was getting shoes to an exploding market. Frank Shorter's win in the Munich marathon had set off an American running boom. If, earlier, it had been win or die for BRS, now it was grow or die. Even venerable firms like Adidas and Puma were having trouble meeting demand. For Phil Knight's company, the tricky thing was balancing small orders from long-standing customers against large orders from new customers without alienating one or the other. The Oregon Waffle never did make it into most retail stores, but its sophisticated successor, the Waffle Trainer, a beveled midsole flat, did.

The Waffle Trainer was the company's first big moneymaker, but its effect on the bottom line was muddied as BRS scrambled to deal with hitting the big time. As part of an effort to improve supply, BRS decided it would make at least some of its shoes in the United States. Renaissance man Jeff Johnson, plunging ever deeper into things he had zero experience doing, supervised the refitting of the old Wise Shoe Company plant in Exeter, New Hampshire. In September 1974, the first American-made Nike came off its assembly line, a Cortez.

That year, company sales were $4.8 million. In 1975, they grew to $8.3 million. Blue Ribbon was turning out product as fast as it could, but was also stretched thin, dependent on bank loans to order the shoes from the factories, dependent on quick sales to pay off those loans.

Exactly how dependent was shown in May 1975. Jeff Johnson was startled to learn that the local Exeter bank wouldn't cash the paychecks he'd just issued because a recent check he'd deposited from Nike's Bank of California account hadn't cleared. This was because another deposit check had bounced out in California. As in a power outage, a short in one wire shut down the whole grid.

This had happened, in part, because as revenues came in, Knight had been repaying loans first to Nissho Iwai, the Japanese trading company that had financed the first Nikes made by Nippon Rubber, and letting other creditors wait until the last possible moment. BRS had been cutting those moments close, but didn't feel they were illegally kiting checks because everyone always got paid. Strictly speaking, however, in sending out checks before deposits came in, kiting was just what they had been doing. The Bank of California examiner saw that, froze all their accounts, and sent in regulators.

Blue Ribbon had more than half a million dollars in outstanding loans from the Bank of California. The bank declared them all in default and immediately due. The bank allowed Blue Ribbon to keep operating, but every week BRS's officers had to show up and get approval to write company checks.

"We had been kicked out of one bank," Knight would recall in 1992. "The second, it was touch and go. The Bank of California had their auditors out, and we couldn't ship anything without their approval. We couldn't cash a check for two or three days."

Nissho Iwai bailed them out of this humiliation in grand fashion. "Nissho was on the hook too for our shoe order loans," said Knight, "but they said, We'll not only give you an extra month to pay all this stuff, we'll take the bank out altogether. They wrote a check for a million bucks to the Bank of California and paid all those loans and said, Gentlemen, you are out of here."

The American banks had all studied BRS's business and set a credit limit based on sales staying about the same. "But Nissho had been following our growth curve," said Knight. "They looked at it differently. They said, 'You know you are going to be a big account five years from now and we want you then.' So it was good business they were doing. I didn't forget that." Knight was still with Nissho Iwai more than thirty years later, a fact of which he was justly proud. "That's kind of an untold story about international business," he would say in 1992. "We'd be cheaper by a little bit if we just dealt with American banks. We choose not to do that. It's not just loyalty. We think that's good business."

Nike's great success would spawn two categories of story, those of unlikely people who joined or invested early and grew rich, and those of people who, for one reason or another, didn't open the door when opportunity knocked. As the company became a huge concern, paying millions in interest and fees to other financial institutions, the Bank of California executives who'd had no faith in the fledgling outfit would have an ever-greater epic to tell—or not tell—about the check-kiters they drove away.

Because of the Munich Games, Prefontaine had not run cross-country in 1972 and because he wouldn't graduate until winter term of the 1973–74 school year, he was eligible to race in the fall of 1973. But his sciatica had limited his training and his confidence was at an all-time low. "I'd never seen Pre act like he did before the NCAA meet in Spokane," Dave Taylor would recall. "He'd injured his back and he was in a panic. He was just a regular person at that meet. He even locked himself in his room at eight that night."

His main rival would be Western Kentucky's Nick Rose, the world junior cross-country champion from Britain. "I'd been racing the way I do best," Rose would say, "just hammering for about four miles and then hanging on the last two." Rose, possessed of a high, rangy stride and great downhill relaxation, flew to a sixty-yard lead at halfway. Runners all over the course recall being astounded to see that gap.

Pre told Taylor later that he was really hurting, "so it was either do or die." He began to gain. Rose knew he was coming "and had this strange feeling I wasn't going to beat him." Pre came alongside with three-quarters of a mile to go and charged on to win his third NCAA cross-country crown.

Behind him, Terry Williams was twenty-second, Dave Taylor thirtieth, Randy James thirty-third, and Gary Barger fiftieth. Oregon won Bill Dellinger's first national team title with 89 points to Texas-El Paso's 157. If this was a dynasty, it hadn't skipped a beat.

Once Prefontaine graduated, he faced a reality that would be unbelievable to later national champions: penury. To run his best, he needed the freedom to train and travel. A full-time, entry-level job in his major field of communications—lugging equipment at a TV station—wasn't compatible with that. So the bulk of his income came illegally, or at least in violation of the amateur code. He would run bursts of European races, where meet promoters would pay in cash or fungible airline tickets. Wedging in additional European races was what hurt his back in 1973.

He did part-time things, such as driving Datsun 240-Zs from LA to Portland, where they sold for a thousand or two more, this financed by an entrepreneurial friend. And he tended bar at The Paddock, his own favorite haunt. The Pad always did great business when Pre was drawing the pitchers.

Bowerman heard about this and sat Pre down for an unscheduled goal-setting session. It didn't take long, because he knew his man by now, knew to lead with the irrefutable. "No one in Oregon," Bill said, "can influence kids the way you can." Once Prefontaine had nodded in prideful agreement, the discussion was essentially over.

However free Pre might feel to lead his own life, said Bowerman, he wasn't free to set an example that, if followed by the youngest of his people, would do them harm. "You're right, Bill," Pre said on very little reflection. "I'll quit. You're right."

Bowerman said later that he and Prefontaine seldom engaged in lengthy talks. "But there wasn't a picture of them," Barbara would observe, "where they weren't looking at each other and saying, 'Hey, who's boss here?'" Each operated by laying out a position and presuming the other would respect it. "When we disagreed about Pre's wanting to be a miler, or his working at the bar," Bill said, "he'd just jump up, run out, come back in fifteen minutes, and say, 'Okay.'"

Shortly after the session with Bill, Nike took Prefontaine on as its first paid track athlete spokesman. Even though his $5,000 a year was in violation of AAU rules against enrichment from sport, and even though Bowerman usually advised everyone to honor those rules until they might be changed, it was Bowerman who directed that the arrangement be made. Pre wrote his own job title, National Public Relations Manager, and had business cards made up. His main activity was joining Geoff Hollister, Olympic decathlete Jeff Bannister, Mac Wilkins, and others in clinics and presentations.

But he also scanned the horizon for deserving runners to help. When in 1975 he saw that an unknown guy from the Greater Boston Track Club had been third in the World Cross-Country in Morocco, Pre fired off some shoes and a letter of congratulations. Bill Rodgers wore those shoes to the first of his Boston Marathon victories, breaking Frank Shorter's American record with 2:09:55.

And Prefontaine never turned down a chance to talk bluntly to at-risk youth. "He became convinced," Mary Creel would remember, "that physical training could cure most of the world's problems. I think that's why he got involved with Nike. He thought they would be the means to spread that word. Obviously, this was Bowerman's influence." Bowerman had certainly done the groundwork with jogging. But Prefontaine's morning ten-mile runs were his own example of being rejuvenated by sheer effort. Why couldn't that work for everyone?

On April 27, 1974, Pre ran his first serious race of the year, a 10,000 at the Twilight Meet, in rain and wind. Mike Manley led him through the mile in 4:28 and then Pre took off. It would be a lonely race. The west stands had been bulldozed, and although 7,000 people were in attendance, they were all huddled in the remaining seats on the far side. Lap after lap, Prefontaine ran 67s, but he ran them by sprinting 32s with the wind in front of the crowd and muscling 35s against the wind on that lonely backstretch.

A lot of Oregonians rose to Pre's front-running battles against the clock because a lot of Oregonians' labor in the woods and mills was so dangerous it could only be done with skill and endurance. The mill workers, steel fabricators, tire-store owners, and filbert farmers (and lawyers, professors, Sunday school teachers, and out-of-their-minds sixth graders) didn't just see a chesty, beetle-browed kid driving into the turns. They saw work being done that they knew was hard unto impossible.

During that 10,000, as he came by on the backstretch, eyes rolled back, mouth agape, moaning, he really seemed to be running into oblivion. Yet when he came past the crowd and it stood up and thundered, he showed that he heard. The rest of us would hear the crowd, be moved to hang on, and try to lift a grateful arm afterward, but Pre always acknowledged his crowd in the moment. He cocked his head *then*, surged for them *then*—and they thundered all the more. He won them by stripping himself naked, absolutely unembarrassed at revealing his need and his agony. He ran an American record 27:43.6 that day, only five seconds slower than Viren's world record in Munich. "I think," he said later, subdued, "this indicates I'm ready."

Jere Van Dyk saw Pre as another Hank Stamper, from Ken Kesey's 1964 masterpiece, *Sometimes a Great Notion*. The "notion" in question is the power—and the sanctity—of an inspired individual to stand fast against a community of fearful naysayers. "For there is always a sanctuary more," Kesey wrote, " a door that can never be forced, whatever the force, a last inviolable stronghold that can never be taken, whatever the attack; your vote can be taken, your name, your innards, even your life, but that last stronghold can only be surrendered. And to surrender it for any reason other than love is to surrender love."

That was Prefontaine. He loved rough, lascivious talk ("envision a satyr," Frank Shorter once said of him), but there was nothing more obscene to Pre than surrender. In June, a few weeks later, Shorter got to see that for himself.

The second annual Hayward Restoration meet was even more loaded with talent than the first. Rick Wohlhuter from the Chicago Track Club warmed up the crowd with a world record 1:44.1 for 880 yards. Pre had invited Shorter to go for a fast time in the three-mile. Race day was windy, so they agreed to alternate halves until the last two laps, and then it would be every man for himself.

They broke away with a 4:16.5 mile and dutifully shared the lead through two miles. "Then Frank didn't hold up his end of the bargain," Pre would growl later. Instead of giving Pre a break, Shorter stayed tucked behind him, forcing him to fight the wind for most of three laps. With 300 to go, Frank compressed all the energy he'd saved into jumping Pre like he'd never jumped him before. As they hit the turn with 220 to go, Shorter had a yawning fifteen-yard lead. The crowd reacted with disbelief and then uttered something like a roar of absolute refusal. It was so loud that Don Kardong, in third, almost stopped. "It was beyond exciting," Kardong would say. "It was terrifying."

That roar got to Pre.

"I almost let him win," he would say later. "I was just thinking it wasn't that big a deal. Then something inside of me said, 'Hey wait a minute, I *want* to beat him,' and I took off. It was the idea of losing in front of my people."

Pre clawed past Frank with forty to go and won in an American record 12:51.4. Shorter ran 12:52.0. "You cheer for that guy," said Frank, deafened and amazed, "and you get something in return."

Prefontaine's obligation to his fans was such that it could physically injure him. That summer in Europe he set three more American records, then come home to train for six weeks before returning. He was looking two years ahead: Because the Olympics usually were held in late summer, he was attempting to learn how to peak later in the year than he'd been accustomed to doing as a collegiate athlete. "He was in awesome shape," Dellinger would recall, "maybe the best he'd ever been in."

As a final tune-up, "to blow out the carbon," as he put it, he always liked to run a fast mile. So on Tuesday, September 3, 1974, he scheduled one and let word pass among fans. A thousand showed. I had intended to be one, but when I saw the roiling wall of field-burning smoke and soot that came in from the north, I was sure Pre would bag it. The valley's rye grass farmers, as was their custom, had torched their fields after the harvest to kill weeds and remove straw. Thousands of acres had gone up just as the wind changed. The day would become known as *Black Tuesday*, one of the worst of such intrusions into the health of Eugene and Springfield. You could not see the length of Hayward Field. But the fans had come out, and because of them Pre ran anyway, clocked 3:58.3 and finished coughing gobbets of blood. His hacking tore muscle fibers under his rib cage.

He was lucky that the damage wasn't worse. Forest-fire crews have been found to have their lung function cut in half from smoke exposure. Pre went to Europe anyway, and in his second race, a two-mile in London against Britain's Brendan Foster, he couldn't breathe with two laps to go and had to step into the infield. In all his career, this was the single race he didn't finish.

The following February, Prefontaine, Bowerman, Savage, Manley, and I all drove up to the state capitol in Salem and testified before the Oregon State Senate. An earlier legislature had enacted a ban on field burning that was to take effect in six months. The seed farmers were lobbying for the ban to be repealed. We urged that the senators enforce it. Pre, being the star, and having the bloodiest tale to tell, was praised effusively by the chairman for doing his civic duty.

Pre said, "Never mind that, sir. I want you to promise me right now in this hearing that you won't cave to pressure from the farmers. Promise me that we'll always be able to breathe clean air in Eugene."

"Thank you, Steve. Thank you."

"Sir, I ask for your word. Your word you'll vote to keep the ban."

"Plenty of time for that, Mr. Prefontaine. Again, I commend you . . ."

"I have been up here before," Pre cut in, "to talk to the prison running club we've got going, and I gotta say you get a lot straighter answers from prisoners than from you politicians!"

Pre was right. The ban would be overturned.

Prefontaine was essentially apolitical, but he was passionate about his sport. He cared about local politics only when it affected air quality, and about air quality only because it affected his training. "He was a good guy in most ways," Mary Creel would say many years later, "but he was the center of his universe and you pretty much had to hop on as he went by."

No one understood that better than Creel herself. But once she hopped on, he wouldn't let her off. Prefontaine had always gone out with other girls because Mary wouldn't sleep with him unless and until they were married, and he was not candid about this with Mary. He wanted it both ways. When Mary discovered that he had dated Oregon coed and runner Nancy Alleman, with whom he was obviously quite close, Pre minimized the relationship. He repeatedly said that he wanted to settle down with Mary, that Mary knew him better than anyone and let him get away with less than anyone. She was a moral standard and a true trusted equal, who loved him for himself and not for his renown.

But Mary was not necessarily going to wait around. When she graduated, she got a job offer in Los Angeles. Pre asked her not to go, saying he needed her nearby. He wanted to marry her eventually, when he was fully ready, but first he had to sow his wild oats. She told him he'd better hope she didn't have three kids by then, accepted the job, and began packing.

Pre did not take her departure mildly. His last words to her were "I'll never let you go!" Mary was furious at his impossible neediness.

Early in 1975, Prefontaine was offered $200,000, the largest contract in the short history of the International Track Association, the professional track circuit that began in 1973 and disbanded before the Montreal Olympics. Pre had little of the traditional distance man's feeling for austerity. "I like to be able to go out to dinner once in a while," he'd say. "I like to drive my MGB up the McKenzie on a weekday afternoon. I like to be able to pay my bills on time."

Still, he turned the contract down. Until the Europeans were well and truly thrashed, he said, "What would I do with all that money?" He had abstained, of course, for one reason—to keep his eligibility to take on Viren in the 1976 Olympics in Montreal.

In January 1975, all the best American distance runners were invited to go through sophisticated physiological and psychological testing at the Aerobic Center in Dallas. We came away knowing some Prefontaine specifics. He had the highest maximum volume of oxygen consumption ever recorded in a runner, 84.4 milligrams per kilogram of body weight per minute. He also had an exchange with psychologist Bill Morgan of Wisconsin that came as close as we ever heard him to putting his motives into words.

"World-class runners have a psychology similar to world-class wrestlers or oarsmen," Morgan explained. "All are lower than the general population in neuroticism, depression, anxiety. This suggests that one prerequisite for success is a psychological profile characterized by stability. Runners are stable to the point of being aloof, even defiant."

Prefontaine gave Morgan a taste of that defiance. Asked for short answers to three simple questions (how he began running, why he continued, what he thought about in races), Pre got impatient with the seeming shallowness of the interview. He delivered a lecture on what running was for him. "A race," he said, "is a work of art that people can look at and be affected by in as many ways as they are capable of understanding."

That was, of course, the credo of the front-runner, who has failed if he hasn't consumed himself completely. "He was trying," concluded Morgan, "for something that only the participants might be able to understand."

After Dallas, what might be called Pre's paradox was conspicuous. The man with by far the most powerful cardiovascular engine also had a history of saying he had little physical talent. The man with the ideal, seventy-seven percent slow-twitch muscle fibers and a heart that hit 210 beats a minute also had a habit of dismissing the importance of all that in effective racing.

During the first long talk he'd ever had with Mary Creel in 1971, he told her that talent was a myth. Ten guys on the team had more talent in their little finger, he said, but he beat them because he could withstand more discomfort. He seemed very much in earnest, seeming to believe that the limits of one's inherent physiology could be overcome by sheer will power.

I believe he was indulging in a natural kind of wish fulfillment for a front-runner, whose sense of sacrifice is such that he needs to believe not only that he is better than the field, but also that he can endure better than the field. Feeling talented doesn't help when the going gets hard, but feeling tough does. If running is largely an act of will and his will is superior, it matters little what kind of engine he has.

But of course the engine does matter. A runner needs a certain basic speed, adaptability to training, and mitochondrial blessings to run well. That Pre was so eager to ignore physiological reality is interesting. Consistently denying one's ability or merit often suggests some degree of self-loathing. I'm not prepared to refute that possibility about Prefontaine, but if he had such feelings (and he was famous for having nervous doubts right before races) they were manageable. When faced with those lofty max VO2 numbers in Dallas, he grudgingly admitted he was gifted.

Ultimately Pre came to accept that running is a balance of physical ability and mental desire. He even adopted the test of talent into his own pursuit of records. "I'd like to come back someday when I'm really in good shape," he said, "and put that oxygen uptake mark way out there."

First he embarked on a quest that enlisted both Bowerman's sympathy and counsel. Pre felt he owed a huge cultural debt to Scandinavia. For five years, he'd toured the tracks of Norway, Sweden, and Finland, seeing how every little town had a meet of its own. When he bought a house on McKinley Street, the first thing he did was build a sauna. He'd brought back plans for European fitness trails, or *parcours*, to put in Eugene parks.

Pre had felt so welcome and understood in the smallest Finnish villages that he conceived a way of repaying its athletes. He'd invite a group of the best to Oregon and have them compete not just in Eugene but all over, from Coos Bay to Madras (which had the closest decent track to Fossil). He'd also get Lasse Viren over to his turf during his usual peak season of May.

Bowerman thought it was a great idea. The AAU track and field administrator, Ollan Cassell, who'd known Pre since 1969, advised him that it needed to be a sanctioned meet or tour and that the US governing body didn't give that right to athletes, only to established meet directors. He should go through the Oregon Track Club, which was putting on the national AAU meet that June.

Instead, Prefontaine adopted the Bowerman view that sometimes it's better to apologize later than ask permission first. He filed all the proper paperwork with the AAU, but before they could deny anything, he sent invitations to ten stellar Finns, including Viren. They accepted. Pre, using a network of high school coaches and tracks he'd developed through Nike, set up five meets all over the state. Presented with this *fait accompli*—and Pre's popularity—Cassell had no choice but to grant the AAU sanction.

Before the Finns arrived, Pre ran a solid 28:09.4 in the April Twilight Meet 10,000 and bragged about his strength. Viren immediately cabled that he was hurt and couldn't come. "Losing him makes everything I've done worthless," said Pre. "But I understand. There were meets in Europe when I didn't show up to run against him."

"I told him that sounding off about how strong he was had been a mistake," Bowerman would recall later, "that if he wanted to get those runners over here to his lair, he had to be more sly. But that was hard for him. He didn't look beyond races. Hell, he didn't look beyond laps."

Prefontaine had wildly overstated what losing Viren meant. It had little effect on another aim. Creel would remember that Pre wanted not just to compete with the Europeans on his own turf, but also to show them what America really was. "All they ever see of the United States is Los Angeles or New York," he said "The big, crowded, hurrying cities. Those places aren't the real America. These guys are going to find out how beautiful the United States is."

Pre had been impressed by the beauty of Scandinavia, Germany, Italy, and France, Creel would say, "but when he compared them to Oregon, he felt they couldn't hold a candle to 'our mountains, our rivers, our ocean.' He wanted the Finns, especially, to know how paradisiacal it is here. He also wanted them to know that there were people in places other than Finland who appreciated the sport."

The monthlong tour was an artistic success. The Finns who did come were treated to the homestyle hospitality that they had provided themselves. Pre even broke the American record for 2000 meters with 5:01.4 in the Coos Bay meet.

But every stop lost money. If he were not to be personally bankrupted by his hands-across-the-seas gesture, he needed to attract at least 5,000 people to the last meet in Eugene, on May 29, 1975. Who would give him a 5000-meter duel worth watching? Pre naturally thought of the man who had come so close a year before, Frank Shorter. In March, at Frank's invitation, Pre had trained with him in Colorado and New Mexico. But Frank had had his wisdom teeth out and had overtrained and been ill. Out of friendship, he came when Pre called. Bobbie and I put him up at our house near Hendricks Park.

Seven thousand people filed in to see their clash, so as they went to the start, Prefontaine knew he was financially solvent. Paul Geis took the first three laps; Shorter led at the mile in 4:17. Prefontaine took over the lead after six laps. At two miles, Pre shot ahead and churned successive laps of 63, 64, and 63, running away with the race, running through the rising shouts of his people, his head cocked to the right, brow knitted tight. This was where he lived, and those long, searing drives never failed to be compelling. He ran the last fifty yards with his eyes shut, squeezing away the suffering. He finished in 13:23.8, only 1.6 seconds slower than his best. Soon the crowd was flowing around him, small boys waving programs, beaming matrons, girls in halter tops.

That night there was a party at Geoff Hollister's house. All the Finnish athletes were there, along with many of the families who had housed them. Prefontaine's parents were there, along with his Marshfield coach, Walt McClure. As the beer flowed and the sandwiches circulated, there was talk of Pre's going to Helsinki and his hospitality being returned. A new AAU rule that if a runner did not race in the nationals he'd be unable to race in Europe during certain "moratorium" periods drew Pre's scorn about the harm the national body was doing American track. "Where is the talent that I competed against in 1969?" he asked. "The shortage is of guys who are out of school and can still figure ways to train and find competition. I'm twenty-four years old and Frank is twenty-seven, and we're *veterans*. That's the shame. That's what's wrong with the American system."

Ray Prefontaine seemed daunted by his son's ferocity. Having heard much of this before, we talked of where the best Dungeness crabs were being caught in Coos Bay. Steve leaned near and whispered to me that he'd never been crabbing. "I've never been fishing either, but for God's sake, don't tell anybody that."

Bobbie and I left the party at 11:00. Frank wanted to stay longer, so Pre said he'd drive him home, and he did at about 12:30. They sat in Pre's car in our driveway and made a date for the three of us to run an easy ten in the morning. Shorter, by then an attorney, promised to brief Pre on legal challenges that might be brought against the AAU's restrictions on international racing.

"Yeah, well, let's go over that tomorrow, when our heads are clear," said Prefontaine, and he drove off down the hill. Frank walked into the house, slipped into bed, and slept soundly.

At 7 a.m. on May 30, we awoke to the shock of our lives, that Prefontaine had been killed in a one-car accident on Skyline Drive, no more than a minute after dropping Frank off. We walked down through neighbors' yards to the scene. The car had been removed by then, but there was broken glass on the street. We saw the accident report and learned he'd struck a natural outcropping of black basalt. He hadn't been wearing his seatbelt. The car had flipped over, coming to rest on that great chest. He had not broken a bone. The weight of his beloved butterscotch MGB had simply pressed the life out of him. If anyone had found Pre then, in the first five minutes, he or she might have saved him with a two-by-four and a brick.

Pre had to have left this world with a fine regard for its absurdities, one being that he was dying on a road he loved to run, on a hill where he made others suffer. His last moments surely recapitulated his finest races, his blacksmith bellows gasping, his fighting down panic, his approaching death's door, his needing the crowd to call him back.

Neal Steinhauer—on his way to the ministry—had talked with him a week before at the Modesto Relays about the seeming disorder of his life and priorities. Steinhauer ever since has hoped that he did enough, hoped that in Pre's last moments his mind turned to the Almighty.

The Coos Bay funeral was extravagant to the point of circus, with Pre's hearse doing a lap of the Marshfield track at about 70 pace. One pallbearer, Jon Anderson, was made so furious by the fear-mongering preacher ("Get right with God. Who among us is safe if our strongest can be taken in an instant?") that he started knocking on the side of the casket. Said another bearer, Mike Manley, "I thought Pre was coming right up out of there."

Bowerman, as he had in Munich, watched with Barbara from high in the stands. Afterward he told us that the Oregon Track Club would hold a memorial on Hayward Field two days later, June 3. Haggard in a way he had not been in

Munich, he said that he would say a few words, but that the rest of the program should be up to the athletes.

The next day, we cast a wide net and assembled all the Prefontaine friends we could think of at our house to see who should say what. We ended up with twenty people in a circle, all pointing at each other and saying, "You knew him better than I did."

Pat Tyson had lived with Pre for two years but felt he went to Frank and me for guidance. We, startled, said we suggested ideas about the AAU but never felt intimate with him. He loved to stay over at Mark Feig and Steve Bence's apartment, but they said he came in so late and got up so early they never saw him. Geoff Hollister, who'd driven all over the state with him doing running talks, never knew until that moment that Pre had started a running club at the Oregon State Prison. We were stunned. Great quadrants of him were not known to more than a few.

The memorial service, we decided, would be the opposite of the funeral. It would be all about him, and it would be fast. It would give him one thing he never got in running: a world record.

At twilight on June 3, 4,000 mourners assembled in the east stands. They received a card saying that the clock would be started, that Pre's fellow Olympians Bowerman, Shorter, and I would speak for ten minutes and leave the field. Then the clock would stop at 12:36, "a time with which Steve Prefontaine would be well satisfied." It was the 63 pace he'd spoken of as a goal, eleven seconds faster than Emiel Puttemans' world record. The scoreboard clock, where Pre's eyes had always gone as he hit the line, was under the control of Bill Dellinger's brother Fred. The seconds began to whip by.

Bowerman began. He was shaky at first, an image of the wrongness of a father burying a son. "Friends," he said, "let us be grateful that we were a part of what Steve Prefontaine, the Champ, stood for, what he enjoyed and what he achieved. Thanks to his mother and dad for giving him those characteristics of truth, honesty, intensity, and physical ability.

"I first knew Pre through Walt McClure—when he was fourteen years old. Walt said, 'Watch this freshman, he's tough and will be a good one.'

"Four years later when he was a frosh, there was the early fall rain. Pre had finished his orientation lecture. Dressed in sweats, he was walking the halls of Mac Court. From inside the arena issued the undertones of the radical student unrest. Catcalls, rude questions, foot shuffling. Pre looked in and said to me, 'I don't believe it!' He walked to the stage and asked, 'May I speak?' He was handed the mike. 'I am a freshman—I chose Oregon—I listened to the orientation—I came to get an education and to run—Listen! You'll learn something—Thanks! I'm glad I came to Oregon.'

"His great races are told better by the press and media. His desire burned to be the best—and he was. Step by step, as he matured he reached his goals. In high school he was state champion and national record holder. In the university he held every American record from 2000-meters, two miles, through six miles and 10,000 meters. In 1976 his goal was Olympic champion and the world records related thereto. He also burned with another great goal: Emancipation, freedom for the US athlete. Tens of thousands of dollars were his for the signing of a professional track contract. No! Help the athlete. Help the sport."

Bowerman told how Prefontaine had done that by challenging track and field's resistance to change. "In the history of our sport," he went on, "no one man had ever been permitted to arrange and bring a foreign athlete or team to the USA. The door was always locked by national red tape and dictatorship. Pre opened the door by persistence and difficult communication. You saw the Finnish athletes. Theirs was the first such visit in this century.

"His legacy to us is truth, honesty, and hard work, work that the good things of track and other sports may be freely enjoyed by athletes and spectators.

"Pre the little champ opened the international door. I pledge to Pre, I know these close family and friends join me, and we invite all true sportsmen to fulfill his great dream—freedom to meet in international sport and friendship."

Frank spoke of how their friendship had unexpectedly blossomed when they had shared the pace in a race and, unlike the year before, Frank actually kept the agreement. "And after that, it seemed I'd passed a test. He was my friend."

Frank told of inviting him to train two months earlier in Taos, New Mexico, for a week of runs above 9,000 feet, altitude being one element that Pre hadn't fully explored. "We were running in blowing snow that had melted and frozen again, and this pelting corn snow was hitting us and blowing in our faces and I had Pre all dressed in goggles and mittens. Steve was a guy who complained under the best of conditions. He was whining, he was asking why, what am I doing here?

"I turned to him and said, 'Steve, you know nobody in the world is training harder than we are right now.' It was the only time I ever ran with him that he got quiet. For the rest of the run, he didn't say a word. We helped each other get better because we knew how to train and not be competitive, when to turn it on and when to turn it off. I've lost a great friend."

I finished with an attempt at summarizing the thoughts of our meeting of friends. "He conceived of his sport as a service," I began, "in the way an artist serves. Without that, he would never have given us all the records. They were out beyond winning or losing, which a runner does for himself. They came from those furious minutes near the end of a race when his relentlessness and our excitement blended into a joyous thunder. All of us who now say, 'I had no idea how much this man meant to me,' do so because we didn't realize how much we meant to him. He was our glory, and we his.

"In Munich he lost. Within an hour, he showed us, not for the first or last time, how meager was our faith. When he came home, we began to see that while the competitive fury was still there, he was no longer driven. He began to channel and refine the prodigious energy that ran in him. He visited schools and spoke so graphically about juvenile delinquency and venereal disease that the teachers blushed. He organized a sports club in the Oregon State Prison. He stormed at state legislators about field burning and said later he preferred the company of the prisoners.

"He answered every single critical letter he ever received. He and his grandfather together built a sauna, of which he was insufferably proud. He continued to give powerful and profane voice to the right of all athletes to be free to compete when and where they chose. Combining that cause with his sense of his roots and people, he brought the team of athletes from Finland to compete around Oregon. And we knew he was happy.

"He was a man of all these parts, and more not mentioned here, and still more that we never knew. It is up to us now to hold him in mind clearly, to remember him exactly as he touched us, infuriated us, and challenged us.

"Time holds him, green and dying, though he sang in his chains like the sea."

When I was done I looked over. "There are still two minutes on the clock," I added. "He could run a half-mile."

The three of us walked across the track and took our seats in the stands. The infield was cruelly empty. As the clock ticked, a spot or two of sun broke through the westerly scudding clouds. People began to rise and a few cried, "Go Pre!" In numbers they stood and applauded. With a minute to go, it was as if he were into his last lap. His people all were up, roaring him home as they had done four nights before. When the clock stopped, there was a visceral "*OOOF!*" and five seconds of dead silence. Then people were pointing, cheering, imagining him on his victory lap. The clock read 12:36.4.

The evocation of Prefontaine was more graphic than we could've imagined. Several people were so emotionally disturbed it was days before they stabilized. Two who would have been devastated anyway were Bowerman and Dellinger.

Bowerman was so distraught that when Blaine Newnham of the *Register-Guard* asked him to speak of how long he'd known Pre and how he coached him, Bill, as he often did, abbreviated and thereby neglected to give Dellinger full credit for his recruiting, coaching, and guidance. Dellinger, just as disturbed, read the article, was hurt, and called Bowerman on its shortcomings: "I thought you taught us all to give credit where credit was due."

Bowerman didn't rectify the omission publicly. But two days later, on June 5, he wrote this to Dellinger: "Dear Bill: I have your note. If I have offended you, it adds to my grief. Of the people I spoke to regarding our community and personal tragedy, only Blaine Newnham interviewed me. I recalled the high points of Pre's career, his background from Coos Bay and Walt McClure briefly. That, as head coach, I did designate the physical coaching to my very able assistant. During that time, philosophy (if that be the correct word) was frequently communicated with the Champ and others, where they seek me.

"If you find offense, it grieves me more.

"Sincerely, Bill."

Dellinger did continue to find offense. They were estranged.

CHAPTER 27

Legacy

THE DEATH OF STEVE PREFONTAINE SPARKED AN OUTPOURING OF LETTERS AND poems of condolence to family, coaches, and newspapers, their authors all struggling to convey what Pre meant to them. Senator Mark Hatfield, seeking to explain the hold Pre had over Oregon's imagination, rose among the master politicians in the United States Senate and celebrated Pre for refusing to be politic.

"I have helped officiate at various meets in Eugene," Hatfield said, "and I know the spirit that fills the University of Oregon track stadium, Hayward Field. The last was during the 1972 Olympic Trials, and the atmosphere was alive with emotions. Pre was the favorite of this crowd in a way few athletes can ever be. We often read of a cocky athlete alienating a crowd. With Pre, confident and cocky as he was, the Oregon track crowds loved him. Perhaps it was for a couple of reasons.

"Pre never was the type that the Amateur Athletic Union or the Olympic fathers, or even the NCAA brass, wanted to parade around as an all-American athlete. Oregon fans had long known that track athletes were not always treated as well as they should be. Oregon fans knew the various squabbling factions cared more for their own petty concerns than they did about the rights and benefits of the athletes. As a result, Pre's willingness to stand up for what he believed in did not cause any loss of his popularity in Oregon. It increased it. Pre was each of us fighting against a bureaucracy caring only about its own preservation.

"A second reason Pre was so loved in Oregon is that everyone knew he had turned down one of the largest offers to compete in professional track. His answer was that he wanted to run in Oregon, for 'his people.' His willingness to go against the grain set him apart. Perhaps people saw in him a spirit they felt they had within themselves. In a state such as Oregon, with our strong traditions of individualism, he stood as a true native son."

The manner of that son's passing would lead to apprehension over how he would be remembered. The day after the accident, the Eugene Police Department announced that his blood alcohol level had tested at 0.16 percent, well above Oregon's (then) legal limit of 0.10. It would break Elfriede Prefontaine's heart that this led many to accept a simpleminded version of her son's death. The legend grew that like James Dean, another charismatic rebel, Steve had gotten drunk, slammed his car into a stone wall, and killed himself.

Because Pre had been sharing beers with us at Hollister's party, none could deny that he had been drinking. And 0.16 percent is a lot, a level assumed to cause real impairment. Yet Frank Shorter—a cautious man, who was such a friend that he would not have hesitated to take the wheel—didn't feel at all concerned about riding with him. "He was in the same condition I was in," said Frank. "We'd had three or four beers and he seemed fine. I trusted him to drive." Pre had simply said he was tired.

It turned out that police had deviated from standard procedure when they had taken a blood sample from the body at the funeral home and released the figure to the press. The normal practice was for the county medical examiner to do a blood alcohol test during the autopsy. The examiner who performed Prefontaine's autopsy, Dr. Ed Wilson, was criticized by the family for (they presumed) revealing the 0.16 level. In a letter to Bill Dellinger, Wilson stated that he never got the vial of blood the police had taken at the funeral home, never tested it, and so had not been responsible for that finding. "This was done in an unusual manner," Dr. Wilson wrote. "I don't remember ever having it happen that way before or since. I was very angry about it."

Because different test methods can affect readings by as much as twenty percent, the change in procedure gave rise to suspicions. Did the police have their own agenda, a wish to emphasize Pre's drunkenness? Dr. Wilson would later say that when he informed police chief Dale Allen that he was unhappy with how the case had been handled, Allen had replied to the effect that he wasn't unhappy that Steve Prefontaine had been shown not to be a god, that he was human like anyone else.

Chief Allen's remark was not inconsistent with the estimation more than a few police officers had of Prefontaine. Pre didn't handle authority well and often bridled at the sight of cops. They often bridled back. Prefontaine's prodigious, incurable, what-you-see-is-what-you-get honesty—honesty that let him perform and enrapture the crowd as he did—also meant that he had never been a hypocrite about his drinking. But there were more important elements to the story than a fishy blood test.

The home closest to the accident belonged to Bill and Karen Alvarado. Their front door opened ten feet from the twisting, two-lane road that is Skyline Drive. The Alvarados had gone to the track meet, visited friends, and come home just after midnight. It was a still, warm evening. They made sandwiches and sat in their bedroom with the windows open to the fragrant woodsy air. They heard a loud sports car engine on the road just below their window. It passed and there was a screech of tires, an impact, and silence. "It was so absolutely still," Karen Alvarado would say, "we knew something was wrong."

She told Bill Alvarado to go see. Within twenty seconds he was downstairs, out the door and onto the street, looking left downhill toward where the sound had been. The rightward curve of the road just prevented him from seeing what had happened. As he peered into the night, he heard a car starting down there, just around the bend. In a moment he was blinded by its headlights. "I thought he'd hit the stop sign," Alvarado recalled ten years later. "I stood in the street and waved my arms. But there was no way he was going to stop and I had to get out of the way in a hurry." As the car shot past, he saw that it was a light-colored MGB. In seconds it was around the turn uphill, out of sight. Alvarado got angry at the driver's having taken off like that. He hopped in his Jeep and followed. He drove up the hill and into Hendricks Park, but never found the pale MGB. It had pulled off onto a side street.

Alvarado, driving slowly in his hunt, took a looping route to get home, around onto Birch, left on Skyline, and at last—four or five minutes after it had happened—found Pre's overturned car. He parked and ran far enough toward his house to yell to his wife that someone was hurt and to call for help. He returned to the car. "I didn't know who it was, but he was still gasping and somehow I managed to lift the car partway off him. But that was all I could do. I couldn't get the car completely off and I couldn't pull him out.

"I'm not a medical person, but I know he was still breathing. If I could have had help lifting the car, if the other car had stopped, we could have saved time and maybe we could have lifted it off of him."

When Alvarado realized he was no good to the man alone, he ran to call for help. While he was gone, the Eugene police arrived. By then, Steve Prefontaine was dead. The first medical person on the scene, Dr. Leonard "Jake" Jacobsen, was a tough, experienced surgeon who'd also taught at the university. He had been called by the Alvarados and gone down a hillside path through the ivy from his home directly above the wreck. He pronounced Pre dead. Later, the two police officers would report they smelled alcohol at the scene. Dr. Jacobsen, a veteran of much trauma, said that was untrue, that it was only vomitus.

The police had come because they had been called by the driver of the MGB that had roared past Bill Alvarado and vanished. When that driver didn't return to the scene, the police located him a few blocks away, at his family home on Kona Street. Twenty-year-old Karl Lee Bylund said he'd arrived at the site after the accident, seen someone pinned underneath, panicked, and driven off to get his father, Richard Bylund, a doctor. Because neither Bylund had returned to render aid, the police were suspicious and treated it as a potential hit and run. But there were no scratches on Bylund's car. A week later, the police reported that Karl Bylund had passed a lie detector test in which he held to his story. The case was closed, listed as a single-car fatality.

But questions lingered. The tow-truck driver noted that the car had been in second gear. The Alvarados had not felt Pre had been speeding past their window. Why had Pre slammed into a rock wall on the far side of a road along which he was moving at moderate speed? Over the years, I came to believe that for the accident to happen as it did, Pre had to have approached that rock wall at a very specific angle. To attain that angle he had to make a forceful, leftward turn of his steering wheel. I concluded that he was taking some kind of evasive action. Something had been in his lane and (since there was steep hillside jutting up to his right) he avoided it by slamming on the brakes and swerving left. This view was shared by David Sonnichsen, a neighbor and researcher who, with the help of the Prefontaine family, spent years interviewing the principals. Sonnichsen, who meticulously established the facts presented in this account, also concluded that the police's disdain for Pre probably did not rise to the level of an actual plot to discredit him or had done so only marginally.

What was Pre trying to miss? It could have been a deer or a raccoon. Given that the Alvarados heard no other car besides Pre's until Bill Alvarado reached the street, it could have been the MGB of Karl Lee Bylund. Alvarado said he heard it start from first gear right before it came around the turn and past him. That was about thirty seconds after the accident. So Bylund might have swung too wide around the turn from Birch onto Skyline and placed himself in Prefontaine's lane. Bylund, although he was asked about it over the years, never changed his story that the car was already overturned when he came upon it.

With time, these findings partially satisfied my own need for a coherent explanation. For me (and for Dr. Jacobsen), the issue of whether Karl Bylund had any part in causing the accident was secondary to his not going back and helping Bill Alvarado help Pre. That failure had potentially fatal consequences. I never met Karl Bylund. Over the years, my feelings about his actions would evolve from uncomprehending fury, through morbid curiosity, to a kind of academic pity at his having to go through life haunted by the knowledge that he could have done more.

The effect of all this was to make us wild to cling to Prefontaine's legacy, to define and protect it. He hadn't left a will, but he might as well have. "I did not want to waste or squander any effort Pre put forward," Shorter would remember.

"I felt if you could keep momentum going on something he cared about, then you should."

Our leader in much of this was Bill Bowerman. Earlier that year, when Hayward Field's new west stands were completed, the annual Restoration meet had been renamed the Bowerman Classic. Bill now scotched that. Pre was "part of the dream to replace the old, condemned stands," Bowerman wrote in a press release. "He was the driving force in the two Restoration meets. Our Oregon Track Club Board concurs that in living memorial to Pre—his inspiration, his ambition—the meet he did so much to make successful should bear his name. Next Saturday evening you may attend the Steve Prefontaine Classic, a first step in a parade of opportunities to share directly in the dreams of Steve Prefontaine."

Bowerman got a note that week from university president Robert Clark. "Your gesture in naming Saturday night's event for him was magnanimous indeed," Clark wrote. "We owe much to Steve, but we owe even more to you for your years of service at the university and for the quality in you that brought Steve Prefontaine and others to us."

The Pre Classic would grow into the finest IAAF Grand Prix invitational in the country. And a living memorial it is, coming at the season he left us, when the roses and peonies are most potent, and blending the two opposites that warred in him, the voluptuary and the ascetic.

A second step, Bowerman felt, was to embed Pre's goals in an institution. To that end, Bill convened Ray Prefontaine, Walt McClure, Jim Grelle, Jon Anderson, Wade Bell (now a CPA), Roscoe Divine (now a lumber broker), attorney Greg Foote, and me. We departed the meeting having fashioned the nonprofit Steve Prefontaine Foundation. Its first major job was to build a running trail the equal of those Steve had enjoyed in Europe.

Bowerman marshaled local producers. Mills donated sawdust. Trucking companies loaned vehicles and drivers. Pre's Trail was to be in Lane County's Alton Baker Park, across the river from the campus. County engineers helped plan the route and used a small federal grant to fund youth crews to lay a base of gravel for drainage. Then Oregon Track Club work parties and school sports teams spread the wood chips. Bowerman doubted that such cooperation would have been possible without everyone knowing for whose dream he or she labored.

Today the trail is six miles of springy cedar bark and wood waste path. Fulfilling Pre's expressed wish, it has a *parcours* of exercise stations. Some loops are so smooth they are good for shock-free, 60-pace interval training. After a few years, we would recall running with Pre himself in favorite sections. It would bring us up short to realize he never saw it, that he knew only the paved bike paths along the river.

Once the trail was finished, the Prefontaine Foundation took on a mission close to Pre's heart—to help the most talented in our sport, wherever they may be, whatever they may need. Pre had observed with disgust that there was little support for gifted young female runners. He'd been wildly protective of 15-year-old Mary Decker, whom he'd met on the AAU national team in 1973. He'd called her often at her home in LA to check on her training and moaned to us that her mother and coach were overworking and over-racing her. So his namesake foundation funded young athletes, especially women, to competitions appropriate to their ability.

Bowerman also used the foundation to help schools and towns around the state upgrade their tracks from muddy cinders to rubber asphalt. He always insisted, when helping with a new track, that the foundation put forward money only if it was matched by the community receiving it, to nurture a sense of ownership. Somehow, donors and matchers always pungled up their halves and the tracks got built.

The last item on Pre's wish list was fixing the governance of American track, specifically to free athletes so they could develop and compete as they saw fit. "The AAU was what we were discussing, sitting in the car that night he died," Shorter would recall, "and I think it was only natural for me to go on with the fight." This was actually a matter of rededication for Shorter and me, because two years earlier, embarrassed by all the snafus at Munich (and coaxed by 1964 Olympic swimming champion Donna De Varona), the USOC had agreed to form the Olympic Athletes' Advisory Council (AAC). Shorter and I were invited to be founding members.

Olympic athletes had never had vote or voice in the USOC unless they were prepared to spend years working their way up through different committees, by which time they were no longer purely athletes. But the new USOC AAC had one unconflicted competitor from every Olympic sport—winter and summer, men's and women's—thirty or more active or recently retired athletes. All had in common the grounding Olympic experience, yet they were vastly different otherwise. That mix of common purpose and cross-pollination made the AAC a rousing group of achievers.

The AAC was no more than advisory at first, but it quickly began urging the Olympic Committee to open all its governing boards and subcommittees to a fixed percentage of athletes. Frank and I had told Prefontaine all about this and said that every top athlete was welcome to attend, but he was always too impatient to go to AAC meetings. He had a million suggestions, however, which usually boiled down to getting some power over the AAU that the NCAA hadn't been able to attain.

We got right on it. In our very first meeting in Chicago in 1973, we were asked to weigh in on a bill then before Congress authored by Senator James Pearson of Kansas that would break up the AAU and set up a central amateur sports association. This body would be empowered to establish rules under which "US Sports Associations" could be issued federal charters as international franchise holders in their respective sports. Significantly, an association would be prohibited from holding more than one charter and would be required to grant active athletes twenty percent of voting power in the association.

USOC President Phillip O. Krumm and Executive Director Colonel F. Don Miller made impassioned speeches to the athletes' group, saying the American Olympic movement had always been free from government money and government strings and that it was desperately important to our way of life to keep it that way. We were on a toboggan run to socialism if we didn't resist this attack. Senator Pearson said the Olympic sports and the AAU were so unlikely to spontaneously improve that Congress had to step in.

The athletes debated and agreed, by a vote of twenty-five to four, to support the bill. Air Force Captain Micki King, the AAC president and 1972 diving champion, went before the full USOC board of directors to deliver that message. She came out white. "If Phil Krumm had had an M-16," she said, "I'd be in my grave." Ignoring its athletes' considered views, the USOC opposed the bill hysterically and it was defeated.

Bowerman was fascinated by these echoes of his own battles in the early 1960s. "Promise me," he said once after I'd briefed him on a meeting, "that you and Frank won't bang your heads against this wall for fifteen years like I have. Life is too short." (One heard that life is too short a lot after Pre died.)

But then, in late 1975, news came that President Gerald Ford was naming the President's Commission on Olympic Sports (PCOS) to hold hearings for a year to fully document what was wrong with American amateur sport and arrive at how to fix it. The one thing Bill's experience had shown was that there could be no reform of the AAU-NCAA power struggle unless it was mandated in federal law. Shorter and I assured Bowerman that the PCOS had the power to recommend just that and to shepherd an act through Congress, if the various powers with clout (especially the NCAA) could be brought on board. Bill said he'd believe it when he saw it, but if we needed him for anything, just to ask.

Another conflict—the Bowerman-Dellinger estrangement—though painfully real, was publicly muted. Bowerman had almost pointedly not included Dellinger in the original leadership group of the Prefontaine Foundation, but there was plenty of overlap. The Pre foundation, the varsity coaches, the OTC all-comers-meet people, the road-run people—all would be there at the Wednesday OTC breakfast meetings, where Dellinger and Bowerman were always elaborately cordial. Dellinger trained his team well and talked it up effectively at Oregon Track Club board meetings. Nonetheless, he was soon at odds with Bowerman over personnel.

Bowerman had coached every track and field specialty, and he invited each athlete to become "a student of his event." He was coach because he knew them all, but one could absorb enough about one's own sport in four years to be regarded as a colleague. Dellinger didn't have quite the breadth to follow suit. More of a running specialist, he depended on assistants for the field events.

To help in coaching Mac Wilkins, Dellinger planned to hire Frank Morris, from an athletic Medford family. "But Frank in his youth ran afoul of the law on some incident that put him on Bowerman's not-good list," Bill Landers would say. "And with Bill that was pretty much a lifetime assignment. So when he learned that Frank could be coming into his life's work he went ballistic." Although Morris may have continued to coach Mac, he was never hired as a permanent assistant.

Bowerman's great strength and great weakness occasionally seemed like two sides of the same coin. Along with his dogged kind of genius and refusal to accept defeat came an equally dogged refusal to tolerate people who disappointed him in some important way. Once one lost his respect, one never regained it. "He disappeared people," was how Jim Grelle had put it. Bowerman would never go that far with Dellinger. Still, these were two proud men, Olympians who held Olympic-level expectations for those they admired and respected.

Their estrangement after Prefontaine's death seemed harder on Dellinger. Bowerman's first champion always felt he owed an unpayable debt to his coach and he didn't want to go through life at odds with him. But Dellinger genuinely felt Bowerman had not done enough to give him due credit for Prefontaine's success. Bowerman, as he did when he believed himself crossed or betrayed, seemed to dismiss any need for reconciliation from his mind. Dellinger saw that and gave up on mending the breach.

The two Bills didn't feud. They simply went on in their own, characteristic ways. Bowerman took refuge in his little research shoe lab, turning out several more of what would amount to hundreds of templates and designs. And he actually became more sociable. He began a regular Tuesday lunch group with Hendrickson, Newland, Chris Christensen, and Bill McHolick. Les Anderson and Wade Bell would drop by, too, and UCLA coach Jim Bush when he was in town.

McHolick dubbed this the Ad Hoc Committee because it rendered cackling, caustic judgment on pretty much every issue of the day, and on its members as well.

Dellinger, for his part, was so shaken by Pre's death that he doubted he could ever grow personally close to an athlete again. He had never hesitated to become friends with runners and throwers, and he connected with Pre as he had with no other. Now Dellinger, in his grief (some part of which was a pang of guilt that he hadn't gotten Pre to cut down more on his drinking), asked himself whether Bowerman might not be right about that. Keeping more distance might have made the blow more like a doctor losing a patient rather than a family losing a son. He didn't feel capable of ever opening himself up as much again.

Miler Matt Centrowitz, however, was being affected by Dellinger's withdrawal. Centrowitz, from Power Memorial High School in the Bronx (Kareem Abdul-Jabbar's alma mater), had been the fastest high school miler in the country in 1973 with 4:02.7. He began at Manhattan College that fall and qualified for the NCAA cross-country meet out in Spokane, Washington, where he met a couple of Oregon runners, including Prefontaine, in his final college race. "Pre showed us around," Centrowitz would recall, "and I met Bill Dellinger that afternoon. My coach and I talked with him about the Oregon training methods. Hard and easy, on the East Coast, was part myth. I was fascinated by that."

Centrowitz transferred to Oregon the following summer and had to support himself through an ineligible, redshirt year in 1974–75. Fortunately, there was work at hand, and a taskmaster. Bowerman gave Centrowitz the job of shellacking the new west stands, assigned his hours, and, because the city boy had never done any painting, taught him the proper way to wield a paintbrush. "He worked with me as an equal," Centrowitz would say, "and trusted me in tracking my hours. I remember him saying, 'You want to round up, now.' He made you feel good about yourself, not just welcome but valued."

Centrowitz never did a specific workout just for Bowerman, but he ran with—and soaked up lore from—Roscoe Divine. "I heard the stories, the rationale, the whys of what we were doing under Dellinger," he would say. Because Centrowitz wasn't varsity eligible and Pre had graduated, they frequently trained together that fall and winter. Matt once asked Pre which of the two Bills was better. "I need them both!" Pre said. "I go to Dellinger for the best workouts. I go to Bowerman whenever I need my head tuned!" Centrowitz found Bowerman more outgoing than Dellinger: "He was more verbal. And those eyes! An amazing presence, whether joking around or tinkering with my shoes. Dellinger was more the reserved, Western distance-runner type."

Except in the liberating presence of Prefontaine. "When Pre was around, Bill Dellinger was happy," Centrowitz would say. "They both were happy. They were like brothers. Theirs was like no coach-athlete relationship I'd ever seen or ever will see. Pool, darts, girls, they played and talked about absolutely everything. So when Pre was there, you saw that side of Bill. But when Pre went away you stopped seeing it." And when Pre died, Centrowitz would say, "we saw the bottom drop out of things."

Centrowitz, who grew up without a father in New York City where the drinking age was eighteen, unwittingly drew Dellinger back into some intimacy with his charges. "At home, my mom sanctioned my drinking, within bounds," Matt would say. "At Oregon, Dellinger did everything he professionally could to discourage me. I'd promise to stop and that would last about a week. I'd come sit down in front of him in a tavern and he'd be so disappointed. I was a determined guy, without a father, who wanted to be around an older guy."

Dellinger later said that if he had not had Centrowitz and the team needing him to be emotionally present for them, it would have taken far longer to come back. Eventually he began to open up again. In return, Matt developed great loyalty to Dellinger. "I knew even then that it was a trade-off," he would say. "I was giving away something on the track in return for something I got in that tavern sitting with Bill. As an adult, I cherish those lessons, that guidance, more than any championship. But that was me. That's for maybe one guy out of ten." Centrowitz's own children would never see him take an alcoholic drink. Neither would the runners he coached.

Dellinger began to hear criticism about his sitting in a bar with a varsity runner, a practice unheard of under Bowerman. Centrowitz went to Dellinger and asked how he could help the situation. "You help by speaking with your performance," Dellinger told him. "You help by making this Olympic team."

Bowerman, meanwhile, had ensured that Hayward Field would once again be the venue for the Olympic Trials. The 1975 AAU meet had been held in a Eugene still under the pall of Prefontaine's absence. But with Bob Newland at the meet's helm, it had been another artistic and financial triumph for the Oregon Track Club.

Thus, three things happened at the next meeting of the USOC Track and Field Committee. First, the 1976 Olympic Trials were awarded to Eugene (and the OTC would be allowed to pay the top athletes' expenses). Second, the women's track Trials were combined with the men's ("which would not only enhance the meet's appeal," said Newland, "but spread fairness in the land."), and third,

Newland himself was elected an assistant manager of the 1976 US men's Olympic track team going to Montreal.

To give the US Olympic marathoners more recovery time between the Trials and the Games, the marathon was held in Eugene in early May, six weeks before the rest of the track events. I felt myself a contender. But a week before the race, trotting back from an effortless interval workout, an odd feeling of weakness crept in. I was barely home when I was shaken with chills and fever. When a dream is taken by pneumonia, it's over quick. One's every gasping breath is so clearly one's last that any regret over not being a three-time Olympian pales.

A week later, I was strong enough to get out of bed, fire the pistol to start the Trials marathon, and go back to bed. Frank Shorter and Bill Rodgers floated stylishly away and took the top two places, Frank winning in 2:11:51. Don Kardong had run every mile with his great friend and Stanford teammate, Antonio Sandoval. Then Kardong sprinted in third, making the marathon team a deep and able group. I told him fate had obviously brought me down so he could be an Olympian. He said, "Then, God, don't breathe on me."

In the track Trials in late June, the women, in the persons of sprinter Evelyn Ashford and miler Francie Larrieu, didn't so much steal the show as prove to Eugene what it had been missing. Lynne Winbigler became Oregon's first female Olympian by winning the discus. On the men's side, the '76 Trials saw the apogee of a man Bowerman had launched, Mac Wilkins. That spring, in the winds of Mt. San Antonio College and Modesto, Mac had four times dropped his discus down beyond the chalk world record line, lengthening it by six feet, to 232 feet 6 inches. He won the trials with a meet record 225 feet 4 inches.

Bill Dellinger had trained two Ducks to be Olympians, Centrowitz in the 1500 and the gifted Paul Geis in Bill's own distance. In the 5000 final, Geis, the 1974 NCAA three-mile champion and a sub-4:00 miler, went with Dick Buerkle's pace until they were alone and the team was selected. Buerkle won in 13:26.6. Geis was third in 13:38.4.

In the 1500 final, Centrowitz's plan was to go hard the last 440. But at the gun, Ohio State's Tom Byers, swept up in the occasion, became the tiger that Bowerman always warned you not to be, the one who sprints the first lap in 55. Byers, running tall and wild, kept right on going, leaving the elongated field behind and passing 800 meters in 1:52.0. This was an impossible pace, 3:30 pace, when the 1500 world record was 3:32.16, held by Tanzania's Filbert Bayi.

Centrowitz had worked hard to be where he was, a distant second, but well ahead of the rest of the astounded field. With 700 to go, Byers began coming back to him so fast it forced a decision. "It was windy on the backstretch," said

Centrowitz. "I was praying he'd keep going and protect me until off the turn with 500 to go, which he didn't do." Centrowitz was tempted to tuck in. "But I didn't want to let the guys who started slower back into the race." So he took the lead with a long 660 to go. In so doing, he made sure that the three Olympians were the ones who stayed sane in the presence of mania. He led past three laps in 2:52.7. In the homestretch, 800-meter record holder Rick Wohlhuter and his Chicago Track Club teammate Mike Durkin edged past. Wohlhuter won by two yards in 3:36.4. Centrowitz repassed Durkin for second and destroyed Prefontaine's school record of 3:38.1 with 3:36.7, the equivalent of a 3:53 mile.

Montreal would be the Olympic debut of Nike, the shoe with the swoosh. Blue Ribbon Sports was now a $14 million company, and coming off a big legal win. In mid-1975, the Onitsuka company had agreed to settle their lawsuit by paying BRS $400,000. The sum basically just covered Phil Knight's legal fees, but the settlement freed the company from an oppressive legal cloud. Already selling Waffle Trainers by the carload, BRS continued to do so—but, as ever, it needed to borrow money to order shoes. That fall, the company applied for a loan from the US Small Business Administration. The SBA loan officer asked both Phil Knight and Bill Bowerman to personally guarantee the loan.

Knight had done this before, but Bowerman never had. So Bill sat with John Jaqua and did some reappraising. He'd leapt into the BRS partnership eleven years earlier more for the chance to make decent shoes than to get rich. He'd never minded profits being plowed back into the company's growth, but he was retired from the university now, on a fixed pension. He had no intention of risking his home above the river if BRS went under. So he and Jaqua worked out a plan whereby Bowerman would sell most of his BRS stock to Knight. This allowed him to keep a slice of the company but avoid personal liability. He parted with forty-four percent of the company for cash, an insurance policy, and a $15,000 per year consulting contract.

Bowerman had no sense of having relinquished any great future hopes. In fact, relieved of worry about his home, he returned invigorated to his R&D projects—and thereby developed a complicated relationship with someone who admired him immensely, Jeff Johnson, back East in Exeter.

Production capacity at the Exeter factory was a meager 200 pairs a day at a time when the company could have sold fifty times that. A second factory was opening in Maine, but the only place to find the requisite volume was overseas.

Overseas manufacturing had its risks, however. In a huge plant, one that might also make shoes for other brands, Nike would have no control over who saw its best ideas—which might start showing up elsewhere. "So our best, most creative stuff we wanted to make in Exeter," Johnson would say. "We also used the factory to train people before sending them out to train the foreign mega-factories."

Meanwhile, in Eugene, Bowerman operated a little development lab out of the rented basement of a medical arts building. Here, Bill kept his own secrets, hiding new things he was working on before receiving visitors with cameras. And, being competitive in all things, he began to feel increasingly pitted against Johnson's research shop in Exeter.

Bowerman's group, which included Bob Newland, orthotist Dennis Vixie, and orthopedic surgeon Stan James, developed two projects before the Montreal Olympic year. One was a series of spikes called the Vainquer, distinguished by a larger spike plate developed by Bill. The trend in spiked racing shoes had been toward smaller spike plates and tighter, snugger toe boxes. Bill asked, Why not spread out the toes, give them room to be a foot the way feet were evolved to work?

Not unlike fish-skin shoes, larger spike plates made great sense in theory. In practice, though, they just felt—odd. The men wouldn't wear them because it felt too much like being barefoot. And the women objected to the width. "At one point," Johnson would say, "I had to do a factory 'stealth run' of shoes with smaller spike plates for our best people in Nikes." Bowerman was not pleased, in part because such stealth seemed designed to keep him in the dark.

Bill's other pet design was a sturdy flat, the LD-1000 Trainer. The shoe featured a flared sole, suggested by Dr. Stan James, to increase stability and reduce torque in the knees. The medical community raved about the idea. "But when the production models arrived from the factory," said James, "I thought Bill was going to have a heart attack. It was an abortion." The heel was so wide that if the shoe came down at any angle other than perpendicular, the flare would hit the ground and lever the foot. "Instead of stabilizing, it accelerated pronation," Johnson would say, "and hurt both feet and knees."

"It was good for doctors," said James. "It was a bonanza for knee doctors." The heels were narrowed in subsequent versions.

Then there was a battle over something that one imagines would have been known by 1976, namely, whether human feet are straight or curved. James and Vixie had perused some anthropological research and found that most people's feet were straighter than the lasts their shoes were built on. So Bill's lab made a straight last (called the Vixie last), on which he fashioned uppers for different models and got some nice shoes. They sent the Vixie last to Johnson in Exeter.

The factory-made shoes turned out to be too narrow because the machines tugged too hard on the uppers. Nobody could get a foot into the shoe. "What had happened in Bill's lab," Johnson would say, "was they had given it a hand job. They'd draped an upper over the last and tugged and smoothed and caressed until it fit. Machines couldn't duplicate that." Bowerman refused to acknowledge the problem.

Johnson sent the same prototype to Knight, who couldn't get it on either. Knight told Johnson to reshape the last enough to allow the manufacture of the shoe Bill had created. Johnson did just that, but Knight, in classic fashion, didn't convey the decision to Bowerman. "So Bill thought that I was trying to undermine him," Johnson would say. In any event, once the shoes were on the market, they met with a lukewarm reception. Most of the best runners, including Frank Shorter, didn't like the straight-lasted shoes because their feet were curved.

In 1976, Johnson came out to Eugene for the Olympic Trials. By then, Bowerman was steaming. Johnson remembered it well. "We at Exeter were the main supplier of all shoe-related stuff Bill needed for his shop, so he'd ask for, say, a box of uppers to be sent to Vixie's lab. So within twenty-four hours we sent them to Vixie's lab. But Vixie wouldn't tell Bill they arrived and Bill would complain to Buck." This went on for other things—spike plates, midsoles.

"Bill complained to Buck that he didn't get them, and who was this Johnson working for because it didn't seem to be us. I never knew there was a problem, but one day during the Trials in Eugene, Knight got Bill, Vixie, and me together under the new stands, turned to Bill, said, 'Go,' and stood back." Bill started in with his list. "I didn't get these uppers . . . " Johnson said he'd sent them out in twenty-four hours to Vixie's lab. Dennis, did you get them? Yes. Vixie said yes to every item on the list until Bill finally said, "I've had enough of this shit," and stormed out. "That has always been one of Buck Knight's favorite stories about our fantastic corporate communication," Johnson would say.

Johnson went back to Exeter thinking it was a hell of a thing to admire a man as much as he did Bowerman and, in his phrase, "always be pissing him off by getting trapped into these misunderstandings." But one morning at 6:30 the phone rang. It was Bowerman, calmly asking about some unremembered aspect of the shoes they were planning. Johnson, realizing it was three hours earlier in Oregon, thought, *God*damn *this man is serious about shoes!* They got along better after that. Bowerman came to appreciate that Johnson was far from just a shoe dog. Johnson, as a coach himself, most appreciated Bowerman for his indifference to those who opposed him on the worth of the hard-easy approach. "Bill simply asked, Who ya gonna believe, those who don't want to change or the evidence before your own eyes?" Jeff would say. "Bowerman seemed born to be brave that way, to stand firm in defense of simple, humiliating truth."

There was abundant humiliation for the world's traditional track powers at the 1976 Olympics. First, the Games were vitiated by a black African boycott over the IOC not booting New Zealand for carrying on rugby exchanges with banned South Africa. Then Montreal became the first Games dominated by doping-assisted regimes.

East Germany—a country of seventeen million the size of Ohio—won forty-nine total medals, eleven of them gold. The United States took forty-six and six. In track and field, East German women took eight golds. The Soviets and Poles took most of the rest. The usually strong US women won not a single event and had only three medallists, Kathy McMillan's silver in the long jump, Kate Schmidt's bronze in the javelin, and the 1600-meter-relay team's 3:22.8 for silver, thirty yards behind East Germany's 3:19.23.

Fifteen years later, after the Berlin Wall was hammered down and East German secret police files were unearthed, it was revealed that virtually every East German athlete, knowingly or not, had been given anabolic steroids as part of his or her training, usually for years. The East German athletes passed all their Olympic drug tests because East German officials brought a lab of their own and tested every entrant the week before. If he or she had not cleared traces of the drugs from his or her system, he or she was said to have suffered a convenient injury and was withdrawn, uncaught. Unless the IAAF could force year-round, surprise testing, any sufficiently organized country would be able to get away with this.

The US men fared a little better in Montreal, but nothing like in years past. Cuba's great stallion, Alberto Juantorena, took the 400 in 44.26 from Fred Newhouse's 44.40 and won the 800 in a world record 1:43.50. Bruce Jenner was magnificent in winning the decathlon with a record 8,618 points, as was Edwin Moses in the 400 hurdles, with a world record 47.64.

Matt Centrowitz had developed an Achilles problem, finished eighth in the 1500-meter prelims, and watched the final from the stands. "When I saw the people who got the medals [great kickers John Walker of New Zealand in 3:39.17, Ivo Van Damme of Belgium in 3:39.27, and Paul-Heinz Wellmann of West Germany in 3:39.33]," he would say, "the next day I became a 5000-meter runner." Centrowitz would go on to win four US national championships in the 5000 and take nine seconds from Pre's best time, with 13:12.91.

Paul Geis was the only US runner to make the 5000 final. He vowed to stay with the leaders as long as humanly possible. With two laps to go, he was right there with Lasse Viren, who'd again won the 10,000 and was going for his second double. Viren ran the last 800 in well under two minutes, held off Kiwi Dick Quax, and won in 13:24.76. Geis was twelfth.

Mac Wilkins stepped into the Montreal discus ring wearing a mountain man's mass of hair and beard. More scathing than Bowerman or Pre in blasting the USOC, he had allowed himself to be quoted saying that the USOC's support of American postgraduate athletes was so abysmal that he hoped a nation that did support its older athletes, East Germany, would win all the medals. Some of this was heartfelt, but some had to do with trying to unnerve the United States' other great thrower, John Powell, with whom he was far from cordial. Wilkins's best friend among the throwers was East Germany's Wolfgang Schmidt. They were an ironic pair, each appreciating what the other had more than the other did himself. Schmidt was always in trouble with the East German authorities for his freethinking ways and would eventually, with Wilkins's help, defect.

In the qualifying round, on his first throw, in still air, with what Schmidt said was the technically best throw he ever saw in his life, Wilkins set an Olympic record of 224 feet. In the final (when prelim marks don't carry over), with one throw to go, Wilkins led with 221 feet 5 inches. Powell stood second with 215 feet 7 inches and Schmidt third with 213 feet 9 inches. Responding to the ultimate pressure, Schmidt uncorked a throw of 217 feet 3 inches to grab the silver from Powell. Wilkins ran over and gave him a big bear hug.

"That was one of the rare times you saw sport cut across nationalism," US shot-putter Maren Seidler would say. "That was the Olympic ideal, right there. And what happened? Both guys got shafted for it." Schmidt's travel was restricted. Wilkins, blasted by super-patriots for being happy that his countryman had been beaten, would have one-tenth the endorsement offers of Bruce Jenner.

Speaking of product placement, Frank Shorter set out to wear Nikes in the Olympic marathon, lacing on a pair of racing flats that Geoff Hollister and Dennis Vixie had customized for him out of three pairs of production models. While warming up, he looked down and saw the uppers separating from the midsole. "I had no other Nikes with me except clunky training shoes," he would recall years later. "Bruce McDonald, the walking coach, just happened to be watching the warm-up field. He also happened to be staying in the same room in the Village. He ran to the Village, which was only a half-mile away, got my old Tigers, ran back, and threw them over the fence." Shorter got to the starting line fifteen seconds before the gun went off.

(Years later Frank would remember that day. "If I had known about Kitami's ploy back when Onitsuka tried to take a controlling interest in Blue Ribbon Sports, I would not have worn Tigers in Montreal," he would declare. "I would have had Nike backups." But old shoe dog Jeff Johnson demurred. "If those shoes were 'cannibalized,' in the sense that Dennis Vixie was cutting and pasting material together, it definitely was better for Frank to run in production shoes, and hang brand loyalty.")

Once past his shoe scare Shorter was ready, I believed, to take a minute and a half from the 2:08:33 world record of Australia's Derek Clayton. But Frank, always supremely lean, was at his best in the heat. That day Montreal provided a chilly, misting rain. He never felt loose. Even so, when he surged ahead after fifteen miles, atop Mont Royal, only one man went with him, a former East German steeplechaser named Waldemar Cierpinski. Frank ran the next, downhill two miles about as fast as he could go, but the other man flew out to a 100-yard lead. On the level again, with six miles to go, Shorter forced himself back up to within fifty meters of Cierpinski. "Then," Frank would say, "he turned around, looked at me, and ran away."

Cierpinski won in 2:09:55. Shorter held second in 2:10:46. Karel Lismont of Belgium (who'd won the silver in 1972) took the bronze by three seconds from a charging Don Kardong, 2:11:13 to 2:11:16. Bill Rodgers, running with a foot injury, was fortieth in 2:25:14. I had talked tactics with Kardong earlier and seconded his plan to start sensibly and run people down late. "You advise yourself and you get fourth," he said afterward. "You advise me and I get fourth. I'm getting a new adviser."

(Twenty years later, Shorter and Kardong would take grim satisfaction when Dr. Werner W. Franke of the German Cancer Research Center in Heidelberg began uncovering documents kept by the East German physicians and coaches who'd conducted the country's doping program. The documents showed that Cierpinski was on androgenic steroids in 1976. "I mean, I always knew," Shorter would say, "and now I knew for sure.")

For the first time in twenty years, Bowerman was not present at the Olympics. In what seems almost an act of renunciation, he stayed home from Montreal and was a classically frustrated TV watcher, not seeing much of the track meet. From now on, the Games would no longer dictate his life and calendar as they had since 1956, his first Games as a coach. This caused Barbara to speculate about fulfillment. "I always thought his secret ambition was to equal or surpass Lydiard's three medallists in one Olympics," she would say, wondering if Bill had any regrets that Otis Davis was the only one of his athletes to win a gold medal during his active coaching career. "If he felt any regrets, I think he would have shaken them off. He lived what he preached to you boys (excuse me, you Men of Oregon!): If at the end of a race you know yourself that you have done your best, you're a winner."

As Bowerman turned his attention to his farm, the needs of his university and community, and those who sought him out for coaching and counseling, he kept a weather eye on the goings-on in the world of sports governance. Progress on that front was heartening in 1976.

All year, the President's Commission on Olympic Sports held hearings, hired a huge staff to organize information, and studied the American Olympic sports governing bodies. In 1977, the PCOS issued a report outlining legislation to end the NCAA-AAU feud and solve a dozen other systemic problems. The proposed law would dissolve multisport rulers such as the AAU and allow the USOC to decide (using specific criteria protecting athletes' rights and coaches' membership) who got to be the recognized national governing body in each sport. In the fall of 1977, the Senate Commerce Committee held hearings on the resulting bill, put forward by Iowa's John Culver and Alaska's Ted Stevens. After the NCAA's Walter Byers was mollified that actual guarantees of athletes' rights wouldn't be in the law of the land, but rather in the USOC constitution, it passed.

The Amateur Athletic Act of 1978 broke up the AAU and insured that athletes and coaches had the rights that Bowerman and Prefontaine had fought for. The IAAF had to accept the new US national governing body because it was a federal decree (the Soviet ministry of sport, for example, dictated to the IAAF who to accept as its representative). Bowerman was overjoyed that the new US track body was required to admit all the NCAA coaches and give them votes proportionate to their numbers. In addition, twenty percent of every committee's members had to be athletes.

The new authority took on a name worthy of its drawing together of old foes, The Athletics Congress, or TAC. The AAU-NCAA war was over. There was only one major issue the act could not address, because it took international cooperation—the question of amateurism and Olympic eligibility.

Even before the 1978 law change, Nike was taking steps to do something for postcollegians, who were essentially abandoned by the college-focused American track family. Back in 1972, when Mac Wilkins was an undergraduate, he wrote a paper on amateurism for Bill, carefully examining the pros and cons of the system and coming to the conclusion that "the time has come for track to save itself by throwing off a dead institution"—namely, the Olympic insistence that athletes make no money from their sport. Bowerman had scrawled on the paper "I like your thinking" and advocated establishing "standards of athletic conduct that operate according to principle, not expediency, an elastic system that grows with a changing culture."

Bowerman might have been writing the prospectus for Nike's next creation.

In November 1977, Nike formed Athletics West, a club designed to provide elite postgrad athletes with the kind of support Eastern Europeans got from their governments. Members would receive coaching, a basic stipend, insurance, travel to big meets, a weight room, an exercise physiologist, and a world-class masseur. Knight declined to name the club for Nike, wishing not to link commercial benefits with the concept.

For head coach, Knight hired a man Bill had recommended to succeed him at Oregon, South Eugene High's Harry Johnson. Thirteen charter athletes came to Eugene from around the country, and a year later, Athletics West broke ground on its own training center and office building in West Eugene. A newsletter was begun. Pre would have ripped it to shreds, though. Its letterhead had a drawing of the moment on the last backstretch of the Munich 5000 when Gamoudi came muscling past him.

In the coming years, Knight would make a compelling case for how important Bowerman was as the conscience of the company. But as with most consciences, Bill tended to gnaw and nag and gnaw some more. Somehow, the bigger Nike grew, the harder it would be for Bill to fit in.

In 1978, when the shock of losing Prefontaine had ebbed somewhat, Mary Creel returned from Southern California and became Phil Knight's secretary, reading his mail and briefing him on all things. She would stay for eight years. Part of her job was to help organize board meetings ("and wait on members hand and foot"), so she saw Bowerman often.

"Bill was really nice to me, because we'd had that time in Munich with Steve," she would say. "But I think he was always uncomfortable coming to Nike. He was less and less happy with the corporation it became." Creel observed the inherent awkwardness of the situation. "Phil had a deep-seated fear of Bill, but at the same time he was essentially Bill's boss. It seemed to me that Phil's attitude was 'I have to tolerate you because I'd be nothing without you, but it's uncomfortable.'"

Knight would agree: "It was awkward—a very complicated set of feelings."

In late summer 1978, Bowerman wrote to John Jaqua describing the philosophical divide he felt. He cited a meeting some six years earlier at which he had asked what the company's objectives were.

"You looked at Buck," Bill wrote, "and he said, 'Make money.' I concur that without it you can't swim, but I said, 'Mine continues to be to make the best possible product at a price that will achieve the objective but keep the customer coming back.' I hear lip service to that, but I observe us not only standing still, but distributing a lot of crap. Obviously there is more confidence in [products developed in] Exeter, Saco, Japan, Korea, and Taiwan than in the input I have made in the past three years. All correctable—but not if Pony, Brooks, Etonic, New Balance Cobra, Famolare, Diadora Autry, and fourteen others cut us up."

"Bill seemed sad to feel more and more a dinosaur," Mary Creel would say, "the crazy inventor that everyone tolerated." Creel would recall Bowerman once showing a design for a workingman's shoe, to which marketing head Rob Strasser said, "You want to see your garbageman wearing Nikes?"

After such a rejoinder, Bowerman would return to his basement shoe lab, his own lair, where he could be fierce in what he perceived as a running R&D battle between Eugene and Exeter. In the fall of 1978, writer and 2:19 marathoner Tom Derderian, who worked for Jeff Johnson in R&D in Exeter, found himself a pawn in that war. As Derderian would tell the story, Bowerman had invited him to Eugene, ostensibly to show him how research was done there. Instead, Derderian spent a week in Eugene being given only menial tasks by Bill.

Athletes on whom Bill had used such methods to haze them into making some sign of respect for his authority might have guessed what was happening, but Derderian was not interested in such rites of passage. One task was to make waffle molds by hand. "When I questioned what the company would gain by my operating nineteenth-century machinery, he got angry," Derderian would recall years later. "He said, 'You don't want to do things my way, so get out of here before I throw you up the stairs.' I certainly did not feel physically threatened, but it was clear that he was angry and irrational and had no intention of working with me, so I left. I wasn't about to have a fistfight with him." Derderian returned to Exeter and reported that he hadn't seen any research going on in Eugene. "I told Jeff Johnson that Bowerman's day had passed."

Oregon varsity miler Mike Friton would begin working in Bill's lab a year later and stay on full-time after graduating in 1981. His take on the Derderian situation offers some insight into Bowerman's methodology.

"In the lab, Bill often tested people before he would work with them," Friton said in 2005. "The test was usually some form of manual labor. He would get you started and then walk away, letting you finish on your own. If you completed the work and did a good job, you were in. This was simple for someone coming from a working-class family, but for those who did not—or who thought themselves above the work—it could be very difficult, if not impossible. Bill often told the story of an athlete from a wealthy South American family who tried out for the track team. When Bill told him that he was expected to have a part-time job to be on the team, the athlete replied, 'Work—work is for fools.' Every time Bill told that story he would laugh so hard it would nearly bring him to tears."

Friton didn't witness the tossing of Derderian, but he heard about it from the tosser. "I recall some of Bill's side of the story," he said. "Bill was expecting Tom days before he showed up. As a result, he thought Tom was more interested in his social agenda than in working with him. Then, when Bill tried putting him to work, he failed the test that would have gotten him through the door."

In late October Derderian wrote Bowerman a letter. Bill never answered it, but he filed it with his favorite patent documents and sole designs. "Dear Mr. Bowerman," Derderian began. "A week ago I left you; you were in a rage, one which shocked me and left me with no rebuttal. Perhaps you have recovered from your anger with me; I recover more slowly. I am Armenian and for us, forgiveness often takes generations." He went on to describe his view of the abortive week and why he had been frustrated ("I needed to know your plan, what you were doing and why, so I could insure that production procedures would remain on design to produce a shoe that would function according to your researched theory and consequent prototypes.").

Of the angry confrontation, Derderian wrote, "At thirty years old I am not your superior, not even your equal, but I am not a college freshman to be taken mockingly to the showers and pissed on." Then he offered a truce: "A working relationship is still possible and I welcome that. . . . I stand ready to aid your efforts in any way. A phone call to me will speed delivery of any equipment and materials I can provide."

Although Bill didn't write back, he must have mentioned the letter to someone. When word reached Woodell, he fired Derderian, who promptly got a job with another shoe company. "Later I learned that many such encounters between Exeter people and Bowerman followed," Derderian would say, "and that it had not been Bowerman's order or suggestion to fire me."

Eventually Derderian went back to Nike—at three times his old salary. "So I figure that disagreeing with Bowerman ultimately was a good career move. I'd like to think that he kept the letter out of admiration for a guy who stood up to him, or out of guilt, but I don't know." (Personally, I think it was Tom speaking so darkly of taking generations to forgive. Bill was going to give him time.)

Phil Knight always knew it was going to be tough. "To this day," he would say years later, "I'm not sure I didn't start this company to please Bill Bowerman. Old teammates have said to me, 'You did it to spend a lifetime with him, not just four years.' And I can't disagree. But then they say, 'Bill must make it seem like *two* lifetimes.' And I can't disagree with that either. Bill basically just railed at us all the time as a company. We made the worst shoes, except for all the others. Barbara once said, 'I don't know how you put up with him.' I said, 'I don't know how *you* do.'"

Barbara later came across sheaves of old letters, which she divided into two stacks. "One was of my pleas and complaints to Bill in the late '70s and early '80s," she would recall. "The other was letters from Bill to Buck—complaining strongly that no one in Beaverton was paying any attention to the excellent advice and shoes he was sending from his basement lab in Eugene. It made me laugh to think that while I was nagging Bill he was nagging Phil and both men were ignoring the nags, with good reason. Both the naggers were well supplied, maybe oversupplied, with everything their hearts desired—yes, even attention and appreciation." Barbara would remember that Bill often remarked, "I have everything I want. Why would I want more?" Since she felt the same, she was moved to wonder at their seeming discontent. "My explanation for those testy notes is that we were pretty normal human beings," she would conclude, "able to find or make up a few trials to fuss about even while we were fully enjoying our 'happily ever after' life on our land in Oregon. I'd like our children to know we were not always crotchety."

Witnesses to Bill's daily life in the late 1970s insist that he never let concern over Nike's direction or R&D head-butting interfere with his radiating contentment. Such irritants were nothing compared with the joys of his burgeoning farm. The sheep were fine lawn mowers and provided wool for Barbara's spinning and knitting. He observed the problems and rewards of the Jaquas' Hereford cattle operation and wondered if he might do better. He raised chickens. He tried to keep a goat, but refused to have any animal smarter than he was on the property, and after it learned to climb trees to outwit him, he served it at a faculty barbecue, calling it venison until it was eaten.

Bowerman spoke and wrote about all this in a tone derived less from Thomas Jefferson than Will Rogers. In 1978, a couple of days before he would receive Derderian so roughly in Eugene, he rose and delivered his greatest Round Table paper, entitled "Gallus Gallus."

"This is not a report for feminists," he began, "Rather, it is research and flight of the imagination concerning men and cocks . . . or roosters. . . . It is my purpose to raise large chickens that lay lots of eggs and do not crap in the carport. . . .

"In keeping book on chickens and isolation of the genes for: one, big birds; two, lots of eggs; three, the mess in the carport, it is necessary to isolate individuals or pairs. But how do you tell who lays and what?

"According to Page Smith in a book named *The Chicken*, if you look at a chicken's vent and it is a dull saffron, the hen is probably not laying. However, if it is roseate red, it is likely a laying hen. I tried this several times. I picked up each hen, turned her tail back and looked. Almost without exception, the vent would wink at me. Not just once but several times.

I stopped this practice because, as Knight Duncan once remarked of an English laird, 'There is nothing queer about Chumly.' I did not want the reputation of being 'queer with chickens.'

"So how do you tell who lays and who goes into the pot? I found another authority. Ulisse Aldrovandi of Verona found in his research that when the hen is held in one hand, if two fingers can be laid at the vent, the hen is a layer. If, however, there is room for only one finger, the prospect is for the pot.

"I tried this method. I picked up a nice hen, presented her backside, and laid my index and third finger in the pelvic crease. The hen got an alarmed expression, squawked, and took flight. After more trials, I learned the Aldrovandi method simply causes the hens' eyes to bug out and they continue to look with some suspicion on the examiner thereafter.

"I isolated a single hen in her apartment for four days. My grandmother said that a hen with a rich, red, full comb is a layer. My testing by the solitary confinement method has proved without a doubt that my grandmother knew more than either Page Smith or Aldrovandi . . . "

For fifteen pages, Bill lavished such style on his methods of selecting eggs for incubation and qualities of breeding stock. "Starting with Rhode Island Reds, a banty for setting and white leghorns, what did I get? The hybrid vigor I am seeking. A rooster which weighs eight pounds. White with a mantle of red. He seems to have received, like Elisha, a double portion of the spirit. Released from a pen, I have seen him service a flock of pullets on the hillside in less time than it takes an Oregon runner to cover a mile."

Bill covered the world records for egg laying and his adoption of a brooder that could accommodate fifty chicks, and revealed that his fascination with genetics went back to his biology professor, Ralph Huestis. "Many people inquire about the apparent superiority of black athletes over whites and whether this has to do with something like a longer Achilles tendon," Bill wrote. "Ralph would reply, 'Not to speak specifically about the tendon or physical characteristics of the races, but this may be evidence of *hybrid vigor*.'" He included a page of Mendelian hereditary probabilities, explaining why it takes five generations for a trait to breed true.

He dilated upon his methods for controlled experiments, keeping the birds in different portable cottages, which he called *galleria* from Columella. He gathered eggs daily, weighing, measuring, dating, and recording them. He found that Pliny the Elder had preceded him in finding that long eggs hatched into a hen and round ones into a rooster. "There is a modern study going on today in Sweden on the production of square eggs. The theory being that a dozen square eggs would pack into a smaller space. I join the hens in being unalterably opposed. Certainly a scientific study would be required to produce not only hens with square vents but also cocks with square . . . no the idea is preposterous!"

He addressed the issue of predators, which included the fox, the opossum, "and even my four-year old grandson," who, Bill said, "has been thoroughly trounced twice by the red rooster!

"About a year ago, I was losing one chicken each night to something large enough to mash down the chicken country condominiums which were designed after a great horned owl settled in on silent wings and took the head off a Jersey Giant pullet. I have made numerous nocturnal defense sallies, armed with buckshot. Only twice have I had the wily rascal in my beam. Finally, in midsummer, the distress calls awakened me. Grabbing my arms I hurried to the defense. I caught the eyes in the flashlight but before I could get the shotgun into position they were gone. I walked around the house, scanned a maple tree, then the lawn. Two coals of fire appeared. Slowly I raised the gun and let fly. The recoil raised the gun and the light. I said to myself, *That so-and-so won't go far!*

"Then, from Lady Barbara's flower planting around the edge of the lawn I heard a hissing. 'Snakes,' I thought. But the light beam revealed a fountain. I had blown a hole in the plastic pipe two inches below the ground. 'Blaspheme and Fire!' I raged.

"I shut off the main line and went to bed."

He ended with a coda of surpassing sweetness.

"Some of the good things that come of researching with chickens include night hunting, coon fried chicken, cockfights, and some of the richest fertilizer known to horticulture.

"I move my portable galleria every six or seven days. It takes about fifteen minutes and is wonderfully good for our shallow soil. It never fails to bring the nostalgia of boyhood and walking through the chicken yard barefoot. No sensation is more memorable than the flow between the toes."

For some time, friends would ask whether he had isolated the toughest gene, the non-carport-crapping one. He would say not quite yet and ask them to walk the edges of the carport and look for droppings that were flat on one side. That would show that some subject was halfway there. Later, Jay Bowerman would say you absolutely could not understand his father's sense of humor without seeing a video of Al, the black-tailed rooster, to the accompaniment of Misty River bluegrass band, servicing a pair of snow-white Nike Cortezes.

The following year, Great Britain's Sebastian Coe broke the 800 (1:42.50), mile (3:49.0), and 1500 (3:32.1) records, becoming the first to own them all. That September, at Geoff Hollister's urging, Coe cooled out in Eugene. Coe's intentions were to rest from running and sample Americana. I took him up to the Bowermans'. After Barbara's lemonade and oatmeal cookies, we all walked through the woods to a hillside pasture in which grazed a few, small, chunky black cattle. "Trying to build a herd of Dexter cows," Bill said. "It's an Irish breed. They're supposed to be small, so they don't eat much, but they still give you a gallon of milk." Bill hoped to eventually take his herd through enough generations to name a new breed *Bos domesticus oregonensis.*

As they walked, Coe stopped suddenly, his hand on his hip. "Since last winter," he said, "I've had occasional pain that goes from my back down my leg."

"It's certainly not a hamstring pull," said Bill, "or you wouldn't have been able to do what you've done." He pressed Coe against a fir, teaching him an abdominal exercise to align the back and pelvis. Coe walked away with pitch on his shirt and an elevated gaze.

"Pretty good," said Bill. "Not swaybacked at all."

Soon he had Coe describing his training in detail. "My father is my coach," Sebastian said, "and the basic foundations have been consistent, although the headings have meandered a bit as we've experimented. Essentially, it has been one hundred percent quality, not quantity. It is speed endurance—that is, seeing how long you can endure speed. In winters I have very seldom run more than fifty miles per week, less in the spring."

"No more than that?" asked Bill, knowing that Coe's predecessor as mile record holder, New Zealand's John Walker, coached by Arch Jelley under Arthur Lydiard's system, did over a hundred in his stamina-building phases. Coe, somehow, had defied middle-distance wisdom that pure speed work was destructive and led to staleness. "How do you stay fresh and strong on so little distance work?" asked Bill.

"My father," Coe said, "says that you might not know the accepted lore of athletics, but if you know people and can sense individual needs, it can make all the difference." At the words *individual needs*, Bowerman's closed his eyes. "Hear, hear," he said.

"Yet," continued Coe, "I wouldn't know why some people can get away with less distance than others. I really haven't a clue."

Bowerman at once subjected Coe to a set of Twenty Questions, honing in on that clue. It soon came out that there was more to Coe's training than just running. He spent ten or eleven hours every winter week in the Loughborough gym under the eye of George Gandy, a lecturer in biomechanics and coordinator of his training.

"It has been described as Coe's commando workout," said Sebastian. "In the fall, it's the use of everything you can think of in the gymnasium, lifting heavy weights twice a week, working every part of the body. After Christmas, we concentrate on every muscle from knees to sternum, using box jumping, speed drills, repeatedly mounting a beam, high knee lifts, bounding on grass or a soft-sprung floor.

"All this was associated two-and-a-half years ago with rapid improvement in my leg speed. It's simple athleticism really, the coordinated transference of weight and force through the body."

Bill concluded that the strength and flexibility Coe brought to the track from such work supported him as well as did the stamina that others gained through long runs. "It was a happy accident that from the first, when I was thirteen, my father felt you ought not smash a kid on the road, so he kept the distance low. As a junior in 1975, I averaged twenty-eight miles per week and ran successfully— third in the European junior 1500—against juniors running eighty or ninety miles."

Bowerman listened with an expression of beatific gratification. He was hearing confirmation of long-cherished beliefs about uniqueness and the need for self-knowledge. "So you've developed a methodology," he said, "that isn't at all dependent on what others do. That takes a certain sort of man."

"Well," said Coe, slightly embarrassed, "sometimes the difficult thing is to hold back when things are going well, to remember that what you're doing is, after all, preparation. That's hard when you're in a competitive group."

"How do you avoid racing when you are in training?"

"I have always trained alone."

"Tell me about your father," said Bowerman. "He's an engineer?"

"Yes. He's production director of a cutlery firm."

"Does he talk to you about body mechanics, balances?"

"When I was a child, he always spoke of lines and angles and carrying oneself efficiently. You see, the day I started running was the day he started coaching. After that, it was bringing his science to bear, studying everything he could find. He's gotten rid, he says, of ninety-five percent of what he's learned. The five percent he's kept is very specific. He has no other runners. People ask if he will coach them and he says, 'I don't know enough about you. I'd have to move in with you.'" Coe grinned. "You don't know my father, but that usually ends it."

"I would very much like to know your father," said Bowerman gravely, sensing that rarest thing for him, a kindred spirit. "I want you to tell him that he is always welcome here. Always."

Also in 1979, Bowerman received a surprise tribute at the annual Nike sales meeting at Sunriver Resort, south of Bend, Oregon. Geoff Hollister and Barbara Bowerman put together what would be the first of a powerful series of videotaped collections of old pictures of Bill, photogenic Bill, in various stages of life and BRS's history. Hollister scored it to Frank Sinatra's "My Way" and everybody cried, including Bill. "You really got me this time, Buck," he rasped.

Buck had gotten a lot of people lately and was driving toward a goal—surpassing Adidas. Since 1976, BRS's sales had doubled every year. In 1979, Adidas's President Horst Dassler said in an interview that Nike had defeated Adidas in the American running-shoe market. "It's not only what we didn't do," Dassler said, "but what someone else did well. Nike did a better job." With its 1980 sales at $270 million, Nike became the number-one athletic-shoe company in the United States.

With no financial clouds over it and many early investors pressing to sell their shares, Knight figured it was time to make BRS a publicly traded corporation. On December 9, 1980, Nike made an initial public stock offering that brought the growing company $28 million in fresh capital. BRS stock opened at $22 a share and stayed there.

Bowerman's shares of the company were now worth $9 million. Bill's clothes, home, and vehicles showed no sign of his new riches. They never would. But he did employ his new liquidity in an old endeavor, confounding people. One cold morning that very week, he appeared at my front door with a briefcase and a printout showing that a thousand dollars invested back in 1966, when I had had my chance, would be $750,000 now. This rendered me speechless.

"But," he said, "you must always know that as long as I'm with the company, there will be these for you." He whipped out a box of Cortezes.

To explain what it meant to be in good standing in his eyes, a tiger, a Man of Oregon, requires explaining why we were both so thrilled by that moment. He was ferociously exultant. He almost skipped up the steps to his car. I felt a sense of rightness that he would do this and I was proud of myself for enjoying Bill's enjoyment. We'd made our choices and we'd lived with them happily, but wasn't it a kick to tease the other about what might have been?

There never would be any unmanly talk about cutting anyone in late because it was too bad everybody couldn't share in this huge success, or that I somehow deserved riches because long ago he had borrowed my foot. A deal is a deal. He would never mention it again. There was no need. The affirmation warms me still. Everyone must have a story like that. Well, everyone should. Granted, it's easier to pull it off when both of you know there are more important things than money.

In early spring of that Olympic year of 1980, steeplechaser Henry Marsh and 5000-meter man Paul Geis had asked Bowerman to take over their training. Both had broken down under the workouts of Harry Johnson at Athletics West. Bowerman gave them counsel for a while but then decided to stop, explaining in a note to Knight, "It was unfair to them as athletes to have different advisors and coaches of Nike pulling at cross-purposes. It was unfair to me to find myself being short-circuited by the AW coach, administrator, physiologist, dietitian, and to some extent the promotion office. It's unfair to Harry Johnson, who finds his empire out of his control."

But Marsh pressed Bowerman to change his mind, indicating that if he did not, Marsh would try to train himself. Geis felt much the same. Convinced that the two runners were ill-served by the Johnson regimen, Bowerman concluded, "I told them I will coach both of them wholly. Anything from Athletics West will be directed to me. Any and all decisions will be made by me regarding these two men. If they are to be screwed up, or can't make it—the cake is mine. If they succeed as hoped, it will be for the Nike ship I gave my effort, and for my pleasure."

Soon it seemed any training was pointless. In January, reacting to the Soviet invasion of Afghanistan, President Jimmy Carter had announced that he would require the US Olympic team to boycott the Moscow Olympics unless the Soviets withdrew by February 20. "The ancient Greeks," Bowerman said, echoing his response to the Munich terror, "believed the Olympic arena so sacred they stopped their wars for them. Now we believe our wars are so sacred we sacrifice Olympics for them."

The most immediate blow in Eugene was to Bob Newland, who had been elected head manager of the US track team. Bowerman and Newland had been conferring often on how Newland could anticipate the team's needs in the Games. Bill was as disappointed as Newland that his old friend wouldn't be making use of all their planning.

In March, the White House brought a group of Olympians to Washington, DC, to be told by Carter and National Security Advisor Zbigniew Brzezinski why the boycott was necessary. A map of the Middle East was on a stand. Brzezinski slapped the end of his pointer on the Strait of Hormuz and said the Soviets in invading Afghanistan had moved a step closer to being able to disrupt the West's oil shipping. The athletes were part of a considered, realpolitik response, so the Soviet action would not be without cost. "Thanks for checking with us first," said 1976 400-meter silver medallist Fred Newhouse.

Afterward, at a disconsolate dinner, pentathlete Jane Frederick asked me to help a movie get made. Eugene had won the Olympic Trials for a third time and they would still be held. Director Robert Towne (author of *Chinatown* and *Shampoo*) wanted to shoot scenes during the Trials for *Personal Best*, a film about four years in the lives of two women pentathletes. Frederick had helped with the screenplay. But, she said, Towne and Warner Brothers had been denied permission by the university and the OTC.

I looked into it. Bowerman said the movie people had visited in the winter. "They promised to keep their cameras off the field," Bill said, "and then were overheard saying, 'We can agree to anything now and then run them on when the time comes.' We ran them off." Besides, the university had had problems with the script.

I called Towne. We'd actually spoken three years before, when I needed advice on coping with a possible TV movie on Pre. The ubiquitous Donna De Varona had brought us together. Towne now said the loose-lipped advance man was no longer with the film. "He didn't understand how crucial is shooting at the Trials. You can't go out to a high school track and fake it."

Towne's desire to make it real moved me to read the script. It had some of the corrosive language he was known for, but nothing in it offended my knowledge of my sport. Its threads were many, including a sexual relationship between the two women, but its core seemed part of every athlete's story: how to summon one's best, how to deal with the ferociousness of competition with people one respects and loves. Towne asked me to ask the university and the OTC to reconsider. In April, to demonstrate his seriousness, he brought actors Mariel Hemingway and Scott Glenn to Eugene.

A new university president, William Boyd, had taken over from Robert Clark. Oregon Vice President Curtis Simic had been the one to rule that the script was objectionable. Boyd read it himself and had my toughest lit professor (and turn judge), Edwin Coleman, read it too. Both loved it. In a delicate shift (so as not to obviously overrule the squeamish Simic), Boyd said the university would give permission if shooting was acceptable to the Oregon Track Club, which meant Bill Bowerman.

I called Bill. He would not agree to hear Towne out. "Ask me anything but that," he said and hung up. A Barbara Bowerman assertion came to mind: "Only two men can get Bill to pull back and re-think something—Otto Frohnmayer and John Jaqua." Jaqua read the script and advised Bill to meet with Towne.

Towne had been in Eugene a week by now and seemed near the end of his rope. Driving up to Bowerman's hillside, he said, "I don't know what to say to him. I have no sense of Bill Bowerman besides the amazing respect he commands." His hands were shaking.

Bowerman met us coolly. He placed us in soft chairs and took a hard, straight one for himself. I gave a little summation, concluding that the decision was now up to him. He turned to Towne.

Towne hesitated, seeming lost, wild-eyed. "I looked at Bowerman," he would say later, "and suddenly I knew that here was that rare man who isn't controlled by bureaucratic fears or others' opinions. I understood that if he decided I was one percent more right than wrong, he would support me."

Towne traced the origins of the project, from meeting Jane Frederick in the UCLA weight room in 1976 to coming to know and be affected by the world of female track athletes. He had written the screenplay with the help of Frederick, javelin bronze medallist Kate Schmidt, and Olympic 100-meter hurdler Patrice Donnelly. He was determined to approach the highest level of reality. He would use world-class athletes in all but two roles. Hemingway, who'd grown up a skier in Idaho, had been training for the pentathlon events of hurdles, shot put, high jump, long jump, and 800 meters for eighteen months.

Bowerman sat impassive, unreadable. Towne churned on, saying that he wanted to do a movie that showed track and field as it had never been shown before and that it was absurd to think of doing it anywhere but in Eugene and at the Trials. "They say I'm crazy in the industry for using real athletes, but I can't understand Eugene's not wanting me to give my best shot at showing something that Eugene loves as much as I do . . . "

Bowerman held up his hand. "You stay off my track," he said, in a tone I knew. "You stay off my infield. And I don't care if you photograph each other buggering yourselves under the stands." It didn't sink in. Even in the car, Towne said, "You really think it's all right now?"

Of course it was. The Oregon Athletic Department even ended up as the agency supplying thousands of extras for the crowd scenes.

I took Towne and Hemingway to the plane. As soon as I got home, the phone was ringing. It was Towne in LA saying, "You know that goof of a swimmer, Denny, who comes in near the end? Mariel and I want you to read for that part."

Once in a lifetime, everyone should have a phone call like that as a test of cardiac fitness. "But I've never . . . I'm shy. I get embarrassed. I became a writer so I wouldn't have to talk."

"You're an athlete," he said. "And the *character* is easily embarrassed." Writhe though I might, authenticity was his hook. If I wanted to help make the film be true, he insisted, I wouldn't resist his judgment in what he knew best.

I made no promises. In May, Towne came up with Patrice Donnelly and had me read through Denny's scenes. "You're in trouble now," he said.

All that could save me was if I photographed too old. Denny was supposed to be in his mid-20s. I was 36. So I had to take a screen test. I flew to LA and reported to Towne's office in the Burbank Studios. "I give you my word that playing Denny will not be contrary to your own character," he said. "Tomorrow you and Mariel will simply do the weight-lifting scene, which is an echo of how I met Jane. It will be my job to spur you, or soften you, or maybe infuriate you, so that what the camera sees is real. But I won't violate you."

A couple of days later, the printed takes were ready. The whole crew trooped up some stairs to projection room six. I was calm, equally able to accept any verdict. "Stop grinding your teeth," said Donnelly.

My first impression as the images lit the screen was that there had been a cruel trick. The jolt was like first hearing your voice played back on a tape recorder as a child, but more potent. The close-ups were excruciating, my eyes seeming on the verge of rolling out of my head. My slow pace of talking seemed a speech impediment. There was laughter. In the last takes I just concentrated on watching Hemingway.

The lights came up and people crowded around. Towne shoved them aside and hugged me hard, saying there was no going back now, that he'd just learned a lot about how to use Hemingway and me. I walked out in a kind of icy, consternated disbelief. Discovered.

Towne's cinematographers shot 105,000 feet of film during the Olympic Trials, almost all of the pentathlon as it proceeded. Jodi Anderson won it with 4,697 points and was hired to join the cast. Scott Glenn, a ropy, hard-muscled man, had come to acting late after a hitch in the Marines. A mountain climber and martial arts student, he asked systematic questions. By the end of the Trials, he really could have been the acerbic, intimidating track coach he played in the film. He and I sat with Bowerman during the steeplechase final, because this was the race for which Bill had been coaching Henry Marsh.

Of all the runners Bill advised, Marsh took his precautions against killing yourself in the early laps most seriously. In that steeple final, he laid back so far that Bill rolled his eyes, worried he was being too casual about all the ground he had to make up. But the steeplechase is different. Slamming through the water jump six times and always having to chop your steps to get aligned approaching the barriers reduces almost everyone to a state where a true kick is out of the question physiologically.

But not for a perfectly peaked Henry Marsh, who was always a superb hurdler. He came on with a powerful last lap and set an American record of 8:15.68, winning from Doug Brown (8:20.60) and John Gregorek (8:21.32).

"Thanks, Bill," Marsh said simply when he reached him.

"It was my pleasure," said Bill, looking it. "My great pleasure."

Oregon varsity distance runners were as strong and deep as ever. In the 5000 final, Eugene sophomore Bill McChesney sprinted away from the field with three laps to go. Matt Centrowitz and Dick Buerkle finally caught up and went one-two in 13:30.62 and 13:31.90. But McChesney held third at 13:34.42. That made two Ducks on the team in Pre's race alone. In the 10,000, Alberto Salazar, who had graduated from Oregon that spring, placed third behind Athletic West's Craig Virgin (who'd taken Pre's national record in the 10,000) and Greg Fredericks.

And in the women's 1500 meters, Oregon sophomore Leann Warren elicited the roar of the meet when she outkicked Francie Larrieu to take third and make the team. Mary Decker won in 4:04.91. Julie Brown was second in 4:07.13 and Warren ran 4:15.16. The number of Ducks on the team made the overarching melancholy of these Trials more personal. These great new talents had no sooner announced themselves than they had reached the end of the line. "All dressed up," as NBC announcer Charlie Jones put it, "and nowhere to go."

For months, these events, and my being dragooned into a movie, made great fodder for Bill and the Tuesday Ad Hoc luncheon group. I would be "the thespian" for years.

After shooting in Eugene, Towne continued in LA and San Luis Obispo. Then, in July, the Screen Actors Guild struck all the major studio productions over the issue of Pay-TV and video-cassette residuals. Towne asked for an exception because *Personal Best*'s athletes, though Guild members, weren't really actors. Both the Guild and Warner Brothers said no. So Towne refinanced the picture, making it an independent production. He could then agree to meet whatever terms the Guild won from the whole industry and resume.

The $11 million this switch cost came from record producer David Geffen. In case he went over budget, Geffen demanded that Towne put up his house and car and, later, the rights to several future scripts. This all caused big gaps in shooting.

In August, I escaped to reality, the Moscow Olympics. I didn't know which was sadder, a Trials that went nowhere or a vitiated Games.

Because Geffen repeatedly shut down shooting while he extracted from Towne the rights to more future work, *Personal Best* wasn't ready for release until early 1982. Bowerman suggested that a premiere in Eugene would be a great benefit for the Prefontaine Foundation. Towne and Warner Brothers, the distributor, agreed, so we arranged for one on February 17, 1982, at the Oakway Cinema.

By that time I had seen the final cut once and was sure Towne had attained the reality he sought. Especially powerful was Scott Glenn's portrayal of the caustic, manipulative, hypercompetitive coach, Terry Tingloff, whom the female characters have to learn from and eventually rise above. I had met such coaches and always thanked my lucky stars that they weren't mine.

Concerns that the lesbian aspect would overwhelm the main themes were unfounded. Towne had written it for its dramatic urgency; the danger, and consequent romance, would be greater. "But it's a natural thing to explore with athletes," he said. "Skill and passion are not unrelated. It's an extension of their being children, of discovering who they are through their bodies, in competition, in love. Anything to do with sex—whether masculine or feminine—is just all on the way to defining what they are about."

Then he issued a Dante-like curse: "People who can't think of anything else but whether the person you love is convex or concave should be doomed to not think of anything else, and so miss the other ninety-five percent of life."

As it happens in the movie, Chris Cahill (Hemingway) and Tory Skinner (Donnelly) break off their affair. Cahill takes up with a skinny swimmer named Denny. When Chris asks him how he feels about her having had a female lover, Denny comes up with a line that for me was an anthem of ho-hum acceptance. "I think," he says mildly, "we both like great-looking girls."

During the Eugene screening I sat with Bill and Barbara Bowerman. He laughed at that line and a lot of others. Both of them kept elbowing me during my scenes, one of which, famously, was nude in the bathroom. At the end there was Hayward Field-grade applause.

When I came back Sunday night, my father met my plane with the Register-Guard of the 19th, two days after the screening. The headline was "He Calls It Personal Worst." The subhead was "Fuming ex-U of O coach wants his name stricken from closing credits." Bill was quoted as saying the film was a discredit to sports in general and a sorry presentation of track and field.

Reporter Fred Crafts went on:

> Bowerman was among about 150 people who attended a special Northwest premier of the movie Wednesday night. Afterward, Bowerman congratulated co-star Kenny Moore, one of his former U of O

runners and told Moore he was "great." But when a reporter asked him Wednesday night for a review of the movie, Bowerman was visibly uncomfortable. He said he liked some of the action sequences, but added that some of the scenes "just didn't seem real." Bowerman skipped a post-screening reception. Instead he went home and fumed about the movie. On Thursday morning, he sought out a reporter to reveal his true reactions.

Bowerman, one of the most respected coaches in track history, was angriest over the portrait of the women's track coach as a boozing, swearing, lusting, shouting, hard-nosed jerk. "I don't know a coach that acts like that, and I know a lot of them," he said. Bowerman said he felt the motion picture could "harm track" by giving young viewers an erroneous impression of training rules. "Maybe I'm just old and very naïve," he said with a sigh. Bowerman lamented that he saw "no humor in the whole thing. There's a lot of humor in sports." When reminded that the audience laughed in several places, Bowerman retorted, "I think they laughed because they didn't know what else to do."

What the hell had happened? Only years later would I be able to marshal this guess. In the night after the screening, the Bowerman mind, whose usual fare was the Muppets and classical music, had slammed headlong into the very reality he denied was there. His outrage focused on the scheming coach played so well by Scott Glenn. Had I known anything about Bowerman's inner coils and conflicts on women, on masculinity and femininity, anything about the lingering residue of his mother's telling him to beware of all men and his resultant putting women on pedestals, I might have understood. He had put those two young women athletes on his pedestal and by God he was going to defend them against that coach. Towne couldn't have concocted a more perfect anti-Bowerman if he'd tried.

Bill did ask Towne to take his name off the movie, but he did it calmly, not with a trumpet blast. Towne sorrowfully did as asked. I went up to see Bill. We had lemonade and looked at the river and talked about it in a roundabout way. There was no need to confront him because his manner was absolutely unchanged toward me. In all the years afterward, he never held it against me.

In spite of the breakthrough heralded by passage of the Amateur Athletic Act of 1978, one bastion of Brundage-era aristocracy was still standing: amateurism. Now that the Moscow boycott had taught American runners that Olympic dreams are iffy at best and subject to the most ignorant interference, the time was ripe to rebel.

Marathoner Don Kardong and race director Chuck Galford had an idea. They called around to all the best distance runners, men and women, and said, Why don't we go all the way? Why don't we start a runner's union and call it the Association of Road Racing Athletes? Why don't we then start a professional road racing tour at different cities around the country and award prize money right out in the open? And if The Athletics Congress kicks us out and we lose our Olympic eligibility, tough, we didn't get to go to the last Olympics anyway. Besides, we'll have our own professional circuit. We'll make an honest living at our booming sport, and we're sure to attract others.

Phil Knight was gung ho to help. His company had ridden the running boom to power and he wanted to use that power to push for reform. A showdown race was picked—the June 28, 1981, Cascade Run-Off 15K in Portland. Nike put up $50,000 for prizes and promised $100,000 for the Nike marathon in Eugene in the fall.

Remarkably, this was all moving too fast for William J. Bowerman. "I may not agree with the rule," he said, "but I'll sure as hell try to live up to it as long as it's on the books. In offering prize money, Nike is endangering amateur track as well as Eugene's chances of hosting championship meets. Knight must have gotten bad advice on this one."

Knight knew exactly what he had done, because he knew how serious the runners were. In the days before the Cascade Run-Off, the nation's finest flocked to Portland. The 100-strong Association of Road Racing Athletes (ARRA) competitors' meeting roared when Bill Rodgers urged unity. New Zealand's Anne Audain, the women's record holder in the 3000 meters, found an analogy for taking prize money. "Hey, come on," she said. "It's like losing your virginity. You're a little misty for a while, but then you realize, wow, there's a whole new world out there!"

Kardong and his ARRA members were tough union men and women, perfectly ready to strike this blow and take the consequences. It was their fire Frank Shorter pointed to when he went to reason with TAC executive director Ollan Cassell two days before the race. Frank said that TAC and the IAAF were going to have zero control after this, that the pro league would succeed and every good American would be in the ARRA and not in TAC. If TAC and the IAAF didn't want to be obsolete tomorrow, Frank said, they would have to accept a deal where the runners got money but were not banned as pros. The mechanism, Shorter said, was the trust fund. Prize money should go through a trust fund that TAC could monitor and say the athletes were being paid for "training expenses."

Only a combination of Rodgers's and Kardong's ardor and Shorter's cool could have gotten Cassell to accept that deal. TAC gave in and the trust fund system was set up that week. It wasn't immediately acknowledged, but that was the end of amateurism in US track and field. The ARRA established a successful pro tour of races and no one was ever thrown out again for taking money earned in competition. It was, as Bowerman had hoped in his note on Wilkins's paper ten years before, a most flexible solution.

With all these noble acts, maybe it was inevitable that Bowerman would be caught up in the petty and personal. In 1981, a new Oregon athletic director had taken over. He was a youngish wrestling coach named Rick Bay who'd been an assistant director of the University of Michigan Alumni Association. First impressions were positive. Coming from a nonrevenue Olympic sport, it seemed he'd surely mesh well with Bill Dellinger and the track community.

It turned out otherwise. One of Bay's first directives was to assign coaches to different offices. In Dellinger's case, this meant leaving the windowed cubicle that Hayward and Bowerman had hallowed for fifty years and setting up camp half in a hallway, half in a glorified closet behind the sports information director's mimeograph machines. Dellinger tried it for a while and voiced his chagrin over his sudden loss of privacy.

In January 1982, he received this memo from Bay:

> *Pursuant to our conversation earlier today, I want to reaffirm my distress and disapproval of your continuing poor attitude regarding my decision to relocate your office and your all too frequent statements that I do not have any concern about Oregon's track and field program.*
>
> *While I recognize you are not happy with your new office space, I made the decision to improve the office situation for the entire department. In any case, my decision is irrevocable, I expect you to respect it and do not want to hear any more about it from you personally or secondhand. . . .*
>
> *In the final analysis, if you truly believe that I have no regard for your program and if you are unhappy with conditions as they now exist in the athletic department, I recommend you look for employment elsewhere. . . . I have no desire to have people on my staff who are unhappy and who reflect a negative attitude. . . .*

While I consider track and field an extremely important part of our program, it along with every other sport must be considered in proper perspective. And while I expect you to be most concerned and protective of your sport, I do not think it appropriate you do so so selfishly that your thinking excludes all the other sports. If you cannot see that we are a team trying to accomplish something together, then I recommend you find a club job where coaching track and field is your only consideration.

In short, if you wish to continue in your present role at the University of Oregon, I expect to see a vastly improved attitude on your part immediately.

Soon after, Dellinger, at the Original House of Pancakes, laid a copy of that memo before Bowerman, whose eyes widened. "Wow," he whistled. "I count twice he says look for another job and once he might fire you anyway." Bowerman thanked him for sharing the memo with him and wished him good luck with this new boss.

When Dellinger had gone, Bowerman sat back and pondered. From that moment on, he would never be able to place any trust in Rick Bay. This was an offense not only to Dellinger and Bowerman but also to Bill Hayward. It could not cut any deeper.

In making this cut, Bay unknowingly elicited a classic Bowerman reaction. Bill occasionally said that the ideal thing, if you could, was to oversolve a problem. He had solved the problem of rotten shoes by starting his own shoe company. Now, he thought, Fine: If this AD won't give Dellinger a decent place to work, I'll give the university a whole new building.

Bowerman placed $350,000 of Nike stock in trust with the Prefontaine Foundation as a financing pledge. The rest of that winter, he and architect Jack Stafford sketched a two-story building that would go at the north end of the track, at the top of the homestretch. The plan called for locker space, weight rooms, a sauna, and a hall of honor to display the trophies and photos of past champions. Particularly spacious were the offices for the men's and women's track coaches.

When Bowerman and Stafford presented the concept to Bay, he thanked them cordially, looked at the drawings, and said it was against his philosophy to allow his track coaches to have offices apart from the department. Bill, remarkably, held his tongue. In their second meeting, Bay suggested that 400 square feet become the Athletic Department's laundry room.

Bowerman came away convinced that Bay was intent on frustrating the purpose of his gift. He realized that his Nike money was casting him in a role he had often lamented—a fat cat alumnus trying to call all the shots. He knew, therefore, to be subtle. He and attorney William Wheatley, a member of John Jaqua's firm, drafted a proposed contract that stated that the facility would cost the university nothing, that its primary use would be for track and field, and that other uses were fine if final approval lay not with Bay but with the university president, now the eminent mathematician Paul Olum. Bay resisted this, saying that limiting his control of the building in any way would be "illegal and immoral."

While Bowerman considered his next move, Dellinger complicated things by joining forces with the Adidas company. A few years before, he'd come up with an idea for absorbing shock in road shoes. He'd taken it to Nike, but they were working on what would become the first air-cushioned shoes, such as the Pegasus, and passed on developing the design. Adidas, however, smarting at being outstripped by Knight and wanting to invade his home turf, snapped it up.

In 1982, full-page ads appeared in the running trades showing a smiling Dellinger holding the "Oregon web" shoe. The text read, "Bill Dellinger has discovered a new use for Newton's Third Law of Motion." Arrows showed how the polyamide netting that went around and through the midsole "acts like a torsion bar" to absorb and redirect up to ten percent of impact shock.

Dellinger had signed a contract with Adidas as far back as 1977 and had been perfectly open about it with Bowerman. The elder Bill congratulated the younger on his royalty rate. Now, Adidas offered the university another $350,000 on top of Bill's money to complete the new building in style. Bowerman hailed the offer, saying the more the merrier. But Bay, apparently still unwilling to accept any constraints on its use, held back from blessing the terms of the gift.

The new building brought Dellinger and Bowerman together only briefly. Dellinger's Adidas shoe might not have bothered Bowerman, but Phil Knight was definitely bothered—because Adidas was sponsoring the team in other ways: With Bay's approval, Dellinger had switched the Oregon men's team from Nike to Adidas warm-up sweats.

Dellinger had essentially decided that Bay was his boss and he had to live with him. Bowerman had not. In November 1982, after no further response from Bay, Bowerman suspended the offer of the new building. Adidas later withdrew its offer as well.

CHAPTER 28

Rajneeshpuram

IN 1979, BILL'S ELDEST SON, JON, BOUGHT A 2,000-ACRE RANCH ALONG THE John Day River near Clarno, twenty-five miles from Fossil. The land is meadow along the river, where the cows have gentle hills to wend and bunchgrass to chew. The first time Bill and Barbara visited, Jon's fields were yellow with sunflowers. Bill loved to sit and let the changing light lead his eye across the immensity, playing over rimrock, sage, juniper, and dusty roads, scanning, checking, moving on.

The land was perfect for Jon. He had been a Marine guard in the US Embassy in Tegucigalpa, Honduras, taken his degree from Oregon, and coached the US women's ski team. But through it all what he really wanted was to cowboy. He had ridden in rodeos for years, and had broken his neck doing it. When he recovered, he was so happy to find himself alive and with a future that he wanted to spend it raising rodeo stock. In 1982, he married Candace Cookson, and on July 9, 1983, they had a daughter. Bill and Barbara's fifth grandchild was named Elizabeth, after Bill's mother. Hers would be an eventful infancy.

Two years before Elizabeth's birth, followers of Indian spiritual master Bhagwan Shree Rajneesh, headed by his secretary, Ma Anand Sheela, bought the 64,000-acre Big Muddy Ranch from Rube Evans for $5.75 million. Its bluffs and bottoms were just across the river from Jon Bowerman's ranch. That summer, Sheela and an advance party of *sannyasins* (disciples) arrived, renamed the property Rancho Rajneesh, and promised Margaret Hill, the mayor of nearby Antelope (population forty-four), that no more than forty people would be employed on it.

It soon emerged, however, that the Rajneeshee had big ideas and substantial resources. They planned to construct a spiritual commune as the center of the Bhagwan's worldwide, 200,000-member movement. In mid-September, Margaret Hill wrote to a land-use watchdog group called 1000 Friends of Oregon with the news that the Rajneeshee's "stated goal was to build a self-contained city for 50,000."

In a state that led the nation in protecting farmland and open range from urban sprawl, this goal was cause for serious concern. Oregon cities were required to maintain growth boundaries, zoning any new development within them. Any change in land use—such as plopping down a big new town on empty grazing land—had to be approved by the state Land Conservation and Development Commission (LCDC).

Henry Richmond, director of 1000 Friends, advised the commune leaders that Rancho Rajneesh was zoned as agricultural land and couldn't be used for commercial or industrial purposes. The closest place with an urban boundary was Antelope, which was the only entity that could approve new buildings without LCDC review. Under the aggressive, well-educated, and relentless Rajneeshee leadership, the commune immediately commenced buying property in Antelope and moving *sannyasins* in.

"Thus began the battle of Antelope," wrote Oregon law professor Garrett Epps in his 2001 book, *To an Unknown God*, "which set the pattern for the commune's contentious dealings with county and state." The Antelope City Council held a vote to disincorporate their town, but the new Rajneeshee residents outvoted the longtime townspeople fifty-five to forty-two.

Not long afterward, in November 1981, the Rajneeshee got permission from Wasco County (the county most of the ranch was in) to incorporate a brand new city, Rajneeshpuram, on the ranch proper. The Rajneeshee lawyers had found a loophole in the land-use laws. Unlike development outside an existing city boundary, incorporating an entirely new city required only county approval, not that of the LCDC.

In mid-1982, about a year after the Rajneeshee arrived in Oregon, Bowerman and Henry Richmond formed Citizens for Constitutional Cities, a nonprofit corporation to fund legal opposition to the ranch. Bill was its first president. "My ancestors," he wrote in a press release, "have lived in Oregon since 1845. My son Jon is a rancher in Wheeler County. Bowermans past, present, and future are deeply committed to this state. Thousands like me have become concerned about the effect this group has had on its neighbors. As an educator and coach at the University of Oregon, I have always welcomed and encouraged new ideas and diverse people to come and live in this great state, irrespective of race, creed, national origin, or religion."

But the battle of Antelope had shown there was cause for concern. "Citizens for Constitutional Cities," Bowerman wrote, "is going to monitor the activities of the Rajneeshee and challenge them in court if necessary to avoid the creation of unlawful cities in this state and protect our citizens from harassment and intimidation in violation of the Oregon and United States Constitutions."

The Rajneeshee response was to assert, in a letter to Henry Richmond, that they were the object of Eastern Oregon religious bigotry. Richmond replied with some heat. "If the early Christians had as much money and as many lawyers, planners, consultants, and public relations operators as you do, the Romans would have been hauled out of the grandstands and fed to the lions instead of the other way around. Who do you guys think you're kidding?"

Bowerman's main concerns were practical: the potential burden on taxpayers of a huge, tax-exempt city, the school and road costs, and its effect on the water rights of surrounding farmers. As it happened, Rancho Rajneesh did pay some taxes. It had a three-part financial structure. One was the Rajneesh Foundation International, a religious entity presided over by Ma Anand Sheela. One was the Rajneesh Investment Corporation, a subsidiary run by Sheela's husband, Jayananda. And one was the Rajneesh Neo-Sannyas International Commune, which ran all the Rajneesh businesses, including a hotel in Portland. Only the foundation was tax-exempt as a church. But that distinction would soon blur.

In musing over the possible impact of the Rajneeshee, Bowerman realized that he knew virtually nothing about them or their master. He and Barbara began a crash course. The guru's original name was Chandra Mohan Jain, and he'd been an assistant professor of philosophy at the University of Jabalpur. In 1960 he began giving public lectures in which he criticized Gandhi for his worship of poverty. Jain preached that India needed capitalism, science, technology, and birth control. His audiences grew. In the early 1970s in Bombay, he founded his Neo-Sannyas International Movement and changed his name to Bhagwan ("The blessed one") Shree Rajneesh. He liked and attracted Westerners; once they had become *sannyasins,* he sent many back to their homes to start Rajneeshee centers.

In 1974, Rajneesh and his first disciple, a woman named Ma Yoga Laxmi, moved to the city of Pune (formerly Poona), bought a villa, and began an ashram. By 1976, the Pune ashram, with 600 permanent residents, had become a major attraction for thousands of Westerners. Rajneesh let Westerners lead therapy groups in which hundreds of people screamed, sang, and threw themselves violently about. "I'm going to bring your insanity out," he said. "Unless you become consciously insane you can never be sane." By 1981, as mentally ill *sannyasins* ended up in Pune hospitals and others were caught smuggling dope, the good people of Pune had had enough. Rajneesh's lectures went downhill, becoming dirty jokes and political attacks. Traditional Hindus were aghast. The Indian government refused permission for the ashram to move and make a fresh start.

In April 1981, Laxmi's aide, Ma Anand Sheela, announced that the guru had gone into silence and would lecture no more. That May he flew to the United States with twenty disciples. His visa application said he was going for medical treatment, but he did not present himself to any US doctors. In Montclair, New

Jersey, Sheela took over from Laxmi as the now-silent guru's secretary. That summer she found the Big Muddy Ranch.

In Oregon, as Rajneesh himself continued to maintain his silence, Sheela called all the shots. But who was this woman? The Bowermans learned she'd been born in India and moved to the United States in her teens. In New Jersey she married an affluent American, Marc Silverman, and returned with him to India where they became disciples at the Pune ashram in 1973. In 1975, she'd started a Rajneesh meditation center in Montclair.

Sheela had bought the Oregon ranch on impulse. She believed in going with her feelings, changed her mind often, and was a great self-dramatizer. According to University of Oregon sociology professor Marion Goldman, who in 1999 published *Passionate Journeys*, her study of the women of Rajneeshpuram, "Sheela could change instantly from charming and flirtatious to abusive and vicious, because she inevitably sought adulation and approval, and became furious when she did not receive them." During the four years she was in Oregon, Goldman would say, Sheela "grew increasingly irrational."

In late 1982, Rube Evans, who'd sold the land to the Bhagwan, called Jon Bowerman to say he needed to sell the 800 acres he owned adjacent to Jon's ranch and asked if Bill Bowerman would be interested. Jon said no, but Evans then called Bill directly, mentioning that Sheela wanted the land. "Dad paid almost a million for that," Jon would say, "to keep the Rajneeshee out of Wheeler County, his boyhood stomping grounds." The property had a comfortable, doublewide trailer, in which Bill and Barbara took up temporary residence. Next Bill bought the trailer camp in Antelope, giving them voting rights there.

Sheela's combativeness seemed to permeate the Rajneeshee ranch. She instituted a police force and armed it to the teeth. The press and public were welcome to tour the ranch, escorted by attractive guides. But *sannyasin* guards along the riverbank would hold up their weapons as frightened rafters and fishermen floated by. The Rajneeshee set up video cameras and taped Antelope residents coming and going. Some older, retired town residents were so intimidated they left.

Because Jon Bowerman objected to such tactics in letters and articles in the local paper, he drew special surveillance. The ridge on the Rajneesh side of the river towers over the Bowerman ranch house. (Bill likened the butte's topography to that of Riva Ridge in Italy.) "They had armed guards watching us here constantly," Jon would recall, "with big spotting scopes by day, searchlights by night. It was like being watched by the East German border guard in Berlin. The lights were as bright as 747 landing lights, and periodically they would shine them at our house."

In 1984, when daughter Elizabeth was six months old, Jon and Candy would wake up to her crying and find strobe lights playing across the walls of her room. When they moved her to the next room, the Rajneeshee shifted the lights downstream so they shone into that one. Jon called the police, but they refused to come at first, saying "it was just lights." Jon said, "Well in that case I guess it's okay if I put them out. With my .30-06 sniper rifle, two shots, guaranteed." The police came and saw the harassment, and the Rajneeshee signed a consent order to desist. "But the next year, when Becky was due," said Jon, "they came back with banks of lights and lit up the whole hillside."

"No one's distress over all this matched Bill's," Barbara Bowerman would say. "He was worried about Jon, Candy, and the two little girls. We could hear target shooting on the other side of the river, and looking down, they always knew when Jon was home and when he wasn't."

During this time the Bhagwan, accompanied by an armed guard in a Jeep, began to be chauffeured at two o'clock every afternoon in a new Rolls-Royce the fifty miles to Madras, the closest town of any size. There, a female devotee would get him a soda and the little convoy would turn around and go back to Rajneeshpuram. At the time, he had amassed twenty-one Rolls-Royces from donors, but the number kept rising (to ninety-three in all). Pulitzer Prize-winning author Frances FitzGerald, who visited Rajneeshpuram in May 1983, noted that these afternoon outings were the only times the Bhagwan's disciples ever saw their guru. "For these pass-bys the *sannyasins* would line up along the roads and greet him with palms pressed together and beatific expressions."

When they weren't lining up to view their guru, the *sannyasins* were working very hard. In two years, the Rajneeshee completed a total of 250,000 square feet of new buildings. They cleared 3,000 acres of land and planted them in wheat, sunflowers, and fruit trees. The ranch produced ninety percent of their vegetables and all their eggs and milk. They dammed Mud Creek Canyon to make a forty-acre reservoir for irrigation and boasted that where Bowerman and the ranchers had worried that the Rajneeshee would lower the water table, they were actually raising it. They had a ten-megawatt power substation, a sewer system, and a phone system. They built a runway and had several aircraft. Their eighty-five school buses constituted the fourth-largest public transportation system in the state. Festivals drew as many as 15,000 outside *sannyasins* to the ranch.

At the time of FitzGerald's first visit, the Rajneesh investment in Oregon was about $50 million. Her findings about the people who had joined the movement explained their power both to raise money and to spend it so effectively. Krishna

Deva, by then the mayor of Rajneeshpuram, was the former David Knapp of Santa Monica, California. A clinical psychologist, he had done his PhD thesis on 300 American Rajneeshee in Pune. "There are various myths about us," he told FitzGerald. "People think that a master-disciple relationship is like a master-slave relationship. They think we are dependent types, avoiding stress and decisions." Quite the contrary, Deva asserted. "By and large, the people here on the ranch are people who have had success in worldly terms, and who see themselves as successes. When they came to Bhagwan, they were people in transition. There was some change involved—some openness happened. But they're not dropouts. They're what I call 'dropups.'"

When Bill and Barbara talked to friends in Eugene about the Rajneeshee, ironies abounded. Bill, of course, was the one who had asked the Oregon team to presume all religious expression as genuinely felt. So he wasn't antireligious. This wasn't a matter of Christian vs. Hindu. It wasn't even separation of church and state that much. But Bill objected to the fact that the Rajneeshee were not living by the Golden Rule; the Rajneeshee seemed not to care about non-Rajneeshee. They had these hotshot lawyers and they were litigious as hell—indeed, Sheela always seemed to be suing someone for slander.

Then Bill got word Sheela wanted to meet him. As Barbara would tell the story, a company in Eugene had been making good money selling the Rajneeshee industrial steel and plastic pipe. "One company executive kept telling Bill they were great people who paid on the barrelhead," Barbara would remember. "He said, 'Come see how nice they are,' and invited us to lunch at the Town Club in Eugene. Sheela and her entourage flew over in their helicopter. They were all dressed in dark red clothes. Sheela was determined to convince Bill she was a nice person, and she kept talking about how nice she was, but her language was not nice. She said, 'Barbara, do you know the men in Antelope are raping our women?' I said, 'Oh, I'm sure that's not true.' Bill sat there like the Sphinx."

As it happened, the Sphinx was corresponding with US Representative Robert Smith, in whose district Rajneeshpuram lay. "Having spent six months in Pakistan," Bill wrote, "I have some feeling for the subcontinent. An Afridi tribesman in the northwest (India) territory told me that in India one does not 'kick the basket when it may be full of cobras.' I have frequently thought of that when the transplanted culture of Raj city comes up. That is an Indian city-state. Enjoying the rights and privileges that all of us are paying for—raising hell with five counties and influencing the lives of most Oregonians. Sitting and waiting is not going to help cure a bad thing that will only get worse if ignored."

Oregon politicians were not indifferent to the problem, but they urged caution. Governor Vic Atiyeh met with Bill and Barbara. When Bill said, "All we ask is that you monitor the hell out of them," Atiyeh said he had to be careful not to appear to be singling out a religion for harassment. "No doubt you sensed my frustration," Atiyeh wrote to Barbara afterward. "The fact that a group suspected of having ill motives is able to hire topflight lawyers who can assist them in keeping within the law, and holds unpopular philosophies, does not put them outside the protection of the law."

All true. But Bowerman and Henry Richmond felt the commune's religious nature brought it over the line separating church and state. And Bowerman had, in one of the most satisfying (one might even say karmic) developments of his life, a friend in the perfect place to pursue that. In 1980, Otto Frohnmayer's son David had been elected attorney general of Oregon.

"I talked with Jon and Bill about the abuses to local people in Antelope and elsewhere," David Frohnmayer would recall, "and I had to be the voice of caution, saying, 'If laws are broken, we'll go right after them.' I didn't want to get the family in trouble by being too aggressive, because Sheela was saying everybody was prejudiced against them. I remember hearing Jon Bowerman mention how easy it'd be to take down the power lines to the ranch, and I said that'd be the worst thing anybody could possibly do."

Then, in September 1983, a legislator requested a legal opinion from Frohnmayer: Was the incorporation of Rajneeshpuram constitutional under the establishment clause of the First Amendment? (The establishment clause, of course, reads "Congress shall make no law respecting an establishment of religion, or prohibiting the free exercise thereof.")

"We researched that opinion exhaustively," Frohnmayer would say. "And as we were doing it, the Rajneeshee made a tactical error. They stopped busing the Antelope-area farm kids to Madras and forced them to go to the Rajneeshpuram school." Bill asked Frohnmayer to listen to a delegation of farmers about their concerns about harassment, and Frohnmayer suddenly realized how high the stakes were.

Frohnmayer asked his respected Boalt Hall constitutional law professor, Dean Jesse Choper, to review the draft opinion. Choper recalled that a recent Supreme Court ruling had language to the effect that it was unconstitutional to "enmesh churches in exercise of substantial government powers." Frohnmayer also got Gerald Gunther at Stanford and Lawrence Tribe at Harvard ("names that would turn the head of any federal judge") to consult and sign on to the opinion. Frohnmayer's research showed that Rajneeshpuram was entirely private land, owned by the nonprofit Neo-Sannyas Foundation, a religious entity. All the construction in the city was for the benefit of the religious group. All administrative offices were filled by *sannyasins*. The question of whether this church was "enmeshed" in government was indisputable.

Frohnmayer issued his opinion on October 6, 1983. He wrote that the city "is the functional equivalent of a religious commune." Not only should it not be allowed to receive state funding, but so long as it was a religious body, the city itself was unconstitutional and must cease to exist.

"I'm outraged beyond words," Sheela wrote in a press release. "The attorney general's statement is in the long tradition of bigotry which this state has exhibited since birth." She concluded that Frohnmayer needed psychiatric help at a Rajneeshee clinic.

Bowerman felt vindicated by the attorney general's opinion, but nothing changed immediately. Frohnmayer sued in state court to disincorporate the city. The Rajneeshee delayed, dragging the case from state to federal court. But because of Sheela's ascending paranoia, the commune took all kinds of other measures. Once, after Otto and MarAbel Frohnmayer had visited Bill and Barbara at Jon's house and driven home to Medford, MarAbel picked up the phone and a questioner demanded to know if they owned the make, model, and license number of the car that had been visiting the Bowermans. When MarAbel said yes, she realized the call was to let them know they were being watched. The voice then began asking all kinds of questions about whether Dave had ever fallen on his head as a baby. "Anything at all to account for this insanity now?" MarAbel hung up, white.

Bill and Barbara began to get spooky envelopes in the mail, stuffed with dark poems describing how they would soon die of poison. "Horrible letters came all the time," Barbara would recall. "Ones telling me about all the women Bill was with. It was just crazy."

Crazy was the word. In November 1983, Sheela, suspicious of everyone, ordered listening devices be placed in the cabins where journalists and other visitors stayed. A few months later, eavesdropping was expanded to the Hotel Rajneesh, her rival Laxmi's quarters, and the entire ranch telephone system. Although the *sannyasins* said it was for the protection of the guru, Sheela had her own reasons: She was vulnerable to charges of immigration fraud and also worried about an internal revolt.

Her solution was to have a close aide, Puja, drug and poison those who knew too much. Puja had created a secret lab on the ranch and experimented with poisoning mice. Soon *sannyasins* who opposed Sheela were falling ill and almost dying. That September, three Wasco County commissioners who had angered Sheela by voting to repeal the city's land-use plan visited Rajneeshpuram. Sheela gave them glasses of water. The commissioner nearly died of poisoning. The second got mildly sick. The third remained healthy.

That fall, in an effort to win two judgeships and the sheriff's office, Sheela had some 4,000 homeless people imported to pack voter registration, bringing the ranch's total to about 7,000 voters. The county seat, The Dalles, had 12,000 voters, so Sheela planned to infect the town's water supply on election day to keep people from voting. As a rehearsal, she and aides put salmonella in ten restaurant salad bars in The Dalles. Seven hundred and fifty people got sick, 400 at Shakey's Pizza alone. Fortunately, all lived. It remains the largest germ-warfare attack in the history of the United States.

And it spurred a record election turnout that November. To prevent fraud, the Oregon Secretary of State had the state assume control of voter registration in Wasco County. "All new voters," wrote author Garrett Epps, "would be required to register in The Dalles, where state attorneys would interview them to decide whether they intended to remain in Oregon after the election, a requirement under the state's voting laws. Perhaps realizing that their street people could never pass such an interview, Sheela denounced the plan as more religious big-otry and announced a boycott of the election." The Rajneeshee elected no friendly sheriff or commissioners.

On February 28, 1985, Congressman Jim Weaver gave a speech on the House floor describing why he was convinced that the salmonella poisoning in The Dalles had been the handiwork of the Rajneeshee. At the time, all health author-ities were equally convinced that the blame lay with restaurant food handlers, and Weaver took some heat in the press.

Weaver had been following Rajneeshee developments closely ever since a visit from Bill Bowerman the year before. Bowerman had come to Weaver to ask him to stop the Bureau of Land Management from going through with a proposed swap with the Rajneeshee. (The Big Muddy region was a checkerboard of sections owned by the BLM and the Rajneeshee.) As chairman of the subcommittee with oversight of such deals, Weaver had kept the proposal on hold for several months, but the BLM still wanted to go through with it.

Meanwhile, matters were coming to a head. "By June 1985," wrote FitzGerald, "Sheela had come to believe that the authorities would soon be coming to arrest her and Rajneesh." She and her inner circle drew up a hit list of Rajneeshpuram enemies, a list that included US Attorney Charles Turner, David Frohnmayer, Portland *Oregonian* reporter Leslie Zaitz, and Helen Byron, a former *sannyasin*, who'd just won a big judgment against Sheela. Sheela and three others obtained false IDs, bought handguns in Texas, and staked out Charles Turner's house in Portland, planning to shoot him in his car. Somehow, he avoided them.

With the BLM still pushing hard to conclude the land swap, Weaver surveyed the Big Muddy by helicopter and jeep in the company of the two Prineville BLM chiefs. "One thing struck me with force," Weaver would remember later for the Eugene *Register-Guard*. "The two BLM officials were fervently for the land swap, arguing all the way for the benefits the land swap would hold for the BLM. Why were they so enthusiastic? Had they made personal arrangements with the Rajneesh?"

For a week Weaver sat in the Bowerman house across from the Big Muddy, poring over maps. One day he and Bill went out on the river with Jon, rowing a boat along the banks and even swimming to shore, where the *sannyasin* guards patrolled with AK-47s.

The next morning, Weaver suddenly realized why the Rajneeshee wanted the land swap: they wanted to build a large resort and housing development along the river, but a promontory of BLM land that went right into the river blocked access to the planned resort area. "I saw how the land swap would give them a road route from their ranch land to the resort location," Weaver would recall. "The value of the land would increase enormously."

It was only a matter of days before the papers were to be signed, but Weaver prevailed upon the regional director to kill the deal, "or I will raise so much hell you'll wish you never heard of the Rajneeshees." The director said he would look into it. "Apparently, what he found did not smell so sweet," Weaver would write, "for the next day he called me and said the swap was terminated."

Two days later, in mid-September, Sheela and fifteen other disciples left the ranch and fled to Europe. The two Prineville BLM chiefs announced their resignations the same day. "One of the most prized mementos of my congressional career," Weaver would say, "is a handwritten note from Bill Bowerman, received a few days after the Rajneesh debouched, saying, 'Thanks, Jim.'"

The guru, rather than cover for his fleeing secretary, opened the ranch up to investigators and even accused her of crimes himself. Sheela and Puja were caught in Germany and extradited back to Portland.

Once on the ranch, federal agents found evidence of Bhagwan's immigration fraud—holding mass weddings for green cards. They presented it to state and federal grand juries. Word reached Rajneesh through his lawyers that he was about to be charged, so he ran for it. On October 27, 1985, he boarded one of two rented Lear jets and took off, headed for Bermuda.

An informant in the commune alerted the Feds, saying the Bhagwan was to switch planes in Charlotte, North Carolina. As Garrett Epps told the story, "At home, Frohnmayer awoke next morning to a call from a gravelly Southern voice that introduced itself as Robert Morgan, a former US Senator who was now the head of the North Carolina State Bureau of Investigation. "Did you get Bhagwan?' Frohnmayer asked.

"'I don't know anything about that,' Morgan drawled, 'but there's a guy here who's some kind of maharajah.'"

Once Rajneesh was back in Portland, his attorneys posted bond so he could return to Rajneeshpuram. He left the United States less than two weeks later, after filing no contest pleas to two counts of immigration fraud and paying prosecution costs of $400,000. He went to India, Nepal, and Crete, unsuccessfully seeking asylum. Eventually he resettled in Pune. In 1989, he changed his name to Osho, and on January 19, 1990, he died.

Sheela, Puja, and Shanti Bhadea pleaded guilty to the attempted murder of Deveraj, the guru's doctor, with an injection of adrenaline; the poisoning of William Hulse and his colleague; causing the outbreak of salmonella poisoning in The Dalles; immigration fraud; and setting fire to the Wasco County planning offices. Sheela and Puja received twenty-year sentences. Sheela paid a half-million dollars in fines and served almost three years in a federal medium-security prison, then departed for Europe.

By the end of December 1985, most of the *sannyasins* had left the ranch. That same month, Dave Frohnmayer won Oregon's suit against the incorporation of Rajneeshpuram. After the ranch was already up for sale, the federal district court enjoined the city from exercising governmental power because there was no effective separation of church and state. In the intervening years, if one wanted to see a special gleam enter the eye of David Frohnmayer, all one had to do was lift a glass and toast that miracle given to us by the founding fathers, the Establishment Clause.

Bill Bowerman, in coming home do battle, had been reacquainted not only with the vistas of his childhood, but with present-day Antelope and Fossil and their people. Bill decided to spend more time in Wheeler County. He looked across to the Big Muddy Ranch, unfurled a yellow pad, and made some notes for an essay on its natural history: "The south end is a geologic treasure. Numerous pre- and post-Columbian Indian pictographs are in the area. The desert highland ridges are habitat of deer, chukars, pheasant, and a few antelope. Yes, and rattlesnakes, but no more cobras."

CHAPTER 29

Builderman

SEVERAL YEARS OF CONCENTRATING ON RAJNEESHPURAM DIDN'T DISTRACT Bowerman from advising selected athletes and pledging more gifts to his university. In some cases, he was gratified by the results, in others exasperated. Judging from his correspondence, Bill was most frustrated by the way his American dream was coming true. Nike was growing so fast it felt less and less like his own creation.

Bowerman's letters on the subject during the 1980s all describe some point in a cycle. First he lists his hopes for projects he's developing in his Eugene lab. Then he writes of finding some resistance to them in the company, either by the Exeter R&D lab or by a bunch of midlevel managers in the Beaverton headquarters he'd never dealt with before. He complains to Knight, Bob Woodell, and the board of directors. He feels this does no good. He asks to be removed from the board. Knight, John Jaqua, and other board members plead that doing so would be a terrible blow to the company. One, former Deputy Secretary of State (and Robin Jaqua's brother) Chuck Robinson, wrote him, "You are a symbol of integrity to the entire athletic world." Bill relents and morosely pursues other ideas, recording his dissatisfactions in detailed memos.

One such document in 1982 listed twenty-three projects he and his Eugene lab people were working on, including racing shoes for Duck middle-distance star Joachim Cruz of Brazil and Kenyan 3:49.4-miler Mike Boit, who was taking his PhD from Oregon. Bill was customizing shoes for thirteen Athletics West runners and also tailoring them for children with braces at a Portland hospital. He was developing an aerobics shoe, a gymnastics shoe, a children's shoe, a shoe for nurses, a boat shoe, a system of straps for Oregon women javelin-throwers' boots (to prevent toe bruising), and, with Dr. Bill McHolick consulting, a "mature women's" shoe. (Designed to accommodate painful bunions, this shoe was so ugly, John Jaqua would say, "that my Robin wouldn't even test it in the privacy of her bedroom.")

Another McHolick idea was a Velcro-strapped shoe to accommodate the swelling feet of diabetes patients. Bowerman was also devising an interval training flat with an intriguing "horseshoe-type spike plate to enable training with cushion and yet prevent slippage." He was working on a prototype high-jump shoe for women and, with Geoff Hollister, a windsurfing aqua sock. With wheelchair-mile world record holder Craig Blanchette, who lived in Springfield, Bill was designing racing suits and the critical pushing gloves used to transfer muscle power to the rubber-coated rings connected to the wheelchair's axle.

Most of these had little mass-market appeal, but even those that did rarely made it into production in the shape or with the alacrity that Bill wanted. In early 1984 he had a host of complaints. His children's and infants' shoe had been researched four years before, but current production models were "dogs." The company had termed Velcro "a passing fad," but it hadn't passed. His gymnastic and aerobic shoes were experiencing "roadblocks."

The Bowerman mind was less and less suited to shrugging off such impediments. Bill felt stymied as the company grew because his nature was so opposite to the corporate. Conflict was inevitable.

Phil Knight had seen this coming, of course. Early on he had vowed to himself never to lose Bill Bowerman, a vow that would define the culture of his company. Knight would make keeping Bowerman a mark of keeping Nike's soul, of defeating the competition with quality. Knight worked to retain Bill's sensitivity to the individual—even as Bill was moaning that the company was losing faith in it—by hiring, training, and promoting employees who didn't mind Bowerman's driven perfectionism. When Knight got notes from Bill wanting to resign (such as one in 1984 saying, "My effectiveness as a Nike employee is somewhere between zero and fifty percent"), he could only hope that one day Bowerman would fully comprehend the effort needed to make the transition from boutique to behemoth.

Knight would lose count of Bill's attempted resignations. "It was a bunch," he'd say in 2005. Each time it happened, Knight would grit his teeth, count to fifteen, and go on. He never let the resignations take effect. "I had been trained by him," said Knight. "I knew him. I loved him. I simply never took it personally. If I had anything to say about it, he was not going to leave."

Time would clarify the best role for Bill in the company. About the so-called power struggle between Exeter R&D and Eugene R&D, Jeff Johnson would have this to say in 2005: "We did different things, and it was a good division of labor. Bowerman was supposed to do his Bowerman thing, which was to be a genius, a process which knows no supervision or deadlines. Exeter was supposed to produce new models and entire lines in a timely fashion."

In the late 1970s, as growth in the athletic-shoe industry shot upward, Exeter set up a dedicated research lab staffed with exercise physiologists, biomechanists, and computer-assisted design and manufacturing equipment. They began foot morphology studies on thousands of athletes to guide the design of shoe lasts. "Exeter had an entirely different charge than Eugene," Johnson would say, "and it would not only have been stupid of us, but silly and enormously petty to think we were in some kind of 'war' for power with Eugene." Although Jeff clearly did not feel his lab was competing with Bill's, Bill was just as clearly inclined to feel the opposite—or at least that was true for several years.

Into all this trotted a tall, lean, observant distance runner. Mark Parker had gone to Penn State and run vast training mileage for Harry Groves, a coach almost as acerbic as Bowerman. He graduated in 1975 and Jeff Johnson hired him to work at Exeter, where he would have eight different jobs in two years. "I did design for Jeff, and I became an all-purpose product guy," Parker recalled.

Johnson was his mentor, but Parker was also deeply affected and inspired by both Pre and Bowerman. In 1980 Parker was sent to Eugene during the week of the Olympic Trials. His primary mission was to meet with author and wrestler Ken Kesey at his farm, to talk wrestling shoes. He then went to call at Bill's Eugene lab.

"When I met Bill he was wearing a green cowboy hat," Parker would recall. "I introduced myself and he said, 'Oh, from Exeter,' as if that was from the devil. A sign above his workbench said, 'Russia has its Siberia. Nike has its Exeter.'"

Parker was about to work a little détente, or at least glasnost. "Bill had a way of coming up and testing you to see what you were made of," Parker would say. "He'd tell you what he thought—this is crap, this is terrific—in order to get your opinion." Parker's conditioning under Harry Groves kept him from being intimidated. Bill especially cared how someone felt about a product's weight, being solidly of the "form must be driven by function" school, a philosophy that Parker also believed in. But Parker told Bowerman that the company had to sell shoes to average folks, not just the most elite athletes. Bill—who might have gagged at hearing this from a salesman—deemed it reasonable coming from a runner. He accepted Parker as a colleague.

"What I eventually came to love about Bill," Parker would say, "was how opinionated he was, and how he applied that brutal candor to our delicate creations." Parker felt Bowerman's constant testing to be at some level deeply enjoyable for both of them. "It got so predictable that I looked forward to it," he would recall. "In the formal setting of a board meeting, you'd be an R&D dog, showing off your sample shoe, and he'd let you go, explaining, explaining, while he'd swivel away and rock in his chair, and finally he'd swivel back, clear the table—it was a ceremony—open his briefcase and pull out a postage scale. You'd feel this eruption building. . . . It made everyone go quiet. Then he'd say, 'Lemme see that.'" Bowerman would weigh the shoe and then ask a barrage of penetrating questions "way beyond the rest of the board." That every Nike designer could picture Bill waiting, rocking, coiled to administer his final exam, kept a lot of half-baked ideas off the table.

Partial to eccentrics, Parker found Bowerman's personality invigorating. "If you let him—if you turned to mush when he was trying to see if you were chopping-block maple—he'd roll right over you," Parker would say. "Bill was a pure person in many respects, and driven to his death to do better surfaces and shoes. To this day, his critical examination is what I subject new products to."

Bill's savage testing remains the Nike way and helped set a lasting tone. "The intensity of the arguments between divisions today, between, say, Soccer and Running," Phil Knight would say in 2005, "is no different than back in the '70s when Johnson got so mad at Woodell over some banking question that he ended up screaming at him, 'You're not good for anything but a doorstop!' Our visiting bankers heard this, saw Woodell in his wheelchair go raging back into his office, and turned white. They were therefore surprised, ten minutes later, when Jeff stuck his head in that office and asked Woodell if he would be over for dinner as usual, and Woodell said sure."

During the early 1980s, Knight realized that some of Bill's testiness had to do with his health. About the time of the 1980 Olympic Trials, Bowerman had noticed a number of disquieting signs. He was losing his balance a lot. His ankle had grown so weak it was hard for him to keep his foot steady on the gas pedal. He ignored the ankle because he'd always surged and slowed and surged on the highway ("If you cared about your stomach," Jim Grelle would recall, "you did not get in a car with Bill behind the wheel."), and anyway, Bill had learned, his father had driven the same maddening way.

But Bill got worse. "One day in the fall of 1980," he recalled some time later, "I had a limp when I went out with Bill McHolick. He asked me what I thought was causing it. I told him I was just getting old. He said he knew a lot of old guys, but not a lot who limped." McHolick inquired further and learned that the limp wasn't the half of it. Bowerman didn't have any feeling in his feet and had lost his night vision.

McHolick gave his old friend no choice but to undergo tests. Bill made the rounds of specialists. An oncologist had seen similar symptoms caused by a bone tumor pressing on the nerves, but Bowerman's bones were clean. "Then we thought something might be wrong with my back," Bowerman would recall, "so we had that X-rayed. The doctor said I had the back of an eighteen-year-old. An eighteen-year-old what he didn't know, but there was nothing wrong with my back. So I went to a Eugene neurologist."

Dr. Raymond Englander tested Bill's reflexes and thought it might be amyotrophic lateral sclerosis, or Lou Gehrig's disease. "You can die in six months with ALS," Bowerman said later, "so I asked him to goose the tests along." Englander referred him to the University of California Medical School, where Dr. Robert Layser found that it wasn't ALS and diagnosed him with "toxic polyneuropathy," meaning something was poisoning his nervous system. But Layser couldn't determine what it was.

A few weeks later, Bill's medical advisers in Eugene sent him to the Mayo Clinic in Rochester, Minnesota. Bowerman endured three more days of tests. They allowed the eminent Dr. Peter Dyck to conclude that his neuropathy had two components, one toxic and one hereditary. He had a predisposition to be sensitive to whatever was doing the damage, but Dyck couldn't pinpoint the toxic agent. "They suggested he research his family history to find out if such a problem ran in the family," Barbara would say, "but there were few ancestors whom he didn't know all about, and none had suffered anything like it."

Bowerman came home and reported all this to McHolick, who had found him a good pair of plastic braces that let him walk with less stumbling. "With every negative for a specific disease," McHolick said later, "the more it seemed it had to do with his environment." So McHolick and Bowerman walked through his typical day, noting what he drank, ate, wore, and touched. "It didn't take long," said Bill, "to find I'd been sniffing glue." For twenty-three years, from 1958 to 1981, Bowerman had been laboring in tight, unventilated quarters, assembling his shoes with rubber contact cement. "He didn't realize," said his old three-miler Vic Reeve, now an eminent forensic chemist, "that what he was working with, acrylamide glue, before it polymerizes, can enter through the skin and cause nerve damage."

"I was killing myself with it," Bowerman would say. "It had two poisons in it [the other was n-hexane in the solvents he employed] and was dissolving the sheaths on my nerves." When he stopped using it, that wintry day of discovery in 1981, some function began to return. "My eyesight was normal in six months," he would remember. "I got some regeneration in my skin, but my muscles never really, fully came back." From then on, he would walk with a pronounced dropped foot, slapping his lead leg down as he had once exaggeratedly done in demonstrating form for his hurdlers.

It was hard to see this without thinking of the price Bill had paid. Bowerman, giver of soft, light shoes to the runners of the world, had in the process rendered himself unable to run in them. He would always be offhand about this—

"inventors," he noted, likening himself to Daedalus, the Greek mythic symbol of human craft, "seem to make the gods nervous"—but the punishment seemed awfully steep for the mundane sin of ignorance.

Bill may not have whined about fate mocking him so, but he was not immune to wishing for a different outcome. In 1983, as he watched one of the first masters (forty-and-over age groups) track meets at Hayward Field, a reporter asked him whether masters competition was not just one more self-absorbed, baby boomer phenomenon.

"They're enjoying it, aren't they?" Bill snapped. "They're not hurting anybody. And they're fit. They're making their whole life experience more vivid. My regret is I can't get out there and run with them. I'm jealous of those elder statesmen. God, I envy them." He remained able to walk the hill to his upper and lower pastures along the McKenzie and hike the five miles of fence line on his and Jon's Wheeler County properties. He swam when he could, but lived such a busy life that that wasn't often.

Another loss weighed upon Bowerman at about this time. One of his great champions departed the world in the prime of life. In late 1982, Bill grieved to learn that Harry Jerome had died.

Harry had helped Bill coach the Duck sprinters in the mid-1960s and taken his master's degree in 1967. He'd retired from racing after the Mexico Olympics and gone to work for Sports Canada, setting up the Premier's Sport Award program to encourage elementary-school fitness. He was also the Canadian national sprint coach.

Jerome was so esteemed as an African Canadian role model that he was knighted by Queen Elizabeth, becoming Sir Harry Jerome. This had tickled Bowerman more than it did Harry. "Harry's full name was Harry Winston Jerome," Bill would say. "He was born in 1940, and he told me once that his father so admired Churchill's magnificent defiance during the London blitz that he'd stuck Winston in his name. How could you not knight a moniker like that?"

On December 7, 1982, Jerome suffered a brain seizure and died on the way to the hospital. He was forty-two. Canada honored him with statues and named Vancouver's finest track meet in his honor.

This, for Bowerman, was far too evocative of losing Pre. He reported the details of Harry's passing to the Ad Hoc group at a mournful Tuesday lunch. Bob Newland would always remember Bill saying athletes dying young felt a little like death passing over him in the war.

"I'm steeling myself," Bill said, "to be the last one to go. I'm doomed to always be giving eulogies for those who should have lived to give mine." Bill McHolick absorbed that and said, "Okay, I want you to say I was the real inventor of the waffle sole and I died in the throes of sexual congress with three cheerleaders."

"Only three? Damn it, McHolick, it's your fault. You're the one who kept me from a timely passing."

In fact, there was much to live for. The most gifted female distance runner in American history, Mary Decker, had moved to Eugene from Boulder, Colorado, in 1979 and proceeded to run up a storm. "I came because Pre had always said I should come," she would say some years later, "and the 1980 Trials would be there, and I had great Nike friends there."

Mary had missed the 1976 Olympics with the pain-locked shins of compartment syndrome. Surgery in 1977 had freed her calf muscles from their constraining fascia, and she returned to blissful running. "It almost seems like the faster I go the easier it is," she said after a 4:17 indoor mile in 1980 in the Houston Astrodome.

After she settled into a house in Eugene, she asked Athletics West administrator and physiologist Dick Brown to coach her. He agreed and soon had Bowerman involved as well. "Bill would come watch my workouts," Mary would recall, "and tell me I was going out too fast in my races. He was always comforting and warm, and very respectful of my talent. I'd heard he had some male chauvinism in his history, but he wasn't like that at all with me." She had heard right, but the chauvinism had evaporated in the face of Doris Brown's, Francie Larrieu's, and her own proof that women could run as hard and devotedly as any man. "I enjoy working with them more than men," Bowerman would say in 1980. "They have fewer bad habits to unlearn." His wink acknowledged that he was the one undergoing the reeducation.

Dick Brown and Bowerman agreed that there was no need for Decker to risk a lot of mileage or run killing intervals. If she remained consistently healthy, her talent would lift her ever higher. And it did. Over the next decade she spoiled the Hayward crowds with her graceful command of all distances from 800 to 10,000 meters. In 1982, she set six world records, two at the mile and the 2000, 3000, 5000, and 10,000 meters. The last was a 31:35.4 run in flats at an all-comers meet in Eugene. *Sports Illustrated* put her on the cover, hands on hips, head cocked, as if to say, "Wanna race?"

A year later, she entered both the 1500 and 3000 in the 1983 World Championships in Helsinki, events that were dominated by the Soviets, including Moscow Olympic 1500-meter champion and world record holder Tatyana Kazankina. Decker's race plans were suggested by Bill. Mary had little experience running in tight packs because no wing of women could ever keep up with her. She had always ranged out ahead, going as hard as she felt capable.

But she was not going to break contact with the Russians in the Helsinki 3000. So Mary would run from the front, where she was comfortable, but not really try to break away. As Pre had in Munich, she would gradually increase the pace late, in her case over the last 600 meters, to sap the kick of all who stayed with her.

In the early laps, Decker looked strong, but Kazankina looked stronger and stalked her all the way. Into the homestretch, Kazankina tore by Decker to a half-yard lead. This elicited a competitive fury Decker had never revealed. She dug down, fought back past Kazankina, and won the world championship in 8:34.62.

It didn't seem that a race could possibly be more dramatic, but the 1500 was. Mary had to be fatigued, and the Soviets now knew how good she was and would use team tactics against her. Bowerman, recalling Grelle and Prefontaine's experiences with rough European tactics, had suggested that Mary should run the 1500 just as she had in the 3000, up front, out of the range of Soviet elbows and spikes. But this promised to be harder, because the faster pace of the metric mile would give those drafting on her a bigger advantage. It was a plan that trusted Decker to know and run within her limits.

So Mary led the 1500 final at a pace that felt fast but not sacrificially so, to preserve her finish. Behind her ran a fresh Zamira Zaitseva, whom all the Russians in the race were working to help win.

Late in the last turn, Zaitseva blasted into the lead. This time Mary's form didn't change. She simply ran tall and sustained her speed. Zaitseva was tightening. Decker came even with ten meters to go. Zaitseva hurled herself at the line, falling, but Decker had won, 4:00.90 to 4:01.19.

Mary was the runner of the meet, and *SI* Sportsperson of the Year. More important to Decker, her Helsinki double made her the favorite for the 1984 Olympics, to be held in her native LA. "It just couldn't get more perfect," she said that winter, in no small part because earlier that year she had met British discus-thrower Richard Slaney. They would marry in 1985.

The best venue for selecting an Olympic team is the track where the Games will be held, so Los Angeles was naturally awarded the 1984 Trials. It would be the first time in twelve years that Eugene didn't stage them. They were barely missed. In June, the NCAA meet returned to Eugene, and the Oregon men, under Bill Dellinger and led by 800- and 1500-meter champion Joachim Cruz, won the team title, Dellinger's first.

That night, 200 of Bowerman's former athletes gathered at the Valley River Inn Ballroom for a tribute to Bill and Barbara organized by Wade Bell, Bob Newland, Bill McHolick, Ray Hendrickson, and Geoff Hollister. All received a striking photo by Brian Lanker of Bill in a green cowboy hat and work overalls, his arms crossed over a mossy fence rail. The program had perhaps too many references to his proclivities in the shower, but there were other gems.

"My memory," said adhesives company president Bob Craig, "includes Bill Bowerman shooting me in the leg with his starter's pistol, which required a tetanus shot at the infirmary."

"Mine," added 4:01 miler Bob Rhen, "was when Bill couldn't remember my name but, wanting to call encouragement in a race, yelled, 'Go, Burns!,' the name of the town I was from."

"For me," said 26-foot long-jumper, Dr. Tom Smith, "it was the look on Bowerman's face when I spent my dorm money on a new Mustang."

Most poignant at the ensuing dance was the sight of Jerry Tarr and his daughter Sheila, who that afternoon had won the women's heptathlon for the University of Nevada at Las Vegas.

Bowerman's role in his men's lives was the topic of much conversation. Some verged on the academic. University of Oregon political science professor Art Hanhardt, who'd had many Men of Oregon in his classes, announced that in his professional opinion, the varsity and Oregon Track Club "cohort" of Jere Van Dyk, Roscoe Divine, Bill Norris, Arne Kvalheim, Mike Deibele, Damien Koch, Dave Wilborn, Mike Manley, Jon Anderson, and me "had kept in touch more closely and been intertwined in each others' lives more than any combat-bonded group I have ever studied." This was greeted with the cry that wounds from Bowerman surely qualified as battle inflicted.

The occasion was the first real consideration by his athletes of Bowerman's place in history. The world of track and field had weighed in years before. The US Track and Field Hall of Fame had first selected him for induction in 1978, two years after admitting Pre, but Bill refused to accept the honor until they first enshrined Bill Hayward, who had of course coached many more Olympic teams than Bill's one. For reasons known only to the Hall of Fame officials, they have yet to induct Hayward, but they inducted Bowerman anyway, in 1981.

Down the years, as was only natural for people he treated so differently, his men developed diverse views on Bowerman's stature. Arne Kvalheim, for example, felt that the American college system—geared for team scores in dual meets and national championships—had worked against Bill's developing truly great athletes, in contrast to the likes of Herb Elliott's Percy Cerutty or Jim Ryun's Bob Timmons, whom Kvalheim characterized as "great coaches for one extremely gifted athlete." Kvalheim considered Bowerman to have been too conservative to produce greatness.

"Bill's strength and his weakness," Kvalheim would say, "was that he didn't let the really gifted athletes work up to their potential, for fear of overtraining. Hence, after Otis Davis he never coached another world record holder or Olympic champion. An incredible number of University of Oregon athletes developed to be good, solid runners, but none of us achieved anything truly great, Pre included."

But Bowerman continued to believe that the thing to do was seek an optimum load for each individual. He continued to practice a moderate approach, and often found that less work brought more benefit.

Once, back in 1970, after miler Mike McClendon kept getting hurt under then-assistant Dellinger's workouts, Bill offered to take him over and got him down to 4:00.3 on fewer than thirty miles per week. Bill said he was as proud of that mile PR as any he'd ever contributed to.

Steeplechaser Henry Marsh, the only runner Bill was still coaching regularly, was both example and exponent of moderate training. After setting his American record in 1980, Marsh had moved back to Utah for his third year of law school, but faithfully called Bill every Sunday night to report on his workouts and receive a new week's worth. This regimen had resulted in Marsh's ranking number one in the world in 1981 and 1982, but he'd suffered weird mishaps in big races. In the 1981 World Cup, he won but was disqualified for being pushed into the infield before the last water jump and having to run around it. In the 1983 World Championships in Helsinki, as he was charging past the leader, he fell over the last hurdle and placed eighth. He was wild, therefore, to redeem himself in the 1984 Olympics.

"Bill and I were meticulous in planning that whole year," Marsh recalled some twenty years later. After winning the Trials in LA Marsh was elated. "And the next day my son was born," he would say. "I was ecstatic, but it was too much. I didn't sleep. I just broke down. I got a virus that dogged me all the way to the Olympics." Still, his training did not seem to have been totally compromised. If he had a good day, he could be a contender.

To be there for Marsh and to see Decker's finest hour, Bill and Barbara went to their first Olympics since Munich. They flew to LA and rented a car, thinking they knew the city well enough after years of visits. But a few days later, Wade Bell got a call in his Eugene office. "Wade," Bill said, "you're an Olympian. You shouldn't miss these Olympics." Bell said they'd be nice to see, but he had too much business to attend to. Bowerman finally admitted they'd been buffaloed by what seemed a dozen new freeways and said that Wade really ought to come drive them around. Bell flew down and took the wheel. They gloried in seeing Duck Joachim Cruz, running for his native Brazil, beat Sebastian Coe to win the 800 in an Olympic record 1:43.0.

But the fortunes of Bowerman-guided entrants weren't happy. The women's 3000-meter final, of course, was darkly historic. It was the first meeting between Decker and young, barefoot South African Zola Budd, running for Britain. Mary's race plan was similar to what had worked in Helsinki, a building acceleration over the last 600 meters. But her preparations were far from ideal. She had concluded the Olympic Trials with a painful Achilles tendon. Dr. Stan James had injected it and ordered her off it for a month. She trained by running in the Easter Seals Pool until eight days before the first round of the 3,000 in the Olympics. She qualified strongly. But her instructions for the final were a little different.

"Unlike in Helsinki," Mary Decker Slaney said with some asperity in 2005, "in Los Angeles I didn't do what Bill had advised at the Worlds. I listened to Dick Brown." Brown had told her before the LA final, "If anyone wants to share the pace, let them."

"I said that," confirmed Brown years later, "because I didn't know how she'd feel out there, and she didn't know either."

That was not, on the face of it, a dumb idea, being an energy-saving measure. As in the rest of life, however, timing is everything. After Decker Slaney had led for four laps, Budd floated past into the lead. Decker Slaney, heeding Brown's advice, didn't react. "I let her by," recalled Slaney, "and she drifted in without being far enough ahead to do it and we made our contact."

For five or six strides their legs tangled before Decker Slaney was tripped by Budd's flying left calf. As Slaney fell, her arm reached forward, and she inadvertently tore the number from Budd's back. She went headlong into the infield, slamming her right leg down in such a way that tremendous force traveled up the femur and into her hip socket, tearing the gluteal muscles. She could not get up, much less continue.

Medical attendants and Richard Slaney ran across the track to her. The photo of her there, snarling her disbelief and rage, was hideously expressive. She, who had been hurt so often, for whom the sensation of raw exhaustion was a joy compared with the misery of not being able to run, was hurt again, three laps from the end of overcoming all that hurt.

The race was won by Romania's Maricica Puica in 8:35.96. Budd, the object of cascading boos, faded to seventh. Bowerman, shaken, watched the replays on the stadium's big screen and said Mary had to be seriously injured. "In retrospect," Bill said later, "we should have appreciated how little experience Mary had racing in the pack, maneuvering in tight quarters. Her main concern with other runners on the track had been in lapping them. We might have done some drills with her, honed her reflexes a little, so that when Budd started to drift in on her, Mary would have reached over and moved her back out."

Sheer fitness, not positioning, would be Henry Marsh's problem in the steeplechase. After his virus he had tried to finesse both workouts and rest and had ended up feeling neither healthy nor in shape. But he was a crisp, efficient hurdler who could lead with either leg, and Bill had sharpened his sense of pace and tactics. "He'd even taught me how to yell at guys to let me through," recalled Marsh, whose seemingly slow starts often simply meant he was running even pace and then catching the pack when it died.

Before the LA final, the omens were not good. Warming up, Marsh caught a spike on a hurdle, fell, and cut a shin. As the runners went to the line, he was still a little dazed and dropped even farther back than usual in the early running. But his technique was solid and his mind undaunted. With two laps to go he came charging up at the leaders. "With three hundred to go I thought I was going to win it," Marsh would say. But when Kenya's (and Washington State's) Julius Korir surged ahead in the middle of the backstretch, Marsh ran out of gas.

Suddenly he was sharing Pre's plight in Munich. In trying so hard to win, he had jeopardized his chance at a medal. Korir won in 8:11.80. Brian Diemer, Marsh's teammate, outkicked him for third, 8:14.06 to 8:14.25.

Bowerman gave him his highest compliment: that he could have done no better. "Bill didn't let on, then or ever," said Marsh later, "but I heard he told friends he was disappointed that I couldn't have had a decent race when I was as fit as I had been. That it didn't come together in LA frustrated Bill."

Marsh had no intention of hanging up his spikes any time soon, a desire to keep going that he laid squarely at the feet of his coach. Unlike coaches who push athletes past their limits, Marsh would say, "Bill asked you to leave each workout feeling that you could have done a little more. That way, you felt good, and good about yourself. Bill never burned anyone out. He always put life in perspective, always factored in family and work. His lessons were always about balance and efficiency. So if you were healthy, you wanted to run."

Strong and desirous in 1985, Marsh improved his American record to 8:09.17. Over his career he would be national steeplechase champion nine times, the last in 1987. For thirteen straight years he ranked in the top ten in the world. He made four Olympic teams, placing sixth in Seoul in 1988. He ran his first sub-4:00 mile at age thirty-one, and did it again at thirty-four.

This extraordinary longevity Marsh vehemently credits to Bowerman's influence. At this writing, he still holds the American steeplechase record and has done so for twenty-five years. Is such sustained achievement the equal of a single skyrocketing year or two such as Herb Elliott had? One imagines Bill getting out his scales and weighing the two. One hears him saying, "It's apples and oranges. It's greatness vs. joyful sanity."

One who channeled his competitive fire into other enterprises was Wade Bell. As his Olympic chauffer duties attest, he was becoming Bowerman's right-hand man. After returning from Mexico City in 1968, he had tried to keep up his running, but hadn't found the hours. He received no inkling from Bill that he was leaving too soon, so he retired from racing, became an OTC official, and for the next ten years was the starter at the all-comers meets for two days every week in July and August (and renowned for disqualifying a six-year-old who false-started twice in the 220). It was Bell who made arrangements when the Ad Hoc Group members traveled in raucous style to wherever the Pac-10 meet happened to be that year.

Bowerman relied on Bell most when the Nike money began to back up on him. It was as if he had foreseen the need for a trusted financial advisor years before, because Bell had gained his expertise in part due to Bill. "I'd graduated in PE," Wade would remember in 2005, "but I wanted not to smell jocks all my life, so after the 1968 Olympics, Bill made arrangements for me to live for a year and a half in the Hendricksons' basement. I got my accounting degree in 1970." That spring, Bell had his chance to go with BRS when Phil Knight asked him to become the company's treasurer. "I want to be a CPA first, like you," Wade said. Bell was certified in 1972, but, because he was so happy with work and family in Eugene, never made it back to Knight.

In 1978, Bell took over as the Bowerman tax accountant, when Bill's modest income was from book royalties and his retirement pension. When Nike went public in 1980, Bell handled Bowerman's gifts of stock to each of his three sons. Jon immediately sold his so he could buy the ranch on the John Day. From 1982 to 1995, Bell maintained an office for Bowerman at his own CPA firm, where Bill could make calls and dictate letters. Bell's stewardship ranged from the protective to the invisible, but was always deft. He even took on some of Bill's tone of voice, Bill's style.

Bell may have been Bowerman's accountant, but it was John Jaqua whom Bill always blamed for advising him not to keep his Nike eggs in one basket, to diversify into other stocks. "He told me later that he thought I probably kept him from being one of the wealthier people in America today," Jaqua would recall, laughing. "But he didn't really mind. He was an innovator, not a tycoon. But if he hadn't diversified, he'd have been twice as wealthy, maybe more. It wouldn't have shown up in his personal life, but he would have had a little greater room for his charities, which gave him great pleasure. A lot of local institutions would have been greater beneficiaries had he not diversified."

As it was, the recipients of Bowerman's largess benefited quite handsomely. Bill's giving did not begin with his offer to build the track office building at Hayward. It began almost as soon as he sold some Nike stock in 1980. "Bill was intensely loyal to his friends," Bell explained in 2005. When he was still coaching the varsity and needed to get a student athlete into a class for three hours' credit and a passing grade, he'd call a friend in the appropriate department and a class would open up. "So later, when Bill had money and the need arose," Bell would say, "he gave money to all their departments in those guys' names."

Bowerman paid, in the name of George W. Shipman, for example, to update the University of Oregon Library's computer system long before Knight gave them such an addition that they named it for him. He gave to the law school in the names of Otto Frohnmayer and Orlando Hollis. He gave to the physics department in the name of Ray Ellickson and to the geology department in the name of Lloyd W. Staples (who set up the Center for Vulcanology). He gave to the school of journalism and communications in the name of his dear friend Glenn Starlin and gave a $50,000 grant (stunning Wade) to the English department. He gave a grant to the Human Performance Center in the name of a professor who died of cancer. Bill also funded a host of presidential scholarships to attract Oregon's brightest scholars.

Nor did the recipient have to be the university itself. "Bill cared about a guy in the math department," said Wade, "who cared about preserving the Mt. Pisgah natural area, so Bill was happy to help with that. And of course when his old war buddy, Bill Boddington, raised funds for the Tenth Mountain Division's building of ski huts in the Rockies, Bill said yes in an instant."

Some people didn't even have to ask. One was former Oregon president Robert Clark. When Clark wrote an article for the alumni magazine on Bill's biology professor Ralph Huestis, Bill paid for it to be reprinted, Clark recalled, "in handsome format." Bill had also liked an essay Clark had written on Thomas

Condon, the geologist, collector of fossils from the John Day country, and early Oregon faculty member. Bowerman approached Clark to write a biography of Condon, and when Clark mentioned the price of the traveling he'd have to do, Bill said that that was no problem; the foundation he'd established would underwrite it. "And so I plunged into the work," Clark would say, "and happily finished while Bill was still living. His foundation subsequently created a lectureship in my honor, administered by the Oregon Humanities Center. I owe much to Bill Bowerman, and his interests were far-ranging."

When his philanthropy became known, Bill was plagued by requests from needy souls and scammers. "I was a target," he would recall. "You've got to have some kind of system, somebody guarding the gate." In 1983, he began the Bowerman Foundation and put Orlando Hollis, the forbiddingly austere former dean of the law school, at the head of its board and Bell as its treasurer. He transferred all his stock destined for gifts to the foundation. "He was always thinking the stock would plummet," Bell would say, "so this was a way to sell and preserve the value until it could be used for the new building that he always wanted to build." In the meantime, the foundation funded more scholarships.

Bowerman referred all appeals to Bell, who would carry the worthy ones to Bill and the board. Barbara Bowerman is on record that Bell saved "untold millions" by reining in Bill's first impulses. Bell, for his part, is justly proud of never, on his own, suggesting a single gift that Bill might want to make. Neither did he ever own a share of Nike stock. "I was not going to have a shadow of conflict of interest," he once said.

The Bowerman team, therefore, was well prepared to reopen negotiations on a new building for the university in 1990, after athletic director Rick Bay departed Oregon for Ohio State. The new AD, Bill Byrne, and the new UO vice president in charge of sports, Dan Williams, were determined to get along with Bowerman. Williams went so far as to interview Roscoe Divine and other Bowerman cronies, asking for tips on managing him. Yet Williams, perhaps because Bowerman learned he was from a small town in Oregon, Astoria, never had a moment of trouble with him.

The tussle over control was finished. The building, all parties agreed, would house track offices. Byrne swore in writing that the coaches could use them. Architects Jack and Jon Stafford came up with a larger, more costly building than the one originally planned, with a wing for what would be the university's International Institute for Sport and Human Performance, a research and information clearinghouse. The Bowerman Foundation rented the site from the university, put up the building just the way Bill wanted it, and gave it back to the university. It cost $2.2 million.

The two-story gray brick structure was completed in 1991—about eight years after it should have been. The university asked what to name it. As Wade Bell would tell the story, Bill met with the foundation's board and Orlando Hollis said, "Bill, it's gotta be the Bowerman building because you built it!" Bill squirmed. He didn't like publicity because it brought people in need. But this time he couldn't get out of it. At the building's dedication, Bill was resplendent in coat and tie, the embodiment of the German meaning of his name—*Builderman*. He spoke of the power of persistence.

One of Bill's motives for picking the site at the top of the stretch was to block the northerly tailwind that had kept several sprinters from legal world records in the 100. So now he adopted as his papal seat the balcony just above the sprint starting line. From then on, the Ad Hoc Group would watch the Pre Classic from there, seated, fittingly, in director's chairs.

But you couldn't sit there in peace unless you had done your part for the Oregon Bach Festival. This had begun in 1970 with a friendship between Oregon music professor Royce Saltzman and the sublime German organist and conductor Helmuth Rilling, established when Rilling came to Eugene for an informal concert. Rilling returned summer after summer, bringing along ever-finer artists and orchestras, and slowly the festival grew.

Saltzman was one of the professors who'd taken Bill's trackmen into classes when needed and he knew that Bowerman and the conductor would have a lot in common. The three of them sat on Bowerman's deck above the river. "It was wonderful for me," Saltzman would recall, "to hear Bill recount the whole Munich experience for Helmuth Rilling, whose childhood was in the war and whose first suit was out of an American CARE package."

The festival always needed money, long before Bill had any to spare, so Bowerman and Bill McHolick took Saltzman fund-raising. It was like nothing he'd ever done.

They'd simply charge into the offices of CEOs and bank presidents whom Bowerman knew and Bill would browbeat them into giving money. "Goddamn it, you're going to buy respectability," Bowerman said to one, who willingly forked over $500 once Saltzman had explained that musicians for the Bach Festival were as world-class as Bowerman and Burley. Another man anted up after Bill told him, as Saltzman would remember it, that "if he didn't do right by us, we were going to stand there and piss on his new leather chair."

But when Nike exploded, Bowerman gave more than he cadged or shamed or squeezed. He sat with Saltzman and Rilling and asked what they needed the most.

Rilling said the funds to attract the finest artists. Bill said, Great, "but don't endow anything. I want you to *use* my money." In 1994, he set up a grant that paid $75,000 a year for ten years. "And in those ten years," Saltzman would say, "the festival reached an extraordinary level of recognition around the country and world."

Bowerman's giving inspired others to follow suit. One of Bowerman's old teammates and friends, who had invested early in BRS and made a fortune, wanted to recognize Bill with a gift to the university. The George Scharf family gave a million dollars in stock to the University of Oregon—a third of it for scholarships, a third for the library, and a third for the Bach festival. One night when Rilling was conducting, Saltzman would recall, "we recognized Bill and Barbara and the Scharfs. Oregon president Paul Olum thanked the donors and gave maestro Rilling a box of Nikes to show where the money came from. Helmuth came out wearing them for the second half of the concert and said, 'The tempo's going to be faster now!'"

As a patron of the arts, Bill looked to aid individuals as well as choral festivals. He once called Saltzman and said, like a coach asking about a recruit, "Heard a student of yours named Sheryl Aydelott in church. What's she going to do with that voice?" Saltzman found out that Aydelott wanted to study voice in New York. Bill said he would pay for two years of study but didn't want her to know, Saltzman would remember. "So we put it under the name of the MarAbel Frohnmayer Scholarship."

At this writing, Aydelott happily remains in New York, her life transformed. But it would be a decade before she knew the truth. "MarAbel was so embarrassed to get these emotional thank-you letters from her," Barbara Bowerman would recall. "She felt so silly writing back. How could she ever say something sincere? Otto roared at the whole thing." Saltzman finally told Aydelott a few years ago, but not before she had come out and sung in two Bach festivals. "Oh, those two scoundrels!" she laughed in 2005, meaning Saltzman and Bowerman. "That grant had a huge impact on my life."

Amidst all his philanthropy, it may seem extraordinary that Bowerman would worry about Nike stock taking a dive. However, his fears were not entirely unjustified. In 1982, the company had been slow to respond to the aerobics boom and was thus passed by Reebok as the nation's largest shoe purveyor. This seemed fundamentally wrong to those who shared the Bowerman feeling for form and function.

"We used to say if we had the best athletes in the best shoes, we couldn't lose," Phil Knight would say. "But guess what? Reebok went by us with what we thought were terrible shoes. They were so soft they ripped apart. We asked women why they wore them. They said they were comfortable. We asked what they did when they ripped. Oh, buy another pair." The day it was announced that Reebok's sales had overtaken Nike's, Knight closeted himself in his office, faced the wall, and sat there, weak and sick and devastated for hours.

Mark Parker—"whose strength was design and appearance," said Knight—led the company back, not by asking consumer focus groups what was best but by finding it out in the lab and then telling people. In advertising.

For one such promotion, after the 1984 Olympics, Nike paid Michael Jordan $500,000 to develop and promote a special line of Air Jordan shoes. Bowerman rolled his eyes. "Bill thought we were overpaying prima donna athletes," Knight would say twenty years later. "Now Michael Jordan sounds a lot like Bowerman when he rails at how high we have to go to pay the new guys."

The Air Jordan shoes and campaigns were amazingly successful and brought the company back to preeminence. "After Reebok," said Knight, "it was the best athletes, best shoes, best ads." Bill may have grumbled about the need for such ads, but he loved the actual results. The essential Nike phrase "Just do it" had certainly been uttered by Bill to all of us.

Everything Bowerman moaned about to the Nike board, including payments to athletes and, much later, questions when Nike was accused of exploiting cheap foreign labor, were muted compared to his passion for shoes. Two things (besides his postage scale) were usually in his briefcase: a super-light spike and a modestly priced training shoe for beginning high school runners. The latter, of course, would undercut the higher price models that Nike was already selling. Bill became accustomed to no one leaping up and saying, That's a shoe we have to make.

There were other slights. Bill went to one Nike board meeting to get a grant restored that would have paid for former UCLA coach Jim Bush to coach inner-city athletes in LA. The board said no and Bill was furious. "The next day," Wade Bell would recall, "Phil announced the address of the new company campus in Beaverton—One Bowerman Drive. Bill came down here and said, 'You know, they tried to buy me off! They turned me down on Jim's grant and tried to appease me by naming a street after me.' I said, 'Bill, do you know how hard it is to name a street? They had to go to the city of Beaverton and get approval, and go to the post office, etc. Believe me, that decision wasn't made that morning so they could put you in a better mood.'"

Bill never mentioned it again. By now he knew the difference between the nettlesome and the eternal, and he got a hell of a reminder at the end of January 1987. Barbara would never forget it.

As he was watching a basketball game on TV, eating a bowl of popcorn, Bowerman suddenly cried out, "Call Tom! Take me to the hospital!" Barbara got son Tom from his nearby cottage and they called Bill McHolick. "Bill said that it was like 'a wire around my chest, cutting into me,'" Barbara would recall. McHolick told them to take Bill to McKenzie Willamette Hospital in Springfield, where McHolick was on the staff. Tom and Barbara did so, Barbara would say, all the while listening to Bowerman giving orders.

At the hospital emergency room, while Barbara filled out papers, the doctors started working on Bill. Soon they told Barbara that he was having an extreme heart attack and they were taking him to Sacred Heart in Eugene. Tom took his mother home and the next morning Bill called her. "His first words were 'I'm fine. I had great fun watching 'em get all this crud out of me,'" she would say. "He found it so entertaining that they gave him a little mirror so he could watch!"

The cardiac surgeons had run a catheter through his blocked artery and told Barbara that it was amazing, but Bill was clogged with plaque in only one place; he was fine otherwise. With no other problems or risk factors, he was allowed to go back home quickly.

But all were sobered. "I am up, but on restricted duty," he wrote to Knight on February 4, 1987. They had been trying to decide how much Bill should be paid for his shoe lab work and consulting. "Since my episode of last Tuesday, the general plan seems moot," wrote Bill. "It is also possible or probable that all parties will be best served by heeding the mortal and immortal messages." Whatever messages Bill heeded seemed to work. John Jaqua would find him "actually better after that attack than before. He had more color, more energy. I think he'd been plugged for quite a while, because after that catheter, all of a sudden he got a lot more color in his face—and a lot more profanity in his speech, which is a good sign. He was definitely healthier."

CHAPTER 30

Immortal Messages

MANY OF THE IDEAS THAT UPLIFTED BILL WERE FROM THE CHRISTIAN SCIENCE services he attended with Barbara. He listened to the sermons with mellow good humor, but never joined the church, perhaps because of its belief that physical healing comes primarily through the power of God and prayer. "Obviously he believed that when somebody was hurt you have got to go and see a doctor," Bill's great friend Bill Landers would say. "You can't just pray about it. Well, you can pray all you want, but you have got to have the thing attended to." Landers marveled at how the Bowerman marriage endured "because often in a situation of differing beliefs you get at loggerheads, you get stuck," he would say. But Barbara didn't press Bill, an approach consistent with her faith that, as she put it, "life is simply all of us expressing intelligence, expressing truth, expressing love."

"It would take a very special person to live with Bill Bowerman," Landers would say. "Barbara was a remarkable woman."

Who brought with her a remarkable set of values. "My belief in fairy tales is literal, but that doesn't mean it's easy," Barbara would say. "Every hero goes through hard work and resolving things." When her sons Tom and Jon looked askance at her relentless positivism, she would tell them, "I am this way because I believed I'm happy. Life *became* one of depth and satisfaction." Of her husband she would say, "Bill is that way because he was determined. He just did it. Shoes, whatever. Even when his spikes were falling off Jimmy Puckett in midsprint, he believed he'd get it. It just fascinates me, this stuff, this drive to know and live one's design. It's the stuff of creation itself."

Bill Bowerman was designed, Barbara agreed, to process. The defining act of his life was preparation, not completion. The house was always unfinished, the big meets were always grounding for bigger, the best shoes could always be made better. The champagne for a great occasion stayed in the closet.

There was no grand, final victory. He was moved by the very evanescence of laurels. They were sacred because they withered, because they symbolized the brevity of earthly triumph. "Winning is nice," he had said in 1972, on the eve of the Munich Games, "but you savor that victory for an evening and you wake up in the morning and it is gone."

And you are still here and in need of meaning. One post-attack communiqué from his heart advised Bill to spend more time with the family. So, he kicked back and relished the sight of all three sons leading great lives by following age-old Bowerman instincts.

The nearest was the youngest, Tom. He'd graduated from the Oregon School of Architecture in 1969 and shown the wanderlust of a Chambers (and the idealism of his mother) by trying his hand at urban planning in a tough place for it—strife-ridden Ulster, Northern Ireland. "Fortunately, he lived," Bill would say, "and came to a new appreciation of his own quiet hillside."

Where, up the road to the Bowerman pond, he assembled a pioneer-style sawmill and cut planks from fallen trees. With these, he built a spare little cottage a little upstream from Bill and Barbara. He found a balance between progressive businesses (managing Eugene rental homes and buildings on the National Historic Register) and causes, such as cofounding the McKenzie River Trust. Eventually Tom would marry Kris Norberg, whom he met when he was hitchhiking up the Oregon coast to see a Seattle girlfriend. Tom never did make it to Seattle. On April 28, 1978, and February 28, 1980, Kris and Tom had sons McKenzie and Will. Bill made baby shoes for the little boys and tried to keep them from the ire of his roosters.

Jay, the middle son, had made a second Olympic biathlon team, for the 1972 Winter Games in Sapporo, Japan, where the team finished sixth in the 4 x 7500-meter relay. Bill had helped him structure his training. "He provided big-picture thoughts about specific races and stages of development and left the individual workouts to me," Jay would recall in 2004. "It must have worked, as I moved from being a mediocre member of the US biathlon skiers to sweeping the nationals, as well as earning a spot on the US cross-country team."

As the environmental director for Sunriver, a high-end resort and residential development along the Deschutes River, fifteen miles south of Bend, Jay expanded the community nature center, providing visitors with looks at spectacular Central Oregon birds, amphibians, and reptiles. He was certified by the state Department of Fish and Wildlife to keep and retrain injured raptors for release into the wild. This meant exercising hawks, owls, and falcons until they could hunt for themselves.

Bill enjoyed watching Jay training golden eagles over the golf course, which he did with a leather falconer's glove, keeping them attached, like flapping, disobedient kites, to a reel of fly line. Once, three gentlemen from Ohio were crouched over their putts. A ground squirrel scampered out of its hole near the green. A great shadow soon loomed over them. They looked up and saw the seven-foot wingspread of Jay's eagle descending at them, talons outstretched. They dove like so many marmots. The bird forgot the squirrel, landed on the green, and advanced toward them, wings out, eyes wild, beak agape. Jay arrived. His father's son, he regarded the cowering golfers and couldn't resist. "There's a reason nobody ever makes an eagle on this hole," he said.

In 1973, Jay married the inestimable Teresa Chin-Tze Wang of Taiwan, and on September 28, 1974, and June 10, 1976, they produced Jayson and Traycee, who embody the classic Bowerman loves of sport and music. Jayson, who can play and make any stringed instrument, works as a luthier in Bend. Traycee grew up a pianist, took her bachelor's in biology and wilderness studies at the University of Montana, and serves as wild salmon coordinator for the Oregon Natural Desert Association. Both teach kayaking and have hurled themselves over cataracts that would strike fear into the hearts of most parents. "Proof of hybrid vigor," their grandfather grinned.

Stock breeding terms tripped lightly from Bill's tongue. One of his preoccupations and joys was attempting to produce what he hoped to be able to call *Bos domesticus oregonensis*. The American Cattle Association informed Bill that after five generations he could apply for certification of a new breed. This would let him sell either bulls or semen, a prospect he relished discussing.

"How do I get the semen?" he would ask. "Remember the Ethiopian miler Hailu Ebba? He took animal husbandry at Oregon State. I asked him about taking semen. He said the easiest way was to put female urine on cattle hide, and when the bull is excited, you deftly trick him with a bottle."

Bill carefully delineated lineages, seeking gentle bulls so he could have one pull a kid's wagon. In 1994, he delivered his last Round Table paper on the subject. It told of a little bull that he had loaned to his son Jon for two years. The bull was a great lover, and fighter, too. "I guess his size was such that he'd go right under Jon's bigger bull," cackled Bill, "and take his legs out from under him. Jon called and said, 'Take him back. He's ruining my reputation.'"

Bill's bovine stories were legion. Wade Bell loved one that Bill told at the Tuesday lunch one day. "This has not been my best morning," Bill began. "It had been raining, and I opened the gate, went in the pasture, slipped, and fell flat on my back. I was all right, but I was stuck.

"I felt around and realized the only way I was going to get up was to turn over in the muck. I did and got a nice coating of manure, front and back. I got in the Jeep covered like a mud baby, drove up to the house, and was heading for the back door into the kitchen when I thought no, that's dumb. So I took off all my clothes on the porch and started hosing off. Which is when Barbara drove up and said, 'I'm not running a nudist colony here!'"

Bill's day almost always included time with his herd, and thus with the observant Mike Friton, who not only worked with Bill in the shoe lab but also lived in a mobile home on the Bowerman property, taking care of the livestock and doing farm chores. "I knew and worked with Bill for eighteen years," Friton would remember in 2005. (When Bowerman's Eugene lab was closed in 1995, upon the death of Bob Newland, Friton moved to the mother ship, the Nike campus in Beaverton.)

Bowerman named many cattle in his herd after members of the Nike board. "He tried to match their personalities," Friton would remember. "One in particular he named Donahue. He was a feisty little red bull that liked to jump the fences. One day Bill invited the actual board member [and distinguished attorney] Richard Donahue out to the house and introduced him to the little bull Donahue. They both seemed pleased and got along okay."

Friton and Bill often drove around the property for hours in Bill's little pickup. "He would reminisce about athletes, the war, and family," Friton would remember. "A few of those stories he repeated often. Over time, I learned to listen more to the pauses than the words themselves. They would signal the mood of his day, as well as the emotion of reflecting on important moments in his life. When I repeat stories about Bill, it's difficult to express the full meaning because the words alone do not contain all of the understanding."

Among the things that Friton and Bowerman had in common was childhood trauma, which Friton believes was "instrumental" in developing Bill's creative approach to the world. "I had the experience of a broken family and witnessing traumatic events," Friton would say. "Bill's defining moments may have been the loss of his twin brother and the breakup of the family. We both had to learn to cope at an early age with tremendous amounts of loss and fear." Friton believes they survived by "relying heavily on our internal creative instincts." Friton also thinks that Bill's years in the military reinforced the process: "I could hear that in many of his stories about the war."

The result, in Bill's Nike lab, was a rousing sort of liberty that also harks back to Barbara's belief that Bill was motivated more by the journey than the destination. "There were no limits or final answers in our endeavor to find a better way of doing things," Friton would say. "I thought a lot about this over the years and discussed it with Bob Newland and Bill. It was a boundless creative response."

Their great, onrushing inquiry wasn't totally anarchic, however, permeated as it was with Bill's sense of rightness. "Character was everything," Friton would say. "Bill insisted that those around him respect certain principles in life, or as he would say, 'Have character.' A great deal of the conflict between Bill and others at Nike was based on his view that they did not value some of these principles."

One of the key principles—and certainly what got Tom Derderian off on the wrong foot—was that Bowerman's time was not to be wasted. "When you set a time to do something with Bill you were expected to be on time or better yet show up early," Friton would remember. "I occasionally did workouts with a few of Bill's club runners, postgraduates from all over the country who came to Eugene hoping to be coached by Bill. The first thing they had to learn was to show up on time. If they were a minute late they could find themselves invisible to Bill for that day. They could be right in front of Bill asking him questions but he would act as if they were not there. The only thing he might say was to show up on time at the next workout. I have seen this reaction bring tears to the toughest of these runners."

Bill Landers agreed about Bill's priorities. "There was a moral compass that shaped Bill's whole life," Landers recalled in 2005. "His mission was to find innovative ways to improve the lives of us fellow voyagers. You see it in his early interest in medicine, his heroism as a warrior, his unflagging curiosity about what makes the human body behave the way it does. And all of this came from the deep moral center of his being. It led to the strong judgmental facet of his personality. He once told me, 'I have neither the time nor patience to waste on trash.' And if you were marked trash it was all over. But if you were not, your sins were forgiven. I think it was this core moral force that attracted people to him because in its most pure form, as his was, it is a rare commodity. People wanted to be judged worthy by him. I know I did, and I suspect you did too. And Phil Knight? Oh, yeah."

Another who could never shake that need was Bill Dellinger. By the early 1990s, Bowerman had grown further at odds with Dellinger over several issues. One was the latter's tie to Adidas. But the most emotional was that when the university constructed palatial new athletic department buildings next to Autzen Stadium, Dellinger moved his office there from the trackside Bowerman Building. "The Bowerman Building was Bill's outreach to Dellinger," Barbara would say. "Bill was heartbroken when he moved across the river."

Bowerman also had let it be known that he felt Dellinger was getting lazy. His proof was that in major cross-country and distance races, the Oregon lemon and green was being blotted out by red and cardinal hordes of splendid Arkansas and

Stanford runners coached by John McDonnell and Vin Lananna. Bowerman got on Dellinger about all the high school talent going elsewhere. Dellinger replied that he had only twelve scholarships for track and field, or three or four per year. Once they were awarded, Dellinger saw little point in constantly calling recruits if he couldn't offer them aid.

Bowerman disagreed and found support from a number of former Oregon athletes. Half-miler Steve Bence said it best: "Stanford and Arkansas had the same limitations as Oregon, yet they were attracting winning athletes. A ton of good kids wanted to go to Oregon at their own expense, or try to find other ways of funding, just to be a part of the heritage. All they needed was a phone call to say that they were welcome." But Dellinger resented anyone telling him how to recruit, especially Bill, who had hated it himself.

Still, their estrangement gnawed at him. Dellinger owed the fact and shape of his life to Bill's lessons. The very thing he had insisted upon when Pre died—the need to give credit where credit is due—would give Dellinger's conscience no rest. Bowerman meant so much to him that Dellinger refused to be written off as obsolete or lazy.

This meant that Dellinger had to take the initiative. So one morning he dressed in old clothes and visited the Bowerman pastures, simply stopping and waving and helping Bill move some irrigation pipe. They talked about times past, and Dellinger noted that it had been about forty years since his win in the 1954 NCAA mile that had been the start of some good things. Bill recalled how excited he had been at that and loosened up a little. Dellinger said this was fun, and would Bill mind his stopping by again? Bill said help yourself. There was always work. So Dellinger did visit, several times over a month or two.

One of those times he told Bill that he had moved his office across the river against his will, that it had been the edict of the new AD. "I hated to go over there, away from the track," he said. Finally there came a day when Bowerman allowed that Dellinger was dealing with things like scholarship limitations or equal funding for women's programs that Bowerman had been lucky not to have to face. It was tougher now, he admitted, tougher to field a strong team with walk-ons. But true teaching was still vital, Bill said, and Dellinger was still good at that. Dellinger, as he departed and for the rest of his days, experienced the relief of knowing he had found it in himself to reach out, to be worthy enough to reconcile with Bill.

In 1991, shortly after Bill turned eighty, Phil Knight commissioned a retrospective of the man whose approval was and had been so essential to so many. He assigned Geoff Hollister (who was becoming guardian of the company's Prefontaine/Bowerman legacy) to throw a reunion dinner in the new Nike campus gym for the Men of Oregon Bill had coached and their families. This was the occasion when all were photographed with Bill in the corner of a sauna, both his keys and Cheshire-cat grin glinting

Hollister interviewed dozens of Bill's champions on video and skillfully cut the results together with iconic photos, Barbara's hilariously dry memories, and a surging score. Dellinger was powerfully abrupt, stating flatly, "Bill was a genius. He would have been successful in any walk of life. Fortunately for us, he ended up in track and field." The more clinically a speaker documented the embarrassments he subjected us to, the better Bill liked it. Knight had asked him what he would prefer, knowing that he could give a rebuttal or knowing that he didn't have to give a speech. Bill said, "No speech."

The occasion was a tremendous success. Knight in later years would hope he had done enough for Bill. Even though there would be other events, in that single one, he had. The evening seemed so significant that it gave rise to the first talk of this book. That summer, Bill Landers and I were summoned to the Bowerman deck, plied with lemonade and cookies, and given our own commission from Bill: to tell the story of his life and times and of the athletes he'd been fortunate to teach and learn from. Landers set about interviewing first Bowerman relatives and friends and then Bill and Barbara.

The transcripts are less an exercise in nostalgia than the thoughts of a problem-solver reflecting on what worked, what didn't, and what was priceless and had to be maintained. Bill stressed that in Eugene the support of the sharpest, most energetic people outside of the university family, the lay community, was crucial. "That filled those stands," he said. "It was the thing to do, to be connected to the track program. When you let that kind of an organization wither and die, you are going to lose it at the other end, the track end."

About a parallel concern he said, "The athletic department now thinks to have a good program you have to spend a lot of money. So they charge more for a track meet and price the little kids out of the market. They also outprice the people who can't afford to take a bunch of little kids. And the best athletes come from families that don't have an extra two to four dollars."

When Landers asked about the secret for team unity, for the hold he had had on young men, Bowerman's first thoughts turned to the team's spring trips. To us sodden, native Oregonians at that time, the very sound of what lay to the south in winter was like a church choir jumping up in your head. Dressed in baggy shorts, an aromatic T-shirt, and a ludicrous hat and/or women's huge hexagonal sunglasses, Bowerman had marched his teams straight from winter-term finals onto chartered buses and headed south, giving wearying, pun-filled commentary on old Medford haunts and the passing Siskiyous. Once near Mt. Shasta, he ordered the bus off the highway and onto a narrow lane into the woods. When the route became impassable, Bowerman and several athletes jumped out.

"Where are you going?" asked the driver.

"Call of nature!"

The bus couldn't turn around. It had to back up a half mile, scraping boulders and saplings, the driver muttering, "Did it have to call you so far?"

"The human race," Bowerman informed the passengers, "possesses a super-abundance of surliness."

He had contacts with generals, who got the team into the plush, whitewashed adobe barracks and Bachelor Officers' Quarters of Hamilton Air Force Base in Marin County. The essential thing, said Bowerman, was that we all lived as one, spending time together apart from workouts. It was necessary to do this because there is no more bizarre assemblage of human designs than a track team. On the spring trip, we learned to interact across the body type and personality divides, ectomorphic runners conversing with mesomorphic throwers, easygoing vaulters with prideful sprinters. Bill yelped in agreement on hearing Dr. George Sheehan's immortal definition of a runner as "a small-boned loner, built for flight and fantasy," but immediately added, "I guess that leaves out Pre."

Nike was hardly the only institution wanting to honor Bill in these years. He graciously turned most down, and kindled the kitchen stove with the parchment and gold leaf. But in April 1993 (after making sure he could bring along Dr. Chris Christensen), he accepted a trip to the Penn Relays in Philadelphia. This was due not to any high regard for the relays—Duck teams had almost never run there—but because his old pal and *Jogging* book coauthor, Jim Shea, was vice president of nearby Temple University and hosted the visit.

"When Bill and Chris arrived the first day," Shea would remember in 2005, "the weather was cold and wet, and Franklin Field near empty. There was a gathering that night in the Penn Athletics building. The meet director, Jim Tuppeny, welcomed a list of guests, and when he got to Bill he said what good fortune it was to have him there, and would Bill please say a few words? That startled our Bill, because the request came out of the blue. No one had mentioned that possibility to him, though, as guest of honor, he probably could have expected it. So Bill took him literally. He said a few words, very few. As a matter of fact, he mumbled. There was a pause, the pregnant variety. All waited. Eventually it was evident nothing more was coming. If some of the Bowerman wisdom was dispensed that evening, everyone missed it."

Shea knew Bill so well that he could speculate on the reasons for this uncharacteristic refusal to switch into gracious recipient mode. "He was wary of this crowd," Shea would say, "with some longstanding reservations."

Bowerman had long regarded Eastern track as wrong in wasting time on winter indoor racing when athletes should be building their strength for the real track season. He may have accepted the invitation purely out of respect for the presence of a few coaches he valued as colleagues. But once there he likely resented spending time with officials who, as Shea would put it, "had been kissing cousins" to the detested Avery Brundage, the man who for so long had defined "amateurism" to exclude so many.

Fortunately, the last day of the great relay carnival was sunny and packed with 50,000 spectators. Bill stood in the infield, leaning on his cane, and observed the logistics of managing thousands of athletes. And at last he relaxed and began to appreciate what an institution the Penn Relays is and how good it is for track and field. He turned to Shea and said, "Isn't this wonderful?"

Out on the infield, he made a friend. One of the patrons and competitors at the Penn Relays over the years has been comedian Bill Cosby. He was quick to take Bill's hand and say how much he admired him. Cosby had attended Temple on a track scholarship and had competed for decades in masters races at 200 and 400 meters. One Cosby routine on an early comedy album was about the onset of death in the last yards of a 440. And twenty years earlier, Cosby had come to Eugene for a Mac Court performance. His grave opening words were "Nothing I can say or do in the next two hours . . . can possibly be more thrilling than what that gentleman with the moustache in the front row did in the Twilight Meet an hour ago—*3:55 flat in a cold wind!*" The crowd rose in ovation for both a thunderstruck Steve Prefontaine and for Cosby's tribal understanding.

So on Franklin's infield, those two old quartermilers, Bowerman and Cosby, had plenty to talk about. "They spoke quietly on a bench," Shea would recall, "deep in discussion, oblivious of the 50,000." But both were natural clowns, too. Soon they were mugging for Shea's camera and accusing each other of stealing each other's name. "I had it first," said Bowerman.

"But my *mother* gave it to me," pleaded Cosby.

"My *grand*mother gave it to me," said Bowerman. "Let me tell you about my grandmother. Ever hear of the Oregon Trail . . . ?"

Even so, Shea couldn't get Bill to stay an extra day in the East. "He took the last plane in and the first one out," Shea said. "Didn't linger. Home to Oregon and comfort."

As Bowerman aged and the number of high school tracks he'd donated edged toward fifty, he sometimes seemed to be stepping back and making sure all was going to be right with his world. In 1994, one event set his mind wholly at ease on at least one front: David Frohnmayer (who'd lost a run for governor and become dean of Oregon's Law School) was made president of the University of Oregon. From that moment on, Bill had no further problems with his alma mater. In an era when the legislature was shrinking support for higher education, two de facto sons of Bill Bowerman, Dave Frohnmayer and Phil Knight, teamed up to strengthen the institution they all cherished.

Within a few years, Knight had given $50 million to the university—$30 million for academics and $20 million for athletics. In 1996, in his biggest one-year injection, he gave $15 million to endow faculty chairs and $10 million to help fund the William W. Knight Law Center, a beautiful new building across Agate from Hayward Field. John Jaqua threw in more than a million to complete and stock the law library. In 1998, the Nissho Iwai American Corporation, Knight's visionary trading company and bank loan guarantor (which had already helped finance the library's $27.4 million expansion) also chipped in.

Bowerman was secure in the knowledge that he'd instilled some of this generosity in Knight and others whose source was Nike's success. He didn't take it as a moral affront when a new athletic director, Bill Moos, arrived in 1995 and went on a building tear. Moos used Knight's gifts as the backbone of a campaign to up the wattage of Oregon's sports facilities. Knight was far from the only donor, but his pledges to match others' gifts amplified their effect.

Bill sighed a little, seeing fortunes expended to help win the favor of fickle eighteen-year-olds from afar ("I think if I were going to war," he said, "I'd rather go with the home folks than with mercenaries."), but he really took issue with bigness only if it brought compromise. He was far more peeved by his company making many of its performance shoes with a lot of weighty bells and whistles. He understood the economics of that, but never stopped working on a light racing spike. Once, when showing me a pair, he winked and said, "I'm being patient. I'm going to be ready with this if the market ever sours so much the company has to go back to its roots."

"His frustrations grew and occasionally flared up through the years," said Nike president Mark Parker in 2005, "when he didn't see the Nike machine snatch up and duplicate his creations with his fervor. But those crude, handcrafted prototypes that Bill always pulled out of that well-worn briefcase had far more impact on the broader Nike product line than he ever realized."

They certainly influenced the narrowest of lines—a shoe for a single competitor. In the 1996 Atlanta Olympics, Bill's rationale for those old prototypes was tested on the feet of Michael Johnson. In the 200-meter final, Johnson bent into the blocks wearing a pair of golden handmade spikes from Nike.

Namibia's Frankie Fredericks led early, but Johnson caught him at 80 meters and lifted into a gear neither he nor anyone else had ever attained. In the stretch, his effort was engraved on his face. Johnson hit the line and looked left at the infield clock. It read 19.32. He had broken his world record by .34 of a second.

Johnson's time was one that statisticians had projected would not be possible until a couple of decades into the next century. Fredericks ran 19.68, the third-fastest time in history, yet was beaten by four meters, the largest winning margin in an Olympic 200 since Jesse Owens defeated Mack Robinson 20.7 to 21.1 in 1936. In 2004, USA Track and Field voted Johnson's 200-meter record the top performance of the previous twenty-five years.

"One of the greatest sources of inspiration for Michael Johnson's world-record-setting golden spikes," Mark Parker would say, "was a pair of handmade shoes Bill made for Kenny Moore thirty years before and kept in the Nike archives."

Michael Johnson's shoes were Bill's last technical hurrah, proving that his high-performance ideas—founded on sheer physics—were still current because they are eternal. Bill was also tickled to see that the running form of Johnson, whose erect torso put off many coaches, was an echo of Bill's greatest long sprinter, Otis Davis.

With those riveting shoes, Johnson and Nike had burned a place in our collective imagination. In similar fashion, in that summer of 1996, a pair of Hollywood studios were setting out to plumb the essence of Bill and his meaning to his athletes.

Within a month of Johnson's historic race, shooting began on two feature films depicting the Bowerman-Prefontaine relationship. The need to preserve Pre's memory was dragging Bill back into a world for which he had only expressed contempt after *Personal Best*.

In the early 1990s, an independent documentary producer named Jon Lutz had moved to Eugene. He kept hearing about the power Pre's story had over people and decided he wanted to tell it. Geoff Hollister and I talked with him, judged him a decent guy, and acted as references so he could buy the film rights from Ray and Elfriede Prefontaine.

When Lutz had purchased both documentary and feature film rights, he brought in director Erich Lyttle, who listened to our stories of Pre and explained the needs of a documentary script. I wrote one, which loosely guided Lyttle and Hollister in filming interviews with many who knew Pre, including Bill. When it was edited, Ken Kesey narrated and *Fire on the Track* premiered on CBS right before the 1993 Pre Classic.

So far so good. But then things got thorny. Lutz next approached Hollywood studios about doing a major dramatic feature about Pre. He found interest from Disney. At about this time, *Personal Best* director Robert Towne, who had since worked with Tom Cruise, had Cruise over for lunch one day and happened to show him seven minutes of Pre running in *Fire on the Track*. Cruise was soon wild to develop a project about him. He seemed to connect with Pre's vulnerabilities as much as his mastery.

Towne said I was the one to write it, and he'd direct. So I took some months away from *Sports Illustrated*, put aside the Bowerman biography, moved to Towne's house in Pacific Palisades, and set to work. In the spring of 1995 we had the first draft of a script.

Throughout all of this, Towne and I had been keeping Jon Lutz, the owner of the family's film rights, aware of Cruise's interest. Towne also pointed out to Lutz that his and Tom's existing contractual arrangements made it better for them to do the film at Warner Brothers. Accordingly, when my script was deemed solid, Warner Brothers offered Lutz a comfortable executive producing deal, in return for the Prefontaine family's film rights.

But Lutz had kept up his talks with Disney, which made a similar executive producing offer. Lutz now had to choose between two deals. Financially, they were about equal. But one was at Disney, with no director or star committed to it, and one at Warner Brothers with a superstar, Tom Cruise, emotionally attached and an Oscar winner, Robert Towne, set to direct. Lutz, who had no experience in big-budget feature film, chose Disney.

Cruise was astounded and furious. He predicted that Disney would make grand promises but greatly compromise its support in the end. He still wanted to make a Warner Brothers film, but would the studio finance it, now that it was known that Disney was making one too? The studio would and did. There were now dueling Prefontaine movies.

Warner Brothers was able to finesse the question of the family's rights because Pre was a public figure and had had many friends who could contribute recollections and anecdotes. The meat of his story could easily be told without his parents' private memories.

But now there occurred a parallel to the making of *Personal Best* fifteen years before. The Oregon Track Club and the University of Oregon, led by Dave Frohnmayer, were fiercely protective of Pre's legacy. Neither would consider permitting filming on campus or joining either warring studio's side until they knew the wishes of one man. Wade Bell summed it up in one sentence: "The script has to be acceptable to Bill."

One Friday in March 1995, I dropped a copy off with Barbara in the Bowerman kitchen. All that weekend, I heard nothing. Towne began to call me every hour from LA asking for news. Finally, on Sunday, I could stand it no longer and drove up. The Bowerman house was deserted. I thought they must still be in church. But then I heard an impossible sound, an infuriating sound in their protected woods: a chain saw. I thought, *I'll be the hero. I'll run up the hill and sneak up behind whomever is stealing Bowerman virgin timber and catch them in the act.*

I did it carefully and well, finally creeping down a slope above the whine, through greening underbrush, closer and closer, until I could see a bunch of shaggy-coated people around a windblown, uprooted old tree, cutting the precious burl out of where the roots met the trunk. It was Jay, his son Jayson, and Bill and Barbara. I moaned like a spirit of the woods and ran toward them. They saw me and whooped. I dropped down into the foxholelike crater the root ball had left. Bill came across it and hugged me hard. Barbara hugged me harder. The script was wonderful, they said, a triumph.

Bill joined the Warner Brothers production, throwing his home open for shooting. The university signed a contract to give the studio exclusive rights to shoot at Hayward Field. But this had little apparent effect on Disney, which plowed ahead with its own project.

After Bill gave his imprimatur, a host of runners who knew Pre picked the same side. But Geoff Hollister, who had worked with Lutz on the CBS documentary, chose the Disney side.

I tried to explain to Geoff what Towne had drilled into me—namely, that every studio film starts out with great promises, but then bean-counting studio executives invariably want to cut the budget or compromise in some other way. At that point, you need a club—a Tom Cruise, someone so vital to the studio's future that it has to honor the original commitments. Hollister, having never experienced this, was unpersuaded. I recall saying, when I realized it was useless, "Well, we competed against each other for years and stayed friends, let's pledge to do that now." He so pledged.

Hollister signed on with the Disney production and tried to maneuver Phil Knight and Nike into backing it. But Knight, with Hollister on one side and Bowerman on the other, said, "I'm Switzerland. I'm neutral." He wished both sides luck. It is one of my chief regrets that I could not have found some way to prevent competing productions. Had all the athletes and admirers of Bill and Pre been working together, we could have spent more time and energy on art than on venom.

Disney lawyers immediately wrote to inform me that in speaking to unnamed people about Pre's life, I was engaging in tortuous contract interference, a felony. Towne's friend, the über attorney Bert Fields, wrote back demanding to know what I was being accused of so he could defend me. If I was interfering with Disney's contracts with anyone, he said, then name those people and provide those contracts so he could advise me to stop it.

The Disney attorneys replied, angrily, but not to the point. They never would, because they couldn't. The only people I'd spoken to who also had contracts with Disney were Hollister and Pre's sister Linda, and I'd told both of them that we wouldn't be talking for a while because of just this legality. Worse than that, Disney attorneys wrote scary letters to the Prefontaine family, saying that any contact with the Warner side would be regarded as a violation of their rights.

At such times, I would think of Pre himself, and pledge to do the best I could to help Towne evoke him on the screen. But before Towne could begin shooting, he had to be a part of another late-life reconciliation extended by Bill Bowerman. Towne had cast Billy Crudup as Pre and Donald Sutherland as Bill. A nervous Sutherland wanted to meet Bill, and Towne wanted that, too, so a lunch was arranged. Bill and Barbara arrived last to the dining room of Eugene's Valley River Inn, where we waited at a table overlooking the Willamette. Barbara would say later that Bill had seemed kind of cool that morning, making her apprehensive about whether he had truly put his old fury over *Personal Best* behind him.

By this time, Robert Towne had Bill Bowerman deep in his neurons, having imagined how it was for him throughout all the stages of Pre's development, the horrors of Munich, and Pre's death. Towne began taking Bowerman and Sutherland through those different scenes almost as if he'd been there himself. Barbara, watching, was astounded to see that Bill had decided that Towne was indeed the man for this job. Bill made no mention of *Personal Best*. He complimented Towne on doing his homework. And he was all soothing grace and warmth with Sutherland, assuring him he'd do fine.

Bowerman didn't ask that a word of the script be changed. He did add one line. Tom Cruise's partner in producing, Paula Wagner, wanted to meet Bill, so she visited a Tuesday Ad Hoc Group lunch at the Town Club and kidded him, saying he had a helluva nerve wrecking Barbara's waffle iron to make shoe soles. She would never have let her husband get away with that. "Paula," Bill replied, "tell your husband there are times when it's better to beg for forgiveness than ask for permission." So we threw that in the script.

We would call the film, in homage to Pre's wild yearnings, *Without Limits*. Bill did pay a call to the set, one Sunday after church. When the 2,000 Eugene extras in the stands got a glimpse of Bill, they stood in ovation. Bowerman walked along the whole backstretch, waving, glowing in the full and transparent knowledge that he deserved it. He was the only star on the set. Sutherland, affirming this, genuflected. Bill then sat down and was mightily impressed to see Crudup doing tough, 26- and 27-second 200s while reenacting Pre's finish against Frank Shorter in the 1974 Restoration Meet three-mile.

The Disney movie, called *Prefontaine*, came out first and proved Cruise prophetic. The budget had been minuscule. The director, Steve James, who had done the magnificent *Hoop Dreams* (and who shared screenwriting credits on *Prefontaine* with Eugene Corr), didn't understand Pre and tried to put him into the mold of what he did know—an athlete using sport to escape a ghetto or a small town.

The film also defamed the character of Bill Bowerman, creating a fictitious 1972 ultimatum from the USOC (the film called it something else) and portraying Bill as giving up his fight for athletes' expenses to avoid being removed as Olympic coach. The facts, of course, were that Bill had smiled and turned over the 1972 Trials' proceeds and refrained from suing the USOC. Had Bill actually been slapped with such an ultimatum, he would have walked to the nearest reporter, announced he'd just been shit-canned, and explained the reasons. Instead, *Prefontaine* showed him going on being Olympic coach, having knuckled under in a way Bowerman never would have. In trying to add "drama," the film trashed Bill's honor.

In February 1997, *Without Limits,* the Warner Brothers movie, was edited enough for viewing by a select audience. John Jaqua's son Jim, who had helped Towne plan the major race sequences, and I showed a working print to Bill and Barbara Bowerman and John and Robin Jaqua, on the Jaqua's TV. Bill was rapt for two hours. When it was over, no one spoke. Robin Jaqua was quietly weeping. Barbara looked to Bill. Bowerman took a moment to compose himself, nodded, and croaked, "That's the way it was. The way it was with the Men of Oregon."

That, for me, was praise enough.

In the years since, *Without Limits* has been immensely rewarding for its makers because of kids' reactions to it. It has become a relay baton with a message tucked inside, handed from one generation of runners to the next, keeping vivid both the story of Pre and the truths Bowerman held to be vital—namely, that we are all physical entities, that we all have the ability to get better (some of us a *lot* better), but to do that we have to accept our limits at any given moment and work within them. Great coaches are great because they see and help transcend those limits. If that is not exactly an immortal message, it should be.

Bill, the mortal Bill, was fading mentally, as were his cronies. Bob Newland had died of liver cancer in 1995. Ray Hendrickson more often lost the thread of his stories. But Bill and the rest of the Ad Hoc Group were so brutal to him when it happened that he'd be buoyed by their savage togetherness. Their motto, voiced by McHolick, was "Hey, Alzheimer's isn't so bad. You meet new friends every day."

Bill developed a few tricks to ward off concerns about his short-term memory. When he was asked a question and wanted to give his brain time, he'd ask, "Do you need to know by dinner?" He never lost his long-term memory, but it was never that hot in the first place. Even when Bill was just in his fifties, Phil Knight once said, "he was always wrong on his facts and right on his principles."

Like one of his heroes, Senator Wayne Morse, Bill had periods late in life when he got too angry and spent too much energy on things that should have been beneath him. Caught in the Olympian dilemma of having tougher standards for self and circle than the wider world can possibly meet, he had to make a shift that every champion eventually faces one way or another. He had to cut the rest of the world some slack.

Being one whose life had involved bringing health to others, Bill did the healthy thing. He genuinely mellowed. His judgmental, quick-to-sue side showed up less often. His underlying, beatific, joy-in-every-sunrise side outshone it. It helped that he went back to Fossil for some of those sunrises.

Bill and Barbara never minded the four-and-a-half-hour drive between their two homes because it plunged them back into so many important times. Barbara even conceived the structure of a symphony that would describe the trip.

"Eugene traffic would be warming up the orchestra," she would write to me in 2001, "then violins for the sound of the McKenzie as you ascend, a regular beat that is the rows of the first trees, then deep woods, dark and Wagnerian, out of which we get trilling flute glimpses of snowy mountains. Then a quiet period, flat, for the opening of the summits, the sky so big. I love that period of expansiveness. Then a little Indian tom-tom passing the towns of Sisters and Madras, for the different drums of the ponderosa trunks. Finally we settle down in the John Day canyons, the flat buttes, and another river theme closes the passage, something like where we began, but ineffably different."

When Bill's sister Beth needed an assisted-living facility, Bill bought an interest in airy, new Haven House in downtown Fossil. However, Beth soon aged right past being able to live there, so they found a nursing home in Madras for her. Bill and Barbara took the rooms in the Haven House facility themselves and rented out their home near Jon's property. They still commuted occasionally to Eugene, but in 1998 Tom needed to remodel the McKenzie View Drive kitchen, so they stayed in Fossil until he was done. They were so content they never moved back.

Bill had always joked to his teams that Fossil's population was a constant 527. When you said come on, it had to fluctuate a little, he'd say, "Nope. Nope. Every time a baby's born, a man leaves town." Now the green sign read "Pop. 430," but with the addition of the Bowermans, the town gave the impression of more.

Bill and Barbara would have been heroes to Fossil if they had simply returned there to live. But after their leadership in the Rajneeshpuram war, they were accorded mythic standing. Bill met all attempts to deify him with leveling humor.

Bill's company was still pleased to make use of him. For years, Nike had had a list of eleven rules. Number eleven was simply, "Remember the man." Steve Bence, who had been on the team with Prefontaine and has since become a key Nike manager, believes that the company is "exceptionally good for a large corporation in taking inspiration from one of its founding members" and credits Phil Knight with keeping Bowerman's spirit alive. The Nike running group created a line of shoes called the Bowerman series, a collection of shoes focused on performance. Bowerman's Cortez is still in the line and selling strongly around the world.

People who got their start in Bill's Eugene lab—Mike Friton, Ellen Schmidt Devlin, soccer player Don Remlinger, and pole-vaulter Tinker Hatfield—would move into influential positions at Nike and carry on his message. Many of Nike's overseas offices would have a conference room called the Bowerman Room, with his image and quotes on the wall. As Bence would say, "We hold up Bowerman as an example of an innovator, visionary, mentor, and teacher."

So at selected times, vanloads of new Nike employees were driven out to take his hand and know that Bill was real. He was usually memorable, too. Jeff Johnson recalled Geoff Hollister taking the Nike running development group to meet with Bill and filming him answering their questions. Bill said at one point, "By using these methods the Men of Oregon won two NCAA titles."

Hollister said, "Bill, it was actually four."

Bill fixed him with a look of suspicion that turned to joy. "The *hell* you say."

In June 1999, Bowerman stepped down as a member of the Nike Board of Directors. Over thirty-one years he had made countless attempts at this. Now, with sales creeping toward six billion dollars a year, Buck had finally permitted it. "Free at last," Bill said. "What's next?"

Six months later, Bill helped Barbara get their Christmas cards out on time. He lingered over a note to Otto and MarAbel Frohnmayer, because Otto was gravely ill with pancreatic cancer. "My dad got the last note Bill ever wrote," Dave Frohnmayer would recall. "We, the family, were all there in Medford that night, Christmas Eve. Barbara had written a lovely letter and there was a short, cogent note from Bill. I read it to Dad and he nodded and understood. Bill died that night and Dad died five weeks later."

Bill died beneath Barbara's favorite photo of him, taken at their wedding. It hung beside the photo he most loved of her, taken that same June day in 1936. She was standing on a pedestal, to display the great train of her dress. On his wedding day Bill was at parade rest, his shoulders back, his hands behind him. His face was calm, with a knowing, almost smug look of victory. One imagines the same look on the face of the departed, at eighty-eight, lying comfortably on the red and blue flowered bedspread, when Barbara came out of the shower and found him gone. "Oh, it's just like you," she said, "to go on ahead, and with absolutely no warning!"

He had pulled it off. Just when many had begun to worry about his taking longer and longer walks in the magnificent corridors of his mind, Bill managed a perfect ending to his life. Barbara sat with him and took his hand and thought back on the seventy years she'd been beside him, his loving girlfriend, wife, planner, organizer. With her energy and buoyant intuition, she had taken every pressure from him that she could, as they had for each other from the beginning, in their first dance. And never, she realized, in all that time, did these two piercingly intelligent beings completely fathom each other's mystery.

Bill was interred not far from the westward-facing slope where J. W. Chambers, as Bill had written, "sleeps in the warmth of the western setting sun." Barbara, who took his death in stride, wished no public memorial service.

In the months and years after Bill died, Barbara slowly went through chests of documents and photos in their McKenzie View homestead. She found the gun and the champagne from the war. "It will stay unopened, " she said of the Mumm.

"It seems sacrilegious otherwise. If we two didn't find an occasion, no force on earth should open it now."

Barbara also found a letter Bill had begun to Knight but never sent. Before they'd moved to Fossil for good, Bill had jotted some thoughts on a legal pad, roughing out a first draft, but didn't have Barbara type it out, meaning to polish it later. "He had to have written it in the last few minutes we were here," Barbara would recall. "But then in the rush of packing it got left behind."

Barbara was struck by its formality. "Usually he'd knock out his notes himself because all he'd say was, 'Buck, you knothead, I won't work with that new bleep you have in charge of communications.' But this was different. This was calm and considered."

It read:

> *The Waffle Farm*
>
> *Dear Buck,*
>
> *I want to tell my "Partner in Sports" how much I admire your leadership and the crew or team you have assembled and direct.*
>
> *The road has had some sharp curves. Yes, and some major obstacles to get around or over.*
>
> *I have never availed myself of the opportunity to express my admiration for your leadership and accomplishments in the growth, from small Blue Ribbon to International Nike Inc.*
>
> *Your leadership has been phenomenal. Barb joins me in appreciation and admiration.*

He had left it unsigned. A few days later, Barbara delivered the entire legal pad to Knight. "Am I going to cry?" he asked her. She nodded, so he took it away to read alone. "That resides in a sacred drawer," he would say later, knowing at last that Bill Bowerman had judged him worthy.

Index